HOW 14

A Handbook for Office Professionals

James L. Clark
Professor Emeritus
Business Department
Pasadena City College

Lyn R. Clark
Chair, Computer Applications
and Office Technologies Department
Los Angeles Pierce College

CENGAGE Learning®

Australia • Brazil • Mexico • Singapore • United Kingdom • United States

CENGAGE Learning

HOW 14: A Handbook for Office Professionals, 14th Edition
James L. Clark and Lyn R. Clark

Vice President, General Manager, Social Science & Qualitative Business: Erin Joyner

Product Director: Jason Fremder

Product Manager: Heather Mooney

Content Developer: Sarah Huber

Product Assistant: Brian Pierce

Marketing Director: Kristen Hurd

Marketing Manager: Jeff Tousignant

Marketing Coordinator: Chris Walz

Production Management, and Composition: Lumina Datamatics, Inc.

Art Director: Linda May

Intellectual Property
Analyst: Terina Bradley
Project Manager: Betsy Hathaway

Manufacturing Planner: Ron Montgomery

Cover and Title page images: Syda Productions/Shutterstock.com, wavebreakmedia/Shutterstock.com, Monkey Business Images/ Shutterstock.com

Chapter Opener Images: Wavebreakmedia/Shutterstock.com, Rawpixel/Shutterstock.com, bikeriderlondon/Shutterstock.com, Eugenio Marongiu/Shutterstock.com, Corepics VOF/Shutterstock.com, Pressmaster/Shutterstock.com, Maridav/Shutterstock.com, GaudiLab/Shutterstock.com

Library of Congress Control Number: 9781305586963

ISBN-13: 978-1-305-58696-3

Cengage Learning
20 Channel Center Street
Boston, MA 02210
USA

Printed in the United States of America
Print Number: 01 Print Year: 2015

Contents

Preface

HOW 14: A Handbook for Office Professionals, 14th edition, has been designed to provide assistance for preparing all types of written business communications. Its content and style focus upon the needs of students—as well as office personnel, business writers, and other business professionals—to produce suitable documents for success in a highly competitive, fast-paced global economy.

HOW 14 presents detailed and precise information for writing, formatting, and transmitting business documents. It serves as a reference to answer specific questions regarding writing style, language conventions, business formats, and document transmission as they relate to the preparation of e-mail messages, business letters, memorandums, reports, manuscripts, proposals, bulletins, résumés, faxes, agendas, itineraries, press releases, and meeting minutes.

A Comprehensive Reference Manual for Business

HOW 14 is succinct, yet comprehensive. It covers thoroughly the principles of business writing style, grammar, punctuation, capitalization, number usage, word hyphenation and division, and abbreviation format in simple, easy-to-understand language. Each rule is illustrated with examples or example sentences related to business circumstances or conditions. In addition, more than 250 word confusions—such as *affect/effect*, *ensure/insure*, and *principal/principle*—are differentiated by simple definitions and discriminating examples.

Content and formats for various business documents are covered thoroughly in *HOW 14*. All the major parts of a business letter, forms of address for domestic and foreign correspondence, and commonly used letter styles are discussed and illustrated, along with the basic formats for writing memorandums. Business writers will find helpful the up-to-date guidelines for citing sources, preparing visuals, setting up listings, providing main and text headings, compiling preliminary pages and bibliographies, formatting a report, and developing an effective business writing style.

Instructions and examples for preparing e-mail messages, itineraries, agendas, press releases, and meeting minutes further enhance the usability of this book as a business writer's resource. To assist readers with the entire document processing cycle, *HOW 14* provides detailed procedures for preparing business documents on computer-based equipment and accessing the Internet to collect information.

New to *HOW 14*

The following information is new to *HOW 14*:

- *New, updated information and examples* throughout the entire reference manual.

- *New and expanded information* on using the Internet to access Web 2.0 resources—social media, blogs, cloud computing, wikis, and other communication resources (see Chapter 14).

Special Features

Several features, besides the Table of Contents and the extensive Index, increase the functionality of *HOW 14* as a reference resource:

1. **Solution Finders**—comprehensive topic indexes at the beginning of each chapter enable readers to locate easily answers to their questions.
2. **Two-color format**—primary rules are printed in red and examples are printed in black so that principles may be located, read, and understood quickly.
3. **Example headings**—boldfaced headings differentiate aspects of each rule so that specific examples and applications may be located immediately.
4. **Spiral binding**—the lie-flat feature of spiral binding permits readers to compare readily their written work (or questions) with the examples.
5. **Glossary of grammatical terms**—a listing with definitions and examples of all the grammatical terms used in this reference manual may be accessed for further clarification of any language principle.

Finding Solutions to Problems

Information you need may be located easily and quickly in *HOW 14* by using a four-step process:

1. Find the chapter you need by turning to the Contents. Locate the chapter by turning to the page number listed.
2. Turn to the Solution Finder, which you will find on the next page.
3. Locate the information you need in the Solution Finder. Each main topic is listed alphabetically followed by subsections of that topic with their corresponding section numbers.
4. Turn to the appropriate section within the chapter by referring to the page-guide references (the section numbers shown at the top right corner of the odd-numbered pages).

If information cannot be located through surveying the contents listed on the back cover, use *HOW*'s comprehensive Index at the end of the reference manual to find the appropriate section.

User Profile

HOW 14 may be used as a classroom text or supplement for instructing students or by general office employees, administrative assistants, business writers, and managers—anyone who deals with the preparation of written business documents.

Students in business communication, business English, word processing, keyboarding, voice-recognition, transcription, legal office, medical office, and office procedures courses—all courses that require the processing of written words—will benefit from using *HOW 14*. It functions as a resource for class assignments, answering questions on writing style, language applications, punctuation, document framework, and document format. Use of *HOW 14* enables students to produce professional business documents. This reference manual continues to be a valuable resource as students enter the business environment and experience actual situations in business writing and document preparation.

Leaders who conduct business communication seminars will find *HOW 14* an indispensable tool for assisting participants in improving their writing skills, language competence, mechanics of expression, and knowledge of document framework and formats.

HOW 14 serves as a reference for all persons in business who are responsible for communicating through the written word. Similar to the indispensable dictionary, this manual compresses other essential reference information into a single source for producing effective business documents. Persons in all fields of business, education, government, law, and medicine will benefit from using *HOW 14* as a reference in preparing written documents for their professional position and their personal business circumstances.

Supplementary Materials

The *Workbook for HOW 14* (ISBN 9781305586970) provides reinforcement for the major principles covered in the reference manual. This 390-page supplement contains exercises that are coordinated specifically with sections in *HOW 14* and are designed to provide learners with realistic applications, not just isolated sentence exercises.

Workbook exercises enable learners to apply the rules governing grammar, punctuation, capitalization, number usage, word confusions, abbreviations, writing style, spelling, proofreading, and editing. In addition, learners receive practice in locating reference sources on the Internet, composing e-mail messages, using correct address formats, formatting business letters and memorandums, and indexing names for filing.

The *Instructor's Manual and Key*, which is available on the *HOW 14* Web site, includes keys to all the exercises in the *Workbook for HOW 14*. In addition, this teaching tool supplies more than 120 instructional Microsoft Word projection documents that contain the major punctuation, grammar, capitalization, and number-usage principles in *HOW 14* and correspond directly with the exercise applications in the workbook. Other teaching materials in the instructor's manual include a familiarization exercise, a series of assessments for the business letter and memorandum applications in the workbook, and PowerPoint presentations for the punctuation principles and other communication concepts covered in *HOW 14*. These resources are available for instructor download instantly from the *HOW 14* Web site at login.cengage.com.

Acknowledgments

Special acknowledgment and thanks are extended to PamWeigand, Eastern Washington University, who has been a continual supporter of the *HOW* series and spent several hours with the authors providing feedback for the publication of *HOW 13.*

We also thank the following reviewers for their assistance in the preparation of this reference book throughout its many editions:

Steve Abram, Kirkwood Community College
Velda Arnaud, Lane Community College
Elsa Barr, Central Community College
Dr. Kimberlee Bartel, Central Washington University
Carole Bennett, Santa Rosa Junior College
Jane Braynard, Santa Rosa Junior College
Dr. G. Jay Christensen, California State University, Northridge
Dr. Lajuan Davis, The University of Southern Mississippi
Pamela Dupin-Bryant, Utah State University
Gwen Eltz, Spokane Falls Community College
Jane Flesher, Chippewa Valley Technical College
Leann Gatewood, Iowa Central Community College
Joyce E. Graham, Rogue Community College
Patti Koluda, Yakima Valley Community College
Julie Lewis, Baker College-Allen Park
Dr. Natalie A. Lupton, Central Washington University
Michael Martel, Ohio University
Jeanette Martin, University of Mississippi
Catherine Peck, Chippewa Valley Technical College
Kathleen Richards, Utah Valley State College
Cynthia Townsend, Baker College
Mary Tucker, Ohio University
Twila Wallace, Central Community College
Shani Watkins, Central Washington University
Linda Wenn, Central Community College
Karen Woolstenhulme, Utah State University
Diana Yohe, Bristol Community College

James and Lyn Clark
E-mail: LynClarkPC@Hotmail.com

1

Grammar and Usage

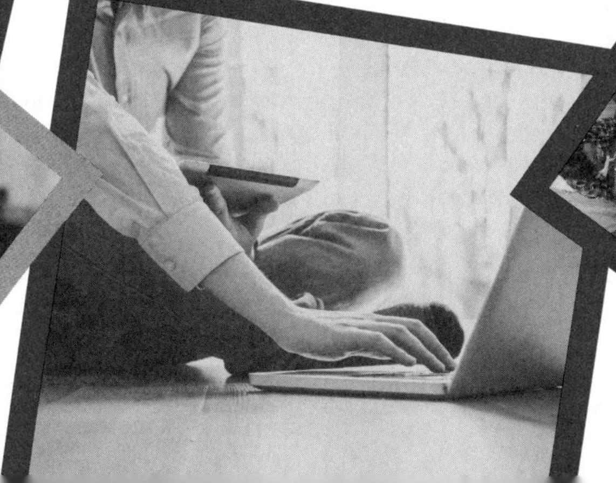

Grammar and Usage Solution Finder

Grammar and Usage Solution Finder *(Continued)*

Overview

The basis for successful communication lies in how people put together words to convey ideas. Knowing how words function in sentences and being able to construct complete sentences enhances a person's communication abilities. Whether speaking or writing, an understanding of how words function in sentences and applying conventional usages for the various kinds of words will contribute to an individual's communication skills.

1–1 Parts of Speech

Words used in sentences may be labeled according to the function they perform. By labeling words, we can easily analyze whether we are using words and constructing sentences correctly. Labels for the various word types, the basic parts of speech, follow:

- **Nouns.** Nouns name—for example—persons, animals, places, objects, feelings, and things. *Michael, cat, Dallas, iPad, love,* and *organization* are examples of nouns.
- **Pronouns.** Pronouns are noun substitutes. They take the place of a noun to avoid continually repeating a word. *She, he, it, they, her, him,* and *them* are examples of pronouns. Examples include *he* or *him* for *Michael* and *it* for *iPad.*
- **Adjectives.** Adjectives modify nouns and pronouns. They may describe, indicate how many, or tell which one. Examples include *effective* advertising, *four* companies, and *their* offices.
- **Verbs.** Verbs are the motors of a sentence. They show action or describe a state of being. Verbs such as *drive, eat, write,* and *study* show action while verbs such as *am, was, look,* and *feel* describe a state of being.
- **Adverbs.** Adverbs describe verbs, adjectives, or other adverbs. They tell *how, when, where, why,* or *to what degree*. Examples include drive *carefully*, arrived *yesterday,* stay *there,* understand *why*, and speaks *too quickly*.
- **Prepositions.** Prepositions are connectors. Most prepositions can be identified by imagining what a plane can do to a cloud. It can fly *over, under, through, in, around*, and so on, a cloud. Prepositions introduce descriptive phrases that relate to other parts of the sentence. Examples are *within* the next few days, *through* your efforts, and *under* these circumstances.
- **Conjunctions.** Conjunctions, too, are connectors. Coordinating conjunctions connect like parts in the sentence and adverbial conjunctions introduce clauses. Coordinating conjunctions include *and, but, or,* and *nor*. Examples of adverbial conjunctions include *because*, *since*, *as*, and *if.*

- **Interjections.** Interjections are words used to express a strong feeling or a sudden emotion. Such words usually stand by themselves followed by an exclamation mark or appear at the beginning of a sentence followed by a comma or an em dash. Examples of interjections include *wow*, *oops*, *yes*, *no*, and *oh*. *No*, all our stores are closed on New Year's Day. *Definitely*! We are always in the market for good ideas.

1–2 Parts of Speech Used in Sentences

a. Every word in a sentence may be identified as one of the eight parts of speech, depending upon the role it plays in the sentence.

sentence containing all parts of speech

Yes, Kevin and I drove to the airport yesterday.

Yes (interjection)	Kevin (noun)	and (conjunction)
I (pronoun)	drove (verb)	to (preposition)
the (adjective)	airport (noun)	yesterday (adverb)

sentence spotlighting nouns, pronouns, adjectives

noun pronoun adjective noun
Please call **Christina** if **you** need **additional information**.

noun noun adjective noun pronoun
Matthew forwarded **copies** of **Jonathan's e-mail** to **me**.

sentence spotlighting verbs and adverbs

verb adverb
For continued good health, **exercise daily**.

verb adverbs
Shannon **talks too loudly** in the office.

sentence spotlighting conjunctions and prepositions

conjunction preposition
Our manager **and** assistant managers will be working **on** alternate shifts.

preposition conjunction preposition
You will receive a call **from** the doctor **or** his assistant **within** the next few days.

sentence spotlighting interjections

interjection
Great! Our division won first place in the company sales contest.

interjection
Oops, I should have notified you earlier about the change in the meeting time.

b. Language customs govern how the parts of speech may be used in sentences. Specific usage principles apply to the various parts as they play their roles in the development of sentences to communicate ideas. A sentence (1) contains a verb (a word showing action or describing a condition), (2) has a subject (a noun or pronoun that interacts with the verb), and (3) makes sense (comes to a closure). Use sentences to express ideas.

(1) Verbs appear by themselves or in a verb phrase. The last verb in a verb phrase is considered to be the main verb.
(2) Subjects are either simple or compound. *Simple subjects* consist of a single noun or pronoun whereas *compound subjects* contain two or more nouns or pronouns linked by *and, or,* or *nor.*
(3) A complete sentence is an *independent clause,* a word group that by itself makes sense.

statements

simple subject **verb**
Four **employees** in our department **attended** the conference. (Makes sense.)

subject **verb**
This latest **proposal** by Kym Freeman **is** excellent. (Makes sense.)

compound subject **verb phrase**
The **seating and accessories** in the reception area **have been moved** to the new offices. (Makes sense.)

questions

simple subject **verb**
Which **student** in your class **wrote** this excellent report? (Makes sense.)

simple subject **verb**
Who among your staff **is** eligible to apply for this position? (Makes sense.)

compound subject **verb phrase**
How many real estate **agents and brokers** from our region **will attend** this conference? (Makes sense.)

requests or commands

verb
Please **complete** the online survey by June 30. (Simple subject you is understood; makes sense.)

verb phrase and adverb *not*
Do not litter in the parks or on the highways. (Simple subject *you* is understood; verb phrase, *do* (*not* = adverb) *litter*; makes sense.)

Nouns

1–3 Nouns[1]

a. Nouns are words that name something—for example, persons, animals, places, things, objects, time, feelings, qualities, actions, concepts, measures, and states of being.

person
A **pharmacist** is on duty 24 hours daily, seven days a week.

How often does our **webmaster** update the posting of career opportunities with our company?

animal
Dr. Shapiro manages a shelter for abandoned **dogs** and **cats**.

We deliver fresh **fish** daily to all Market Depot stores in the city.

place
The **mall** in our **neighborhood** is often too crowded on weekends.

Plan to arrive at the **airport** at least two hours before your scheduled departure.

thing
All the **data** for this **project** is stored on the **network**.

Which **company** was eventually awarded the **contract**?

object
How did you crack the **face** of your **cell phone**?

Move the **computer** to the **desk** in my office.

time
Payment for these purchases is due within 30 **days**.

Our new payroll system should be operational next **month**.

feeling
Everyone in the room sensed Mr. Smith's **anger** as he spoke.

The mother's **love** and **adoration** for her newborn shone in her face.

quality
I appreciate your **thoughtfulness** and **generosity**.

Such **irresponsibility** must be reported to the supervising physician.

---

[1] The rules and spellings in this chapter are based on Merriam-Webster, Incorporated. (2014). *Merriam-Webster's Collegiate Dictionary* (11th ed.). Springfield, MA: Merriam-Webster, Incorporated. For a complete, up-to-date online resource, visit Merriam-Webster at http://www.m-w.com. Individuals who have purchased *Merriam-Webster's Collegiate Dictionary*, 11th ed., may obtain a digital download and also register for a free one-year subscription to the online versions of multiple Merriam-Webster dictionaries.

action
Posted signs forbid **swimming** in this part of the lake.

Golfing is an individual sport enjoyed by both men and women.

concept
Our country was founded on **freedom** of **expression**.

Please report any **progress** you have made in locating the heirs.

measure
Johnson Industries' assets total more than **$700 million**.

Three **yards** of fabric are required to re-cover each chair.

state of being
Is she being treated for her **illness** by a specialist?

Complacency in this changing industry could easily lead to **bankruptcy**.

b. Any noun that names a particular one is capitalized. These capitalized nouns are known as *proper nouns*. Nouns that do not name specific ones are known as *common nouns*, and they are not capitalized.

proper nouns
Yesterday **Mayor Anderson** announced a 1 percent increase in city sales tax.

Repairs on **Pacific Coast Highway** are still in progress.

You will have our decision before **December 31**.

Much of this information is available through the **Internet**.

common nouns
Yesterday the **mayor** announced a 1 percent increase in city sales tax.

Repairs on the **highway** are still in progress.

You will have our decision before the 31st of next **month**.

Most of this information is available through online **resources**.

c. Although most common nouns consist of single words, many contain two—or even three—words. These *compound nouns* appear as regular entries in the dictionary and are defined as nouns. Some compound nouns are hyphenated, but most are separate words without hyphens (*open compounds*) or written solid (*closed compounds*).

closed compound nouns
John is the main **speechwriter** for our state governor.

Is your firm handling the Andersons' **lawsuit**?

open compound nouns
Have you invested in the **stock market** since its sharp decline?

Ask the **vice president** to sign this purchase order.

hyphenated compound nouns
Our company is sponsoring a **fund-raiser** for the employee's family.

The **vice-chancellor** must approve all faculty appointments.

1-4 Noun Plurals[2]

a. Most nouns form their plurals by adding *s*. However, nouns ending in *s, sh, ch, x,* or *z* form their plurals by adding *es*.

nouns adding s

account	accounts	executive	executives
report	reports	message	messages

nouns adding es

bus	buses	branch	branches
business	businesses	tax	taxes
brush	brushes	waltz[3]	waltzes

b. Common nouns ending in *y* form the plural in one of two ways. If the letter preceding the *y* is a vowel, just add *s*. However, if the letter preceding the *y* is a consonant, drop the *y* and add *ies*[4]

y preceded by a vowel

attorney	attorneys	monkey	monkeys
delay	delays	valley	valleys

y preceded by a consonant

company	companies	facility	facilities
policy	policies	photocopy	photocopies
factory	factories	territory	territories

[2] Noun plurals, other than regular ones ending in *s* or *es*, are shown in the dictionary immediately after the singular form of the word. Spellings for noun plurals are based on Merriam-Webster, Incorporated. (2014). *Merriam-Webster's Collegiate Dictionary* (11th ed.). Springfield, MA: Merriam-Webster, Incorporated. For a complete, up-to-date online resource, visit Merriam-Webster at http://www.m-w.com. Individuals who have purchased *Merriam-Webster's Collegiate Dictionary*, 11th ed., may obtain a digital download and also register for a free one-year subscription to the online versions of multiple Merriam-Webster dictionaries.

[3] An exception to this rule is the word *quiz*. For the plural form, add *z* before adding *es*—*quizzes*. The same exception applies to *whiz*, as in *computer whiz* or *math whiz*. For the plural form, add *z* and *es*—*computer whizzes* or *math whizzes*.

[4] An exception to this rule is the word *money*. For the plural form, follow the general rule or drop the *ey* and add *ies*. Either *moneys* or *monies* is correct.

c. **Musical terms ending in *o* form the plural by adding *s*. Other common nouns ending in *o* may form the plural by adding *s* or *es*. The correct plural form for all words ending in *o* is shown in the dictionary after the singular form of the word. If two plural forms are shown for a word, use the first one—unless the second form is otherwise preferred.**

musical terms

pianos solos sopranos altos cellos banjos

***common nouns ending in* os**

macros ratios portfolios studios memos logos

***common nouns ending in* oes**

cargoes tomatoes heroes potatoes vetoes mottoes

d. **Nouns ending in *ff* form the plural by adding *s*. Nouns ending in just *f* or *fe* may add *s*, or they may drop the *f* or *fe* and add *ves*. Nouns taking the irregular plural form by adding *ves* are shown in the dictionary. If the dictionary does not show the plural form, just add *s*. If the dictionary shows two plural forms, use the first one.**

***plural nouns ending in* ffs**

bailiff	bailiffs	plaintiff	plaintiffs
tariff	tariffs	sheriff	sheriffs

***plural nouns ending in* fs *or* fes**

belief	beliefs	chef	chefs
chief	chiefs	safe	safes
proof	proofs	strife	strifes

***plural nouns ending in* ves**

half	halves	shelf	shelves
knife	knives	thief	thieves
self	selves	wife	wives

e. **The plurals of proper nouns are formed by adding *s* or *es*. Those proper nouns ending in *s, sh, ch, x,* or *z* form the plural by adding *es*. All others form the plural by adding *s*.**

proper nouns adding* es *for plural forms

Winters	the Winterses	Finch	the Finches
Ross	the Rosses	Bendix	the Bendixes
Bush	the Bushes	Mendez	the Mendezes

proper nouns adding* s *for plural forms

Dixon	the Dixons	Kelly	the Kellys
Garcia	the Garcias	Russo	the Russos
Halby	the Halbys	Wolf	the Wolfs

f. Many nouns of foreign origin have both an English plural and a foreign plural. Consult your dictionary, and use the plural form that appears first.

foreign-derived nouns with preferred English plurals[5]

appendix	appendixes	hors d'oeuvre	hors d'oeuvres
auditorium	auditoriums	index	indexes (book)
bureau	bureaus	memorandum	memorandums
formula	formulas	plateau	plateaus
gymnasium	gymnasiums	ultimatum	ultimatums

foreign-derived nouns with preferred foreign-derived plurals

alumna	alumnae	emphasis	emphases
alumnus	alumni	nucleus	nuclei
analysis	analyses	parenthesis	parentheses
basis	bases	phenomenon	phenomena
crisis	crises	stimulus	stimuli
criterion	criteria	syllabus	syllabi
curriculum	curricula	synopsis	synopses
datum	data	synthesis	syntheses
diagnosis	diagnoses	terminus	termini
ellipsis	ellipses	thesis	theses

g. Some nouns form their plurals by changing letters within the word or adding letters other than *s* or *es*. These irregular plurals are shown in the dictionary in the same entry with their singular form.

child	children	mouse	mice
foot	feet	tooth	teeth
man	men	woman	women

h. Some nouns have the same form in both the singular and the plural. Other nouns are used only with singular verbs, and still others are used solely with plural verbs. These irregular constructions are explained in the dictionary entry that defines the word.

---

[5] Preferences for English and foreign noun plurals are based on entries shown in Merriam-Webster, Incorporated. (2014). *Merriam-Webster's Collegiate Dictionary* (11th ed.). Springfield, MA: Merriam-Webster, Incorporated. For a complete, up-to-date online resource, visit Merriam-Webster at http://www.m-w.com. Individuals who have purchased *Merriam-Webster's Collegiate Dictionary*, 11th ed., may obtain a digital download and also register for a free one-year subscription to the online versions of multiple Merriam-Webster dictionaries.

nouns with the same singular and plural forms

Chinese	gross	mumps	series
cod	headquarters	odds	sheep
corps	Japanese	politics	species
economics	measles	rendezvous	vermin
fish	moose	salmon	Vietnamese

nouns always used with singular verbs

aeronautics	genetics	mathematics	news

nouns always used with plural verbs

belongings	earnings	premises	scissors	winnings
credentials	goods	proceeds	thanks	

i. Form the plural of hyphenated or open compound nouns on the main word. For (1) hyphenated compounds not containing a main word and (2) compound nouns written as a single word, form the plural at the end.

plural formed on main word

attorney**s**-at-law	grant**s**-in-aid	notar**ies** public
bill**s** of sale	graphic design**s**	personnel manager**s**
co-owner**s**	leave**s** of absence	sister**s**-in-law
going**s**-over	lieutenant colonel**s**	vice-chancellor**s**

plural formed at end

bookshel**ves**	get-together**s**	stockholder**s**
come-on**s**	go-between**s**	teaspoonful**s**
database**s**	printout**s**	trade-in**s**
follow-up**s**	stand-in**s**	workm**en**

Some compounds have irregular plural forms. Check your dictionary to verify the plural forms of compounds you do not use regularly.

irregular plural forms

chaise longue	chaise longue**s**	passerby	passer**s**by
filet mignon	filet**s** mignon**s**	time-out	time-out**s**

j. The plurals of numerals, most capital letters, words referred to as words, and abbreviations composed of initials are formed by adding *s* or *es*. For clarity, though, all isolated lowercase letters and the capital letters *A*, *I*, *M*, and *U* are made plural by adding an apostrophe before the *s*. Italicize plural numerals, letters, abbreviations, and words referred to as such.

***plural formed with* s**

Mr. Matthews wants this assignment completed without any further **ifs**, **ands**, or **buts**.

Make a list of **dos** and **don'ts** for the care of this copier.

There are vacancies for two **RNs** on our team.

How many members of your accounting staff are **CPAs**?

Please ensure that these **c.o.d.s** are sent out by the end of the week.

plural formed with* s *or* es *and referred to as such

Please request our receptionist to write her ***1s*** and ***7s*** more legibly, since I often have difficulty distinguishing between them.

If you receive many more ***Cs*** during the next two semesters, you may have difficulty entering our graduate program.

Ms. Graham, our new copy editor, does not use her ***whiches*** and ***thats*** correctly.

On the last ballot, did the ***noes*** outnumber the ***yeses***?

Always express in lowercase letters the ***a.m.s*** and ***p.m.s*** with clock time.

plural formed with an apostrophe and* s *and referred to as such

To ensure that your writing is legible, be sure to dot your ***i's*** and cross your ***t's***.

Your son received three ***A's*** on his last grade report.

Be careful not to use too many ***I's*** in your business writing.

Why do the ***M's*** appear smudged in this document?

k. When referring to two or more individuals with the same name and title, make either the name or the title plural, but not both. For two or more individuals with either a different title or a different name, use the singular form.

same name and title

the **Messrs.** Johnson	*or*	the Mr. **Johnsons**
the **Drs.** Berger	*or*	the Dr. **Bergers**
the **Mses.** Tyler	*or*	the Ms. **Tylers**
the **Mesdames** Jones	*or*	the Mrs. **Joneses**
the **Misses** Binsley	*or*	the Miss **Binsleys**

different name or title

Mr. Bentley and **Mr.** Thompson have accepted your invitation for lunch on May 15.

Two of the finalists for the position are **Ms.** Stevenson and **Mr.** Stevenson!

You may obtain this information from either **Mrs.** Anderson or **Ms.** Corey.

1–5 Noun Possessives[6]

To determine ownership and identify possessive nouns, locate what is owned and who owns it. Place what is owned and the owner in an ownership phrase. By inverting the order of two nouns that appear together and inserting *belonging to, of,* or *for,* you can check for ownership and determine where an apostrophe might be needed.

a. All "owner" nouns *not* ending with a pronounced *s,* whether singular or plural, form the possessive by adding *'s.*

what is owned ——→ owner	possessive form
briefcase of the **attorney**	**attorney's** briefcase
toys belonging to the **children**	**children's** toys
cell phone belonging to **Janet**	**Janet's** cell phone
purses for **women**	**women's** purses
laws of **Illinois**	**Illinois's** laws
mayor of **Des Moines**	**Des Moines's** mayor
paycheck of **Ms. DuBois**	**Ms. DuBois's** paycheck
restaurant belonging to **Francois**	**Francois's** restaurant

(Note: The final *s* in words such as *Illinois*, *Des Moines*, *DuBois*, and *Francois* is not pronounced; therefore, *'s* is used with these possessive forms.)

b. "Owner" nouns ending with a pronounced *s* form the possessive by simply adding an apostrophe unless an additional syllable is pronounced in the possessive form. If an additional syllable is pronounced, add *'s.*

no extra pronounced syllable

what is owned ——→ owner	possessive form
benefits for **veterans**	**veterans'** benefits
the cooperation of two **cities**	two **cities'** cooperation
the home belonging to the **Coxes**	the **Coxes'** home
the pen belonging to **Mr. Simons**	**Mr. Simons'** pen

extra pronounced syllable

what is owned ——→ owner	possessive form
grades of the **class**	the **class's** grades
the wallet belonging to **Mr. Harris**	**Mr. Harris's** wallet
testimony of the **witness**	the **witness's** testimony

---

[6] See Section 2–55 for additional examples.

c. In cases of joint ownership (when owners share ownership), show possession only on the last noun. Where individual ownership exists, show possession on each noun.

joint ownership

The Martinezes and the **Williamsons'** store is located on Bixby Circle.

Candice and **Justin's** supervisor was transferred to Salt Lake City.

Our law firm will draw up Mr. Simms and **Ms. Ross's** partnership agreement.

Clark and **Clark's** reference manual is required for this class.

individual ownership

John's and **José's** commission checks were drawn for incorrect amounts.

My **mother's** and **father's** clothes were damaged in the fire.

Mr. Granados' and **Ms. Stone's** applications for admission to the police academy have been accepted.

All the **accountants'** and the **administrative assistants'** offices have been moved to the new building.

d. The possessive form of compound nouns is shown at the end.

business belonging to my **mother-in-law**	**my mother-in-law's** business
the meeting of **stockholders**	the **stockholders'** meeting
offices of **attorneys-at-law**	**attorneys-at-law's** offices
computer belonging to the **systems manager**	**systems manager's** computer
inheritance for his two **stepsons**	his two **stepsons'** inheritance

e. Use the possessive form before a gerund (verb + *ing* used as a noun).

Lisa's assisting us with this project will ensure that it will be completed by the deadline date.

There is no record of the **witness's answering** these questions under oath.

f. Use an apostrophe with the possessives of nouns that refer to time—minutes, hours, days, weeks, months, and years.

time nouns—singular

peace for a **minute**	a **minute's** peace
activities for the **day**	the **day's** activities
notice of a **month**	a **month's** notice
mail from this **morning**	this **morning's** mail
calendar for **tomorrow**	**tomorrow's** calendar
schedule for **Friday**	**Friday's** schedule

time nouns—plural

work for four **hours**	four **hours'** work
interest for two **weeks**	two **weeks'** interest
trial for three **months**	three **months'** trial
experience for five **years**	five **years'** experience

g. Use an apostrophe with the possessives of nouns that refer to distance.

She lives just a **stone's** throw from the theater district.

The truck missed hitting a tree by an **arm's** length.

h. Do not use an apostrophe to form possessives for inanimate (nonliving) things or objects except for time or distance. Instead, use a simple adjective or an *of* phrase.

Words such as *company, team, organization, association, committee, herd,* and *flock* are not considered inanimate because they refer to groups of people or other living groups.

simple adjective
The **camera** lens has a scratch. (Not *The camera's lens has a scratch.*)

The **computer** keyboard needs to be replaced. (Not *The computer's keyboard needs to be replaced.*)

of *phrase*
When did you crack the **face of your cell phone**? (Not *When did you crack your cell phone's face?*)

The attorney read aloud the **stipulations of the will**. (Not *The attorney read aloud the will's stipulations.*)

group composed of people or another living group
Most of the **company's** profits in 2015 were from Internet e-commerce.

The **college's** offerings have expanded significantly during the past few years.

Nearly 100 acres of the **herd's** grazing lands were destroyed by the fire.

i. In some possessive constructions, the item or items owned do not directly follow the ownership word or are not named. The ownership word, however, still shows possession with an apostrophe.

item owned does not directly follow the ownership word
The only computer station to be replaced is **Kasey's**. (Kasey's computer station.)

On Tuesday we will meet at the **Lopezes'** to discuss listing for sale their condominium. (The Lopezes' condominium.)

item owned not named
Mr. Halby left the **attorney's** more than an hour ago. (The attorney's office.)

Did you leave your iPad at the **Gallaghers'**? (The Gallaghers' home.)

Verbs

1–6 Verbs

a. **A verb is often described as the motor of a sentence—verbs make sentences "go." Verbs show action or describe a state of being at a certain point in time. Examples of action verbs are *run, swim, talk,* and *write.***

Nonaction verbs, those that describe a state of being, include words such as *seem, feel,* and *smell.* The most commonly used nonaction verbs, however, are derived from the verb *be—am, is, are, was, were,* and *been.*

b. **In their infinitive form, verbs are preceded by the preposition *to.***

action verbs	nonaction verbs
to call	to be
to demonstrate	to appear
to apply	to taste

c. **Verbs appear alone or in phrases with helpers (for example, *has, have, was, did*). The last word in a verb phrase is the main verb. Word groups must contain a verb or a verb phrase to be complete sentences.**

verb in sentence

Darryl **directs** all his e-mail messages to his cell phone.

Please **return** these defective hard drives to the vendor.

Vista Industries **is** one of our best customers.

verb phrase in sentence

We **have received** several contracts from Gourmet Cookery.

Bradford Architects **has been commissioned** to design the suites in the new medical building.

Our office staff **is** presently **processing** your order.

How much money **did** our company **invest** in this condominium project?

d. **Verbs have a variety of parts to signify tenses—that is, to describe points in time. The main parts of a verb used to form tenses include the present part, the past part, the past participle, and the present participle.**

1–7 Formation of Parts for Regular Verbs

Most verbs, which are regular verbs, form their parts in this way:

(1) The present part has the infinitive form without the accompanying *to.*
(2) The past part adds *ed* to the present form.

(3) The past participle uses the past part with at least one verb helper.
(4) The present participle adds *ing* to the present form and uses at least one verb helper.

infinitive	**present**	**past**
to ask	ask	asked
to collect	collect	collected
to interview	interview	interviewed

past participle	**present participle**
(have, was) asked	(was, has been) asking
(has, had been) collected	(am, have been) collecting
(were, have been) interviewed	(are, will be) interviewing

sentence examples

You will need **to collect** more evidence before we can present this case to the district attorney's office. (Infinitive.)

Blair **collects** stamps from countries all over the world. (Present part.)

The courier **collected** all our mail for overnight delivery about an hour ago. (Past part.)

My assistant **has collected** prospectuses from five major suppliers of health insurance programs. (Past participle with a helping verb.)

Our Research Department **is collecting** additional information from consumers. (Present participle with a helping verb.)

1–8 Formation of Parts for Irregular Verbs

a. Many verbs do not form their past part, past participle, and present participle in the usual manner. *All such irregular verb forms are shown in the dictionary; they are listed directly after the present form of the verb.* Verbs without such a listing are regular verbs, and their parts are formed in the regular way described in Section 1–7.

b. A number of irregular verbs form their parts in the same way.

(1) Most verbs ending in *e* form their past part and past participle by adding *d.* These same verbs form the present participle by dropping the *e* and adding *ing.*
(2) Another group of verbs double the final consonant before adding the regular endings to the past part, past participle, and present participle.

***verbs ending in* e**

Infinitive:	to change	to enclose	to complete
Present part:	change	enclose	complete
Past part:	changed	enclosed	completed
Past participle:	(has) changed	(have) enclosed	(have) completed
Present participle:	(is) changing	(are) enclosing	(is) completing

verbs that double the final consonant

Infinitive:	to trim	to stir	to clip
Present part:	trim	stir	clip
Past part:	trimmed	stirred	clipped
Past participle:	(has) trimmed	(has) stirred	(have) clipped
Present participle:	(is) trimming	(are) stirring	(is) clipping

c. Some irregular verb forms do not follow a particular pattern in forming the past part and the past participle. A list of parts for some such commonly used irregular verbs follows:

Present Part	*Past Part*	*Past Participle*	*Present Participle*
am	was	been	being
arise	arose	arisen	arising
become	became	become	becoming
begin	began	begun	beginning
bite	bit	bitten	biting
blow	blew	blown	blowing
break	broke	broken	breaking
bring	brought	brought	bringing
burst	burst	burst	bursting
buy	bought	bought	buying
catch	caught	caught	catching
choose	chose	chosen	choosing
come	came	come	coming
dig	dug	dug	digging
do	did	done	doing
draw	drew	drawn	drawing
drink	drank	drunk	drinking
drive	drove	driven	driving
eat	ate	eaten	eating
fall	fell	fallen	falling
fight	fought	fought	fighting
fly	flew	flown	flying
forget	forgot	forgotten	forgetting
forgive	forgave	forgiven	forgiving
freeze	froze	frozen	freezing
get	got	got	getting
give	gave	given	giving
go	went	gone	going
grow	grew	grown	growing
hang (an object)	hung	hung	hanging
hang (a person)	hanged	hanged	hanging
hide	hid	hidden	hiding
know	knew	known	knowing
lay	laid	laid	laying
lead	led	led	leading
leave	left	left	leaving
lend	lent	lent	lending
lie (to recline)	lay	lain	lying
lie (to tell an untruth)	lied	lied	lying
lose	lost	lost	losing
make	made	made	making
pay	paid	paid	paying

Present Part	*Past Part*	*Past Participle*	*Present Participle*
ride	rode	ridden	riding
ring	rang	rung	ringing
rise	rose	risen	rising
run	ran	run	running
see	saw	seen	seeing
set	set	set	setting
shake	shook	shaken	shaking
shrink	shrank	shrunk	shrinking
sing	sang	sung	singing
sink	sank	sunk	sinking
sit	sat	sat	sitting
speak	spoke	spoken	speaking
spring	sprang	sprung	springing
steal	stole	stolen	stealing
strike	struck	struck	striking
swear	swore	sworn	swearing
swim	swam	swum	swimming
take	took	taken	taking
tear	tore	torn	tearing
throw	threw	thrown	throwing
wear	wore	worn	wearing
write	wrote	written	writing

sentence examples

APC's summer clearance sale **begins** August 1.

We **began** work on this construction project early last March.

Orders, as a result of our national television campaign, **have begun** to flood our telephone lines.

Our Web site sales **are beginning** to exceed our catalog sales.

1–9 Simple Tenses

Verb parts are used to form tenses that place an action or a condition in a time frame. The verb part itself may express tense, or a verb part with helpers (a verb phrase) may be needed to identify the time frame. The most commonly used tenses are the simple tenses—the *present*, the *past*, and the *future*.

a. The present tense is used to indicate an ongoing action or a currently existing condition. Use the present part or a conjugation (changes in spelling to accommodate person) of the present part to form this tense.

(1) Place an *s* at the end of the present part when it is used with any singular subject except *I* and *you*.

(2) Place *es* at the end of the present part for verbs ending in *s*, *sh*, *ch*, *x*, and *z* when it is used with any singular subject—except *I* and *you.*[7]

(3) Use just the present part with any plural subject.

[7] The verbs *do* and *go* add *es* also; that is, the singular form of *do* for *he*, *she*, and *it* is *does*. The corresponding form for *go* is *goes*.

present tense formations for most verbs

to eat	**to provide**	**to sit**
I eat	I provide	I sit
you eat	you provide	you sit
he eats	he provides	he sits
John eats	John provides	John sits
she eats	she provides	she sits
Mary eats	Mary provides	Mary sits
it eats	it provides	it sits
the cat eats	the company provides	the cat sits
we eat	we provide	we sit
you eat (pl.)	you provide (pl.)	you sit (pl.)
they eat	they provide	they sit
the children eat	the parents provide	the patients sit

***present tense formations for verbs ending in* s, sh, ch, x, *and* z**

to wish	**to teach**	**to relax**
I wish	I teach	I relax
you wish	you teach	you relax
he wishes	he teaches	he relaxes
John wishes	John teaches	John relaxes
she wishes	she teaches	she relaxes
Mary wishes	Mary teaches	Mary relaxes
it wishes	it teaches	it relaxes
the company wishes	the program teaches	the cat relaxes
we wish	we teach	we relax
you wish (pl.)	you teach (pl.)	you relax (pl.)
they wish	they teach	they relax
the children wish	the schools teach	the travelers relax

use of present tense

Our representative **visits** all pharmacies in this area regularly.

The All-Clean cleaning crew **waxes** our office floors weekly.

Johnson Industries **establishes** offices in all countries in which it **does** business.

He **goes** to the doctor regularly for checkups.

a. The *past tense* describes a single past action or event. Simply use the past part of a verb to express the past tense.

The decorator **selected** gray carpeting for the computer training room.

Our office manager **received** your signed contracts yesterday.

Cameron **bought** this digital equipment from an Internet site.

b. The *future tense* describes expected or anticipated occurrences. To form the future tense, use the present part with the helping verb *will*.

The receptionist **will call** you next week to confirm your appointment.

The committee **will review** your proposal by March 1, and I **will notify** you of the committee's decision by March 8.

Our company **will** not **submit** a bid for this project.

1–10 Perfect Tenses

The perfect tenses—the present, past, and future—use the past participle of the verb along with a helping verb formed from *have*.

a. The *present perfect tense* describes an action or a condition that began in the past and has continued until and including the present. This tense is formed by using *has* or *have* with the past participle of the verb.

Carson and Ashley **have worked** in the Accounting Department since 2011.

The Incredible Magellan **has performed** regularly in the Tiki Room for the past three years.

Dalton Industries **has** already **paid** heavy fines for environmental-impact violations.

b. The *past perfect tense* describes a past action that occurred before another past action. Use *had* as a helping verb with the past participle of the main verb to form this tense.

Our client **had paid for this policy** just three weeks before he **died**.

Although the manufacturer **had shipped** the merchandise two weeks ago, it **arrived** too late for our sale.

We **accepted** Armstrong Enterprises' offer only after we **had contacted** three other vendors.

c. The *future perfect tense* describes an action that will take place before another future action. Use the helping verbs *will have* with the past participle of the main verb to form this tense.

By the time we **publish** this book, we **will have spent** more than $60,000 in fees to freelance writers.

If **allowed to continue**, this project at its conclusion **will have cost** United States' taxpayers more than $3 billion.

You **will have** already **completed** the semester before your scholarship funds **arrive**.

1–11 Progressive Tenses

The progressive tenses show action in progress during the present, past, and future. Use the present participle of the verb along with a *being* verb helper—*am, is, are, was, were,* or *be*.

a. **The *present progressive tense* describes an ongoing action during the present time. The *being* verb helper *am, is,* or *are* is used with the present participle to form this tense.**

I **am writing** a report for my business communications class.

Encino Hospital **is sponsoring** a 10K run to benefit its cancer wing.

Several employees **are relocating** to our main office in Salt Lake City.

Are you **planning** to take any additional online classes?

b. **The *past progressive tense* relates an ongoing action that occurred in the past. The *being* verb helper *was* or *were* is used with the present participle of a verb to form this tense.**

I **was planning** to join a soccer league this season until I learned that my new position will require considerable travel.

Until the end of last year, we **were** still **manufacturing** replacement parts for this model wheelchair.

c. **The *future progressive tense* forecasts an ongoing future action. To form this tense, use the helping verbs *will* and *be* with the present participle of the verb.**

We **will be hiring** employees for this new restaurant location approximately three weeks before construction is completed.

Our auditors **will be reviewing** Price Investment Corporation's books for at least another two months.

1–12 Passive Voice Constructions

Unlike other verb constructions, the passive voice does not necessarily identify who does what. Instead, the person or thing performing the action may be cloaked in ambiguity.

In business communications the passive voice is often used to soften the impact of a negative idea or to avoid placing blame for an oversight or error. It is also used simply to provide variety in sentence construction. Although grammar checkers (software programs) may flag passive voice constructions, they are not grammar errors.

To form a passive voice construction, use the past participle of the verb with one of the following *being* verb helpers: *is, are, was, were, be,* or *been*.

Our cosmetic line **is sold** through franchised dealers only.

Unfortunately, the shipment **was damaged** in transit.

On December 31 eviction notices **were mailed** in error to all the building tenants.

The account **was closed** because of nonpayment.

Each online order **is acknowledged** by a message to the customer's e-mail account.

All depositors **have been notified** that the insured deposits of Universal Bank **were transferred** to Western bank.

1–13 Use of *Lay* and *Lie*

a. Broadly defined, the verb *lay* means "to place or put" and the verb *lie* means "to recline." Forms of these two verbs are often confused in usage. The principal parts of *lie* and *lay* follow:

Present Part	*Past Part*	*Past Participle*	*Present Participle*
lie	lay	lain	lying
lay	laid	laid	laying

b. Use a form of *lie* when the subject of the verb is performing the action, that is, the subject is what is lying. Otherwise, if the subject of the sentence is not the person or thing doing the lying, use a form of *lay*.[8]

Always use a form of *lay* when the past participle appears with a *being* verb helper (*is, are, was, were, be, been*).

***subject is performing the action*—is lying**
The new *fashion mall* **lies** at the base of the La Crescenta Foothills.

Tony **lay** unconscious for nearly half an hour before the ambulance arrived.

Our *computer system* **has lain** idle for nearly three hours.

At this pet hospital, the *dogs* **were lying** in clean, well-maintained cages.

***subject of verb is* not lying**
Jennifer **lays** all new magazines on tables in the reception area. (*New magazines* are lying on tables—not subject of verb; *Jennifer* is the subject.)

Before leaving the office, Morgan **laid** the contracts on your desk. (*Contracts* are lying on the desk—not subject of verb; *Morgan* is the subject.)

Our shipping clerks **have** always **laid** these electronic devices horizontally in their packing boxes. (*Electronic devices* are lying in packing boxes—not subject of verb; *shipping clerks* is the subject.)

Retail stores throughout the country **are laying** plans to capture their share of holiday purchases. (*Retail stores*, not *plans*, is the subject of the sentence.)

***always a form of* lay (being *verb + past participle*)**
Sandbags have **been laid** along the riverfront to protect the homes from the impending floods.

---

[8] Use of the verb *lay* with three of its parts—*lay, laid*, and (*has, have*, or *had*) *laid*—is often easily identified by substituting a form of the verb *put*. If *put* or one of its forms makes sense, then the use of *lay* or one of its forms is correct. Otherwise, a form of *lie* is more than likely to be correct.

When **was** the carpeting **laid** in the model homes?

Each morning by 10 a.m. the mail **is** opened and **laid** on Mr. Parker's desk.

1–14 Principles of Agreement

a. The verb of a sentence must agree in person and number with the subject. To identify a subject, omit any prepositional phrases that separate the subject and the verb.

E-mail **messages** in your company account **are** open for scrutiny. (Omit prepositional phrase *in your company account.*)

The **stock** of cartridges for our printers **is running** low. (Omit prepositional phrases *of cartridges* and *for our printers.*)

b. A pronoun that represents the subject must agree in number and gender with the subject.

Addison submitted **his** monthly expense form last week.

Remind **every salesperson** to provide us with **his** or **her** cell phone number.

Avery and **Cameron** have already submitted **their** home-loan application to Chase Bank.

The **company** increased **its** production because **it** foresaw an increased demand for computer games during the holiday season.

c. Compound subjects joined by *and* generally require the use of a plural verb. When compound subjects are joined by *or* or *nor*, the form of the verb is determined by the part of the subject that is closer to the verb. If one part is plural and the other is singular, place the plural part, where possible, closer to the verb.

***compound joined by* and**
My **daughter and son-in-law subscribe** to *TIME* and *Bloomberg Businessweek.*

Letters and packages for overnight delivery **leave** our office on a regularly scheduled basis.

Mr. Muñoz and his two assistants are temporarily out of the office.

***compound joined by* or *or* nor**
Either Dakota or **I am** responsible for opening the store on weekends.

Neither Blair nor **Cory was** available to meet with the client on Friday.

Ms. Kligman or her **assistants are** reviewing the manuscript. (Not *Her assistants or* Ms. Kligman is *reviewing the manuscript.*)

Candy or **flowers are** typically given on Valentine's Day. (Not *Flowers or* candy is *typically given on Valentine's Day.*)

d. Subjects joined by *and* take singular verbs in only two cases: (1) when the parts separated by *and* constitute a single person or thing and (2) when the compound is preceded by *each, every,* or *many a(an).*

single person or thing

Our **tax attorney and accountant has** prepared all the reports needed for the Internal Revenue Service.

Her **nurse and companion works** six days a week.

Bacon and eggs is the most popular breakfast item on our menu.

This **horse and carriage was** used throughout the television series *The Shannon Family.*

***compound preceded by* each, every, *or* many a (an)**

Each home and condominium was inspected by the general contractor before it was released for occupancy.

Every man, woman, and child is responsible for carrying his or her belongings during the tour.

Many a student and instructor has requested additional tickets to our Theater Department's production of *Mamma Mia.*

e. Indefinite pronouns such as *each, every, everyone, everything, somebody, anybody, either,* and *neither* take singular verbs.

Each of these books **is** available electronically for download.

Everyone was pleased with the hotel accommodations.

Everything in these files **needs** to be transferred to microfiche.

Neither of them **was** present at the meeting.

f. When the word *there* precedes the verb, select the singular or plural verb form based on the number of the noun that follows. If the noun is singular, then use a singular verb; if it is plural, use a plural verb.

The same rule applies to those words such as *some, all, none, most, a majority, one fourth,* and *part* that indicate portions. When they function as subjects, the number of the noun that follows governs whether a singular or plural verb is correct.

there *preceding a singular verb form*

There **is** one **applicant** for the position that stands out from the rest.

There **appears** to be only one **reason** why our bid was rejected.

there *preceding a plural verb form*

There **are** three **applicants** for this position.

There **appear** to be several **reasons** why our bid was not accepted.

portion preceding a singular verb form

Some of the **money has** been invested in U.S. Savings Bonds.

Part of your **order has** been shipped.

One third of our **clerical staff needs** additional training on this new system.

portion preceding a plural verb form

All the **materials were** shipped to you yesterday.

So far only **one half** of the **apartments have** been painted.

The majority of our **employees receive** a bonus annually from our incentive plan.

g. The words *a number* used as a subject require a plural verb. *The number* used as a subject requires a singular verb. Keep in mind that descriptive adverbs and adjectives may separate the article *a* or *the* from the word *number*.

a number *subject, plural verb*

A number of the applicants **are** from out of state.

A surprisingly large **number** of customers **have** purchased the lightweight laptop instead of the tablet.

the number *subject, singular verb*

The number of employees selecting MDA medical insurance **has** increased substantially since 2012.

The large **number** of customer inquiries received from our recent Facebook posting **was** far greater than we had anticipated.

h. To express the subjunctive mood (a situation or condition that is untrue or highly unlikely), use *were* instead of *was* after *if, as if, as though,* or *wish*. The verb *was* is used only if the situation after *if, as if,* or *as though* could be true.

use of* were *for untrue conditions

If I **were** you, I would update my application before the deadline date. (A condition that is untrue—I cannot be you.)

If you **were** Darren, which of the two colleges would you select? (You are not Darren—a condition that is untrue.)

use of* were *for an unlikely situation

I **wish** I **were** able to answer that question for you. (However, I cannot answer the question.)

Mr. Evans took charge **as though** he **were** the owner of the store. (However, Mr. Evans is not the owner of the store.)

***use of* was**

If Hayley **was** here, she did not sign her weekly time sheet. (Hayley could have been there.)

The customer acted **as if** he **was** irritated with our payment policy. (The customer certainly may have been irritated.)

i. Avoid splitting an infinitive, that is, placing any words between *to* and the verb form.

Be sure **to document thoroughly** in your report any findings related to the greatest job growth rates in Phoenix. (Avoid *to thoroughly document.*)

None of us seemed **to understand fully** the reasons for the change in policy. (Avoid *to fully understand.*)

j. Collective nouns such as *committee, jury, audience, group, team, class, board, crowd,* and *council* may take either singular or plural verbs, depending upon the situation in which the noun is used. If the individual members of the collective noun are operating as a unit, use a singular verb; if the individual members are acting separately, use a plural verb.

In most cases the use of a plural verb with a collective noun results in an awkward-sounding construction. To avoid such situations, restructure the sentence to use a plural-noun subject.

elements of collective noun acting as a unit
When a live **audience gives** performers a standing ovation, you may be sure that the audience considers them outstanding.

Has the standards **committee** finished its report?

elements of collective noun acting separately
The **jury were** arguing loudly. (Alternative: The jury members were arguing loudly.)
The **board are** still discussing various outcomes that may affect their decision. (Alternative: The board members are still discussing various outcomes that may affect their decision.)

restructured sentence with plural-noun subject
Unfortunately, the **members** of the council **do** not agree on the purpose of the newly formed committee.

After the game the team **members were** seen arguing with one another on national television.

k. A relative pronoun clause (a clause commonly beginning with *who* or *that*) must agree in gender and number with the noun or pronoun it modifies.

Ms. Nelson is a **person** who **is** concerned about maintaining **her** good health.

Our manager is the kind of **man** who **is** always considerate of **his** employees.

All **children** who **attend** this school are required to maintain **their** grade average at or above the *C* level.

Have you listened to all the **messages** that **have** accumulated in your message center during the past three days?

Our weekly budget **meeting**, which **was** scheduled for November 11, has been canceled for this week.

l. Relative pronoun clauses (*who* and *that* clauses) preceded by such phrases as *one of those doctors* or *one of the doctors* generally agree with the plural noun—in this case, *doctors*. Phrases such as *one of those* (or *the*) *executives, one of those* (or *the*) *books*, and *one of those* (or *the*) *assistants* are in the same category. The entire group is described by the clause; therefore, plural forms must be used.

In sentences in which *one of those* ____ or *one of the* ____ is limited by the word *only*, the relative clause does not refer to the entire group. Singular forms are correct in these instances.

one of those _____—*plural forms*

Drew is one of those business **executives** who **travel** extensively for **their** company.

He is one of the **salespersons** in our region who regularly **visit** all **their** customers.

Top of the Mountain is one of those **books** that **have** a surprise ending.

Dana is one of the **managers** who **work** in our Springfield office.

one of those _____*limited by* only—*singular forms*

Drew is the **only one** of the business executives who **travels** extensively for **her** position.

He is the **only one** of our salespersons who regularly **visits** all **his** customers.

Top of the Mountain is the **only one** of these books that **has** a surprise ending.

Dana is the **only one** of the managers who **reports** to our Springfield office.

Pronouns

1–15 Pronouns

a. Pronouns are noun substitutes; they take the place of nouns. Business writers use pronouns to add variety and interest to their writing.

sentence without pronouns
When you see Devon, please ask Devon to sign Devon's time card for this week.

sentence with pronouns
When you see Devon, please ask **him** to sign **his** time card for this week.

b. Pronouns perform one of four functions: they may (1) substitute for a person or thing, (2) refer back to a noun used previously in the sentence, (3) substitute for an unspecific person or thing, or (4) act as an adjective by modifying a noun.

substitute for a person or thing (personal pronoun)
Michael has been ill for three days; **he** should schedule an appointment to see Dr. Sasunian.

Because **Mrs. Aguon-Garrido** is in charge of this program, please give your expense report to **her**.

The board **members** can only blame **themselves** for these problems.

Our **company** has opened stores in bordering states; however, **it** has been unable to show any profit from these new operations.

reference to a noun named previously in the sentence (relative pronoun)
Please order a copy of the **book** about World War II **that** Sean recommended.

Courtney interviewed two **students** from Australia **who** are interested in our accounting program.

substitute for an unspecific person or thing (indefinite pronoun)
Do you know **anyone** who might be interested in this employment opportunity?

Neither of these applicants has responded to our invitation for an interview.

personal pronoun used as an adjective
His desktop computer has a CD-RW drive and a DVD drive.

The briefcase found in the elevator is **hers**.

1–16 Personal Pronouns

a. Personal pronouns may be expressed in three ways; these ways are referred to as *case forms*. The three case forms for personal pronouns are the *subjective*, the *objective*, and the *possessive*.

b. The subjective-case[9] personal pronouns follow:

I	she	we	who
he	you	they	it

[9] The subjective case is also known as the *nominative case*.

A subjective-case pronoun is used as follows:

(1) For the subject of a verb
(2) For the complement of a *being* verb (*am, is, are, was, were, be, been*)
(3) After the infinitive *to be* when this verb does not have a subject (a noun or pronoun) directly preceding it

subject of a verb
She *has been promoted* three times within the past four years.

They *will arrive* from Montreal at 10 a.m. on Wednesday and *return* the following Wednesday.

Chandler, Aaron, and **I** *have been appointed* to the committee.

complement of a* being *verb
The person who answered the telephone *was* not **I**.

"This *is* **she**" or "This *is* **he**" is the appropriate response when a telephone caller asks for you by name.

The visitors could have *been* **they**.

infinitive* to be *without a subject
Taylor is often thought *to be* **I**.

The doctor on duty during your shift is certain *to be* **he**.

c. The objective-case personal pronouns follow:

me	her	us	whom
him	you	them	it

Use an objective-case pronoun when the pronoun is one of the following:[10]

(1) The direct or indirect object of a verb
(2) The object of a preposition
(3) The subject of any infinitive
(4) The object of the infinitive *to be* when it has a subject
(5) The object of any infinitive except *to be* when it does not have a subject

direct object of a verb
Mr. Shaw *will meet* **her** at the airport tomorrow.

Please *ask* **him** to supply this missing information from the application.

Ms. Orsini *asked* Kelly and **me** to serve as members of the selection committee.

---

[10] Use a shortcut to determine whether a subjective-case pronoun or an objective-case pronoun is correct. First apply the three rules related to the subjective-case pronoun (Section 1–16b). If none of these rules apply, then an objective-case pronoun is correct.

indirect object of a verb

Please *fax* **me** *a receipt* as soon as you receive the payment.

We *will send* Meredith or **him** *these copies* before Friday.

object of a preposition

When was the shipment sent *to* **us**?

Two of the customers asked *for* **her**.

Between **you** and **me**, I do not believe the project will be completed by May 1.

subject of an infinitive

Our department manager expects **her** *to complete* the audit by June 30.

We thought **them** *to be* somewhat overconfident about their being awarded the contract.

object of* to be *with a subject

I wanted the **winner** *to be* **her**.

Ms. Stevenson thought **the Johnsons** *to be* **us**.

They expected **Maria** *to be* **me**.

***object of an infinitive other than* to be**

Our office will not be able *to mail* **them** until Monday.

We asked Adrian *to help* **us** with the decorations for the banquet.

d. The possessive-case personal pronouns follow:

my	mine	their	theirs
his, her	his, hers	its	its
your	yours	whose	
our	ours		

All possessive-case pronoun forms are written without apostrophes. They should not be confused with contractions.

possessive pronouns—no apostrophes

Its wrapping had been torn before the package was delivered.

Is this **your** signature on the check?

The idea to sell our products online was **theirs**.

Whose cell phone was left in the conference room?

contractions—apostrophes

It's (It is) still raining very heavily here on the West Coast.

Let us know if **you're** (you are) going to the convention.

If **there's** (there is) a logical reason for the delay, please inform the passengers.

Who's (Who is) in charge of ordering supplies for our copier?

e. Use the possessive case immediately before a gerund (verb + *ing* used as a noun).

His leaving the company so suddenly was quite a surprise.

We would appreciate **your responding** to our invitation by Friday, March 18.

Her texting while driving was cited as the cause of the accident.

f. A pronoun after *than* or *as* may be expressed in either the subjective or objective case, depending on whether the pronoun is the subject or object of the stated or implied verb.

subjective case
Are you as concerned about our manager's decision as **I am**? (Stated verb *am*.)

He has been with the company two years longer than **I**. (Implied verb *have*.)

objective case
Our supervisor compliments Brandon more than he compliments **me**. (Stated subject and verb *he compliments*.)

She works for Mr. Reece more often than **me**. (Implied subject, verb, and preposition *she works for*; . . . than *she works for* me.)

g. Pronouns used in apposition take the same case as those nouns or pronouns with which they are in apposition.

We, Dylan and **I**, have been subpoenaed for jury duty.

Corey told Karen to submit her expenses to one of our accounting **supervisors**, Jesse or **me**.

h. Pronouns followed by an identifying noun (such as *we employees* or *us employees*) are treated as if the noun were not there in determining the proper case form. Therefore, mentally omit the noun in such pronoun-noun combinations (restrictive appositives) to select the correct form.

subjective case
Within the next week, **we ~~employees~~** must decide whether we will move with the company to Columbus. (Subject of verb phrase *must decide*.)

The persons filing the petition in this case are **we ~~students~~**. (Complement of *being* verb *are*.)

objective case
Dalton Industries has offered **us ~~employees~~** the opportunity to purchase company stock at prices below the market value. (Indirect object of verb *offered*.)

None of **us ~~students~~** have received enrollment information for next semester. (Object of preposition *of.*)

i. **Pronouns ending in *self* or *selves* emphasize or reflect a noun or pronoun used previously. They should not be used in place of objective-case pronouns.**

emphasizes previous noun or pronoun
Wendy herself was not pleased with the results of the advertising campaign.

He himself could not justify his exorbitant budget request.

reflects a previous noun or pronoun
Darren addressed the envelope to **himself**.

The council members voted **themselves** an annual salary increase of $6,000 each.

objective case pronoun used correctly
Some of these packages are for **me**. (Not *Some of these packages are for* myself.)

Alexandra was disappointed that the cosmetic samples were not for **her**. (Not *Alexandra was disappointed that the cosmetic samples were not for* herself.)

j. **Rules for using the pronouns *who, whoever, whom, whomever,* and *whose* are the same as those that apply to the other personal pronouns. *Who* and *whoever* are used for the subjective case; *whom* and *whomever,* for the objective case; and *whose,* for the possessive case.**

To decide easily whether to use *who* or *whom,* use the following procedure. See how the example sentence leads to the correct choice.

(1) Identify the sentence that contains the who?/whom? clause; for example, John is the person who/whom I believe Ms. Wilkes will hire.
(2) Isolate the clause in which the pronoun appears: *who/whom I believe Ms. Wilkes will hire.*
(3) Eliminate any extra clauses: *I believe.* The *who/whom* clause is now *who/whom Ms. Wilkes will hire.*
(4) Place the clause in subject-verb order if it does not already appear so: *Ms. Wilkes will hire who/whom.*
(5) Mentally substitute *he* for *who* and *him* for *whom* to help you distinguish between the subjective and objective cases: *Ms. Wilkes will hire him.*
(6) Use *whom*, the correct choice for the example sentence: *John is the person whom I believe Ms. Wilkes will hire.*

***subjective case*—who *or* whoever**

Who removed this accounting software from our network? (Subject of verb—*[he]* removed.)

Please give me a list of **who** will be seated at the head table. (Subject of verb—*[he]* will be seated.)

I do not know **who** the caller may have been. (Place the clause in subject-verb order.) (Complement of *being* verb *been*—the caller may have been *[he]*.)

Please let me know **who** the winner is. (Place the clause in subject-verb order.) (Complement of *being* verb *is*—the winner is *[he]*.)

Who do you think will be selected for the position? (Omit extra clause *do you think*.) (Subject of verb phrase—*[he]* will be selected.)

The mayor must approve the appointment of **whoever** is nominated. (Subject of verb phrase—*[he]* is nominated.)

The vice president will allow you to select **whoever** you think is qualified. (Omit extra clause *you think*.) (Subject of verb—*[he]* is qualified.)

***objective case*—whom *or* whomever**

Whom did Mr. Chin recommend for promotion? (Place clause in subject-verb order.) (Direct object—Mr. Chin did recommend *[him]*.)

He is a person with **whom** we have had business dealings for more than 25 years. (Place clause in subject-verb order.) (Object of preposition—we have had business dealings with *[him]*.)

Ask Mr. Worley **whom** he selected to replace José. (Place clause in subject-verb order.) (Direct object—he selected *[him]*.)

We do not know to **whom** we should award the contract. (Place clause in subject-verb order.) (Object of a preposition—we should award the contract to *[him]*.)

Whom do you think the Detroit Spitfires will hire as the team's new manager? (Omit extra clause *do you think*.) (Place clause in subject-verb order.) (Direct object—the Detroit Spitfires will hire *[him]*.)

Our manager will need to interview **whomever** you recommend before we can offer that person a contract. (Place clause in subject-verb order.) (Direct object—you recommend *[him]*.)

The board will allow you to select **whomever** you wish for the internship program. (Place clause in subject-verb order.) (Object of an infinitive—you wish to select *[him]*.)

***possessive case*—whose**

Whose sales reports have not yet been submitted to the home office?

We do not know **whose** recommendations will be adopted to implement our new cost-savings plan.

k. Pronouns must agree in gender and number with any nouns or other pronouns they represent.[11]

A **customer** must first register **his** or **her** complaint with an assistant manager.

Both **Ms. Burke** and **Mr. Snow** placed **their** orders yesterday.

The **puppy** caught **its** tail in the door.

The **company** will conduct **its** annual inventory next week.

1–17 Relative Pronouns

a. Relative pronouns introduce dependent clauses that refer back (relate) to a noun in the main clause of the sentence. Relative pronoun forms are *who, whom, that,* and *which*.

b. Use *who* and *whom* to refer to a person or persons. To distinguish between *who* and *whom*, apply the procedures outlined in Section 1–16j.

***subjective case*—who**

Mr. Vasquez is the *applicant* **who** was selected for the position. (Refers back to *applicant*.) (Subject of verb—*[he]* was selected.)

The *person* **who** served as chair of the finance committee was Ms. Bell. (Refers back to *person*.) (Subject of verb—*[she]* served.)

Cassidy is the *sales representative* **who** I believe is the best candidate to replace Leslie as district sales manager. (Refers back to *sales representative*.) (Omit extra clause *I believe*.) (Subject of verb—*[she]* is the best candidate.)

Next month our *advertising manager*, **who** has held this position for more than 20 years, will retire. (Refers back to *advertising manager*.) (Subject of verb—*[he]* has held.)

***objective case*—whom**

Mr. Vasquez is the *applicant* **whom** Ms. Jones selected for the position. (Refers back to *applicant*.) (Direct object of verb—Ms. Jones selected *[him]*.)

Our new *college president*, **whom** the board appointed just yesterday, has already called a meeting of campus administrators. (Refers back to *president*.) (Direct object of verb—the board appointed *[him]*.)

You are a *person* **whom** I know Ms. Ferraro would be pleased to hire. (Refers back to *person*.) (Omit extra clause *I know*.) (Object of infinitive—Ms. Ferraro would be pleased to hire *[him]*.)

c. Use *that* or *which* to introduce a dependent clause that refers back to a place, thing, or idea in the main clause—any noun that does not

[11] Refer to Section 1–14 for additional information on principles of agreement.

represent a person. Careful writers use *that* to introduce restrictive dependent clauses (essential to the meaning) and *which* to introduce nonrestrictive dependent clauses (additional information).

(1) Restrictive dependent clauses provide essential ideas that refine the information contained in the main clause; that is, they specify *which one*.

(2) Nonrestrictive dependent clauses provide extra information that does not alter the substance of the main clause; in other words, the information is not needed to identify *which one*. Nonrestrictive clauses are separated from the main clause with a comma or a pair of commas.

restrictive dependent clause requiring **that**

Include on the order form the quantity and catalog number of each *item* **that** you order. (Refers back to *item*.) (Specifies only items that are ordered.)

The *prices* **that** are listed in this sale brochure are guaranteed only until June 30. (Refers back to *prices*.) (Specifies which prices—the ones listed in this sale brochure.)

nonrestrictive dependent clause requiring **which**

The Model No. 431 noise-canceling microphone, **which** you ordered last week, has been replaced by the Model No. 642. (Refers back to *microphone*.) (Clause not needed to identify which microphone—provides extra idea.)

Please credit our account for the three Toshiba laptop computers, **which** were charged to our account in error. (Refers back to *computers*.) (Clause not needed to identify which computers—provides additional information.)

1–18 Indefinite Pronouns

a. Indefinite pronouns do not represent a specific person, place, or thing.

b. Simple indefinite pronouns include the following words used as subjects or objects:

each	every	either
neither	all	another
any	both	few
many	more	most
none	one	other
several	some	

c. **Compound indefinite pronouns end with *-body, -one,* or *-thing*.**

____body	____one	____thing
anybody	anyone	anything
everybody	everyone	everything
nobody	no one	nothing
somebody	someone	something

d. **Simple indefinite pronouns used as subjects may require singular or plural verbs. Compound indefinite pronouns used as subjects require singular verbs.**

simple indefinite pronoun as subject
Each of our patients **has been** informed of our pending relocation.

Neither of the elevators **is** large enough to transport this conference table.

Few of the visitors to Las Vegas **have used** our restaurant coupons.

None of the construction projects **are scheduled** for completion before early next year.

compound indefinite pronoun as subject
Nearly **everybody was** late for the meeting because of the unexpected snowstorm.

Everything on these invoices **has been** received.

e. **Any other pronouns representing an indefinite pronoun must agree in number and gender with the indefinite pronoun.**

Neither of the winners has claimed **his** or **her** prize.

Would **everyone** please return **his** or **her** evaluation form by May 15.

Adjectives

1–19 Adjectives Modify Nouns

Adjectives modify nouns or pronouns. They answer such questions as *what kind*? *how many*? *which one*?

what kind?

cement floor	**laptop** computers	**noise-canceling** microphone

how many?

four orders	**several** months	**three dozen** eggs

which one?

your answer	**those** flight attendants	**Preston's** report

1–20 Use of the Articles *A* and *An*

Use the article *a* before a word that begins with a consonant sound, a long *u* sound, or an *h* that is pronounced. Use *an* before words that begin with a pronounced vowel sound (except long *u*) or before words that begin with a silent *h*.

***use of* a**

a newspaper	a uniform	a hillside
a restaurant	a union	a history class
a large undertaking	a usual occurrence	a hidden entry

***use of* an**

an answer	an unusual request	an hour
an opportunity	an upper floor	an heir
an effective solution	an ultimate goal	an honest person

1–21 Adjective Comparison

a. **Adjectives may be used to compare two or more nouns or pronouns. Use the comparative form (*-er* or *more, less*) to compare two persons or things and the superlative form (*-est* or *most, least*) to compare three or more.**

b. **Most one-syllable adjectives ending in *e* add *r* for the comparative and *st* for the superlative.**

Most one-syllable adjectives ending in consonants add *er* for the comparative and *est* for the superlative, but some double the final consonant before adding *er* or *est.*[12]

***most one-syllable adjectives ending in* e**

simple	*comparative*	*superlative*
nice	nicer	nicest
fine	finer	finest
tame	tamer	tamest

His television set has a **large** screen.

His television set has a **larger** screen than mine.

His television set has the **largest** screen offered for sale in today's market.

---

[12] Single-syllable adjectives that end in *e* or that double the final consonant before adding *er* (comparative form) or *est* (superlative form) are considered irregular. These irregular forms are shown in the dictionary after the simple form.

most one-syllable adjectives ending in a consonant

simple	*comparative*	*superlative*
sweet	sweeter	sweetest
mild	milder	mildest
proud	prouder	proudest

Do you have an explanation for this month's **high** travel expenses?

Why are this month's travel expenses so much **higher** than last month's?

This month's travel expenses are the **highest** we have experienced this year.

some one-syllable adjectives ending in a consonant

simple	*comparative*	*superlative*
sad	sadder	saddest
trim	trimmer	trimmest
drab	drabber	drabbest

Do you expect to make a **big** profit on this stock?

Which of these stocks do you think will yield a **bigger** profit?

Mr. Doyle's **biggest** profit on investments this year came from pharmaceutical stocks.

c. Most two-syllable adjectives and all adjectives containing three or more syllables use *more* or *less* and *most* or *least* to construct comparative and superlative forms.

Forms for those two-syllable adjectives that do not follow this pattern are shown in the dictionary after their simple form. These words include *costly, friendly, happy, healthy, heavy, kindly, merry, lonely, lovely, pretty*—all ending in *y*. For two-syllable adjectives ending in *y*, change the *y* to *i* and add *er* for the comparative form or *est* for the superlative form.

***two-syllable adjectives with* more, most, less, *or* least**

simple	*comparative*	*superlative*
useful	more useful	most useful
	less useful	least useful
suitable	more suitable	most suitable
	less suitable	least suitable

Our receptionist maintains a **pleasant** demeanor as she greets each client, regardless of how congested our office might be.

Greg has a **more pleasant (less pleasant)** manner than Tom in dealing with irate customers.

Andrea is the **most pleasant** (**least pleasant**) assistant with whom I have ever worked.

***two-syllable adjectives ending in* y**

simple	*comparative*	*superlative*
friendly	friendlier	friendliest
	less friendly	least friendly
lonely	lonelier	loneliest
	less lonely	least lonely

Our state purchased a **costly** accounting system last year.

Our state's highway program is **costlier** (**less costly**) than its conservation program.

Our state's welfare program is the **costliest** (**least costly**) one in the nation.

***three-syllable adjectives with* more, most, less, *or* least**

simple	*comparative*	*superlative*
comprehensive	more comprehensive	most comprehensive
	less comprehensive	least comprehensive
practical	more practical	most practical
	less practical	least practical

Harper's Bazaar showcases **expensive** women's clothing.

This color laser printer is **more expensive** (**less expensive**) than the one offered by Best Buy Electronics.

The Evans line is the **most expensive** (**least expensive**) grade of linens we carry.

d. Irregular forms for adjective comparison appear in the dictionary. They are listed after the simple forms. A list of commonly used irregular adjective forms follows:

simple	*comparative*	*superlative*
bad, ill	worse	worst
good, well	better	best
far	farther, further	farthest, furthest
little	littler, less	littlest, least
many, much	more	most

e. Use *other* or *else* when comparing one person or object with the other members of the group to which it belongs.

Our London office earns more revenue than any of our **other** international branch offices. (Not *any of our international branch offices.*)

Cody is more diligent than anyone **else** in the class. (Not *anyone in the class.*)

f. **Some adjectives cannot be compared in the regular sense because they are absolute. A partial list of such adjectives follows:**

alive	finished	round
complete	full	straight
dead	perfect	unique

Absolute adjectives may show comparison by use of the forms *more nearly* or *most nearly*.

The water cooler in the employees' lounge is **full**.

The water cooler in your office is **more nearly full** (not *fuller*) than the one in ours.

The water cooler in the Office of Human Resources is the **most nearly full** (not *fullest*) one on this floor.

The police report is **accurate**.

The *Daily News*' report of the accident was **more nearly accurate** (not *more accurate*) than the one appearing in the *Tribune*.

The *Daily News*' report of the accident was the **most nearly accurate** (not *most accurate*) one that appeared in the media.

1–22 Independent Adjectives[13]

When two or more adjectives appearing before a noun modify the noun independently, separate these adjectives with commas.

His **direct, practical** approach to solving problems has created a high degree of respect for him among his staff.

We returned that **boring, poorly written** manuscript to its author last week.

Donna-Mae handled the problem in a **sure, calm, decisive** manner.

1–23 Adjectives with Linking Verbs

Use adjectives, not adverbs, after linking (nonaction) verbs. Common linking verbs include *feel, look, smell, sound,* and *taste*.

I **feel bad** that you did not receive this well-deserved promotion. (Not *badly*.)

Cakes from Federico's Bakery always **taste delicious**. (Not *deliciously*.)

The offices **smelled terrible** after the reception room fire. (Not *terribly*.)

---

[13] See Section 2–8 for a detailed explanation of the use of the comma with independent adjectives.

1–24 Compound Adjectives[14]

a. **Adjectives containing two or more words that are shown hyphenated in the dictionary are known as *permanent compounds.*[15] These words are always hyphenated when they are used as adjectives.**

Your **up-to-date** files have been very helpful in compiling this data.

My present job is only **part-time**, but I will begin looking for a **full-time** job in September.

As one of the oldest players in the league, Steve doesn't seem to know when he is **well-off**.

b. **When two or more words appearing before a noun function as a single-thought modifier, place hyphens between the words even though these words do not appear hyphenated in the dictionary. These compound adjectives are *temporary compounds* and are hyphenated only when they appear before the noun or pronoun they modify.**

temporary compound adjective before the modified noun
Upon reading your **well-documented** report, the city council voted to establish a new community center.

Very little of the **high-priced** merchandise was sold during our clearance sale.

Do not exceed the **65-mile-an-hour** speed limit.

You may advertise this opening as a **$60,000-a-year** position.

temporary compound adjective following the modified noun
Your report is certainly **well documented**.

This merchandise is too **high priced** for our store.

The speed limit on this freeway is **65 miles an hour**.

Our manager's salary is at least **$60,000 a year**.

Adverbs

1–25 Functions and Forms of Adverbs

Adverbs modify verbs, adjectives, or other adverbs. They answer such questions as *when? where? why? how? to what degree?*

---

[14] See Section 5–2 for detailed rules regarding the formation of compound adjectives.

[15] All hyphenations for compound adjectives in this reference manual are based on those shown in Merriam-Webster, Incorporated. (2014). *Merriam-Webster's Collegiate Dictionary* (11th ed.). Springfield, MA: Merriam-Webster, Incorporated. For a complete, up-to-date online resource, visit Merriam-Webster at http://www.m-w.com. Individuals who have purchased *Merriam-Webster's Collegiate Dictionary*, 11th ed., may obtain a digital download and also register for a free one-year subscription to the online versions of multiple Merriam-Webster dictionaries.

a. Most adverbs end in *ly*.

accidentally	daily	finally
carefully	definitely	steadily
cautiously	diligently	usually

b. Some adverbs may either end in *ly* or take the adjective form of the word.[16]

Please drive **slowly** (or **slow**) on this icy road.

Your order will be processed as **quickly** (or **quick**) as possible.

You may call **directly** (or **direct**) to our home office on this line.

c. Other adverbs do not take an *ly* form. Such adverbs include the following:

again	late	not	there
almost	never	now	very
here	no	soon	well

1–26 Adverb Comparison

a. One-syllable adverbs and some two-syllable adverbs are compared by adding *er* or *est*. For comparisons between two items, use *er;* for comparisons among more than two items, use *est*.[17]

comparison of two

You live **closer** to the college than I.

My assistant left **earlier** than I.

comparison of more than two

Of all the students in the study group, you live **closest** to the college.

Who is scheduled to arrive the **earliest**—Kirby, Bryce, or Morgan?

b. Most adverbs containing two syllables and all adverbs containing more than two syllables form the comparison by adding *more* or *most* (or *less* or *least*) to the positive form. Use *more* (or *less*) in comparing two items and *most* (or *least*) in comparing more than two items.

comparison of two

The Supra X model rides **more smoothly** than the Fortura.

Please drive **more carefully** to avoid another citation.

Surf soap is **less widely** used on the East Coast than in the South.

---

[16] For adverbs that may end in *ly* or just take the adjective form, both forms are shown in the dictionary.

[17] Two-syllable adverbs that show comparison by adding *er* or *est* are considered irregular. Therefore, these forms are shown in the dictionary following the simple form.

comparison of more than two
Denver has been mentioned **most often** as the likely site for our next convention.

This class is among the **most unusually conducted** ones I have ever taken.

Surf soap is the **least widely** used of all the major brands.

1–27 Adverb Placement

a. Place adverbs or adverbial phrases as closely as possible to the words they modify. The misplacement of an adverb or a dangling adverbial (participial) phrase can cause confusion, result in an awkward-sounding sentence, or change the meaning of a sentence.

changed meaning
Only Tyler was invited to attend the leadership training seminar.

Tyler was invited to attend **only** the leadership training seminar.

awkward construction
Our costs have **nearly** risen 20 percent this year. (Awkward)

Our costs have risen **nearly** 20 percent this year. (Correct)

We have the opportunity **rarely** to hire such a creative graphic artist. (Awkward)

We **rarely** have the opportunity to hire such a creative graphic artist. (Correct)

confused meaning
Hoping to attract more customers during the holiday season, many items were placed on sale. (Are the items hoping to attract more customers? Confused meaning.)

Hoping to attract more customers during the holiday season, the manager placed many items on sale. (Tells who was hoping to attract more customers.)

Working the late shift last week, the restaurant seemed more crowded than usual. (Was the restaurant working the late shift? Confused meaning.)

Working the late shift last week, Alexis thought the restaurant seemed more crowded than usual. (Tells who was working the late shift last week.)

I noticed a significant discrepancy in the income figures looking through the spreadsheet. (Were figures looking through the spreadsheet? Confusing.)

Looking through the spreadsheet, I noticed a significant discrepancy in the income figures. (The person doing the looking is now clear.)

b. Avoid splitting an infinitive with an adverb; place the adverb after the infinitive.

We will need **to evaluate carefully** all the architects who have bid on this project. (Avoid *to carefully evaluate*.)

If you wish **to discuss** this possibility **further**, please call me. (Avoid *to further discuss*.)

1–28 Adverbs vs. Adjectives

Use an adverb after a verb that shows action; use an adjective, however, after a nonaction (or linking) verb.

Verbs relating to the senses (*feel, look, smell*) may function as nonaction verbs. In some cases you may test such occurrences by substituting a form of *to be* (*am, is, are, was, were*). If the sentence reads smoothly, use the adjective form for any descriptive word that modifies the verb.

action verb
You **did well** on your six-month performance evaluation.

The pedestrian **crossed** the street **cautiously**.

Most of the council members **opposed bitterly** the rezoning of this residential area.

The professional soccer team **was beaten badly** in yesterday's game.

nonaction or linking verb
If we do not brew fresh coffee every two hours, it begins to **taste bitter**. (. . . is bitter.)

The employees' lounge **smells terrible**. (. . . is terrible.)

Paul **looked angry** after he received the news. (. . . was angry . . . .)

I **feel bad** about Mr. Johnson's predicament.

The entrée at the Sunday evening banquet **was delicious**.

1–29 Double Negatives

Use only one negative word or limiting adverb to express a single idea.

I did **not** receive **anything** (not *nothing*) from our insurance agent. (*Or* I have received **nothing** from our insurance agent.)

Do **not** discuss the pending merger with **anybody** (not *nobody*). (*Or* Discuss the pending merger with **nobody**.)

I **can** (not *can't* or *cannot*) **scarcely** believe that our college president would make such a statement.

We **were** (not *weren't* or *were not*) **hardly** in the office when Ms. Kawamura gave us the good news.

He **had** (not *hadn't* or *had not*) **barely** finished computing the results when the Board of Directors requested him to report his findings.

Prepositions

1–30 Prepositions as Connectors

a. Prepositions link descriptive words to other words or ideas in a sentence. The most commonly used prepositions are *of* and *for*. Occasionally used ones are *about, during, except,* and *but* (meaning *except*). Other commonly used prepositions, those listed below, can easily be identified by picturing what an airplane can do in relation to clouds: the airplane can fly ________ the clouds.

above	down	over
after	from	through
alongside	in	to
among	inside	toward
around	into	under
at	near	up
before	off	upon
behind	on	with
below	opposite	within
between	outside	without

b. Prepositions begin a phrase that ends with a noun or a pronoun. This phrase is related to another word in the sentence—it describes, limits, or modifies the word in some way by clarifying *who, what, when, where, how, why, which one,* or *to what degree*.

Everyone **in your class** passed the state nursing examination. (*In your class* is related to *everyone*—specifies who.)

Our staff **of accountants** is available to assist you. (*Of accountants* is related to *staff*—specifies what.)

When you need plumbing service, you may call us **at any time**—day or night. (*At any time* is related to *call*—specifies when.)

You may park your car **behind the building**. (*Behind the building* is related to *park*—specifies where.)

Through the architect's efforts, we obtained the city building permits to begin the project. (*Through the architect's efforts* is related to *obtained*—specifies how.)

1–31 Prepositional Phrases

In determining subject-verb agreement, generally ignore any prepositional phrases that separate the subject and the verb. (See Section 1–14l for subject-verb agreement principles related to prepositional

phrases appearing before relative pronoun clauses [clauses beginning with *who* or *that*]).

One of your clients **is** waiting in the outer office. (Omit *of your clients* to match "One . . . is.")

A large **quantity** of bathing suits **has** been ordered for the sale. (Omit *of bathing suits* to match "quantity . . . has.")

Our current **supply** of paper goods and linens **was** damaged when the kitchen flooded. (Omit *of paper goods and linens* to match "supply . . . was.")

1–32 *In, Between,* or *Among?*

When a preposition has a single object, use *in*. For two separate objects, use *between;* for three or more objects, use *among*.

***preposition* in**
Did the auditor discover any discrepancies **in** our accountant's report?

The judge noted several discrepancies **in** the defendant's testimony.

***preposition* between**
Between you and me, I believe this stock will split before the end of the year.

There were several discrepancies **between** the two witnesses' reports.

***preposition* among**
Please distribute these printer cartridges **among** the various departments on the third floor.

Among themselves the board members had consented previously to withdraw their bid to acquire this software company.

1–33 Prepositions Used with Certain Words

Certain words require particular prepositions, depending upon the meaning to be conveyed. Other words often acquire prepositions incorrectly. A list of commonly used correct combinations follows:

Agree **on** or **upon** (mutual ideas or considerations—to reach an understanding)

Agree **to** (undertake an action)

Agree **with** (a person or his or her idea)

All **of** (Use *of* when followed by a pronoun; omit *of* when followed by a noun. *All of us . . . . All the people . . . .*)

Angry **about** (a situation or condition)

Angry **at** (things)

Angry **with** (a person or a group of persons)

Both **of** (Use *of* when followed by a pronoun; omit *of* when followed by a noun. *Both of them . . . . Both the managers . . . .*)

Buy **from** (Not *off* or *off of*)

Compare **to** (Use to show a likeness.)

Compare **with** (Use to look for differences as well as similarities.)

Comply or compliance **with** (Not *to*)

Conform **to** (To act in accordance with prevailing standards)

Conform **with** (To be similar or in agreement)

Convenient **to** (a location)

Convenient **for** (a person)

Correspond **with** (a person—by writing)

Correspond **to** (a thing)

Different **from** (Not *than*)

Discrepancy **in** (one thing)

Discrepancy **between** (two things)

Discrepancy **among** (three or more things)

From (a person) (Not *off* a person)

Help (doing something) (He could not *help* laughing at . . . .) (Not *help from*)

Identical **with** (Not *to*)

Inside (Not *inside of*)

Off (a thing) (Not *off of*)

Opposite (Not *opposite to* or *opposite of*)

Outside (Not *outside of*)

Plan **to** (Not *plan on*)

Retroactive **to** (Not *retroactive from*)

Take **off** (a thing)

Take **from** (a person)

Conjunctions

Conjunctions join words or groups of words within a sentence. While some conjunctions join equal ideas, others join contrasting ideas or introduce dependent clauses.

1–34 Coordinating Conjunctions

a. The most commonly occurring coordinating conjunctions—*and, but, or,* and *nor*—are used to join like or equal ideas within a sentence. These ideas may be words, phrases, or clauses.

words
Please place a copy of the **proposal** *and* the **contract** in each client's file.

You may obtain additional information from **Mr. Parr**, **Ms. Dow**, *or* **me**.

phrases
Please post these notices **on all bulletin boards** *and* **in student gathering places** throughout the campus.

Ms. Ross has agreed to **edit the manuscript** *and* **follow it through all the production stages**.

clauses
If you accept our offer, **we will sign a guarantee of completion by May 1** *and* **you will be protected against any losses until that date**.

Our advertising funds for this year have been spent, *but* **we are interested in considering your proposal for next year's budget**.

b. Because coordinating conjunctions join equal ideas, the ideas they join must be expressed in the same way; that is, they must have *parallel structure*. Parallel structure requires that the connected ideas have the same format. For example, if the first idea begins with a noun or pronoun, so must any others. If the first idea begins with an infinitive, then all others must begin with an infinitive. Be sure to match each idea—gerund with gerund, verb with verb, prepositional phrase with prepositional phrase, and so forth.

parallel structure with gerunds
You may obtain your free trial subscription by **calling** our toll-free number *or* **visiting** our Web site.

We would appreciate your **making** this payment at your local Department of Motor Vehicles office by May 1 *and* **sending** us a copy of the receipt issued at the time of payment.

parallel structure with verb phrases (past participles)
The contractor has **leveled** the site *and* **poured** the foundation.

We have **notified** our delinquent customers of their status, **requested** immediate payment of all overdue amounts, *and* **halted** any charge orders in progress.

parallel structure with clauses (subject and verb)
As soon as we receive your loan approval, **the bank will release** the money *and* **we will open** an escrow account.

Our local **chamber of commerce has endorsed** this project, *but* **chambers of commerce** in surrounding cities **are opposed** to it.

1–35 Conjunctions Used in Pairs

a. Use *either . . . or* for positive statements; use *neither . . . nor* for negative statements. The same grammatical construction should be used after each part.

***positive statements,* either . . . or**
Either Ms. Saunders **or** Mr. Ramirez will inspect the property.

Be sure to specify a room with **either** an ocean view **or** a mountain view when you make your hotel reservations.

***negative statements,* neither . . . nor**
Certified Car Rental has **neither** an Explorer **nor** a Suburban available for rent next week.

Neither the patient's husband **nor** her children have been notified about the apparent success of the surgery.

b. Use the same grammatical construction after each part of the conjunctive pair *not only . . . but also.*

Our company manufactures **not only** commercial restaurant appliances **but also** household kitchen appliances. (Not *Our company* not only *manufactures commercial restaurant appliances* but also *household kitchen appliances.*)

Jeremy is well liked by **not only** his coworkers and our customers **but also** his supervisors. (Not *Jeremy is* not only *well liked by his coworkers and our customers* but also *his supervisors.*)

c. In comparisons use *as . . . as* for positive ideas and *so . . . as* for negative ideas.

***positive ideas,* as . . . as**
Our Model 1028A cell phone has become **as** popular **as** our Model 1218A.

I believe that Ms. Saito's understudy is **as** talented **as** she.

***negative ideas,* so . . . as**
Our Model 1028A cell phone is not **so** popular **as** our Model 1218A.

Watermelons are not **so** expensive **as** they were last year.

1–36 Subordinating Conjunctions

Words such as *if, as, when, since,* and *because* (subordinating conjunctions) may be used to introduce word groups (dependent clauses). A partial list of subordinating conjunctions follows:

if	because	while
as	since	before
when	although	after

a. When a subordinating conjunction with its corresponding clause introduces a sentence, place a comma after the introductory clause.

If you wish any additional information, please e-mail me or call me at (800) 555–3782.

Before you sign the contract, you should speak with some of All-State Fencing's former clients.

b. When a subordinating conjunction with its corresponding clause follows a main clause, separate the two clauses with a comma only if the subordinating conjunction introduces an additional or a nonessential (nonrestrictive) idea.

no comma separating clauses—essential (restrictive) idea
We will ship the porcelain figurines **as soon as we receive authorization from your credit card company**.

You should verify this information **before you purchase these bonds**.

comma separating clauses—additional (nonrestrictive) idea
We will conduct our annual inventory on January 15, **after the store closes at 6 p.m.**

My clients have agreed to settle this matter out of court, **although I advised them against doing so**.

1–37 *As* vs. *Like*

***As* is a conjunction and is used when the construction following it is a clause (a word group containing a subject and a verb). *Like* is a preposition and is used when the construction results in a prepositional phrase (begins with a preposition [*like*], contains no verb, and ends with a noun or pronoun).**

as *introducing a clause*
The shipping clerk did not package the order **as** (not *like*) **I had expected he would**.

As (not *like*) **you indicated in your e-mail message**, we cannot expect to show a profit during our first quarter of operation.
We will have these recruitment brochures printed by Friday, just **as** (not *like*) **I promised you.**

like *introducing a prepositional phrase*
We need to hire more qualified agents **like Terry**.

Please order another desk **like the one** you have in your office.

1–38 Conjunction Literacy

Besides distinguishing between the use of *as* and *like* (see Section 1–37), use the following conjunctions accordingly:

But, not *and*, to join and contrast two ideas. (I called Cameron immediately, **but** he was not in his office.)

Because, not *being that*, for a clause of reason. There is no such conjunction as *being that*. (**Because** Dr. Rose will be on vacation, we need to reschedule your appointment.)

Pretend that, not *pretend like*, to introduce a clause. (The company can no longer **pretend that** it does not have a declining market.)

Read that, not *read where*, to introduce a clause. (I **read that** interest rates will continue to remain at this low level for another six months.)

Reason . . . is that, not *reason . . . is because*, to introduce a clause. (The **reason** you have not heard from me sooner **is that** I have been out of the office for the past week.)

Interjections

1-39 Use of Interjections

Interjections express sudden emotion or strong feeling, but they do not contribute substantially to the meaning of the sentence. When used alone, interjections are followed by an exclamation mark. When used within a sentence, they are followed by a comma and the sentence generally ends with an exclamation mark. Examples of interjections used alone follow:

Absolutely not!	Never!	Well!
Ah!	No!	Whew!
Great!	Oh!	Wow!
Indeed not!	Terrific!	Yes!

interjections used alone

Whew! I'm certainly glad the work for this tax period is behind us.

Absolutely not! Only employees with security clearances are permitted in this area.

interjections in sentences

Oh, you can't expect us to have this Web site completed and uploaded by tomorrow!

No, we cannot make any exceptions to this company policy!

Sentences

1-40 Complete Sentences

a. **Simple sentences consist of a single independent clause that contains (1) a subject and (2) a verb or verb phrase. They express only one complete thought that makes sense.**

The **manager** of our Fairfield branch **has been employed** by the company for seven years. (Simple subject, *manager*; verb phrase, *has been employed*; makes sense.)

Partnerships and corporations in this state **are** not eligible for this tax deduction. (Compound subject, *partnerships and corporations*; verb, *are*; makes sense.)

b. Compound sentences may take several forms. One form contains two independent clauses joined by a coordinating conjunction—*and, but, or,* or *nor*. Each independent clause has a subject, has a verb or verb phrase, and makes sense. Each could stand alone as a simple sentence.

***joined by coordinating conjunction* and**
Our regional **representative will be** at Macy's next week, **and she will demonstrate** our new line of Creative Illusions cosmetics. (Simple subjects, *representative* and *she*; verb phrases, *will be* and *will demonstrate*; each makes sense.)

***joined by coordinating conjunction* but**
Neither of our vice presidents **will be** in the office this week, **but** our **general manager** for East Coast operations **is** available to answer your questions. (Subjects, *neither* and *general manager*; verb phrase and verb, *will be* and *is*; each makes sense.)

c. Other forms of compound sentences contain two independent clauses joined by either (1) a semicolon or (2) a semicolon and a transitional expression such as *therefore, however, for example,* or *of course*—usually followed by a comma (see Section 2–19). Each independent clause has a subject, has a verb or verb phrase, and makes sense. It could stand alone as a simple sentence.

joined by a semicolon
The **loan** on your home **has been transferred** to American Home Bank; **you should receive** a payment booklet from this lender within the next week. (Simple subjects, *loan* and *you*; verb phrases, *has been transferred* and *should receive*; each makes sense.)

joined by a semicolon and a transitional expression
Professors and administrators at our college **are covered** under the same retirement program; **therefore**, **administrators**, too, **are** eligible for retirement at age 55. (Compound and simple subjects, *professors and administrators* and *administrators*; verb phrase and verb, *are covered* and *are*; each makes sense.)

d. Complex sentences include an independent clause and a dependent clause, each of which contains both a subject and a verb or verb phrase. The independent clause can stand alone as a complete sentence because it makes sense, but the dependent clause cannot.

Dependent clauses commonly begin with (1) a relative pronoun such as *who, whom, that,* or *which* or (2) a subordinating conjunction

such as *if, as, when, because, since, although,* and *while*. The dependent clause may begin, interrupt, or conclude the sentence.

complex sentence with a relative pronoun clause
Our Web site was designed by Ms. McDonald, **who has been with our company for only seven months.**

None of the people **whom we interviewed** were willing to accept the position at the salary offered.

The software **that you recommended** is no longer available for purchase online.

Tyler is frequently late, **which may be the reason for his dismissal.**

complex sentence with a subordinating conjunction
As soon as we receive your check, we will process your application for admittance.

You may, **if you set up an electronic account**, pay your bills online at our secure Web site.

Our sales have increased substantially **since the new television commercials have aired.**

e. Compound-complex sentences contain two independent clauses and one dependent clause.

We have discontinued our line of Pillow-Touch mattresses **because deliveries from the manufacturer to our customers have been slow**, but we plan to replace this line with one of equal or better quality.

We received more than 30 applications for this opening; but **after I read all the résumés**, I realized that not one of the candidates was qualified for the position.

1–41 Sentence Fragments

a. Confine the use of sentence fragments to informal business writing, and use only sentence fragments that *represent* a complete thought.

And now to the point.

If only I had known!

What a relief!

b. For the most part, use concluding punctuation marks (periods, question marks, and exclamation marks) only after complete sentences. You may, however, in informal writing use these marks after sentence fragments that represent a complete thought (see Section 1–41a for examples).

Not: **In the near future.**

But: **In the near future**, we will introduce several new product lines.

Not: **Although the present contract has expired.**

But: **Although the present contract has expired**, both union members and management are governed by its provisions until a new contract is in place.

Not: **The biggest money-saving event of the year.**

But: Be sure to take advantage of our annual clearance sale, **the biggest money-saving event of the year**.

2

Punctuation

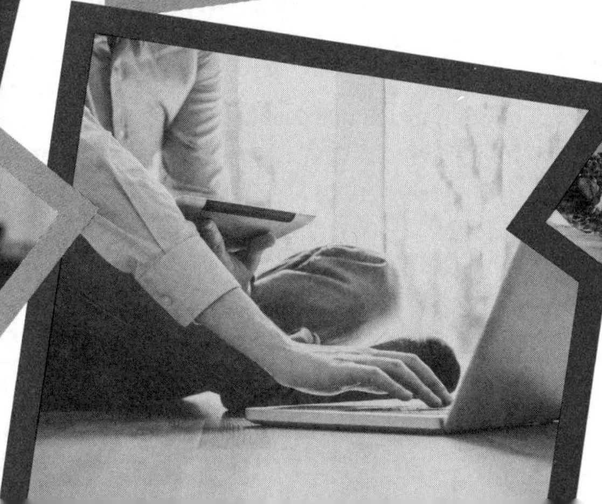

2 Punctuation

Punctuation Solution Finder

Ampersand

Apostrophe

Asterisk

Brackets

Colon

Comma

Punctuation Solution Finder *(continued)*

Dash

Diagonal

Ellipsis

Exclamation Mark

Parentheses

Period

Question Mark

Quotation Marks

Semicolon

Underscore

Comma

2–1 Series

a. Three or more equally ranked parts—words, phrases, or short clauses—within a sentence make up a series. The last part in the series is connected by a conjunction (*and, or,* or *nor*). Place a comma after each part in the series except the last one. Be sure to use a comma before the conjunction (*and, or, nor*).[1]

words

You will be eligible to win an iPhone, an iPad, or a digital camera for answering this online questionnaire.

Google, Bing, and Yahoo! Search are the three most popular Internet search engines.

Next year's budget will permit our company to hire a webmaster, a network administrator, and an additional administrative assistant.

We accept cash only—checks, bank cards, or purchase orders are not accepted for payment.

phrases

Our staff needs additional training in providing customer service, searching the Internet, and preparing PowerPoint presentations.

You may order this fashionable jewelry armoire by calling (800) 413-5555, accessing our Web site at www.furnituremart.com, or visiting one of our retail stores in your city.

Kingston Industries developed several new medications, expanded its territories for greater national coverage, and established three additional branch offices to obtain a greater market share in the pharmaceutical industry.

short clauses

Tyler sold the new vehicle, I approved the contract, and Sheri obtained the financing.

Carter pulled the driver from the burning car, Sylvia called 911, and a passerby halted oncoming traffic.

b. Do not use commas when the parts of a series are all joined by conjunctions.

words

Your monthly phone plan includes voice mail **and** texting **and** call-waiting.

---

[1]Some periodicals and literary writers prefer to omit the comma before the conjunction in a series. For business writing, however, use the comma (commonly referred to as the *Oxford comma*) before the conjunction to promote ease of reading and clarity.

Before boarding the aircraft, you must present a passport **or** a valid driver's license **or** a government-issued picture identification card.

phrases
Citywide Management Services will lease the office space **and** collect the monthly rental payments **and** maintain the premises.

c. **Although generally avoided, *etc.* is sometimes used to indicate "and so forth" at the end of a series. If used, set off *etc.* with commas; do not use the word *and* before *etc.***

within a sentence
Managing your checking account, savings account, loan account**, etc.,** through our online banking service is an available option.

end of a sentence
Our president plans to visit all the branch offices next year—Dallas, Los Angeles, Chicago, London, Paris, Rome**, etc.**

d. **Use a comma before an ampersand (&) in an organizational name only if the organization uses the comma in its official name.**

no comma
Jones, Hill **&** Howard will move into its new offices on May 1.

comma
Our company has retained Duncan, Phelan, Liggett**, &** Phelan to perform an internal audit.

2–2 Parenthetical Expressions

a. **Set off by commas transitional words and expressions that are considered unnecessary for the grammatical completeness of a sentence and that *interrupt its natural flow*. A partial list of such parenthetical expressions follows:**

according to our records	by the way	in effect
accordingly	consequently	in essence
after all	even so	in fact
all in all	finally	in general
all things considered	for example	in my opinion
also	fortunately	in other words
as a matter of fact	furthermore	instead
as a result	hence	in summary
as a rule	however	in the first place
at any rate	in addition	in the meantime
at the same time	incidentally	likewise
besides	in conclusion	moreover
between you and me	indeed	namely

needless to say
nevertheless
no
no doubt
obviously
of course
on the contrary
on the other hand
on the whole
otherwise
perhaps
periodically
secondly
so
that is
then
therefore
thus
too
under the circumstances
unfortunately
what is more
without a doubt
yes

beginning of a sentence
Consequently, the software you ordered will be available for download on July 1.

end of a sentence
Kevin answered all the client's questions, **needless to say**.

within a sentence
A large crowd, **nevertheless,** remained until the football game ended.

b. Sometimes words and phrases used as parenthetical expressions *do not interrupt* the flow of a sentence. In such cases no commas are used with the expression.

beginning of a sentence
Perhaps we should schedule the sales meeting at a hotel that is closer to the airport.

end of a sentence
Our vice president plans to visit potential store locations in Oregon **too**.

within a sentence
She was **indeed** concerned about the error in the financial report.

c. An exclamation at the beginning of a sentence is a parenthetical expression that requires a comma.
Oh, what a surprise to see Ms. Hawkins on the six o'clock news!
Whoa, we did not expect the price of our stock to drop to this level!

d. Set off by commas, dashes, or parentheses enumerations or explanations used as parenthetical expressions *within a sentence*.

(1) Use commas when the enumerated or explanatory information has no internal commas.
(2) Use dashes when the information contains internal commas.
(3) Use parentheses when the information is considered to be incidental to the rest of the sentence.

commas
Only one company, **Empire Plumbing,** bid on the contract.

dashes

This client reported income from several sources—**namely, salary, interest, dividends, and rentals**—on his last income tax return.

parentheses

Our vice president toured several Ohio cities **(Cleveland, Columbus, and Toledo)** to locate a suitable plant site.

e. A parenthetical expression that introduces an enumeration or an explanation *after a complete thought* may be set off by either (1) commas or (2) a semicolon and a comma. If the enumeration or the explanation itself is a complete thought or contains internal commas, use a semicolon and a comma. Otherwise, use commas.

commas

Next week we will receive bids from two major computer manufacturers to equip the company training facility, **namely,** Hewlett-Packard and Dell.

Plan to cut expenses at least two ways during the next quarter, **for example,** by reducing your advertising and your convention budgets.

semicolon and comma

A kitchen remodel generally requires purchasing new appliances; **namely,** a stove, an oven, a dishwasher, and a refrigerator.

f. Short introductory prepositional phrases (two or three words) essential to the meaning of a sentence should not be mistaken for parenthetical expressions. These phrases answer specifically questions such as *when, where, why,* or *how* and are not followed by a comma. See Section 2–10c for further information on punctuating introductory prepositional phrases.

In the future you may wish to make your airline reservations online. (Tells when)

At the conference we met agents from all parts of North America, Europe, and Asia. (Tells where)

For that reason your account has been turned over to an agency for collection. (Tells why)

In this way you will be able to cut your travel costs significantly. (Tells how)

g. Parenthetical expressions that are used as adverbs do not require commas.

However brilliant his work may be, Mr. Andrews will not be promoted until his disposition improves.

Obviously concerned about the drop in sales, our regional manager called a meeting of all sales personnel.

2–3 Direct Address

In written documents use commas to set off the name, title, or affiliation of a person when addressing that person directly. Speaking directly to individuals or groups in written works by using their name requires that you set off their name with commas. For words used in direct address within a sentence, capitalize only (1) proper nouns and (2) personal and professional titles.

beginning of a sentence
Ladies and gentlemen, please consider these investment opportunities.

Ms. Delgado, you have been promoted to vice president of operations.

within a sentence
Will you please, **Mr. Morgan,** send us your check for $237.80 by July 1.

The books you ordered, **Professor,** have been shipped to the college bookstore.

Please examine carefully, **residents of Valley Village,** how this proposal will affect your property value.

You, **fellow golfing enthusiast,** will now be able to cut strokes from your game with this new Leading Edge driver.

end of a sentence
Please place any new applications we receive in my in-box, **Marie**.

You also should be concerned about this issue, **fellow American**.

2–4 Appositives

a. **Appositives are word groups that rename, describe, or explain the nouns or pronouns they follow. These descriptive words usually add extra information and are set off by commas. (See Sections 2–4b and 2–4c for exceptions.)**

within a sentence
All expense claims must be submitted to Ms. LaGrasta-Sundy, **our sales manager,** for approval.

Our vice president, **Mr. Voddon,** will be in Belgium all next week.

end of a sentence
We were advised to contact a claims representative in one of your nearby branch offices, **the Costa Mesa office**.

You have reservations on the 6:45 p.m. flight, **the last flight to Portland today**.

b. Restrictive appositives—word groups that are *needed to identify* a person or thing referred to earlier—are not set off by commas. These descriptive word groups tell *which one* or *which ones* and are essential to the meaning of the sentence.

necessary for identification—tells which one or which ones

The book ***Web Site Design and Development*** has been selected as the textbook for my course.

Your student **Vladimir Paransky** is on the Dean's Honor Roll.

We **board members** are responsible for ensuring that each child in our community receives a quality education.

unnecessary for identification—which one is known

Mark Wooldridge's latest book, ***Digital Photo Journalism*****,** is available through most online bookstores.

Your best student**, Sandra Dubin,** is on the Dean's Honor Roll.

c. Closely related one-word appositives or those forming parts of proper names do not require commas.

closely related one-word appositives

My sister **Anna** has received two promotions within the past year.

I **myself** plan to attend the organizational meeting in Nashville.

State legislation sets forth guidelines in this area for us **teachers**.

proper name

His last two novels dealt with the lives of Alexander **the Great** and Richard **the Lionhearted**.

d. Set off by commas college degrees and abbreviations written after individuals' names; the abbreviations *Jr.* and *Sr.* and Roman numerals, however, are not set off by commas unless the individual chooses to include them.

An abbreviation such as *Inc.* or *Ltd.* that appears after a company name is also set off by commas if the particular company includes them.

commas with college degree or abbreviation after name of individual

Melanie Jadaon**, Doctor of Divinity,** will deliver the invocation at this year's graduation ceremony.

Please schedule an appointment with William J. Clark**, DDS, MD,** to have your wisdom teeth extracted.

The author of *Executive Decision Making* is Dorothy W. Rupert**, PhD**.

Our firm has retained Alan Strozer**, Esq.**[2]

---

[2] The abbreviation *Esq.* may be used after the name of a lawyer. Courtesy or professional titles are not used with the abbreviation *Esq.* since it replaces the courtesy title (*Mr., Mrs.,* or *Ms.*) and the professional title *Attorney-at-Law*.

no commas with Jr., Sr., or a Roman numeral after name of individual
Our sales representative in South Africa is Lowell T. Harrison **Jr.**

Thomas Oliver **Sr.** has requested a copy of the lease agreement.

Donald J. Ellington **III** has just been appointed secretary of state.

commas with abbreviations after company names
Republication, reproduction, or redistribution of Cengage Learning, **Inc.,** content—including by framing or similar means—is prohibited without the prior written consent of Cengage Learning.

One of the largest jobbers on the West Coast is Clothiers, **Ltd.**

no commas with abbreviations after company names
Ricon MED **Inc.** installed the wheelchair lifts in our hospital vans.

Your crystal order from Cash & Co. **Ltd.** will be shipped from Ireland within the next week.

e. **Place in italics words or expressions referred to simply as words or expressions. If an italic font is not available, underscore or place in quotation marks the words or expressions.**

italics
Too many writers use the word ***insure*** when they really mean ***ensure***.

underscored
The word **convenience** is often misspelled in business documents.

quotation marks
The phrase **"Thanking you in advance"** is an outdated expression that should not be used in business documents.

2–5 Dates and Time Zones

a. **Dates containing combinations of weekday, calendar date, and year require commas. Place a comma *after each element* used unless, of course, the last element concludes a sentence. Remember *always* to place a comma *after* the year when a calendar date and year appear within the sentence.**

Commas are not used with a calendar date expressed alone.

calendar date expressed alone
On **June 17** the Internal Revenue Service audited our books.

calendar date and year
On **June 17, 2015,** the Internal Revenue Service audited our books.

weekday and calendar date
On **Wednesday, June 17,** the Internal Revenue Service audited our books.

weekday, calendar date, and year
On **Wednesday, June 17, 2015,** the Internal Revenue Service audited our books.

b. Expressions of month and year are written without commas.

The Internal Revenue Service audited our books in **June 2015**.

In **March 2018** we will release our new line of cleaning products.

c. Set off by commas any time zones used with clock times.

Our flight will leave Denver at 9:35 a.m., **MST,** and arrive in New York City at 3:18 p.m., **EST**.

We received your fax from Japan at 10:40 a.m., **PDT**.

2–6 Addresses

a. Separate by commas parts of an address that are written in sentence form.

name and complete address
Please send the check to Ms. Donna-Mae Villanueva, Manager, Accounting Department, American Paper Company, 2996 Grandview Avenue, NE, Suite 312, Atlanta, Georgia 30305-3245, by May 1.

complete address only
Mr. Buckley may be reached at 625 Hilgard Avenue, Apt. 5, Los Angeles, California 90025.

b. Use commas to set off a state following the name of a city. Likewise, use commas to set off a country following the name of a city. Remember to use the second comma after the state or country name when it appears in the middle of a sentence.

within a sentence
Will you request to be transferred to Nashville, **Tennessee,** next year?

Please e-mail this order to Frankfurt, **Germany,** today.

end of a sentence
This large order is from a new customer in Tacoma, **Washington**.

Is this tour scheduled to visit Sydney, **Australia**?

2–7 Coordinating Conjunctions

a. The words *and, but, or,* and *nor* are coordinating conjunctions. Place a comma before any of these words that separate two independent clauses (complete thought units) in a compound sentence. No comma is used if both clauses are not totally independent and could not stand alone as separate sentences. (See Section 2–18 for use of a semicolon instead of a comma.)

two independent clauses
Eight applicants have accepted our invitation for an interview, **and** we will schedule them next week.

Twenty-four orders still remain unfilled, **but** we will close for the holiday weekend as scheduled.

You may have the interest added to your account, **or** we can send you a check biannually for the interest earned.

We have not purchased anything from this distributor during the past month, **nor** have we requested an extension of our credit line.

You may, Mr. Villano, obtain up-to-date flight schedules from our Web site, **and** you may make your reservations at the same time.

no second independent clause
My staff plans to collect the data by July 15 but cannot guarantee to have the final report completed in time for this month's board meeting.

Our regional manager recognizes the sales potential in the Detroit area and realizes that another sales representative needs to be assigned to this city.

b. In imperative sentences (command statements), the subject *you* is understood. Separate with a comma two independent clauses, whether one or both are in the imperative form.

Ship the printers to me at Three Rivers Occupational Center, **but** send the invoice to the business manager at our district office.

Please call Dr. Malamed's office tomorrow morning, **and** the receptionist will schedule an appointment for you.

c. When a simple adverb, an introductory phrase, or a dependent clause precedes and applies equally to two clauses, the second clause is not a totally separate thought unit. Consequently, no comma is placed before the conjunction.

simple adverb
Please call the doctor's office tomorrow morning and arrange to have your appointment rescheduled for next week. (The adverb *please* refers to both *call* and *arrange*. Therefore, the second clause is not an independent thought unit and a comma is not required.)

introductory phrase
During the next month, several board members will visit selected sites in Kansas City and they will choose one on which to build a warehouse. (*During the next month* applies equally to both clauses. Consequently, the second clause is not an independent thought unit and a comma is not required before *and*.)

Punctuation 2

dependent clauses
As soon as we receive your e-mail response, we will notify our distributor and he will ship your order the next day. (In this case *As soon as we receive your e-mail response* applies to both clauses; therefore, no punctuation mark is needed before *and*.)

When Mr. Anderson arrives, ask him for his new address and give him a copy of our most recent catalog. (Subject *you* is understood in both clauses. *When Mr. Anderson arrives* applies to both clauses. Therefore, the second clause is not an independent thought unit and no punctuation mark is required before *and*.)

d. **Omit the comma in short compound sentences connected by *and*. For simplicity, *short* in these cases may be interpreted to mean "compound sentences containing up to 12 or 13 words."**

Purchase a USB drive **and** use it to back up this directory.

John wrote the letter **and** he signed it for his supervisor.

We received the inquiry yesterday **and** my assistant responded to the client immediately.

2–8 Independent Adjectives

Use commas to separate two or more independent adjectives that modify a noun. No commas are needed, though, when the first adjective modifies the second adjective and the noun as a unit.

To identify independent adjectives (1) reverse the adjectives, (2) read the adjectives independently, and (3) read the sentence with the word *and* between the adjectives. If the sentence makes sense and means the same thing with the adjectives read in these ways, then commas should be placed between them.

independent adjectives
Our dental office has three **well-organized, efficient** assistants.

Enclose a **stamped, addressed** envelope with your inquiry.

Just as business moves forward with **24-hour, 7-day** global operations, so does education with **anytime, anywhere** offerings in online classes.

first adjective modifies second adjective and noun

The posters were lettered in **large <u>bold print</u>**.

She received several **attractive <u>job offers</u>**.

The room contained **old <u>local newspapers</u>** dating back to the 1990s.

Does the press release describe Liza's **dazzling <u>blue evening gown</u>**?

2–9 Introductory Clauses

a. Introductory clauses begin a sentence, contain a subject and a verb, and usually start with one of the following words:

as	are most common	after	provided	until
if		although	since	whenever
when		because	so	while
		before	unless	

Place a comma after an introductory clause.

If your architectural firm wishes to be considered for this project, please submit your preliminary drawings and bid by October 1.

Although Alex received a substantial inheritance, he did not manage the money and properties wisely.

b. Occasionally an introductory clause may contain an implied verb and/or subject. This shortened form is treated the same as any other introductory clause. Place a comma after the shortened form.

As agreed, our charges for this catered event will be solely on a per-person basis. (As we agreed, ...)

If so, completion of this rapid transit project could be delayed another six months. (If that is so, ... *or* If this is so, ...)

c. Occasionally an introductory clause may follow another introductory word group. In such cases place a comma only after the introductory clause.

I suggest that **before you file the client's tax return,** you check with Meredith on this issue.

Our credit manager decided that **if these customers pay their overdue balances,** we will reinstate their credit privileges.

d. When an introductory clause is followed by two main clauses, place a comma only after the introductory clause.

When Connor addresses prospective clients, he explains clearly all our investment options and he answers all questions patiently and courteously.

If you are interested in Remco's employment opportunities, visit our Web site at www.remco.com and complete an online application.

e. When a sentence contains two introductory clauses, place a comma only after the second clause.

If the committee authorizes the purchase of a new network server and after you obtain the appropriate signatures, please submit all the specifications on our standard purchase order form.

2–10 Introductory Phrases

a. An introductory infinitive phrase begins a sentence and starts with the word *To,* which is followed immediately by a main verb. Place a comma after an introductory infinitive phrase. Note that all introductory phrases containing a verb form are followed by a comma.

To stay healthy, maintain a well-balanced diet and exercise daily.

To answer your question, I will need to refer to past sales trends.

To settle the dispute between the employee and the bank, the court sent the case to arbitration.

b. An introductory participial phrase begins a sentence and starts with a verb form ending in *ing* or *ed*. Place a comma after an introductory participial phrase as it contains a verb form.

Beginning in 2018, all our employees will use mobile devices for their primary mode of communication.

Interested in learning how e-commerce might increase sales, Jordan plans to attend the E-COM convention next month in Boston.

c. An introductory prepositional phrase begins a sentence; it starts with a preposition and ends with an object. A partial list of prepositions that may begin an introductory prepositional phrase follows:

about	among	behind	during	on	until
above	around	below	for	over	up
after	at	between	from	through	upon
along	before	by	in	under	with

Place a comma after an introductory prepositional phrase—unless it is short (only two or three words) and does not contain a verb form.[3] A short introductory prepositional phrase that contains a verb form is followed by a comma.

more than three words
Within the next hour, you should receive an e-mail confirmation from the Sunset Village Hotel.

Between July 1 and August 31, the Palm Desert Grill will be closed on Sundays and Mondays.

During the past few days of litigation, both sides have made significant concessions.

two or three words—verb form
After *winning*, members of the soccer team always meet at Pizza Parlor for a celebration.

[3]Some authorities suggest placing a comma after all introductory prepositional phrases.

Before *calling* you, I verified the meeting time and place.

By *enrolling* today, you are assured that your child will receive a place at Pinecrest Nursery School in September.

two or three words—no verb form
By noon all maintenance on our network will have been completed.

On February 1 our laboratory released information to the press about the Federal Drug Administration approval of our new cancer drug.

With this software you can easily capture text and images from the Internet.

After a short introductory prepositional phrase (two or three words) that does not contain a verb form, use a comma if the comma is necessary for clarity.

After the class, discussion on this issue will continue until 3 p.m. in Conference Room 14. (Not *class discussion* . . . .)

In my office, files dating back to 2007 are stored in three of the cabinets. (Not *office files* . . . .)

Until next Monday, morning deliveries will be accepted only between 8:30 a.m. and 10:30 a.m. (Not *Monday morning* . . . .)

d. An introductory phrase that follows another introductory word group is treated as if the opening introductory word group were not included. Mentally omit the opening expression, and punctuate the introductory phrase according to the rules in Section 2–10a–c.

infinitive phrase
Mr. Adams explained that **to meet our production deadline,** all employees would need to work overtime during the next two weeks.

participial phrase
Obviously **trying to resolve their differences,** Ms. Bates called Laura and Beth into her office.

prepositional phrase, more than three words
We expect that **during this growth period,** many investors will attempt to acquire our successful e-commerce enterprise.

John anticipates that **within the next week,** we will receive the new furniture for the reception area.

prepositional phrase, contains a verb form
We realized later that **before e-mailing everyone,** we should have checked to see if the conference room was available on August 24.

Our plant manager believes that **by implementing new technologies,** the company will be able to reduce its production costs.

prepositional phrase, two or three words without a verb form
We are hopeful that **within the month** the union and our company management will have reached agreement on all contractual issues.

We assure you that **by tomorrow** your order will be ready for shipment.

e. A phrase that begins a sentence and acts as the subject is not followed by a comma. Likewise, an opening phrase that is part of the predicate is not followed by a comma.

beginning phrase that acts as a subject
To answer your question would require several days' research.

Helping his employees prepare for advancement does not rank high among Mr. Green's management attributes.

beginning phrase that is part of the predicate
From the intensive police investigation came some new evidence that led to the apprehension of the suspected arsonists. (Normal order: *Some new evidence that led to the apprehension of the suspected arsonists came from the intensive police investigation.*)

Among the group of dignitaries from Seattle were a number of school children and their parents. (Normal order: *A number of school children and their parents were among the group of dignitaries from Seattle.*)

2–11 Restrictive and Nonrestrictive Phrases and Clauses

Restrictive phrases and clauses modify and contribute substantially to the main idea of a sentence and are essential to its meaning. They tell *who, what,* or *which one* and are not set off with commas.

Nonrestrictive phrases and clauses add an additional idea and do not significantly change or contribute to the main idea of a sentence. They are nonessential word groups; that is, they are not needed by the main clause to tell *who, what,* or *which one.* Set off nonrestrictive phrases and clauses from the rest of the sentence with commas. Notice that phrases and clauses directly following proper nouns are nonrestrictive.

a. Relative clauses (those beginning with *who, whose, whom, which,* or *that*) are either restrictive (no comma) or nonrestrictive (comma required).

restrictive and essential to meaning
Job applicants **who are proficient in using all components of Microsoft Office** can obtain well-paying positions. (Tells *which kind* of job applicants.)

nonrestrictive and not essential to meaning
Ms. Washington, **who readily uses all components of Microsoft Office,** can obtain a well-paying job. (Provides additional idea—clause following a proper noun.)

In the first example, the clause "who are proficient in using all components of Microsoft Office" limits the type of job applicants who "can easily obtain well-paying positions." In the second example, "who readily uses all components of Microsoft Office" is of no assistance in identifying Ms. Washington but is merely an additional idea. Therefore, this example is a nonrestrictive clause that is set off by commas.

restrictive and essential to meaning
All employees **who have been employed by the company for at least three months** are eligible for health insurance benefits. (Tells *which* employees.)

nonrestrictive and not essential to meaning
Steve, **who has been employed by the company for three months,** is eligible for health insurance benefits. (Provides additional idea that is not needed to identify *Steve*—clause following a proper noun.)

b. **Careful writers will use *that* for restrictive clauses (no comma) and *which* for nonrestrictive clauses (comma required).**

restrictive
The video **that you requested us to purchase for your class** has yet to be closed-captioned. (Tells *which* video.)

Our insurance programs **that appeal to adults with young families** should be featured in this commercial. (Tells *which* insurance programs.)

nonrestrictive
Unlike HTML (hypertext markup language), **which is a fairly rigid set of standards,** XML (extensible markup language) is designed for flexibility. (Provides additional idea.)

We have canceled our winter sales meeting, **which was scheduled from December 11 to 13 in Miami.** (Provides additional idea.)

c. **Dependent adverbial clauses (clauses beginning with words such as *if, as, when, since, because,* etc.) that follow the main clause may be restrictive (no comma) or nonrestrictive (comma required). Restrictive clauses (1) answer such questions as *when, why, how,* or *whether* or (2) limit the main idea of the sentence. Nonrestrictive clauses add an additional idea that does not, however, alter the meaning of the main clause.**

restrictive and essential to meaning
Monthly sales in Orange County have increased significantly **since the advertising campaign began**. (Tells *when.*)

Our college bookstore discontinued selling textbooks last year **because the bookstore could not compete with online book prices.** (Tells *why.*)

You will add 5,000 bonus miles to your frequent flyer account **if you answer our online questionnaire**. (Tells *how*.)

We can still promise you the discount price **if we receive your order on or before November 10**. (Tells *whether*.)

You may order these sale items from our Web site **as long as our current supply of merchandise lasts**. (Limits main idea.)

nonrestrictive and not essential to meaning
Our client bid on this commercial property, **although he feels his bid will not be accepted.** (Provides additional idea.)

Costs of raw materials have risen more than 10 percent during the last quarter, **as our company president predicted earlier this year**. (Provides additional idea.)

d. A dependent clause or a short independent clause used to provide an extra idea within a sentence is nonrestrictive. Set off such clauses with commas (or dashes for emphasis).

interrupting dependent clause
On February 7, **when you arrive for your first appointment,** please give your packet of completed forms to the receptionist.

I can, **if you wish,** give you a list of dentists in your area who accept our insurance plan.

This year's line of holiday greeting cards—**although the cards are larger and more exquisite**—is less expensive than last year's.

interrupting short independent clause
Ms. Lee, **I believe,** is the only applicant who resides in Utah.

We will, **I hope,** be able to obtain our passports by July 1.

e. Participial, infinitive, or prepositional phrases appearing within a sentence may be restrictive (no commas) or nonrestrictive (commas required), depending upon whether or not they tell *who, what, what kind,* or *which one.* Phrases that answer these questions are restrictive (no commas).

participial restrictive
All current employees **planning to participate in the company stock option program** must sign up by August 1. (Tells *which ones*.)

participial nonrestrictive
Mr. Fletcher, **planning to participate in the company stock option program,** has signed up to attend the August 10 seminar on stock options. (Provides additional idea—phrase following a proper noun.)

infinitive restrictive
We plan **to sign up for the program** by August 1. (Tells *what*.)

infinitive nonrestrictive
Hill & Hill's stock option program offers employees an excellent investment opportunity, **to mention only one aspect of the company's benefits program**. (Provides additional idea.)

prepositional restrictive
The advertising mailers **for our July sale** will be available May 25. (Tells *which ones.*)

Clients **like the Pollards** make the real estate business a pleasure. (Tells *what kind.*)

Word confusions **like *cite*, *site*, and *sight*** are often misused in business writing. (Tells *what kind.*)

prepositional nonrestrictive
We are planning, **in response to numerous requests,** to market our holiday ornaments online as well as maintain our current store location. (Provides additional idea.)

Some residential real estate clients, **like the Pollards,** make working in real estate sales a pleasure. (Provides additional idea.)

Small tool manufacturing companies, **like Belmont Tools and ABC Tool Manufacturers,** are showing little profit in this tight economy. (Provides additional idea.)

Large, worldwide hotel chains—**like Marriott, Hilton, and Hyatt**—provide toll-free numbers for guests to book reservations. (Provides additional idea.)

2–12 Contrasting, Limiting, and Contingent Expressions

Contrasting, limiting, or contingent expressions are set off by commas. Words often used to introduce contrasting and limiting expressions include *not, never, but, seldom,* and *yet.*

contrasting expression
Our company has found online surveys, **not telephone interviews,** to be the most effective means for assessing customer satisfaction.

limiting expression
The producers will give us four tickets for opening night, **but only for the theater critics on our staff**.

contingent expression
The sooner we receive your room preferences, **the sooner** we will be able to confirm your hotel reservations.

The more money you deposit, **the greater return** you will receive on your investment.

The higher the resolution you set for the monitor, **the better the picture quality** you may expect in the display.

2–13 Omitted Words

Commas are often used to indicate the omission of words when the context of the sentence makes the omitted words clearly understood.

Three new sales associates were hired by the Oxnard store; two, by the Ventura store. (Two *new sales associates were hired* by the Ventura store.)

Last week I used speech-recognition software to prepare four long reports; this week, two long reports. (This week *I used speech-recognition software to prepare* two long reports.)

Our car insurance premium is due on May 1; our homeowner's insurance, May 10; and our life insurance, May 15. (Our homeowner's insurance *premium is due on* May 10, and our life insurance *premium is due on* May 15.)

2–14 Commas for Clarity

a. Separate by a comma two identical verbs that appear together in a sentence.

Whoever **wins, wins** an all-expense paid vacation to Hawaii for two.

Whatever irregularities **occurred, occurred** without my knowledge.

b. Separate by a comma words repeated for emphasis.

He had been warned **many, many** times about his frequent absences before he was terminated.

The district manager has not visited our store for a **long, long** time.

c. Set off by a comma a word or phrase at the beginning of a sentence that could be read incorrectly with the words that follow.

Ever since, she has been employed by Disney Studios in Burbank.

The month before, the corporation expanded its operations to Brazil.

In our business, letters are written primarily to sell goods and services and to collect money.

d. Place a comma between the last name and the first name of a name written in inverted form.

Irwin, Carl　　Koller, Lyn M.

2–15 Short Quotations

a. Set off a short quoted sentence from the rest of the sentence by a comma. When the quoted sentence is broken into two parts, commas are required before and after the interjected thought.

beginning quotation
"End-of-the-year bonuses will be awarded once our accountant has verified the December sales," said Mr. Schneider.

interrupted quotation
"End-of-the-year bonuses will be awarded," said Mr. Schneider, "once our accountant has verified the December sales."

ending quotation
Mr. Schneider said, "End-of-the-year bonuses will be awarded once our accountant has verified the December sales."

b. Substitute a question mark or an exclamation mark for the separating comma in a beginning quotation when the quotation is a question or an exclamation—unless the beginning quotation is interrupted.

question mark
"Does United Parcel Service accept employment applications only online?" asked Sandra.

interrupted question
"Does United Parcel Service," asked Sandra, "accept employment applications only online?"

exclamation mark
"These internships in the entertainment industry are a great opportunity for our students!" exclaimed Mr. Ono.

interrupted exclamation
"These internships in the entertainment industry," exclaimed Mr. Ono, "are a great opportunity for our students!"

c. No comma is needed to set off a quotation or part of a quotation that is woven into a complete sentence or one that is not a complete thought.

woven into sentence
Our building management company guarantees that **"any needed air-conditioning repairs will be completed within 24 hours."**

Jason reported that **". . . no staff vacancies will be filled until May."**

incomplete sentence
The representative from Atlantic Mutual advised me to **"submit a résumé before the end of the week."**

Please mark the sides of this box **"Glass, Handle with Care."**

He merely answered **"yes"** to all the questions.

d. When a comma and a quotation mark fall at the same point in a sentence, *always* place the comma inside the closing quotation mark. Periods, too, are *always* placed inside the closing quotation mark.
"We continue to give customers wireless access to our many services," reported Tyler Moore, E-Bank's chief executive officer.

Her last article, "Treasures of the Grand Canyon," appeared in last month's issue of *Travelers' Guide*.

Brian reminded us, "Be sure to e-mail your response by November 1."

e. For placement of question marks and exclamation marks with closing quotation marks, see Sections 2–44a and 2–46c.

2–16 Numerals

a. When expressed in United States format, numerals of more than three digits require commas.

1,320 63,481 963,481 1,293,070 23,092,946 450,500,000

b. Separate by a comma two independent figures that appear consecutively in a sentence.

Do not separate by a comma two consecutive numbers that function as adjectives to describe the same noun. Instead, write the first number in words and the second one in figures. If the first number cannot be expressed in *one or two words*, place it in figures also.

independent figures
Of the **$412,000, $247,483** of the home loan remains to be paid.

During **2015, $8,783,000** in sales was financed through our credit card program.

By June **1, 47** applicants had submitted online résumés for this position.

two numbers modifying a noun, word-figure form
We will need **thirty 13-gallon** wastebaskets for offices in the new building.

Each package contains **twelve 2-inch** nails.

Please order **twenty-four 100-watt** bulbs for lamps in the reception areas.

two numbers modifying a noun, figure-figure form
The prescription was for **150 10-milligram** tablets.

When the carton fell, **127 40-watt** light bulbs were broken.

Please obtain a quote to duplicate this PowerPoint presentation on **250 650-MB** CDs.

c. Commas are omitted in years, house numbers, zip codes, telephone or fax numbers, decimal fractions, metric measurements, and any label-numeral combinations. In metric measurements use a space to separate all numerals containing more than four digits.

year
1893 1998 2016

house number
6201 Winnetka Avenue 12378 Laurel Canyon Boulevard

zip code
Northridge, CA 91325 Bothell, WA 98041-3011

telephone or fax number
(212) 555-9768, Ext. 4412 *or* 212-555-9768, Ext. 4412

decimal fraction
0.4769

metric measurement
1400 kilometers 12 600 kilometers

label-numeral combination
Serial No. 9226263 page 1072 Room 3210 Invoice 43798

d. Volume numbers and page references are separated by commas.

Please refer to Volume XII, page 119.

The article appeared in Volume VII, February 2015, page 87.

e. Measurements (such as weights, capacities, dimensions, etc.) are treated as single units and are not interrupted by commas.

weight
The Wilsons' new baby weighed **7 pounds 6 ounces** at birth.

dimension
The patient is **5 feet 10 inches** tall.

Our reception area is **25 feet 10 inches** by **18 feet 6 inches**.

time period
Is our flight time still estimated to be **3 hours 15 minutes**?

Semicolon

2–17 Independent Clauses without Coordinating Conjunctions

a. Place a semicolon between two or more closely related independent clauses (complete thoughts that could stand alone as separate sentences) that are not connected with a coordinating conjunction (*and, but, or, nor*).

two independent clauses
Too many orders are delayed leaving our Milwaukee warehouse; Ms. Nguyen will check into our shipping procedures there.

Plan to attend the next sales leadership conference of the American Management Association International; you will find this conference to be well worth your time.

three independent clauses
Mr. Lieberman drafted the contract specifications last week; Ms. Brooks consulted the firm's attorneys on Monday; Mr. Ahrens signed and sent the contract out for bid on Thursday.

b. Short and closely related independent clauses may be separated by commas. *Short clauses* may be defined generally as containing six or fewer words.

two short independent clauses
Pittsburgh Bank issued the checks, TSI mailed them to the clients.

three short independent clauses
The monitor flashed, it emitted sparks, it went blank.

He came in, he looked around, he left.

2–18 Independent Clauses with Coordinating Conjunctions

Two independent clauses linked by a coordinating conjunction (*and, but, or, nor*) are generally separated by a comma. Lengthy, complicated sentences containing internal commas in either or both clauses, however, may be punctuated with a semicolon between the two clauses.

clauses separated by a comma
We were pleased with the results of the survey**, and** you will receive a copy of the summary.

Carmen had planned to take vacation time next week**, but** several clients needed her immediate assistance.

You may mail your payment, **or** you may take it to one of the fast, convenient express registers located throughout our stores.

clauses separated by a semicolon
Several large orders were recently placed and filled through the new Dayton office; **and** Ms. Baca, our national sales manager, commended the warehouse staff for its diligence in processing these orders promptly.

You, of course, need not attend the committee meeting scheduled for September 4; **but** I believe, Mr. Newton, you will find reading the minutes helpful before you address the Board of Directors next week.

2–19 Independent Clauses with Transitional Expressions

A partial list of common transitional expressions follows. In addition, those words and phrases listed in Section 2–2a may be considered transitional expressions.

accordingly	however	moreover	otherwise
besides	indeed	nevertheless	so
consequently	in fact	notwithstanding	then
furthermore	in other words	on the contrary	therefore
hence	likewise	on the other hand	yet

Two independent clauses (complete thoughts) separated by a transitional expression require a semicolon. Place the semicolon after the first independent clause. Place a comma after a transitional expression with two or more syllables or where a strong pause is needed after a one-syllable expression.

transitional expression with two or more syllables
Stellar's recent promotion of its satellite communications network has influenced large numbers of television viewers to switch to satellite reception; **consequently,** some companies providing cable reception are experiencing a revenue decline.

transitional expression with one syllable
All departments will operate on the same budget allotments next year; **thus** your staff should not plan to acquire all the digital imaging equipment and software requested.

USB drives will no longer be permitted for external storage; **hence,** all files are to be posted on a company FTP site.

2–20 Series Containing Internal Commas or Complete Thoughts

a. Items in a series are usually separated by commas. However, when one or more of the items contain internal commas, use semicolons to separate the parts.

Offices in Hartford, Connecticut; San Francisco, California; and Little Rock, Arkansas, all exceeded their quotas for this quarter.

Our online courses serve nontraditional adult students; provide flexible, convenient learning options; and satisfy students' needs for continual lifelong learning.

b. Three or more independent clauses (complete thoughts) comprising a series are separated by semicolons. Only very short clauses may be separated by commas.

series of independent clauses
Nearly 10,000 flyers were distributed to prospective clients in 2009; more than 18,000 flyers were distributed in 2014; and next year we plan to mail 12,000 new brochures as well as distribute 25,000 flyers.

series of independent clauses with internal commas
Brett Harris, President, will welcome the stockholders at 10 a.m.; Ashley Williams, Vice President of Marketing, will report on past year's sales at 10:30 a.m.; and Dana Murillo, Treasurer, will provide a complete financial picture at 11 a.m. using PowerPoint slides.

series of short independent clauses
The tenant called yesterday, the manager investigated his complaint, and the air-conditioning will be restored today.

2–21 Enumerations and Explanations

a. **Certain words and phrases are used to introduce enumerations or explanations that follow an independent clause (complete thought). Some common introductory expressions follow:**

for example (e.g.)　　for instance　　that is (i.e.)　　namely (viz.)

If the enumeration or explanation following the introductory expression *contains commas* or *forms another complete thought*, use a semicolon after the opening independent clause and a comma after the introductory expression.

enumeration containing commas
A number of factors have contributed to the sharp increase in production costs during the past six months; **namely,** price increases in raw materials, wage increases for electrical workers, and overtime payments to supervisors.

explanation forming another complete thought
To open its Birmingham plant, Caldwell Industries advertised for a number of new employees; **that is to say,** not all its employees were willing to transfer from Syracuse to the new location.

b. **Some independent clauses followed by expressions that introduce enumerations or explanations require a comma, not a semicolon, after the independent clause. If the enumeration or explanation that follows the introductory expression does *not* contain commas or form another complete thought, use commas after the independent clause and the introductory expression.**

enumeration without internal commas
As a member of our user group, you are eligible to purchase computer peripherals through our discount program, **for instance,** a scanner or a printer.

explanation forming an incomplete thought
You may wish to call Ms. Hendrix for further advice, **for example,** to inquire which accounting software would be best suited for your small business.

c. **Enumerations or explanations used as parenthetical expressions within a sentence are not set off by semicolons. Use commas when the enumerated or explanatory information has no internal commas; use dashes or parentheses when the information contains internal commas.**

commas
Your accounting procedures, **for example, reconciling accounts receivable,** can be streamlined by using our software.

dashes
Current economic conditions have forced us to postpone updating our multimedia equipment—**e.g., digital video cameras, digital still cameras, and portable data projectors**—to stay within our budget allocations.

parentheses
Your recommendations **(namely, downsizing our human resources staff, scanning all incoming résumés, and computerizing our testing program)** were approved unanimously by the board.

d. Complete thoughts that introduce enumerations or explanations without an introductory expression are followed by a colon, not a semicolon.
The following employees have requested vacations in July**:** Christina López, Darren Brubaker, Duncan Haledon, and Jamie McCloskey.

Several new software concepts for workplace access are being investigated by our company**:** retina scanners, fingerprint scanners, and face-recognition systems.

Only 87 teachers attended the ARTA state conference**:** apparently many of our members did not receive their brochures in time to plan for this event.

2–22 Semicolon Placement

Always place the semicolon *outside* the closing quotation mark or the closing parenthesis.

outside closing quotation mark
Last month Mr. Parsons promised, "I will mail you a check the 1st of next month"**;** but we have received no money or explanation from him.

parentheses
Our accounting supervisor was ill last week (with the flu)**;** consequently, our end-of-the-month reports will reach the home office a week late.

Colon

2–23 Formally Enumerated or Listed Items

a. Use a colon after an independent clause (complete thought) that introduces a formal listing or an enumeration of items. Words commonly used in introductory independent clauses include *the following, as follows, these,* and *thus*. Sometimes, however, the introduction is implied rather than stated directly. Use a colon following both direct and implied introductions.

direct introduction
The Accounting Department has requested the following new equipment and furniture: two desktop computers, one laser printer, two computer stations, one printer stand, and two ergonomic computer chairs.

Observe these rules for a successful job interview:

1. Obtain information beforehand about the company.
2. Dress appropriately.
3. Appear interested in the company and the job.
4. Answer questions courteously.
5. Thank the interviewers for their time.

implied introduction
Several kinds of laptop computers were on display**:** Hewlett-Packard, Dell, Sony, and Toshiba.

In determining whether to use a colon or a semicolon for introducing enumerated items, use the colon when the enumeration is not preceded by a transitional introductory expression such as *namely, for example, e.g., that is,* or *i.e.* If an introductory expression immediately precedes the listing, use a semicolon before the expression and a comma after it. (See Section 2–21a for examples.)

b. The colon is *not* used to introduce listings in the following situations: (1) an intervening sentence separates the introductory sentence and the listing; (2) the items follow a "being" verb or are the object of a verb; (3) the items are the object of a preposition; and (4) the listing is preceded immediately by an enumerating expression.

no colon: intervening sentence
The following new dinnerware patterns will be available January 1. They will be introduced to our dealers next month.

1. Golden Harvest
2. Apple Melon
3. Sunburst
4. Fiesta

no colon: following a "being" verb
The words most commonly misspelled **were** *convenience, occasionally, accommodate, consequently,* and *faculty.* (Not ". . . were: *convenience,* . . . .")

no colon: acting as the object of a verb
Popular Web browsers **include** Chrome, Firefox, Internet Explorer, Safari, and Opera. (Not ". . . include: Chrome . . . .")

no colon: object of a preposition
The first lessons introduce the new Microsoft Excel user **to** the Tab Bar, the Ribbon, and the Quick Access Toolbar. (Not ". . . to: the Tab . . . .")

Department meetings are scheduled **for** January 3, February 4, March 7, and April 9. (Not ". . . for: January 3, ...")

no colon: listing after enumerating expression
Please order some additional supplies; **namely,** 8.5- by 11-inch white laser printer paper, legal-size envelopes, and letter-size manila file folders.

2–24 Explanatory Sentences

Use a colon to separate two sentences when the second sentence explains, illustrates, or supplements the first.

explanation
During the next three months, we will gross approximately 50 percent of our annual sales: major toy purchases occur during September, October, and November.

illustration
This year's new model, the Manacetti, was designed for buyers who want an economy car: advertising brochures promise efficient gas mileage, low maintenance costs, and reliability.

supplement
A number of new customers complained about the delay in receiving credit approval: they expected to have their charge accounts approved in time for holiday shopping.

2–25 Long Quotations

Long one-sentence quotations are placed in quotation marks and introduced by a colon.

Quotations containing two or more sentences (and usually more than three lines) are placed in a separate paragraph without quotation marks. Indent the left and right margins, and separate the quotation from the main text by single blank lines before and after the quotation.

long one-sentence quotation
Carmen Garcia, Westco's human resources manager, pointed out in her annual report: "Graduates from the University of Southern California's School of Business have been placed in a number of our divisions, and they have risen to middle-management positions within a three-year period."

long quotation of two or more sentences
A brief introduction to Speech Applications Language Tags (SALT) may be found on the Microsoft Web site:

> SALT (Speech Application Language Tags) is an extension of HTML and other markup languages (cHTML, XHTML, WML) that adds a powerful speech interface to Web pages, while maintaining and leveraging all the advantages of the Web application model. These tags are designed to be used for both voice-only browsers (for example, a browser accessed over the telephone) and multimodal browsers.[4]

This platform permits multimodal and telephony-enabled access to information, applications, and Web services from PCs, telephones, ...

2–26 Special-Purpose Uses for the Colon

a. In business letters a colon is placed after the salutation when the mixed punctuation format is used (see Section 11–8).

Dear Bill: Dear Ms. Madison: Gentlemen:

b. Use the colon to separate hours and minutes in expressions of time.

The budget meeting will be held at **8:30 a.m.** on Thursday, October 9, in Room 316.

Mr. Greeley is scheduled to address the Spokane Chamber of Commerce at **12:15 p.m.**

c. In expressing ratios, use the colon to represent the word *to*.

Do the label instructions recommend proportions of **3:1** or **4:1**?

The council members voted **2:1** against the proposed zoning change.

d. The colon is often used to separate elements in literary references.

between title and subtitle
Dr. Mary Ellen Guffey's latest book, *Business Communication: Process & Product*, 8th ed., is now in stock at our college bookstore.

between place of publication and publisher in footnotes and bibliographies
Clark, James L., and Lyn R. Clark. *HOW 14: A Handbook for Office Professionals.* 14th ed. Mason, Ohio**:** Cengage South-Western, 2017. (Bibliographical entry.)

between volume and page number in footnotes and bibliographies
6. Kristin F. Armstrong and John R. Jacobs, "Developing Company Web Sites: Strategies for Making Yours 'User Friendly,'" *The Bulletin for the Association of Webmasters* 5 (October 2014): 47–52. (Sample footnote entry.)

---

[4] *Speech Application Language Tags (SALT)*, Microsoft Corporation, 2014, http://msdn.microsoft.com/en-us/library/ms994629.aspx (December 23, 2014).

biblical citation
The minister quoted Isaiah **24:1** (Chapter 24, verse 1).

2–27 Colon Format and Use with Other Punctuation Marks

a. In computer-generated copy, space once or twice after a colon that introduces enumerated items, an explanatory sentence, or a long quotation. Placing two spaces after a colon in business documents promotes ease of reading. Whichever format you choose, be consistent throughout the document.

Please send me copies of these documents: the Wongs' lease agreement, their move-in deposit receipt, and the latest tenant rules and regulations.

b. Place the colon outside closing quotation marks and closing parentheses.

closing quotation mark
Please distribute to the following staff members copies of Donna Haile's latest article, "Closing the Sale Effectively"**:** Mina Balejian, Charles Ballesteros, Paul Kellogg, and Kyung Kim.

closing parenthesis
Three contractors are being considered for the housing project (Sierra Canyon Estates)**:** Wyeth & Sons, Burnside Developers, and Feldman Construction Company.

c. Use the following formats for vertical listings introduced by a colon:

(1) Capitalize the first word in each item of a vertical listing.
(2) Conclude each item in the listing with a period only if the items are complete sentences.
(3) Single-space the items in a vertical listing.
(4) Double-space between the items if any item occupies more than one line. If all the items consist of a single line, you may *either* leave one blank line between each item *or* single-space the listing.
(5) Place one blank line before and after a listing.
(6) Use the margins of the main text or indent the listing from the left and right margins in business letters and memorandums.[5]
(7) Number, accent with bullets, or leave untagged items in a listing.

complete sentences, numbered items, standard margins
We have discontinued our Model 1040 microwave oven for the following reasons:

1. Popularity of our Model 1040 oven has decreased continually during the past 18 months.

---

[5]See Section 12–9 for guidelines governing the format and preparation of horizontal and vertical listings in reports and manuscripts, as well as in business letters and memorandums.

2. Manufacturing cost and price differ only slightly from our standard-size microwave, the Model 1041.
3. Two other models smaller than our standard-size one, Model 1038 and Model 1039, have been more popular.

incomplete sentences, bulleted items, indented margins

A computer may be connected to the Internet through one of the following:

- DSL
- Cable modem
- Wi-Fi
- T line
- Satellite

incomplete sentences, unnumbered items, indented left and right margins

Effective July 1 new premium rates will be in force for the following types of policies:

Jewelry riders on homeowners' policies
Liability coverage for drivers under 25 years of age
Earthquake riders on all casualty policies
Term life insurance for males 65 and older

2–28 Capitalization with Colons

a. When a colon is used to introduce a horizontal listing of items, the first letter after the colon is not capitalized unless it begins a proper noun. Capitalize the first letter of each item in a vertical listing.

lowercase letter in horizontal listing

Place the following items in Alex's in-box: **t**he original invoice, the duplicate invoice, and the shipping copy.

proper noun capitalized

Four cities have been identified as possible sites for our new location: **O**gden, Utah; Utica, New York; Jackson, Mississippi; and Cedar Rapids, Iowa.

capitalized letters in vertical listing

You may pay for your Hawaiian Village Time-Share package in a number of ways:

Personal check
Credit card—VISA, MasterCard, or American Express
Eighteen monthly installments of $737.50

Do not miss the opportunity to get in on the ground floor of this . . . .

b. Do not capitalize the first letter after a colon when the second sentence explains or supplements the first unless the letter begins a proper noun.

lowercase letter begins second sentence
Your account has been frozen temporarily**: o**utstanding charges of $938.44 still remain unpaid.

proper noun capitalized
Matthew Horne was awarded the $1,500 prize**: M**att's Web site was judged by a panel of three experts to be the best student entry in Web site design.

c. **Capitalize the first word after a colon when the colon introduces a formal rule or principle stated as a complete sentence.**

Use correct formats in composing e-mail messages**: A**lways include a subject line to identify the content of your message.

Ms. Sullivan emphasizes adherence to the following policy**: I**n case of absence, employees are to notify the Human Resources Department by 7:30 a.m. on the day of absence.

d. **When two or more sentences follow a colon, capitalize the first letter of each sentence.**

Several suggestions emerged from the discussion**: T**o begin with, an architect should be retained to determine the extent of damage to the building. **T**hen three contractors should be asked to provide estimates for repairing the damage. **F**inally, lending resources should be investigated to determine the best means for financing the repairs.

e. **Capitalize the first letter of sentences or phrases introduced by words such as *Note, Attention, Warning, Caution,* or *For Sale.***

Warning: All cars parked illegally will be towed away at vehicle owner's expense.

Caution: Please hold children by hand.

For Rent: Large three-bedroom house with family room, fireplace, air-conditioning, and pool. Phone (617) 555–3542.

f. **Capitalize the first word of a quotation that follows a colon.**

Mr. Lopez informed the board about expansion plans for this year**: "S**ince the property on Tampa Avenue closed escrow last month, construction of our new branch office will begin early this spring in time for a September opening."

Dash

2–29 Parenthetical Expressions, Appositives, and Summaries

a. **Parenthetical expressions and appositives are usually set off from the rest of the sentence by commas. When the parenthetical expression or appositive contains internal commas, however, substitute dashes (or parentheses) for the separating commas.**

Where possible, use an em dash—a character that appears as a solid line and is twice the length of a hyphen. If access to an em dash is unavailable through an extended character set,[6] form the dash by typing two hyphens with no space before, between, or after (see Section 2–32).

parenthetical expression with internal commas
Last month Ms. Abajian—with the hope of locating store sites, recruiting new employees, and establishing additional sources of supply—visited several other New York cities.

appositive with internal commas
A number of Web sites—for example, Amazon.com, Schwab.com, and eBay.com—have set the precedent for a revolutionary pattern in American purchasing trends.

b. Use a dash to set off a brief summary from the rest of the sentence.

Thanksgiving Day, Christmas Day, and New Year's Day—these are the only holidays our stores will be closed.

Black, navy, and bone—the Sling purse is available in these colors.

c. To achieve greater separation, use dashes instead of commas to set off abrupt parenthetical expressions or those requiring emphasis. Appositives requiring emphasis may also be separated from the rest of the sentence with dashes instead of commas.

abrupt parenthetical expression
Her main interest—notwithstanding job security—was to obtain employment in an organization with opportunities for advancement.

emphatic parenthetical element
Several orders were rerouted to the Madison office—not to the Eau Claire office.

emphatic appositive
We will need some heavy-duty equipment—bulldozers and graders—to complete the first phase of the project according to schedule.

d. For emphasis use a dash in place of a comma or a semicolon to introduce an example or an explanation.

example requiring emphasis
Insurance coverage purchased five years ago may no longer be adequate—for example, with current inflationary trends, your fire and theft insurance may not cover the replacement costs of your property and its contents.

---

[6] Word processing programs provide access to extended character sets. Extended characters are letters, number styles, symbols, and foreign language characters that are not on the standard keyboard but are needed to produce documents.

explanation requiring emphasis
Our sales of multimedia software have increased 40 percent since 2014—namely, from $1 million to $1.4 million.

e. **Afterthoughts or side thoughts generated from the text, but not necessarily part of it, may be separated from the rest of the sentence by a dash or a pair of dashes.**

afterthought
Mrs. Muñoz will install our new accounting software this afternoon—at least Brett believes she has planned to do so then.

side thought
Several items from our new product line—I do not know which ones—will be featured at our exhibit in New Orleans next month.

2-30 Hesitations in Verbal Reports

Use dashes to indicate hesitations, faltering, or stammering in reports of conversations, testimonies, or speeches.

Mr. Weston: Well—perhaps a computerized inventory-control system will solve some of the current problems.

2-31 Source of Quotations

Place a dash before the source of a quotation when the source is listed after the quotation.

"With the current influx of new businesses, we can anticipate a significant decrease in our state's unemployment rate during the next nine months."

—H. J. Scott

"The difference between the right word and the almost right word is the difference between lightning and the lightning bug."

—Mark Twain

2-32 Format and Placement of Dash

a. **For documents prepared with desktop publishing or word processing software, use an em dash (not a hyphen or an en dash) to form the dash. The em dash is the length of two hyphens and may be accessed through the extended character set of most applications software. Leave no space before or after the em dash.**

If the em dash is unavailable, form the dash by typing two consecutive hyphens; leave no space before, between, or after the hyphens.

A dash may end a line, but it may not begin a new line.

em dash
Several influential community organizations—the Kiwanis Club, the Chamber of Commerce, and the Rotary Club—sponsored Courtney Burrows for the vacant seat on the city council.

dash formed with two hyphens
Three cities--Albuquerque, Little Rock, and Fort Worth--are still under consideration for our new plant site.

end of line
Contract negotiations—after reaching an impasse on December 20—
were resumed on January 5.

b. Only one punctuation mark may precede an opening dash—a period in an abbreviation. Closing dashes may be preceded by a period in an abbreviation, a question mark, or an exclamation mark.

opening dash after abbreviation
The first performance is scheduled to begin at 7 p.m.—additional performances are at 9 p.m. and 11 p.m.

closing dash after question mark
The Consumer Guide—are you familiar with this magazine?—has rated the Landis surround-sound system as "No. 1."

c. For documents prepared with desktop publishing or word processing software, use an *en* dash (not an em dash) to represent the word "to" or "through" with a number sequence. The en dash is slightly longer than a hyphen and may be accessed through the extended character set of most applications software.

If the en dash is not available, substitute a hyphen.

en dash with a number sequence
The Waco County Fair will be held **May 1–15** at Canby Downs.

An excellent description of these gemstones may be found on pages **87–104** of *Jewelry Shopping Guide*.

hyphen with a number sequence
Alice's Café will be closed **July 16-August 5** for renovation.

Refer to pages **11-13** in your user's manual for instructions on how to reset the date on your Fromax digital camera.

Period

2–33 End of Sentence

Place a period at the end of a declarative sentence, an imperative statement or command, an indirect question, or a polite request. Polite requests end with a period, even though they may appear to have the format of a question. A polite request (1) asks the reader to *perform a specific action* and (2) is *answered only* by the reader's

doing or not doing what the writer has requested. (See Section 2–41e for additional information and examples.)

declarative sentence
Your Sensora Web-enabled FotoPhone will be available August 1.

We have received introductory offers for an Internet connection from Time Warner and AT&T.

imperative statement
Please lock all entrances and engage the security system before you leave the store.

Remember that this offer is valid only until December 31.

indirect question
Several customers have inquired whether these plastic storage containers are dishwasher safe.

A number of our employees have asked about working overtime hours during the holiday season.

polite request
Would you please sign and return the enclosed escrow papers by June 15.

May I have your tax identification number so that we can issue payment for your consulting services.

2–34 End of Independent Phrase

Conclude independent phrases with a period. An independent phrase implies a complete thought and is not connected directly to the following sentence.

Now, to the point. Until we can determine the cause of the continual sales decline in the South Bend area, we will be subject to sustaining additional losses.

Yes, for the most part. Our salespeople have increased their sales since the new incentive program was established.

2–35 Abbreviations and Initials

a. **Abbreviated words are usually followed by a period. (See Section 2–39a for spacing following the period.) However, abbreviated forms for business and government organizations, associations, radio and television stations, federal agencies, and certain professional designations (*CLU, CPA, CPS, PLS*) do not contain periods.**

period after abbreviation
Fischer and Company **Inc.** has been handling our investment portfolio.

periods after abbreviations
The furniture is being shipped **f.o.b.** from Charleston, South Carolina.

Zip codes may be located on the **U.S.** Postal Service Web site.

no periods with certain abbreviations

Will the former president of **IBM** be available to address our national convention?

MSN is Microsoft's portal—offering news, sports, games, entertainment, weather, and other such features.

b. Place a period after an initial. Leave one space between the period and the next word or another initial.

Lindsey **K.** Morgan, one of our regional managers, has applied for a transfer to New York City.

Please fax this confirmation for hotel reservations to **R. W.** Hall.

2–36 Outlines

a. The outline feature of word processing software automatically sequences characters before each item in an outline. The software offers several outline models from which to choose. The setup and amount of space between the sequencing character and the item are determined by the kind and location of tabs set in the document. Guidelines for alphanumeric and decimal outlines follow:

(1) Use periods after letters and numbers (except those enclosed in parentheses) in alphanumeric outlines. Leave the equivalent of two blank spaces before beginning the content of the item.

(2) Use periods after whole numbers in decimal outlines. Leave the equivalent of two blank spaces after the last typed character before beginning the content of the item.

alphanumeric outline

```
I.  Xxxxxx
    A.  Xxxxxx
    B.  Xxxxxx
        1.  Xxxxxx
        2.  Xxxxxx
            a.  Xxxxxx
            b.  Xxxxxx
                (1)  Xxxxxx
                (2)  Xxxxxx
                     (a)  Xxxxxx
                     (b)  Xxxxxx
                          1)  Xxxxxx
                          2)  Xxxxxx
                              a)  Xxxxxx
                              b)  Xxxxxx
```

II. Xxxxxx
III. Xxxxxx
IV. Xxxxxx

decimal outline

1. Xxxxxx
    1.1. Xxxxxx
    1.2. Xxxxxx
        1.2.1. Xxxxxx
        1.2.2. Xxxxxx
            1.2.2.1. Xxxxxx
            1.2.2.2. Xxxxxx
                1.2.2.2.1. Xxxxxx
                1.2.2.2.2. Xxxxxx
                    1.2.2.2.2.1. Xxxxxx
                    1.2.2.2.2.2. Xxxxxx
                        1.2.2.2.2.2.1. Xxxxxx
                        1.2.2.2.2.2.2. Xxxxxx
2. Xxxxxx
3. Xxxxxx

b. No punctuation mark is placed after an incomplete thought in outlines and listings. Use periods only after complete sentences.

no periods—incomplete sentences

A. Broadband connections to the Internet for home users
    1. Direct Subscriber Line (DSL)
        a. Uses the extra bandwidth in a telephone line to provide continuous Internet connectivity
        b. Provides greater security than cable connections
        c. May experience slower than optimum speed depending upon the distance to the nearest telephone office
    2. Cable
        a. Offers speeds about twice the maximum speed of DSL and four times that of satellite Internet
        b. Uses a coaxial cable to connect users to the Internet
        c. Stays connected at all times
        d. May have slower connection speeds during peak hours when many people are online
    3. Satellite
        a. Allows users to have high-speed Internet in rural or remote areas where other forms of broadband are not available
        b. Costs more for the Internet service provider (ISP) to deliver the signal to a home computer from space so the higher costs are passed on to the user

c. Requires a large set-up fee
d. Has a slower speed than other broadband options

periods—complete sentences

A. Two processes separate our surfboards from the rest.
   1. Lamination of fiberglass to wooden surfaces contributes to vessel buoyancy.
   2. Sealing of surfaces prevents moisture absorption.

2–37 Decimals

Use periods to signify decimals.

Only **24.6** percent of the customers responding to our survey rated our service as "Excellent."

Electronics Depot is advertising the i-C 7-inch tablet, 16 GB, Quad Core, for **$79.99** during its weekend sale.

2–38 Ellipses

An ellipsis (a series of three periods with a space before, between, and after the series) is used for emphasis in advertising material or for showing omissions in quoted material. In showing omissions, indicate the completion of a thought with an additional period or other closing punctuation mark directly after the last word. (See Section 2–52 for further information on the use of ellipses.)

emphasis

Try our R-lax Massager . . . for relief from tension headaches . . . for ending miserable aches and pains . . . for a happier, tension-free you.

omission

The president read from the consultant's report: "Next year's operations should be conducted according to the enclosed report. . . . Operations personnel should . . . implement the recommended procedures."

2–39 Period Format

a. **No space is placed between a decimal point and a number or after a period within an abbreviation. Within a sentence, however, place one space after an initial or the concluding period in an abbreviation. In copy prepared on a word processor, allow one or two spaces after a period at the end of a sentence.**[7]

---

[7] For desktop publishing some authorities recommend one space after a period that concludes a sentence. To promote ease of reading in documents written for business, others use two spaces after a period that concludes a sentence. Spacing after a concluding period is discretionary, and word processing software can be defaulted to permit one or two spaces.

decimal—no space
The rise in building costs may be attributed to the **12.5** percent increase in the price of steel and lumber since 2013.

period within abbreviation—no space
Be sure to quote these furniture prices **f.o.b.**

initial—one space
Cameron **T.** Miller has been promoted to national sales manager.

abbreviation within sentence—one space
Dr. Sussman has scheduled **Mrs.** Hoffman for surgery at 7 **a.m.** on November 28 in Encino Hospital.

end of sentence—one space
Please submit proof that the property taxes have been **paid.** As soon as we receive a copy of your canceled check, we can close escrow.

end of sentence—two spaces
Please submit proof that the property taxes have been **paid.** As soon as we receive a copy of your canceled check, we can close escrow.

b. Use only one period to end a sentence, even though the sentence may end with an abbreviation.

If you wish, we can send this order c.o.d**.**

Your flight to Washington, DC, leaves at 7:28 a.m**.**

c. Always place a period inside the closing quotation mark.

At the meeting Ms. Jennings emphasized to all department heads, "No purchase requests will be funded after June 30**.**"

Our foods editor is interested in publishing your article, "Cooking with Garlic**.**"

d. Place a period inside the closing parenthesis when the words in parentheses are a complete sentence. When the words in parentheses are not a complete thought and are part of another sentence, place the period outside the closing parenthesis.

complete sentence in parentheses
More than 300 employees were laid off shortly after the merger. (The new management decided to downsize the company**.)**

incomplete sentence in parentheses
Two major marketing strategies were implemented after Dylan Consulting completed its analysis (August 2014**).**

Question Mark

2-40 Direct Questions

Conclude a direct question that requires an answer with a question mark.

Has Mrs. Shannon replied to our last e-mail message?

Of the more than 100 employees attending the board meeting, how many would you estimate were disappointed with the salary proposal?

2-41 Statements with Questions

a. **When a sentence contains a statement followed by a direct question, conclude the sentence with a question mark. Separate the statement from the question with a comma, dash, or colon, depending upon the nature of the statement.**

question mark with comma
I recommend that we contact at least three other vendors before selecting a permanent source of supply, wouldn't you agree?

question mark with dash
The council members seemed pleased with the architectural renderings for the proposed performing arts center—what is your appraisal?

question mark with colon
Each of us should consider the following question: what can we do to improve the profit picture for next year?

b. **Conclude a statement that contains a short, direct question with a question mark.**

You have filed your income tax return, have you not, for the past taxable year?

Our monthly payments are current—aren't they—for the leased offices in the Bradley Building?

c. **Conclude with a question mark a statement that is meant as a question.**

You have already finished reconciling today's receipts?

The conference has been delayed until April?

d. **Place a period, rather than a question mark, after an indirect question.**

Mr. Dinh asked when our Albany office will send us the information.

Ms. Casavilca inquired about placing two of her advanced students in our Accounting Department as trainees in an internship program.

e. **Polite requests phrased as questions are followed by periods rather than question marks because they are considered to be commands or "please do" statements. A polite request (1) asks the reader to perform a specific action and (2) anticipates that the reader will perform the requested action instead of responding "yes" or "no." Both components *must* be present for a period to be used; otherwise, a question mark is correct.**

polite request requiring period
Would you please complete the enclosed medical information form and bring it with you on June 17 for your appointment with Dr. Hayes.

May I please have your response by November 15.

Won't you take ten minutes now to complete our online questionnaire and at the same time enter your name in a drawing to win an iPad.

May we count on your support with a "yes" vote on Proposition A.

direct question requiring question mark
Would you be willing to sponsor a runner (with a small financial contribution) in the San Diego Marathon for the fight against leukemia? (Specific action that requires a "yes" or "no" response.)

May we visit your office next week to show you how the Ultima 1120 data projector will enhance your PowerPoint presentations? (Specific action that requires a "yes" or "no" response.)

Wouldn't you like to be the winner of a sleek Toshiba Satellite laptop computer? (Does not require reader to return a "yes" or "no" response; however, no *specific* action is requested.)

May we count on your support in this election? (Does not require reader to return a "yes" or "no" response; however, no *specific* action is requested.)

May I compliment you on your outstanding performance in meeting this year's sales quota? (No "yes" or "no" response is required; however, no *specific* action is requested.)

2-42 Expressions of Doubt

Signify doubt in expressing factual statements by enclosing a question mark in parentheses.

The national sales manager's last visit to our plant was in 2013 **(?)**.

Our administrative assistant earns $4,500 **(?)** a month.

2–43 Series of Questions

When a sentence contains a series of questions, place a question mark at the end of each question. Only the first letter of the sentence is capitalized unless a question in the series begins with a proper noun or is a complete thought. Leave one space after a question mark that appears within a sentence; leave one or two spaces after the concluding question mark (depending upon the style used throughout the document).[8]

series of incomplete questions
Who requested copies of the police report—the judge? the insurance company? the plaintiff's attorney?

What are the primary features of the Sigma XM 1200? the Sigma XM 1250? the Sigma XM 3000?

series of proper noun questions
Will the cruise ship make sightseeing stops in Montego Bay? Acapulco? Cabo San Lucas?

series of independent questions
Several topics were discussed at last week's company retreat: What style trends will dominate the market during the next decade? What comfort demands will the public make on furniture manufacturers? How much will price influence consumer furniture purchases?

2–44 Question Mark Placement and Format

a. Question marks may be placed either inside or outside the closing quotation mark or parenthesis. Use the following guidelines for determining question mark placement:

(1) Place the question mark inside the closing quotation mark or parenthesis when a complete question is contained within the quotation or parenthetical remark.
(2) Place the question mark outside the closing quotation mark or parenthesis if the entire sentence—not just the quotation or parenthetical remark—comprises the question.
(3) Use only the first question mark—the one appearing inside the closing quotation mark—if a quotation within a sentence and an entire sentence are both questions.
(4) Use only one concluding punctuation mark at the end of a sentence.

---

[8]Some desktop publishing authorities recommend only one space after the concluding punctuation mark; others use two spaces to promote ease of reading in business documents. The use of one or two spaces after a concluding punctuation mark is governed by the preference of the document originator, and word processing software may be defaulted to implement this preference.

complete question contained in quotation marks
"Will the entire original New York cast be present for the opening night in Philadelphia?" asked a local reporter.

The store manager then inquired, **"Who authorized these payments?"**

complete question contained in parentheses
We received official notification yesterday **(did your notice arrive yet?)** that all tenants must vacate the building by February 1.

Yesterday someone told me that Wilson Edwards has been promoted to vice president of sales for the Eastern Region. **(Has the Board of Directors announced its decision already?)**

question encompasses entire sentence
Have you read the article "International Business—Investment Opportunities Abroad"**?**

Will you be able to ship this order by May 15 (earlier if possible)**?**

both quotation and entire sentence questions
Did the president ask, "When will the directors hold their next meeting?"

b. In word processing copy, leave one space after a question mark that appears within a sentence and one or two spaces after a question mark that appears at the end of a sentence.[9]

one space after questions within sentence
Should I place these telephone directories in the reception desk drawers**?** in the file cabinet**?** in the storeroom**?**

one space after ending question mark
When is your flight scheduled to depart**?** What time do you wish to arrive at the airport**?** What type of airport transportation do you prefer**?** May I please have your e-mail reply or phone response by tomorrow morning?

two spaces after ending question mark
When is your flight scheduled to depart**?** What time do you wish to arrive at the airport**?** What type of airport transportation do you prefer**?** May I please have your e-mail reply or phone response by tomorrow morning?

---

[9]Some desktop publishing authorities suggest using only one space after a concluding punctuation mark; others use two spaces in business documents to promote ease of reading. The choice of one or two spaces remains with the document originator, and word processing software may be defaulted to implement this choice.

Exclamation Mark

2–45 Use of Exclamation Mark

To express a high degree of emotion, use an exclamation mark after a word, phrase, clause, or sentence.

word
What! You mean the hearing has been postponed again?

phrase
How original! The designer obviously used complementary colors and imagination to create the pattern in this fabric.

clause
If he attends! He'd better attend, or Mr. Ray will find a new assistant.

sentence
Yes, Dylan finally received the promotion she had been promised!

2–46 Exclamation Mark Format and Placement

a. **Exclamation marks should be used sparingly in business documents. Placing exclamation marks at the end of two consecutive sentences or thought units should be avoided. Instead, use a comma, a period, or a question mark with an exclamatory thought.**

exclamation with comma
Oh, we can't possibly meet the contract deadline without a large number of our employees working overtime!

exclamation with period
Impossible! There are no indications that the network has a virus.

exclamation with question mark
What a shock! How could our cash reserves have disappeared so quickly?

b. **In word processing copy, leave one or two spaces after the exclamation mark before beginning the next word.[10]**

c. **Exclamation marks may be placed either inside or outside the closing quotation mark or parenthesis. Use the following guidelines for determining exclamation mark placement.**

(1) Place the exclamation mark inside the closing quotation mark or parenthesis when a complete exclamatory remark is a quotation or is enclosed in parentheses.

[10] Some desktop publishing authorities recommend only one space after an ending punctuation mark; others use two spaces to foster reading ease. Document originators may use either style as long as they are consistent throughout the document.

(2) Place the exclamation mark outside the closing quotation mark or parenthesis if the entire sentence, not just the quotation or parenthetical element, comprises the exclamatory expression.
(3) Use only one concluding punctuation mark at the end of a sentence.

complete exclamatory expression in quotation marks
To free the trapped employee, the fire captain shouted, **"Break down the door!"**

complete exclamatory expression in parentheses
He obtained advice from another architectural firm **(what a mistake that was!)** to assist him in selecting the project contractor.

Management was surprised by the employees' reactions to the new system. **(Only 14 percent welcomed the change!)**

exclamatory expression encompasses entire sentence
I cannot believe the mayor's statement, "Only two members of the city council voted in favor of a rapid transit system for our city"!

If you wish to take advantage of the convention hotel rates, you will have to act immediately (before the block of rooms is sold out)**!**

Quotation Marks

2–47 Direct Quotations

Direct quotations contain the exact wording used by a writer or speaker. Follow these guidelines for punctuating short, direct quotations in business documents.

(1) Place one-sentence quotations and short two-sentence quotations within quotation marks.
(2) Use commas to introduce most one-sentence quotations. Long one-sentence quotations and quotations of two sentences or more are introduced by a colon.
(3) Quotation marks are not used for indirect quotations, which do not use the exact wording of the source.

direct quotation
"Americans' persistent demand for foreign products has driven the trade deficit to a record high," said Roger Watson, a renowned economist.

Roger Watson warned, **"Other countries are financing our debt, but they will not continue to do so forever."**

"Although this stock has split three times since 1999," explained Ms. Hadley, **"you cannot anticipate that it will continue to do so."**

The state architect's report denied our request for approval: **"Approval for this project is being withheld until plans are revised for updating (1) the infrastructure to support the proposed additional wing to the building and (2) the specifications for the ramp at the building entrance are brought into compliance with Federal Disabilities Act mandates."**

Mr. Miller's report recommended the following: **"Because interest rates have declined, we should investigate refinancing our building. We should contact several lenders to see if their plans would be to our advantage."**

indirect quotation
Perry Goldman, our production manager, forecasts that costs will increase another 10 percent unless we update our manufacturing process.

2-48 Long Quotations

Quotations of three or more sentences (usually four or more lines) in business documents are written without quotation marks, single-spaced, and formatted as separate paragraphs. They are indented from the left and right margins (0.5 inch) and separated from the main text by single blank lines at the beginning and the end.

The speaker also brought out the importance of effective management communication when she made the following statement:

> To exercise the function of leadership, there must be effective communication. If a leader cannot communicate, there is no leader because information cannot pass between the two groups. For instance, in management one cannot delegate duties and authority without effective communication.

Effective communication is paramount to effective leadership in . . . .

2-49 Short Expressions

a. **When short expressions such as jargon, words used in humor or irony, technical words used in a nontechnical way, coined expressions, or slang words are used in a document, they are placed in quotation marks.**

words used in irony
The board has set 2018 as a **"reasonable date"** for the completion of all the projects in the $6.5 billion bond program.

slang words
Mr. Simpson has difficulty working with others on the production team because he always wants to be **"in the driver's seat."**

technical words used in a nontechnical way
Ms. Evans announced that **"all systems are go"** for the new Scottsdale golf course and condominium project.

b. Place in quotation marks the definitions of words or expressions. Italicize the word or expression defined.

defined word
According to some economists, a ***recession*** is actually a **"short depression."**

defined expression
The French term ***faux pas*** means **"a social blunder."**

c. References to the words *marked, labeled, stamped,* or *signed* are placed in quotation marks.

Please mark all cartons **"Glass—Handle with Care."**

Stamp the envelope **"Addressee Unknown, Return to Sender."**

The letter was signed **"Sam Norris"** but contained no return address on either the letter or the envelope.

2-50 Titles of Literary and Artistic Works

Titles of various kinds of literary or artistic works—such as magazine or newspaper articles, chapters of books or pamphlets, unpublished manuscripts, episodes in television series, acts in plays or musicals, short poems, lectures, songs, and themes—are placed within quotation marks.

Names of books, magazines, pamphlets, newspapers, and other complete published or artistic works that contain subdivisions, however, are placed in italics. (See Section 3-6 for further information and examples of titles placed in italics.)

book and chapter title
The chapter **"Webmaster Onboard"** contained in ***Web Site Design and Maintenance*** was helpful in specifying the duties and responsibilities of our webmaster.

musical and song title
Of all the songs from the musical production ***Man of La Mancha***, **"The Impossible Dream"** is probably the most well recognized.

episode in television series
For the past four years, **"To Serve Man"** has been aired on our network's Thanksgiving Day marathon of selected episodes from the ***Twilight Zone***.

lecture title
The last lecture, **"Purchasing Your First Home,"** attracted a larger audience than we had anticipated.

2 Punctuation

2-51 Quotations within Quotations

Use single quotation marks to signify a quotation within a quotation. If your software does not support single quotation marks, use the apostrophe key.

For quoted material within single quotation marks, return to using double quotation marks.

quotation within a quotation
The report stated, "According to the U.S. Chamber of Commerce, **'The problem of air and water pollution must be solved within the next decade if our cities are to survive.'"**

quotation within single quotation marks
The newspaper article quoted the defendant's attorney as saying, "When I asked my client, 'Did you endorse the check **"Robert S. Parry"** and then proceed to cash it?' he replied, 'No, I did not.'"

2-52 Ellipses

An ellipsis—a series of three periods with a space before, between, and after the periods—is used to show an intentional omission of quoted material:

(1) If the omission begins the quoted sentence, use an ellipsis to begin the quotation.
(2) If the omission occurs within a sentence, use an ellipsis to substitute for the omitted words.
(3) If the omission occurs at the end of a sentence, use an ellipsis and then add the closing punctuation mark for the sentence.
(4) If one or more sentences have been omitted after the quoted sentence or sentences, first conclude the last sentence with the appropriate punctuation mark and then follow with an ellipsis to show the omission.

omission at beginning of quotation
The instructions stated, " **. . .** and remove blades before washing." (Remember to leave one space between the opening quotation mark and the first period in the ellipsis, one space between the periods, and one space after the closing period in the ellipsis.)

omission within sentence
A posted sign warns nonresidents about parking in this private lot: "Violators will be towed **. . .** cars will be released only upon payment of a $500 fine."

end-of-sentence omission
According to the written guarantee, "All repairs not under warranty will be made at manufacturer's costs **. . . .**"

Sean asked each applicant, "In Excel can you set up worksheets, generate charts, use database functions, create pivot tables, . . . ?"

one or more sentences omitted
The instructions stated explicitly: "Ship these international orders by June 1. . . . Our European distributors must have their merchandise by July 1." (Close the sentence with a period. Place one space before each period in the ellipsis; place one space after the final period in the ellipsis before beginning the next sentence.)

The marketing manager wrote in her September 9 e-mail, "Will you be able to attend the conference in Baltimore? **. . .** We will need to set up our display booths on October 9." (Use a closing punctuation mark followed by an ellipsis. Place one space before each period. After the final period in the ellipsis, place one space before beginning the next sentence.)

2–53 Capitalization with Quotation Marks

a. Capitalize the first word of a complete sentence enclosed in quotation marks.

"**Y**ou may make an appointment to renew your driver's license at our Web site," said the recorded voice at the other end of the telephone.

Courtney asked, "**W**hen will our campus be set up for wireless Internet access?"

b. Capitalize incomplete thoughts enclosed in quotation marks only if the quoted words themselves are capitalized. First, last, and main words[11] in quoted expressions preceded by *stamped* or *marked* are usually capitalized.

capitalized
This check was returned by the bank marked **"Insufficient Funds."**

"Handle with Care" was stamped on the package.

Did you mark the claim check **"Paid in Full"**?

not capitalized
Ms. Brown suggested we place **"a minimum priority"** on this project.

The advisory council was surprised to learn from the consulting architect's report that current funding for the renovation of these historic buildings has **"a projected $31 million shortfall."**

---

[11]*Main* words are all words EXCEPT (1) the articles *a, an,* and *the;* (2) the coordinating conjunctions *and, but, or,* and *nor;* (3) prepositions; (4) the word *to* in an infinitive (*to* write); and (5) the word *as*—unless any of these words are the first or last words.

2–54 Quotation Mark Placement

a. Commas and periods are always placed inside the closing quotation mark; semicolons and colons, outside the closing quotation mark.

period
The purchase requisition stipulates, "Cancel this order if the merchandise cannot be delivered by July 1."

comma
"We must find ways to lower our operating costs," said Mr. Hunter.

semicolon
The consultant's report specified, "The company should perform a thorough analysis of its information processing system"; however, no procedures have been initiated for such an analysis.

colon
Mrs. Daley suggested that we adopt the following policy "unless a better one can be formulated": (1) Employees may select vacation times according to company seniority and (2) employees, whenever possible, may resolve among themselves any schedule conflicts.

b. Follow these procedures for using question marks or exclamation marks with quotation marks:

(1) When a complete question or exclamation is contained within the quotation, place the question mark or the exclamation mark inside the closing quotation mark.
(2) When the entire sentence comprises the question or exclamation, place the appropriate mark outside the closing quotation mark.
(3) When both the quotation and the entire sentence are questions, use only the first question mark—the one inside the closing quotation mark.

complete question within quotation
The auditor asked, **"Do you have the receipts for these expenditures?"**

entire sentence comprises question
Which issue of *Business Today* contains the article "Speech Technology Revolutionizes Internet Strategies"?

complete exclamation within quotation
"Do not," exclaimed Mr. Rey, **"leave the lights burning all night!"**

entire sentence comprises exclamation
Our new sales manager appears to be a real "go-getter"!

question within a question
Did you receive Eric's e-mail that asked, "Who was responsible for engaging the security system last night?"

Apostrophe

2-55 Possessives

a. **When a noun, singular or plural, does not end with a pronounced *s*, add an apostrophe and *s* (*'s*) to form the possessive case.**

singular noun
Yes, I located the purchase requisition on my **assistant's** desk.

Lisa's appointment has been rescheduled for November 23.

Most of the **company's** profits were earned during the first quarter.

plural noun
Women's fashions this summer season are featuring bright colors.

Most of our discounted **children's** toys have already been sold.

These sweaters are made from 100 percent **sheep's** wool.

b. **When a noun, singular or plural, ends with a pronounced *s*, add an apostrophe (') to form the possessive case. However, an apostrophe and *s* (*'s*) may be added to singular nouns if an additional *s* sound is pronounced.**

singular noun with pronounced s sound—add ' only
Ms. Simons' income and credit rating qualify her to buy this property.

Most of these museum pieces were found among **Athens'** ruins.

plural noun with pronounced s sound—add ' only
Customers' accounts more than 90 days overdue are referred to an agency for collection.

One of our real estate agents sold the **Lopezes'** home today.

singular noun with additional s sound—add 's
Your **class's** scores on this state examination were exceptionally high.

Ask **Mr. Jones's** assistant for a copy of the report.

Were you present in court during the **witness's** testimony?

c. **Use an apostrophe to show possession with (1) nouns that represent people, animals, and other living entities (animate objects) or (2) nouns related to time, distance, value, or celestial bodies. For other types of nouns (inanimate objects), use an *of* phrase to show possession.**

animate possessive
The **employees'** representative will meet with me on February 15.

Preserve your **hair's** color and luster with Canterbury's Protein+ conditioning shampoo.

Were any of the **horse's** hooves lacerated during the race?

Can you ensure that the **tree's** roots will not crack the swimming pool deck?

Our **company's** steadily declining profits led to the replacement of its executive officers. (The word *company* is animate because it is composed of animate objects—people.)

time possessive
This past **year's** income statement showed a gain of nearly 9 percent.

Six **months'** interest on your bank card alone amounted to $1,218.60.

Yesterday's mail was still lying unopened on her desk when this **morning's** mail arrived.

distance possessive
The Kingston Hotel is just a **stone's** throw from the airport.

Although the suspect rushed by within **arm's** length, we were unable to supply a description to the police.

value possessive
Our office manager ordered several thousand **dollars'** worth of supplies and equipment.

We owe the customer 50 **cents'** change.

celestial possessive
During the summer months, the **sun's** rays can be extremely harmful.

Is **Mars'** atmosphere suitable for human survival?

inanimate possessive
The **terms of the loan** were extended six months. (Not *loan's terms.*)

Who broke the **base of the statue**? (Not *statue's base.*)

d. Form the possessive of compound nouns by having the last word show possession.

Ann was appointed her **mother-in-law's** custodian by the courts.

Our meeting will be held at the **chairman of the board's** home.

My two **sisters-in-law's** business is doing well.

e. When two or more nouns have joint ownership (own one thing together), only the last noun shows possession. When the nouns represent individual ownership (each owns something separately), however, each noun must show possession.

joint ownership
Tom and Karen's administrative assistant has worked at Synco Corporation for three years. (Tom and Karen share the same administrative assistant—joint ownership.)

The Harrises and the Bradys' boat was damaged in the storm. (The Harrises and the Bradys own the same boat—joint ownership.)

individual ownership
Leslie's and Carson's offices have been relocated to the new wing of the Richmond Building. (Leslie and Carson have different offices—individual ownership.)

The Schaeffers' and the Gonzalezes' homes are on the same street. (The Schaeffers and the Gonzalezes live in different homes—individual ownership.)

f. Express the possessive form of indefinite pronouns such as *anyone, everyone, someone, anybody, everybody, somebody,* and *nobody* by using the same rules that apply to possessive nouns.

Anyone's vehicle parked illegally in a space reserved for disabled individuals will be towed away.

Somebody's keys were found in the employee parking lot this morning.

g. The possessive forms of personal or relative pronouns (such as *its, yours, hers, theirs,* or *whose*) do not include apostrophes. These pronouns are often confused with verb contractions, all of which contain apostrophes.

possessive pronoun
Although the company experienced **its** greatest sales volume last year, it still has not shown a profit.

The bill was introduced by Senator Adams, **whose** term of office will end in December.

contraction
It's (It is) one of our most profitable lines.

We met with Keith, **who's (who is)** the developmental editor for this project.

h. Express the possessive form of abbreviations by using the same rules that apply to possessive nouns (Sections 2-55a and 2-55b).

abbreviation not ending with pronounced s
The **CPA's** report was short, yet comprehensive.

NASA's Mars Curiosity rover was launched on November 26, 2011, and landed on Mars on August 5, 2012.

abbreviation ending with pronounced s
Barker Bros.' annual sale has been extended for another week.

All **RNs'** and **LVNs'** identification badges are reissued annually.

You may download copies of income tax forms from the **IRS's** Web site. (Use *'s* instead of just an apostrophe because of the extra pronounced *s* sound.)

2 Punctuation

i. Use the possessive form of a noun or a pronoun before a gerund (a verb form ending in *ing* that is used as a noun).

noun
Ryan's placing among the top 10 percent of his high school graduating class ensured his admittance to Armstrong University.

pronoun
We would appreciate **your returning** the enclosed form by March 31.

j. When a possessive noun is followed by an explanatory expression (an appositive), use an apostrophe only in the explanatory expression. When this form of writing sounds awkward, as it does in most cases, show possession by using an *of* phrase.

apostrophe
Ms. Norton, **our advertising manager's**, office is being renovated.

of ***phrase***
The office **of our advertising manager,** Ms. Norton, is being renovated.

k. Many organizations with plural possessives in their names have omitted the apostrophe; organizations with singular possessives have tended to retain the apostrophe. Use an apostrophe in an organizational name only if the organization itself does so.

plural possessive
Your loan approval from **Farmers** Bank arrived this morning.

singular possessive
Did Allison find her lost **Macy's** credit card?

l. Sometimes the possessed item is not stated explicitly in a sentence; instead, it is understood or implied clearly. In such cases the ownership word still requires an apostrophe to show possession.

Next month our investment club will meet at **Kevin's**. (Kevin's *apartment*, Kevin's *home*, or some other place belonging to Kevin.)

Be sure to arrive at the **doctor's** by 9 a.m. (Doctor's *office.*)

The briefcase found in the elevator was **Mr. Ruiz's**. (Mr. Ruiz's *briefcase.*)

Deliver this floral arrangement to the **Briggses'** before noon. (The Briggses' *home.*)

This year's sales are considerably higher than last **year's**. (Last year's *sales.*)

2–56 Additional Uses of the Apostrophe

a. Use the apostrophe to form contractions.

single-word contraction

acknowledged **ack'd** national **nat'l** cannot **can't**

two-word contraction

you are **you're** is not **isn't** I have **I've**

b. The apostrophe is used for clarity to form the plural of all isolated lowercase letters and the single capital letters *A, I, M,* and *U.*

plural of lowercase letter

The word *professor* is spelled with two ***s's***, not two ***f's***.

Remind the children to cross their ***t's*** so that they are easily distinguishable from their ***l's***.

***plural of capital letters* A, I, M, *and* U**

Last semester Maria earned three ***A's***, which placed her on the dean's list.

The ***M's*** in this font style are especially difficult to read.

c. The apostrophe may be used for the single quotation mark to signify a quotation within a quotation.

Adam reported, "The president opened the forum with **'We're going to drive QuickWrite's sales back up to and beyond its former high!'**"

d. Use the apostrophe to signify the omission of figures in expressing a year.

Job prospects for the class of **'17** look favorable—especially for applicants with computer, math, and communication skills.

e. In technical material the apostrophe may be used as a symbol for *feet.*

15' × 18' (room) 5' 9" (height) 100' × 140' (area)

Parentheses

2–57 Nonessential Expressions

Parentheses are used to set off and subordinate nonessential expressions that would otherwise confuse the reader because they (1) give supplementary information that has no direct bearing on the main idea or (2) call for an abrupt change in thought. References and instructions are two examples of expressions that are often enclosed in parentheses.

abrupt change in thought

I e-mailed Mr. Bradley **(I tried to call him, but there was no answer)** and asked him to contact us before August 30.

2 Punctuation

reference
All purchases over $5,000 must be approved by the vice president of business services. **(See Bulletin 8 dated March 2.)**

instructions
Please mail 200 copies of our annual report to each of our European offices. **(Send them by Priority Mail® International.)**

2–58 Numerals

Numerals in legal, business, and professional documents are often shown in parentheses to confirm a spelled-out figure.

All repair work is guaranteed for ninety **(90)** days.

The approved bid was for five thousand dollars **($5,000)**.

Purchase requisitions in excess of nine thousand nine hundred ninety-nine dollars **($9,999)** must be approved by the vice president.

On March 4 our client received a check for two thousand eight hundred forty-three dollars and seventy-five cents **($2,843.75)**.

2–59 Enumerated Items

Enclose in parentheses numbers or letters used to enumerate lists of items within a sentence. (See Section 2–36a for the use of parentheses with alphanumeric outlines.)

numbers
Please supply me with the following data for last year: the number of **(1)** new hires, **(2)** retirements, **(3)** voluntary resignations, and **(4)** terminations by the company.

letters
This Web site supplies up-to-date employment information for Los Angeles County: **(a)** occupations with fastest job growth, **(b)** wages by occupation, and **(c)** employment by industry.

2–60 Parentheses with Other Punctuation Marks

a. **Words, phrases, and clauses enclosed in parentheses in the middle of a sentence function as part of the sentence in applying rules of punctuation and capitalization.**

word
Are you planning to go to Fort Lauderdale **(Florida)** for the American Management Association convention?

phrase
Ms. Parsons will gross nearly $900,000 **(compared with a $600,000 average)** in sales this year!

clause
Our new webmaster **(he joined our company on March 1)** will meet with the department managers to set up a company intranet.

b. When an incomplete thought enclosed in parentheses ends a sentence that requires a period, a question mark, or an exclamation mark, place the closing punctuation mark outside the closing parenthesis.

According to our legal counsel, this promotion violates laws in two states **(only Minnesota and Wyoming).**

c. When a complete thought enclosed in parentheses follows a sentence, the two parts are treated separately. Place a closing punctuation mark (period, question mark, or exclamation mark) at the end of each sentence—with the final closing punctuation mark appearing inside the closing parenthesis.

Yes, your order was shipped on April 17. **(You should receive it within five or six working days.)**

Did any members of our staff attend the ATLW conference this year? **(This year's conference was held in Honolulu.)**

d. If an interrupting word, phrase, or clause shown in parentheses requires a question mark or an exclamation mark, use such a mark of punctuation only if the sentence ends with a different mark.

parenthetical question
Our vice president **(do you know Alex Lesino?)** will arrive here tomorrow to review our operations.

When will our revised price list **(has your copy arrived)** become effective?

parenthetical exclamation
Are you aware of the recent large-scale price increases **(I can't believe them!)** in single-family homes?

Living conditions **(you can scarcely call them that)** are absolutely deplorable in this section of the city!

e. Place commas, semicolons, and colons outside the closing parenthesis.

comma
If you plan to attend our manager's retirement banquet (May 16**),** please send your reservations to Terry Thomsen by Monday, May 12.

semicolon
His report deals primarily with the importance of our country's major transportation systems (railroads, inland waterways, motor trucks, pipelines, and air transportation**);** therefore, little emphasis was given to rising transportation costs.

colon

On February 1 Ms. Haddad will introduce two new product lines (for women's fashion departments)**:** the Sportswoman Series and the Sun and Surf Coordinates.

Brackets

2–61 Use of Brackets

a. Use brackets to insert an explanation, a correction, or a comment in quoted material. To show that an error in quoted material appeared in the original document, enclose the term *sic* (meaning "so" or "this is the way it was") in brackets.

Ms. Simons stated in her report: "With new equipment to speed up the production process **[she did not specify what new equipment was needed]**, substantial reductions can be realised **[sic]** in both labor and overhead costs."

b. Brackets may be used within parentheses to indicate yet another subordinate idea.

The auction of Rita Rothchild's possessions (including jewelry, furs, furniture, movie costumes **[from 1958 through 1988]**, china, silverware, and other memorabilia) is scheduled for July 17 and 18.

2–62 Use of Angle Brackets

Some authorities suggest using angle brackets to enclose the addresses (URLs) of Internet sites or e-mail addresses when contiguous punctuation may confuse the reader. This practice is generally not suggested for audiences familiar with Web site and e-mail address formats.

Have you had an opportunity to visit the Los Angeles Community College District employment Web site, <http://www.laccd.edu/district_resources/employment.htm>?

2–63 Brackets with Other Punctuation Marks

The placement of other punctuation marks with brackets follows the same principles outlined for parentheses in Section 2–60.

Asterisk

2–64 Use of the Asterisk

Asterisks may be used to call the reader's attention to footnotes in a document when they appear infrequently and occur at widely spaced intervals. The asterisk follows other punctuation marks—except a dash, a closing parenthesis, or a closing bracket.

after most punctuation marks
A recent government report states, "Air traffic is expected to double within the next decade."*

before dash, closing parenthesis, or closing bracket
We are studying the works of Ray Bradbury*—one of our leading contemporary science fiction writers.

A number of companies that have hired outside consultants to develop cost-cutting procedures have reported successful results. (Several articles supporting the effectiveness of outside consultants have recently appeared in leading professional journals.*)

Prominent national magazines (such as *TIME*, *Newsweek*, and *Bloomberg Businessweek* [May and June issues*]) have published informative, interesting articles on issues related to social-networking Web sites.

Diagonal

2-65 Use of Diagonal

Use a diagonal (also called a "solidus," "slash," or "virgule") between (1) letters in some abbreviations, (2) numerals in fractions not available through the extended character set of a word processing program, and (3) the expression *and/or* to show that the terms are interchangeable. No space appears before or after the diagonal.

abbreviation
Please address the package to Mrs. Monica Simonian, **c/o** Mr. Jorge Martinez, Display Manager, Nelson Paper Company, 860 SW Market Street, Portland, Oregon 97208.

fraction
Our state sales tax will increase ½ percent on January 1.

To reupholster the reception room sofa will require **12 ⅝** yards of fabric.

The precision requirement for this engine part is within **1/1000** of a millimeter.

Since the remaining fabric on this bolt is only **1 15/16** yards, it should be discounted and sold as a remnant.

and/or
Authorization for future equipment purchases may be obtained from Ms. Silva **and/or** Mr. Paransky.

Underscore

2–66 Use of the Underscore

The underscore is generally not used in computer-generated or printed copy. Other font attributes—italics, bolding, bolded italics, and varied font sizes—substitute for the underscore. Underscoring may occasionally be used as a font attribute. In such cases use continuous lines with no spacing between words. The ending punctuation mark is not underscored unless it is the concluding period in an abbreviation.

underscoring used as a font attribute
Parking citations will be issued to any employee parked in spaces reserved for customer parking.

concluding punctuation mark after underscored words
Merchandise may be returned for exchange or refund within 30 days.

concluding punctuation mark after underscored abbreviation
During the summer months, our store hours will be Tuesday through Saturday from 10 a.m. until 4 p.m.

Ampersand

2–67 Use of the Ampersand

a. **The ampersand (&), a symbol that represents the word *and*, is used primarily to express the official name of some business organizations.**

ampersand in company name
Candice's first experience as a pharmaceutical representative was with Johnson **&** Johnson.

Foster, Jacobs **&** Newman is handling the settlement of the Hutchinson estate.

use of* and *in company name
All merger talks with Merritt **and** Sons have been delayed until the end of our fiscal period.

b. **When an ampersand appears in a series, use a comma before the ampersand only if the organization does so in its official name.**

no comma before the ampersand
The law offices of Levitt, Myers **&** Cohen represented the plaintiff in this case.

comma before the ampersand
Fall fashions from Liz, Lee**,** **&** Co. should arrive in our store by the middle of July.

3

Capitalization

Capitalization Solution Finder

Capitalization Solution Finder *(continued)*

3–1 Beginning Words

a. Capitalize the beginning words of sentences, quoted sentences, independent phrases, lines of poetry, and items in an outline.

sentence

We are in the process of changing the label design for our pasta products.

Because of its outstanding dental hygienist program, some of our students have decided to attend West Los Angeles College.

Have you considered using our free online bill-paying service?

quoted sentence

The contract stipulates, **"Employees** may change medical insurance providers only during the open enrollment period."

independent phrase

Now, for the most important topic.

poetry

By the rude bridge that arched the flood,
Their flag to the April's breeze unfurled,
Here once the embattled farmers stood,
And fired the shot heard round the world.

—Emerson

outline

1. **Contents** of carton
   a. **Instructions** for assembly
   b. **Parts** for Royal mini cycle
   c. **Tools** needed for assembly
   d. **Diagrams** illustrating assembly

b. The first word of an incomplete quoted thought that is woven in with the rest of the sentence is not capitalized unless it is (1) a proper noun, (2) introduced by an identifying term such as *marked* or *stamped*, or (3) capitalized because of another rule of capitalization.

lowercase

The staff was directed **"not** to speak to the press about the pending merger."

proper noun

The newscaster's comment was simply **"Jon** Greeley takes all!"

***introduced by identifying term* marked *or* stamped**

The patient's check was returned by the bank and marked **"Insufficient Funds."**

Request our Shipping Department to stamp all these packages **"Fragile—Handle with Care."**

another rule of capitalization
Remind students that these survey questionnaires are machine-readable forms and the instructions specify **"No. 2** pencils only."

c. **In business letters addressed to specific individuals, groups of individuals, or companies, capitalize the first word and any nouns contained in the salutation. For letters directed to undetermined individuals, capitalize the first word and all main words[1] in the salutation.**

Capitalize only the first word of a complimentary close.

standard salutation—first word and all nouns
Dear **M**r. **S**chleicher: **G**entlemen: **M**y dear **F**riend:

Dear fellow **A**merican: **L**adies and **G**entlemen: **D**ear **C**lient:

salutation to undetermined individual—first word and all main words
To **W**hom **I**t **M**ay **C**oncern:

To **S**tockholders of **R**ecord on **M**ay 1, 2016:

complimentary close
Sincerely yours, **C**ordially yours, **Y**ours very truly,

d. **The first word following a colon is generally not capitalized. Capitalize the first word, however, when the following words (1) begin with a proper noun, (2) consist of two or more sentences, (3) begin a vertical listing, (4) present a rule, or (5) require emphasis.**

first word not capitalized
To landscape the model homes, our crew will require the following**: sod,** ground cover, and low-growing plants.

Our Houston branch is experiencing a delay in filling its orders**: the** warehouse fire set back its schedule by at least three weeks.

proper noun following colon
Three colleges are involved in the project**: Kennebec** Valley Community College, Copiah-Lincoln Community College, and Spokane Community College.

two or more sentences following colon
Here are two questions to consider**: Will** expanding our factory operations be economically feasible at this time? **Will** future market demand support any increased production?

---

[1]*Main* words are all words EXCEPT (1) the articles *a, an,* and *the*; (2) the coordinating conjunctions *and, but, or, nor,* and *for*; (3) all prepositions; (4) the word *to* used in an infinitive (*to* write); and (5) the word *as*—unless any of these words are the first or last words.

vertical listing following colon

Please send us copies of the following documents:

1. **Lease** agreement with Property Management Associates
2. **Statement** of income and expenses for 2016
3. **Budget** of projected income and expenses for 2017

formal rule following colon

Apply the following punctuation rule for all articles published in *Business Monthly*: **For** items in a series (words, phrases, or clauses), place a comma after each item in the series including the one before the word *and*.

Use the following style to prepare all correspondence for our company: **Format** letters in modified block style with blocked paragraphs and mixed punctuation.

item of special emphasis following colon

Note: **Several** of our employees consistently access nonwork-related Web sites during working hours.

Wanted: **Full-time** salesperson to work weekdays 8 a.m. until 5 p.m.

e. The first word of a complete thought contained in parentheses *within a sentence* is not capitalized—unless the word is a proper noun. A complete thought contained in parentheses appearing immediately after a sentence is treated as a separate unit, and the first word is capitalized.

first word not capitalized within sentence

Several minor changes (**these** were recommended by Mr. De La Garza) will be made in the final copy.

parentheses within sentence—proper noun capitalized

Your suggestions (**Ms.** Berger approved all of them) will be incorporated into the marketing survey.

parentheses after end of sentence—first word capitalized

Twelve students who are majoring in production management wish to tour our Logan plant. (**The** students are seniors from Utah State University.)

3–2 Proper Nouns and Adjectives[2]

a. Proper nouns (words that name a particular person, place, or thing) and adjectives derived from proper nouns are capitalized. Capitalize the names of persons, cities, states, countries, rivers, mountains, streets, parks, colleges, buildings, shopping centers, malls, developments, organizations, ships, airplanes, specific events, and other such entities.

---

[2] The capitalization principles that follow are based primarily on those suggested by The University of Chicago Press. (2010). *The Chicago Manual of Style* (16th ed.). Chicago: The University of Chicago Press. *The Chicago Manual of Style Online* is available at http://www.chicagomanualofstyle.org/home.html and may be accessed in its entirety for an annual fee.

proper noun

Our field representative for your area is located in **Warren, Ohio**.

Have you visited our new offices in the **Atlantic Building** on **South Broad Street**?

The **Ventura County Fair** will be held in **Fallbrook Park** this year.

We flew to **Fort Lauderdale, Florida,** on a **Boeing 757** to meet our ship, the **Regal Princess**, for a cruise through the **Panama Canal**.

Which architectural firm was awarded the contract to design the **Fashion Square Mall**?

Next month **Derek** and **Beth** will raft down the **Colorado River**.

How much is the toll for the **Golden Gate Bridge**, which spans **San Francisco Bay**?

adjective derived from proper noun[3]

Football, basketball, and baseball are typical **American** sports enjoyed by both children and adults.

Be sure to order **Roquefort** dressing and grated **Swiss** cheese for the salad bar.

Where can I find a listing of **Internet** access providers for our area?

How many **Canadian** dollars do you anticipate we will need while we are on this tour?

Our decorator showroom, The Gallery, always carries an extensive line of **Victorian** furniture.

b. When well-known descriptive terms, such as nicknames, are used in place of proper nouns, they are capitalized.

My territory includes all sales districts west of the **Rockies**. (Rocky Mountains)

Most of his recent business trips have been to the **City of Brotherly Love** and the **Big Easy**. (Philadelphia and New Orleans)

The assassination of **JFK** in 1963 stunned the nation. (John F. Kennedy)

Big Blue is among the few information technology companies whose history dates back to the nineteenth century. (IBM)

c. Sometimes proper nouns, such as the names of widely used commercial products, become common nouns through popular usage. As a result, they are not capitalized. Always capitalize, however, specific brand or trade names of products. Any words that describe a type or kind of product (such as *refrigerator, vacuum cleaner,*

[3] The capitalization of all adjectives derived from proper nouns is based on entries shown in Merriam-Webster Incorporated. (2015). *Merriam-Webster's Collegiate Dictionary Online*. Springfield, MA: Merriam-Webster Incorporated. http://www.merriam-webster.com/info/copyright.htm

3 Capitalization

television, computer, or _printer_) are not capitalized unless they represent a coined derivative that is considered part of the trade name.[4]

common noun meaning

Addresses without a **zip code** on this mailing list are undeliverable as bulk mail.

Would you like me to **xerox** these forms for you?

Before computer-aided design software became available, these drawings were all done in **india** ink.

Our restaurant serves **french** fries with all its sandwiches.

Copies of the **braille** alphabet may be obtained from the Braille Institute of America.

Reproductions of this statue can be made from plaster of **paris**.

How many **china** patterns does Regency carry in its line?

You will find dining at Adagio's Ristorante an **epicurean** delight.

The demand for our cars with **diesel** engines is declining steadily.

brand or trade name with common noun product

Our store no longer carries **Kleenex facial tissues** exclusively.

Your new **Jacuzzi whirlpool bath** will be delivered and installed on Tuesday, March 8.

Please provide the client with an auxiliary backup drive for this **Dell computer**.

Manufacturing of the **Panasonic plasma television** ceased in 2013 as newer technologies dominated the television market.

product name part of trade name

Your **Amana Radarange** (microwave oven) will give you many years of service.

For Father's Day our store experienced a heavy demand for **Sony Handycams** (camcorders).

Almost every day for lunch, Kevin has either a **Filet-O-Fish** sandwich or an order of **Chicken McNuggets**. (Registered product names from McDonald's)

---

[4]Check an up-to-date dictionary to determine which proper nouns have become common nouns and are no longer capitalized. The examples shown here are based on entries from Merriam-Webster Incorporated. (2015). *Merriam-Webster's Collegiate Dictionary Online*. Springfield, MA: Merriam-Webster Incorporated. http://www.merriam-webster.com /info/copyright.htm.

3–3 Abbreviations

Most abbreviations are capitalized only if the words they represent are capitalized. Exceptions to this rule are the abbreviations of academic degrees, professional designations, and certain coined business expressions. Refer to Section 6–11 for the proper format of abbreviations commonly used in business.

lowercase words represented by lowercase abbreviations

Please send the 4 dozen cardboard file boxes **c.o.d.** (*collect on delivery*)

Our office is open weekdays from 9 **a.m.** until 5:30 **p.m.** (*ante meridiem* and *post meridiem*)

capitalized words represented by capitalized abbreviations

You may be requested to prepare your résumé in **ASCII** format for online transmission. (*American Standard Code for Information Interchange*)

Ms. Chin was awarded a bachelor of arts degree from **UCLA** in 2011. (*University of California, Los Angeles*)

exceptions

Our university offers **BS** and **MS** degrees in psychology through the College of Letters, Arts, and Sciences. (*bachelor of science* and *master of science*)

Buena Vista Medical Clinic has an opening for an additional **RN**. (*registered nurse*)

Subscription **TV** is available through your local cable company or a satellite company servicing your area. (*television*)

3–4 Numbered or Lettered Items

Capitalize word-numeral and word-letter combinations except in references to pages, paragraphs, lines, verses, sizes, and vitamins.

The word *number* is abbreviated except when it appears at the beginning of a sentence.

capitalized word-numeral and word-letter combinations

Your electronic ticket is for **Flight 143** from Chicago to Denver on April 8.

Before sending payment, check **Invoice 187324** to verify that all the items have been received.

The class has been moved to **Room 132** in the Harper Building.

Definitions of grammatical terms used in this reference manual are contained in **Appendix A**.

lowercased word-numeral and word-letter combinations

Refer to **page 6**, **paragraph 2**, of the contract for the schedule of project completion.

Lack of **vitamin A** can result in visual defects.

the word* number *abbreviated within a sentence

Have you had an opportunity to restock our supply of **No.** 10 white envelopes?

My homeowner's policy, **No.** HO387092, should cover this loss.

Your Invoice **No.** F23146 was paid on February 14 by Check **No.** 871.

the word* number *written out at the beginning of a sentence

Number 982-RC patio sets should arrive from the manufacturer within the next week.

3–5 Personal and Professional Titles[5]

a. Capitalize the courtesy titles *Mr., Ms., Mrs., Miss, Master,* and *Dr.* when they precede and are used in conjunction with persons' names.

Capitalize also a title representing a person's profession, company position, military rank, service rank, religious station, or political office when it precedes and is used directly with a person's name *in place of a courtesy title.*

Capitalize a title representing family relationship or nobility when it appears before the name of an individual and is used directly with the name.

courtesy title

Two board members, **Mr.** John Crossley and **Dr.** Joseph Perret, are unable to attend the March 4 meeting.

Both **Ms.** Korzan and **Mrs.** Scher-Padilla have agreed to serve on the selection committee for our Houston sales representative.

Please inform **Master** Todd Jaffarian that he has been selected as a finalist in the "eight-year-old" category of our children's contest.

professional title

Has **Professor** Donna Anderson agreed to critique the manuscript?

title indicating company position

Although **President** Newton attended the stockholders' meeting, she asked **Vice President** Larry Kraus from our Charlotte branch to present last year's earnings report.

military or service rank title

Major Michael Zimmerman has requested a transfer to Edwards Air Force Base.

Police matters of this type are under **Captain** Murillo's jurisdiction.

---

[5] The principles presented here are based upon those contained in The University of Chicago Press. (2010). *The Chicago Manual of Style* (16th ed.). Chicago: The University of Chicago Press, online edition.

religious title

Please ensure that **Archbishop** Lucatorto receives copies of these district reports.

The **Reverend** William Gillespie will be the guest minister for next Sunday's services.

Marvin and Stephanie have requested that **Rabbi** Cogan perform the marriage ceremony.

political title

When will **Senator** Reeves return to Washington, DC?

Has **Governor** Brown released a statement to the press about next year's budget?

Mayor Alex Rivera will meet with the city council on Monday.

title showing family relationship

As soon as **Aunt** Laura's house is sold, her attorney will establish a trust fund.

These U.S. Savings Bonds were given to the children by **Grandpa** Peterson.

title of nobility

Several recent magazine articles have dealt with the life of **Prince** William and his family.

This furniture style dates back to the era of **Queen** Victoria.

b. A person's title—professional, business, military, service, religious, political, family, or one pertaining to nobility—is not capitalized when it is followed by the person's name used as an appositive.

She consulted her **doctor, Linda Montgomery,** after the accident.

You will need to obtain approval from the **executive vice president, F. Ross Byrd**.

Please consult the **captain, John Blakely,** before recommending any changes in this precinct's boundaries.

Such decisions are made solely by the **governor, Paul Nieman.**

Rebecca Dentino inherited the property in Troy, Michigan, from her **uncle, Gino Marcus.**

c. In running text do not capitalize a title that appears after a person's name. Titles that appear after persons' names in a displayed list are capitalized.[6]

---

[6]The principles presented here are based upon those contained in The University of Chicago Press. (2010). *The Chicago Manual of Style* (16th ed.). Chicago: The University of Chicago Press, online edition. Some business and government organizations choose to capitalize the titles of their officials even if the title appears after the name or without the name. In doing so, they should be consistent in their application of this variation.

title after name in running text
Mike Rawlings, **mayor** of Dallas, is the former CEO (chief executive officer) of Pizza Hut.

Johnny Isakson, **senator** from Georgia, was elected for another six-year term, which ends in January 2017.

Captain Harrison, our **company commander**, has been alerted that our unit may be placed on active duty next month.

You may wish to invite Janet Horne, **president** of AMCO Products, to address the convention participants on May 11.

Carl Irwin, **director of marketing**, has developed several innovative ideas for promoting our weight-loss program.

If you wish additional information, please contact Svetlana Holt, **professor of business**, at Simpson Community College.

Did Dr. David Schultz, **rabbi** of Temple Beth Torah, accept our invitation to give the invocation at the graduation ceremony?

title after name in a displayed listing
The company's leadership team includes the following CEO staff members:

Kevin Sweeney, **President and Chief Executive Officer**
David Goodman, **Vice President and Chief Information Officer**
Denise Fenton, **Executive Vice President**
Brian McDougall, **Senior Vice President, Human Resources**
George Morrison, **Executive Vice President, Global Operations**
John Dow, **Executive Vice President and Chief Financial Officer**
Roger Obermeier, **Vice President, Research and Development**
Harriet Scott, **Senior Vice President and General Counsel**

d. When a person's title is used in place of his or her name, the title is generally not capitalized. However, in cases of family relationships and direct address, capitalize the title if it *replaces the name*.

Do not capitalize common nouns such as *sir, madam, ladies,* or *gentlemen* used in direct address.

title used in place of name—not capitalized
Has the **president** announced who will fill the vacancy left by the **secretary of state**?

Since the **governor** will be in Washington, DC, the **lieutenant governor** has agreed to open the bicentennial celebration honoring the founding of our city.

The **president** directed her **executive assistant** to inform all the department managers that the **vice president of human resources** has resigned.

family title used in place of name—capitalized
I believe **Grandpa** is eligible for some of these veterans' benefits.

Do you think **Mother** has a copy of my birth certificate?

family title used as common noun—not capitalized
Both my **mother** and my **father** have personal Web sites.

title capitalized in direct address
When will final grades for this course be available, **Professor**?

Yes, **Doctor,** we have confirmed your flight reservation for August 3.

If you wish to change your schedule, **Captain**, please notify me.

common noun not capitalized in direct address
I believe, **ladies and gentlemen**, that all our sales personnel will meet their quotas this year.

e. **In business correspondence always capitalize a person's title when it appears in an inside address, a signature line, or an envelope address.**

Ms. Delieu Scopesi, **Director of Research and Development**

Dr. Francisco Rodriguez, **Chancellor**, Los Angeles Community College District

f. **When the title of an executive officer is used in that organization's formal minutes, bylaws, or rules, it is capitalized.**

The **Treasurer's** report was read and approved.

The **President** is responsible for negotiating all labor contracts.

g. **Descriptive terms such as *ex, elect, late,* and *former* are not capitalized when they are combined with a title.**

ex
Since **ex-**President Frank J. Smith left the company, it has begun to show a profit.

elect
Councilman-**elect** Richard Ahrens will be sworn in on January 2.

late
The **late** President Eisenhower was an avid golfer.

former
Last month **former** President Bush addressed a student group at the University of Texas.

3–6 Published and Artistic Works Containing Subdivisions

a. Capitalize the first letter of the main words in the title of a published or an artistic work. Main words are generally all words except the following:

(1) Articles (*a, an, the*), conjunctions (*and, but, or, nor, for*), and all prepositions (e.g., *over, with, through, around, at*) unless they appear as the first or last words of the title or as the first word of a subtitle following a colon or a dash.

(2) The word *to* in infinitives (e.g., *to write, to exercise, to study*) unless it appears as the first word in the title or subtitle.

(3) The word *as*—regardless of the speech part it represents—unless it appears as the first word in the title or subtitle.

b. Italicize the titles of complete published and artistic works that contain subdivisions. Use italics for the titles of books, magazines, newspapers, booklets, pamphlets, compact discs, plays, musicals, operas, musical albums, Web sites, and other similar works that contain subdivisions such as chapters, articles, columns, acts, episodes, songs, or links.

Italicize also the titles of movies and television series.

book

Your copy of *The American Heritage Dictionary of the English Language* arrived yesterday.

A Day Late and a Dollar Short is available online at Amazon.com.

The setting for the novel *The Moon Is Down* is presumed to be a small town in Norway.

book with subtitle

This topic is addressed on page 32 of *HOW 14: A Handbook for Office Professionals*, 14th edition.

Travels with Charley: In Search of America was one of John Steinbeck's later books.

magazine

Did you receive the June issue of *Better Homes and Gardens*?

Renew online your subscription to *MAKE: Technology on Your Time*.

newspaper

An article in yesterday's *The Wall Street Journal* discussed sales trends in the consumer electronics industry.

Our hospital placed an advertisement in the *Los Angeles Times* for registered nurses and certified nursing assistants.

pamphlet or booklet

Distribute copies of *How to Write Effective E-mail Messages* to all members of our administrative staff.

A copy of *Your Attitude Is Showing* will be given to all new employees.

Print at least 5,000 copies of our employee booklet, *Employee Programs and Benefits*, for worldwide distribution to our employees.

compact disc
Esta Lancome, as part of its February gift-with-purchase promotion, has included a free CD entitled *How to Keep It Natural.*

play or musical
Neil Simon's play *I Ought to Be in Pictures* premiered at the Ahmanson Theatre in Los Angeles.

Yesterday we saw the last performance of *The Sound of Music*; next month *The Phantom of the Opera* will open.

The musical *Les Misérables* continues to attract theatergoers worldwide.

movie title
Next month local theaters will schedule children's matinees for showings of Disney's *Snow White and the Seven Dwarfs.*

The movie *Gone with the Wind* is considered to be a classic among American films.

television show
Since 1989 *The Simpsons* has been a popular television series.

Web site
Have you tried to locate this information through *Google*?

3–7 Subdivisions of Published and Artistic Works

a. Capitalize the main words[7] and place in quotation marks the titles of individual chapters, sections, articles, columns, acts, episodes, or songs contained in complete published and artistic works. Such works include books, magazines, booklets, pamphlets, newspapers, Web sites, CDs, DVDs, plays, musicals, and operas.

chapter in a book
Chapter 4, "Information Systems and Applications," has contributed greatly to the success of *Contemporary Management Principles.*

section in pamphlet
Please review the section "Submitting Your Application Online" before you apply for a job through the Internet.

---

[7] *Main* words are all words EXCEPT (1) the articles *a, an,* and *the*; (2) the conjunctions *and, but, or, nor, and for;* (3) all prepositions; (4) the word *to* in infinitives (*to say, to enter, to look,* etc.); and (5) the word *as*—unless any of these words are the first or last words.

article in a magazine
Did you read "Phones Use GPS to Show You the Way" in this month's issue of *Electronics World*?

column in a newspaper
Potter's "Financial Outlook" predicted yesterday that investors will see a rising stock market during the next quarter.

section in a CD or DVD
Ella Carter's first hit song, "Keep on Moving," is included in her latest CD, *Ella's Favorites.*

act in a play or musical
During the second act, "Homecoming," many people in the audience were tearful.

episode in a television series
"The Enemy Within," is next week's scheduled CBS broadcast of *NCIS.*

link in a Web site
Just click the "Apply Online" link on the Pierce College home page (www.piercecollege.edu) to apply for admission.

b. For a published work, capitalize the first letter of subdivisions such as *preface, contents, glossary, appendix,* and *index* when they refer to a specific work.

specific work
Definitions of grammatical terms are contained in the **A**ppendix.

Consult the **I**ndex to find the pages that contain instructions for using the LOOKUP functions in Excel.

general reference
The **i**ndex follows any **a**ppendixes that may be included in a book.

3–8 Published and Artistic Works without Subdivisions

Capitalize the first letter of the main words in any title. (See Section 3–6 for an explanation of *main words.*)

Place in quotation marks the titles of radio programs, poems, songs, paintings, sculptures, and essays—any such published or artistic works that do not contain subdivisions with subtitles.

radio program
Our talk show, "Opinion—From the Queen City," has been well received by Cincinnati radio listeners.

poem
Jennifer Durand's poem "A Mother's Love" has been published in poster format.

song
Two well-known songs from the musical *The King and I* are "Getting to Know You" and "I Whistle a Happy Tune."

3–9 Unpublished Works

a. Place the titles of unpublished essays, manuscripts, reports, theses, and dissertations in quotation marks. Capitalize the first letter of the main words[8] in the title.

title of a report
Copies of "Progress Report on Street Maintenance and Repair" will be distributed to city council members next week.

title of a thesis or dissertation
Casey Wong's thesis, "Differences in Accounting Practices of Three Major Accounting Firms Compared with Accounting Theory Taught in the Three Leading Accounting Textbooks," was approved by the committee last week.

b. Capitalize the main words and place in quotation marks the titles of lectures and sermons.

Capitalize the main words and place the subject lines of memorandums and e-mail messages in quotation marks when they are referred to in textual material.

lecture or sermon
Dr. Strozer's last presentation, "Religion, Politics, and Education," concluded with a challenge the audience could not overlook.

subject line of memorandum or e-mail message
According to John Baudry's July 28 e-mail, "Production Schedule Timeline," the Model 690 scanners should be ready for shipment to retail outlets by September 1.

3–10 Headings and Text Headings

a. In all published or unpublished written works, capitalize the main words in primary headings, secondary headings, centered text headings, and side (or margin) text headings. Capitalize parts of a hyphenated word. (See Section 3–6 for an explanation of *main words.*)

---

[8] *Main* words are all words EXCEPT (1) the articles *a, an,* and *the*; (2) the conjunctions *and, but, or, nor,* and *for;* (3) all prepositions; (4) the word *to* in an infinitive (*to purchase, to sign, to negotiate,* etc.); and (5) the word *as*—unless any of these words are the first or last words.

The **A**ge of the **U**niverse
Up-to-**D**ate **T**ravel **N**ews
Time **I**s **M**oney
Evolution of the **C**omputer
Principles of **E**-**M**ail **M**essaging
Communication **t**hrough the **A**ges
Document **C**reation with **V**oice **I**nput
Developments on the **H**orizon

b. In published and unpublished written works, capitalize only the first word and any proper nouns in paragraph text headings.

Investment in Europe and other foreign markets. During the past year, the company has established offices in Frankfurt, London, Paris, Mexico City, and Tokyo. With an overseas staff of 23 and a home office staff of 6 dedicated to enlarging our foreign markets, we expect to . . . .

3–11 Computer Software Program Titles

Capitalize the main words in computer software program titles. Note that in some cases main words are capitalized and written without an intervening space. Follow the format used by the manufacturer. (See Section 3–6 for an explanation of *main words.*)

software title written as separate words
Did you use **Microsoft Word** to prepare this manuscript?

Our law firm has just upgraded its operating system to **Windows 10**.

software title written without spaces
What version of **QuickBooks** is your company presently using?

My administrative assistant used **InDesign** to prepare these marketing brochures.

3–12 Punctuation Format for Literary and Artistic Titles

a. Titles of literary and artistic works are often used in appositive expressions; that is, they are used to rename a previously mentioned noun. In cases where the title is not needed to identify the work, set it off from the rest of the sentence with commas. No commas are used when the title is needed for identification.

title unnecessary to determine which article
Mark's latest article, "Marketing Strategies in the Automotive Industry," recommended a startling departure from current practices.

title necessary to determine which book
The book *Escape to Riches* should soon make the best-seller list.

b. Always place periods and commas *before* the closing quotation mark; always place semicolons and colons *after* the closing quotation mark.

period and comma before closing quotation mark
Hawaii is the location of our next episode, "Mousetrap."

Your March 13 report to the Board of Directors, "Computerized Accounting Procedures in the Banking Industry," has been helpful to me in planning our new system.

semicolon and colon after closing quotation mark
A number of our clients have requested reprints of your article "Increasing the Value of Your Portfolio"; the reprints will be mailed tomorrow.

These newscasters may be heard nightly on "Kansas City Reports": Rob McCoy, Elsa Newcomb, Steve Markham, and Lisa Darnell.

c. Follow these guidelines for placing a question mark or an exclamation mark with the closing quotation mark of a title:

(1) If a question or an exclamation mark concludes a quoted title that appears in the middle of a sentence, place the question or the exclamation mark before the closing quotation mark. The question or the exclamation mark substitutes for the second comma when a title is an appositive.
(2) If the question or the exclamation mark in a title appears at the end of the sentence, no other form of punctuation is required.
(3) If the sentence, not the title, is a question or an exclamation, place the ending punctuation mark outside the closing quotation mark.

quoted title phrased as question—middle of sentence
William Stanfield's lecture "Is Your Network Really Secure?" was a startling revelation to the network administrators present.

Did you read the article "How Secure Is Wi-Fi?" that appeared in this month's issue of *Business World*?

quoted title phrased as question—appositive in middle of sentence
Your latest article, "Are You Earning the Most from Your Investment Dollars?" will appear in next month's newsletter to our clients.

Jamie Wilson's last presentation, "How Can You Measure Your Communication Effectiveness?" was well received by the seminar participants.

quoted title phrased as question—end of sentence
This week's feature article was entitled "What Is Earthquake Readiness?"

Who wrote the article "Can Company Blogs Improve Internal Communication?"

quoted title separate from question
What percent of our subscribers read "Talk of the Town"?

3–13 Academic Courses and Subjects

a. Capitalize the names of numbered courses and specific course titles.

names of numbered courses
Professor Krimm's section of **Computer Science 101** has 14 students on the waiting list.

To earn an associate in arts degree, you must satisfactorily complete **History 11, Psychology 1,** and **Music 30**.

specific course title
You are scheduled to teach two sections of **The Internet for Business** next semester.

Last semester Christina took **Speech 125, Introduction to Public Debate**.

b. Capitalize only proper nouns in the names of academic subject areas.

subject area
I suggest, Sally, that you take an **accounting** class next semester.

Our college offers more than 25 different **mathematics** courses.

subject area containing proper noun
How many students earned an *A* in your **business English** class?

Before you leave for Paris, you may wish to take a course in **conversational French**.

3–14 Academic Degrees

a. References to academic degrees are generally not capitalized unless they are used after and in conjunction with the name of an individual.

general reference
Eric Nguyen will be awarded a **bachelor of science** degree this June.

She earned her **master's** last summer.

after person's name
Ann Drew, **Doctor of Divinity**, will deliver the opening address.

b. Capitalize abbreviations of academic degrees appearing after a person's name. Remember, though, that the *h* in *PhD* appears in lowercase form.[9]

Make your check payable to John M. Erickson, **MD**.

[9]Some authorities still prefer to use periods with abbreviations of academic degrees. Examples of periods with abbreviations of academic degrees include *Ph.D., M.D., M.A.,* and *B.S.*

Florence McKenzie, **PhD**, will join our clinic as a staff psychologist.

William Clark, **DDS, MD**, is an excellent oral surgeon.

We have asked Susan White, **DBA**, to be our guest speaker.

3–15 Organizations

a. Capitalize the main words in the names of all organizations—business, civic, educational, governmental, labor, military, philanthropic, political, professional, religious, and social.

Articles (*a, an, the*), conjunctions (*and, but, or, nor, for*), all prepositions, the word *to* in infinitives, and the word *as* are not capitalized unless they are the first word.

Granada **H**ills **C**hamber of **C**ommerce
National **C**ouncil of **C**hurches **USA**
Arizona **D**epartment of **M**otor **V**ehicles
Children's **H**ome **S**ociety of **F**lorida
United **S**tates **D**epartment of **D**efense
The **A**merican **S**ociety for the **P**revention of **C**ruelty to **A**nimals
Illinois **S**tate **B**oard of **E**ducation
Sears, **R**oebuck and **C**o.
American **C**ancer **S**ociety
The **P**helps **G**roup
Metro-**G**oldwyn-**M**ayer **S**tudios **I**nc.
DIRECTV, **I**nc.

b. When the word *the* precedes the organizational name and is officially part of the name, it must be capitalized.

Our client is insured by **The** Prudential Insurance Company of America.

c. When the common noun element of an organization's name is used in place of the full name, it is generally not capitalized. In formal documents and in specific references to national government bodies, however, capitalize the shortened form.

general communication

Full-time employees of the **company** are entitled to ten days' paid sick leave each year.

The **board of education** convened yesterday for a special meeting to consider the budget crisis.

Two members from our local **chamber** received special recognition from the **state senate** for outstanding community service.

How many members of the **city council** will support our proposal for low-cost housing in the inner city?

formal communication

As executive director of the **Association**, I am authorized to sign the convention contracts.

On July 1, 2014, the **Company** acquired Western Mutual Bank, which had 23 branches throughout the state.

national government bodies
Michael Johnson, our former mayor, has been elected to the **House**. (United States House of Representatives)

The president still needs to appoint two additional **Cabinet** members. (President's Cabinet)

Will **Congress** reconvene next week? (United States Congress)

Who is presently majority leader of the **Senate**? (United States Senate)

This issue is now before the **Supreme Court**. (Supreme Court of the United States)

d. Government terms such as *federal, government,* and *nation* are often used in place of their respective full names. Because they are used so often and are considered terms of general classification, they are not capitalized.

federal
Security measures have been heightened in all **federal** buildings.

government
Since the **government** is concerned about inflation and its effect on the economy, it often uses economic measures to control pricing.

Student loans such as these are fully guaranteed by the **federal government**.

nation
Through the strength and courage of its people, the **nation** has been able to overcome a number of crises.

e. Capitalize the main words in the official name of a division or a department within a business organization. When a division or a department is referred to by its function because the official or specific name is unknown, do not capitalize this reference.

Always capitalize main words in a division or a department name used in a return address, an inside address, a signature block, or an envelope address.

official or specific name
Please notify the **Department of Human Resources** by 8 a.m. if you will be absent from work that day.

All contracts in excess of $25,000 must be approved by the **Board of Directors**.

Last month three members of our **Accounting Department** retired.

We will send a copy of our findings to your **Department of Research and Development**.

Please send a technician from the **Information Technology Department** to solve our network problem.

official or specific name unknown
You can increase the productivity of your **accounting department** by using the new release of our software.

Ask a member of your **advertising department** to contact one of our account executives so that your company can take advantage of this rare opportunity.

return address, inside address, signature block, or envelope address
Mr. Arthur Chu, Manager, **Credit Department**

f. Capitalize the main words in the names of departments, bureaus, divisions, offices, and agencies in government organizations.

We are forwarding your application to the **Department of Health and Human Services** today.

Please contact the **Bureau of Indian Affairs** for further information.

Copies of the proposed freeway route are available from the **Division of Highways**.

This case is under investigation by the **Office of Internal Affairs**.

g. Capitalize the main words in the names of specific departments, divisions, and offices within educational institutions. Capitalize also the main words in the names of schools or colleges within universities.

educational departments, divisions, or offices
This year La Costa Community College's music festival, sponsored by the **Music Department**, will be held March 27–29.

Does Professor Andrea Davidson teach in the **Social Science Division**?

Departmental budget requests for the next academic year must be submitted to the **Office of Business Services** by April 30.

university schools or colleges
I have been admitted to the MBA program in the **School of Business and Economics** at Kentview State University.

The major in which you are interested is offered in the **College of Letters, Arts, and Sciences**.

3–16 Geographical Locations

a. Capitalize the names of places—for example, specific continents, countries, islands, states, cities, streets, mountains, valleys, parks, oceans, lakes, rivers, canals, bays, and harbors. When a geographical term (such as *city, street, bay,* or *island*) appears directly after a place

name, it is considered part of the name and is capitalized. Terms used in this way are capitalized in both singular and plural forms.

specific place

Our products are distributed throughout **North America**.

Does any airline have a nonstop flight from **Los Angeles** to **Baltimore**?

Clients residing in the **Hawaiian Islands** will soon be serviced by our new branch office in **Honolulu**.

The article dealt with recreational facilities on the **Colorado River**.

We sponsor tours for visitors to **Yellowstone National Park**.

Many of our shipments are routed here through the **Panama Canal**.

Property taxes in **Marin County** have risen steadily during the past five years.

specific places—geographical term in plural form

Our company provides riverboat excursions on both the **Mississippi and Missouri Rivers**.

Most of the new earthquake faults have been discovered in the **San Bernardino and San Gabriel Mountains**.

The main entrance to the Century Plaza Shopping Mall is located on Broadway between **15th and 16th Streets**.

A geographical term appearing before the name of a place is generally not capitalized. Capitalize the term only if (1) it is part of the official name or (2) it is used by the governing bodies of that place as part of an official name.

geographical term appearing before specific place—not capitalized

Most of our business is conducted within the **state** of Utah.

The **city** of Albuquerque will be the site for our next convention.

The estimated 2020 population for the **county** of Ventura is 947,556.

geographical term appearing before specific place—capitalized

Our regional warehouse is located in the **City of Industry**. (Geographical term part of city name.)

The **City of Albuquerque** has approved a new budget plan. (Geographical term used by governing body as part of its official name.)

Governor Quinn delivered a 2015 budget for the **State of Illinois** and a five-year blueprint that will secure the state's finances for the long term. (Geographical term used by governing body as part of its official name.)

b. Capitalize nicknames of geographical locations and names of regional areas that have evolved as a result of usage.

geographical nicknames

The **Aloha State** attracts tourists from all parts of the world. (Hawaii)

How many times each year do you travel to the **Motor City**? (Detroit)

In 2016 the Summer Olympics were held in **The Marvelous City**. (Rio de Janeiro)

Your tour of Australia includes six days in the **Harbour City**. (Sydney)

regional names emerging from usage

Offices of the Better Business Bureau have served the residents of **Upstate New York** for more than 75 years.

Merchants from the **Inland Empire** have banded together to support this worthwhile project.

Many residents of the **Bay Area** are concerned about the pollution occurring in San Francisco Bay.

Industrious immigrants became the first business owners in the **Lower East Side**.

c. **Capitalize points of the compass when they are used as simple or compound nouns to designate *specific geographic regions.* Points of the compass are not capitalized, however, when they are used to indicate *direction* or *general localities.***

specific regions

Firms connected with the aerospace industry are heavily concentrated in the **West** and **Southwest**.

All our offices are on the **East Coast**.

Most of the granite sold and installed by our company is imported from the **Middle East**.

The parade and the festival are scheduled to be held in **East Los Angeles**.

Sales in our **Southern Region** have increased 15 percent during the past year.

Within the next month, we will expand our operations into **East Texas**.

directions

Your new territory, as regional manager, will include all states **east** of the Mississippi River.

The consultant's report recommended that our new plant be located directly **northwest** of Louisville.

To avoid the harsh winter weather, many retirees travel **south** or **west** during the snow season.

By taking the **eastbound** on-ramp, you will be able to drive to the downtown area of Madison.

general localities

The **southern** section of our state is suffering a severe drought.

Our delivery service is confined to the **east** side of Miami.

Customers from the **northwest** sector of the city have registered more complaints than customers from any other sector.

Our analysis revealed that most of our sales were from customers in the **western** states.

This new weather stripping is guaranteed to protect you against the severity of **northern** winters.

d. Capitalize words derived from simple or compound nouns representing *specific* regions.

A number of **Midwesterners** have inquired about our Mexi-Pepper franchises.

Southern Californians are known for their casual lifestyle.

Our most recent survey solicited responses only from **Easterners**.

Nashville is known for its **Southern** hospitality.

3–17 Dates, Time Periods, and Events

Capitalize days of the week, months of the year, holidays (including religious days), specific special events, and specific historical events or periods.

The names of seasons, decades, and centuries are generally not capitalized. If, however, a season is combined with a year, capitalize the season.

day of week and month

Our committee will meet the first **Monday** in **March**, **June**, **September**, and **December**.

holiday

Will our restaurant be closed on **New Year's Day** this year?

Each year **Veterans Day** is observed on November 11 or the nearest weekday.

specific special event

Our company will celebrate its **Silver Anniversary** next year.

Administrative Professionals Week is traditionally observed during the last full week of April, Sunday through Saturday.

This year the **Roseville County Fair** will be held from September 4 through September 27.

How many of our staff members will be attending **Computer Expo** this year?

historical period

In this **Information Age**, the Internet has emerged as a major communication medium and information source.

The stock market crash of 1929 brought the **Roaring Twenties** to a dismal end and catapulted our country into the **Great Depression**.

During the **Industrial Revolution,** children were often forced to work long hours under intolerable conditions.

season

Our most popular sales item during this **spring** season has been the Model 650 patio set.

None of the **winter** coats we ordered have arrived yet.

If you wish to enroll for the **fall** semester, please submit your application by August 15.

We have received your application for admission for the **Winter 2017** quarter.

decade

During the past year, a number of movies portraying life in the **eighties** have been released.

Both Microsoft and Apple Computer were founded in the **mid-1970s**, thus initiating the microcomputer industry.

century

Technological developments during the **twentieth century** have advanced the human race further than all other developments during our previous history.

Many of Mr. Donovan's employees believe that he operates his business on **nineteenth-century** management principles.

3–18 Ethnic and Religious References

a. Capitalize ethnic-related terms—references to a particular language, race, or culture. Generic terms such as *black, white,* and *brown* when used in reference to race are generally not capitalized.

language

A knowledge of both **German** and **English** is required for this job opening in Frankfurt.

race or ethnicity

The 2015 population estimates indicated that this area is highly populated by **Asians**.

Several **African-American** leaders have asked to address the city council on this issue.

The predominant native language of **Hispanics** is Spanish, but a significant number claim Portuguese as their native tongue.

culture
Cinco de Mayo is observed with many festivities in the **Mexican-American** community.

A large number of restaurants in Glendale specialize in serving **Middle Eastern** cuisines.

b. Capitalize references to specific religious groups.

Massive opposition from **Catholic**, **Protestant**, and **Jewish** clergy led to the defeat of this proposed legislation.

A **Mormon** temple will be built on this site in 2018.

3–19 Celestial Bodies

Capitalize the names of celestial bodies—planets, planet satellites, stars, constellations, and asteroids. Do not capitalize the terms *earth, sun,* and *moon,* however, unless they are used as the names of specific bodies in the solar system.

capitalized
We have been studying the orbital paths of **Mars** and **Earth**.

Can you pick out the **North Star** or the **Big Dipper** among the many stars in the sky?

When will **Earth** next pass between the **Sun** and the **Moon**?

The background of the scene embraces a darkened sky highlighted only by an array of stars and **Saturn** with its bright rings.

lowercase
Rays from the **sun** can damage your skin and subsequently cause skin cancer.

None of the pieces from the satellite found their way back into the **earth's** atmosphere.

The Old Farmer's Almanac at its Web site provides the dates and times (based on Eastern Standard Time or Eastern Daylight Time) of full **moons** for the current year.

4

Number Formats

Solution Finder for Number Formats

4 Number Formats

General Format

4–1 Rules for General Numbers[1]

a. ***Always*** **express in word form a number that begins a sentence. When the number cannot be written in one or two words, however, change the word order of the sentence so that the number does not begin the sentence. Then write the number in figures. This number rule takes precedence over all others.**

number written in words
Thirty-one employees are willing to work overtime next week to assist with taking inventory.

sentence order rearranged for figure form
The online survey was answered by **183** customers who had purchased products using our secure Web site. Or The online survey obtained responses from **183** customers who had purchased products using our secure Web site. (Not *One hundred eighty-three* [or *183*] customers who had purchased . . . answered the online survey.)

b. **Write numbers *one* through *ten* in words. Write numbers above *ten* in figures, except those used to begin a sentence (see Section 4–1a). This rule applies only to general numbers—numbers not governed by any other number-usage rule.**

number* ten *or below
Of the **ten** applicants, only **two** were qualified for the position.

***number above* ten**
During the past month, we have released **16** new wireless phone products for our broadband subscribers.

Twenty-one new wireless phone products are scheduled for release during the early part of next year.

c. **Write in either figures or words approximations above *ten* that can be expressed in one or two words. Keep in mind that figures are more emphatic and conform to the conventions established for expressing general numbers.**

approximation written in figures
Nearly **900** people sent letters, e-mails, or faxes to the governor to protest the proposed sales tax increase.

approximation written in words
Yes, fewer than **sixty** members registered for the conference.

---

[1]*General numbers* in this manual refers to numbers that are not governed by any other number-usage convention. Percentages, money amounts, weights and measures, addresses, and telephone numbers are among the kinds of numbers not considered to be "general numbers" because they are governed by separate usage protocols.

d. Hyphenate numbers below *100* that are written in word form if they are written as two words; that is, hyphenate compound numbers *21* through *99* when they are spelled out.

Twenty-six homes that were severely damaged in the hurricane are insured by our company.

e. Round numbers in the millions or billions are expressed in a combination of figures and words. Only *one million* used as an approximation is written in all word form; otherwise, it is written *1 million.*

round number
Captain Bustillo has flown more than **2 million** miles since he has been with our airline.

round number with fraction
Our company manufactured **3½ billion** pens for worldwide distribution last year.

round number with decimal
By 2020 the population of Houston is expected to reach **7.2 million** people.

one million *as an approximation*
How many United States cities have populations exceeding **one million**?

1 million *as an exact figure*
The company will recover all its research and development costs once it has sold **1 million** of these handheld, voice-activated Internet computers.

4–2 Related Numbers

a. Numbers used in a comparable or corresponding manner in the same document are considered related numbers and should be expressed in the same form. Therefore, write numbers *one* through *ten* in figures when they are used with related numbers above *ten.*

Of the **72** boxes in the shipment, only **3** were crushed as a result of the accident.

During July the agents in our office sold **21** private residences, **7** condominiums, and **1** apartment complex. (Note that items appearing in a series are always considered to be related.)

b. Use all figures to express round numbers in the millions or billions that appear with (1) related numbers below a million or (2) related numbers that cannot be expressed in a combination of words and figures.

***combined with number below* 1 million**
Sales of our digital cameras rose from **970,000** last year to more than **2,000,000** this year.

combined with number over* 1 million *written in figures
According to the 2010 census, the population of our county has risen from nearly **2,000,000** to **2,875,500** residents during the past decade.

c. **Consider separately unrelated numbers used in the same sentence to determine whether they should be expressed in words or figures.**

unrelated numbers in same sentence
All **21** laser printers were ordered for faculty in **nine** departments on the new campus.

To accommodate **120** people for this banquet, set up **15** tables with **eight** place settings at each table.

combination of related and unrelated numbers in same sentence
Our warehouse inventory of **22** dishwashers, **17** refrigerators, **8** washing machines, and **6** dryers must be distributed among our **three** stores. (Items in a series are always related.)

The large carton holds **four** packs, each containing **12** cans of soda; the smaller carton holds **six** packs, each containing **6** cans of soda. (*Packs* is related to *packs*; *cans* is related to *cans*.)

Numbers Expressed in Figure Form

4-3 Money

a. **Dollar amounts—*$1 or more*—are expressed in figures. Omit the decimal and zeros in expressing whole dollar amounts, even if they appear with mixed dollar amounts.**

dollar amounts expressed in figures
With a two-year subscription to Air-Wireless, you can own this new Microlite WebPhone for only **$99.95**.

omission of decimal and zeros
Available accessories range in price from $2.99 to **$120**.

Purchases included items for **$9**, $26.50, $79.95, **$120**, and **$206**.

b. **Amounts of money *less than $1* are expressed in figures followed by the word *cents*—unless they are used with related amounts of *$1 or more*. Treat unrelated amounts of money appearing in the same sentence separately.**

***amounts less than* $1**
The transit company increased bus fares from **75 cents** to **90 cents**.

related amounts of money
To mail the three reports, I paid **$.85, $1.40**, and **$2** in postage.

unrelated amounts of money
The sales tax on this **$10** binder was **75 cents**.

c. **Express round amounts of money in millions or billions of dollars in combined figure and word form except when they are used with (1) related dollar figures below a million or (2) related amounts that can be expressed in figures only.**

round amounts
Cost estimates for the new technology building accelerated from **$15 million** to **$18½ million**.

Nearly **$3.5 billion** in assets provides the customer confidence that makes Liberty Mutual the largest federal savings bank in the country.

related to amount less than **$1 million**
We estimate that **$850,000** will be needed to retool the Wilmington plant and **$2,000,000** will be needed for the Van Nuys plant.

related to amount that can be expressed in figures only
Our domestic sales decreased from **$12,658,000** last year to less than **$12,000,000** this year.

d. **Amounts of money in formal legal documents are expressed in words followed by the figure amount contained in parentheses. Capitalize the main words. The word *and* is used only to introduce cents included in money amounts written in word form.**

round dollar amounts
The Company shall pay up to **Five Thousand Dollars ($5,000)** within 30 days upon receipt of a valid release statement.

The amount of indebtedness incurred by the defendant was **Ten Thousand Five Hundred Eighty-three Dollars ($10,583)**.

dollar amount with cents
A check for **Two Thousand Four Hundred Sixty-one Dollars and Forty-eight Cents ($2,461.48)** was received from Westin Industries on May 3.

4–4 Decimals and Percentages

a. **Express in figures all numbers that contain a decimal. To prevent misreading, place a *0* (zero) before a decimal that does not contain a whole number or begin with a *0*.**

decimal with whole number
Our miles-per-gallon test of one hybrid car resulted in **58.67** in city driving.

This model printer will handle only standard-width **8.5-inch** paper.

***decimal beginning with* 0**
According to our government contract, this part must be manufactured within **.004** inch of specifications.

***decimal not containing whole number or beginning with* 0**
This year **0.2** percent of our microphones were returned because of defective workmanship.

b. Write percentages in figures followed by the word *percent*. The percent symbol (%) is used only for statistical or technical tables or forms.

percent *used in sentence format*
Last month our company was able to decrease its energy consumption by **7 percent**.

This year's travel expenses have increased only **1 percent** over last year's.

A **12½ percent** pay increase will be granted to all office employees, effective July 1.

Our state legislature is expected to levy a **0.5 percent** increase in sales tax this year—from **7 percent** to **7.5 percent**.

% used in statistical tables or forms

47.5%	60%	99.9%	5.63%	3%	0.8%

4–5 U.S. Standard Weights and Measures

a. For quick comprehension express in figures the amount something weighs or measures. Weights and measures (inches, feet, yards, miles, ounces, pounds, tons, pints, quarts, gallons, each, dozen, gross, reams, pecks, bushels, degrees, acres, etc.), however, are written out fully in words. Abbreviations or symbols representing these units are limited to use in business forms or statistical materials.

general use
Trucks in excess of **2 tons** must take an alternate route.

Use **1-inch** screws for this job.

According to the latest weather forecast, the predicted high for tomorrow is **93 degrees**.

The installer estimated that **164 square yards** of carpeting will be needed for our office suite.

This carton is **4 pounds 3 ounces** in excess of the U.S. Postal Service weight limitation.

use for forms and statistical materials

5 doz.	10 yd.	92°	4#	8 ft.	75 lb.	12 ea.

b. The following tables provide equivalents for various standard measures of length, weight, and capacity:

(1) Standard measures of length may be expressed in mils, inches, feet, yards, rods, furlongs, miles, and leagues.
(2) Standard weights may be expressed in grains, drams, ounces, pounds, hundredweights, and tons.
(3) Standard capacities may be expressed in teaspoons, tablespoons, ounces, cups, pints, quarts, gallons, pecks, and bushels.

standard measures of length

1 mil	=	.001 inch
1 inch	=	1,000 mils
12 inches	=	1 foot
3 feet	=	1 yard
16.5 feet	=	1 rod
40 rods	=	1 furlong
8 furlongs or 5,280 feet	=	1 mile
3 miles	=	1 league (land)

standard measures of weight

1 grain	=	.036 drams
1 dram	=	27.34 grains
16 drams or 437.5 grains	=	1 ounce
16 ounces or 7,000 grains	=	1 pound
100 pounds	=	1 hundredweight
2,000 pounds	=	1 ton

standard measures of capacity

3 teaspoons or 0.5 ounce	=	1 tablespoon
2 tablespoons	=	1 ounce
16 tablespoons or 8 ounces	=	1 cup
2 cups or 16 ounces	=	1 pint
2 pints, 4 cups, or 32 ounces	=	1 quart
4 quarts or 128 ounces	=	1 gallon
8 quarts	=	1 peck
4 pecks	=	1 bushel

4–6 Metric Weights and Measures

a. The most common metric measurements are based on grams, liters, and meters. Prefixes indicating fractions and multiples of these quantities follow:

fractions

deci (1/10) centi (1/100) milli (1/1000)

multiples

deka (× 10) hecto (× 100) kilo (× 1000)

b. Express metric measurements in figures. For general correspondence spell out the units of measure.

Use a space to separate numbers of five or more digits into groups of three. No space or comma is used with four-digit figures.

regular metric measures
When will our European distribution center begin using **1.75-liter** plastic bottles for its large-size fruit juices?

In the international market, purchasers will need at least twenty-four **4-centimeter** screws to assemble this computer station.

four-digit figures
The driving distance from Rome to Paris is more than **1500 kilometers**.

Please order **1200 kilograms** of flour and **1000 kilograms** of sugar for delivery to our bakeries throughout Germany.

five-digit figures
His 5-acre parcel of land is equal to approximately 2 hectares, that is, approximately **20 000 square meters**.

c. Although units of measure are spelled out in general correspondence, they may be abbreviated in technical writing, medical reports, or any kind of form.

general correspondence

12 millimeters	6 liters	90 kilometers

technical writing, medical reports, or forms

50 mm (millimeters)	500 mg (milligrams)
32 km (kilometers)	100 cc (cubic centimeters)

d. The following tables show equivalents for metric and standard measures of length, weight, and capacity:

equivalents for measures of length

Metric to Standard	*Standard to Metric*
1 kilometer = 0.6214 (5/8) mile	1 mile = 1.609 kilometers
1 meter = 1.0936 yards	1 yard = 0.9144 meter (exact)
1 meter = 39.37 inches	1 foot = 0.3048 meter (exact)
1 centimeter = 0.3937 (2/5) inch	1 inch = 2.54 centimeters (exact)

equivalents for measures of weight

Metric to Standard	*Standard to Metric*
1 ton (or tonne) = 1.1023 tons	1 ton = 0.90721 ton (or tonne)
1 kilogram = 2.2046 pounds	1 pound = 453.592 grams
1 kilogram = 35 ounces	1 ounce = 28.35 grams
1 gram = .035 ounce	

equivalents for measures of capacity

Metric to Standard	*Standard to Metric*
1 hectoliter (hl) = 2.838 bushels	1 bushel = 35.239 liters
1 liter (L) = 0.264 liquid gallon	1 liquid gallon = 3.785 liters
1 liter (L) = 1.057 liquid quarts	1 liquid quart = 0.946 liter
1 liter (L) = 0.908 dry quart	1 dry quart = 1.101 liters
1 milliliter (ml) } = .034 fluid ounce 1 cubic centimeter (cc) }	1 ounce = 29.537 milliliters

e. Two common scales measure temperature: Fahrenheit and Celsius. In Fahrenheit 32 degrees is the point at which water freezes and 212 degrees is the point at which water boils. In Celsius water freezes at 0-degree temperature and boils at 100 degrees.

(1) To convert Celsius temperatures to Fahrenheit, apply the following formula: (Celsius temperature × 1.8) + 32.

(2) To convert Fahrenheit temperatures to Celsius, use this formula: (Fahrenheit temperature − 32) ÷ 1.8.

(3) The following table illustrates some common conversions:

Fahrenheit to Celsius		*Celsius to Fahrenheit*	
32	0	0	32
40	4	5	41
45	7	10	50
50	10	15	59
55	13	20	68
60	16	25	77
65	18	30	86
70	21	35	95
75	24	40	104
80	27	45	113
85	29	50	122
90	32	100	212
95	35		
100	38		
212	100		

Normal body temperature is **98.6 degrees Fahrenheit** or **37 degrees Celsius.**

The high temperature yesterday in Madrid was **31°C—**or **88°F.**

4–7 Numbers Used with Words, Abbreviations, and Symbols

a. Numbers used in word-number combinations are placed in figures. Page numbers, model numbers, policy numbers, and serial numbers are just a few instances in which numerals are used with words. Words preceding the numerals are usually capitalized—except the words *page, paragraph, line, size,* and *verse.* (See Section 3–4 for capitalization format.)

model number

Perhaps we should purchase a ProDisk 150 GB **Model ST856932** external drive to back up our data on Dropbox.

Do you have any Sanasonic **Model No. 8371** DVD players in stock?

policy and serial numbers

Enclosed is a copy of your new auto insurance policy, **Policy 78-93642811-D**.

Your software license, **Serial No. A380 BCP9 X2M6 TVEL 87B4**, will be required for you to install Excel on your laptop.

paragraph and page number

The Elton scanner is pictured on **page 56** of the enclosed catalog.

Plant safety rules are contained in the employee handbook beginning with **paragraph 3** on **page 72.**

b. Capitalize and abbreviate the word *number* when it introduces a number. Use figures to express the number. When the word *number* begins a sentence, however, do not abbreviate it.

word* number *capitalized and abbreviated

We are considering replacing our camera equipment with your **No. 1070** digital series.

The following checks were returned by your bank: **Nos. 321, 323,** and **326**.

word* number *at beginning of sentence

Number 42 is the table at which we normally seat parties of eight or ten.

Numbers 392, 972, and **1041** were among the winning raffle tickets.

c. Symbols are generally avoided in business writing. However, for forms (such as orders and invoices), charts, tables, and other documents in which space is limited, symbols are used liberally. Numbers expressed with symbols are written in figures.

2/10, N/30 8% #455

Time

4–8 Dates

a. When the day is written after the month, use cardinal figures (*1, 2, 3,* etc.). Ordinal figures (*1st, 2nd, 3rd,* etc.) are used for expressing days that appear before the month or that stand alone.

month followed by day
October 31, 2018, is the closing date for bids on this construction project.

If you cannot file your income tax return by **April 15**, you may "e-file" your application for an automatic extension through the IRS Web site.

day appearing before month
According to the contract, full payment is due by or before the **30th of June**.

Will our new offices be ready for occupancy by the **1st of October**?

day used alone
Your reservations at the Maui Beach Hotel for the **9th** through the **16th** have been confirmed.

Rental payments for this office are due by the **1st** of each month.

b. Dates in most domestic business correspondence are expressed in terms of month, day, and year. A comma separates the day and the year. In military and international correspondence, dates are generally written day, month, and year without an intervening comma.

domestic business correspondence
December 17, 2018

military or international correspondence
17 December 2018

4–9 Clock Time

a. Use figures with *a.m., p.m., noon,* or *midnight* to express clock time. Omit the colon and zeros with even times, even if they appear with times expressed in hours and minutes.

The terms *noon* and *midnight* may be used with or without the figure *12.* When these terms are used with other clock times containing *a.m.* and/or *p.m.*, however, include the figure *12.* Never use *a.m.* or *p.m.* following *12, noon,* or *midnight.*

a.m., p.m., noon, midnight *with figures*
Our flight was scheduled to depart at **8 p.m.**, but it did not leave until **11:30 p.m.**

The daily museum tour begins at **10:45 a.m.** and ends at **12 noon.**

Afternoon shifts are scheduled from **3:30 p.m.** until **12 midnight**.

noon *and* midnight *with the figure* 12

Items on the breakfast menu may not be ordered after **12 noon**.

Employment opportunities are available on the night shift, which begins at **12 midnight**.

The Westfield branch of the U.S. Postal Service is open Saturdays from **8 a.m.** until **12 noon**.

Burger Roundup is open daily from **8 a.m.** until **12 midnight**.

noon *and* midnight *without the figure* 12

May we please have your answer before **noon** on Thursday.

All envelopes containing federal income tax payments must be postmarked before **midnight**, April 15, to avoid a penalty.

b. Either word or figure form may be used with *o'clock*. Use *o'clock* only with even clock hours (clock times not containing minutes).

To arrive at the airport on time, we must leave the office by **nine o'clock** (or **9 o'clock**).

c. When even clock hours of the day are expressed without *a.m., p.m., noon, midnight,* or *o'clock,* use word form. Either word or figure form may be used, however, when both hours and minutes are expressed.

exact hour

The last performance of *Mama Mia!* at the Civic Arts Center is scheduled to begin at **seven** on Sunday evening.

Our dental office is closed daily between **twelve** and **one**.

hour and minutes

The committee meeting finally adjourned at **5:30** (or **five-thirty**).

Computer access to our network shut down at **9:05** (or **five after nine**) this morning, but it was restored shortly before **10:30** (or **ten-thirty**).

d. Phrases such as "in the morning," "in the afternoon," or "at night" may follow clock times expressed alone or with *o'clock,* but these phrases may not be used with clock times expressed with *a.m.* or *p.m.*

Coffee breaks for the convention are scheduled at **ten in the morning** and at **three in the afternoon**.

By **3** (or **three**) **o'clock in the afternoon**, our campus is almost deserted; but by **7** (or **seven**) **o'clock in the evening**, it is filled with students attending night classes.

e. **World time, also known as "international time," is based on a 24-hour clock. Greenwich Mean Time[2] keeps track of world time. The day begins at midnight with 00:00:00 (hours, minutes, seconds) and progresses through 23:59:59.**

Besides being the United States military time standard, world time is used for international flight schedules. Usually it is expressed in hours and minutes with the day and date.

Your flight is scheduled to leave Los Angeles on **Monday, June 12**, at **18:05** and arrive in Copenhagen on **Tuesday, June 13**, at **17:15**.

Our Qantas flight from Chicago to Sydney will be 21 hours 30 minutes—the flight will leave Chicago at **17:40** on **Sunday, January 25**; arrive in Los Angeles at **20:10** the same day; depart for Sydney at **22:30**; and arrive in Sydney at **08:10** on **Tuesday, January 27**.

4–10 Periods of Time

a. **General periods of time specifying seconds, minutes, hours, days, weeks, months, and years are treated the same as any other general number. Numbers *ten* and below are written in word form, and numbers above *ten* are written in figure form.**

general references to clock time
Each candidate's response to the questions in this television debate is limited to **two minutes**.

We offer **24-hour** plumbing service to all residents in Bixby County.

general time period—days, weeks, months, or years
During the past **nine months**, our store has experienced a significant sales increase in Lego action figures.

Jensen Auto Works has been in this location for **32 years**.

The grocery workers' strike lasted **112 days**.

b. **Express in figures time-period data related to specific loan lengths, discount rates, interest rates, payment terms, credit terms, or other such information dealing with business contracts or terms.**

According to the loan documents, full payment is due within **90 days**.

All invoices paid within **10 days** of the invoice date are eligible for a **1** percent discount.

Your application for a **9** percent loan for **6 months** has been approved.

---

[2]For more information on world time and world time zones, visit *Greenwich Mean Time* on the Web located at http://wwp.greenwichmeantime.com/ (January 16, 2015).

4–11 Ages and Anniversaries

Ages and anniversaries that can be expressed in one or two words are generally written in word form; those that require more than two words are written in figures. Figures are also used when an age (1) appears directly after a person's name; (2) is used in a legal or technical sense; or (3) is expressed in terms of years, months, and sometimes days. Note that no commas are used to separate the years, months, and days in the expression of ages.

general expression of ages and anniversaries

Mark will be **twenty-nine** on May 31; his son will be **three** the same day.

Although Mrs. Wong has celebrated her **sixty-fifth** birthday, she will not retire this year.

Next month we will celebrate our manager's **twenty-fifth** anniversary with the company.

Our city will celebrate its **150th** anniversary in 2018.

age after name

Ms. Ida Bergstrom, **47**, was promoted to executive vice president last week.

age used in technical or legal sense

The legal voting age in the United States is **18**.

At **25**, with a good driving record, you will be eligible for our company's reduced insurance rates.

Employees may retire and be eligible for Social Security benefits at age **62**.

age in years, months, and days

According to our records, the insured was **48** years **9** months and **23** days of age upon cancellation of the policy.

Addresses and Telephone Numbers

4–12 Addresses

a. **House numbers are expressed in figures except the house number *One*. No commas are used to separate digits in house numbers.**

One Alpha Avenue	**4** Headquarters Plaza North
2432 East Jefferson Boulevard	**18564** Clearbrook Street

b. **Express in word form street names *ten* or below with ordinal numbers (*First, Second, Third,* etc.). Street names above *ten* are written in ordinal figures—numerals with an added *st, nd, rd,* or *th*.**

street name* ten *or below

Our New York City offices are located on **Fifth** Avenue.

Mail your payments to our office at 360 East **Third** Street, Winston-Salem, North Carolina 27101-4036.

street name above **ten**
To receive your rebate, fill out this form and send it to AVCO, Inc., 540 **23rd** Street, Denver, Colorado 80205-2145.

The applicant's former address is listed as 3624 West **59th** Place.

c. Apartment numbers, suite numbers, box numbers, and route numbers are expressed in figure form.

2193 Gerald Avenue, Apt. **12**
Bristol Financial Tower, Suite **300**
Post Office Box **1320**
Rural Route **2**

d. ZIP Codes are expressed in figures (without commas) and typed a single space after the state. Address lines containing ZIP + 4 are written in the same manner as those containing five-digit ZIP Codes. Separate the extra four digits from the first five digits with a hyphen.

sentence format
Redirect this order to Fairfield Electronics, 1586 North Cicero Avenue, Chicago, Illinois **60651**.

Ms. Foster requested that the books be sent to her at Pasadena City College, 1570 East Colorado Boulevard, Pasadena, California **91106-2003**.

inside address or envelope address
Mrs. Sidney Harrington
7820½ South Ninth Avenue
Moonachie, NJ **07074**

Mr. José Luis Fernandez
1073 23rd Street, Apt. 2
Inglewood, CA **90305-1004**

Ms. Eleanor Chu, Vice President
Parke-Dunn Pharmaceutical Company
74 West Michigan Mall, Suite 300
Battle Creek, Michigan **49017-3606**

4–13 Telephone and Facsimile (Fax) Numbers

Telephone and fax numbers within the United States are expressed in figures and contain ten digits—a three-digit area code that appears first followed by a seven-digit local number. Some telephone numbers may have an extension number. Use the following guidelines to express telephone and fax numbers:

(1) For the standard format, begin by enclosing the area code in parentheses. Place the local telephone or fax number after the area code, and separate the first three digits from the last four digits with a hyphen.

(2) As an alternative format, omit the parentheses and separate the area code from the local telephone or fax number with a hyphen. Continue with the local telephone or fax number directly after

the area code, and separate the first three digits from the last four digits with a hyphen.

(3) As another alternative format, separate with periods the area code, the first three digits of the local number, and the last four digits of the local number.

(4) An extension number is introduced by the abbreviation *Ext.* and follows the telephone number. If an extension number interrupts a sentence, place a comma before and after it. However, if an extension number ends a sentence, use a single comma to separate it from the telephone number.

telephone or facsimile (fax) number in standard format

If you have any questions about our products or services, just call us at **(210) 553-7831**.

Please ask Dr. Wagner to fax the prescription for this prosthesis to **(818) 363-6534**.

telephone or facsimile (fax) number in an alternative format

Call our toll-free number, **800-885-3322**, to place your order.

You may fax a copy of your proposal to me at **427-555-7821**.

Details about this investment opportunity are available from your J. W. Barnes broker at **800.713.4421**.

area code, telephone number, extension

Ask Jill to call **(213) 347-0551, Ext. 244**, for an appointment.

You may reach me any weekday at **(617) 555-7139, Ext. 3712**.

Formats

4–14 Number Format

a. In numbers expressed as figures, separate groups of three digits by commas. Exceptions include years, house numbers, telephone numbers, fax numbers, ZIP Codes, serial numbers, page numbers, decimal fractions, and metric measurements. Metric measurements of five or more digits are separated into groups of three with spaces.

commas in figures with more than three digits

2,312	43,487	585,921	3,247,500	1,680,921,900

no commas in certain figures

June 2018	Check 1783	(413) 555-8397
page 1027	Serial No. 4621987-HG	4218 Lake Street
0.5325	Evansville, IN 47701-1957	1200 kilometers

space in metric measures with five or more digits

We deliver more than **12 000** liters of bottled water daily to stores.

b. When two independent figures appear consecutively (one directly after the other) in a sentence, separate the figures with a comma.

Between 2012 and **2015, 12** new office buildings were built in our city.

Of the **217, 183** homes in the development have already been sold.

Two consecutive numbers that act as adjectives modifying the same noun are *not* separated by a comma. Instead, write the first number in words and the second one in figures. (The second number is generally a form that would be written in numerals if it were to appear alone.) If the first number cannot be expressed in *one or two words*, place it in figures also.

two numbers modifying a noun, word-figure form
Each carton contains **four 1-gallon** containers of low-fat milk.

Our contract is for **three 25-second** commercials daily.

Your order for **eighteen 42-inch** bolts of silk prints was shipped today.

Please order an additional **twenty-four 60-watt** bulbs.

The restaurant-size carton contains **thirty-six 8-ounce** servings.

The contractor will build **forty 5-bedroom** homes in this tract.

two numbers modifying a noun, figure-figure form
Please purchase **150 49-cent** stamps from the post office.

Security Bank has approved your loan to purchase a **2014 40-foot** manufactured home.

The patient's prescription is for **125 50-milligram** tablets.

c. Separate volume numbers from page references with commas.

This information is contained in **Volume VII, page 326**.

d. Weights, capacities, and measures that consist of several words are treated as single units and are not separated by commas.

weight as a single unit
The Nelsons' newborn weighed **6 pounds 9 ounces** at birth.

capacity as a single unit
This ceramic pitcher holds **3 quarts 1 cup**.

measure as a single unit
The hotel manager ordered new carpeting for the ballroom, which measures **122 feet 8 inches** by **58 feet 10 inches**.

Your flight time from New York to Phoenix is **4 hours 20 minutes**.

e. The plural of a figure is formed by adding *s*.

There is one too many **4s** in this serial number.

The **1900s** will be noted for humanity's first successes in space travel.

Special Forms

4–15 Fractions

a. Simple fractions that can be expressed in two words are written in word form. Fractions written in word form are not hyphenated unless they are used as compound adjectives.[3]

simple fraction used as a noun
By August the sales staff had already met **three fourths** of its quota for the year.

Only **one third** of our clients returned the questionnaire by the deadline date.

simple fraction used as a compound adjective
A **two-thirds** majority vote is needed to ratify the union contract.

Our investment syndicate wishes to purchase a **one-fourth** interest in the proposed new financial center.

b. Use figures to express (1) long and awkward fractions, (2) fractions combined with whole numbers, or (3) fractions used for technical purposes.

long and awkward fraction
Our study indicated that **21/200** of a second is needed for the average person to begin reacting in emergency situations.

fraction combined with whole number
Allston's new plant and warehouse is located **5½** miles from the center of Seattle.

fraction for technical use
The Maintenance Department is temporarily out of ⅝-inch roundheaded sheet metal screws.

c. Follow these guidelines to create fractions in a word processing program:

(1) Use the extended character set of your word processing program to insert common fractions that are written in figures. Those usually available are ¼, ½, ¾, ⅓, ⅔, ⅛, ⅜, ⅝, and ⅞.
(2) Use a diagonal and font attributes to create fractions written in figures that are not found in extended character sets of word processing programs. Key and format the first number in superscript; return to the normal font and key a diagonal; then key the second number at the normal position on the line and resize it to match the number formatted as superscript.

---

[3] "Table of Numbers," footnote 5, Merriam-Webster, Incorporated. (2014). *Merriam-Webster's Collegiate Dictionary* (11th ed.). Springfield, MA: Merriam-Webster, Incorporated, p. 852.

(3) Leave no space between any whole number appearing with a fraction that has been constructed using extended character sets or font attributes.

(4) Key all fractions in normal type size using the diagonal construction in word processing programs that do not contain extended character sets or permit font attributes. In mixed numbers keyed in normal type, leave one space between the whole number and the fraction.

fraction keyed through an extended character set

The east wall of the family room has ½-inch oak paneling.

mixed number keyed through an extended character set

Markets in the Dallas-Fort Worth area ordered **3⅜** tons of beef last week from our distributor.

Our employees averaged **35¾** hours of sick leave in 2015 as compared with **27¼** hours this past year.

fraction or mixed number keyed using font attributes

These $^{15}/_{16}$-inch screws have been manufactured specifically to assemble our Model 8320 computer stations.

To be reupholstered, the two dining chairs will require **2**$^{11}/_{16}$ yards of fabric.

The supply closet requires **30**$^{9}/_{10}$ square feet of flooring.

fraction or mixed number keyed in normal type

We will need only **5/6** yard of lace to finish the wedding dress.

According to the contract, all these parts must be manufactured within **1/100**-inch of specifications.

Each of these panels is exactly **35 9/16** inches wide.

4–16 Ordinals

a. Ordinal numbers (*first, second, third,* etc.) that can be written in one or two words are generally expressed in word form except those appearing in (1) dates before the month or standing alone and (2) numbered street names above *ten*.

general use

Mr. Woo was elected to represent the **Sixty-third** Congressional District.

The **twentieth** century will be noted for the birth of the Internet and providing American households access to worldwide resources.

dates

The remaining amount on this loan must be paid by the **1st** of June.

Your monthly rental payments are due the **15th** of each month.

Please submit your monthly expense report by the **1st** of the month.

numbered streets

Our State Street store will move to 470 East **Third** Street during the last two weeks of August.

The new theater complex will be built on the corner of Hampshire and **22nd** Streets.

b. Ordinals expressed in figure form end in *st, nd, rd,* or *th.*

The note on this hillside property is due the **1st** of June.

May we have your response by the **22nd** of November.

This year marks the **123rd** anniversary of our city.

Our new offices are located at 1560 **12th** Avenue.

4–17 Roman Numerals

a. Use capital letters when keying Roman numerals for chapter or outline divisions.

When creating outlines with the outline feature of a word processing program, adjust the tab settings so that the periods align for Roman numerals as well as for other divisions in the outline.

Use capital letters for expressing years written in Roman numerals.

table of Roman numerals

Arabic Numeral	*Roman Numeral*	*Arabic Numeral*	*Roman Numeral*
1	I	16	XVI
2	II	17	XVII
3	III	18	XVIII
4	IV	19	XIX
5	V	20	XX
6	VI	30	XXX
7	VII	40	XL
8	VIII	50	L
9	IX	60	LX
10	X	70	LXX
11	XI	80	LXXX
12	XII	90	XC
13	XIII	100	C
14	XIV	500	D
15	XV	1,000	M

chapter divisions
We appreciate receiving your insightful review of **Chapter IX**, "Internet Resources."

divisions in an outline
I. Hardware requirements

II. Network capabilities

III. Software requirements

IV. Training programs

year expressed in Roman numerals
Chiseled at the top of the archway was the year the old stone church had been built—**MDCLXXXVI**. (1686)

b. The preliminary sections of a report (such as the transmittal letter, the table of contents, and the list of tables) are numbered with lowercase Roman numerals. Number the pages consecutively using *i, ii, iii, iv, v,* and so on.

5

Hyphenating and Dividing Words

Hyphenating and Dividing Words Solution Finder

Hyphenating Words

5–1 Compound Nouns and Verbs

Often two or more words act as a single idea. Nouns and verbs in this class may be written as separate words, written as single words, or hyphenated. When in doubt about a combination, consult an up-to-date dictionary to determine the exact form of compound nouns and verbs.[1]

separate words, nouns

Web site	market research	income tax	air conditioner
cell phone	credit card	time sheet	voice mail
cash flow	profit sharing	waiting room	health care

single words, nouns

checkbook	workforce	salesperson	paycheck
spreadsheet	afterthought	courthouse	moneymaker
caregiver	coworker	goodwill	lifestyle

hyphenated words, nouns

sister-in-law	attorney-at-law	by-product	self-confidence
double-talk	fund-raiser	write-in	air-conditioning
runner-up	trade-in	follow-up	e-mail

separate words, verbs

to back up	to cut back	to hand out	to follow through
to set up	to mark down	to step down	to call in
to stand out	to trade in	to slip up	to sign on

single words, verbs

to upgrade	to pinpoint	to downsize	to underline
to handwrite	to upload	to handpick	to mastermind
to highlight	to undercut	to landscape	to overrate

hyphenated words, verbs

to e-mail	to air-condition	to triple-space	to cross-examine
to ill-treat	to second-guess	to double-check	to piece-dye
to spot-check	to force-feed	to rubber-stamp	to double-date

[1]All spellings and hyphenations used in this manual are based on Merriam-Webster, Incorporated. (2014). *Merriam-Webster's Collegiate Dictionary* (11th ed.). Springfield, MA: Merriam-Webster, Incorporated. For a complete, up-to-date online resource, visit Merriam-Webster at http://www.m-w.com. Individuals who have purchased *Merriam-Webster's Collegiate Dictionary*, 11th ed., may register for a free one-year subscription to the online version of the 11th edition.

5–2 Compound Adjectives

When two or more words appearing together act as a single idea to describe a noun or pronoun, these words function as a compound adjective. In many cases compound adjectives are hyphenated; in other cases they are not.

a. **A number of compound adjectives are listed and shown hyphenated in the dictionary. These adjectives may be considered permanent compounds. They are hyphenated whenever they are used as adjectives in a sentence, no matter where they appear in the sentence—before or after the nouns or pronouns they modify.**

permanent compound adjective before a noun or pronoun—hyphenated

able-bodied men and women
clear-cut decision
fork-tender filet mignon
full-time employees
hands-off policy
hard-core football fans
life-size models
machine-readable text
narrow-minded manager
no-fault insurance
one-sided opinion
public-spirited citizens
ready-made suits
small-scale investments
snow-white fabrics
soft-spoken individual
time-consuming tasks
up-to-date records
well-known personalities
well-to-do clients
word-of-mouth advertising
worn-out tires

permanent compound adjective following noun or pronoun—hyphenated

The advertising for our successful business is just **word-of-mouth**.

All the dinosaur models on display are **life-size**—each one made from Lego.

Will this software automate those tasks that are too **time-consuming**?

Since we installed the new accounting program, all our accounts receivable records have been **up-to-date**.

Our clothing line is **well-known** throughout the world.

Mailing addresses on all envelopes from our company are **machine-readable**.

All the job openings posted on our Web site are **full-time**.

b. **Sometimes compound nouns (nouns that contain more than one word) are used as single-thought adjectives to describe other nouns or pronouns. When these combinations are shown as *open compounds* (not hyphenated) in the dictionary, they are not hyphenated when used as compound adjectives.**

compound noun used as compound adjective—no hyphen

charge account customer
department store personnel
finance company records
grass roots movement
health care provider
high school principal
human resources management
income tax forms
life insurance premiums
real estate office
savings account passbook
stock market information
voice mail messages
word processing software

Income tax forms may be downloaded from the Internal Revenue Service Web site.

If you wish, you may pay your **life insurance** premiums on a monthly basis.

Please list your **health care** provider at the bottom of the medical information form.

Our **charge account** customers always receive advance notice of all sales.

c. **Many single-thought word groups that function as compound adjectives are not shown in the dictionary. Such word groups are known as *temporary compounds.* These temporary compounds are hyphenated only when they appear before—not after—the nouns or pronouns they modify.**

temporary compound before noun or pronoun—hyphenated

Many handheld electronic devices have **speech-recognition** capability to send text messages.

All **city-owned** property is exempt from these county taxes.

We retained a **well-established** legal firm to represent our interests.

Capture that **never-to-be-forgotten** event with pictures taken by PhotoPro!

The mayor's **not-too-cordial** attitude toward the press was evident.

temporary compound following noun or pronoun—no hyphen

All the software programs on this list are **speech recognition**.

None of the properties in this area are **city owned**.

Cox & Cox has been **well established** in Austin, Texas, for 30 years.

Your wedding day should be one that is **never to be forgotten**.

Mr. Winters' greetings this morning were certainly **not too cordial**.

Combinations of numbers and words that are usually plural are written in singular form and hyphenated when they appear as temporary compound adjectives before a noun or pronoun. The

combinations retain their plural form and are not hyphenated when they appear after the noun or pronoun they modify.

temporary compound in singular form before noun or pronoun—hyphenated
The **160-foot** driveway leading to the house will need to be paved before our clients will purchase the property.

Most of our clients are interested in purchasing a **four-bedroom** home in a quiet, residential neighborhood.

The Butlers' **6-pound-11-ounce** daughter was born on April 5.

The state highway patrol enforces strictly the **65-mile-per-hour** speed limit on this highway.

temporary compound following noun or pronoun—no hyphen
The driveway leading up to the house is **160 feet** long.

The Holtzes' new home has **four bedrooms**.

At birth the Butlers' daughter weighed **6 pounds 11 ounces**.

The speed limit on this highway is **65 miles per hour**.

d. **When *two separate* proper nouns or *two separate* common nouns are combined to form single-thought adjectives before other nouns or pronouns, hyphenate these compounds.**

separate proper nouns used as an adjective—hyphenated
This morning's issue of *The Wall Street Journal* carried several articles on **Chinese-American** trade relations.

Your **New York-London** flight has been delayed for three hours.

separate common nouns used as an adjective—hyphenated
All the applicants have experience in **union-management** relations.

Our classes may not exceed a 15:1 **student-teacher** ratio.

e. **Two or more words that represent a *single* proper noun are not hyphenated when they are used as an adjective.**

Our company has been negotiating with a **Middle Eastern** firm for the past six months.

How many **University of Florida** alumni have you been able to locate in Salt Lake City?

f. **Adverbs ending in *ly* that are combined with adjectives to form a single modifier are not hyphenated.**

Although holiday shopping is in full swing, we experienced a **surprisingly slow** weekend.

Katelyn Matsuyama is an **exceptionally gifted** graphic artist.

g. Hyphenate two separate colors contained in a compound adjective. Other compound modifiers, however, containing a color and another kind of adjective are not hyphenated—unless the combination is a permanent compound shown hyphenated in the dictionary.

two separate colors
The **burgundy-gray** combination in this fabric will complement the carpeting we have selected.

Ahni Morey used **red-orange** hues effectively to portray the Hawaiian sunset in these paintings.

other adjective combined with color
In this large tank, the **bluish green** water magnifies the colorful fish.

For the summer season, designers will be featuring **lime green** and **hot pink** accessories.

Ask our sales representatives to wear **dark gray** or black suits while they are in the exhibit area.

Place these artists' prints against a **snow-white** background to accentuate their deep color contrasts. (The adjective *snow-white* is shown hyphenated in the dictionary.[2])

h. Use suspending hyphens when a series of hyphenated adjectives has a common ending.
Have these color announcements printed on **8½- by 11-inch** photo paper.

Please order a supply of **$\frac{1}{16}$- and $\frac{1}{8}$-inch** drill bits.

These awards are for **eleventh- and twelfth-grade** students.

All construction bids for this hillside development are based on **one-, two-, and three-level** family dwellings.

i. Amounts in the millions and billions, percentages, and words used with numerals or letters are *not* hyphenated when they function as compound adjectives.

amounts in the millions and billions
According to the U.S. Census Bureau and the U.S. Bureau of Economic Analysis, in November 2014 the United States had a **$39 billion** deficit in trade of goods and services.

More than **3 billion** people worldwide use the Internet; **279.8 million** people in the United States alone use the Internet.

percentages
Between July 1 and July 31, you will receive a **10 percent** discount on all orders placed through our Web site.

---

[2] Merriam-Webster, Incorporated. (2014). *Merriam-Webster's Collegiate Dictionary* (11th ed.). Springfield, MA: Merriam-Webster, Incorporated.

We will experience a ½ **percent** increase in our state sales tax effective May 1.

words used with numerals or letters

Kendall will be rated in as a **Grade 1** administrative assistant.

How many **vitamin C** tablets are in the giant-size bottle?

When is our shipment of Sultan **Model 2863** tablets scheduled to arrive?

j. Simple fractions are hyphenated *only* when they are used as compound adjectives.[3]

compound adjective

Hayden sold his **one-fourth** ownership in the company for $2.5 million.

Amendments to the bylaws require a **two-thirds** majority approval.

simple fraction as noun

Only **one third** of the stockholders responded to the questionnaire.

The Board of Directors voted to reinvest **one half** of this year's profits in sustainable building design and construction projects.

5–3 Prefixes

a. Some prefixes are hyphenated; others are not. Use the following guidelines for hyphenating prefixes:

(1) Words beginning with *ex* (meaning "former") and *self* are hyphenated.
(2) Words beginning with *pre*, *re*,[4] and *non* are generally not hyphenated.
(3) Words beginning with *co* and *vice* may or may not be hyphenated. Use your dictionary to check the hyphenation of words with either of these beginnings.

ex *and* self

Lucian Reynolds, the **ex-mayor** of Oceanside, is now a stockbroker.

The **ex-chairperson** of our committee still has last year's records.

Successful salespeople usually project **self-confidence**.

Employee **self-satisfaction** contributes to raising both morale and productivity.

---

[3]"Table of Numbers," footnote 5, Merriam-Webster, Incorporated. (2014). *Merriam-Webster's Collegiate Dictionary* (11th ed.). Springfield, MA: Merriam-Webster, Incorporated, p. 852.

[4]The words *re-collect* meaning "to collect again," *re-cover* meaning "to cover anew," *re-create* meaning "to create again," *re-lease* meaning "to lease again," *re-present* meaning "to present again," *re-press* meaning "to press again," *re-sign* meaning "to sign again," *re-sort* meaning "to sort again," and *re-tread* meaning "to tread again" are exceptions to this rule. Note that without the hyphens these words would have completely different meanings.

pre, re, *and* non

Use the template that is **preformatted** for thirty 1-inch-by-2¼-inch address labels for this mailing.

When will the **preemployment** interviews be held?

Please **recheck** carefully all the receipts from our Corona store.

The tires on this truck need to be **realigned**.

Tuition **reimbursements** are unavailable for classes taken at **nonaccredited** colleges and universities.

Do you wish to initiate legal proceedings against Fox One-Hour Photo for **nonpayment** of its account?

co

co-edition	coauthor
co-occurrence	codefendant
co-owner	coinsurance

vice

vice-chancellor	vice admiral
vice-consul	vice president
vice-regent	vice squad

b. When a prefix is added to a proper noun, place a hyphen between the prefix and the proper noun.

Our survey showed that many firms operating in the South today date back to **pre-Civil War** times.

If you cannot ensure a **mid-May** delivery date, please cancel the order.

For some Americans an Independence Day celebration without fireworks would be **un-American**.

5-4 Numbers

a. Hyphenate compound numbers from *21* to *99* when they appear in word form.

Eighty-three of our agents responded to our e-mail query, but we are still awaiting a reply from **twenty-six** more.

b. For numbers greater than *99* expressed in word form, hyphenate only the compound numbers. In formal legal documents, begin each number with a capital letter.

Three hundred forty-seven children are in our summer camp.

The lessee shall pay a sum of **Two Thousand Eight Hundred Seventy-five Dollars and Twenty-four Cents** ($2,875.24) to the lessor.

c. Simple fractions not used with units of measure are expressed in word form. Hyphenate these fractions *only* when they function as compound adjectives.

simple fraction used as noun
At least **one third** of our present construction projects are implementing green technology; for example, all are scheduled for the installation of solar panels.

Approximately **three fourths** of our company vehicles are leased from Statewide Mobile Service.

simple fraction used as compound adjective
Richmond, Inc., has purchased a **one-half** interest in the Mesa Canyon Shopping Mall.

A **two-thirds** majority vote is needed to pass this bond measure, which will appear on the November ballot.

d. When a number-word combination functions as a *single unit* to describe a noun (a compound adjective), (1) express the word part of the compound adjective in singular form and (2) separate the parts of the compound adjective with a hyphen. Only in percentages, amounts in the millions and billions, and capitalized word-numeral combinations are the hyphens omitted.

number-word compound adjective—hyphenated
Our **three-year** lease for these offices will expire on August 31.

Police officers are citing drivers who ignore the **15-mile-per-hour** postings in school zones.

Cars, SUVs, and vans are charged **50-cent** tolls along this turnpike.

One of our recent graduates just started a **$4,500-per-month** job.

The Joneses' **7-pound-8-ounce** baby was born on January 1.

percentage—no hyphen
Your division experienced a **15 percent** sales increase during the last quarter.

amount in the millions—no hyphen
Ridgewood, Inc., announced a **$2.4 million** profit for the current year.

capitalized word-numeral combination—no hyphen
Your Evansdale **Model 380** curio cabinet should arrive in our store within the next three weeks.

e. In word processing copy, use an *en* dash (if possible) to represent the terms *to* or *through* between two numerals. If an *en* dash is not available, use a hyphen to replace these terms.

As you requested, your vacation this year has been scheduled from July **3–18**.

Refer to pages **70–75** for further instructions.

End-of-Line Word and Word-Group Divisions

Where possible, avoid dividing words at the end of a line because complete words are easier to read, easier to understand, and neater in appearance. Sometimes, however, word divisions at the end of a line are necessary to avoid overly uneven line lengths or, in justified copy, awkward-appearing lines with large spaces between words.[5]

5–5 Words and Word Groups Never to Be Divided

Some words and certain word groups may not be divided under any circumstances:

a. Do not divide one-syllable words, including those that end in *ed*.

one-syllable words

freight straight threats thought through bread

one-syllable* ed *words

called changed weighed planned striped shipped

b. Do not set off a single-letter syllable at either the beginning or the end of a word.

beginning of a word

i tinerary a warded e nough i dentify o mitted u niform

end of a word

radi o bacteri a health y rati o criteri a photocop y

c. Do not set off a two-letter syllable at the end of a word. At least three characters of a divided word must appear on the next line.

present ed	compa ny	month ly
build er	week ly	debt or

d. Do not divide abbreviations unless a hyphen already appears within the abbreviation. Divide hyphenated abbreviations only after the hyphen.

not divided

UNESCO	AAMCN	USA	AOL	UCLA	PhD
EdD	BA	Sept.	bdrm.	c.o.d.	equiv.

may be divided

AFL-CIO KMET-TV NBEA-WBEA

---

[5]Observe the following rules to divide words and certain word groups correctly at the end of a line. Some of these rules should be followed strictly; others are flexible in their application, especially in desktop published copy.

5 Hyphenating and Dividing Words

e. **Do not divide month and day; *a.m., p.m., noon,* or *midnight* from clock time; percentages from the word *percent*; page numbers from page references; or other such closely related word-and-numeral combinations.**

If you are using a word processor, place a nonbreaking space between the components of the combination to keep all parts on the same line. Key a nonbreaking space in Microsoft Word by holding down the Ctrl and Shift keys and tapping the space bar.

month and day

February 6 September 30 December 12

a.m., p.m., noon, *or* midnight *with clock time*

9 a.m.	7:30 a.m.	1 p.m.
4:05 p.m.	12 noon	12 midnight

***percentage with the word* percent**

0.5 percent 1 percent 8.25 percent 60.5 percent

page number with page reference

page ix page 76 page 351 page 1184

other word-and-numeral combinations

6 ounces	Room 3250	Model 1287A	No. 7352-1869-4
Check 213	8.5 inches	219 miles	12 yards
75 cents	Suite 400	Chapter 5	size 10

f. **Do not divide contractions or numerals.**

contractions

wouldn't doesn't haven't you've you're o'clock

numerals

$12,387 1,135,450 2 billion 3,350 $4,250 $3.5 million

g. **Do not divide the last word in more than two consecutive lines.**

h. **Do not divide the last word in a paragraph or the last word on a page.**

5–6 Words to Avoid Dividing If Possible

Observing the following rules is certainly desirable, but situations may occur where end-of-line word divisions are unavoidable. Apply these rules—unless doing so would result in an extremely ragged right margin.

a. **Avoid dividing words that contain six letters or fewer.**

forget person better number listen filter

b. **Avoid dividing a word after a two-letter prefix.**

in corporate	un necessary	re warding
de pendent	en large	im portant

5 Hyphenating and Dividing Words

5–7 Rules and Guidelines for Dividing Words

Divide words *only* between syllables. Use an up-to-date dictionary to locate the correct syllabication of words to be divided.[6]

Words containing several syllables often require forethought to determine the appropriate place to separate the word. Use the following guidelines to determine where to divide a word:

a. Divide hyphenated and single-word compounds at their natural breaks.

hyphenated compound

vice-/chancellor[7]   self-/esteem   Governor-/elect   brother-/in-/law

single-word compound

nation/wide   sales/person   data/base   week/day

b. Where possible, divide words after a prefix or before a suffix.

prefix

non/profit   super/visor   mis/informed   pre/liminary

suffix

corpora/tion   employ/ment   conscien/tious   willing/ness

c. Divide words between double letters *except* when the root word itself ends with the double letters and is followed by a suffix.

divided between double letters

bul/letin   accom/modate   neces/sarily   vacil/late

divided after double letters

business/like   fulfill/ment   helpless/ness   install/ing

d. Divide words between two vowels pronounced separately.

reconcili/ation   concili/ative   continu/ation   gradu/ation

e. Divide words *after*, not before, a single vowel pronounced as a syllable except when the vowel is part of a suffix.

single vowel

congratu/lations   bene/ficial   apolo/gize   clari/fication

suffix vowel

accept/able   allow/able   collaps/ible   forc/ible

---

[6]All word divisions shown in this reference manual are based on the syllabication shown in Merriam-Webster, Incorporated. (2014). *Merriam-Webster's Collegiate Dictionary* (11th ed.). Springfield, MA: Merriam-Webster, Incorporated.

[7]The slash (/) as used here and in the following sections of this chapter signifies an appropriate place for dividing a word or a word group at the end of a line.

5-8 Guidelines for Dividing Word Groups

Certain word groups are preferably divided in specific places. Use the following guidelines to separate dates, names of individuals, addresses, numbered items, copy containing dashes, and copy containing ellipses. If you are using word processing software, place a nonbreaking space between any parts in the word group that should appear on the same line. Key a nonbreaking space in Microsoft Word by holding down the Ctrl and Shift keys and tapping the space bar.

a. Divide dates between the day and the year, *not* between the month and the day.

February 14, / 2017	*not*	February / 14, 2017
December 9, / 2018	*not*	December / 9, 2018

b. Full names of individuals are ideally divided directly before the last name, but they may be divided before a middle name. Do not, however, divide a name (1) after a courtesy title, (2) before a middle initial, or (3) before an abbreviation.

Names preceded by long professional titles may also be divided between the title and the first name or between words in the title.

divided before last name

Ms. Marley / Sanders	*not*	Ms. / Marley Sanders
Dr. Cayden K. / Gelobedian	*not*	Dr. / Cayden K. Gelobedian Dr. Cayden / K. Gelobedian
Mr. Jason / Montgomery Jr.	*not*	Mr. / Jason Montgomery Jr. Mr. Jason Montgomery / Jr.

divided before middle name or last name

Karen / Lynelle / Clark Jordan / Christopher / Savage

divided after long title or between words in a long title

Associate / Professor / Alice H. / Duffy

Lieutenant / Colonel / Frank / Ritzkowski

c. Avoid, where possible, dividing a street address directly after the house or building number. Street addresses are preferably divided between the street name and the street type (*Street, Avenue, Boulevard, Lane,* etc.). If the street name contains more than one word, the street address may also be divided between words in the street name.

division of single-word street name

1571 Charleston / Avenue	One Blythe / Drive
20 Wilshire / Boulevard	4810 36th / Street

5 Hyphenating and Dividing Words

division possibilities of street name containing more than one word

4300 Coldwater / Canyon / Avenue

817 East / Jersey / Street

17325 San / Fernando / Mission / Boulevard

3624 West / 59th / Place

d. Divide city and state lines in addresses between (1) the city and state or (2) the state and ZIP Code. They may also be divided between words in those cities and states containing more than one word.

Dubuque, / Iowa / 52001 San / Diego, / California / 92109-2134

Poughkeepsie, / New / York / 12601-1032

e. A numbered or lettered horizontal listing may be divided directly before the number or letter, but not directly after.

The college president offered these three reasons for our hiring practices: (1) enrollment declines, (2) fewer full-time faculty openings in the college, and (3) no mandatory retirement age for professors.

f. A sentence with a dash may be broken after the dash, but not directly before it.

The vice president agrees that your recommendation is excellent—
a step in the right direction.

When our peak sales subside at the end of the year—in December—
we plan to move our offices to Portland.

g. A sentence may be divided directly after an ellipsis, not directly before. At least one word of the sentence must appear on the same line before the ellipsis.

If you are using word processing software, place a nonbreaking space before and between the periods in an ellipsis to prevent the periods from word wrapping incorrectly to the next line. Key a nonbreaking space in Microsoft Word by holding down the Ctrl and Shift keys and tapping the space bar.

As the article stated, "The mayor's campaign issues focus on . . .
crime prevention in our city."

According to the *Newsweek* article, "As the number of Internet access providers continues to grow, prices for these services will drop. . . .
Such factors will result in substantially fewer providers."

6

Abbreviations, Acronyms, and Symbols

Abbreviations, Acronyms, and Symbols Solution Finder

6 Abbreviations and Symbols

Abbreviations and Acronyms[1]

6–1 Use of Abbreviations and Acronyms

a. **An *abbreviation* is "a shortened form of a written word or phrase used in its place," for example, *amt.* for *amount* or *Feb. 14* for *February 14*. An *acronym* is "a word formed from the initial letters of the major parts of a compound term" or "an abbreviation formed from the initial letters of a compound," for example, *RAM* for *random-access memory* and *ASAP* for *as soon as possible.* Those acronyms formed from the initial letters of a compound are often referred to as *initialisms*.**

b. **Use abbreviations and acronyms only when you are confident that the reader understands their meaning. Except for commonly used terms, confine your primary use of abbreviations to (1) business forms; (2) suitable technical documents; and (3) tables, charts, graphs, and other such visual aids. Limit your use of acronyms in running text. If used, write out the words and place the acronym in parentheses the first time the words are used.**

Before filing this tax return, please check with the **Internal Revenue Service (IRS)** on the legitimacy of this deduction. Several recent **IRS** rulings in this area may affect the client's ability to use these losses as a deduction.

c. **Use consistently the same form for an abbreviated word or sequence of words throughout your document.**

Applications for undergraduate admissions to **Louisiana State University (LSU)** are due by November 30. Students planning to attend **LSU** must apply for admission before submitting a housing application. (not *Louisiana State*)

d. **Generally omit periods in acronyms written in all capital letters. Use periods with most abbreviations that appear in all lowercase letters. Abbreviations with combinations of capital and lowercase letters may or may not contain periods.**

acronyms written with all capital letters

Have you received any information regarding the **MBA** program at **UCLA**?

The closest **IBM** office to you in the **UK** is located in London.

6 Abbreviations and Symbols

---

[1]The guidelines for expressing abbreviations contained in this chapter are based on The University of Chicago Press. (2010). *The Chicago Manual of Style* (16th ed.). Chicago: The University of Chicago Press, pp. 487–527. Spellings of abbreviations are primarily based on Merriam-Webster, Incorporated. (2014). *Merriam-Webster's Collegiate Dictionary* (11th ed.). Springfield, MA: Merriam-Webster, Incorporated.

abbreviations written with all lowercase letters
Please order additional letterhead, envelopes, copy paper, felt-tips, **etc.**, from Vista Office Supplies.

The meeting is scheduled from 10 **a.m.** until 2 **p.m.**; lunch will be served to all the participants.

abbreviations written with capital letters and lowercase letters
At your request our office is sending a copy of your medical records to **Dr.** Erik Simonson.

Tomorrow's *Donna Sullivan Show* will feature an interview with Andrea Robinson, **PhD**, about her new book, *Your Dress Size Is Really 8.*

6–2 Names and Titles

a. Middle names of individuals are often represented by an initial. Sometimes individuals prefer to use an initial to represent their first name. In both cases capitalize the first letter of the name followed by a period and one space.

The abbreviations *Mr., Ms., Mrs.,* and *Dr.* are used for courtesy titles.

middle or first name abbreviated with initial
The host on *Early Morning America* will interview Jon **A.** Freeman on Monday.

B. Scot Underwood has been elected to the board of Litchfield Corporation.

Have you read any of the works of **T. S.** Eliot?

courtesy titles—with full names

Mr. Thomas C. Wrigley	**Mrs.** Ann Knight
Ms. Lena R. Sabawi	**Dr.** Jeremy Cole

b. Write out a civil, educational, military, or religious title used before and in conjunction with a person's full name or last name only. Abbreviate lengthy titles (those containing more than one word), however, when they appear before a person's *full* name and brevity is required.

title written out—with full name
This semester **Professor** Donna-Mae Villanueva is teaching the advanced communications class.

title written out—with last name only
This initiative has been placed on the ballot through the efforts of **Governor** Brown.

The keynote convention speaker will be **Lieutenant Governor** Anderson.

title abbreviated—with full name
You may contact **Lt. Col.** Isidore Goodman for further information. (Lieutenant Colonel)

I believe that **Asst. Dist. Atty.** William M. Gallagher has been assigned to this case. (Assistant District Attorney)

c. **Abbreviate and capitalize professional designations (*CPA, CLU, RN, RPT,* etc.) that follow a person's name. The designations are written without periods or spaces. Place a comma before and after an acronym appearing within a sentence and before an acronym at the end of a sentence.**

professional designation within a sentence
Horst Tarnowski, **CPA**, will be in charge of the audit for Canterbury Industries. (certified public accountant)

Michelle Allen, **CE**, will demonstrate our new face cream line at this year's Beauty Expo. (certified esthetician)

Has Kelsey Collins, **RPT**, applied for the opening at Valley Hills Hospital? (registered physical therapist)

professional designation at the end of a sentence
The surgery floor supervisor during that shift is Michael Yano, **RN**. (registered nurse)

The position has been filled by Robin Wong, **CAP**. (certified administrative professional)

You may wish to have this insurance policy examined by Riley Jefferson, **CLU**. (chartered life underwriter)

d. **Abbreviate and capitalize academic degrees (*MD, PhD, EdD, MBA, BA,* etc.) that follow a person's name. Modern usage suggests writing academic degrees without periods or spaces, although many traditionalists still prefer to use periods with academic degrees. Omit the periods unless they are needed for clarity, tradition, or consistency.**

Place a comma before and after an abbreviated academic degree appearing within a sentence and before one at the end of a sentence.

academic degree—modern usage
Your appointment with Marc Cohen, **DDS**, has been postponed until June 30. (doctor of dental surgery)

This journal article on spinal cord injuries was written by Dorothy Salazar, **MD**. (doctor of medicine)

academic degree—traditional usage
Direct all student complaints to Curtis Washington, **Ph.D.**, our vice president of student services. (doctor of philosophy)

Our Social Service Department has offered the position to Toby Bramham, **M.A.** (master of arts)

e. For individuals holding a doctor's degree, use either the courtesy title *Dr.* before the name or an academic degree (*MD, PhD, EdD, DDS,* etc.) after the name. Do not use a title and an academic degree with the same meaning for an individual. Academic degrees and courtesy titles with different meanings may be used for a single individual.

courtesy title and academic degree with the same meaning

Dr. Jeffrey Weisel is scheduled to perform the surgery next Thursday.

Jeffrey Weisel, **MD**, is scheduled to perform the surgery next Thursday.

courtesy title and academic degree with different meanings

Professor Diana Simonian, **PhD**, has consented to be a guest lecturer at our college.

Ms. Jordan Acuña, **RN**, was transferred to the Critical Care Unit at Westside Hospital as of May 1.

f. Abbreviate and capitalize personal titles that follow a person's name. Conclude the abbreviations *Jr.* and *Sr.* with a period. Personal titles are considered part of the name and are therefore written without commas.

Roger W. Armstrong **Jr.** was recently elected to the Springfield Board of Education.

A suite at the Atlas Hotel has been reserved for Charles T. Wellington **Sr.**

Please send a copy of the report to Robert Lucio **III** by April 1.

Andrew Miller **Sr.**, MD, and Andrew Miller **Jr.**, DDS, have offices in the same medical building.

6–3 Organizations

a. The names of business, educational, government, professional, military, labor, philanthropic, and other organizations or agencies may be abbreviated. No periods or spaces are used to separate the individual letters.

business organizations

AA	American Airlines, Inc.
ARCO	Atlantic Richfield Company
GE	General Electric Company
GMC	General Motors Corporation
HP	Hewlett-Packard Company
IBM	International Business Machines Corporation

educational organizations

ERIC	Educational Resources Information Center
NYU	New York University
PCC	Pasadena City College
UCLA	University of California, Los Angeles

governmental organizations

FBI	Federal Bureau of Investigation
FCC	Federal Communications Commission
FDA	Food and Drug Administration
FTC	Federal Trade Commission
HUD	Department of Housing and Urban Development
ICC	Interstate Commerce Commission
OSHA	Occupational Safety and Health Administration
SEC	Securities and Exchange Commission
SSA	Social Security Administration
UNESCO	United Nations Educational, Scientific, and Cultural Organization
USDA	U.S. Department of Agriculture
USPS	U.S. Postal Service

professional organizations

ABA	American Bankers Association; American Bar Association
ABC	Association for Business Communication
AIA	American Institute of Architects
AIB	American Institute of Banking
AMA	American Medical Association
IAAP	International Association of Administrative Professionals
NBEA	National Business Education Association

other organizations

AAA	American Automobile Association
AFL-CIO	American Federation of Labor and Congress of Industrial Organizations
BBB	Better Business Bureau
NAACP	National Association for the Advancement of Colored People
YMCA	Young Men's Christian Association
YWCA	Young Women's Christian Association

b. Television and radio station call letters are written in all capital letters without periods or spaces.

ABC	CBS	CNN	HBO	MTV	PBS
NBC	KABC	KERA	KAAL	KNUU-AM	WDPT-FM
WABC	WAXY				

c. In the names of business firms, abbreviations such as *Co., Corp., Inc., Ltd.,* and *Mfg.* are used only if they are part of the official organizational name. Commas, too, are used only if they are part of the official organizational name.

We are still awaiting the remainder of our order from Century **Mfg. Co.**

Brockton Computers, **Inc.**, submitted the lowest bid to update our network.

6–4 Dates and Time

a. Spell out days of the week and months of the year. Abbreviate them only in lists, tables, graphs, charts, illustrations, or other such visual displays where space is limited.

days and months spelled out in text
Our grand opening is scheduled for **Friday, October 9**.

By **Wednesday, January 21**, we must have our annual report ready to be mailed to stockholders.

days of the week abbreviated in visual displays

Sun.	Mon.	Tues.	Wed.	Thurs.	Fri.	Sat.
Su	M	Tu	W	Th	F	Sa

months of the year abbreviated in visual displays

Jan. Feb. Mar. Apr. May June July Aug. Sept. Oct. Nov. Dec.

or

Jan Feb Mar Apr May Jun Jul Aug Sep Oct Nov Dec

b. The abbreviations *a.m.* (ante meridiem) and *p.m.* (post meridiem) indicate clock time before noon (a.m.) and after noon (p.m.). Use lowercase letters followed by periods for these abbreviations. No space follows the first period.

Would you prefer to take the flight at 8:45 **a.m.** or the one at 2 **p.m.**?

All our department meetings are scheduled at 1:30 **p.m.**

c. United States time zones—*EST* (eastern standard time), *CST* (central standard time), *MST* (mountain standard time), *PST* (Pacific standard time), *AST* (Alaska standard time), and *HST* (Hawaiian standard time)—are usually abbreviated. Time zones for daylight saving time are abbreviated *EDT, CDT, MDT, PDT,* and *ADT*. Hawaii does not have daylight saving time.

Operators are available from 8 a.m. until 10 p.m., **EST**, to take telephone orders.

John's flight is scheduled to arrive in Denver at 2:38 p.m., **MDT**.

d. The abbreviations *BC* (before Christ) and *AD* (anno Domini) are sometimes used in expressing dates. *AD* precedes the year and *BC* follows the year. Both are shown in capital letters without periods. They may also appear in small caps with or without periods.

BC *after the year*
Professor Reinhardt has substantiated that these artifacts date back to 600 **BC**. (or 600 BC or 600 B.C.)

AD *before the year*
The Spanish legions, under the leadership of Galba, conquered Rome in **AD** 68. (or AD 68 or A.D. 68)

6–5 Standard Units of Measure

Common units of measure—distance, length, temperature, volume, and weight—are usually spelled out in business documents. Abbreviations, however, may be used on invoices, packing slips, and other business forms where space is limited. Place periods after one-word abbreviations and use the singular form. Omit the periods in abbreviations representing more than one word.

general business documents
All perishable goods shipped over 100 **miles** should be kept below 40 **degrees Fahrenheit**.

business forms, one-word abbreviations
16 **ft.** 8 **in.** (16 feet 8 inches) 6 **lb.** 12 **oz.** (6 pounds 12 ounces)

72°**F** (72 degrees Fahrenheit) 3 **doz.** pens (3 dozen pens)

business forms, multiple-word abbreviations
120 **wpm** (120 words per minute) 65 **mph** (65 miles per hour)

6–6 Metric Units of Measure

a. Write out metric units of measure in standard business documents. However, in forms, tables, technical writing, and scientific writing, they are often abbreviated. These abbreviations are written without periods, and the singular and plural forms are the same. Common abbreviations for measurements related to distance, weight, and volume follow:

prefixes

deka	**da**	(× 10)	deci	**d**	(1/10)
hecto	**h**	(× 100)	centi	**c**	(1/100)
kilo	**k**	(× 1000)	milli	**m**	(1/1000)
mega	**m**	(× 1 000 000)			
giga	**g**	(× 1 000 000 000)			

6 Abbreviations and Symbols

common units of measure

meter	**m**	centimeter	**cm**	kilometer	**km**
gram	**g**	kilogram	**kg**	milligram	**mg**
liter	**l**	milliliter	**ml**		
kilobyte	**KB**	megabyte	**MB**	gigabyte	**GB**

cubic centimeter	**cc**	square meter	**sqm**

b. Although the abbreviation for *liter* is a lowercase *l*, some authorities suggest using a capital *L* because the lowercase letter *l* and the numeral *1* (one) in many fonts look the same. Therefore, to avoid confusion, the capital *L* is suggested as a substitute.

1 **L** milk *but* 1 **ml** vaccine (abbreviation is clear)

c. Temperatures in the metric system are expressed on the Celsius scale. This term is abbreviated *C* without a period.

37°**C** 25°**C**

d. Express abbreviations related to kilometers per hour with a diagonal.

The maximum speed limit on our city expressways is 105 **km/h** (65 mph).

Slow down to 40 **km/h** (25 mph) in the residential areas.

6–7 Business and General Terms

a. Write the word *number* in full when it is not followed by a numeral. Use the abbreviation *No.* when a numeral directly follows the word—unless the word begins the sentence. Always spell out and capitalize the word *Number* when it begins a sentence.

The catalog **number** for the Klear-Vue Slimline CD jewel case is **10-587**.

When may we expect our order of **No. 1423** ProShot digital cameras?

Please order two **Model No. 2024NW** color laser printers.

Number 138-B replacement shelves must be ordered directly from the manufacturer.

b. Most commonly abbreviated business, computer, and Internet terms are written in all capital letters with no spaces or periods separating the letters. (See Section 6–11 for an additional listing of business and computer terms.)

capitalized abbreviation of business terms

COD	(collect on delivery)
FYI	(for your information)
FOB	(free on board)
LIFO	(last in, first out)
SOP	(standard operating procedures)
TQM	(total quality management)

capitalized abbreviation of computer terms

CPU	(central processing unit)
FTP	(file transfer protocol)
OCR	(optical character recognition)
RAM	(random-access memory)
WYSIWYG	(what you see is what you get)

capitalized abbreviation of Internet terms

DSL	(digital subscriber line)
HTML	(hypertext markup language)
ISP	(Internet service provider)
PDF	(Portable Document Format)
WWW	(World Wide Web)

c. Capitalize and abbreviate the word *extension* (*Ext.*) used with a telephone number. Place a comma before and after the combination when it appears within a sentence and before the combination when it concludes the sentence.

For more information call (213) 439-1884, **Ext.** 2830, any weekday between 8 a.m. and 5 p.m.

Please respond to this invitation by telephoning (800) 555-8237, **Ext.** 373.

d. Commonly abbreviated terms derived from Latin expressions are keyed in lowercase letters and followed by a period at the close of each abbreviated word; complete words such as *et* and *pro* in abbreviated terms do not require periods. Other abbreviated terms are keyed in all capital letters without periods.

lowercase abbreviations from Latin expressions

e.g.	(for example)	viz.	(namely)
et al.	(and others)	ibid.	(in the same place)
i.e.	(that is)	loc. cit.	(in the place cited)
etc.	(and so forth)	op. cit.	(in the work cited)
cf.	(compare)	a.m.	(after midnight until noon)
pro tem.	(temporarily)	p.m.	(after noon until midnight)
id.	(the same)	ca.	(approximately; around)

capitalized abbreviations from Latin expressions

PS	(postscript)	AD	(year after Christ)
NB	(note well)	BC	(year before Christ)

6–8 Plurals

Apostrophes are not used to form the plurals of abbreviations; most plural abbreviations are formed by adding only *s* to the singular form. However, some words—those related to length, area, weight, volume, and capacity—use the same abbreviation for the singular and plural forms.

plural formed by adding s

hr., **hrs.**	mo., **mos.**	IOU, **IOUs**
mgr., **mgrs.**	pkg., **pkgs.**	CPA, **CPAs**
yr., **yrs.**	memo, **memos**	RN, **RNs**

singular and plural forms identical—units of measure

1 deg., **70 deg.**	1 ft., **14 ft.**	1 in., **10 in.**
1 lb., **15 lb.**	1 qt., **3 qt.**	1 cu. in., **2 cu. in.**
1 yd., **3 yd.**	1 doz., **4 doz.**	1 sq. mi., **5 sq. mi.**

6–9 Addresses and Geographical Expressions

a. For addresses in business correspondence, street designations such as *Boulevard, Street, Avenue, Lane, Place,* and *Road* are written in full. *Boulevard,* however, may be abbreviated (*Blvd.*) if space is limited when expressing a long street name.

street designation spelled out

Ms. Gita Brooks
130 Barrington **Avenue**
Iowa City, IA 52240

Paramount Real Estate Company
6840 Washington **Boulevard**
Columbus, OH 43266-0309

boulevard *abbreviated with long street name*

Mr. Joseph F. Campanelli
1140 Martin Luther King **Blvd.**
San Francisco, CA 94127

b. Simple compass directions (*North, South, East, West*) that appear before a street name are spelled out. Compound directions such as *Northwest* or *Southeast,* however, are abbreviated when they appear either before or after the street name.

simple direction before street name

470 **East** Fountain Avenue

compound direction with street name

7500 Capitol Avenue, **NE**

3420 **SW** 43rd Street

c. **The U.S. Postal Service recommends that the names of states be abbreviated on all mailings by using the official state designations. (They are displayed in capital letters with no periods or spaces.) These two-letter state designations are shown in Section 6–12 and on the page opposite the inside back cover.**

Because modern optical scanning equipment no longer requires the use of the two-letter designations, either the full state name or the two-letter state designation may be used, depending on which form more nearly balances with the other lines of the address. If both forms provide balance, use the two-letter state designation.

two-letter state designation
Los Angeles Pierce College
6201 Winnetka Avenue
Woodland Hills, **CA** 91371

state name spelled out
Diamond Publishing Company, Inc.
1100 West Kensington Avenue, Suite 400
Ridgewood, **New Jersey** 07541-1863

d. **Since 1974 the U.S. Postal Service has recommended a format for addressing envelopes that uses all capital letters, abbreviations, and no internal punctuation marks. As yet, this format has not been widely accepted for individually prepared correspondence or even computer-generated form correspondence; its use has been limited mainly to standard bulk mailings.**

format recommended by U.S. Postal Service
JANE L MILLER
MILLER ASSOCIATES
1960 W CHELSEA AVE STE 2006
ALLENTOWN PA 18104-2378[2]

e. **Geographical abbreviations containing all capital letters are written without periods or spaces including the abbreviated form for *United States of America*. However, the abbreviated form for the shortened version *United States* is written with periods and no space between the letters.**

For geographical abbreviations containing a combination of capital and lowercase letters, place a period and a space after each abbreviated word.

capital letters

USA	(United States of America)	UK	(United Kingdom)
GB	(Great Britain)	ROC	(Republic of China)

[2]United States Postal Service. (2015, January). "Business Mail 101, Delivery Address." Retrieved from http://pe.usps.com/businessmail101/addressing/deliveryAddress.htm (as of January 2015).

capital and lowercase letters

So. Nev. (Southern Nevada) Ire. (Ireland)

***abbreviated form for* United States**

U.S. (United States)

U.S. currency (United States currency)

U.S. Postal Service (United States Postal Service)

U.S. Census Bureau (United States Census Bureau)

6–10 Abbreviation Format

a. The capitalization of abbreviations is generally governed by the format of the original word or words. Proper nouns are always capitalized, but common nouns generally appear in lowercase letters. A number of common noun abbreviations, however, are capitalized through popular usage.

capital letters for proper noun

UNESCO promotes international cooperation among its members in the fields of education, science, culture, and communication. (United Nations Educational, Scientific and Cultural Organization)

lowercase letters for common noun

atty. (attorney) mgr. (manager)

pkg. (package) agt. (agent)

capital letters for some common nouns

Sales this year for portable **DVD** players have declined from last year's sales.

You may obtain high-speed Internet access from your **TV** cable company.

b. Abbreviations that appear in all capital letters are generally formatted without periods or spaces. Exceptions are (1) the geographic term *U.S.* and (2) initials in a person's name.

general rule—no periods and no spaces

The story was first aired on **CBS** television.

Have you sent your résumé to **IBM**?

Before sending your tax return to the **IRS**, be sure to check it carefully for accuracy.

Angela Ramos, **RPT**, is the physical therapist who treated Ms. Spangler.

Will Briana Buenzli, **CLA**, be the new legal assistant in our firm?

I believe Mr. Fujimoto earned his **MBA** from Columbia.

Our new store location is 1760 Fillmore Street, **NW**, in Springfield.

All garments made in the **ROC** show their origin on the label.

reference to U.S.—periods with no spaces
Their travel agency in Bonn, Germany, had the best exchange rate for **U.S.** dollars.

Within the next month, the **U.S.** Food and Drug Administration should approve this new cancer drug.

initials—periods and spaces
Please deliver this report to Ms. **J. T.** Kelley.

Only Gerald **H.** Monroe applied for the position.

c. Abbreviations written with capital and lowercase letters may (1) contain no periods or spaces, (2) end with a period, or (3) contain both periods and spaces. Follow these guidelines:

(1) Multiple-word abbreviations condensed into a single entity contain no periods or spaces.
(2) Abbreviations beginning with a capital letter followed by all lowercase letters end with a period.
(3) Abbreviations containing more than one part have both periods and spaces.

abbreviations condensed into a single entity—no periods and no spaces
Sharon Lund O'Neil, **PhD**, was offered the position. (Modern style)

The board has appointed Devon O'Hanlon, **EdD**, to chair the task force. (Modern style)

abbreviations containing only initial capital letter—period
Please answer this inquiry from Cary Davidovich, **Esq.**

abbreviations containing more than one part—periods and spaces

So. Calif. (Southern California)	N. Mex. (New Mexico)
Brig. Gen. (Brigadier General)	Mng. Ed. (Managing Editor)

d. A period generally follows each letter or group of letters representing a word in abbreviations containing all lowercase letters. No space is used between periods and letters in compound abbreviations.

No periods are used in (1) abbreviations of metric measurements and (2) compound abbreviations representing measures per time or measures per capacity.

general rule—periods

p.m.	(post meridiem)	mgr.	(manager)
a.m.	(ante meridiem)	qt.	(quart or quarts)
ft.	(foot or feet)	amt.	(amount)

metric measurements—no periods

mm	(millimeter)	ml	(milliliter)
cm	(centimeter)	kg	(kilogram)
mg	(milligram)	cc	(cubic centimeter)

measures per time or capacity—no periods

rpm	(revolutions per minute)	mpg	(miles per gallon)
wpm	(words per minute)	mph	(miles per hour)

e. If an abbreviation containing a period falls at the end of a sentence that requires a period, use only a single period. In a question or an exclamation, place a closing question or exclamation mark directly after the period appearing in the abbreviation.

period
Please provide a quick lunch for the committee—sandwiches, drinks, chips, **etc.**

question mark
Will Mr. Anzel arrive at our offices before **8 a.m.?**

exclamation mark
Please deliver these documents by courier to Jon Martin, **Esq.!**

6–11 Abbreviations of Terms Commonly Used in Business

Abbreviation	*Term*
AA	associate in arts (degree)
acct.	account
AD, AD, A.D.	anno Domini (Latin: "in the year of our Lord")
ad, advt.	advertisement
addnl.	Additional
Adm.	admiral (military rank—capitalized when used as a title with a person's name)
adm., admin.	administration, administrative
afft.	affidavit
agcy.	agency
agt.	agent
AI	artificial intelligence
a.k.a.	also known as
AKDT	Alaska Daylight Time
AKST	Alaska Standard Time
a.m.	ante meridiem (Latin: "before noon")
amt.	amount
ans.	answer
AP	accounts payable
approx.	approximate, approximately
APR	annual percentage rate (of interest)
Apr., Apr	April
apt.	apartment
AR	accounts receivable, acknowledgment of receipt

6
Abbreviations and Symbols

Abbreviation	*Term*
ARM	adjustable rate mortgage
AS	associate in science (degree)
ASAP	as soon as possible
ASCII	American Standard Code for Information Interchange
assn., Assn.	association
assoc., Assoc.	associate, associated, association
asst.	assistant, assorted
AST	Alaska Standard Time
ATM	automated teller machine
att.	attached, attachment, attention, attorney
attn.	attention
atty.	attorney
Aug., Aug	August
AV	audiovisual, ad valorem (Latin: "according to the value")
av., avg.	average
Ave.	Avenue
BA, AB	bachelor of arts (degree)
bal.	balance
BBA	bachelor of business administration (degree)
bbl.	barrel, barrels
BC, BC, B.C.	before Christ
BIOS	Basic Input/Output System
bit	binary digit
bl.	bale, bales, barrel
BL	bill of lading
bldg.	building
blog	Weblog
BO	back order, branch office
bps	bits per second
bros., Bros.	brothers
BS	bachelor of science (degree)
BS	balance sheet, bill of sale
bu.	bushel, bushels
c	copy
C	Celsius
CAD/CAM	computer-aided design/computer-aided manufacturing
CAI	computer-aided instruction
cap.	capacity, capital, capitalize, capitalized
CAP	certified administrative professional
Capt.	captain (military or government service rank—capitalized when used as a title with a person's name)
CAT	computer-aided transcription
cc	cubic centimeter
cc, CC	courtesy copy
CC	common carrier, community college
CD	certificate of deposit, compact disc
CD-ROM	compact disc read-only memory
CDT	Central Daylight Time

Abbreviation	*Term*
CE	certified esthetician
CEO	chief executive officer
CFO	chief financial officer
cg	centigram
chg.	change, charge
CIF	cost, insurance, and freight
CLU	chartered life underwriter
cm	centimeter
c/o	care of
co., Co.	company
c.o.d., COD	collect on delivery
Col.	colonel (military rank—capitalized when used as a title with a person's name)
COLA	cost-of-living adjustment
comm.	commission, committee, communication, community
cont., contd.	continued
COO	chief operating officer
corp., Corp.	corporation
CPA	certified public accountant
cpi	characters per inch
cps	characters per second
CPS	certified professional secretary
CPU	central processing unit
cr.	credit
CST	Central Standard Time
CT	Central Time (same as Central Standard Time)
ctn.	carton
cu.	cubic
cwt.	hundredweight
DA	deposit account, district attorney
DA	doctor of arts (degree)
DBA	doctor of business administration (degree)
DBA, d/b/a	doing business as
DBMS	database management system
DC	doctor of chiropractic (degree)
DD	doctor of divinity (degree)
DDS	doctor of dental surgery (degree)
Dec., Dec	December
depr.	depreciation
dept.	department
disc., dis.	discount
dist.	district
distr.	distribute, distribution
div.	dividend, division
DJIA	Dow Jones Industrial Average
DO	doctor of osteopathy (degree)
d.o.b.	date of birth
doz., dz.	dozen
DP	doctor of podiatry (degree)

Abbreviation	*Term*
DP	data processing
DPM	doctor of podiatric medicine (degree)
dpi	dots per inch
dr.	dram, drams
Dr.	doctor
Drs.	doctors
DST	daylight saving time
DSL	digital subscriber line
dstn.	destination
DTP	desktop publishing
dup.	duplicate
DVD	digital video disc
DVM	doctor of veterinary medicine (degree)
ea.	each
ed.	editor, edition, education
EdD	doctor of education (degree)
EDP	electronic data processing
EDT	Eastern Daylight Time
EFT	electronic funds transfer
e.g.	exempli gratia (Latin: "for example")
e-mail	electronic mail (verb, noun)
enc., encl.	enclosure
EOM	end of month
Esq.	Esquire
EST	Eastern Standard Time
ETA	estimated time of arrival
exp.	expense, experience, express
Ext.	extension
F	Fahrenheit
FAS	free alongside ship
FAQ, FAQs	frequently asked question(s)
fax	facsimile
Feb., Feb	February
FIFO	first in, first out (inventory)
f.o.b., FOB	free on board
Fri., Fri, F	Friday
frt.	freight
ft.	foot, feet
FTP	file transfer protocol (Internet)
fwd.	forward
FY	fiscal year
FYI	for your information
g, gm	gram
gal.	gallon, gallons
GB	gigabyte (billion bytes)
GDP	gross domestic product
gen.	general
Gen.	general (military rank—capitalized when used as a title with a person's name)

Abbreviation	*Term*
GIGO	garbage in, garbage out
GM	general manager
Gov.	governor (capitalized when used as a title with a person's name)
gov., govt.	government
GNP	gross national product
gr.	gross
GUI	graphical user interface
hdlg.	handling
HDTV	high-definition television
HMO	health maintenance organization
hp	horsepower
HQ	headquarters
HR	human resources (department)
hr.	hour
hrs.	hours
HST	Hawaii-Aleutian Standard Time
HTML	hypertext markup language
http	hypertext transfer protocol
ID	identification
i.e.	id est (Latin: "that is")
in.	inch, inches
inc., Inc.	incorporated, Incorporated (capitalized when used in specific organizational names)
incl.	include, included, including, inclusive
info	information
ins.	insurance
int.	interest
intl.	international
inv.	invoice
invt.	inventory
I/O	input/output
IOU	I owe you
ips	inches per second
IQ	intelligence quotient
IRA	individual retirement account
ISP	Internet service provider
IV	intravenous, intravenously
Jan., Jan	January
JD	doctor of jurisprudence, doctor of law (degrees)
Jul., Jul	July
Jun., Jun	June
K	Kelvin, kilobyte, kilometer, thousand
KB	kilobyte, kilobytes (thousand bytes)
kg	kilogram, kilograms
km	kilometer, kilometers
km/h	kilometers per hour
l or L	liter

Abbreviation	*Term*
l., ll.	line, lines
LAN	local area network
lb.	pound, pounds
LC	letter of credit, Library of Congress
LCL	less-than-carload lot
LIFO	last in, first out (inventory)
LLB	bachelor of laws (degree)
lpm	lines per minute
Lt.	lieutenant (military or government service rank—capitalized when used as a title with a person's name)
Lt. Gov.	lieutenant governor (capitalized when used as a title with a person's name)
ltd., Ltd.	limited, Limited (capitalized when used in an organizational name)
LVN	licensed vocational nurse
m	meter
MA	master of arts (degree)
Maj.	major (military rank—capitalized when used as a title with a person's name)
Mar., Mar	March
max.	maximum
MB	megabyte, megabytes (million bytes)
MBA	master of business administration (degree)
MC	master of ceremonies, mistress of ceremonies, emcee
MD	doctor of medicine (degree)
mdse.	merchandise
MDT	Mountain Daylight Time
memo	memorandum
Messrs.	Misters
mfg., Mfg.	manufacturing, Manufacturing (capitalized when used as part of an organizational name)
mfr.	manufacture, manufacturer
mfrs.	manufacturers
mg	milligram, milligrams
mgr.	manager
mgmt., mgt.	management
MHz	megahertz
mi.	mile, miles
min.	minimum, minute, minutes
MIS	management information systems
misc.	miscellaneous
ml	milliliter, milliliters
mm	millimeter, millimeters
MO	mail order, money order
mo.	month
mos.	months
Mon., Mon, M	Monday
MPA	master of public administration (degree)

Abbreviation	*Term*
mpg	miles per gallon
MPH	master of public health (degree)
mph	miles per hour
Mr.	Mister
Mrs.	Mistress
MS	master of science (degree)
MSP	moved, seconded, and passed
MST	Mountain Standard Time
MSW	master of social work (degree)
mt.	mount, mountain
mtg.	meeting
n/30	net (payment due) in 30 days
n/a	not available, not applicable
NA	North America, not applicable, not available
nat., natl.	national
n.d.	no date
No.	number
Nos.	numbers
Nov., Nov	November
NSF	not sufficient funds
nt. wt.	net weight
OAG	Official Airline Guide
OC (also OTC)	over-the-counter
OCR	optical character recognition
Oct., Oct	October
OD	doctor of optometry (degree)
OD	overdraft, overdrawn
OK	okay
opt.	option, optional
org.	organization, organized
orig.	original
OS	operating system (computer), out of stock
OTC (also OC)	over-the-counter
oz.	ounce, ounces
p., pp.	page, pages
PC	personal computer
pd.	paid
PDT	Pacific Daylight Time
PERT	program evaluation and review technique
PhD *or* Ph.D.	doctor of philosophy (degree)
phone	telephone
photo	photograph
PIN	personal identification number
pkg.	package
P and L	profit and loss
p.m.	post meridiem (Latin: "after noon")
PO	post office, purchase order
POE	port of entry

Abbreviation	*Term*
pp., p.	pages, page
ppd.	postpaid, prepaid
PR	public relations
pr.	pair, pairs
pres.	president
PS	postscript
PST	Pacific Standard Time
PT	physical therapy
pt.	part, pint, pints, point
qt.	quart, quarts
qtr.	quarter
qty.	quantity
RAM	random-access memory
R&D	research and development
rec.	receipt, received
reg.	registered, regular
req.	requisition
ret.	retail, retired
retd.	returned
rev.	revised, revision
RFD	rural free delivery
rm.	ream, reams
rm.	room
ROM	read-only memory
rpm	revolutions per minute
RSVP	répondez s'il vous plaît (French: "respond, if you please")
rwy.	railway
S/	signed by
Sat., Sat, Sa	Saturday
SASE	self-addressed, stamped envelope
sec.	second
sec., secy.	secretary
sec., sect.	section
Sept., Sep	September
Sgt.	sergeant (military or government service rank—capitalized when used as a title with a person's name)
shtg.	shortage
SO	shipping order, special order
SOP	standard operating procedure
sq.	square
SSN	Social Security number
std.	standard
stmt.	statement
Sun., Sun, Su	Sunday
TAT	turn-around time
Thurs., Thu, Th	Thursday
TIN	taxpayer identification number
Tues., Tue, Tu	Tuesday

Abbreviation	*Term*
TV	television
UPC	Universal Product Code
URL	uniform resource locator (Web site address)
VAT	value-added tax
VIP	very important person
vol.	volume
VP	vice president
vs., v.	versus
wam	words a minute
WAN	wide area network
WATS	Wide-Area Telecommunications Service
Wed., Wed, W	Wednesday
whsle.	wholesale
wk.	week, work
wks.	weeks
w/o	without
WP	word processing, word processor
wpm	words per minute
wt.	weight
www	World Wide Web
WYSIWYG	*w*hat *y*ou *s*ee *i*s *w*hat *y*ou *g*et (pronounced *whiz-ee-wig*)
yd.	yard, yards
yr.	year
yrs.	years
YTD	year to date
ZIP	zone improvement plan

6–12 Abbreviations of States and Territories

State or Territory	*Two-Letter Postal Designation*	*Standard Abbreviation*
Alabama	AL	Ala.
Alaska	AK	—
American Samoa	AS	—
Arizona	AZ	Ariz.
Arkansas	AR	Ark.
California	CA	Calif.
Colorado	CO	Colo.
Connecticut	CT	Conn.
Delaware	DE	Del.
District of Columbia	DC	DC
Florida	FL	Fla.
Georgia	GA	Ga.
Guam	GU	—
Hawaii	HI	—
Idaho	ID	—
Illinois	IL	Ill.
Indiana	IN	Ind.
Iowa	IA	—

State or Territory	Two-Letter Postal Designation	Standard Abbreviation
Kansas	KS	Kans.
Kentucky	KY	Ky.
Louisiana	LA	La.
Maine	ME	—
Maryland	MD	Md.
Massachusetts	MA	Mass.
Michigan	MI	Mich.
Minnesota	MN	Minn.
Mississippi	MS	Miss.
Missouri	MO	Mo.
Montana	MT	Mont.
Nebraska	NE	Neb., Nebr.
Nevada	NV	Nev.
New Hampshire	NH	NH
New Jersey	NJ	NJ
New Mexico	NM	N. Mex.
New York	NY	NY
North Carolina	NC	NC
North Dakota	ND	N. Dak.
Ohio	OH	—
Oklahoma	OK	Okla.
Oregon	OR	Ore., Oreg.
Pennsylvania	PA	Pa.
Puerto Rico	PR	PR
Rhode Island	RI	RI
South Carolina	SC	SC
South Dakota	SD	S. Dak.
Tennessee	TN	Tenn.
Texas	TX	Tex.
Utah	UT	—
Vermont	VT	Vt.
Virgin Islands	VI	VI
Virginia	VA	Va.
Washington	WA	Wash.
West Virginia	WV	W. Va.
Wisconsin	WI	Wis., Wisc.
Wyoming	WY	Wyo.

6–13 Two-Letter Postal Designations for Canadian Provinces and Territories

Province or Territory	Designation
Alberta	AB
British Columbia	BC
Manitoba	MB
New Brunswick	NB
Newfoundland and Labrador	NL
Northwest Territories	NT

Province or Territory	*Designation*
Nova Scotia	NS
Nunavut	NU
Ontario	ON
Prince Edward Island	PE
Quebec	QC
Saskatchewan	SK
Yukon Territory	YT

Contractions

6–14 Contractions

a. Contractions are similar to abbreviations in that they are shortened forms. Unlike most abbreviations, however, contractions always contain an apostrophe to indicate where letters have been omitted. The use of single-word contractions is generally limited to business forms and tables. Some common single-word contractions follow:

ack'd	(acknowledged)	rec't	(receipt)
ass't	(assistant)	add'l	(additional)
gov't	(government)	cont'd	(continued)
nat'l	(national)	'15	(2015)

b. A second kind of contraction occurs with verb forms. By using an apostrophe to indicate where letters have been omitted, two words may be combined into one. The use of verb contractions is generally limited to informal business writing. Some commonly used verb contractions follow:

aren't	(are not)	should've	(should have)
can't	(cannot)	that's	(that is)
couldn't	(could not)	there's	(there is)
didn't	(did not)	they're	(they are)
doesn't	(does not)	wasn't	(was not)
don't	(do not)	we'll	(we will)
hasn't	(has not)	we're	(we are)
haven't	(have not)	weren't	(were not)
he's	(he is)	what's	(what is)
I'll	(I will)	where's	(where is)
I'm	(I am)	who's	(who is)
isn't	(is not)	won't	(will not)
it's	(it is)	wouldn't	(would not)
I've	(I have)	you'd	(you would)
let's	(let us)	you're	(you are)
she's	(she is)	you've	(you have)
shouldn't	(should not)		

Symbols

6–15 Symbols on the Standard Computer Keyboard

a. Avoid using symbols in running text except the dollar sign ($) in amounts of money, the asterisk (*) in unnumbered footnotes, and the ampersand (&) in company names. Limit the use of symbols to business forms, statistical material, tables, charts, graphs, and other documents or visuals where space is limited.

dollar sign, asterisk, and ampersand in running text

Unauthorized charges of **$247.56**, **$153.29**, and **$73.20** appeared on last month's credit card statement.

Use **ASCII*** characters to prepare your résumé for this online career center.

We have retained **Leavitt, Kahn & Moss** to handle this legal matter for our firm.

symbols in forms, statistical materials, and visuals

4 @ $7.95 #833 37# 46% 6'1" tall 20:1

b. Use standard keys on the computer keyboard for the following commonly used symbols:

Symbol	*Description*	*Examples*
/	abbreviated word separator	c/o, w/o
&	and (ampersand)	Johnson & Sons Inc. AT&T
@	at, each at (e-mail address)	12 @ $59.95 lynclarkpc@hotmail.com
×	by	8 × 10 inches
"	ditto (same as quotation marks)	six 2-GB USB pocket drives two 4-GB " " "
/	divided by (diagonal)	July Sales/Annual Sales $27,500/3
$	dollar, dollars	$2,843.62
=	equals	Price + Tax = Cost
'	foot/feet (apostrophe)	14' × 16' room, 5' 6" tall
/	fraction separator (diagonal)	1/2, 2/3, 3/4
>	greater than	100 > 90
"	inch/inches (quotation marks)	8 1/2" x 11"
<	less than	90 < 100
–	minus	Price – Discount, 75 – 50
'	minute, minutes (apostrophe)	60' sessions

6 Abbreviations and Symbols

×	multiplied by	12 × 12 = 144
*	multiplied by (asterisk)	12 * 12 = 144
#	number	#568712, #3 pencil
%	percent	87.2%
+	plus	Principal + Interest, 8 + 4
#	pound, pounds	24# paper
:	ratio (colon)	3:1 ratio
"	second, seconds (quotation marks)	5" intervals, every 5"
*	unnumbered footnote (asterisk)	. . . for diacritical marks.*
/	word separator (diagonal)	and/or

6–16 Symbols Not on the Standard Computer Keyboard

Many commonly used symbols do not appear on the standard computer keyboard. Contemporary word processing programs, though, have extended character sets and provide access to many of these symbols. With just a few keystrokes or mouse movements, you can access the following symbols:

Symbol	*Description*	*Examples*
¢	cents	85¢
©	copyright	Copyright © 2017 by Cengage Publishing Company
™	trademark	The Computer Inside™
®	registered	Kinko's®, Pentium®
°	degree, degrees	72°
÷	divided by	144 ÷ 12 = 12
–	en dash	pages 41–47, March 11–14
—	em dash	We have three colors in this style—red, blue, and black
¼	fractions	¼, ½, ¾, 4⅓, 27⅔
≥	greater than or equal to	≥ 1,000
≤	less than or equal to	≤ 10,000
é	letter with diacritical mark	résumé, La Cañada, Fräulein
¶	paragraph, paragraphs	¶11, ¶¶ 23–29
||	parallel to	Main Street || Hill Street
±	plus or minus	±$50
Σ	sum	Σn = 286

7

Words Often Confused and Misused

Words Often Confused and Misused Solution Finder[1]

All entries in this chapter appear in alphabetical order.

A/An

A (ARTICLE; used before a word beginning with a consonant sound or a long ū sound)—We will need the services of ***a t***echnician to solve this network problem. Please ask the student nurses to wear ***a w***hite uniform. ***A u***nion representative met with us yesterday.

An (ARTICLE; used before a word beginning with a vowel sound other than long ū)—As treasurer of our tax-exempt organization, you are responsible for preparing ***an a***nnual report to the Internal Revenue Service. Please make ***an e***ffort to meet with Señor Lopez while you are in Puerto Rico. Have you established ***an i***ndividual retirement account? We have not yet received ***an o***ffer on this property. The doctor suspects that Mr. Adams may have ***an u***lcer.

A lot/Allot/Alot

A lot (ARTICLE + NOUN; a combination meaning "many" or "much")—***A lot*** of our German clients will be attending our user conference. We have spent ***a lot*** of time investigating your proposal.

Allot (VERB; to allocate or assign)—The contract did not ***allot*** enough time for the completion of a building project of this magnitude. How much of the advertising budget should we ***allot*** for Internet ads next year?

Alot (misspelling of *a lot*)

A while/Awhile

A while (ARTICLE + NOUN; a combination meaning "a period of time")—***A while*** ago we sent you several brochures describing our master bedroom suites. It has been ***a while*** since we received an order from you. I have already waited quite ***a while*** to receive a response from the Internal Revenue Service on this matter.

Awhile (ADVERB; meaning "*for* a short time")—I believe we should continue this advertising campaign ***awhile*** longer. Exercise ***awhile*** each day to maintain your good health. After using speech-recognition software ***awhile***, you will wonder why you didn't rely on voice input sooner.

Accede/Exceed

Accede (VERB; to agree or consent)—The leasing company will ***accede*** to the tenants' request for new carpeting only if they sign another one-year lease. If the applicant does not **accede** to the city's demands, his license will not be renewed.

Exceed (VERB; to surpass a limit)—Lending companies cannot charge clients interest fees that ***exceed*** the legal limit. Most accidents occur when drivers ***exceed*** the posted speed limit.

---

[1]Audible pronunciations for all words in this chapter may be obtained online without charge at the Merriam-Webster Web site—http://www.m-w.com.

Accelerate/Exhilarate

Accelerate (VERB; to speed up)—The contractor will need to ***accelerate*** the schedule if he plans to meet the deadline for this project. We must ***accelerate*** our progress in providing speech access to the Internet if we wish to increase our sales for high-end cell phones.
Exhilarate (VERB; to make cheerful; to refresh or stimulate)—News that our office was No. 1 in sales ***exhilarated*** the entire staff. The crisp, fresh air at Blue Pines Resort ***exhilarated*** all of us who attended the retreat.

Accept/Except

Accept (VERB; to take or receive)—Sunrise Market does not ***accept*** two-party checks or checks written on out-of-state banks. Please ***accept*** our apologies for the delay in shipping your order.
Except (PREPOSITION; with the exclusion of, but)—Jubilee's two-for-one dinner coupon is valid every day ***except*** holidays. Everyone in the company ***except*** Tyler Moore has received his or her overtime bonus payment for November.

Access/Excess

Access (NOUN; admittance or approachability. VERB; to pass to and from a place freely; to approach or communicate with a person or thing)—Do you have remote ***access*** to your company e-mail account? Because of the wildfires, all ***access*** to Porter Ranch was cut off. How many people in your organization have ***access*** to the company president? Employees with a security clearance may ***access*** all offices in the building. Only authorized personnel may ***access*** these student files. Bank customers may now ***access*** their accounts through our online services.
Excess (ADJECTIVE; pertaining to a surplus. NOUN; a surplus, beyond ordinary limits)—You may return all ***excess*** flooring materials for full credit within 60 days of purchase. Avoid placing ***excess*** information in these one-page advertisements. An ***excess*** of nine cartons remained after the workers laid the tile floor. John has been performing duties in ***excess*** of those listed for his job classification.

Ad/Add

Ad (NOUN; an abbreviated form of *advertisement*)—We sold the entire lot of these municipal bonds by running an ***ad*** in Sunday's edition of the *Los Angeles Times*.
Add (VERB; to increase by uniting or joining)—These new computers and software updates will ***add*** to the productivity of our staff.

Adapt/Adept/Adopt

Adapt (VERB; to adjust or modify)—Our agency must ***adapt*** readily to this rapidly changing real estate market. We must ***adapt*** our advertising campaigns to capture the new generation of college graduates.
Adept (ADJECTIVE; skilled; proficient)—Mark is particularly ***adept*** at writing successful grant proposals. All our customer service representatives are ***adept*** at dealing with irate callers.
Adopt (VERB; to take and follow as one's own)—The Harrises have filed a petition to ***adopt*** their foster child. We will ***adopt*** Mrs. Williams' proposal to update the computerized version of our current accounting system.

Add: see Ad.

Addict/Edict

Addict (NOUN; one who is habitually or obsessively dependent; a devotee)—Our clinic has noted success with the rehabilitation of drug ***addicts***. Many of today's teenagers are pop music ***addicts***.

Edict (NOUN; a proclamation of law; an order or a command)—According to the news article, an American citizen's ownership of Peruvian coastal property has been challenged by a Peruvian government ***edict***. When did our manager issue this ***edict***?

Addition/Edition

Addition (NOUN; the process of uniting or joining; an added part)—Increased production quotas have resulted in the ***addition*** of factory floor space in two of our facilities. When will the new ***addition*** to your home be completed?

Edition (NOUN; a particular version of printed material)—Only the fourteenth ***edition*** of this reference manual is now available from the publisher.

Adept: see Adapt.

Adherence/Adherents

Adherence (NOUN; a steady attachment or loyalty)—Strict ***adherence*** to these safety procedures is required of all personnel. Because of Britons' ***adherence*** to the British monarchy, the monarchy has continued to flourish.

Adherents (NOUN; loyal supporters or followers)—The many ***adherents*** to the space program believe in its importance to the human race. Senator Fleming's recent bill that was introduced to the state senate pleased ***adherents*** of educational reform.

Adopt: see Adapt.

Adverse/Averse

Adverse (ADJECTIVE; opposing; unfavorable)—Rising housing costs have had an ***adverse*** effect on real estate sales and new home developments. Air traffic at Kennedy Airport has been interrupted by ***adverse*** weather conditions for the past three days.

Averse (ADJECTIVE; unwilling; reluctant)—Most of my clients are ***averse*** to investing in high-risk bonds. Sandra is not ***averse*** to working overtime to meet specific deadlines.

Advice/Advise

Advice (NOUN; a suggestion, an opinion, or a recommendation)—I should have followed your ***advice*** and declined the job offer. He could have avoided further legal problems had he followed his attorney's ***advice***.

Advise (VERB; to counsel or recommend)—Mr. Canton is qualified to ***advise*** you on the courses you will need to complete the marketing major. Did you ***advise*** her not to sign the contract in its present form?

Affect/Effect

Affect (VERB; to influence or to produce a significant influence upon)—Increased costs will ***affect*** our pricing policies on all merchandise. Lack of exercise and

poor eating habits can ***affect*** your health adversely. Has the labor shortage in our industry ***affected*** your company's ability to locate qualified personnel?
Effect (VERB; to bring about or cause to happen; to create)—Rising costs of raw materials will ***effect*** large price increases in our products. Our government plans to ***effect*** a change in the rate of inflation by tightening bank credits. When will the state legislature ***effect*** legislation to ban smoking in all public places? The Springfield Board of Education has already ***effected*** several new policies regarding the allocation of federal funding.
Effect (NOUN; a result or consequence)—The company's new vacation policy has had an apparent ***effect*** on boosting employee morale. What ***effect*** will this inflationary trend have on our state's economy?

Aggravate/Irritate

Aggravate (VERB; to make something worse or more serious; to produce inflammation in)—Bringing in legal counsel at this time would only ***aggravate*** the situation further. These problems have been ***aggravated*** by the hospital administrator's neglect. By scratching the infected area, you will ***aggravate*** it. The prescribed topical medication seems only to ***aggravate*** the patient's symptoms.
Irritate (VERB; to create an annoying condition)—If we do not refund the purchase price, we will surely ***irritate*** the customer. Do not ***irritate*** the professor with your continual interruptions.

Aid/Aide

Aid (VERB; to help or assist. NOUN; assistance)—The United States ***aids*** many other countries. Your contribution of $25 will ***aid*** needy, homeless children. All applications for financial ***aid*** are due by August 1. The teachers appreciated the mothers' ***aid*** during the state testing process.
Aide (NOUN; a person who assists another)—Please ask your ***aide*** to deliver these papers to Dr. Powell's office by Friday afternoon. Sunset Villas has several open positions for nurse's ***aides***.

Aisle/Isle

Aisle (NOUN; a passageway for inside traffic)—After each showing, the ***aisles*** of the theater are littered with empty popcorn containers and candy wrappers.
Isle (NOUN; a piece of land surrounded by water, an island)—This script centers around two teenagers marooned on a tropical ***isle***. The state of Hawaii has a number of beautiful tropical ***isles.***

All ready/Already

All ready (ADJECTIVE; prepared)—Our college is ***all ready*** to offer distance learning courses in business law, international business, and small-business management next semester. The project team is ***all ready*** to begin work on the design of the new building.
Already (ADVERB; by or before this time)—Orders for our August sale have ***already*** been placed with the suppliers. We had ***already*** mailed the check before the invoice arrived.

All right/Alright

All right (ADJECTIVE; satisfactory or agreeable)—Changing your vacation dates from June to July seems to be ***all right*** with our supervisor.
Alright (an informal spelling of *all right* that is not appropriate for business writing)

All together/Altogether

All together (ADVERB + ADVERB; wholly as a group; counted or summed up)—We must work ***all together*** if the company is to meet the contract deadline. The books lay ***all together*** in a heap after the earthquake. ***All together****, there were* 21 bids.
Altogether (ADVERB; entirely or completely; in all; on the whole)—This problem is ***altogether*** different from the one we faced last year. For this computer system, we spent ***altogether*** more than $3,000. Although we did not reach our goal of $3 million in sales, our company's progress may ***altogether*** be considered successful.

All ways/Always

All ways (ADJECTIVE + NOUN; a combination meaning "by all methods")—We must try ***all ways*** possible to expand news coverage for our rapidly growing list of online subscribers.
Always (ADVERB; at all times, continually)—Our employment agency is ***always*** looking for qualified office personnel with experience in Word, Excel, and PowerPoint. Marissa is ***always*** borrowing supplies from other students.

Allot: see A lot.

Allowed/Aloud

Allowed (VERB; permitted)—Our company is ***allowed*** to sell its cosmetic line only through contracted retail outlets. Persons under 21 are not ***allowed*** to gamble in Las Vegas.
Aloud (ADVERB; with a speaking voice so as to be heard)—Ask Beth to read the poem ***aloud***. The president's resignation was read ***aloud*** to all board members present.

Allude/Elude

Allude (VERB; to mention or refer to indirectly)—Did the student ***allude*** to his reason for withdrawing from the class? The manager ***alluded*** to Paul's frequent absences, but he did not specify the number or the dates in his evaluation. As proof of Americans' concern for conservation and economy, I ***allude*** to the increased popularity of hybrid vehicles during recent years.
Elude (VERB; to evade or escape from)—The senator has been able to ***elude*** severe criticisms of his program by anticipating and counteracting objections. The fleeing robbers were able to ***elude*** the police only briefly.

Almost/Most

Almost (ADVERB; nearly)—***Almost*** everyone in the audience was teary as the movie ended. By the end of the third quarter, this company had sold ***almost*** 600,000 copies of its low-end voice-recognition software through online sources.
Most (ADJECTIVE; the greatest in amount or number)—***Most*** of the food had been eaten by the end of the evening. John Zayac received the ***most*** votes in the election for Academic Senate vice president.

Alot: see A lot.

Aloud: see Allowed.

Already: see All ready.

Alright: see All right.

Altar/Alter

Altar (NOUN; a structure used for worship)—The wedding flowers are to be placed on the ***altar*** by 6 p.m.
Alter (VERB; to change)—Please ***alter*** your teaching schedule so that you will be available to attend the monthly meeting of department chairs. To fit the bride, this wedding dress will have to be ***altered.***

Alternate/Alternative

Alternate (VERB ['ȯl-tər-ˌnāt]; to change from one to another repeatedly. NOUN ['ȯl-tər-nət]; one that substitutes for another. ADJECTIVE ['ȯl-tər-nət]; substitute; every other)—Our conferences ***alternate*** between the northern and southern parts of the state. Jack Smith has agreed to serve as my ***alternate*** on the budget committee. For the next few months, motorists will be required to use an ***alternate*** route to the downtown area. Dr. Malamed schedules annual physicals on ***alternate*** Fridays.
Alternative (NOUN; a choice between two or among several. ADJECTIVE; offering or expressing a choice)—We were left with only two ***alternatives***: either accept the lease conditions or find another location. None of the ***alternatives*** presented by the committee were acceptable to the general manager. The available ***alternative*** sites for our new location are less desirable than the one we had originally selected.

Altogether: see All together.

Always: see All ways.

Among/Between

Among (PREPOSITION; ordinarily refers to more than two persons or things)—Making the best choice from ***among*** so many qualified candidates is a difficult task. Distribute the supplies equally ***among*** the three departments.
Between (PREPOSITION; ordinarily refers to two persons or things; refers to more than two persons or things when they function one-on-one in a group)—***Between*** work and family life, the Chadwicks have little time for hobbies. The customer had little difficulty deciding ***between*** the two computers. The differences ***between*** the airfares to Cincinnati quoted by American, Delta, and United are significant. Use a vanilla filling ***between*** the layers in this five-tier wedding cake.

Amount/Number

Amount (NOUN; used with singular nouns and mass items that cannot be counted)—The large ***amount*** of dirt remaining after the excavation has yet to be removed. Only a small ***amount*** of the wedding cake was eaten. The bank manager has not yet determined the ***amount*** of money missing from the safe. Because of the power failure, a significant ***amount*** of the frozen food had deteriorated.

Number (NOUN; used with plural nouns and items that can be counted)—Only a small ***number*** of spaces have been allotted for visitor parking. In 2015 the ***number*** of children in each classroom was reduced by three. Although the sign at the express checkout shows "10 items or fewer," a ***number*** of people with more than ten items persist in using this checkout.

An: see A.

Anecdote/Antidote

Anecdote (NOUN [ˈa-nik-ˌdōt]; a story or a brief account of an event)—Many speakers begin their presentations with an ***anecdote***, a short description of an interesting, amusing, or biographical incident. We all chuckled at Tom's ***anecdote*** about the customer who insisted upon returning a product our store has never sold.

Antidote (NOUN [ˈan-ti-ˌdōt]; a remedy that counteracts a harmful substance or circumstance)—Dr. Martin has consented to write an article about the ***antidote*** he developed for common household poisons. The only ***antidote*** I have found for employees who are habitually late and take extended lunch breaks is to replace them.

Annual/Annul

Annual (ADJECTIVE; yearly)—The company's ***annual*** report will be mailed to all stockholders of record next week. Most companies providing online computer protection packages charge ***annual*** fees ranging between $32 and $75.

Annul (VERB; to void or abolish)—Our lawyers recommended that we agree to ***annul*** the contract because its terms are not stated clearly. Because the defendant had not disclosed significant information about his background before the marriage, the judge agreed to ***annul*** the marriage.

Antidote: see Anecdote.

Anxious/Eager

Anxious (ADJECTIVE; worried or apprehensive)—Although I am enthusiastic about this project, I am ***anxious*** about its outcome. Donna is ***anxious*** about taking the upcoming real estate brokers' examination.

Eager (ADJECTIVE; anticipating with enthusiasm)—I am ***eager*** to learn if I have been admitted to our state university. Mr. Adams is ***eager*** to begin his new job with Girard Enterprises next week.

Any one/Anyone

Any one (ADJECTIVE + PRONOUN; any one person or thing in a group [always followed by *of*])—***Any one*** of our sales executives is qualified to assist you with selecting the hybrid vehicle that best suits your needs. I would be pleased to assist ***any one*** of the new employees in our department.

Anyone (PRONOUN; any person at all)—***Anyone*** having information about the whereabouts of this fugitive, please call your local police. If you know ***anyone*** who has these qualifications, please ask that person to e-mail a résumé to our manager of human resources.

Any time/Anytime

Any time (ADJECTIVE + NOUN; an amount of time)—Yesterday's schedule was so filled with appointments that we did not have ***any time*** for lunch. We have

not had ***any time*** today to review the various department's requests for next year's funding.
Anytime (ADVERB; whenever; at any time whatsoever)—Please call me ***anytime*** you have questions about company policies or procedures. ***Anytime*** we can be of service, just call our toll-free number and a service representative will assist you. Drop by our offices ***anytime***. Yes, you may take your vacation ***anytime*** during July or August.

Any way/Anyway

Any way (ADJECTIVE + NOUN; any method)—Is there ***any way*** we can step up production to advance our July 1 release date?
Anyway (ADVERB; in any case)—Considering the low bids of our competitors, I don't believe we would have received the contract ***anyway***.
Anyways (an informal form of *anyway* that is not appropriate for business writing)

Appraise/Apprise

Appraise (VERB; to estimate the value or nature of something)—Before we can liquidate this company, we must hire an outside firm to ***appraise*** its assets. As I ***appraise*** the situation, the current manager shows no initiative in attempting to increase store sales.
Apprise (VERB; to inform or notify)—Please ***apprise*** all employees immediately of this change in our safety policies. Has the apartment manager ***apprised*** the tenants of their rent increase, which will be effective March 1?

As/Like

As (CONJUNCTION; used to introduce a clause [a word group that contains a subject and a verb])—I will get the patient's file to you by Friday, ***as*** (not *like*) *I promised*. Please format this month's report in the same style ***as*** (not *like*) *you formatted* last month's. Our manager always acts ***as if*** (not *like*) *he knows* more than anyone else.
Like (PREPOSITION; used when the sentence requires a preposition meaning "similar to" [followed by a noun or pronoun and any modifiers])—This adhesive compound feels ***like*** *wet cement*. I have never met anyone else ***like*** *him*. These cookies taste ***like*** *the chocolate chip cookies* my mother used to make.

Ascend/Ascent/Assent

Ascend (VERB; to move up)—Will participants on this tour have sufficient time to ***ascend*** the stairs to the fort and learn about its history firsthand? Frederick Bourne began as a stenographer in the Singer Company and ***ascended*** to the company presidency.
Ascent (NOUN; a rising or going upward)—The continual ***ascent*** of gasoline prices has prompted many people to purchase hybrid vehicles. The excited crowd of onlookers watched the manned rocket's ***ascent*** into space until it disappeared in the sky. Hiking Mount Washington can be an exhilarating experience, but surviving the ***ascent*** requires maintaining physical stamina and following safety guidelines.
Assent (NOUN; agreement or acquiescence. VERB; to agree or to consent)—The jury finally reached ***assent*** on a verdict after eight hours of deliberation. You must

obtain ***assent*** from a patient before providing any medical information to family members. The National Cancer Institute has provided a guide for parents regarding children's ***assent*** to participation in clinical trials. Do you believe the voters will ***assent*** to this $5 billion bond proposal? If the vice president ***assents*** to the committee's proposal, it will be funded. The department heads readily ***assented*** to the technology plan you have outlined in this report. The cast ***assented*** to the audience's clamor for an encore.

Assistance/Assistants

Assistance (NOUN; help or aid)—The project could not have been completed by September 1 without your ***assistance***. If you need financial ***assistance***, please fill out these forms.
Assistants (NOUN; people who aid or help a superior)—The consultant's staffing report indicates that our general manager should have three ***assistants***.

Assure/Ensure/Insure

Assure (VERB; to promise; to make a positive declaration)—I ***assure*** you that the loan will be repaid according to the terms specified in the note. Please ***assure*** the patient that this procedure is not painful.
Ensure (VERB; to make certain)—To ***ensure*** the timely completion of this project, please hire additional qualified personnel. If you cannot ***ensure*** that this order will be delivered by October 15, we will need to place it with another vendor. Security guards are here 24 hours daily, seven days a week, to ***ensure*** a safe environment in our expansive building complex. The director ***ensured*** that sufficient funds were available to cover the expenses before approving the travel request.
Insure (VERB; to protect against financial loss)—We ***insure*** all our facilities against fire, flood, and earthquake damage through Great Western Indemnity. Have you updated your fire coverage so that you are ***insured*** sufficiently to cover current replacement costs?

Attendance/Attendants

Attendance (NOUN; being present or the act of attending)—At least one half of the committee members must be in ***attendance*** for the committee to have a quorum. In checking the candidates' employer references, please inquire about their ***attendance***.
Attendants (NOUN; those who attend to others to perform a service)—The two ***attendants*** had difficulty parking all the cars for such a large crowd. Major airlines are required to hire flight ***attendants*** for the safety and the security of their passengers.

Averse: see Adverse.

Awhile: see A while.

Bad/Badly

Bad (ADJECTIVE; not reaching an acceptable standard [an adjective or subject complement used *after* such nonaction verbs as *is*, *was*, *feel*, *look*, or *smell*])—Sales *were* ***bad*** today. I *feel* ***bad*** that your transfer request was denied.

Profits for the first quarter *look* ***bad*** in view of the additional expenses incurred by our sales staff. The air in this office *smells* ***bad***.

Badly (ADVERB; in a bad manner; to a great degree [used with transitive or action verbs])—The defeated candidate behaved ***badly*** before thousands of television viewers. The home team was defeated ***badly*** in last night's game. We need ***badly*** the advice of a tax attorney before we invest any money in this project.

Bail/Bale

Bail (NOUN; a guarantee of money necessary to set a person free from jail until the trial)—***Bail*** in your client's case has been set at $50,000.

Bale (NOUN; a large bundle)—One ***bale*** of used clothing was lost in transit. How many ***bales*** of hay do you order monthly to feed your horses?

Bare/Bear

Bare (ADJECTIVE; uncovered; empty; plain; or mere)—The paint had chipped and peeled so badly that the ***bare*** wood was showing. Our supply cabinet will soon be ***bare*** if we do not send a requisition to Central Supply this week. Every year our work group retreats for three days to a ***bare*** wooden cabin in the mountains. I had time to cover only the ***bare*** facts involved in this dispute.

Bear (VERB; to support; to carry; or to bring forth)—Unfortunately, the senior partner has had to ***bear*** the brunt of the financial losses. Our travel agency has hired guides who have donkeys to ***bear*** the luggage and provisions. As a result of the surgery, the patient was able to ***bear*** children.

Base/Bass

Base (NOUN; the bottom part of something or a foundation)—The small, secluded village lies at the ***base*** of the volcano. When did the ***base*** of this marble column crack?

Bass (ADJECTIVE; pertaining to a low-pitched sound; having the low range of a bass [a musical instrument])—We could use his ***bass*** voice in our quartet. Do you play the ***bass*** violin?

Bazaar/Bizarre

Bazaar (NOUN; a fair for the sale of articles)—Our Lady of Lourdes Church will hold its annual ***bazaar*** during the Memorial Day weekend.

Bizarre (ADJECTIVE; strikingly out of the ordinary)—Floyd's Fashions has often been described as carrying ***bizarre*** clothing lines and accessories.

Bear: see Bare.

Because of/Due to

Because of (PREPOSITION; by reason of)—***Because of*** the increased interest in our new phone plan, we are extending our store hours during the sale. Several flights from Chicago O'Hare International Airport were canceled yesterday ***because of*** snowstorms in the Midwest.

Due to (PREPOSITION; as a result of)—(an outdated form of *because of* that is not appropriate for business writing)

Berth/Birth

Berth (NOUN; the place where a ship lies at anchor; a place to sit or sleep on a ship or vehicle. VERB; to bring into a berth)—How many ***berths*** does your port have for ships from major cruise lines? The only sleeping accommodations not yet reserved on the train are upper ***berths***. When will the Caribbean Princess next ***berth*** in Puerto Rico?

Birth (NOUN; the emergence of a new individual from the body of its parent)—Present hospital policy permits only two family members to be present during the ***birth*** of a child.

Beside/Besides

Beside (PREPOSITION; by the side of)—Please place the new scanner on the table ***beside*** Ms. Carter's computer. We must ensure that an electronic night table has been placed ***beside*** each bed in all the rooms of our new hospital wing before we can open the wing.

Besides (PREPOSITION; in addition to)—What other Internet service providers ***besides*** Time Warner have you contacted? Who ***besides*** Zachary has applied for the promotional opportunity in our department?

Between: see Among.

Bi-/Semi-

Bi- (PREFIX; two)—Our newsletter is published ***bi***monthly: January, March, May, July, September, and November.

Semi- (PREFIX; half)—Bulletins to the staff are issued ***semi***monthly, on the 1st and 15th of each month.

Biannual/Biennial

Biannual (ADJECTIVE; occurring twice a year)—The stockholders' ***biannual*** meetings are held in January and July.

Biennial (ADJECTIVE; occurring once every two years)—According to our committee's charter, the ***biennial*** election of officers will be held in November. Our association's ***biennial*** conventions are scheduled for 2016, 2018, and 2020.

Bibliography/Biography

Bibliography (NOUN; a list of works consulted by an author in the production of another written work)—Be sure to include in the ***bibliography*** all the sources you used for the report—books, magazines, newspapers, electronic databases, Internet resources, and so on.

Biography (NOUN; a history of a person's life written by someone else)—This book is an exceptionally well-written ***biography*** of Henry Ford, the automobile magnate. Has anyone written and had published a comprehensive ***biography*** of Elvis Presley?

Billed/Build

Billed (VERB; charged for goods or services)—You will be ***billed*** $39.95 on the 15th of each month for your pest-control service.

Build (VERB; to construct)—We plan to ***build*** a new, larger plant in Louisiana within the next two years.

Biography: see Bibliography.

Birth: see Berth.

Bizarre: see Bazaar.

Boarder/Border

Boarder (NOUN; one who is provided with regular meals and lodging)—Homeowners in residential areas are limited in the number of ***boarders*** they may solicit for commercial purposes.
Border (NOUN; an outer part or edge; boundary)—Which ***border*** did you select for the cover page of the report? If you plan to cross the ***border*** into Arizona, do not bring any live plants. During heavy traffic times, crossing the ***border*** between California and Mexico may take several hours.

Bolder/Boulder

Bolder (ADJECTIVE; more fearless or daring)—During a drought the coyotes become ***bolder*** and seek prey in the outlying parts of the city. Perhaps the university needs a ***bolder*** leader to serve as president.
Boulder (NOUN; a large rock)—Damage to the insured's vehicle was apparently caused by a loose ***boulder*** falling from the hillside onto the highway.

Born/Borne

Born (ADJECTIVE; brought forth by birth; originated)—This patient was ***born*** on February 14, 1964. One can hardly believe that the multibillion-dollar microcomputer industry was ***born*** in a Silicon Valley garage barely four decades ago.
Borne (VERB; past participle of *bear*)—Mrs. Talbert has already ***borne*** five children, and she is currently expecting her sixth. Our school district has ***borne*** these financial burdens for more than ten years.

Bouillon/Bullion

Bouillon (NOUN ['bü(l)-ˌyän]; a clear soup)—Our chef uses beef ***bouillon*** as the basis for his seven steak gumbo.
Bullion (NOUN ['bul-yən]; uncoined gold or silver in bars or ingots)—Government officials discovered nearly $10 million in gold ***bullion*** hidden in the deserted warehouse.

Boulder: see Bolder.

Breach/Breech

Breach (NOUN; a violation of a law or an agreement; a hole or a gap; a break in friendly relations)—The judge ruled that a ***breach*** of contract transpired when the building was not ready for occupancy by the date agreed upon. Has the contractor repaired the ***breach*** between the kitchen ceiling and the cabinet above the refrigerator? If contract negotiations are to continue, we must narrow the ***breach*** between union and management representatives.
Breech (NOUN; the part of a firearm or a cannon that is located behind the barrel; the hind end of the body. ADJECTIVE; the position of the fetus in the uterus poised to come out buttocks or feet first)—They had difficulty firing the old

cannon because the ***breech*** seemed to have rusted. The two first graders were told to be seated on their ***breeches*** as the teacher scolded them. If a baby is still ***breech*** at full-term, the baby will more than likely be delivered cesarean.

Bring/Take

Bring (VERB; to carry toward [a place])—Please ***bring*** (not *take*) all your receipts when you meet with our accountant.
Take (VERB; to carry away; to carry from one place to another)—You may ***take*** any one of these samples. Please ***take*** these brochures to our Springfield office.

Build: see Billed.

Bullion: see Bouillon.

Calendar/Colander

Calendar (NOUN; a schedule of days and months for a period of time)—Be sure to mark on your ***calendar*** the dates of our monthly department meetings. Please order the coming year's desk ***calendars*** for our staff.
Colander (NOUN; a strainer)—Use a ***colander*** to drain the pasta thoroughly before placing it in the sauce.

Callous/Callus

Callous (ADJECTIVE; insensitive, without feeling)—Mr. Coe's ***callous*** remark concerning one of the applicant's disability caused his removal from the hiring committee.
Callus (NOUN; hard, thick skin)—The patient's ***callus*** was caused by his consistently leaning on the left side of his armchair. Pointed-toe, high-heeled shoes may cause permanent ***calluses*** on your toes.

Can/May

Can (VERB; to have the ability to do something)—You ***can*** develop a Web site without knowing hypertext markup language (HTML).
May (VERB; to express permission or possibility)—Yes, you ***may*** schedule your vacation for the week of July 15. ***May*** we have these files converted from Microsoft Word to InDesign by October 1?

Canvas/Canvass

Canvas (NOUN; a type of firm, closely woven cloth)—All the cushion covers on our patio sets are made of high-quality, durable ***canvas***. Use these ***canvas*** coverings to protect the new cars as they arrive on the lot.
Canvass (VERB; to survey or solicit in an area)—Do you have a volunteer who will ***canvass*** the residences on Jersey Street? We will ***canvass*** registered voters to see if support for this measure can be secured. John has been ***canvassing*** the neighborhood for volunteers to participate in the Neighborhood Watch program.

Capital/Capitol

Capital (NOUN; a city in which the official seat of government is located; the wealth of an individual or a firm; a capital letter)—The ***capital*** of Wisconsin is Madison. Much of our company's ***capital*** is tied up in computers and software. Begin each word in our company name with a ***capital***.

Capital (ADJECTIVE; punishable by death; foremost in importance)—Treason is a ***capital*** crime in most countries. The forthcoming election is ***capital*** in the minds of the school board members.
Capitol (NOUN; the building in which the United States Congress meets [always capitalized])—Senator Cano must be in the ***Capitol*** by 9 a.m. on Tuesday for the hearings. The ***Capitol*** is a major tourist attraction in Washington, DC.
Capitol (NOUN; a building in which a state legislature meets [capitalized only when used in full name of building])—The ***capitol*** was surrounded by angry pickets waving placards. Is your office located in the California State ***Capitol***?

Carat/Caret/Carrot/Karat

Carat (NOUN; a unit of weight for gems)—The total diamond weight in this ring is 2.17 ***carats***.
Caret (NOUN; a proofreading symbol similar to an inverted *v* that is placed at the bottom of a line to show insertions in edited copy)—Ask the editor to place a ***caret*** between the two words where the company name is to be inserted.
Carrot (NOUN; a vegetable)—A ***carrot*** can be just as delicious raw as it is cooked.
Karat (NOUN, GENERALLY USED AS AN ADJECTIVE; a unit of weight for gold)—All the 18-***karat*** gold chains in our store are imported from Italy.

Cease/Seize

Cease (VERB; to stop or come to an end)—Please ***cease*** shipment of any further orders to Home Décor until its outstanding balance has been paid. When does his eligibility for financial aid ***cease***?
Seize (VERB; to take possession of; to take)—Did the Internal Revenue Service ***seize*** the company's assets for nonpayment of taxes? You may wish to ***seize*** this opportunity to request a salary increase.

Ceiling/Sealing

Ceiling (NOUN; the overhead inside lining of a room; upper limit)—Because of former leaks in the roof, the ***ceiling*** in the reception area needs to be repainted. ***Ceilings*** on rent increases are controlled by the city council.
Sealing (VERB, present participle of *seal*; to close securely with a coating)—We will be ***sealing*** and mailing all our holiday cards on December 4. If you have an asphalt driveway, you can make it last longer and keep it looking attractive by ***sealing*** it annually.

Censor/Censure

Censor (VERB; to examine materials and delete objectionable matter. NOUN; one who censors)—We will need to ***censor*** scenes from this movie to make it appropriate for television viewing. Parents are still expected to judge and ***censor*** inappropriate Web sites for their children's viewing. Do you know when the ***censor*** will finish reviewing the script for this movie, either to endorse our rating or provide us with another rating?
Censure (VERB; to criticize or condemn. NOUN; condemnation)—The city council ***censured*** the mayor for awarding the contract to his brother-in-law's firm. After the facts were disclosed, Senator Dillon was subjected to public ***censure***.

Census/Senses

Census (NOUN; an official count of population within a specified geographical area)—The United States conducts an official ***census*** every ten years. Not until the 2020 ***census*** has been completed will we be able to substantiate any growth projections for our county from 2010 through 2020.

Senses (NOUN; the specialized functions of sight, hearing, smell, taste, and touch; conscious awareness or rationality)—Our client's ***senses*** of hearing and touch were impaired as a result of the accident. He finally came to his ***senses*** and transferred to a branch closer to his home.

Cent/Scent/Sent

Cent (NOUN; a coin known as a *penny*)—At the end of the day, your tallies always balance to the last ***cent***.

Scent (NOUN; a distinctive smell or odor)—Every morning the ***scent*** of freshly baked bread from Webby Bakery permeates our industrial complex. The trained police dog was able to follow the ***scent*** of the bank robber, who had escaped on foot.

Sent (VERB; the past tense and past participle of *send*)—Your order was ***sent*** by United Parcel Service yesterday.

Cereal/Serial

Cereal (NOUN; a breakfast food made from grain)—The patient's diet calls for a daily serving of wheat ***cereal***.

Serial (ADJECTIVE; arranged in a series)—In case of fire or theft, the ***serial*** numbers of all our equipment should be on file in your office.

Choose/Chose

Choose (VERB; to select or make a choice)—An advantage of telecommuting is that you can ***choose*** your own work schedule. Do you know whom the general manager will ***choose*** to become his executive assistant?

Chose (VERB; past tense of *choose*)—After careful consideration I ***chose*** the option to telecommute rather than battle the gridlock facing drivers traveling to the downtown area. The general manager ***chose*** Ms. Randall to be his executive assistant.

Chord/Cord

Chord (NOUN; three or more musical tones sounded at the same time)—The pianist played several ***chords*** before the soloist began singing "I Love You Truly."

Cord (NOUN; a long, slender, flexible material usually consisting of several strands that are woven or twisted together; a stack of wood cut for fuel that measures $4 \times 4 \times 8$ feet)—Tie these two packages together with a ***cord*** before you deliver them. Be sure to place the electrical ***cord*** for the laptop in its carrying case. Every winter we order at least one ***cord*** of wood for our fireplace.

Cite/Sight/Site

Cite (VERB; to quote or mention; to summon to a court appearance)—Dr. Rosenthal can ***cite*** many authorities who have researched the problem of pollution in major United States cities. When writing a report, be sure to ***cite*** your sources. In her training session, Andrea ***cited*** several critical procedures for identifying fraudulent online purchases. Did the police officer ***cite*** you for speeding while you were in a company vehicle? Our manager was recently ***cited*** for using a handheld cell phone while driving.

Sight (VERB; to see. NOUN; a view or spectacle)—Did you ***sight*** Ms. Preston among the group of reporters? The young pitcher was unable to ***sight*** his parents among the crowd sitting in the bleachers. Onlookers watched the launch and then stared at the manned space shuttle until it was out of ***sight***. The Statue of Liberty is a popular tourist ***sight*** in New York City. Rome's Coliseum is certainly a magnificent ***sight***.

Site (NOUN; a location)—This 20-acre land parcel is a perfect ***site*** for the proposed housing project. Police have yet to reveal the ***site*** of the crime. With this software you will be able to create your own Web ***site***.

Close/Clothes/Cloths

Close (VERB; to shut; to stop or end)—We ***close*** the safe at 5 p.m. every afternoon. Our accountant ***closes*** our books at the end of each month.

Clothes (NOUN; wearing apparel)—The previous tenant still needs to remove his ***clothes*** from the apartment.

Cloths (NOUN; pieces of fabric)—Use only these ***cloths*** to clean the screens of our new monitors. Our cleaning crews will need specially treated ***cloths*** to wipe the whiteboards in all the classrooms.

Coarse/Course

Coarse (ADJECTIVE; rough texture; crude in manners)—This fabric is too ***coarse*** to be used for reupholstering the chairs in our reception area. We still need 2 cubic yards of ***coarse*** sand to complete the patio. The new director's ***coarse*** demeanor has created considerable apprehension among the staff.

Course (NOUN; a particular direction or route; part of a meal; a unit of learning)—We are committed to a ***course*** of action that will reduce expenses without downsizing staff. The ***course*** of this cruise ship begins in Valparaiso, proceeds through the Strait of Magellan, and ends in Buenos Aires. Which menu item did you select for the main ***course***? You need only three more ***courses*** to graduate.

Colander: see Calendar.

Collision/Collusion

Collision (NOUN; a crash)—Fortunately, no one was hurt in the ***collision***. The freeway was closed for three hours because of the five-car ***collision***.

Collusion (NOUN; an agreement to defraud)—No one suspected the seller, the broker, and the escrow officer of ***collusion*** in the sale of this unstable hillside property. ***Collusion*** among home buyers, real estate agents, and lenders has been cited as contributing largely to foreclosures and declines in the real estate market.

Command/Commend

Command (VERB; to order or direct. NOUN; an order)—The sergeant ***commanded*** his troops to return to base by 0600. This police dog has been trained to obey only its owner's ***commands***.

Commend (VERB; to praise or compliment)—Please ***commend*** the sales staff for its fine job in promoting our product line at the Dallas convention.

Successful managers remember to ***commend*** colleagues as well as staff members for jobs well done.

Complement/Compliment

Complement (VERB; to complete or make perfect. NOUN; something that fills up, completes, or makes perfect)—The paintings you selected for the reception area will ***complement*** the office decor. You may wish to select one of our fine wines to ***complement*** your meal. Please ensure that the display window has a full ***complement*** of our Hansell-Zürich watches.

Compliment (VERB; to praise or flatter. NOUN; an admiring remark)—Mr. Rose did ***compliment*** me on the fine job I had done. You may wish to ***compliment*** Jacquinita on her excellent presentation at TechEd. Andrew received many ***compliments*** on the sales brochure he designed for our new line of bedroom furniture.

Complementary/Complimentary

Complementary (ADJECTIVE; serving mutually to blend, fill out, or complete)—None of these wall coverings are ***complementary*** to the carpeting we have selected.

Complimentary (ADJECTIVE; favorable; given free)—We appreciate receiving your ***complimentary*** e-mail about the exceptional service you received in our Cabazon store. To receive your ***complimentary*** copy of this recipe booklet, merely fill out and return the enclosed postcard.

Confidant/Confident

Confidant (NOUN; a trusted friend)—Robert Lewis has been the senator's closest ***confidant*** for many years.

Confident (ADJECTIVE; sure of oneself)—Sharon was ***confident*** she would pass the state licensing examination to become a registered nurse. I am ***confident*** you will succeed in this program if you allow yourself enough time to study.

Conscience/Conscious

Conscience (NOUN; the faculty of knowing right from wrong)—I believe his ***conscience*** prevented him from accepting the illegal campaign contributions. Let your ***conscience*** guide you in making this decision.

Conscious (ADJECTIVE; aware or mentally awake)—Yes, we are ***conscious*** of the declining market in our industry. Most of our patients are ***conscious*** during this type of surgery.

Console/Consul

Console (NOUN; a cabinet)—The popularity of our Model 4750 entertainment center may be attributed to its attractive ***console***.

Consul (NOUN; an official representing a foreign country)—Travel information may often be obtained from the ***consul*** of the country you wish to visit. Who is the United States ***consul*** in Mexico?

Continual/Continuous

Continual (ADJECTIVE; a regular or frequent occurrence)—***Continual*** complaints from customers in the Vancouver area warrant our inquiry into the activities

of the Seattle office. If you need ***continual*** assistance to complete this course successfully, please request a tutor.
Continuous (ADJECTIVE; without interruption or cessation)—The ***continuous*** humming of the new air-conditioning system is disturbing everyone in the office. If you enjoy slumbering to the ***continuous*** breaking of waves against the Hawaiian shoreline of Kaanapali Beach, our hotel has just the accommodations for you.

Convince/Persuade

Convince (VERB; to bring a person to your point of view)—Do you think you can ***convince*** the board that our losses this year are related directly to a slowdown in the economy? I could not ***convince*** the president that the company needs to explore additional marketing options.
Persuade (VERB; to induce a person to do something)—An effective banner on a popular Web site may ***persuade*** visitors to that site to purchase your products. Were you able to ***persuade*** your manager to restore a portion of the budget cuts?

Cooperation/Corporation

Cooperation (NOUN; the act of working together)—With the full ***cooperation*** of all employees, we will be able to meet the June 30 contract deadline. May I please have your ***cooperation*** to ensure that all employees comply with the safety regulations.
Corporation (NOUN; one type of business organization)—We are looking into the possibility of forming a ***corporation***. ***Corporations*** throughout the United States are continually seeking qualified applicants to fill openings in their organizations.

Cord: see Chord.

Corespondent/Correspondence/Correspondents

Corespondent (NOUN; person named as guilty of adultery with the defendant in a divorce suit)—Who was named as ***corespondent*** in this divorce case?
Correspondence (NOUN; letters or other written communications)—When did we receive the last e-mail ***correspondence*** from Mr. Flores?
Correspondents (NOUN; message or letter writers; news reporters)—Be sure to have one of our ***correspondents*** answer these customers' letters within the next three days. African ***correspondents*** have reported that several countries are still suffering severe food shortages.

Corporation: see Cooperation.

Corps/Corpse

Corps (NOUN ['kōr]; a body of persons having a common activity or occupation)—A ***corps*** of students has been soliciting funds for the stadium lights. Representatives from the Marine ***Corps*** will visit our campus next week.
Corpse (NOUN ['kȯrps]; a dead body)—The identity of the ***corpse*** is still unknown.

Correspondence: see Corespondent.

Correspondent: see Corespondent.

Costumer/Customer

Costumer (NOUN; one who deals in or makes costumes)—Allison Parker was the ***costumer*** for the Valley Playhouse production of *Cats*.
Customer (NOUN; one who purchases a commodity or service)—Does the ***customer*** wish to send the wrapped wedding gift to the bride or just take the gift with her?

Council/Counsel

Council (NOUN; a governing body)—We are scheduled to present the request for a zoning change to the city ***council*** tomorrow morning. How often does the student ***council*** meet during each semester?
Counsel (VERB; to give advice. NOUN; advice)—Our staff ***counsels*** at least 80 students each day. In this situation your attorney gave you excellent ***counsel***.

Course: see Coarse.

Credible/Creditable

Credible (ADJECTIVE; believable)—Dr. Wyndham's stories describing his many experiences and achievements are certainly interesting, but not quite ***credible***. The excuses offered by Charlene for her many absences are hardly ***credible***.
Creditable (ADJECTIVE; worthy of praise or esteem; reliable)—Ms. Kawakami's perfect attendance record is certainly ***creditable***. Keep in mind that not all Internet resources are ***creditable***.

Customer: see Costumer.

Deceased/Diseased

Deceased (ADJECTIVE; dead)—Two of the company's founders are already ***deceased***.
Diseased (ADJECTIVE; sick)—Be sure to spray all these ***diseased*** rose bushes with insecticide.

Decent/Descent/Dissent

Decent (ADJECTIVE; in good taste; proper; adequate)—Students are expected to use only ***decent*** language in the classroom. A ***decent*** solution to this problem would be to compensate the customer for his inconvenience. Did the company offer you a ***decent*** salary?
Descent (NOUN; moving downward; ancestry)—The view of the city from the sky was breathtaking as the plane began its ***descent*** into the Denver airport. Mr. Sirakides is of Greek ***descent***.
Dissent (NOUN; differences or disagreement)—There seems to be considerable ***dissent*** among the council members concerning the resolution to expand our city's police department. Chronic ***dissent*** among our agents will not be tolerated.

Defer/Differ

Defer (VERB; to put off or delay)—Our company has decided to ***defer*** moving its offices until next spring.
Differ (VERB; to vary; to disagree)—State laws in this area ***differ*** from state to state. Doctors' views ***differ*** about the best treatment for the common cold.

They ***differ*** on not only religious beliefs but also political philosophies. I ***differ*** with Adam that sales last quarter were the highest in the company's history.

Deference/Difference

Deference (NOUN; respect and esteem; a yielding to someone else's wishes; in consideration of)—Winning an Olympic gold medal calls for worldwide ***deference***. In ***deference*** to many shoppers' requests, our store will remain open until 9 p.m. during the summer months. The restaurant will remain closed for 24 hours in ***deference*** to the chef and his family during this period of grief.
Difference (NOUN; state of being different, a dissimilarity)—There is very little ***difference*** in product quality between these two brands. Above all, as you learn the ***differences*** between these two vehicles, please consider carefully the smoothness of the ride.

Deprecate/Depreciate

Deprecate (VERB; to play down; to disapprove of or to downgrade; belittle)—His opponent's speech attempted to ***deprecate*** the governor's accomplishments during the past four years. The purpose of the contractor's speech before the city council was solely to ***deprecate*** the present zoning practices. Nick continually ***deprecates*** others' plans to stimulate sales.
Depreciate (VERB; to lessen the value of)—The tax code allows us to ***depreciate*** this new equipment over a five-year period. After the last major earthquake, property values in our area ***depreciated*** from 15 to 60 percent.

Descent: see Decent.

Desert/Dessert

Desert (NOUN; an arid, barren land area)—Palm Springs was once a ***desert*** occupied only by Agua Caliente Indians. Luxurious retirement developments continue to emerge in the Arizona ***desert***.
Dessert (NOUN; a sweet course served at the end of a meal)—Apple pie and ice cream is a traditional American ***dessert***. Restaurants usually offer a variety of chocolate ***desserts***.

Device/Devise

Device (NOUN; an invention or mechanism)—The automatic collating and stapling ***device*** on the copier worked perfectly during the demonstration. Each laptop has an installed electronic ***device*** that can track its location should the laptop be lost or stolen.
Devise (VERB; to think out or plan)—Were you able to ***devise*** an overtime plan that would be equitable to all employees? If we are to remain in this competitive market, we will need to ***devise*** new strategies for product development and marketing.

Dew/Do/Due

Dew (NOUN; drops of moisture)—The heavy ***dew*** that was forecast for this morning was instead a heavy layer of fog, which caused the airport officials to delay all flights.
Do (VERB; to perform or bring about)—What can we ***do*** to promote our products in the international marketplace?

Due (ADJECTIVE; immediately payable)—Your payments are ***due*** by the 10th of each month.

Die/Dye

Die (VERB; to pass from physical life)—During the summer months, water your grass during the morning and the evening hours so that it will not ***die***. If our nursery personnel do not water and feed the houseplants properly, they will ***die*** before they can be sold.
Dye (VERB; to change a color with a coloring substance. NOUN; a coloring substance)—We can custom ***dye*** this carpeting to your color choice. All the ***dyes*** we use for coloring fabrics are colorfast.

Differ: see Defer.

Difference: see Deference.

Disapprove/Disprove

Disapprove (VERB; to reject; to withhold approval)—Our district manager will ***disapprove*** any tuition reimbursement request that has not received approval prior to taking the course. I ***disapprove*** of the manner in which Lisa's supervisor has been handling her excessive absences.
Disprove (VERB; to prove false)—How can we ***disprove*** the witness's false testimony? This new evidence will ***disprove*** that my client falsified any accounting records.

Disburse/Disperse

Disburse (VERB; to pay out; to distribute methodically)—Our accountant devised a new system to ***disburse*** sales commissions more rapidly. The property will be ***disbursed*** according to the provisions set forth in Mr. Williams' will.
Disperse (VERB; to scatter; to cause to become widely spread)—The crowd ***dispersed*** rapidly after the football game. Those factories that ***disperse*** pollutants into the environment will continue to be subjected to heavy fines. Please ***disperse*** this information to consumers nationwide.

Discreet/Discrete

Discreet (ADJECTIVE; showing good judgment in conduct and speech; unnoticeable)—Ms. Doyle is ***discreet*** in discussing patients' cases with other hospital personnel. With a ***discreet*** gesture, Julianne's assistant reminded her that her next client was waiting.
Discrete (ADJECTIVE; separate)—The conglomerate consists of nine ***discrete*** companies. We are exploring several ***discrete*** possibilities for distributing our cosmetics in Europe and parts of Asia.

Diseased: see Deceased.

Disinterested/Uninterested

Disinterested (ADJECTIVE; free from selfish motive or interest; unbiased)—All the judges for this competition have been certified to be ***disinterested*** parties. Only ***disinterested*** persons may umpire a Little League baseball game. You may wish to have a ***disinterested*** observer evaluate the child's behavior.

Uninterested (ADJECTIVE; not interested)—Employees who are ***uninterested*** in the success of the company are certainly not candidates for promotion. The district attorney was ***uninterested*** in pursuing the case any further.

Disprove: see Disapprove.

Dissent: see Decent.

Do: see Dew.

Done/Dun

Done (VERB; past participle of *do*)—Our company has not ***done*** any further research in this area. We have ***done*** all we can for today to locate the missing record.

Dun (VERB; to make persistent demands for payment. NOUN OFTEN USED AS ADJECTIVE; a variable drab color, usually a neutral brownish gray)—Ms. Green's main responsibility is to ***dun*** slow-paying customers. Cred-Co continues to ***dun*** me for hospital services that I did not receive. Before we move into these offices, you will need to hire a painting contractor to transform these ***dun*** walls into a brighter, more pleasing atmosphere. The ***dun***-colored sand of the California beaches glistened in the sunlight.

Due: see Dew.

Due to: see Because of.

Dun: see Done.

Dye: see Die.

Edict: see Addict.

Edition: see Addition.

Effect: see Affect.

E.g./I.e.

E.g. (PREPOSITION + NOUN; Latin abbreviation meaning *for example*)—Michael already has seven write-ups during the three months he has been with the company; ***e.g.***, he has three write-ups for absences without prior notification. Our company specializes in office furniture sales; ***e.g.***, desks, computer stations, file cabinets, bookcases, printer tables, chairs, and reception area furniture.

I.e. (PRONOUN + VERB; Latin abbreviation meaning *that is*)—You may telephone your order anytime; ***i.e.***, we have operators on duty 24 hours a day every day.

Elicit/Illicit

Elicit (VERB; to draw out or bring forth)—Did the seminar speaker attempt to ***elicit*** questions from the audience? The speaker's remarks ***elicited*** cheers from the audience.

Illicit (ADJECTIVE; unlawful)—One of our agents has been cited for ***illicit*** business practices. Two members of the state legislature were publicly censured for ***illicit*** use of public funds.

Eligible/Illegible

Eligible (ADJECTIVE; qualified to be chosen)—To be ***eligible*** for these employment opportunities, applicants must be at least 21 years of age. If you are ***eligible*** for financial aid, please complete the attached forms.
Illegible (ADJECTIVE; unreadable)—The handwriting on this student's paper is ***illegible***. The print on these rain-soaked documents is ***illegible***.

Elude: see Allude.

Emigrate/Immigrate

Emigrate (VERB; to move from a country)—When did your family ***emigrate*** from Costa Rica? The Johnsons ***emigrated*** from Norway in 1996.
Immigrate (VERB; to move to a country)—How many Canadians were permitted to ***immigrate*** to the United States last year? Two of the Snyders' children have ***immigrated*** to Australia.

Eminent/Imminent

Eminent (ADJECTIVE; prominent, distinguished)—A number of ***eminent*** scholars are among the faculty at Pepperdine University. Mr. Mendez is an ***eminent*** authority on labor law in the United States.
Imminent (ADJECTIVE; impending, likely to occur)—Copy machine breakdowns are ***imminent***; consequently, we must have a comprehensive service policy on this equipment. Hurricanes are ***imminent*** in the Caribbean area.

Ensure: see Assure.

Envelop/Envelope

Envelop (VERB; to wrap, surround, or conceal)—***Envelop*** each tamale in a corn husk before boiling it. The chief said his firefighters would ***envelop*** the fire by morning. Each day a layer of early morning fog ***envelops*** the city.
Envelope (NOUN; a container for a written message)—Please send us your check in the return ***envelope*** provided for your convenience.

Every day/Everyday

Every day (ADJECTIVE + NOUN; each day)—I will e-mail you ***every day*** to give you a status report on the development of our speech-enabled smartphone. ***Every day*** you delay making your reservations for the convention, the less chance you have of staying at the convention hotel. Our college president receives at least 60 e-mails ***every day***.
Everyday (ADJECTIVE; ordinary)—Serious customer complaints seem to be an ***everyday*** occurrence in the Litchfield office. All our ***everyday*** china patterns are displayed on our Web site.

Every one/Everyone

Every one (ADJECTIVE + PRONOUN; each person or thing in a group [always followed by *of*])—***Every one*** *of* us is proficient in the use of speech-recognition, word processing, spreadsheet, and presentation software.
Everyone (PRONOUN; all people in a group)—***Everyone*** on the executive staff is expected to be present for the stockholders' meeting.

Example/Sample

Example (NOUN; something serving as a pattern to be imitated)—Please illustrate each of these principles with a meaningful ***example***. Mark is an ***example*** of the kind of employee we need to hire for this new position.
Sample (NOUN; a representative part or a single item from a larger whole)—You will need a larger ***sample*** to validate the results of this study. When purchasing See's candy, each customer is offered a free ***sample***.

Exceed: see Accede.

Except: see Accept.

Excess: see Access.

Executioner/Executor

Executioner (NOUN; one who puts others [usually criminals] to death)—The ***executioner*** wore a black hood.
Executor (NOUN; person appointed to carry out the provisions of a will)—Whom have you named as ***executor*** of your will? The court will need to approve the new ***executor*** recommended for this probate.

Exhilarate: see Accelerate.

Expand/Expend

Expand (VERB; to enlarge)—The new plan to ***expand*** our storage facilities was approved. If you plan to ***expand*** the square footage of your kitchen, you will be limited by the amount of space available in your side yard.
Expend (VERB; to use up, pay out, or spend)—Ms. Smith ***expends*** too much time dealing with insignificant matters instead of meeting major objectives. If you do not ***expend*** these moneys by June 30, they will revert to the general fund.

Expansive/Expensive

Expansive (ADJECTIVE; capable of expanding; extensive)—The ***expansive*** force of September fires in Southern California is controlled with the assistance of "Super Scoopers," which can dump from 1,600 to 2,000 gallons of water on the raging infernos. An ***expansive*** commercial development is planned for this 200-acre site.
Expensive (ADJECTIVE; costly)—The consultant's recommendations were too ***expensive*** to implement. Some of these ***expensive*** designer accessories may be purchased at discount malls.

Expend: see Expand.

Expensive: see Expansive.

Explicit/Implicit

Explicit (ADJECTIVE; expressed clearly)—The accompanying booklet gives ***explicit*** instructions for assembling this computer desk. You will need to be more ***explicit*** in describing conditions that require building maintenance or repair.
Implicit (ADJECTIVE; being understood, although unexpressed; unquestionable)—Although the project manager did not state so in his progress report, I recognized an ***implicit*** appeal for additional engineers to assist with this complicated project.

By not voting, you give ***implicit*** consent to whatever the other homeowners decide. I have ***implicit*** trust in our stockbroker's recommendations.

Extant/Extent

Extant (ADJECTIVE; currently or actually existing)—Please provide me with a three-year budget for all ***extant*** and projected programs. All ***extant*** building projects have been subjected to a large increase in materials costs.
Extent (NOUN; range, scope, or magnitude)—Unfortunately, we will be unable to assess the ***extent*** of the storm damage until next week. When will you be able to determine the ***extent*** of the accident victim's injuries?

Facetious/Factious/Fictitious

Facetious (ADJECTIVE; humorous or witty, often in an inappropriate manner)—His seemingly ***facetious*** remark was perceived by some to be an insult. John's ***facetious*** remark about his opponent indicated that he perceived her to be a strong competitor for the open seat on the president's council.
Factious (ADJECTIVE; creating a faction or dissension)—***Factious*** disputes among the partners eventually led to the dissolution of the legal firm. A ***factious*** minority on the committee attempts continually to disrupt its meetings.
Fictitious (ADJECTIVE; nonexistent; imaginary; false)—The author of this novel has assured us that all its characters are ***fictitious***. This suspect has been known to operate under a number of ***fictitious*** names.

Facility/Faculty

Facility (NOUN; something that is built, installed, or established to serve a particular purpose)—This new ***facility*** will be ready for occupancy on July 1. Recent bond issues passed by our community include not only new buildings for our college but also renovations to outdated classroom ***facilities***.
Faculty (NOUN; the teaching staff of an educational institution)—How many of our full-time ***faculty*** teach online courses? This parking lot has been reserved for ***faculty*** only.

Fair/Fare

Fair (NOUN; an exhibition. ADJECTIVE; marked by impartiality and honesty; mediocre)—Our annual county ***fair*** usually begins during the first week of September. Further legislation was passed recently to enforce ***fair*** employment practices. He did a ***fair*** job.
Fare (VERB; to get along or succeed. NOUN; price charged to transport a person)—Our company did not ***fare*** well in its last bidding competition for state contracts. How did you ***fare*** on the recent state nursing exam? The airline ***fare*** from Chicago to New York has increased considerably during the past month.

Farther/Further

Farther (ADJECTIVE; a greater distance [always a measurable amount of space])—The driving distance from the plant to the warehouse is ***farther*** than I had anticipated. You will need to scroll ***farther*** down the Web page until you see the link *Submit order*.
Further (VERB; to help move forward. ADVERB; to a greater degree or extent. ADJECTIVE; additional)—The Arden Foundation contributed $5 million to ***further***

research in spinal cord injuries. Stock market prices declined even ***further*** after the president's announcement. Refer to my July 8 memo for ***further*** details.

Feat/Fete

Feat (NOUN ['fēt]; an act of skill, endurance, or ingenuity)—Human beings under stress have been known to perform ***feats*** beyond their normal capabilities. The Fehmarn Belt Bridge, connecting Denmark and Germany, is an amazing ***feat*** of engineering.

Fete (VERB; ['fāt]; to honor or commemorate. NOUN; a large elaborate party)—A banquet is being planned to ***fete*** our company president upon his retirement in September. The ***fete*** to honor our company president will be held on August 19.

Fever/Temperature

Fever (NOUN; a rise of body temperature above the normal 98.6 degrees)—When the child was brought into the emergency room, he had a ***fever***—a temperature 2.4 degrees above normal. How long has the patient been running a ***fever***?

Temperature (NOUN; degree of hotness or coldness measured on a definite scale)—Normal body ***temperature*** is 98.6 degrees. Be sure to record the patient's ***temperature*** in his chart. The high ***temperature*** in Las Vegas today reached 120 degrees, a record breaker for this time of the year.

Fewer/Less

Fewer (ADJECTIVE; used with items that can be counted and plural nouns)—We had ***fewer*** sales this month than we had anticipated. Reserve this checkout for customers with ten or ***fewer*** items. ***Fewer*** than half the employees elected to purchase stock options. With ***fewer*** opportunities for financial aid, ***fewer*** students will pursue advanced degrees.

Less (ADJECTIVE; used with mass items that cannot be counted and singular nouns)—You will get by with ***less*** work if you follow my suggestions. As a result of our implementing green technology, ***less*** money was spent on utilities this past year. ***Less*** than half the cake had been eaten by the end of the wedding reception.

Fictitious: see Facetious.

Finally/Finely

Finally (ADVERB; in the end)—The defective DVD drive was ***finally*** replaced by Computab. When do you project these sketches will ***finally*** be ready to submit to the client?

Finely (ADVERB; elegantly or delicately; in small parts)—Visitors to the museum always admire the ***finely*** embroidered tapestries. Your car engine has been ***finely*** tuned by our expert mechanics. You may purchase these ***finely*** chopped nuts in 8- and 16-ounce packages.

Fiscal/Physical

Fiscal (ADJECTIVE; relating to financial matters)—Income tax returns are usually based upon the ***fiscal*** period from January 1 to December 31 of a given year. The ***fiscal*** year for our college district begins on July 1 and ends on June 30.

Physical (ADJECTIVE; concerned with the body and its needs)—Every individual should do a minimum amount of ***physical*** exercise daily. Company well-being programs are devoted to maintaining both the ***physical*** and the mental health of employees.

Flagrant/Fragrant

Flagrant (ADJECTIVE; glaring, scandalous)—The developer's ***flagrant*** disregard for community safety prompted the city council to disapprove its request for a zoning change. The vice president's awarding this major contract to his son-in-law's firm was a ***flagrant*** violation of company policy.
Fragrant (ADJECTIVE; sweet smelling)—Ann received a ***fragrant*** bouquet of flowers from the staff. The ***fragrant*** aroma of these perfumes will persist throughout the day into the evening.

Flair/Flare

Flair (NOUN; a natural talent or aptitude)—Ms. Strehike has a ***flair*** for making people feel at ease when they enter her office.
Flare (VERB; to blaze up or spread out. NOUN; a signal light)—Gusty winds could easily cause the fire to ***flare*** out of control. ***Flares*** in the road guided motorists around the accident.

Flaunt/Flout

Flaunt (VERB; to make a gaudy or defiant display)—Although Mrs. Paige is one of the most affluent Hartford residents, she does not ***flaunt*** her wealth.
Flout (VERB; to mock or show contempt for; to defy)—If Seth continues to ***flout*** the conventions of business etiquette, he will not be considered for a management position. As a new driver, the teenager continued to ***flout*** the posted speed limit.

Flew/Flu/Flue

Flew (VERB; past tense of *fly*)—Our plane ***flew*** to the West Coast in record time.
Flu (NOUN; abbreviated form of *influenza*)—Nearly 15 percent of our employees were absent last week because of the ***flu***. When will the ***flu*** shots for this season become available?
Flue (NOUN; a duct in a chimney)—If the ***flue*** is closed, smoke from a burning fire cannot escape through the chimney.

Flout: see Flaunt.

Flu: see Flew.

Flue: see Flew.

Foreword/Forward

Foreword (NOUN; prefatory comments, as for a book)—William J. Clark, the new president of the Oxnard University Public Library, wrote the ***foreword*** for the 2016 publication of *The Oxnard University Book of Twenty-First-Century Political Quotations.*
Forward (ADVERB; to or toward what is ahead)—Our company, since its beginnings, has moved ***forward*** at a rapid pace in research and development.

Formally/Formerly

Formally (ADVERB; in a formal manner)—At our next meeting, you will be introduced ***formally*** to the other members of the committee.

Formerly (ADVERB; in the past)—Marie Martin was ***formerly*** the president of a large metropolitan area community college.

Former/Latter

Former (ADJECTIVE; first of two things; belonging to an earlier time)—Paul's ***former*** suggestion appears to be the better one. As a ***former*** employee, Ellen Anderson is always invited to attend the company social functions.
Latter (ADJECTIVE; second of two things; nearer to the end)—Of the two lease options available, the ***latter*** one seems to be more economical. Mail deliveries in your area are scheduled for the ***latter*** part of the day.

Forth/Fourth

Forth (ADVERB; forward)—The president requested that any objections to his relocation plan be brought ***forth*** by June 30.
Fourth (ADJECTIVE; a numeric term that represents the ordinal form of *four*)—The ***fourth*** member of our golf foursome was late in arriving.

Fortunate/Fortuitous

Fortunate (ADJECTIVE; having good luck)—We were ***fortunate*** to obtain the services of Ladd, Ladd & Company to render the architectural drawings for our new building. I feel ***fortunate*** to have obtained this management position with Barnesdale & Associates.
Fortuitous (ADJECTIVE; accidental; happening by chance)—Only through these ***fortuitous*** circumstances were we able to purchase our airline tickets at such a reduced price. An increased budget and additional time to complete filming resulted in a ***fortuitous*** coincidence that led to *Savvy Sally* becoming a multimillion-dollar movie success.

Forward: see Foreword.

Fourth: see Forth.

Fragrant: see Flagrant.

Further: see Farther.

Good/Well

Good (ADJECTIVE; meaning *of favorable quality* in describing a noun or pronoun; meaning *fit, wholesome,* or *healthy spirit* in describing a person's well-being)—Has Jason received the ***good*** news that he has been promoted to day supervisor? If we continue to have ***good*** weather conditions, this building project will be completed before the deadline date. I always feel ***good*** after finishing my exercises at the gym. I feel ***good*** about my decision to change careers.
Well (ADVERB; meaning *satisfactorily, skillfully* in describing an action; ADJECTIVE, meaning *fit, healthy* in describing a person's health)—Our soccer team has done ***well*** this season. The majority of our nursing graduates do ***well*** on their state board examinations. Our assistant manager works ***well*** under pressure. My assistant did not look ***well*** today. Jenny did not feel ***well***, so she went home.

Grate/Great

Grate (VERB; to reduce to small particles by rubbing on something rough; to cause irritation; to grind noisily. NOUN; a frame of parallel or crossed bars, especially blocking a passage)—In the future please use a food processor to ***grate*** the cheese for our pizzas. Who will ***grate*** the cabbage for the coleslaw? His continual talking could ***grate*** on anyone's nerves. If you continue to ***grate*** your teeth, you could become a candidate for TMJ disorder. Caution users to clean the barbecue ***grate*** after each use. Be sure to place a ***grate*** over this excavation when you have finished removing the dirt.
Great (ADJECTIVE; large in size; numerous; eminent or distinguished)—From the cruise ship, we often sight a ***great*** white whale. A ***great*** many people have expressed an interest in purchasing our Model 314 speech-enabled smartphone. Many ***great*** performers from stage and screen will be present at our annual benefit.

Hail/Hale

Hail (VERB; to greet or summon; to acclaim. NOUN; rain that falls in the form of small ice balls)—On rainy afternoons you may find it difficult to ***hail*** a taxi in downtown Chicago. The firefighters were ***hailed*** as heroes for rescuing the trapped teenagers from the burning building. Unfortunately, the unexpected ***hail*** in April damaged some of our strawberry crops.
Hale (ADJECTIVE; healthy)—Let's hope you will return from this adventuresome vacation ***hale*** and hearty.

He/Him/Himself

He (PRONOUN; the subject of a clause or a complement pronoun)—***He*** is the best candidate for the position. Although ***he*** usually works on Tuesdays, ***he*** is ill today. The person in our choral group with the best singing voice has always been ***he***. If I were ***he***, I would investigate this opportunity more thoroughly.
Him (PRONOUN; a direct object, an indirect object, or an object of a preposition)—The president asked ***him*** to head the project. Answer ***him*** directly. I sent ***him*** an e-mail last week about the meeting. Doris Waters gave ***him*** the information yesterday. The choice is between you and ***him***. These flowers are a thank-you from Jackie and ***him***.
Himself (PRONOUN; a reflexive pronoun used to emphasize or refer back to the subject)—He ***himself*** had to solve the problem. Although I can assist, Steve ***himself*** needs to research this case. Rick Bogart addressed the envelope to ***himself***. Mark continually asked ***himself*** if there was any way he could have prevented the accident.

Healthful/Healthy

Healthful (ADJECTIVE; beneficial to health of body or mind; promoting one's well-being or good health)—Our programs are individually tailored to inspire you to achieve a ***healthful*** lifestyle. Millions of Americans consider vitamin supplements to be ***healthful***. Mary tries to eat only ***healthful*** foods. Doctors recommend daily exercise as a ***healthful*** activity.
Healthy (ADJECTIVE; being well or fit; enjoying health and vigor of body, mind, or spirit)—Be sure to keep only ***healthy*** plants in our nursery section. Our boarding

kennels accept only ***healthy*** animals. Most of our clients have selected the one-year membership program to remain ***healthy*** and maintain their physical fitness.

Hear/Here

Hear (VERB; to perceive by the ear)—Yes, I can ***hear*** you clearly through the intercom. We are unable to ***hear*** conversations in the next room because of the excellent soundproofing. You may ***hear*** the correct pronunciation of words at the Merriam-Webster Web site.

Here (ADVERB; in this place or at this point)—Install the telephone line ***here***. It was ***here*** on the agenda that the chair interrupted the discussion to have the meeting resume after lunch.

Her/Herself/She

Her (PRONOUN; a direct object, an indirect object, or an object of a preposition)—I saw ***her*** yesterday. When Paulette arrived, Mr. Schultz greeted ***her***. Barbara offered ***her*** a chair. Did you send ***her*** the application? The check is for ***her***. The report was written by Tracy and ***her***.

Herself (PRONOUN; a reflexive pronoun used to emphasize or refer back to the subject)—Wendy ***herself*** wrote and edited the audit report using speech-recognition software. Does Allison ***herself*** have the answer to the riddle she posed? Kristen often talks to ***herself***. Sandy sent a copy of the e-mail to ***herself***.

She (PRONOUN; the subject of a clause or a complement pronoun)—***She*** locked the store and set the alarm yesterday at 6 p.m. Every morning ***she*** opens the bank safe just before business hours. The person who designed this spreadsheet was ***she***. It was ***she*** who answered the phone when I called.

Here: see Hear.

Herself: see Her.

Hew/Hue

Hew (VERB; to cut with blows from a heavy cutting instrument)—State law requires owners to obtain a permit to ***hew*** any trees on properties in this area. Which famous faces have been ***hewed*** on Mount Rushmore? Misty Trail, part of the 17-mile ascent to the top of Yosemite's Half Dome, has steps roughly ***hewed*** into the rock to assist hikers through this wet area.

Hue (NOUN; color or gradation of color; aspect)—Pepe's, a popular Mexican family restaurant, serves all its items in colorful ceramic dishes of varying ***hues***. The ***hues*** of the rainbow glistened in the sunlight. Individuals from every socioeconomic ***hue*** support their local professional sports teams.

Him: see He.

Himself: see He.

Hoard/Horde

Hoard (VERB; to store or accumulate for future use)—Please do not ***hoard*** stationery and other supplies in your office. Recent reports of rice shortages caused shoppers to strip grocery store shelves and ***hoard*** supplies of rice.

Horde (NOUN; a multitude, a large crowd)—A ***horde*** of jazz enthusiasts were waiting for the box office to open so they could purchase prime seats for the October 15 concert. ***Hordes*** of tourists poured into Las Vegas last weekend to take advantage of the discounted packages offered by many hotels.

Hoarse/Horse

Hoarse (ADJECTIVE; low, husky sound; having a rough or harsh voice)—Your voice is too ***hoarse*** to make these telephone calls today. Tony shouted himself ***hoarse*** during the football game.
Horse (NOUN; a large animal)—For this commercial we will need at least eight ***horses***.

Hole/Whole

Hole (NOUN; an opening or an open place)—Burglars had entered the jewelry store by cutting a ***hole*** through the outer wall.
Whole (ADJECTIVE; complete, entire)—Too many inexperienced managers make decisions before knowing the ***whole*** story.

Holy/Wholly

Holy (ADJECTIVE; sacred)—Visitors continually flock to Jerusalem's ***holy*** shrines.
Wholly (ADVERB; completely)—Do you agree ***wholly*** with the committee's plan to invest additional funds in the proposed shopping mall?

Horde: see Hoard.

Hue: see Hew.

Human/Humane

Human (ADJECTIVE; characteristic of people)—Please remember that all of us are guilty of possessing ***human*** frailties. Our organization seeks to protect ***human*** rights throughout the world.
Humane (ADJECTIVE; marked by compassion, sympathy, or consideration)—The treatment of elderly people in this convalescent facility is certainly less than ***humane***. New laws have been enacted to ensure the ***humane*** treatment of cats and dogs whether or not they are domestic pets.

Hypercritical/Hypocritical

Hypercritical (ADJECTIVE; excessively critical)—Many of his coworkers believe Mr. Reed to be ***hypercritical*** of new employees. Your ***hypercritical*** six-month evaluation of Ms. Chase appears to have no basis.
Hypocritical (ADJECTIVE [ˌhi-pə-ˈkri-ti-kəl]; falsely pretending)—Because Brenda-Sue befriended other staff members and then gossiped about their shortcomings, she was fired for her ***hypocritical*** behavior. ***Hypocritical*** managers hamper the effectiveness of the organization in reaching its goals and should be terminated.

I/Me/Myself

I (PRONOUN; a subject of a clause or a complement pronoun)—***I*** received information about this promotional opportunity yesterday. ***I*** agree with you. If you were ***I***, what would you do under these circumstances? Yes, it was ***I*** who received the promotion.

Me (PRONOUN; a direct object, an indirect object, or an object of a preposition)—E-mail ***me*** as soon as you receive a response from the client. Barbara e-mailed ***me*** yesterday. Please send ***me*** this information by the first of next week. Pat gave ***me*** the sales report last week. None of this mail is for ***me***. The fruit basket sent to our new manager is from Sally, Nathan, and ***me***.
Myself (PRONOUN; a reflexive pronoun used to emphasize or refer back to the subject)—I ***myself*** wrote the entire script. Although I had assistance in preparing this report, I ***myself*** must double-check the reference notations. I can blame only ***myself*** for losing this sale. I sent a blind copy of this e-mail message to ***myself***.

Ideal/Idle/Idol

Ideal (ADJECTIVE; perfect, model)—From all that I have observed, Ms. Andrews appears to be the ***ideal*** administrative assistant for your office. Your proposal outlines an ***ideal*** method for rotating our inventory.
Idle (ADJECTIVE; doing nothing)—The production line was ***idle*** for almost a week.
Idol (NOUN; an object for religious worship; a revered person or thing)—Was the church ***idol*** vandalized? Money is often the ***idol*** of ambitious, greedy people.

I.e.: see E.g.

Illegible: see Eligible.

Illicit: see Elicit.

Immigrate: see Emigrate.

Imminent: see Eminent.

Implicit: see Explicit.

Imply/Infer

Imply (VERB; to suggest without stating)—Did the manager ***imply*** that he is dissatisfied with our sales efforts? The inclusion of links on this Web site does not ***imply*** an endorsement of any goods or services advertised. Your entry into this 10K charity run ***implies*** acceptance of the sponsor's rules.
Infer (VERB; to reach a conclusion; to derive by reasoning)—From the results of this survey, we can ***infer*** that our advertising efforts in Miami have been aimed at the wrong population. From your smile may I ***infer*** that you are pleased with these portraits? The panel of judges cannot be expected to ***infer*** from the grant application what should be stated explicitly.

In behalf of/On behalf of

In behalf of (PREPOSITION + NOUN + PREPOSITION; in the interest or benefit of)—Because Ms. Shields was scheduled to be out of town, she requested Mr. Gross to present the award ***in behalf of*** the company. This scholarship has been awarded to Thomas Brooks ***in behalf of*** the USC Alumni Association.
On behalf of (PREPOSITION + NOUN + PREPOSITION; in support or defense of)—Our law firm deals with clinical negligence and medical products liability litigation ***on behalf of*** claimants. In this way, regulatory bodies—for example, the Better Business Bureau—have begun to act ***on behalf of*** consumers. Dr. Phillips spoke ***on behalf of*** Ms. Jones at the hearing.

Incidence/Incidents

Incidence (NOUN; an occurrence; a rate of occurrence)—There has yet to be an ***incidence*** of theft within the company. The low ***incidence*** of traffic accidents during this holiday weekend may be attributed to our television safety campaign.

Incidents (NOUN; events or episodes)—A number of ***incidents*** have occurred recently that require us to review our safety policies and practices. Our agency also investigates reported ***incidents*** of possible child abuse.

Incite/Insight

Incite (VERB; to urge on or provoke action)—The senator's speech attempted to ***incite*** students to become more politically active and sensitive to public issues. Poverty, depression, and starvation ***incited*** riots throughout the war-torn country.

Insight (NOUN; keen understanding)—Bob's ***insight*** and patience resolved the issue before it developed into a major problem. This series of articles provides an ***insight*** into the workings of the television industry.

Indigenous/Indigent/Indignant

Indigenous (ADJECTIVE; native to a particular region)—I believe that this tree is ***indigenous*** to the Pacific Northwest. Use locally ***indigenous*** plants and trees to conserve water in this hot, dry desert region.

Indigent (ADJECTIVE; poor, needy)—He entered the United States as an ***indigent*** refugee from Eastern Europe and is now a network administrator. Our local Salvation Army provides Thanksgiving meals each year for ***indigent*** families.

Indignant (ADJECTIVE; insulting, angry)—Successful store managers must know how to deal with ***indignant*** customers. His comment was intended to be humorous, but instead it elicited an ***indignant*** response.

Infer: see Imply.

Ingenious/Ingenuous

Ingenious (ADJECTIVE; marked by originality, resourcefulness, and cleverness)—Your ***ingenious*** plan could save our company thousands of dollars annually. The Hawaiian Edge pineapple slicer is an ***ingenious*** device—once you own it, you will wonder how you ever lived without it.

Ingenuous (ADJECTIVE; showing innocent or childlike simplicity; natural)—Mayor Warren's ***ingenuous*** smile and warm personality have contributed immeasurably to his successful political career. All Leland Stanton's novels portray an ***ingenuous*** authenticity in the development of its characters.

Insight: see Incite.

Insure: see Assure.

Interstate/Intrastate

Interstate (ADJECTIVE; between states)—Since expanding our operations to Maine and Vermont, we must abide by all laws governing ***interstate*** commerce. Our trucking corporation operates ***interstate***, serving seven Western states.

Intrastate (ADJECTIVE; within a state)—Our company, an Indiana corporation, is concerned solely with ***intrastate*** sales. This new statute applies only to companies operating ***intrastate***.

Irregardless/Regardless

Irregardless (an incorrect usage for *regardless* that is not acceptable for speaking or writing)

Regardless (ADVERB; despite everything)—We must vacate these premises by July 31, ***regardless***!

Regardless of (PREPOSITION; without taking into account; in spite of)—***Regardless of*** price, which one of these models has the best performance record? We have opened an account for Ritter's Clothing Store ***regardless of*** its slow payment record.

Irritate: see Aggravate.

Isle: see Aisle.

It's/Its

It's (PRONOUN + VERB; contraction of *it is*)—Although this model television set has become very popular, ***it's*** not our best seller. If you feel ***it's*** too expensive to send sales representatives to Europe, we should delay doing so.

Its (PRONOUN USED AS ADJECTIVE; possessive form of *it*)—The company had ***its*** stockholders' meeting in Atlanta last week. Our network needs to have some of ***its*** switches replaced.

Karat: see Carat.

Later/Latter

Later (ADVERB; after the proper time)—The shipment arrived a week ***later*** than we had anticipated.

Latter (ADJECTIVE; the second thing of two things mentioned)—Your ***latter*** suggestion is more likely to be adopted by the hiring committee (*see also* **Former**).

Lay/Lie

Lay (VERB; to put or place; a transitive verb that needs an object to complete its meaning; *lay, laid, laid,* and *laying* are the principal parts of this verb)—Please ***lay*** all newly signed contracts on my desk. I ***laid*** the signed contracts on your desk yesterday. During the past week, I have ***laid*** four contracts on your desk signed by Fred Miller. We are ***laying*** the foundation for the new building this week. (See Section 1–13 for additional information on the use of *lay* and *lie*.)

Lie (VERB; to recline; an intransitive verb that does not have an object; *lie, lay, lain,* and *lying* are the principal parts of this verb)—Where may the patient ***lie*** down? He ***lay*** in the hospital waiting room for more than three hours before a doctor examined him. These contracts have ***lain*** on Ms. Lee's desk since Monday. Mrs. Hartman is ***lying*** down. (See Section 1–13 for additional information on the use of *lie* and *lay*.)

Lead/Led

Lead (NOUN or ADJECTIVE ['led]; a metallic element)—The warning label informs consumers that these crystal glasses contain ***lead***. How many feet of ***lead*** pipe did the contractor order for this apartment house complex?
Led (VERB; past tense of *lead* ['lēd], meaning "to provide direction")—Before his retirement Mr. Andrews ***led*** this company from a $3 million deficit to a $6 million annual profit. The guide ***led*** the tourists through tunnels that had been carved into the Rock of Gibraltar during World War II.

Lean/Lien

Lean (VERB; to rest against; to be inclined toward. ADJECTIVE; not fat)—Ask the children not to ***lean*** against these railings. Most of our employees seem to ***lean*** toward receiving additional medical benefits rather than salary increases. We use only first-quality ***lean*** ground beef in our hamburgers.
Lien (NOUN; a legal right or claim to property)—If the company refuses to pay, we will be forced to place a ***lien*** against its property. A legal ***lien*** remains in force as long as the owner retains possession of the property.

Leased/Least

Leased (VERB; property rented for a specified time period)—Our company has ***leased*** this suite of offices for the past seven years. All the units in this new apartment complex have been ***leased***.
Least (ADJECTIVE; smallest, slightest, or lowest)—This year we showed the ***least*** profit since our company was established in 1992. At the ***least*** provocation, our supervisor shouts angrily at both customers and employees.

Led: see Lead.

Lend/Loan

Lend (VERB; to give for temporary use with the understanding that the same or equivalent will be returned)—Has the bank agreed to ***lend*** us additional funds to expand our warehouse facilities? Did you ***lend*** one of our laptops to someone in another department?
Loan (NOUN; something given for a borrower's temporary use)—Your $23,000 car ***loan*** will be fully repaid with your August 1 payment. Your application for a 30-year ***loan*** on the Clearbrook Street property has been approved.

Less: see Fewer.

Lessee/Lesser/Lessor

Lessee (NOUN; one to whom a lease is given)—As specified in the lease, the ***lessee*** must pay a monthly rent of $1,200 by or before the 1st of each month.
Lesser (ADJECTIVE; smaller; less important)—Although the judge ruled in favor of the plaintiff, he awarded a ***lesser*** amount in damages than we had anticipated. Solving the school district's financial problems seems to be of ***lesser*** importance to the board members than getting reelected.
Lessor (NOUN; one who grants a lease)—The ***lessor*** for all our company cars is Allied Car Leasing Service.

Lessen/Lesson

Lessen (VERB; to make smaller)—Chris Timmins recommended that we ***lessen*** our efforts in the manufacture of small appliances.

Lesson (NOUN; a unit of study; something from which one learns)—How many ***lessons*** are contained in the Excel section of your new *Introduction to Microsoft Office* textbook? This experience was a good ***lesson*** for Juanita in how making assumptions can result in miscommunication.

Lesser: see Lessee.

Lessor: see Lessee.

Levee/Levy

Levee (NOUN; the bank of a river; a boat landing place)—The river overflowed the ***levee***. The ***levee*** was washed away during the heavy floods.

Levy (NOUN; an order for payment. VERB; to collect payments by legal authority)—To pay for the flood damage, the governor ordered a 1 percent ***levy*** on gasoline sales. Will the state legislature ***levy*** additional taxes to reduce the state's indebtedness?

Liable/Libel/Likely

Liable (ADJECTIVE; legally responsible, obligated)—The court ruled that the company was ***liable*** for all damages resulting from the accident. In rear-end collisions, the driver ***liable*** is usually the one who collides into the back end of another vehicle.

Libel (NOUN; a false or damaging written statement about another)—Don censored one statement in the reporter's article because he feared the newspaper could be sued for ***libel***.

Likely (ADJECTIVE; probable. ADVERB; probably)—He is a ***likely*** candidate for the position. If you continue to be habitually late and absent, you are ***likely*** (not *liable*) to be fired.

Lie: see Lay.

Lien: see Lean.

Lightening/Lightning

Lightening (VERB [GERUND]; illuminating or brightening; lessening or alleviating)—***Lightening*** the kitchen and the living areas requires us to revise the design drawings to include ceiling lights in these areas. Please select paint colors that will result in ***lightening*** the reception area. Only by ***lightening*** her workload can we expect to retain Ms. Burton.

Lightning (NOUN; the flashing of light produced by atmospheric electricity)—Flashes of ***lightning*** streaked across the sky during the storm.

Like: see As.

Likely: see Liable.

Loan: see Lend.

Local/Locale

Local (ADJECTIVE; limited to a particular district)—Most businesses in the ***local*** area are members of the Granada Hills Chamber of Commerce. Free delivery is available within the ***local*** area.

Locale (NOUN [lō'kal]; a particular location)—This parcel of land is an ideal ***locale*** for a new housing development. Unless we can find a suitable ***locale*** for a new branch office, we will have to postpone our expansion plans.

Loose/Lose

Loose (ADJECTIVE; not fastened, not tight or shut up)—A ***loose*** connection was the probable cause of the power failure on the fifth floor of the Fisher Building. These ***loose*** floor tiles are a safety hazard.

Lose (VERB; to fail to keep; to mislay)—We do not want to ***lose*** any of our accounts in the Philippines because of this temporary materials shortage. If you ***lose*** your keys, please notify Joe Drew in Plant Facilities.

Magnate/Magnet

Magnate (NOUN; a powerful or influential person)—As the first ***magnate*** of the automobile industry, Henry Ford changed the lifestyle of people throughout the world. Conrad Hilton, a hotel ***magnate***, founded the international chain of hotels that bear his name.

Magnet (NOUN; something that has the ability to attract)—Picking up the spilled paper clips with a ***magnet*** was an easy task. Our fall closeout sale was like a ***magnet***, bringing potential customers into our store from all parts of the city.

Main/Mane

Main (ADJECTIVE; principal or most important part)—Our ***main*** selling feature is still customer service.

Mane (NOUN; the heavy hair on the neck of a horse or lion)—The horse's ***mane*** had become entangled in the wire fence.

Manner/Manor

Manner (NOUN; method; a customary or particular way)—Unless this cell phone service provider changes its ***manner*** of doing business, it will lose many more customers. Chancellor Young's congenial ***manner*** has endeared him to both faculty and students alike.

Manor (NOUN; a main house or mansion)—Although the décor of the ***manor*** dates back to the early twentieth century, its interior is still well maintained and elegant.

Marital/Marshal/Martial

Marital (ADJECTIVE; pertaining to marriage)—Employment application forms may not request applicants to disclose their ***marital*** status.

Marshal (NOUN; a military or law enforcement rank; the head of a ceremony)—If you wish to have a ***marshal*** serve these legal papers, you must pay an additional $75 fee. Jack Williams was asked to serve as honorary ***marshal*** of the Independence Day parade.

Martial (ADJECTIVE; warlike, military)—Several bands played ***martial*** music at the Veterans Day commemoration.

May: see Can.

May be/Maybe

May be (VERB; a verb phrase [a helping verb and a main verb] derived from the infinitive *to be*)—This ***may be*** the last year we will lease these facilities. Your package ***may be*** delayed because of the severe storms in the Northeast.
Maybe (ADVERB; perhaps)—***Maybe*** you could ask the sales representatives to e-mail this information to you as they call upon their various accounts. We had hoped, ***maybe***, that you would reconsider our department's proposal to upgrade its accounting software.

Me: see I.

Medal/Meddle

Medal (NOUN; a metal disk; an award in the form of a metal disk)—This morning I found a gold religious ***medal*** lying on the sidewalk outside the church. The firefighter received a ***medal*** for his heroic efforts.
Meddle (VERB; to interfere)—Please ask your assistant not to ***meddle*** in the dispute between Sandra and her supervisor. You will need to remind the employees in your department not to ***meddle*** in the personal affairs of their coworkers.

Miner/Minor

Miner (NOUN; a person who works in a mine)—The ***miner*** had been trapped in the underground cavern for nearly 24 hours before the rescue team reached him.
Minor (NOUN; a person under legal age. ADJECTIVE; a lesser thing)—Please post a sign that reads "No ***minors*** allowed." Your forgetting to fax the proposal yesterday proved to be of ***minor*** consequence.

Mode/Mood

Mode (NOUN; style or preferred method)—What ***mode*** of transportation will you use to reach the airport?
Mood (NOUN; feeling or disposition, a prevailing attitude)—Before you ask Mr. Atkinson for a salary increase, be sure he is in a good ***mood***. The ***mood*** of the crowd gathered outside City Hall still seems calm.

Moral/Morale

Moral (ADJECTIVE; pertaining to right and wrong, ethical)—Too many ***moral*** issues were apparent in this investment strategy for our company to become involved.
Morale (NOUN; a mental condition)—Announcement of an across-the-board 7 percent pay increase instantly boosted employee ***morale***.

Morning/Mourning

Morning (NOUN; the time from sunrise to noon)—Would you be able to schedule an appointment for me to see Dr. Rose on Friday ***morning***?
Mourning (NOUN; showing signs of grief)—Please allow the family to observe this period of ***mourning*** without any interruptions concerning business matters.

Most: see Almost.

Mourning: see Morning.

Myself: see I.

Naval/Navel

Naval (ADJECTIVE; relating to a navy)—Last week Mr. Marsh's son accepted an assignment with ***naval*** intelligence.

Navel (NOUN; a depression in the middle of the abdomen. ADJECTIVE; a type of orange)—According to Dr. Chin, the incision will leave a small scar directly below the ***navel***. On Friday our Produce Department will receive a large shipment of ***navel*** oranges from Florida.

Number: see Amount.

On behalf of: see In behalf of.

Ordinance/Ordnance

Ordinance (NOUN; a local regulation)—Many cities have an ***ordinance*** banning excessive noise after 10 p.m. Local ***ordinances*** set the curfew times for children under 18 years of age and vary among cities.

Ordnance (NOUN; military weapons)—We should know by the end of the month when we will receive the ***ordnance*** needed for the practice maneuvers scheduled during the summer months.

Overdo/Overdue

Overdo (VERB; to exaggerate or do in excess)—Exercise is healthful if one does not ***overdo*** it.

Overdue (ADJECTIVE; late)—Your payment is 15 days ***overdue***.

Pair/Pare/Pear

Pair (NOUN; two of a kind; made of two corresponding parts)—These sale bags of potato chips are packaged in ***pairs***. The ***pair*** of shoes the customer attempted to return showed signs of considerable wear, so the return was refused.

Pare (VERB; to reduce in size or trim; to peel)—All department heads have been instructed to ***pare*** their budgets by at least 10 percent. Be sure to ***pare*** the carrots before cooking them.

Pear (NOUN; a fruit)—Our market carries three brands of canned ***pears***.

Partition/Petition

Partition (NOUN; something that divides)—All workstations in our new office complex will be separated by ***partitions***. The conference rooms in our hotel have soundproof sliding ***partitions*** to accommodate groups ranging from 25 to 100 people.

Petition (NOUN; a formal written request)—Have you signed the ***petition*** to create curb cutouts at all major intersections in the downtown business district? Her attorney filed the divorce ***petition*** yesterday.

Passed/Past

Passed (VERB; past tense or past participle of *pass*, meaning "to go by" or "circulate")—Once you have ***passed*** the intersection, look for our store on the west side of the street. Lisa ***passed*** out copies of the job announcement to all eligible employees in the company.

Past (NOUN or ADJECTIVE; time gone by or ended)—Our weak profit picture is all in the ***past***. From ***past*** experience we have learned not to extend credit to this company.

Patience/Patients

Patience (NOUN; calm perseverance)—Jamie's ***patience*** in working with disabled children is certainly to be admired. Accessing the Internet with a slow connection requires considerable ***patience***.

Patients (NOUN; people undergoing medical treatment)—Is George Allison one of Dr. Hedge's ***patients***? Last night three of the ***patients*** on this floor were transferred to the Intensive Care Unit.

Peace/Piece

Peace (NOUN; truce; tranquility)—As long as hostilities persist, there can be no ***peace*** among these nations. Since Ms. Seraydarian began the project, she has not had a moment's ***peace***.

Piece (NOUN; a part of a defined quantity)—Each of the three beneficiaries inherited a ***piece*** of the prime property. Please ensure that each child receives a ***piece*** of birthday cake.

Peak/Peek

Peak (ADJECTIVE or NOUN; highest point; top)—Our ***peak*** sales period is from September through November. KPFK's transmitter is located at the ***peak*** of Mount Wilson.

Peek (NOUN; a glance)—Some of the buyers have already had a ***peek*** at the new fall fashions by major designers. Following is a quick ***peek*** of what lies ahead in technology.

Peal/Peel

Peal (NOUN; a loud sound or succession of sounds. VERB; to give out a loud sound or succession of sounds)—The flash of lightning was followed by a loud ***peal*** of thunder. ***Peals*** of laughter could be heard coming through the closed conference room doors. Bells ***pealed*** from the church tower signaling that the wedding ceremony was over.

Peel (VERB; to remove by stripping. NOUN; skin or rind)—Ask the customer to ***peel*** off the mailing label and affix it to the enclosed postcard. You may wish to ***peel*** the tomatoes before adding them to the salad. Do any of these recipes require the use of lemon ***peel***?

Pear: see Pair.

Peek: see Peak.

Peel: see Peal.

Peer/Pier

Peer (VERB; to gaze. NOUN; one belonging to the same social group)—Do customers often ***peer*** into the bakery shop window before entering the store? Allison ***peered*** at the computer screen, searching for the information Google indicated would be there. Most teenagers imitate the behavior of their ***peers***. Students with physical disabilities are included in classes with their able-bodied ***peers***.

Pier (NOUN; a structure extending into navigable waters)—The new ***pier*** will have shops and restaurants as well as spaces for sidewalk vendors. Is fishing permitted off this ***pier***?

Persecute/Prosecute

Persecute (VERB; to harass persistently)—If your new supervisor continues to ***persecute*** you, contact your union representative at Ext. 3543. Although the countryside was picturesque and peaceful, we were persistently ***persecuted*** by mosquitoes during the management retreat.

Prosecute (VERB; to conduct legal proceedings against someone)—The district attorney may not have enough evidence to ***prosecute*** the case. Was the bus driver ***prosecuted*** for any offense?

Personal/Personnel

Personal (ADJECTIVE; private; individual)—Be careful about disclosing ***personal*** information over the Internet. Please remove all your ***personal*** belongings from the apartment by June 30. Each employee has a ***personal*** parking space.

Personnel (NOUN; employees. ADJECTIVE; relating to employment)—All ***personnel*** have been notified that the company will be acquired by Certified Investment Corporation, effective July 1. Only company ***personnel*** are permitted to enter beyond this point. Your annual performance evaluation will be placed in your ***personnel*** file.

Perspective/Prospective

Perspective (NOUN; a mental picture or outlook)—I believe his ***perspective*** is distorted by greed. We must evaluate these online instructional materials from the ***perspective*** of our learners. To obtain a broader ***perspective***, we need to include in our focus group community leaders from every cultural hue.

Prospective (ADJECTIVE; likely to be or become, expected)—Have you been able to locate a ***prospective*** buyer for the property on Lake Street? All ***prospective*** tenants must provide written authorization to perform a credit check. What are the ***prospective*** benefits to be derived from the reorganization of our marketing channels?

Persuade: see Convince.

Peruse/Pursue

Peruse (VERB; to read hastily or casually)—Each morning at breakfast I ***peruse*** the newspaper for any items of interest to our industry. Before meeting with the realtor, I suggest you ***peruse*** the online real estate listings in your area. Make your holiday shopping easier by ***perusing*** our online catalog.

Pursue (VERB; to follow in order to overtake; to proceed with a course of action)—As he used his cell phone to notify the police, the onlooker continued to ***pursue*** the hijacker. May I suggest you ***pursue*** this sales lead further. Has Tammy decided on a career she wishes to ***pursue***?

Petition: see Partition.

Physical: see Fiscal.

Piece: see Peace.

Pier: see Peer.

Plaintiff/Plaintive

Plaintiff (NOUN; one who initiates a lawsuit)—The attorney for the ***plaintiff*** in this case has petitioned the court for an extension. Did the ***plaintiff*** agree to settle this case out of court?

Plaintive (ADJECTIVE; expressive of suffering or woe)—In a ***plaintive*** voice, the witness described how the gunmen carried out the robbery. The dean of admissions and records finally sent a ***plaintive*** plea to the college president to purchase contemporary database software.

Pole/Poll

Pole (NOUN; a long, slender object that is usually cylindrical)—The salesclerk will need to use a ***pole*** to bring down any of the toddler dresses hanging from the top of the wall. Power and telephone ***poles*** are being replaced by underground utilities, but the American landscape is traditionally covered with wooden power ***poles*** fashioned after the basic infrastructure of the telegraph network.

Poll (NOUN; counting of opinions or votes cast; place where votes are cast [usually *polls*])—Our latest ***poll*** shows that consumers prefer liquid dishwasher detergent over powdered dishwasher detergent. An informal ***poll*** of our employees showed that the majority believe the acquisition of Econo-Security Systems was a good investment. Be sure to urge all registered voters to go to the ***polls*** next Tuesday.

Populace/Populous

Populace (NOUN; the masses; population of a place)—The winning candidate must have the support of the ***populace***. Hurricane warnings urged the evacuation of the Ponte Vedra Beach ***populace***.

Populous (ADJECTIVE; densely populated)—Our fast-food chain establishes new restaurants only in ***populous*** areas. International airports are usually located in a country's most ***populous*** cities.

Pore/Pour

Pore (VERB; to read studiously or attentively. NOUN; a small opening in a membrane)—How long did the auditors ***pore*** over these books before discovering discrepancies in the entries? We spent hours ***poring*** over brochures to plan our vacation. Hot water will open the ***pores*** of your skin, and cold water will close them.

Pour (VERB; to dispense from a container; to move with a continual or continuous flow)—Please ask the servers to ***pour*** the water after the guests are seated. Even before the game ended, spectators began to ***pour*** out of the stadium.

Pray/Prey

Pray (VERB; to make a request in a humble manner; to address a god)—I ***pray*** that these bureaucrats will give consideration to my suggestion. Children may not be required to ***pray*** in public schools.

Prey (VERB; to have an injurious or destructive effect. NOUN; victim)—Marbella should not let this experience continue to ***prey*** on her mind. Do not become ***prey*** to the get-rich-quick schemes of con artists.

Precede/Proceed

Precede (VERB [pri-'sēd]; to go before)—Mrs. Andrews' breakout session will ***precede*** the convention's opening general session. The backspace key on the computer keyboard deletes the character that ***precedes*** the cursor.

Proceed (VERB [prō-'sēd]; to go forward or continue)—Please ***proceed*** with your analysis of the utility company's financial statements. Our Legal Department has been directed to ***proceed*** with a court case against Canyon Home Builders.

Precedence/Precedents

Precedence (NOUN ['pre-cə-dən(t)s]; priority)—Please give ***precedence*** to training middle management in the use of speech-recognition software. This new project takes ***precedence*** over any other project we have been assigned.

Precedents (NOUN ['pre-cə-dənts]; things done or said that can be used as an example)—There are no legal ***precedents*** in our state for this particular case. What ***precedents*** have been set in the banking industry related to retirement benefits accruing from acquired financial institutions?

Presence/Presents

Presence (NOUN; condition of being present; stately or distinguished bearing of a person)—Please ensure the ***presence*** of all supervisors and managers at this leadership seminar. Everyone was impressed by the confidence and ***presence*** with which the new president addressed the faculty.

Presents (NOUN; gifts or things given)—Company employees donated a record number of ***presents*** to needy children this year.

Prey: see Pray.

Principal/Principle

Principal (NOUN; a capital sum; the head of a school)—Your monthly loan statement shows a breakdown of the ***principal*** and the interest paid the previous month. As ***principal*** of Lindberg High School, Mrs. Brereton is proud of the many seniors who attend college after graduation.

Principal (ADJECTIVE; highest in importance)—The ***principal*** reason for offering employees tuition reimbursement is to encourage them to upgrade their skills.

Principle (NOUN; an accepted rule; a basic truth or belief)—This applicant's knowledge of accounting ***principles*** is questionable. Our country was founded on the ***principle*** that all persons are created equal.

Proceed: see Precede.

Propose/Purpose

Propose (VERB; to suggest)—I ***propose*** that we borrow sufficient funds to purchase all the new equipment at once.
Purpose (NOUN; a desired result)—The ***purpose*** of this meeting is to discuss procedures for increasing our sales through e-commerce.

Prosecute: see Persecute.

Prospective: see Perspective.

Purpose: see Propose.

Pursue: see Peruse.

Quiet/Quite

Quiet (ADJECTIVE; peaceful; free from noise)—Our client wishes to purchase a three-bedroom home in a ***quiet*** residential neighborhood. The ***quiet*** operation of this color laser printer is one of its main sales features.
Quite (ADVERB; completely or actually)—Our salespeople seem to be ***quite*** satisfied with the new commission plan.

Raise/Raze/Rise

Raise (VERB; to lift something up; to increase in amount; to gather together; to bring into existence; a transitive verb that needs an object to complete its meaning; *raise, raised, raised,* and *raising* are the principal parts of this verb)—When you are in a meeting, remember to ***raise*** your hand if you wish to be recognized. Please do not ***raise*** your voice. The company ***raised*** our sales quota 10 percent last month. We have ***raised*** $450 for Mrs. Morgan's retirement gift. A number of our stockholders are ***raising*** questions about the proposed merger.
Raze (VERB; to tear down to the ground)—When does the company plan to ***raze*** this old warehouse and build a new one in its place? The dilapidated, abandoned shopping center was ***razed***; the city constructed in its place housing for low-income senior citizens.
Rise (VERB; to go up or to increase in value; an intransitive verb that does not have an object; *rise, rose, risen,* and *rising* are the principal parts of this verb)—Our sales should ***rise*** above $1 million for this quarter. The rocket ***rose*** 30,000 feet before it exploded. Our sales have ***risen*** for the third month in a row. Production has been ***rising*** steadily since the new equipment was installed.

Rational/Rationale

Rational (ADJECTIVE ['rash-nəl]; based on reason)—There must certainly be a ***rational*** explanation for the strange noises in the attic. One could hardly call the customer's behavior ***rational*** as he began to shout and insult the sales manager.

Rationale (NOUN [ˌra-shə-ˈnal]; an explanation of belief or practice, an underlying reason)—Do you understand management's ***rationale*** for closing this outlet store, which is presently showing a profit? Many investors do not understand American Bank's ***rationale*** for acquiring the ailing Citywide Lending conglomerate.

Real/Really

Real (ADJECTIVE; actual, true; genuine)—By providing us with competent temporary employees during this tax season, your staffing agency has been of ***real*** assistance. The diamonds in this necklace do not look ***real***.

Really (ADVERB; very, certainly)—Susan was ***really*** disappointed that Robert did not accept the position.

Reality/Realty

Reality (NOUN; that which is real, that which exists)—The public must face the ***reality*** that the state cannot continue to offer its present level of services without increasing taxes.

Realty (NOUN or ADJECTIVE; real estate)—The last ***realty*** company that tried to sell my property could not find a qualified buyer.

Receipt/Recipe

Receipt (NOUN; a written acknowledgment of receiving goods or money)—No cash refunds can be made without a ***receipt***. If you do not save your ***receipts***, you will have difficulty obtaining refunds or exchanging merchandise.

Recipe (NOUN; a set of instructions)—Mama Lucia's has always kept secret the ***recipe*** for its delicious spaghetti sauce.

Regardless: See Irregardless.

Regime/Regimen/Regiment

Regime (NOUN; a mode of management rule; a regular pattern of occurrence that is the same as *regimen*, but usage preferences suggest *regime* is used primarily to describe modes of government)—Looking back to the end of the Communist ***regime*** in Eastern Europe, please recommend readings that provide an unbiased account of incidences that led to the collapse of the USSR. Since the early 90s, indigenous peoples have become an important symbolic population for Latin American legal and political ***regimes***. All airline travelers are subjected to the same regulatory ***regime*** before boarding aircraft.

Regimen (NOUN; a systematic plan, especially for maintaining or improving health; a particular system of government that is the same as *regime*, but usage preferences suggest *regimen* is used primarily to refer to systematic health and beauty routines)—The daily ***regimen*** of professional athletes includes a strenuous exercise program. Studies are lacking that compare this weight-loss ***regimen*** with other weight-loss programs. This patient has already undergone two chemotherapy ***regimens***.

Regiment (NOUN; a military unit usually consisting of a number of battalions)—Our son's ***regiment*** is scheduled to return to the United States by the end of June.

Residence/Residents

Residence (NOUN; the place where one lives)—This house has been the clients' ***residence*** for the past 30 years. How long has Houston been your city of ***residence***?
Residents (NOUN; people who live in a place)—Several of the retirement home ***residents*** reported that the heater in their room emits only cold air. The ***residents*** of Nashville have elected a new mayor.

Respectably/Respectfully/Respectively

Respectably (ADVERB; in a correct or decent manner)—The vagrant was dressed ***respectably*** for his court appearance.
Respectfully (ADVERB; in a manner denoting high regard; a word used in the complimentary close of a letter to show high regard for the addressee)—Please remember to treat all our customers ***respectfully***. Letter closing: ***Respectfully*** yours.
Respectively (ADVERB; each in turn or in order)—Janice Jackson, John Zelinsky, and Al Turnbull were first-, second-, and third-place winners, ***respectively***.

Ring/Wring

Ring (VERB; to give out a resounding sound)—Do not allow your cell phone to ***ring*** during the performance; please set all cell phones and pagers to "silent." Our office telephones ***ring*** continually throughout the day.
Wring (VERB; to squeeze or twist)—The care instructions for these garments caution consumers to "Hand wash only. Do not ***wring*** dry; blot dry with towel." My heart ***wrings*** with anguish at the plight of these abandoned children.

Rise: see Raise.

Role/Roll

Role (NOUN; the proper function of a person or thing; a part or character assumed)—Ms. Silva is quite successful in her ***role*** as mediator for grievances within the company. What ***role*** will you play in this theatrical production?
Roll (VERB; to move by turning or rotating. NOUN; something wound around a core; a list of names)—Ask the plumber to ***roll*** back the bathroom carpeting before attempting any plumbing repairs. Please order 3 dozen ***rolls*** of transparent packaging tape from Hillsdale Stationers. How many students are on your ***roll***?

Rote/Wrote

Rote (NOUN; mechanical or repetitious procedure)—All fourth-grade children are expected to know the multiplication tables *one* through *ten* by ***rote***. Our school advocates learning by independent inquiry and discovery-based problem solving instead of learning by ***rote***.
Wrote (VERB; past tense of *to write*)—We ***wrote*** to all our clients last week informing them of our merger with American Financial Corporation.

Rout/Route

Rout (NOUN ['raủt—sounds like *out*]; a disorderly assembly or disastrous defeat)—The football game turned into a ***rout*** after the opposing team scored 28 points during the first quarter.

Route (NOUN ['rüt]; a course taken in traveling from one point to another)—Our delivery ***routes*** were changed based upon the consultant's recommendations. Internet e-mail takes a variety of ***routes*** as it travels from server to server to reach its destination.

Sample: see Example.

Scene/Seen

Scene (NOUN; the place of an occurrence; an exhibition of anger; a subdivision of a play)—The ambulance arrived at the ***scene*** of the collision shortly after the 911 call came in. How would you handle a hostile customer who was creating a ***scene***? My favorite ***scene*** in *Mamma Mia* is when Donna first sees her three former boyfriends who have arrived for the wedding.

Seen (VERB; past participle of *to see*)—I have not ***seen*** our sales manager for three days. No, I have not ***seen*** our sales figures for the last quarter.

Scent: see Cent.

Sealing: see Ceiling.

Seize: see Cease.

Semi-: see Bi-.

Senses: see Census.

Sent: see Cent.

Serial: see Cereal.

Set/Sit

Set (VERB; to place; to position; to arrange; a transitive verb that generally needs an object to complete its meaning; *set*, *set*, *set*, and *setting* are the principal parts of this verb)—Please ***set*** the package on my desk. He ***set*** the clocks ahead one hour for daylight saving time. I have ***set*** the times for all your medical appointments this week. We are ***setting*** higher quotas for our sales personnel this year.

Sit (VERB; to be seated or occupy a seat; an intransitive verb that does not have an object; *sit*, *sat*, *sat*, and *sitting* are the principal parts of this verb)—***Sit*** here, Ms. Brown. Please ***sit*** in the reception area until the nurse calls you. I ***sat*** for more than an hour awaiting his return. He has ***sat*** in that chair all day watching television. If Mr. Weaver calls, tell him I am ***sitting*** in on a meeting of the department heads.

Sew/So/Sow

Sew (VERB; to fasten by stitches with thread)—Please have someone in the Alterations Department ***sew*** a button on this coat.

So (ADVERB; to that degree. CONJUNCTION; with the result that; in order that; therefore)—We are ***so*** interested in entering the Brazilian market that we have set up an office in Rio de Janeiro. The department chair opened another accounting class ***so*** all students on the waiting list were accommodated. Please complete the enclosed form and mail it in the return envelope ***so*** *we* may update our files. Our company is moving its offices to Spokane, ***so*** we are now in the process of recruiting new personnel in this city.

Sow (VERB; to scatter seed)—This equipment can ***sow*** more seed in a day than any 15 farmhands.

Shall/Will

Shall (HELPING VERB; denotes future time in the first person in formal writing)—I ***shall*** give your request the utmost consideration. We ***shall*** initiate legal proceedings on November 1.
Will (HELPING VERB; used with all three persons in business style)—I (or We) ***will*** call you tomorrow. You ***will*** receive your refund when you return the merchandise. He (or She or They) ***will*** finish the project according to schedule unless he (or she or they) encounter(s) bad weather conditions.

She: see Her.

Shear/Sheer

Shear (VERB; to cut; to strip)—When do you plan to ***shear*** the sheep this spring so that we can ship the wool for processing? The mechanic had to ***shear*** off the bolts before he could remove the wheel.
Sheer (ADJECTIVE; transparently thin; utter; steep)—None of these ***sheer*** fabrics are suitable for the kind of draperies we have in mind. Attending this seminar was a ***sheer*** waste of time. A number of mountain climbers have successfully scaled these ***sheer*** cliffs.

Shone/Shown

Shone (VERB; past tense and past participle of *to shine*)—The sun ***shone*** brightly throughout the day. If flashing red lights had been ***shone*** through the dense fog, this series of accidents might have been avoided.
Shown (VERB; past participle of *to show*)—The PowerPoint presentation describing our new products has been ***shown*** to all our salespeople and is available for their use in sales presentations.

Should/Would

Should (HELPING VERB; denotes future time in the first person in formal writing; used to express obligation; used to express expectation)—We ***should*** appreciate your returning the signed contracts by Friday, March 23. Our spa ***should*** investigate showcasing its services on Facebook. The cast ***should*** return from its European tour by September 1.
Would (HELPING VERB; used with all three persons in business style)—I (or We) ***would*** appreciate receiving a copy of this month's sales report. She (or He or They) said that she (or he or they) ***would*** be willing to work overtime if the project is not finished by 5 p.m. Did you say you ***would*** be interested in having a demonstration of our new Model 5610 all-in-one printer?

Shown: see Shone.

Sight: see Cite.

Sit: see Set.

Site: see Cite.

So: see Sew.

Soar/Sore

Soar (VERB; to fly aloft or about; to rise or increase dramatically)—The proliferation of drones ***soaring*** through the air is increasingly pointing out the need for regulations regarding this new technology. News of the merger will cause the price of our stock to ***soar***.

Sore (ADJECTIVE; painfully sensitive)—If you overdo an exercise program, your muscles will be ***sore*** for several days. Last year's financial losses have become a ***sore*** point for our company president.

Sole/Soul

Sole (NOUN; the undersurface of a foot. ADJECTIVE; being the only one)—When you walk, distribute your weight evenly between the ***sole*** and the heel of your foot. John is the ***sole*** heir to his father's fortune.

Soul (NOUN; the immaterial essence of an individual; a living example of moral principle)—Most contemporary religions believe that the ***soul*** of an individual continues on after his or her physical death. Mr. Perry is the ***soul*** of honesty and integrity.

Some/Somewhat

Some (ADJECTIVE; an indefinite amount)—Before we move into our new offices, we will need to have a contractor make ***some*** structural alterations. ***Some*** clients have requested more information about our utility stock offerings.

Somewhat (ADVERB; to some degree)—Our sales force feels that your sales projections for next year are ***somewhat*** optimistic. Our staff is ***somewhat*** disappointed in the vice president's choice of manager for our department.

Some time/Sometime/Sometimes

Some time (ADJECTIVE + NOUN; a period of time)—Our staff will need ***some time*** to review your proposal before we can make a decision. ***Some time*** ago I received an e-mail from you describing your update for Snagit.

Sometime (ADVERB; an indefinite time, anytime)—Your order should be delivered ***sometime*** early next week. The president and his executive staff will inspect the plant operations ***sometime*** within the next two weeks.

Sometimes (ADVERB; occasionally)—***Sometimes*** our firm needs to hire personnel from temporary agencies. Although I would always like to approve your vacation requests, ***sometimes*** our work schedule does not permit me to do so.

Somewhat: see Some.

Sore: see Soar.

Soul: see Sole.

Sow: see Sew.

Staid/Stayed

Staid (ADJECTIVE; sedate, composed)—Our usually ***staid*** supervisor surprised us with her rendition of "Hello, Dolly!" in the company talent show. A ***staid*** individual like Mr. Bradley is needed to handle this delicate situation.

Stayed (VERB; past tense and past participle of *to stay*)—She ***stayed*** long after regular hours to finish the report.

Stationary/Stationery

Stationary (ADJECTIVE; not movable or not moving)—Only two of the interior walls in this office suite are ***stationary***. All the hair stylists' stations in this salon are ***stationary***. The population of this county has remained ***stationary*** during the past three years.

Stationery (NOUN or ADJECTIVE; writing material or related to writing materials)—Prepare this letter on Mr. Parks' personal ***stationery***. Our order for additional ***stationery*** supplies is scheduled to arrive tomorrow.

Statue/Stature/Statute

Statue (NOUN; a carved or molded image of someone or something)—Meet me in front of the ***statue*** of Lincoln at 2 p.m. Our company specializes in the manufacture and distribution of religious ***statues***.

Stature (NOUN; the height of an object or a body; status gained by attainment)—The ***stature*** alone of the pyramids is overwhelming. Dr. Sunayama is a person of great ***stature*** within the community.

Statute (NOUN; a law enacted by a legislature)—A recently enacted ***statute*** prohibits the use of handheld cell phones while driving. ***Statutes*** in this state prohibit gambling in any form.

Stayed: see Staid.

Straight/Strait

Straight (ADJECTIVE; free of bends, curves, or angles. ADVERB; in a direct manner)—Use a ruler with a ***straight*** edge to draw these lines. Ms. Torti always seems able to go ***straight*** to the source of a problem.

Strait (NOUN; a narrow space or passage connecting two bodies of water)—The ship and its cargo were damaged while going through the ***strait***. This cruise is scheduled to pass through the ***Strait*** of Magellan.

Suit/Suite

Suit (NOUN ['süt]; an action filed in court; a set of garments)—A & Z Computer Corporation has already filed a ***suit*** against Compco for patent infringements. Be sure to wear a dark-colored business ***suit*** for the interview.

Suite (NOUN ['swēt]; a group of things forming a unit; a set)—Were you able to reserve a ***suite*** for the week of April 3 at the Hyatt Regency? (Here *suite* refers to a group of rooms.) How many pieces are featured in this bedroom ***suite***? (In this example *suite* refers to pieces of furniture in a set.)

Sure/Surely

Sure (ADJECTIVE; an adjective or subject complement meaning "certain" or "positive")—Nancy was ***sure*** she had made the right decision to accept the position with Latham, Clayton & Montgomery after just one week working at the firm.

Surely (ADVERB; certainly or undoubtedly)—Our employees will ***surely*** be pleased with the new benefit package in their contract.

Take: see Bring.

Tare/Tear/Tier

Tare (NOUN ['ter—sounds like *care*]; a deduction from the gross weight of goods and their container made to allow for the weight of the container, the weight of the container itself)—The ***tare*** on this shipment is 210 pounds.
Tear (NOUN ['tir]; a saline fluid that flows from the eye, usually signifying distress or extreme joy)—A ***tear*** flowed down the child's face as she viewed her brother in the hospital bed.
Tear (VERB ['ter]; to pull apart or rip. NOUN ['ter]; a rip)—When you open the envelope, be careful not to ***tear*** its contents. The customer returned the sweater because it had a ***tear*** in the sleeve.
Tier (NOUN ['tir]; rows, levels, or ranks placed one above the other)—Our company's season ticket seating is located on the first ***tier*** of the stadium.

Temperature: see Fever.

Than/Then

Than (CONJUNCTION; used to show comparison)—Ms. Espinoza has more experience ***than*** I in writing contract proposals. This construction project is taking longer ***than*** we had anticipated.
Then (ADVERB; at that time)—Once all the data has been gathered, you may ***then*** begin organizing the report. After you have applied for admission to the college, only ***then*** may we process your application for financial aid.

That/Which

That (PRONOUN; refers to animals or things; introduces a restrictive or essential subordinate clause)—All dogs ***that*** are found wandering in the streets will be impounded. We have in stock, Ms. Wells, all the items ***that*** you ordered.
Which (PRONOUN; refers to animals or things; introduces a nonrestrictive or nonessential subordinate clause)—The security staff recommended that we acquire a watchdog, ***which*** would be kept inside the plant at night. Our new credit system, ***which*** will be installed next week, will cost almost $50,000.

Their/There/They're

Their (PRONOUN USED AS ADJECTIVE; the possessive form of *they*)—As a result of ***their*** recommendation, we installed an Apex Security System in our main warehouse. All ***their*** accountants are certified public accountants (CPAs).
There (ADVERB; at that place or at that point)—Please be ***there*** promptly at ten o'clock in the morning. My goal was to have lost 15 pounds by April 1, but I am not ***there*** yet.
They're (PRONOUN + VERB; the contraction of *they are*)—Although the union representatives rejected our first offer, ***they're*** willing to consider our second proposal. ***They're*** still on vacation.

Theirs/There's

Theirs (PRONOUN; possessive form of *they*)—This copy of the contract is ***theirs***. ***Theirs*** was the only car left in the parking lot.

There's (PRONOUN + VERB; contraction of *there is* or *there has*)—***There's*** still much to be done before we can open our new store. ***There's*** been too much time and money spent in attempting to obtain a zoning change for this property.

Them/They

Them (PRONOUN; a direct object, an indirect object, or an object of a preposition)—I asked ***them*** to wait outside. I sent ***them*** a statement last week. I waited for ***them*** all morning.
They (PRONOUN; subject of a clause or a complement pronoun)—***They*** are meeting with the Board of Directors this afternoon. The two persons who cochaired the committee were ***they***.

Then: see Than.

There: see Their.

There's: see Theirs.

They: see Them.

They're: see Their.

Threw/Through/Thru

Threw (VERB; past tense of *to throw*)—As I reviewed all the documents in the files, I ***threw*** away those documents that were no longer needed. The pitcher ***threw*** a curveball, which resulted in the last strike.
Through (PREPOSITION; in one end and out the other; movement within a large expanse; during the period of; as a consequence of)—While you are in Atlanta, will your schedule permit a tour ***through*** the plant? The pigeons flew gracefully ***through*** the air. You may order this software at a 15 percent discount from June 15 ***through*** June 30. We have retained this account ***through*** your diligent efforts.
Thru (a variation of *through* that is not acceptable for business writing)

Tier: see Tare.

To/Too/Two

To (PREPOSITION; function word to indicate direction toward. THE SIGN OF AN INFINITIVE; e.g., *to go*)—Please return these materials ***to*** me when you have finished reviewing them. She wanted ***to*** see for herself the condition of the plant cafeteria.
Too (ADVERB; also; to an excessive extent; very)—I was there ***too***. Please e-mail me a copy of your résumé ***too***. Because the office was ***too*** noisy, I had difficulty hearing you on the telephone. ***Too*** many of our employees have applied for vacation days during our busiest season. My client did not seem ***too*** interested in purchasing a home in this area. Students' rooms on the third floor of the dormitory are ***too*** messy.
Two (NOUN; the number between ***one*** and ***three***)—There was just too much work for the ***two*** of us to finish by five o'clock. The ***two*** finalists will compete for the part of Donna next week.

Tortuous/Torturous

Tortuous (ADJECTIVE; winding, twisting)—In Maui the ***tortuous*** road leading to Hana Bay has been the scene of many accidents. For this performance the gymnasts performed ***tortuous*** movements to emulate jungle snakes.
Torturous (ADJECTIVE; causing pain)—Recovering from knee surgery can be a ***torturous*** experience. Filling out all these forms is a ***torturous*** task.

Toward/Towards

Toward (PREPOSITION; in the direction of)—Set up these workstations so that all the screens on the computer monitors face ***toward*** the west wall.
Towards (secondary form of *toward*; use *toward* instead of *towards* in business writing)

Uninterested: see Disinterested.

Us/We

Us (PRONOUN; a direct object, an indirect object, or an object of a preposition)—The vice president took ***us*** on a tour of the plant. The manager gave ***us*** a copy of the annual report. The reception was planned for ***us***.
We (PRONOUN; the subject of a sentence or a clause; a complement pronoun)—***We*** must decide upon a definite course of action by 3 p.m. The singers selected to perform for this special broadcast were ***we***.

Vain/Van/Vane/Vein

Vain (ADJECTIVE; unduly proud or conceited)—Tim would be more popular with his coworkers if he were not so ***vain***.
Van (NOUN; a covered truck)—Our hospital ***van*** is used primarily for transporting patients.
Vane (NOUN; a thin object used to show wind direction)—The weather ***vane*** indicated that the wind was coming from a westward direction.
Vein (NOUN; a tubular vessel that carries blood to the heart; mode or style)—The laboratory technician was able to locate easily a ***vein*** in the elderly patient's arm to draw sufficient blood for the tests ordered by the doctor. Although Mr. Bates had been warned about his unfriendly attitude toward other employees, he continued to behave in that ***vein***.

Vary/Very

Vary (VERB; to change)—The new advertising manager said that for the time being he would not request us to ***vary*** any procedures.
Very (ADVERB; extremely)—These figures are ***very*** difficult to verify from the available information.

Vein: see Vain.

Vice/Vise

Vice (NOUN; immoral habit; personal fault)—Drug abuse by America's populace is a ***vice*** that must be curtailed. Cigar smoking is his only ***vice***.
Vise (NOUN; a clamp. ADJECTIVE; strong hold or squeeze)—Please order a ***vise*** for our new carpenter. He shook my hand with a ***vise***-like grip.

Waive/Wave

Waive (VERB; to relinquish; to refrain from enforcing)—Do you ***waive*** your right to a jury trial? You must petition the dean of academic affairs to ***waive*** this requirement.
Wave (VERB; to swing something back and forth or up and down)—The angry customer was determined to ***wave*** his bill in everyone's face.

Waiver/Waver

Waiver (NOUN; the relinquishment of a claim)—Please sign the enclosed ***waiver*** to release our company from any further responsibility for your injury.
Waver (VERB; to shake or fluctuate)—I believe Mr. Doyle is beginning to ***waver*** concerning our request to update our accounting software.

Wave: see Waive.

Waver: see Waiver.

We: see Us.

Weather/Whether

Weather (VERB; to bear up against. NOUN; the state of the atmosphere)—We are pleased that you were able to ***weather*** the high rate of employee turnover during the summer months. Tomorrow's ***weather*** will bring us scattered showers and a high temperature of 50 degrees.
Whether (CONJUNCTION; an introduction of alternatives)—We will not know until next week ***whether*** our company or Artistry in Motion will be awarded the contract.

Well: see Good.

Whether: see Weather.

Which: see That.

Who/Whom

Who (PRONOUN; the subject of a subordinate clause or a complement pronoun)—I was the person ***who*** invited you to attend. Do you know ***who*** was hired to fill the vacancy in our department? None of us on the staff have been informed ***who*** the new manager may be. I cannot tell you ***who*** the caller might have been. (See Section 1–16j for additional information on the use of *who* and *whom*.)
Whom (PRONOUN; a direct object or an object of a preposition)—No one yet knows ***whom*** the vice president has recommended to become his successor. ***Whom*** have you hired as your assistant? From ***whom*** did you receive this information? Here is the address of the person with ***whom*** we met for legal assistance. (See Section 1–16j for additional information on the use of *who* and *whom*.)

Whole: see Hole.

Wholly: see Holy.

Whom: see Who.

Who's/Whose

Who's (PRONOUN + VERB; a contraction of *who is*)—Please let me know ***who's*** taking over your responsibilities during your leave of absence.

Whose (PRONOUN USED AS ADJECTIVE; possessive form of *who*)—Mr. Long is the vice president ***whose*** position was eliminated.

Will: see Shall.

Would: see Should.

Wring: see Ring.

Wrote: see Rote.

Your/You're

Your (PRONOUN USED AS ADJECTIVE; possessive form of *you*)—***Your*** assistant provided me with a copy of the minutes from our last committee meeting.

You're (PRONOUN + VERB; contraction of *you are*)—If ***you're*** interested in contacting the authors of *HOW 14*, please e-mail us at lynclarkpc@hotmail.com.

8

Elements of Writing Style

Elements of Writing Style Solution Finder

Developing an Effective Writing Style

Your writing style effectiveness is governed by how well you can communicate ideas. Effective written communication is often thought to be an art, but in reality it is a combination of art and a number of applied skills—using language effectively, organizing ideas, and analyzing an audience. Writing style effectiveness can be learned through practice and the application of basic writing principles. Learn to use words effectively; construct meaningful, interesting sentences; group sentences into related paragraphs; and organize the presentation into a smooth-flowing composition that leads the reader seamlessly from one idea to the next. Apply the following principles to improve your communication effectiveness.

Using Words Effectively

8–1 Short, Simple Words

a. Use short, simple words in your written communication. Simple words are easier to read and to understand.

simple word substitutes

about	*for*	approximately
aware	*for*	cognizant
change	*for*	modification
equal	*for*	commensurate
improve	*for*	ameliorate
pay, salary	*for*	remuneration
understand	*for*	comprehend
use	*for*	utilize

simple words in sentences

Poor: Are you **cognizant** that contract negotiations have had an **auspicious** beginning?

Better: Are you **aware** that contract negotiations have had a **favorable** beginning?

Poor: If a better opportunity **materializes**, we will **terminate** our negotiations with Tele-Corps.

Better: If a better opportunity **arises**, we will **end** our negotiations with Tele-Corps.

b. Substitute simple words for wordy phrases.

simple words as substitutes

when	*for*	until such time as
if	*for*	in the event that
to	*for*	in order to
now	*for*	at the present time
since	*for*	in view of the fact that
while	*for*	during which time

simple words in sentences

Poor: **In spite of the fact that** Robert has little **experience in the field of teaching**, he shows considerable promise.

Better: **Although** Robert has little **teaching experience**, he shows considerable promise.

Poor: **I wish to take this opportunity to thank you** for completing the online questionnaire.

Better: **Thank you** for completing the online questionnaire.

c. Use technical terms only when you are sure that the reader understands them. When using an abbreviation, either (1) write out the complete form and place the abbreviation in parentheses after the complete form or (2) write the abbreviation and place the complete form in parentheses after the abbreviation.

technical term

How many **Universal Serial Bus ports** are located on the front panel of the central processing unit of your Model XP5 Alpha desktop system? (Recipient understands the term.)

abbreviation

Fall applications for **California State University, Northridge (CSUN),** are due April 1. On-campus residence facilities are limited; therefore, students who wish to reside in the **CSUN**-sponsored housing facilities must submit their request at the time they submit their application.

The new contract, which has been posted on the company Web site, is in a **PDF (Portable Document Format)** file and may be read with Adobe Acrobat Reader. Other recently posted **PDF** files contain procedures for selecting a benefits package and policies related to paid vacation time and illness days.

8–2 Modern Language

a. Use modern, up-to-date language in place of outdated expressions that commonly appear in written business communications.

modern substitutes for outdated expressions

attached	*for*	attached hereto
because	*for*	due to *or* due to the fact that
enclosed	*for*	enclosed please find
for	*for*	in the amount of
please	*for*	kindly
sending separately	*for*	sending under separate cover

modern substitutes in sentences

Poor: **Thanking you in advance** for approving my petition.
Better: **I would appreciate** your approving my petition.

Poor: I **trust** that we can count on you to accept the chairmanship of the Salary Committee.
Better: I **hope** that we can count on you to accept the chairmanship of the Salary Committee.

b. Rely on modern terms that eliminate gender bias. When referring in a general way to groups of men and women, use the plural form if possible to avoid the use of any singular pronouns (*his* or *her* and *him* or *her*).

modern substitutes to eliminate gender bias

salesperson	*for*	salesman, saleslady
chair, chairperson	*for*	chairman
flight attendant	*for*	stewardess, steward
server	*for*	waiter, waitress
firefighter	*for*	fireman
police officer	*for*	policeman
humanity	*for*	mankind
supervisor	*for*	foreman
technician	*for*	repairman
birth name	*for*	maiden name

gender bias eliminated in sentences

Poor: All the stones in the jewelry we manufacture are **man-made**.
Better: All the stones in the jewelry we manufacture are **synthetic**.

Poor: Fans were gathered at the stage door to obtain the **actress's** autograph.
Better: Fans were gathered at the stage door to obtain the **performer's** autograph.

gender bias eliminated in group references

Poor: **Each employee** will receive a new identification badge that includes the name of **his** or **her** department.

Better: **All employees** will receive a new identification badge that includes the name of **their** department.

Poor: **Every attorney** in this firm must meet **his** or **her** quota of billable hours by December 31.

Better: **Attorneys** in this firm must meet **their** quota of billable hours by December 31.

8–3 Bias-Free Language

a. When referring to a person either by name or position, do not mention the person's race, ethnicity, or religion.

Poor: The **new Hispanic mayor** of Los Angeles will address the state legislature next week.

Better: The **new mayor** of Los Angeles will address the state legislature next week.

Poor: **Tom Washington, the black supervisor**, reported the discrepancy immediately to the vice president.

Better: **Tom Washington** reported the discrepancy immediately to the vice president.

b. When referring to a person, do not mention the person's age.

Poor: **Carmen González, 47**, has been promoted to vice president of marketing.

Better: **Carmen González** has been promoted to vice president of marketing.

c. In general references to an individual with a disability, do not mention the person's disability. Refer to disabilities only when they are relevant to the meaning of the sentence.

Poor: This patio set has been reserved by **the lady in a wheelchair**.

Better: This patio set has been reserved by **another customer**.

Poor: **Bob Smith, who is deaf**, earned an *A* on the first history test.

Better: **Bob Smith** earned an *A* on the first history test.

But: The parking slots painted with a blue wheelchair symbol are reserved exclusively for **persons with disabilities** who have a placard or a special license plate issued by the state.

But: **Hearing-impaired** students may request an interpreter for each class from the Office of Special Services.

8–4 Specific Nouns and Adjectives

a. Whenever possible, use specific nouns and adjectives in your sentences. Specific words provide a vivid picture in the reader's mind and reduce the need for additional explanations.

requires additional explanation

Originator:	"May I purchase a new printer for our department?"
Respondent:	"Black-and-white or color printer?"
Originator:	"Color printer."
Respondent:	"Laser or ink-jet?"
Originator:	"Laser."
Respondent:	"Brother, Dell, Hewlett-Packard, or Xerox?"
Originator:	"Hewlett-Packard."
Respondent:	"Which model, and how much does it cost?"
Originator:	"HP LaserJet Enterprise 500 color Printer M551n that costs $569.99."
Respondent:	"By the way, for what department?"

needed information supplied initially

May the Accounting Department purchase a Hewlett-Packard LaserJet 500 color Printer M551n printer, which costs $569.99 (plus sales tax and shipping), to replace the eight-year-old black-and-white laser printer currently in the department?

b. Avoid general statements when specific words will provide appropriate, exacting information. Always provide the day, date, time, and location in meeting notices. Whenever a response is expected and timing is important, give a date by when the response is needed.

general statements to be avoided

Poor: Please let us know **at your earliest convenience** whether you prefer a room with two double beds or a king-size bed.

Better: Please let us know **by Friday, March 8**, whether you prefer a room with two double beds or a king-size bed.

Poor: To process your loan application before **the projected closing escrow date**, we will need this information **as soon as possible**.

Better: To process your loan application **before the projected June 8 escrow closing date**, we will need this information by **May 10**.

information for meeting notices

The next **Technology Committee** meeting will be held on **Wednesday, October 11, from 1:15 until 2:30 p.m. in Room 300, the General Conference Room.**

8–5 Positive Words and Negative Words

a. Experienced writers use positive words as much as possible and avoid negative words or words with negative connotations. Readers respond more favorably to messages that reflect a positive tone (and use positive words) even though they may be conveying disappointing or negative news.

b. Use words such as the following in your messages:

appreciate	thank you	possible	please
pleased	improve	satisfaction	timely
careful	pleasure	advantage	reliable
grateful	fortunate	benefit	welcome

c. Avoid using the following words and similar ones in your messages:

blame	careless	complaint	defective
delay	dissatisfied	error	failure
fault	impossible	mistake	negligent
poor	trouble	unsatisfactory	wrong

8–6 Synonyms

a. Add interest to your writing by using synonyms. Colorless and overused words are not incorrect; however, often synonyms can provide a more vivid picture for the reader.

colorless and overused words

good	fine	bad	super
nice	little	big	lovely
awful	great	fantastic	said

synonym substitutes

The president **said** that	The president **forecasted** that . . . .
Our **fine** artists will	Our **creative** artists will . . . .
. . . a **good** sales campaign.	. . . an **effective** sales campaign.
. . . a **nice** supervisor.	. . . a **well-liked** supervisor.
. . . a **little** wire.	. . . a **thin** wire.

b. Use synonyms to avoid repeating the same term throughout your message. Consult a thesaurus to assist you with locating suitable synonyms.

Poor: Our **employment** agency locates **employment** for full-time, part-time, and temporary **employees**. Although we predominantly find **employment** for accountants, we also offer services to individuals in related areas of **employment**.

Better: Our **employment** agency locates **jobs** for full-time, part-time, and temporary **applicants**. Although we predominantly find **positions** for accountants, we also offer services to individuals in related **occupations**.

Creating Sentences

8–7 Sentence Patterns[1]

a. Use a variety of sentence patterns to add interest to your messages.

(1) *The simple sentence.* Simple sentences express a single idea. They are complete thoughts that contain a subject and a verb and make sense. Simple sentences are the most frequently used type in business messages, but they can result in choppy writing if overused. Use a simple sentence to emphasize an idea.

simple sentence
All salespersons in our division have met their quotas for this month.

John submitted this week's ad to our local newspapers.

Were you invited to the grand opening of our Dayton office?

(2) *The compound sentence.* Compound sentences consist of two closely related simple sentences that are joined by a conjunction, a semicolon, or a transitional expression. They are used to give equal emphasis to two related ideas and to add variety to a person's writing style.

compound sentence
All arrangements for our user conference have been confirmed, and we have received registration fees from all the participants.

Your staff identification card has been replaced; you may pick it up in the Business Office.

We have e-mailed this information to our clients; however, not all our clients have responded.

(3) *The complex sentence.* Complex sentences consist of an independent clause (simple sentence) and a subordinate clause. They are used to show a close relationship between two ideas while emphasizing one idea over the other.

complex sentence
Because your application was received after the deadline date, your name has been placed on a waiting list for admittance to the physical therapy technician program.

Although we invested thousands of advertising dollars, our Portland campaign increased sales by only 2 percent in the targeted area.

---

[1]For an explanation of and additional information on sentence patterns—simple sentences, compound sentences, complex sentences, and compound-complex sentences—see Chapter 1, Grammar and Usage, Section 1–40.

Please respond to our executive secretary if you will be able to attend this seminar.

(4) *The compound-complex sentence.* Compound-complex sentences consist of two independent clauses (simple sentences) and at least one subordinate clause. Such sentences are used to give equal emphasis to two closely related ideas but at the same time include at least one additional idea requiring lesser emphasis.

compound-complex sentence
Morgan agreed to transfer to the company's new location, but Jordan decided to accept the severance package because his family did not wish to relocate.

This stock is continuing to decline; we should sell our shares before we lose more money.

If you accept this promotion, you will undergo six months' training at full salary and you must commit to remain with the company for at least three years.

Note the difference between the following two paragraph examples.

paragraph consisting solely of simple sentences
We received your fax this morning. Thank you for your order. You will receive a 10 percent discount during our sale. We will ship your order within the next two days. We will charge your credit card $193.50 for the cost of the merchandise, the tax, and the shipping charges.

paragraph edited to achieve sentence variety
Thank you for your faxed order, which arrived this morning. Your order will be shipped by May 12, and a 10 percent discount will be applied during this sale period. Total charges to your credit card for the merchandise, tax, and shipping amount to $193.50. (Complex sentence, compound sentence, simple sentence)

b. Besides using simple, compound, complex, and compound-complex sentences to add interest to your writing style, begin your sentences with a variety of grammatical constructions such as nouns, pronouns, verbs, adjectives, adverbs, prepositions, or conjunctions:

(1) Nouns and pronouns that act as subjects of a sentence

(2) Infinitives and verbs that are used to command or suggest

(3) Articles (*a, an, the*) and other adjectives that act as modifiers

(4) Adverbs that relate to a following verb or that provide transition

(5) Prepositions that begin introductory phrases

(6) Conjunctions that begin introductory clauses and that are used to correlate ideas

noun or pronoun as the subject of a sentence

Retailers throughout the country are experiencing peak holiday sales.

Chris has been promoted to manager of the Marketing Department.

You are invited to attend the grand opening of our Wilshire store, which will be held on Friday, October 1.

I will notify you when your order arrives at our store.

infinitive

To receive information about our software updates, please enter your e-mail address.

To complete the annual sales report, we must receive December's figures from the Accounting Department.

To purchase the property at this time would not be advisable.

To close the Westwood store before December would be a serious mistake.

verb used to command or suggest

Accept any legitimate offer over $375,000.

Lock all the doors and set the alarm if you are the last one to leave the salon.

Distribute this information to all employees who are eligible for medical benefits.

Let me know the results of the survey as soon as you have had an opportunity to analyze the data.

article or other adjective

The company cannot afford to purchase additional property at this time.

An important factor we must consider is the impact of gas prices on consumer demand for SUVs.

Charity organizations such as the Foundation for the Junior Blind operate solely on contributions.

Local governments are experiencing financial setbacks from the declining prices of homes and condominiums in this state.

Tony's office has been moved to the third floor.

Our property tax this year increased 15 percent.

Any questions you may have about the installation of this software should be directed to our Technical Support Department.

regular adverb or transitional adverb

Occasionally we offer this china pattern at a discounted price on our Web site.

Usually this class is offered during spring semesters only.

Please hold children by hand on the escalator.

Therefore, you may use your store credit in any one of our 32 locations.

Consequently, only three of the four applicants recommended for hire will be processed.

preposition that begins an introductory phrase
On July 1 our college district will begin a new budgeting cycle.

For the past month, our Human Resources Department has been trying to locate a qualified replacement for my former administrative assistant.

By focusing on strategies to increase our client base, we can then begin to anticipate additional revenue.

With only a few hundred dollars, the Sutter family began this successful hotdog chain.

conjunction that begins an introductory clause
As soon as we receive your completed credit application, we will begin processing your request for an equity loan.

If anyone in your department is interested in attending this conference, please let me know.

When Microsoft released Windows 10, our company began developing a plan to upgrade to this operating system.

Because two of the applicants have exceptional qualifications for the posted position, we have decided to offer both of them a contract.

correlating conjunctions
Both the production editor **and** her assistant will review the manuscript.

Neither the mayoral incumbent **nor** his primary challenger accepted the invitation from our station for a television debate.

Not only the Spanish-style architecture **but also** the surrounding landscape has made this building the most aesthetically pleasing one in the industrial complex.

Either sign and return the enclosed contract by May 31 **or** return the trial Kelby Robo-Clean system you received on May 1.

8–8 Active and Passive Voice

a. In the active voice, the subject of the sentence has done, is doing, or will be doing the action. The active voice is more commonly used in business messages than the passive voice; however, both forms have their uses.

The **design team** at Nelson & Associates **worked** many hours to provide these miniature display models of the Technology Center.

Many **employees** in our Customer Service Department **speak** more than one language fluently.

Next month two **staff members** located in our Phoenix office **will transfer** to the Tucson office.

b. In the passive voice, the subject of the sentence is acted upon. It has been done to, is being done to, or will be done to. This sentence construction requires a *being* verb helper (e.g., *is, are, was, were, been*) with the past participle of the verb, which allows the "doer" to hide in a cloak of ambiguity.

Passive: For a variety of reasons, the **project** under construction **was assigned** to the Houston office instead of the Dallas office.
Active: For a variety of reasons, the **vice president assigned** the project under construction to the Houston office instead of the Dallas office.

Passive: All **applications** for admission received after May 15 **are being denied**.
Active: The **dean of admissions is denying** all applications for admission received after May 15.

Passive: A $25 late-payment **fee will be charged** for payments received after the 15th of the month.
Active: Our **Credit Department charges** a $25 late-payment fee for payments received after the 15th of the month.

c. Writers generally prefer the active voice to communicate their ideas directly and vividly. Most sentences are written in the active voice because the active voice is more emphatic and interesting than the passive voice.

(1) Use the active voice as the prevalent construction for your sentences. Because the active voice is more direct, straightforward, and natural, sentences using this style are easier to read and to understand.

(2) Use the active voice to emphasize an idea. Information written in the active voice stands out more vividly in the reader's mind.

(3) Use the active voice to convey positive ideas and information. Because the active voice is the voice of emphasis, you will want to emphasize positive ideas and positive information.

emphasize an idea
You will receive a corrected copy of the invoice by Friday.

By Monday, March 1, our **network manager will have installed** the update for all Office 2013 programs.

Twelve of the seminar participants **registered** to receive more information about our investment opportunities.

convey positive ideas and information

The **Board of Directors has approved** your request to transfer to the San Francisco office.

Congratulations! The **president selected** you to be her executive assistant.

The **computers** you ordered from Comp-U-Tab **arrived** this morning.

d. The passive voice is often thought of as the voice of de-emphasis. Although de-emphasis is part of its role, the passive voice has other uses.

(1) Use the passive voice to convey a negative idea. Avoid "placing blame" on a person or a group by not mentioning who does what. Because the passive voice is less vivid, the effect on the reader is viewed as being less severe. Use of the passive voice often provides the right approach for sensitive situations.

(2) Use the passive voice to achieve variety in your writing style. Messages written entirely in the active voice do not distinguish between important ideas and ideas of lesser importance. Also, messages written entirely in the active voice are often not as interesting as those that use a combination of the active voice and the passive voice.

passive voice to convey a negative idea

Active: We are returning your check because you forgot to sign it.
Passive: The enclosed check is being returned for signature.
Active: Our manager denied Stephen's request for a salary advance.
Passive: Stephen's request for a salary advance was not approved.
Active: We sell Cut 'n Curl products only through authorized retailers.
Passive: Cut 'n Curl products are sold only through authorized retailers.
Active: We cannot refund the purchase price because you purchased the camera more than 60 days ago.
Passive: Because the camera was purchased more than 60 days ago, the purchase price cannot be refunded.
Better: Because the camera was purchased more than 60 days ago, this sale is not eligible for a refund. (Combination of passive and active voice)

passive voice to achieve variety in writing style

I appreciate your setting up the Research Committee meeting for Thursday, October 21. Yes, I will report on the progress of the customer survey. **All the surveys have been collected**, and our staff has begun to analyze the data. I hope to be able to report some preliminary findings at the meeting.

This afternoon **I was denied access to SAP** so I could not view my current budget information. **My user ID was not recognized by the system**. Because the Help Desk referred me to my network administrator, I am e-mailing you. Can you help me gain access to SAP? I would certainly appreciate your assistance.

Welcome to Lakefield College! **Your application for admittance has been accepted**. You are one of the 750 students (from 4,500 applicants) **who have been selected** for the freshman class. We feel confident that you will benefit and enjoy your educational experience here at Lakefield.

8–9 Emphasizing and De-emphasizing Ideas

a. Use various ways to emphasize an idea. In some cases individual sentences may be effective; in other situations you may need to use a paragraph or a listing. Besides saying that an idea is important or repeating it, use the following techniques to emphasize an idea:

(1) Place the idea in a simple sentence.

(2) Use the active voice.

(3) Confine the idea to a one-sentence paragraph.

(4) Use direct address to tie in the idea with the reader's name.

(5) Place the idea in boldface type.

(6) Place the idea at the beginning or at the end of a paragraph.

(7) Use a listing to emphasize important aspects of an idea.

idea emphasized in a simple sentence
Sales in our office have decreased 7.8 percent since last year.

May I please have your response before 10 a.m. tomorrow.

idea emphasized using the active voice
Our company vice president has resigned to accept a position with one of our competitors.

Please sign and return this form by Friday, September 12.

idea in a one-sentence paragraph
If you wish to make a change in your medical insurance carrier, you must fill out, sign, and return the enclosed form in the envelope provided by Friday, October 15.

idea used with the reader's name
You may, Tom, wish to consider the impact of rising gasoline prices before you make your decision.

Travel expense for our representatives, Ellen, is the major consideration in selecting the city for our next national sales meeting.

idea placed in boldface type
Sale prices on the merchandise listed in the enclosed catalog will be valid only until January 31.

To be eligible for this discount, you will need to register online at our Web site.

idea placed at the beginning of a paragraph
Please let me know if you will be available to coordinate the business communication sessions. You may either e-mail me (stw9482916048@aol.com) or call me (818-555-3471). I look forward to hearing from you.

Our new branch office will be located in Phoenix. After researching several locations, the Board of Directors selected this Arizona city to establish a new office. Phoenix is one of the fastest-growing cities in the United States, and it presents a financial opportunity for Farrow Home Mortgage.

idea placed at the end of a paragraph
Employees at Atlas Corporation are expected to arrive at 8 a.m. and work their shift, which ends at 4:30 p.m. Our records show that you are continually late, arriving sometimes between 9 a.m. and 9:15 a.m. You have been warned about being habitually late. The next time you do not arrive by 8 a.m., you will be eligible for dismissal.

During the past year, construction costs have risen 12 percent compared to previous years' annual increases ranging from 2 to 3 percent. Increases have been attributed to the expansion of construction worldwide, which has resulted in severe competition for available resources—steel, lumber, and personnel. Building projects that were costed out last year fall short by today's pricing standards. As a result, the new Science Center planned for our South Campus has a $12.3 million shortfall.

ideas placed in a listing
Selection criteria for the scholarship awards follow:

(1) Academic record
(2) Campus activities
(3) Community service

To set up a wireless network within your home or small business, you will need the following:

- A cable or DSL connection to the Internet
- A wireless access-point router
- Wireless network cards for all computers with wireless connectivity

b. Written messages must sometimes convey negative news or information that is contrary to the reader's expectations. Use voice, sentence structure, and paragraph organization to soften the impact created by the conveyance of negative ideas and information.

(1) Use the passive voice to express a negative or unpleasant idea. The passive voice is helpful when your purpose is to sound less offensive.

(2) Phrase the negative information positively when possible.

(3) Use the subjunctive mood to refuse a request.

(4) Camouflage the negative or unpleasant idea in a complex sentence.

(5) Locate the negative idea in the middle of a paragraph.

passive voice for a negative idea

Your recent application for a charge account has not been approved.

Because the evening dress has been worn, it is not eligible to be returned for a refund.

A review of your academic record for the past three semesters has resulted in your being placed on probation beginning next semester.

negative idea phrased positively

You may still buy the Model 400 printer and charge the purchase to your account even though the printer is no longer available at the sale price.

Glenn Shoes are no longer available in our retail stores, but you may purchase them online at www.glennshoes.com.

Our wireless Internet access components are sold only through authorized dealers.

subjunctive mood to refuse a request

I wish substituting your experience for the master's degree requirement were possible, but the state minimum qualifications for the assistant professor of accounting position require an earned master's degree.

If I were an attorney, I would be pleased to answer your question. May I suggest . . . .

I wish I were able to provide you with the information you requested, but privacy laws prohibit my releasing any information about a college student's course progress to anyone other than the student—even to the student's parent.

If I were not going to be out of the country on company business during April, I would have eagerly accepted your invitation to conduct a session at the marketing conference on April 17.

If retrieving the specific information you requested from our database were possible, I would have been pleased to do so. However, ...

I wish I were available to attend the Research and Development Committee meeting on October 15, but I have already agreed to attend the Marketing Committee meeting scheduled at the same time.

negative idea in a complex sentence
If we had received your letter of application and résumé earlier, we would have been able to grant you an interview—before the position was filled. (Scenario: A qualified candidate has requested an interview for an advertised position that has been filled.)

Because the company has suffered severe losses during the past three years, our consultants have recommended that the company consolidate several of its divisions and close three of its branch offices. (Scenario: The company will be downsizing.)

As soon as 50 percent of the work on this project has been completed, we will issue a check for $11,000—which will bring the company payments up to 50 percent of the contract pricing agreement. (Scenario: The contractor has requested an additional payment but has completed less than 50 percent of the project.)

negative idea in the middle of a paragraph
The company is in the process of reorganizing its departments and divisions, and the Marketing Department will be merged with the Sales Department to form the Sales and Marketing Department. By consolidating these two departments, the company will be able to operate more efficiently. Many positions in the Marketing Department overlap those in the Sales Department, **so a number of employees will be transitioned, effective June 30**. Of course, the company will offer an attractive compensation, retraining, and alternate-location program to employees who remain with the company until June 30.

8–10 Parallel Structure for Balanced Ideas

a. Sentences are considered to have parallel structure when matching ideas are expressed in similar ways. If the first idea begins with a noun or pronoun, so must all others. If the first idea begins with a verb, then all others must begin with a verb. Be sure to match each idea—noun with noun, verb with verb, and so forth.[2]

---

[2]For additional information and examples of parallel construction, refer to Chapter 1, Sections 1–34b and 1–35a, b.

Use the principles of parallel structure for the following circumstances:

(1) To join two equal ideas with a coordinating conjunction (*and, but, or,* or *nor*)

(2) To express a series of ideas connected by a coordinating conjunction

(3) To correlate two ideas using correlative conjunctions (*both . . . and, either . . . or, neither . . . nor,* or *not only . . . but also*)

(4) To express ideas in a listing

two ideas joined by a coordinating conjunction
If the company wishes to expand its operations, it will need to **maintain** its sales in Indiana *and* **increase** its efforts in surrounding states.

Should we meet our contract deadline by **requesting** present employees to work overtime *or* **hiring** additional workers from a temporary agency?

series of ideas joined by a coordinating conjunction
Working for DGM Consultants has been **interesting**, **challenging**, *and* **rewarding**.

May I please have more information about the **responsibilities**, **qualifications**, **salary range**, *and* **application procedures** for the sales position you have available.

You may pay for the time-share **with** a credit card, **by** check, *or* **through** our installment plan.

To avoid the projected $9.6 million shortfall, we can **close** one of our stores, **delay** our warehouse expansion, *or* **increase** our indebtedness.

two ideas joined by a correlative conjunction
Both **the** Editing Department *and* **the** Marketing Department will move their offices to Colorado.

Both **a** personnel clerk *and* **an** administrative assistant will be hired for the project.

Either **your** manager *or* **my** manager will receive the vice presidency.

Mr. Johnson will *either* **allocate** additional funds to the project *or* **suspend** its operation until spring.

We accept *neither* **personal checks** *nor* **credit cards** for payment.

He *neither* **offered** a reasonable explanation *nor* **extended** an apology for his apparent rudeness.

We have received telephone calls and e-mail messages from *not only* **faculty** and students *but also* **citizens** in the community.

The board at its last meeting *not only* **authorized** the purchase of the new warehouse site *but also* **appropriated** the $6 million to purchase it.

Not only **was the meeting room** not set up *but also* **dirty dishes were** still on the tables from the last meeting held there.

ideas in a listing

We have set three goals for next year: (1) **increase** sales by 8 percent, (2) **expand** our operations into Oregon and Nevada, *and* (3) **develop** plans to move the offices to a larger complex.

Follow these steps to authorize direct deposit for your paycheck:

(1) **Obtain** a Direct Deposit Authorization form from the Payroll Office.

(2) **Fill** out the form completely and sign it.

(3) **Mail** the form directly to the Human Resources Department, South Florida Community College, 600 West College Drive, Avon Park, Florida 33825.

b. Balance articles, verbs, prepositions, and comparisons within sentences. Follow these guidelines:

(1) In a coordinate or series, repeat the appropriate article (*a, an, the*) for each item.

(2) In a coordinate or series, be sure the main verb is in the correct form when two verbs share the same helper. If two separate verb forms appear in the same sentence, ensure that each one is stated correctly.

(3) In a coordinate or series, some words may require certain prepositions to be grammatically correct. Ensure that such words are each followed by their correct preposition.

(4) In a comparison, include all words necessary for understanding.

balanced articles

Poor: Please bring **a** laptop *and* data projector to the meeting.
Better: Please bring **a** laptop *and* **a** data projector to the meeting.

Poor: Please fax a copy of **the** original offer, acceptance, *and* contract to my office.
Better: Please fax a copy of **the** original offer, **the** acceptance, *and* **the** contract to my office.

Poor: For the concert we still need **a** piano *or* organ player.
Better: For the concert we still need **a** piano *or* **an** organ player.

Poor: The company has contracted with an employment agency to hire **a** personnel analyst, accountant, *and* graphic artist.
Better: The company has contracted with an employment agency to hire **a** personnel analyst, **an** accountant, *and* **a** graphic artist.

balanced verbs

Poor: Ms. Sherman **will go** to Newark on Monday *and* **is attending** the writers' conference there.

Better: Ms. Sherman **will go** to Newark on Monday *and* **attend** the writers' conference there.

Poor: We never **have**, *and* probably never **will**, **recommend** this kind of risky investment.

Better: We never **have recommended**, *and* probably never **will recommend**, this kind of risky investment.

balanced prepositions

Poor: The Board of Directors has great **respect** *and* **belief in** our president's ability to turn this company into a market leader.

Better: The Board of Directors has great **respect for** our president *and* **belief in** his ability to turn this company into a market leader.

Poor: Effective managers strive to **listen** *and* **work closely with** their staff.

Better: Effective managers strive to **listen to** *and* **work closely with** their staff.

balanced comparisons

Poor: Stephen has more clients than **any** lawyer in our firm.

Better: Stephen has more clients than **any other** lawyer in our firm.

Poor: She is absent more than **anyone** in our department.

Better: She is absent more than **anyone else** in our department.

Poor: I appreciate your assistance just **as much**, if not more than, anyone else in the department.

Better: I appreciate your assistance just **as much as**, if not more than, anyone else in the department.

Organizing Sentences into Cohesive Paragraphs

8–11 Paragraph Design

a. A paragraph is a group of related sentences joined for a specific purpose—to present a single idea. In business messages, from e-mails to reports, paragraphs are separated from each other with a single blank line or a paragraph indent. By placing ideas in paragraphs, the message is easier to read and to understand.

b. Paragraphs may vary in length from 1 line to 16 lines. Average paragraph length should be 4 or 5 lines. The length of a single paragraph depends upon its purpose and the number of sentences needed to achieve that purpose. Remember, though, the longer the paragraph, the more imposing it is to the reader.

8–12 Paragraph Unity

Group related sentences into a single paragraph. Ensure that each sentence in the paragraph relates to a single idea.

unity—paragraph relates to time, location, and content of meeting
The Finance Committee meeting is scheduled for Tuesday, August 22, from 2:30 p.m. to 4 p.m. in Conference Room 400. Attached to this e-mail are the minutes from last month's meeting and the agenda for August 22.

unity—paragraph relates to the recipient's presentation
Your presentation is the first order of business on the agenda, and I will have a laptop and a data projector available for your use. One of our technical specialists from Information Technology will set up the equipment and remain during your presentation in case you need assistance. Is there any other way I can help you prepare for this presentation?

8–13 Sentence Order Based upon Organizational Plans

a. Most paragraphs in business messages are written according to the *deductive plan*. The first sentence gives the main idea, and the remaining sentences support the main idea by providing explanations or details.

The new payroll procedures will go into effect July 1. You will be paid by direct deposit on the last working day of the month, and "pay stubs" will be mailed to your address on record in the Human Resources Department. After the first salary payment, please report any payroll discrepancies to the Single Point of Contact (SPOC) at your location.

b. The *inductive plan* for organizing paragraphs is especially useful when you are conveying negative news or attempting to influence the reader. Also, you may wish to use the inductive plan to add variety and interest to your messages. The inductive plan begins with explanations or details that lead up to the concluding statement.

The company's new payroll procedures will go into effect July 1. All employees will be paid by direct deposit on the last working day of the month, and "pay stubs" will be mailed. Currently we do not have on record a bank account for the direct deposit of your pay. **Because payroll checks will no longer be issued, employees who have not registered for direct deposit will receive their salary payments on debit cards**.

c. A third plan for organizing your paragraphs is called the *inductive-deductive plan.* It is particularly useful for conveying negative ideas. The paragraph begins with an explanation that leads to the main idea. The main idea is then followed by additional details.

The Accounting Department is in the process of updating its payroll system, which has been in use since 1998. This new system will reduce the number of payroll errors we have experienced lately. To set up the new payroll system, the network administrator needs two days to convert from the old system to the new one. **Therefore, payroll checks for last month will be issued on February 3 instead of February 1**. Beginning March 1, payroll checks will be issued as usual—the first day of the month. We are confident that this new system will result in fewer payroll errors and ensure our issuing payroll checks in a timely manner.

8–14 Paragraph Coherence

a. To obtain coherence within a paragraph, group related sentences and create a logical sequence within the group. Use one of the organizational plans described in Section 8–13. Ensure that each sentence flows smoothly and directly from the previous one.

b. Use transitional expressions as necessary to strengthen the link between ideas.

(1) To signal an additional idea, use words such as *also, besides, furthermore, in addition,* and *moreover.*

(2) To signal a contrasting idea, use words such as *after all, however, nevertheless, on the other hand,* and *otherwise.*

(3) To signal a comparison of ideas, use words such as *likewise* and *similarly.*

(4) To signal the result of a previous idea, use words such as *accordingly, as a result, consequently, therefore,* and *thus.*

(5) To signal a summary statement, use words such as *for example, in other words,* and *in summary.*

additional idea

In addition, we anticipate that Data Select will release an updated version of its software next year.

Furthermore, you will be eligible for additional benefits once you have been with AAA Insurance Underwriters for six months.

contrasting idea

We will continue, **nevertheless**, to move forward with our plans to open three additional offices.

You may, **however**, be able to purchase this book directly from the publisher.

comparison of ideas

Likewise, all my attempts to contact this client personally have been unsuccessful.

Similarly, the bids for all the new buildings on our campus have come in over budget.

result of a previous idea

Each employee, **consequently**, has been assigned a specific parking space on Level 2 of the new parking structure.

Therefore, we are in the process of moving the convention to another city.

summary statement

In other words, access to the company's intranet will resume Monday morning, November 6, at 8 a.m.

In summary, Great American Bank will be acquired by United Mutual, effective August 1.

Placing Paragraphs in Effective Order

8–15 Message Organization

a. The direct approach (deductive order) and indirect approach (inductive order) that apply to the sequence of sentences in paragraphs also apply to the ordering of paragraphs.

(1) In the direct approach, the opening paragraph clearly reveals the purpose of the message. The paragraphs that follow the opening paragraph provide details or provide additional information related to the opening paragraph. Most messages use this organizational approach.

(2) For sensitive and persuasive messages, the indirect approach is the better choice. It is the reverse of the direct approach. The message begins by presenting relevant information and details before revealing clearly the purpose of the message, thus showing the reader how the decision or request flows naturally from the information presented.

direct approach

Thank you for your interest in the United Bank Platinum Business card. We have enclosed an application and information on the unique features of this card.

As a United Bank Platinum Business cardholder, you will receive an array of special benefits just for business customers like you. Not only will you earn miles that can take you to National Airlines' destinations worldwide but also you will receive special discounts, free annual account summaries, Account Online, 24-hour concierge service, and other amenities to help you manage your business.

To ensure the fastest possible processing of your application, please provide all the information requested. You will hear from us within 30 days after we receive your signed application. We hope to welcome you soon as a new card member.

indirect approach

I appreciate receiving your invitation to participate in Pierce College's Career Fair on May 16. Your Career Fair is certainly well-known throughout the Valley and the surrounding area.

One of our major clients, Preston Industries, is coordinating a conference in Phoenix for my staff and for key members of Preston Industries' management team. Many of the attendees will be traveling from various areas of the country for this important meeting, which is scheduled from May 14 through May 17. Unfortunately, these meeting dates overlap the date set for the Career Fair.

Please consider me for next year. I would enjoy participating in your Career Fair in the future.

b. Another method for organizing messages is to place paragraphs in chronological order. The chronological approach relates a series of events in the sequence in which they occurred.

A meeting with Swenson and Associates on July 15 revealed a $47.5 million shortfall in the building projects for Westfield College. The college's senior staff was charged with reducing the scope of the building program to meet the current budget. With the assistance of Swenson and Associates, the senior staff devised five scenarios. Four of the five scenarios proposed elimination of an entire building.

The five scenarios were showcased on August 25 to the Westfield College Council (WCC), the advisory body to the college president, who will make the final decision. Advocates for the various scenarios addressed the WCC as interested parties looked on. Only questions from members of the WCC were acknowledged.

By September 2 the five scenarios had been posted on the Westfield College Web site, along with a discussion bulletin board. All employees were notified of the posting and the discussion bulletin board through an e-mail message on September 5. The Westfield College Council will make its recommendation on September 15.

8–16 Message Coherence

Like sentences in individual paragraphs, the paragraphs in a message must flow logically and naturally from one to the next. Message effectiveness relies on coherence—the relationship an idea has to the previous idea to reach a logical conclusion. Use the following guidelines to achieve message coherence:

(1) Organize the paragraphs in your message according to the direct approach, the indirect approach, or the chronological approach. (See Section 8–15.)

(2) Check to ensure that the last sentence of the previous paragraph leads the reader smoothly into the following paragraph.

(3) Use transitional expressions to signal the continuation of ideas and any abrupt changes in thought. (See Section 8–14b.)

8–17 Purpose and Anticipated Outcome of a Message

a. Determine if the purpose of the message is to (1) inform, (2) persuade, or (3) convey negative news or controversial information.

(1) Messages that inform or convey good news are considered routine and use a direct approach. They state the purpose in the opening paragraph and explain the details in the remainder of the message.

(2) Messages that persuade use an indirect approach by providing the reader with background information or justifications for a request before actually stating the purpose. These kinds of messages usually conclude with an appeal for action.

(3) Messages that convey negative news or information that is contrary to a person's self-interest require a delicate approach. In fact, in the workplace these kinds of messages are often delivered in person.

If written, negative-news messages use an indirect approach. They begin with a neutral statement, which is followed by an explanation justifying the need to convey information that is adverse to the recipient's interest. The news itself is expressed in such a way as to reduce its negative impact. (See Section 8–9b.) The message should always end on a neutral or positive note.

messages that inform

Congratulations! Exceeding your sales quota by 10 percent during the last quarter has earned you an additional $1,000 bonus. (Continue the message with any necessary details.)

The Advertising Media Committee meeting has been rescheduled for Thursday, March 3, at 1 p.m. and will be held in the Executive Conference Room, Room 683. (Continue the message with any necessary details.)

messages that persuade

This morning the Accounting Department's network printer was sent out for repair. The repair estimate ($387) for this eight-year-old black-and-white document printer approaches the price of a new one.

Because additional reports are often requested by the Board of Directors and other departments, the Accounting Department has needed to use color printing for some of its spreadsheets. This capability is not available in the department's current printer. However, an HP LaserJet Enterprise 500 color Printer M551n that costs $569.99 (plus tax and shipping) would fulfill our needs.

Funds for printer replacement or repair are not available in the Accounting Department budget; therefore, I would appreciate your authorizing the purchase of a new printer through the company's contingency fund. I look forward to receiving your approval.

messages that convey negative news

I appreciate receiving your budget requests for the next fiscal year. As the company plans ahead to increase sales and profits, it must increase budgets to accommodate its growth expectations.

The budget committee is committed to providing departments with increased operating expense budgets, but all the requests submitted by department heads cannot be fulfilled. In this tight economy, company resources must be allocated according to the annual goals and the critical path analysis developed by the planning staff. Department budget allocations for the next fiscal year have been made according to these criteria.

Enclosed is next year's budget for the Marketing Department. Although only several of the requested increases have been authorized, the entire budget represents an 8 percent increase over last year's budget.

Thank you for your excellent management of the Marketing Department and all your efforts to increase company sales and profits.

b. Design your message based upon its purpose and its anticipated outcome.

9

Spelling, Proofreading, and Editing

Spelling, Proofreading, and Editing Solution Finder

Editing

Preparing for Proofreading and Editing

Proofreading

Spelling

Preparing for Proofreading and Editing

Printed reference materials and online resources provide access to the information needed by today's fast-paced business environment. Reference materials are abundant. Numerous kinds and extensive listings are available in libraries, in bookstores, from software vendors, and on the Internet. Some are valuable tools; others are not.

The following sections provide a selective listing of printed materials and online resources that may prove helpful for creating, editing, and proofreading documents. The sources listed may be (1) purchased from bookstores or software vendors, (2) located at local public or college libraries, or (3) accessed on the Internet.

9–1 Dictionaries

a. Although word processing programs provide a spell-checker, this feature has limitations. It does not differentiate between words that sound alike but are spelled differently, flag words that are used incorrectly, or assess whether a term should be spelled as one or two words (e.g., *mark down* or *markdown*). Dictionary entries provide spellings, syllabication, pronunciation guides, definitions, irregular verb forms, irregular adjective forms, and synonyms—all useful information for proofreading and editing documents.

b. Dictionaries are generally published in paperback-pocket format, collegiate editions, desk editions, or complete unabridged versions. Collegiate editions—because of their compact, comprehensive nature and frequently updated printings—are considered the best source for office use. Update your office dictionary every three years, and select an authoritative one such as those listed below:

Merriam-Webster's Collegiate Dictionary (print), with free download of the collegiate edition and one-year online subscription to the unabridged edition. 11th ed. Springfield, MA: Merriam-Webster, Incorporated.

Webster's New World College Dictionary (print), with CD-ROM. 5th ed. Boston: Houghton Mifflin Harcourt.

c. Consider whether specialized dictionaries are needed in your office. Besides the regular array of foreign language–English dictionaries, investigate the usefulness of dictionaries that define business terms, computer terms, legal terms, and medical terms.

Downing, Douglas, Michael Covington, Melody M. Covington, Catherine Anne Barrett, and Sharon Covington. *Dictionary of Computer and Internet Terms*. 11th ed. Hauppauge, NY: Barron's Educational Series, Inc., 2012.

Garner, Bryan A., ed. *Black's Law Dictionary*. 10th ed. Eagan, MN: Thomson West, 2014.

Scott, David L. *The American Heritage Dictionary of Business Terms.* Boston: Houghton Mifflin Harcourt, 2009.

Stedman, Thomas Lathrop. *Stedman's Medical Dictionary for the Health Professions and Nursing,* with illustrated CD-ROM. 7th ed. Hagerstown, MD: Lippincott Williams & Wilkins, 2011.

Stedman's Plus Medical/Pharmaceutical Spellchecker 2015 Standard Edition. 23rd ed. Hagerstown, MD: Lippincott Williams & Wilkins, 2015. *Multimedia CD.*

9–2 Thesauri

During the editing process, use a thesaurus to locate substitutes for any words that may be overused. A partial listing of thesauri follows:

Merriam-Webster Online. "Thesaurus" option. Boston: Merriam-Webster, Incorporated, 2015. Accessed February 11, 2015. http://www.merriam-webster.com/.

Oxford American Writer's Thesaurus. 3rd ed. New York: Oxford University Press, 2012.

Roget's International Thesaurus. 7th ed. New York: HarperCollins, 2010.

Thesaurus.com. Dictionary.com. 2015. Accessed February 11, 2015. http://www.thesaurus.com/.

9–3 Encyclopedias

a. For people involved in international communication, encyclopedias furnish background information about countries' political systems, history, and customs. In addition, encyclopedias provide a concise synopsis on virtually thousands of topics.

b. The following sources[1] may prove valuable in collecting facts and information as well as verifying them through the editing process:

Encyclopædia Britannica Online. Online access for annual fee. Chicago: Encyclopædia Britannica, Inc., 2015. http://www.britannica.com. Accessed February 12, 2015.

World Book Online. Online access for annual fee. Chicago: World Book, Inc., 2015. http://www.worldbook.com/ Accessed February 12, 2015.

9–4 Almanacs

Almanacs, published annually, describe significant events of the past year; provide information about government officials, states, the United States, and other nations; and supply facts on weather and other topics.

The Old Farmer's Almanac 2015. Dublin, NH: Yankee Publishing, Inc., 2014. (Published annually)

Central Intelligence Agency. *The CIA World Factbook 2015.* New York: Skyhorse Publishing, 2014. (Published annually)

Janssen, Sarah. *The World Almanac and Book of Facts 2015.* New York: World Almanac Books, 2014. (Published annually)

---

[1]All Web site addresses appearing in *HOW 14* were active links at the time of publication.

9–5 Atlases

Atlases provide maps of cities, states, countries, continents, and the world. Accompanying a wide variety of maps is often information about population, weather, terrain, agricultural production, and economic orientation. If necessary, consult atlases such as the following during the editing process:

National Geographic Atlas of the World. 10th ed. Washington, DC: National Geographic, 2014.
Concise Atlas of the World. 6th ed. New York: Dorling Kindersley Limited, 2013.
New Concise World Atlas. New York: Oxford University Press, Inc., 2013.
Oxford Atlas of the World. 21st ed. New York: Oxford University Press, Inc., 2014. (Published annually)

9–6 Style Manuals

a. Style manuals govern the presentation style of reports and manuscripts. Three styles dominate the preparation of reports and manuscripts:

(1) The Modern Language Association (MLA) style is endorsed by those writing in the fields of language and arts.

(2) The American Psychological Association (APA) style is endorsed by those writing in the social sciences.

(3) *The Chicago Manual of Style* prescribes a traditional style usable for business, researchers, and students.

b. The following listing gives the latest authoritative published sources for preparing manuscripts or reports according to the MLA style, the APA style, or the Chicago style. Two other sources—popular among students and businesspeople—have also been included.

The Chicago Manual of Style. 16th ed. Chicago: The University of Chicago Press, 2010.
Clark, James L. and Lyn R. Clark. *HOW 14: A Handbook for Office Professionals.* 14th ed. Mason, OH: Cengage South-Western, 2017.
MLA Handbook for Writers of Research Papers. 7th ed. New York: The Modern Language Association of America, 2009.
Publication Manual of the American Psychological Association. 6th ed. Washington, DC: American Psychological Association, 2010.
Turabian, Kate L. Revised by Wayne C. Booth, Gregory Colomb, Joseph M. Williams, and the University of Chicago Press Editorial Staff. *A Manual for Writers of Research Papers, Theses, and Dissertations.* 8th ed. Chicago: The University of Chicago Press, 2013.

Spelling

Proofreading and editing have taken on new roles as spell-checkers and grammar checkers have become integral parts of word processing programs. In many ways the burden of proofreading and editing has been lightened, but only to add different approaches and tasks.

The process of producing documents with correct spellings has been automated to a great extent. However, standard dictionaries and other resources still play a major role in proofreading and/or editing documents for spelling and usage errors. For example, is the correct spelling in the sentence *every day* or *everyday?* The increasing popularity of speech-recognition software has added yet another dimension to the proofreading and editing process. Although all dictated words are spelled correctly, the words dictated may not always match the words printed on the screen. Words that sound alike but are spelled differently (to, too, two) require correction—as do words that are misunderstood entirely.

9–7 Use of the Dictionary to Locate Correct Spellings

a. Use a recognized collegiate or desk dictionary to locate any spellings of words you do not know or about which you are unsure. As an alternative to a print version, however, you may wish to access the online version of *Merriam-Webster* and use its premium collegiate dictionary service. (See Section 9–1b.)[2] Be consistent in verifying the spelling of words by consulting the same reference source for spellings throughout the document. Whether using a print edition or an online version of a dictionary, use the following guidelines:

(1) When the dictionary offers two spellings for a word in the same entry, use the first spelling.

judgment   Not *judgement*   canceled   Not *cancelled*

(2) When verifying the spelling of words, match the word with its correct counterpart in the dictionary. For example, if the word is used as a noun in the sentence, then compare it with the noun spelling of this

[2]The dictionary used for all spellings in this manual is *Merriam-Webster's Collegiate Dictionary*, 11th ed., published by Merriam-Webster, Incorporated, 2014. Merriam-Webster maintains a free-access dictionary and thesaurus Web site at http://www.m-w.com. Premium online access to the unabridged dictionary is available for a minimal annual fee or free for one year with the purchase of the collegiate text edition.

word in the dictionary. As an illustration of differences in spellings, note that *under way* used as an adverb is two words but *underway* as an adjective is one. Similar situations occur with many other words.

mark up (verb)	markup (noun)
break down (verb)	breakdown (noun)
set up (verb)	setup (noun)
double-space (verb)	double space (noun)

(3) The spellings of irregular plural nouns and irregular verb forms appear in the dictionary directly after the main word in the entry. Therefore, when in doubt about the formation of these words, consult your dictionary for their spellings. (See Sections 1–4 and 1–13 for additional information and examples related to irregular plural nouns and verb forms.)

irregular plural nouns

company	companies	tomato	tomatoes
half	halves	child	children
analysis	analyses	alumnus	alumni

irregular verb forms

bring	brought	brought
sing	sang	sung
run	ran	run
lie	lay	lain
see	saw	seen

(4) The spellings of irregular adjective and adverb comparisons appear in the dictionary directly after the main word in the entry. Check your dictionary to verify these spellings. (See Sections 1–21 and 1–26 for rules and additional examples of adjective and adverb comparisons.)

irregular adjective comparisons

costly	costlier	costliest
good	better	best

irregular adverb comparisons

early	earlier	earliest
far	farther	farthest

b. To locate easily the spellings of unfamiliar words in the dictionary, acquaint yourself with the various letter combinations that represent sounds in the written English language. Both consonants and vowels may have different letter combinations that represent the same sound. The chart below presents just a few of the sounds and combinations with which you should become familiar.

Sound	*Letter Combinations to Represent the Sound*
ā	***a***lienate, ***ai***de, g***au***ge, st***ea***k, f***ei***gn, w***eigh***t
ak	***ac***tual, ***acc***olade, ***ack***nowledgment, ***acq***uiesce, ***aq***ueduct
ar	***aer***osol, ***air***borne, ***ar***eas, ***arr***ogant
as	***as***piration, ***asc***ending, ***ass***ertive
aw	f***a***ther, ***au***dacity, t***augh***t, ***aw***esome, ***o***stracize, ***ough***t
ē	***e***dict, ***ea***sement, d***ee***m, rec***ei***pt, p***eo***ple, f***i***asco, p***ie***ce
er	simil***ar***, ***er***adicate, ***ear***nings, ***err***oneous, f***ir***mly, w***orr***isome, t***our***nament, ***ur***banization
f	***f***elony, e***ff***icient, ***ph***onetic, rou***gh***age
g	***g***rimace, ***gh***astly, ***gu***ardian
h	***h***azardous, ***wh***olly
ī	***ai***sle, h***eigh***t, ***i***dentify, t***ie***d, th***igh***, h***y***draulic
j	ju***dg***ment, ***g***ermane, exa***gg***eration, ***j***eopardize
k	***c***oincide, a***cc***ountant, ***ch***emistry, ***k***ilometer, ***q***uandary
m	***m***iraculous, pa***lm***istry
n	***gn***aw, ***kn***otty, ***mn***emonic, ***n***arrative, ***pn***eumonia
ō	b***eau***, ***o***dor, fl***oa***t, d***oe***skin, p***ou***ltry, d***ough***nut, sn***ow***
oi, oy	sp***oi***l, ann***oy***ance
oo	n***eu***tral, fl***ew***, ad***ieu***, t***o***mb, l***oo***se, l***ou***ver, thr***ough***, n***u***trition, tr***ue***, s***ui***t
ow	ann***ou***nce, fl***ow***er
r	***r***etrieve, ***rh***ythm, ***wr***est
s	***c***ertainty, ***ps***ychologist, ***s***alable, ***sc***intillate
sh	ma***ch***inery, espe***ci***ally, ***s***urely, con***sc***ience, ***sch***nauzer, nau***se***ous, ***sh***rewd, preci***si***on, substan***ti***al
t	***pt***omaine, ***t***ranslate
ū	b***eau***tiful, f***eu***d, sk***ew***ed, ***u***niform, f***ue***l, ***yu***letide
w	ch***o***ir, q***u***arterly, ***w***asteful, ***wh***ich

9–8 Use of Word Processing Spell-Checkers

a. Use the spell-check feature of your word processing program to check the spelling of any document you have created. All words in the dictionaries of your word processor will be used to correct the words you have keyboarded.

(1) Any word not in the dictionary of your word processor will be flagged and must be verified through a standard dictionary, a reputable online reference site,[3] or other sources. Spellings of names of individuals and many other proper nouns fall into this category.

(2) Frequently used technical terms or proper nouns not appearing in the main dictionary of a word processor may be added to a dictionary. By clicking the *Add* option during a spell-check, the word is added to your supplemental dictionary. Right-clicking on the word

[3]The Merriam-Webster free online dictionary may be accessed at http://www.m-w.com.

and then selecting the *Add* option from the drop-down menu also adds the word to your supplemental dictionary. Be careful, though, not to add misspellings to your dictionary.

(3) Occasionally a word in the spell-checker of your word processor may not agree with the spelling of the same word in the dictionary reference you are using. In such a case, use the spelling of the word as shown in your dictionary reference.

b. Most word processors provide a "spell-as-you-go" feature and a "correct-as-you-go" feature, which may simplify the proofreading process.

(1) *The "spell-as-you-go" feature.* A wavy red line under a word signals keyboarders that they have entered a word that is misspelled according to the dictionaries of the word processor. For standard words the person keyboarding may right-click on the word to obtain a list of choices to correct the spelling of the underlined word.

(2) *The "correct-as-you-go" feature.* A limited number of misspellings along with their correct spellings are stored in a list. When the keyboarder enters the misspelling exactly as shown in the list, it is corrected automatically; for example, *adn* to *and.* Misspellings and corrections may be added to the list. This feature is useful if a keyboarder often misspells a certain word or wishes to use letters, words, numbers, or symbols as shortcuts for longer word combinations; for example, *pc* for *Pierce College.*

c. Commercially sold spell-checkers that are compatible with the installed spell-checkers in word processing programs are available for specialized vocabularies; for example, medical and legal terminology. If you frequently prepare documents using extensive medical or legal terminology, do an online search to locate vendors who sell spell-checkers in either of these specialized fields.

9–9 Use of Online Resources

For up-to-date spellings of emerging terminology or words with spellings that appear to be in transition, such as computer and Internet terms, consult a reputable online dictionary reference.

(1) Merriam-Webster provides a Web site at which you may access free of charge an English dictionary, an English thesaurus, a Spanish-English dictionary, and a medical dictionary to obtain spellings and definitions. The Web site address is http://www.m-w.com. Accessed February 15, 2015.

(2) *Stedman's Online* is a subscription online resource for a medical dictionary; a health professions and nursing dictionary; a dental dictionary; a pocket medical dictionary; and a medical abbreviations, acronyms, and symbols dictionary. The Web site address is http://stedmansonline.com/. Accessed February 15, 2015.

(3) *TheFreeDictionary* provides a one-stop Web site at which you may access free of charge a legal dictionary, a medical dictionary, and other reference resources. http://legal-dictionary.thefreedictionary.com/. Accessed February 15, 2015.

Proofreading

Proofreading is the process of checking a document against an original to ensure that it conforms to the original in all respects. Proofreaders are responsible for checking a prepared document to correct only spelling errors, typographical errors, and any additions or omissions that do not conform with the original document. The proofreader does not make changes in wording or content.

9–10 Proofreading On-Screen Documents

a. Use the spell-check feature of your word processing program before beginning the proofreading process. Follow these guidelines to check spelling in the document:

(1) Enable the "check-spelling-as-you-type" feature of your word processing program. Any words not in the dictionaries of your word processor will appear with a wavy red underline.

(2) Correct a word with a wavy red underline by right-clicking on it. Select the correct spelling from the drop-down list that appears. If the word is not listed, check your original copy or an up-to-date dictionary for the correct spelling.

(3) Correct proper nouns and technical vocabulary by checking their spellings with the original copy. Spellings of technical words not in the dictionary of the word processor should be verified with the dictionary or another appropriate source such as a medical dictionary, legal dictionary, dictionary of business terms, or dictionary of computer terms.

b. Check for consistency of style throughout the document before actually beginning to read the text.

(1) Assess the appropriateness of margins (top, bottom, left, and right).

(2) Check the line spacing between paragraphs, before and after main or text headings, within letter closing lines, and so on.

(3) Inspect to ensure that the document contains no widow or orphan lines (single lines of a paragraph at the top or bottom of a page). To avoid such occurrences within a multiple-page document, activate the widow-orphan line protection feature of your word processing program. At the same time, check to ensure that the last word on the page is not broken with a hyphen and carried over to the following page.

widow line—last line of a paragraph at top of page or column

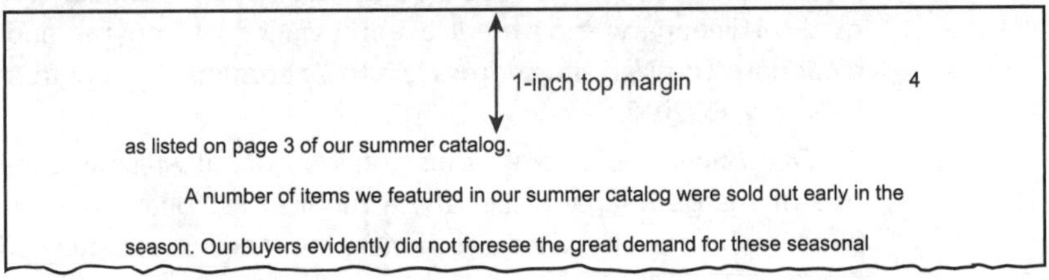

orphan line—first line of a paragraph left at bottom of page or column

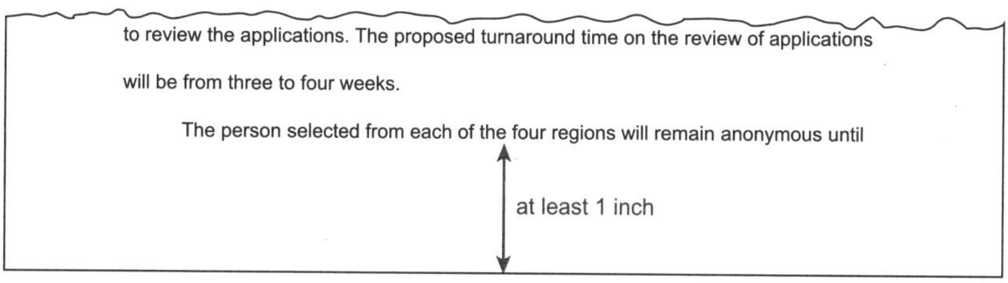

(4) Inspect to ensure that no isolated text headings appear at the end of a page. At least two lines of text from the paragraph following the heading must accompany it on the same page. Use the keep-lines-together feature of your word processing program to force any isolated headings to the next page.

(5) Check the line endings to ensure that certain phrases such as calendar month and day, the word *page* and a number, the abbreviation *No.* and a corresponding number, the word *Model* and any corresponding numbers and/or letters, and other such word-with-number-or-letter combinations appear on a single line. Place a nonbreaking space between any parts in the word group that should appear on the same line. (See Section 5–8.)

(6) Check the line beginnings to ensure that dashes or ellipses do not begin the line.

(7) Evaluate the general appearance of the document through the print preview feature of your word processing program. Check headers, footers, and page numbering carefully.

c. **Read the text for accuracy. Check it carefully against the original copy. Place the original copy on a copy stand next to your screen. Read a group of words in the original copy; then compare those words with the corresponding ones on the screen. Continue this process until you have proofread the entire document. Use the following criteria to evaluate the keyboarded document:**

(1) Are any letters transposed or omitted? Are all words spelled correctly? The spell-check feature of your word processing program will have located most spelling errors, but it will not have detected such errors as using *form* for *from*, *an* for *and*, or *effect* for *affect*.

(2) Have any letters, words, sentences, or paragraphs been omitted? Pay close attention to ensure that no *s*'s have been dropped from plural nouns or *ed*'s from the past tense or the past participle of verb forms. Ensure that no words, sentences, or paragraphs have been skipped.

(3) Have any words, phrases, or sentences been repeated? Repeated words are flagged by your word processing spell-checker, but repeated phrases or sentences are not detected electronically.

(4) Are all names and unfamiliar words spelled correctly? When proofreading names and unfamiliar words or terminology, first verify the

number of letters in the word in the original copy and make sure the same number of letters appear in the document being proofread. Then, check the spelling meticulously—letter by letter.

(5) Have all figures been typed correctly? Are all calculations correct? Double-check all figures carefully with the original source. For long numbers verify the number of digits and then compare the digits in groups of three. If the numbers are in a column with a total, use a calculator to check the total in the original document and then check the same total in the document being proofread.

d. Print the document only when you are satisfied that it has been proofread properly and all aspects are correct.

9–11 Proofreading Printed Copy

a. Check for consistency of style throughout the document before actually beginning to read the text.

(1) Assess the appropriateness of margins (top, bottom, left, and right).

(2) Check the line spacing between paragraphs, before and after main or text headings, within letter closing lines, and so on.

(3) Inspect to ensure that the document contains no widow or orphan lines (single lines of a paragraph at the top or bottom of a page). See Section 9–10b for illustrations of widow and orphan lines. At the same time, ensure that the last word on the page is not hyphenated and carried over to the following page.

(4) Inspect to ensure that no isolated text headings appear at the end of a page. At least two lines of text from the paragraph following the text heading must appear on the same page.

(5) Check the line endings to ensure that word groups that may not be divided appear on a single line; for example, calendar month and day, the word *page* and a number, the abbreviation *No.* and a corresponding number, and other such word-with-number-or-letter combinations. Place a nonbreaking space between any parts in the word group that should appear on the same line. (See Section 5–8.)

(6) Check the line beginnings to ensure that dashes or ellipses do not begin the line.

(7) Evaluate the general appearance of the document. Check headers, footers, and page numbering carefully.

b. Using the original copy as a model, proofread the printed document for accuracy. Read the document carefully, and ask yourself the following questions to correct any keyboarding errors:

(1) Are any letters transposed or omitted? Are all words spelled correctly? The spell-check feature of the word processing program will have located most spelling errors, but it will not have detected such errors as using *you* for *your*, *to* for *too*, or *lose* for *loose*.

(2) Have any letters, words, sentences, or paragraphs been omitted? Pay close attention to ensure that no *s*'s have been dropped from plural nouns or *ed*'s from the past tense or the past participle of verb forms. Ensure that no words, sentences, or paragraphs have been skipped.

(3) Have any words, phrases, or sentences been repeated?

(4) Are all names and unfamiliar words spelled correctly? When proofreading names and unfamiliar words or terminology, first verify the number of letters in the word in the original copy and make sure the same number of letters appear in the document being proofread. Then, check the spelling meticulously—letter by letter.[4]

(5) Have all figures been typed correctly? Are all calculations correct? Double-check all figures carefully with the original source. For long numbers verify the number of digits and then compare the digits in groups of three. If the numbers are in a column with a total, the easiest method of proofreading is to use a calculator to check the total in the original document and then check the same total in the document being proofread.

c. **When proofreading hard copy, make your corrections with a colored pen or pencil. Use the pen-and-forefinger technique to maintain attention.**

(1) Hold the pen in the hand with which you will be making corrections, and place the copy to be proofread on that side.

(2) Place the original on the opposite side, and use the forefinger of that hand to follow along as you compare the two copies.

(3) Keep your eyes focused on the line being proofread.

d. **When proofreading hard copy, use the standardized proofreaders' marks shown in Section 9–12 and also on the inside back cover of this manual to show your corrections.**

9–12 Standardized Proofreaders' Marks to Show Corrections

a. **Standardized proofreaders' marks are used to show corrections in handwritten, typewritten, computer-generated, or printed copy. These symbols are used so that anyone who reads the document will interpret the corrections in the same way. Use the following marks and symbols to make changes in words or word groups:**

[4]The printed version of *Merriam-Webster's Collegiate Dictionary*, 11th ed., contains sections on symbols, foreign words and phrases, biographical names, and geographical names.

Instruction	*Mark or Symbol*	*Example*	*Marginal Note*
Boldface word(s).	~~~~	received by November 1	bf
Capitalize letter.	≡	to the Retailers association	cap
Capitalize letters.	≡≡	from Unesco	caps
Change word(s).	—	~~In view of the fact that~~ Because you have	
Close up space.	⁀‿	You can, never the less, receive	
Delete letter.	/	occassion	
Delete stroke or letter.	/ℓ	policy/ and send us an fax	
Delete word(s).	—ℓ	a ~~postal~~ money order for $50	
Hyphenate word(s).	=	up=to=date records	
Insert a space.	#	Inaddition, you will be	
Insert apostrophe.	∨	its a good deal	
Insert colon.	⊙ (:)	follows pen, ink, and paper.	
Insert comma.	^,	On Tuesday, May 23 we	
Insert em dash.	1/M	comments all are welcome!	
Insert en dash.	1/N	January 14 16	
Insert here (caret).	^	Insert at this place.	
Insert parentheses.	( )	end of this month April 30.	
Insert period.	⊙	by 10 am tomorrow	
Insert question mark.	(?)	Do you agree.	
Insert quotation marks.	∨ ∨	article, Access on the Web, that	
Insert semicolon.	^;	now therefore, you	
Insert word(s).	^	your latest income tax form	
Italicize word(s).	—	The Wall Street Journal	ital
Join to word.	⁀	in our microcomputer laboratory	
Lowercase letter.	/	of the Association	lc
Lowercase letters.	/‾	the UNITED STATES OF AMERICA	lc

Instruction	*Mark or Symbol*	*Example*	*Marginal Note*
Restore word(s).	....	our ~~furniture~~ warehouse in Toledo	stet
Roman type.	—	book titles in *italic* type	rom
Small capital letters.	═	our red tag sale on	sm caps
Spell out word or number.	◯	(3) stores on Fifth (Ave.)	sp
Transpose letters.		all thier profits.	tr
Transpose words.		to legibly print your name	tr
Underscore word(s).	—	We <u>cannot</u> overemphasize	u'score

b. Use the following symbols to move words or word groups:

Instruction	*Mark or Symbol*	*Example*	*Marginal Note*
Align horizontally.	═	In the past two years	
Align vertically.	‖	‖(1) New courses (2) New curriculum	
Center.	] [	]PROOFREADERS' MARKS[	
Combine paragraphs.	no ¶	no ¶ You may also wish to	
Double-space copy.		As a result of this investigation, we have decided to reduce expenses.	ds
Indent 0.5 inch.	.5"	.5" During the last month	
Insert line space.	>	COMPUTER SALES SUMMARY > February 2013.	+1#
Move as shown.		(for the next year)	
Move to next line.		give the contract to Mr.	
Move to the left.	[	[You may wish to	
Move to the right.	]	You] may wish to	
New paragraph.	¶	¶ Many customers do not	
Single-space copy.		As a result of this investigation, we have decided to reduce expenses.	ss

Editing

The proofreading process involves the comparison of a document with an original to assess the correctness of the prepared copy. Editing is a more challenging process because editors do not have "correct" copies upon which they may rely to determine whether the copy they are reading has been prepared properly. Editors themselves are responsible for determining the accuracy and appropriateness of all language and formatting.

9–13 Preparing to Edit

a. If possible, use the document word processing file to spell-check the document electronically. If you are the document originator or preparer, use the "spell-as-you-go" feature of your word processor to flag potential spelling errors. These potential spelling errors are shown with a wavy red underline. You may correct common errors from a drop-down menu by right-clicking on the underlined word and then selecting the correct word from the list that appears.

b. If possible, use the document word processing file and the grammar checker of your word processor to flag any potential grammar errors. Follow these guidelines in using an electronic grammar checker:

(1) Keep in mind that you will need to make judgments when using a grammar checker. Not all flagged items are errors, and often the suggested corrections are incorrect.

(2) Use a reliable reference such as *HOW 14* to verify any grammatical constructions about which you are unsure. Although electronic grammar checkers can be helpful to the expert grammarian, they can be a hindrance to the novice because of their high incidence of error.

(3) Use the "correct-grammar-as-you-go" feature if you are the document originator or preparer. A wavy blue or green line under a word or sequence of words signifies a potential grammar error. Right-clicking on the potential error produces a drop-down menu that provides an opportunity to correct the error or investigate further the reason the grammar checker has flagged the error. Before making any corrections, verify that the identified word sequence is an error.

c. Whether you edit documents from the word processing file or printed copy will depend on whether you are the document originator or you are editing another person's document. Other considerations are the length of the document, the availability of an electronic or print version, and personal preferences.

If you are editing from a word processing file created by another person, more than likely the document originator will prefer your accessing the Review feature of your word processing program to track the changes. The document originator can then view changes

and accept or reject them. You, too, may prefer to track your editing changes if you edit the electronic version of a document you have created.

You may prefer to edit the document from printed copy or printed copy may be the only medium available to you. In that case you will use proofreaders' marks and symbols to indicate changes.

d. Assemble all the materials you will need to edit a document:

(1) An up-to-date (printed within the past three years) collegiate or desk dictionary; for example, *Merriam-Webster's Collegiate Dictionary*, 11th ed.[5]

(2) An up-to-date (published within the past three years) reference manual; for example, *HOW 14: A Handbook for Office Professionals*, 14th ed.

(3) An up-to-date (published within the past five years) thesaurus (See Section 9–2.)

(4) Reference sources from which the document was created; for example, rough drafts, authorization letters, file copies, and meeting notes

(5) Any other published references that may relate to the document; for example, mailing lists, telephone directories, maps, encyclopedias, books, magazines, and newspapers

(6) Addresses (URLs) of any Internet references or resources that may be needed

9–14 Editing the Document

a. Because the editor does not just "check" a document against another source, you will probably need to read the material several times. As an editor, you must evaluate the overall effectiveness of a document in terms of its attaining the goal for which it was written. Therefore, you will wish to read the material critically with several criteria in mind:

(1) Are there any omissions in ideas or content? All important ideas should be included in the document as well as any information to substantiate the ideas. Check to make sure the document is complete in every respect.

(2) Is the document well organized so that the reader can easily follow the ideas as they are presented? The editor needs to ensure that ideas are placed in logical order and that each sentence flows smoothly and lucidly from the previous sentence. Coherent writing results in clarity and allows the reader to understand easily the purpose and contents of the document. (See Section 8–17.)

---

[5]Merriam-Webster provides to purchasers a free download to entries in this dictionary and premium online access to its unabridged dictionary for one year: http://www.m-w.com.

(3) Is the document correct in every way—content, format, grammar, spelling, punctuation, capitalization, and number expression? Be sure to check the accuracy of all the data. In addition, make sure that all the conventions of correct language usage have been observed and that the document has been formatted appropriately. (See Section 9–11.)

(4) Is the content easily understood? Examine the document to ensure that the ideas are presented vividly and with ample illustrations so that the reader can picture concretely what the writer had in mind.

(5) Have all the ideas been expressed in as few words as possible? Look at each sentence to make sure that it does not contain extra wording. Evaluate sentences and paragraphs to see whether they contribute to achieving the overall purpose of the document. Any excess words, sentences, or paragraphs should be deleted.

(6) Are all abbreviations, number expressions, and other format considerations handled in the same way? Check for inconsistencies in these areas and in the contents of the document.

(7) Are the tone and language appropriate for accomplishing the purpose of the document? Check to make sure that letters are written in a friendly and a courteous manner. Reports, in contrast, should have a more formal tone. Match the formality of tone and language with the purpose of the document.

b. Activate *Track Changes* in the Review feature of your word processing program to show insertions, deletions, and formatting changes made to the document if you are editing a document from your word processing program. Use proofreaders' marks and symbols to indicate changes made during the editing process if you are editing from printed copy. These marks and symbols are explained and illustrated in Section 9–12 and on the inside back cover of this manual.

c. Consider double-spacing rough drafts of documents that are to be edited from printed copy. Double spacing not only makes the document easier to read but also makes changes easier to interpret.

9–15 Editing Documents Created with Speech-Recognition Software

a. Speech-recognition programs enable document originators to voice type text into word processing programs, e-mail templates, calendaring programs, spreadsheets, databases, and presentation programs. Users may also navigate the Internet with voice commands.

(1) Continuous voice dictation permits document originators to enter text without using the keyboard; words appear on the computer screen as they are spoken.

(2) Speech-recognition software not only permits continuous voice dictation for text entry but also enables the document originator to issue voice commands to edit, navigate, and format documents.

b. Major developers of speech-recognition software include Nuance (Dragon NaturallySpeaking) and Microsoft (software incorporated into the Windows operating systems beginning with Vista). Prices for Dragon NaturallySpeaking range from moderate to high, with the more expensive versions containing additional features and enhancements. Features of voice input include the following:

(1) Voice-input software is capable of producing text from continuous speech and implementing program commands by voice. Minimally the software may be used to compose documents in Microsoft Word, dictate e-mail messages in a variety of systems, and navigate the Internet. Dictated words are spelled correctly because the dictionary of the software has a large vocabulary. Users, however, must be skilled in making occasional corrections for words that sound alike but are spelled differently; for example, *their* and *there* or *principal* and *principle*. Users may expand the vocabulary of the program to include industry-specific terms or frequently dictated proper nouns. Developers boast of dictation speeds up to 160 words per minute and accuracy performances of 96 to 99 percent in transferring the spoken word to text.

(2) Some voice-input editions provide audio playback for the text dictated, read documents and e-mail messages aloud in a human-sounding voice, and transcribe sound files from handheld recorders—permitting a remote voice-to-text system. Documents may be dictated anywhere, anytime on a pocket-size digital voice recorder. Upon plugging in the mobile recorder to your desktop computer and transferring the voice files to your speech-recognition program, the software will transcribe your documents into any one of a wide selection of text-based programs—where you can review, edit, and format them.

(3) High-end speech-recognition editions add new dimensions to the software. In addition to allowing specialized and/or multiple vocabularies, high-end speech-recognition programs may have a variety of advanced features such as exporting and importing user files, saving dictation for outside correction, creating macros, providing custom templates, permitting direct dictation in additional application programs, or supporting scripting.

c. Speech-recognition programs require a training time for each user. Training times vary, depending upon the software package and the voice of the user—anywhere from 15 minutes to an hour. As each user continues to dictate into the program and follows the recommended procedures for correcting transcription errors, the transcription accuracy of the program improves.

d. Speech-recognition software plays a major role in originating documents in medical, legal, business, and government offices. Although documents created with speech-recognition software do not contain spelling errors or "typos," they still require editing.

e. Documents created with speech-recognition software are subject to most of the same criteria as documents created using a keyboard. However, because the software occasionally substitutes other words for those dictated, exchanges singular and plural forms, and misinterprets past and past participle forms, special attention must be given to correcting these kinds of errors. The following guidelines can assist you in editing documents created with speech-recognition software:

(1) Read the text carefully for meaning. Because speech-recognition software is generally perceived to attain between 96 and 99 percent accuracy, undetected word-recognition errors may result in nonsense-sounding sentences.

(2) Pay close attention to word endings. Speech-recognition software may add or omit the *s* at the end of nouns and verb forms. Similarly, the software may add or omit the *ed* at the end of a verb form. Only by reading the text slowly and carefully for meaning can such errors be detected.

(3) Check carefully for errors in number recognition and format. These kinds of errors can easily occur and go unnoticed. Use the same strategies recommended in Section 9–11b for proofreading numbers.

(4) Double-check the spelling of proper nouns. Although speech-recognition software "learns" the spelling of unusual proper nouns and differentiates among the various spellings of other proper nouns, it may occasionally substitute an incorrect spelling.

(5) Do not rely on the Read Back feature of your speech-recognition software to assist you with the proofreading or editing process. The Read Back feature merely reads back the words exactly as they appear on the screen—errors and all. The copy is not read as it was dictated.

(6) Use any available voice files to assist you with the proofreading or editing process. If the document was created on a mobile digital voice recorder, replay the voice recording of the document as you edit it. This recording will assist you in recognizing words misinterpreted by the speech-recognition software.

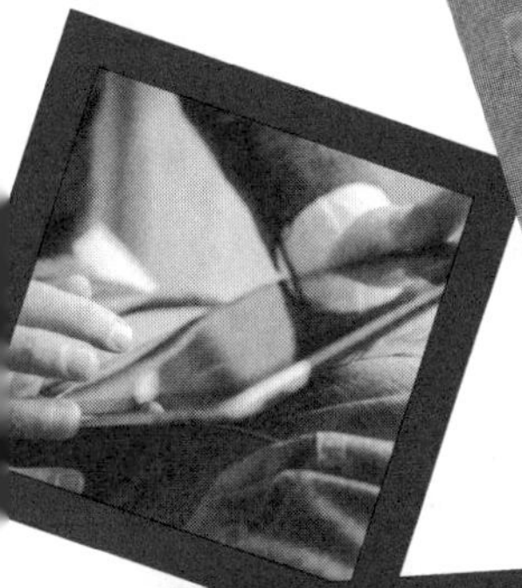

10

Address Format and Forms of Address

Address Format and Forms of Address Solution Finder

General Address Format

10–1 General Address Format

a. Use combinations of the following to address general business correspondence: full name of person with appropriate courtesy title, professional title, company name, street address, city, state, and ZIP Code (five digits or nine digits, depending upon the availability of the nine-digit code).[1]

Coordinate the person's name, title, and company name so that line endings in the inside address are as nearly even as possible. Use the two-letter postal state designation or spell out the state name to achieve further a balanced appearance. (See Section 6–9c.)

Use the same format for the inside address of the letter and the envelope used to mail it.

addressed to individual

Ms. Marie LaGrasta-Sundy
8730 Beach Boulevard, Apt. 2
San Clemente, CA 92672-2036

Dear Ms. LaGrasta-Sundy:

Mr. Anthony A. Livingston
1378 West Laurel Canyon Avenue
Des Moines, Iowa 50310-1436

Dear Mr. Livingston:

addressed to individual within company

Mr. Shawn T. Stein, Manager
Policy Issue Department
General Insurance Company of America
600 Prospect Avenue, Suite 600
Hartford, Connecticut 06105-2920

Dear Mr. Stein:

Ms. Jill R. Binsley
Vice President of Operations
Bank of America
5420 Bayshore Boulevard
Tampa, Florida 33611-4122

Dear Ms. Binsley:

addressed to company

F. M. Tarbell Company
2740 SW Troy Street
Portland, OR 97219-2553

Ladies and Gentlemen:

Cinamerica
Post Office Box 20077
Encino, CA 91416-0077

Ladies and Gentlemen:

b. An address may have a maximum of six lines and a minimum of two lines.

maximum six-line address

Ms. Brenda Forbes-Gallagher
Chief Operations Manager
Quality Control Department
Neware Aluminum Accessories
3600 Chelwood Park Blvd., NE
Albuquerque, NM 87111–5416

---

[1] The nine-digit zip code for an address may be obtained from a link on the home page of the U.S. Postal Service: https://www.usps.com/. Accessed February 16, 2015.

minimum two-line address
Phillips Foods, Inc.
Morristown, NJ 07960–3305

Names and Titles

10–2 Courtesy Titles

a. Abbreviate the courtesy titles *Mr.* and *Mrs.* when they are used with the names of individuals. The courtesy title *Ms.* ends with a period, although it is not an abbreviation.

In the salutations of business letters, use the courtesy title with the last name only.

courtesy title with full name
Mr. Marvin Weston **Mrs.** Sharlene Pollyea **Ms.** Frances Shannon

courtesy title in salutation
Dear **Mr.** Weston: Dear **Mrs.** Pollyea: Dear **Ms.** Shannon:

b. When the name of an individual does not signify whether the person is a man or a woman, omit the courtesy title. Use the same format for the salutation in a business letter.

name does not signify gender

Chris V. Stauber	Cary Antonovich	T. R. Najjar
Casey R. Elliott	Lynn Sebastian	B. Kelly Clemens
Cory Williams	Jaime Bennett	Duong Nguyen

salutation for name that does not signify gender

Dear T. R. Najjar:	Dear Chris V. Stauber:
Dear Cory Williams:	Dear B. Kelly Clemens:

c. When addressing a woman, use the courtesy title *Ms.* unless *Mrs.* (or *Miss*) is specified by the addressee. Use the courtesy title *Miss* for young girls under the age of 13.

woman does not indicate a title preference
Ms. Laura Rankin **Ms.** Ellen Togo

girl under the age of 13
Miss Kristen Fielding **Miss** Claudia Martinez

d. The courtesy title *Master* is used for addressing young boys, usually below the age of 13.

Master William J. Clark **Master** Charles Bentley

e. **The abbreviated courtesy title *Esq.* (*Esquire*) is sometimes used after the surname of a lawyer. In such cases no courtesy title precedes the name.**

David R. Grossman, **Esq.** Allison H. Davis, **Esq.**

f. **Female correspondents who have a courtesy title preference other than *Ms.* should indicate this preference in the signature lines of their correspondence by enclosing the title in parentheses before their names. Correspondents who have names that do not signify gender may also indicate a courtesy title preference by enclosing it in parentheses before their names in a signature line.**

***female with courtesy title preference other than* Ms.**
(Mrs.) Susan K. Willett (Dr.) Barbara Wilson

male or female whose name does not indicate gender
(Ms.) K. C. Roberts (Ms.) Lonnie Abrams

(Mrs.) Chris Dobrian (Mrs.) Lee Haberman

(Mr.) Dana Lopez (Mr.) Leslie Mitchell

10–3 Professional Titles

a. **Except for *Dr.* and long professional titles consisting of two or more words, write out and capitalize professional titles when they precede the names of individuals. *Professor, Dean, The Reverend, Governor, Senator, Colonel, Lieutenant,* and *The Honorable* are examples of titles that are capitalized and written in full.**

Doctor *abbreviated*
Dr. Alan Strozer **Dr.** Shannon T. Goar

professional title written out
Professor Marie Flatley **The Honorable** Brian K. Stanfield

long professional title abbreviated
Brig. Gen. Leonard C. Williams (Brigadier General)

Lt. Col. Ret. Robin A. Anderson (Lieutenant Colonel Retired)

b. **In addressing business correspondence or completing signature lines, capitalize and write out professional titles that follow an individual's name.**

single-line address format
Mr. Kevin McDonald, **Dean** Ms. Patrice A. Halby, **Vice President**

two-line address format
Ms. Melanie L. Fielding
Plant Superintendent

Mr. Adam T. Livingston Jr.
Assistant Vice President

single-line signature format

(Dr.) Jennifer Loucks, **Chair**

(Mrs.) Joyce Moore, **President**

William A. Murillo, **Manager**

Rebecca L. Dentino, **Supervisor**

two-line signature format

John S. Minasian
Chairman of the Board

(Mrs.) Brenda Browning
Collections Manager

(Ms.) Orolyn L. Ruenz-Clark
Vice President of Operations

Bradley C. Johnson
Customer Service Representative

c. Capitalize professional titles *not* appearing in address format or signature lines only when they precede and are used directly with an individual's name in place of a courtesy title. Do not capitalize titles following an individual's name.

title preceding name

President Peter Meggison will deliver the main address.

One of the senators from Michigan, **Senator** Gary Peters, will be the luncheon speaker.

title following name

Peter Meggison, **president** of A & P Enterprises, will deliver the main address.

The Honorable Gary Peters, **senator** from Michigan, will be the luncheon speaker.

d. Only one courtesy or professional title with the same meaning should appear with a single name. Use *Dr.* or *MD,* but not both titles with the same name.

titles with the same meaning

Dr. Jason V. Glaser *or* Jason V. Glaser, **MD**

Dr. Cheng Wong *or* Cheng Wong, **DDS**

titles with different meanings

Dr. Susan Cornner, **Professor**

e. Do not capitalize professional titles that substitute for individuals' names.

The **general** has canceled his weekly staff meeting.

Did the **governor** appear for the press conference?

10-4 Company Names

Spell out company names in full unless the company itself uses abbreviations in its official name.[2] *Inc.* and *Ltd.* usually appear in abbreviated form, but some companies write these words in full.

company name written in full

Pacific Mutual Life Insurance Company

Merriam-Webster, Incorporated

Schultz and Sons

Neilson Corporation

company name containing abbreviation

Consolidated Factors, **Ltd.**

International Computer **Corp.**

McKnight, Larson **&** Crosby

Lyons Investment Group **Inc.**

Places

10-5 Buildings, Units, and Mailbox Numbers

a. **Capitalize the names of buildings and the names of any units within buildings. Place the unit, suite, or apartment location after the building name, but separate the two with a comma.**

If an address contains a unit location without a building name, place it after the street address. Separate the street address and the unit location with a comma. Use numerals for all unit numbers.

building name with unit location

Plaza Medical Center, **Suites 450–460**

Michigan State Capitol, **Office 243F**

Tishman Building, **Suite 600**

Bayview Apartments, **Unit 7**

unit location without building name

220 Main Street, **Suite 100**

5670 Fair Oaks Avenue, **Unit 12**

18564 Clark Street, **Apt. 4**

5426 SW 43rd Street, **#205**

b. **Many large organizations assign mailbox numbers to employees who receive mail regularly. Place the mailbox number directly after the street address; separate it from the address with a comma.**

2000 Kingsley Boulevard, #182

6201 Winnetka Avenue, Mailbox 26

10-6 Street Addresses

a. **Use numerals to express house or building numbers. Only the house or building number *one* is written in word form.**

***house or building number* one**

One Lakeview Terrace

One Riverwalk Place

---

[2]The official name of a company may be determined from its printed letterhead or from any of its contracts. It also may be obtained from the company's Web site.

house or building number in numerals

8 Burbank Lane | **420** Fourth Avenue, Apt. 112

17225 Prairie Street | **10239-3** White Oak Avenue

b. Spell out simple compass directions (*North, South, East,* and *West*) that appear in a street address. Compound compass points (*Northeast, Northwest, Southeast,* and *Southwest*) in an address are abbreviated. Any compound compass directions following the street address are preceded by a comma.

simple compass point in street address

3214 **West** 47th Street | 2160 Century Park **East**

1090 **North** Grand Boulevard | 640 Manchester Street **South**

compound compass point within street address

3028 **NE** 19th Street | 127 **SW** Madison Street

compass point following street address

1603 F Street, **NW** | 3750 Broxten Avenue, **SE**, Apt. 18

c. All street-number names *ten* and below are written in words using ordinal numbers—*First, Second, Third,* and so on. Street-number names above *ten*, however, are written in numerals. Use ordinal numbers (*11th, 12th, 13th,* etc.) when expressing these street names.

street-number name* ten *or below

1482 **Sixth** Avenue | 742 East **First** Street

***street-number name above* ten**

890 South **21st** Street | 3624 West **59th** Place

2036 **42nd** Street | 9680 **123rd** Street

d. Spell out street designations such as *Boulevard, Avenue, Street, Place, Drive,* and *Lane.* Only the street designation *Boulevard* may be abbreviated (*Blvd.*) with exceptionally long street names.

street designation spelled out

18394 Lankershim **Boulevard**

street designation abbreviated

9263 North Coldwater Canyon **Blvd.**

e. Spell out where possible mailing designations such as *Rural Route* or *Post Office Box* that are used in place of street addresses. Abbreviate the mailing designation only with long addresses.

postal designation spelled out

Post Office Box 450 | **Rural Route** 2, Box 1620

postal designation abbreviated

PO Box 1629, Terminal Annex

f. Apartment, suite, and unit numbers are expressed in numerals and are generally included on the same line as the building name. In addresses without building names, these numbers appear on the same line with the street address. The term *Apartment* may be abbreviated when it appears on the same line as the street address.

With long street addresses, apartment numbers may be placed on the following line. The term *Apartment* in these cases is spelled out.

apartment, suite, or unit number with building
Redlands Medical Building, **Suite 540** Oaks Professional Plaza, **Unit 14**

unit or apartment number with street address
6176 Arroyo Road, **Unit 2** 4150 East 21st Street, **Apt. 6**

no specific designation with street address
16932 Wilshire Boulevard, **C-110** 8900 Main Street, **5B**

apartment number on line following street address
8564 Kensington Street, SW
Apartment 230

10–7 City, State, and ZIP Code

a. Spell out in full the names of cities.

Saint Louis New York Fort Worth Los Angeles

b. Use the two-letter post office designation or spell out in full state names. Select either style based upon (1) the degree of formality of the correspondence or (2) the one that provides better balance for setting up the entire address. Should both be equally suitable, use the two-letter postal designation. Use the same form for the inside address and the envelope used to mail the correspondence.

A list of two-letter state and territory designations for the United States may be found in Section 6–12 and on the page opposite the inside back cover.

state two-letter postal designation
Ms. Jessica Morton
108 Academy Avenue
Weymouth, MA 02188-4204

Mr. Richard A. Chui
9540 Barr Drive, Apt. 204
Indianapolis, IN 46229-1214

state name written in full
Mr. William R. Stephenson
1257 American Legion Highway
Richmond, Virginia 23231-1931

Mrs. Shirley Schnair-Goldman
1124 Jefferson Boulevard
Flint, Michigan 48507-4201

c. ZIP Codes are keyed a single space after the state.
Atlanta, GA 30331-8732 *or* Atlanta, Georgia 30331-8732

Address Format for Foreign Correspondence

10–8 Address Format for Foreign Correspondence

a. Addresses for foreign correspondence contain combinations of the following:

(1) Full name of addressee with appropriate courtesy title

(2) Professional title of addressee

(3) Company name

(4) Street address

(5) City and any city numbering codes or section name

(6) State or region, if applicable

(7) Destination country

b. Sequencing of the address parts varies among countries. For mail sent from the United States, however, always place the name of the destination country in all capital letters as the last line of the mailing address. Where elsewhere possible, follow the conventions of the destination country.

(1) Some countries place the name of the addressee first but place the city information before the street address.

(2) Some countries place the house number after the street name or the postal code before the city name.

(3) Some countries follow the familiar street address, city, state, and postal code format used in the United States.

Mr. Atsushi Ishiki
1-6-302 Wutsukusigaoka
1 Chome—C1Z Midoriku
Yokohama
JAPAN

Alexandria
Stanly
237 Zaky Badway Mohamed St.
Mrs. Iman Gaber El-Desoky
EGYPT

c. If possible, use courtesy titles that reflect the language of the country. *Herrn, Frau,* and *Fräulein* (German); *Señor, Señora,* and *Señorita* (Spanish); and *Monsieur, Madame,* and *Mademoiselle* (French) are just a few examples of foreign courtesy titles that represent the English *Mr., Mrs.,* and *Miss.*

In most foreign countries, a comparable term for *Miss* is used for young women. Adult women are addressed with the courtesy title comparable to the English *Mrs.,* regardless of their marital status.

Use English courtesy titles in those cases where the comparable title is unknown or impractical to reproduce on English-based keyboards. However, use the extended character sets of your word processor to form the characters that are supported by the software. Abbreviate or spell out foreign courtesy titles according to the style predominantly used in the country.

French
Le Lien
c/o M. Lucien Aubert
14, rue Roger-Radisson
69322 Lyon
FRANCE

Portuguese
Srta. Kristina Chagas Tavares
Rua 706, n^E=152/178
Balneário Camboriú, SC
CEP 88330
BRAZIL

d. When addressing foreign correspondence, use the English version of a country name (*GERMANY*, not *DEUTSCHLAND*) to ensure the correspondence is routed to the correct country from the United States. For city names, however, use the foreign spelling to hasten delivery within the country (*Köln*, not *Cologne*; *Wien*, not *Vienna*; *Venezia*, not *Venice*). If possible, use all the appropriate letters and diacritical marks in spelling names, streets, cities, and other parts of the address. Consult the geographical reference section of your dictionary for assistance in selecting the correct name and its spelling.[3]

Herrn Paul-Erich Rünz
Diplomat-Kaufman
Gemarkenstraße 290
5000 Köln 80—Dellbrück
GERMANY

Online Address Formats

10–9 Internet Addresses

Companies, government offices, educational institutions, organizations, and individuals have established Web sites—computer "pages" on which they provide information, sell products or services, and/or recruit employees. Each page has an address so it can be reached easily by merely typing in the address. An Internet address is known as a *uniform resource locator—URL*, pronounced "you are el." A description of URL parts follows:

(1) A typical Internet address (URL) might appear as https://www.cia.gov /library/publications/the-world-factbook/ in a listing.

(2) The first part, ***http://***, indicates the type of protocol needed to retrieve the information at the site. In this case ***http*** represents *hypertext transfer protocol.* The *s* following *http shows* that this site is a secure site. World Wide Web sites are accessed by Web browsers such as Internet Explorer, Firefox, Chrome, and Safari using the *http* protocol.

---

[3]The spellings shown here are based on those contained in *Merriam-Webster's Collegiate Dictionary*, 11th ed. (Springfield, MA: Merriam-Webster, Incorporated, 2014). Note that in this dictionary the foreign spelling is shown after the English spelling in the primary reference and also listed separately in a secondary reference.

(3) The ***www*** following the protocol type symbolizes *World Wide Web.* The name of the host computer, ***cia*** (Central Intelligence Agency), is followed by its identifier, ***gov,*** which distinguishes the Web site as a government entity. Note the common URL identifier extensions in the following table:

Identifier	*Definition*
com	commercial organization
edu	educational site
gov	government organization
mil	military
net	organization administering a network
org	miscellaneous organization

(4) At the Web site of the Central Intelligence Agency, ***library, publications,*** and ***the-world-factbook*** are accessed.

(5) Keying in the address bar **https://www.cia.gov/library/publications/the-world-factbook/**,[4] therefore, will take you directly to the contents of *THE WORLD FACTBOOK.* This site provides information on 267 world entities and is updated weekly.

10–10 E-Mail Addresses

Just as everyone has an address for mail delivery by the U.S. Postal Service and private mail carriers, anyone who wishes to send and receive mail through the Internet must have an e-mail (electronic mail) address.

(1) An e-mail address is divided into two basic parts: the user name and the user domain. The user name is the combination of letters and/or numbers assigned to a specific user upon signing up with an online service or other e-mail provider. The user domain identifies the location of the computer that receives the user's mail—the online service or other e-mail provider.[5]

(2) The user name and the user domain are separated by @ (an "at" sign). Examples of e-mail addresses follow:

E-mail Address[6]	*Explanation*
ClarksHOW@socal.rr.com	The user name is *ClarksHOW* (James and Lyn Clark); the e-mail and online service provider is Time Warner (Southern California), an access provider that is classified as a commercial organization.
jdoe@plantronics.com	The user name is *jdoe* (John Doe); the e-mail provider is Plantronics, a commercial organization.

[4]Normally you may omit typing *http://* when entering a Web site address in the address box of your browser.

[5]See Section 10–9 for an explanation of extensions *com, edu, gov, mil, net,* and *org.*

[6]All e-mail addresses shown here are fictitious and are used only as illustrations.

E-mail Address	*Explanation*
allison.jones@sdsu.edu	The user name is *allison.jones* (Allison Jones); the e-mail provider is San Diego State University, an educational site.
bsmith@csupomona.edu	The user name is *bsmith* (B. Smith); the e-mail provider is California State Polytechnic University, Pomona—an educational site.
JLConnor87@earthlink.net	The user name is *JLConnor87* (Jason L. Connor); the online service and e-mail provider is EarthLink, an access provider that is classified as an organization administering a network.
lyndiamilton@netzero.net	The user name is *lyndiamilton* (Lyndia Milton); the online service and e-mail provider is NetZero, an access provider that is classified as an organization administering a network.
az678@lafn.org	The user name is *az678* (Michael Morris); the e-mail/Internet service provider is Los Angeles Free Net, a miscellaneous organization.
sbrooks@cccaoe.org	The username is *sbrooks* (Susan Brooks); the e-mail provider is California Community College Association for Occupational Education, an organization.

Forms of Address

10–11 Personal and General Professional Titles

The following table lists the proper forms of address, salutation, and complimentary close for correspondence addressed to a general individual, two or more general individuals, certain professionals, and a company:

Addressee	*Address on Letter and Envelope*	*Salutation and Complimentary Close*
Man	Mr. (Full name) (Local address)	Dear Mr. (Last name): Sincerely,
Married woman	Mrs. (Husband's first name, last name) (Local address)	Dear Mrs. (Last name): Sincerely,
	Mrs. *or* Ms. (Wife's first name, last name)[7] (Local address)	Dear Mrs. *or* Ms. (Last name): Sincerely,

[7]This form is also used for a woman who is separated or divorced from her husband.

10 Address Format

Addressee	*Address on Letter and Envelope*	*Salutation and Complimentary Close*
Single woman	Ms. (Full name) (Local address)	Dear Ms. (Last name): Sincerely,
Woman, marital status unknown	Ms. (Full name) (Local address)	Dear Ms. (Last name): Sincerely,
Widow	Mrs. (Husband's first name, last name) (Local address)	Dear Mrs. (Last name): Sincerely,
	Mrs. *or* Ms. (Widow's first name, last name) (Local address)	Dear Mrs. *or* Ms. (Last name): Sincerely,
Two or more men	Mr. (Full name) Mr. (Full name) (Local address)	Dear Mr. (Last name) and Mr. (Last name): *or* Dear Messrs. (Last name) and (Last name): *or* Gentlemen: Sincerely,
Two or more women	Mrs. (Full name) Mrs. (Full name) (Local address)	Dear Mrs. (Last name) and Mrs. (Last name): *or* Dear Mesdames (Last name) and (Last name): *or* Mesdames: Sincerely,
	Mrs. (Full name) Ms. (Full name) (Local address)	Dear Mrs. (Last name) and Ms. (Last name): Sincerely,
	Ms. (Full name) Ms. (Full name) (Local address)	Dear Ms. (Last name) and Ms. (Last name): *or* Dear Mses. (Last name) and (Last name): Sincerely,
One woman and one man	Ms. (Full name) Mr. (Full name) (Local address)	Dear Ms. (Last name) and Mr. (Last name): Sincerely,
Married couple	Mr. and Mrs. (Husband's full name) (Local address)	Dear Mr. and Mrs. (Last name): Sincerely,

Addressee	Address on Letter and Envelope	Salutation and Complimentary Close
Married couple with different last names	(Title) (Full name of husband) (Title) (Full name of wife) (Local address)	Dear (Title) (Husband's last name) and (Title) (Wife's last name): Sincerely,
Professional married couple with same title and same last name	(Title in plural form) (Husband's first name) and (Wife's first name) (Last name) (Local address)	Dear (Title in plural form) (Last name): Sincerely,
Professional married couple with different titles and same last name	(Title) (Full name of husband) (Title) (Full name of wife) (Local address)	Dear (Title) and (Title) (Last name): Sincerely,
President of a college or a university	Dr. *or* (Mr./Mrs./Ms.) (Full name), President (Name of institution) (Local address)	Dear President (Last name): Sincerely, *or* Dear Dr. *or* (Mr./Mrs./Ms.) (Last name): Sincerely,
Vice president of a college or a university	Dr. *or* (Mr./Mrs./Ms.) (full name), Vice President (Name of institution) (Local address) *or* Dr. *or* (Mr., Mrs./Ms.) (full name) Vice President, (Area of Responsibility) (Name of institution) (Local address)	Dear Dr. *or* (Mr./Mrs./Ms.) (Last name): Sincerely,
Dean of a school or a college in a university	Dr. *or* (Mr./Mrs./Ms.) (Full name), Dean School *or* College of (Name) (Name of institution) (Local address)	Dear Dean (Last name): Sincerely,
Dean in a college	Dr. *or* (Mr./Mrs./Ms.) (Full name) Dean of (Title) (Name of institution) (Local address)	Dear Dr. *or* (Mr./Mrs./Ms.) (Last name): Sincerely,
Professor	Professor (Full name) (Name of department) (Name of institution) (Local address) *or* Dr. (Full name), Professor (Name of department) (Name of institution) (Local address)	Dear Professor (Last name): Sincerely, Dear Dr. (Last name): Sincerely,

10 Address Format

Addressee	*Address on Letter and Envelope*	*Salutation and Complimentary Close*
Professor, Assistant or Associate	Dr. *or* (Mr./Mrs./Ms.) (Full name) Assistant (*or* Associate) Professor (Name of department) (Name of institution) (Local address)	Dear Dr. *or* (Mr./Mrs./Ms.) (Last name): Sincerely,
Physician	(Full name), MD (Local address) *or* Dr. (Full name) (Local address)	Dear Dr. (Last name): Sincerely,
Lawyer	(Mr./Mrs./Ms.) (Full name) Attorney-at-Law (Local address) *or* (Full name), Esq. (Local address)	Dear (Mr./Mrs./Ms.) (Last name): Sincerely,
Service personnel	(Full rank, full name, and abbreviation of service designation) (*Retired* is added to rank if applicable.) (Unit assignment) (Local address)	Dear (Rank) (Last name): Sincerely,
	Example for a lieutenant colonel, United States Air Force: Lieutenant Colonel Cory Adams, USAF Headquarters Squadron, 22nd Bomb Group March Air Force Base Riverside, California 92506	Dear Colonel Adams: Sincerely,
	Example for a retired brigadier general, United States Marine Corps: Brig. Gen. Ret. Casey Rhodes, USMC (Local address)	Dear General Rhodes: Sincerely,
Company or corporation, men	(Full name of organization) (Local address)	Gentlemen: Sincerely,
Company or corporation, men and women	(Full name of organization) (Local address)	Ladies and Gentlemen: Sincerely,
Company or corporation, women	(Full name of organization) (Local address)	Ladies: Sincerely,

10–12 Government Officials

The following table shows the proper forms of address, salutation, and complimentary close for specific government officials:

Addressee	*Address on Letter and Envelope*	*Salutation and Complimentary Close*
President of the United States	The President The White House 1600 Pennsylvania Avenue, NW Washington, DC 20500	Dear (Mr./Madam) President: Respectfully,
Former president[8]	The Honorable (Full name) Former President of the United States (Local address)	Dear (Mr./Mrs./Ms.) (Last name): Sincerely,
President-elect	The Honorable (Full name) President-Elect of the United States (Local address)	Dear (Mr./Mrs./Ms.) (Last name): Sincerely,
Wife of the president	Mrs. (Full name) The White House 1600 Pennsylvania Avenue, NW Washington, DC 20500	Dear Mrs. (Last name): Sincerely,
Assistant to the president	The Honorable (Full name) Assistant to the President The White House 1600 Pennsylvania Avenue, NW Washington, DC 20500	Dear (Mr./Mrs./Ms.) (Last name): Sincerely,
Vice president of the United States	The Vice President Old Executive Office Building Washington, DC 20501	Dear (Mr./Madam) Vice President: Respectfully,
Chief justice of the United States	The Chief Justice of the United States The Supreme Court of the United States One First Street, NE Washington, DC 20543	Dear (Mr./Madam) Chief Justice: Sincerely,
Associate justice	Mr./Madam Justice (Full name) Associate Justice of the United States The Supreme Court of the United States One First Street, NE Washington, DC 20543	Dear (Mr./Madam) Justice: Sincerely,
United States senator	The Honorable (Full name) Office of Senator (name) United States Senate Washington, DC 20510 *or* The Honorable (Full name) United States Senator (Local address)	Dear Senator (Last name): Sincerely,

[8]This form of address may be adapted to address other former high-ranking government officials.

Addressee	Address on Letter and Envelope	Salutation and Complimentary Close
United States senator-elect	(Mr./Mrs./Ms.) (Full name) Senator-Elect, United States Senate (Local address)	Dear (Mr./Mrs./Ms.) (Last name): Sincerely,
United States representative	The Honorable (Full name) United States House of Representatives Washington, DC 20515 *or* The Honorable (Full name) Representative in Congress (Local address)	Dear Representative (Last name): Sincerely, *or* Dear (Mr./Mrs./Ms.) (Last name): Sincerely,
Cabinet member	The Honorable (Full name) Secretary of (Name of department) Washington, DC 00000	Dear (Mr./Madam) Secretary: Sincerely,
	The Honorable (Full name) Postmaster General Washington, DC 20260	Dear (Mr./Madam) Postmaster General: Sincerely,
	The Honorable (Full name) Attorney General Washington, DC 20503	Dear (Mr./Madam) Attorney General: Sincerely,
Deputy secretary, assistant secretary, or undersecretary	The Honorable (Full name) Deputy Secretary of (Name of department) Washington, DC 00000	Dear (Mr./Mrs./Ms.) (Last name): Sincerely,
	The Honorable (Full name) Assistant Secretary of (Name of department) Washington, DC 00000	Dear (Mr./Mrs./Ms.) (Last name): Sincerely,
	The Honorable (Full name) Undersecretary of (Name of department) Washington, DC 00000	
Head of independent office, commission, or agency	The Honorable (Full name) Comptroller General of the United States General Accounting Office Washington, DC 20548	Dear (Mr./Mrs./Ms.) (Last name): Sincerely,
	The Honorable (Full name) Commissioner, (Name of commission) Washington, DC 00000	Dear Commissioner (Last name): Sincerely,
	The Honorable (full name) Director, Bureau of the Budget Washington, DC 20503	Dear (Mr./Mrs./Ms.) (Last name): Sincerely,

Addressee	*Address on Letter and Envelope*	*Salutation and Complimentary Close*
Federal judge	The Honorable (Full name) Name of Court (Address, city, state, and ZIP Code)	Dear Judge (Last name): Sincerely,
American ambassador	The Honorable (Full name) American Ambassador (Address and city) (Country)	Sir: *or* Madam: (Formal) Very truly yours, *or* Dear (Mr./Madam) Ambassador: (Informal) Sincerely,
American consul general or American consul	(Mr./Mrs./Ms.) (Full name) American Consul General (*or* American Consul) (Address and city) (Country)	Dear (Mr./Mrs./Ms.) (Last name): Sincerely,
Foreign ambassador in the United States	(His/Her) Excellency (Full name) Ambassador of (Country) (Local address)	Excellency: (formal) Very truly yours, *or* Dear (Mr./Madam) Ambassador: (Informal) Sincerely,
Governor of state	The Honorable (Full name) Governor of (Name of state) (Address) (City), (State) 00000	Dear Governor (Last name): Sincerely,
Lieutenant governor	The Honorable (Full name) Lieutenant Governor of (Name of state) (Address) (City), (State) 00000	Dear (Mr./Mrs./Ms.) (Last name): Sincerely,
President of state senate	The Honorable (Full name) President of the Senate of the State of (Name of state) (Address) (City), (State) 00000	Dear Senator (Last name): Sincerely,
Speaker of a state assembly, a house of delegates, or a house of representatives	The Honorable (Full name) Speaker of the (Name of state) (Name of body) (Address) (City), (State) 00000	Dear (Mr./Mrs./Ms.) (Last name): Sincerely,
Chief justice of a state supreme court	The Honorable (Full name) Chief Justice of the Supreme Court of (Name of state) (Address) (City), (State) 00000	Dear (Mr./Madam) Chief Justice: Sincerely,

Addressee	*Address on Letter and Envelope*	*Salutation and Complimentary Close*
Associate justice of a state supreme court	The Honorable (Full name) Associate Justice of the Supreme Court of (Name of state) (Address) (City), (State) 00000	Dear Justice (Last name): Sincerely,
State attorney general	The Honorable (Full name) Attorney General of the State of (Name of state) (Address) (City), (State) 00000	Dear (Mr./Madam) Attorney General: Sincerely,
State secretary of state	The Honorable (Full name) Secretary of State of (Name of state) (Address) (City), (State) 00000	Dear (Mr./Madam) Secretary: Sincerely,
State senator	The Honorable (Full name) (Name of state) State Senate (Address) (City), (State) 00000	Dear Senator (Last name): Sincerely,
State representative, assemblyperson, or delegate	The Honorable (Full name) (Name of state) House of Representatives (*or* State Assembly *or* House of Delegates) (Address) (City), (State) 00000	Dear (Mr./Mrs./Ms.) (Last name): Sincerely,
Mayor	The Honorable (Full name) Mayor of (Name of city) (Address) (City), (State) 00000	Dear Mayor (Last name): Sincerely,
President of a board of commissioners or a city council	The Honorable (Full name), President (Name of city) (Name of board or council) (Address) (City), (State) 00000	Dear (Mr./Mrs./Ms.) (Last name): Sincerely,
City and county officials	The Honorable (Full name) (Position title, e.g., Member, Los Angeles City Council) (Address) (City), (State) 00000	Dear (Mr./Mrs./Ms.) (Last name): Sincerely,
Judge	The Honorable (Full name) Judge of the (Name of court) (Local address)	Dear Judge (Last name): Sincerely,

10–13 Religious Dignitaries

The following table shows the proper forms of address, salutation, and complimentary close for specific religious dignitaries:

Addressee	*Address on Letter and Envelope*	*Salutation and Complimentary Close*
Catholic clergy		
Cardinal	His Eminence (Given name) Cardinal (Last name) Cardinal of (Diocese) (Local address)	Your Eminence: (Formal) *or* Dear Cardinal (Last name): (Informal) Sincerely,
Archbishop	The Most Reverend (Full name) Archbishop of (Diocese) (Local address)	Your Excellency: (Formal) *or* Dear Archbishop (Last name): (Informal) Sincerely,
Bishop	The Most Reverend (Full name) Bishop of (City) (Local address)	Your Excellency: (Formal) *or* Dear Bishop (Last name): (Informal) Sincerely,
Monsignor	The Right Reverend Monsignor (Full name) (Local address) *or* The Very Reverend Monsignor (Full name) (Local address)	Right Reverend Monsignor: (Formal) *or* Dear Monsignor (Last name): (Informal) Sincerely, Very Reverend Monsignor: (Formal) *or* Dear Monsignor (Last name): (Informal) Sincerely,
Priest	The Reverend (Full name), (Initials of order, if used) (Local address)	Reverend Sir: (Formal) Dear Father (Last name): (Informal) Sincerely,
Mother superior	Mother (Full name), (Initials of order, if used) Superior, (Name of convent) (Local address)	Dear Mother (Full name): Sincerely,
Nun	Sister (Full name), (Initials of order, if used) (Name of convent) (Local address)	Dear Sister (Full name): Sincerely,
Monk	Brother (Full name), (Initials of order, if used) (Local address)	Dear Brother (Full name): Sincerely,

Addressee	Address on Letter and Envelope	Salutation and Complimentary Close
Jewish clergy	Rabbi (Full name) (Local address)	Dear Rabbi (Last name): Sincerely,
Protestant clergy Bishop	The Right Reverend (Full name) Bishop of (Name) (Local address) *or*	Right Reverend Sir: (Formal) *or* Dear Bishop (Last name): (Informal) Sincerely,
	The Reverend (Full name) Bishop of (Name) (Local address)	Reverend Sir: (Formal) *or* Dear Bishop (Last name): (Informal) Sincerely,
Dean	The Very Reverend (Full name) Dean of (Name of church) (Local address)	Very Reverend Sir: (Formal) *or* Dear Dean (Last name): (Informal) Sincerely,
Minister	The Reverend (Full name) (Title, if any) (Name of church) (Local address)	Dear Reverend (Last name): *or* Dear (Dr./Mr./Mrs./Ms.) (Last name): Sincerely,
Chaplain	Chaplain (Full name) (Full rank, service designation) (Post office address of organization and station) (Local address)	Dear Chaplain (Last name): Sincerely,
Lay clergy	Deacon (Full name) (Name of church) (Local address)	Dear Deacon (Last name): Sincerely,
	(Brother/Sister) (Full name) (Name of church) (Local address)	Dear (Brother/Sister) (Last name): Sincerely,

10–14 Undetermined Individual or Group

Although addressing correspondence to an undefined or undetermined individual or group should generally be avoided, circumstances sometimes provide no other alternative. In these cases the letter contains no inside address. The phrase *To Whom It May Concern*: replaces the standard salutation, and the complimentary close is either *Sincerely yours,* or *Yours very truly,*.

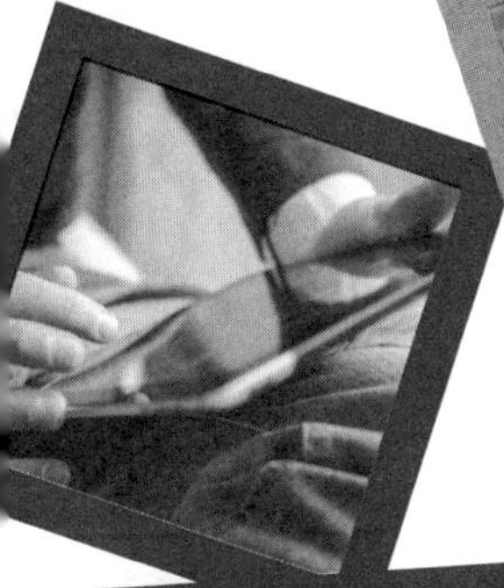

11

E-Mail Messages, Business Letters, and Memorandums

E-Mail Messages, Business Letters, and Memorandums Solution Finder

Addressing Envelopes

E-Mail Messages

Folding and Inserting Correspondence

Letter Format and Placement of Major Parts

E-Mail Messages, Business Letters, and Memorandums Solution Finder

11 Business Messages

E-Mail Messages

E-mail (electronic mail) is a system that permits people to communicate through computers and networks. Members of the system have an electronic "mailbox" and an "address" to which messages are directed and from which they may send messages. Messages sent to the mailbox by other e-mail participants are stored until recipients open their mailboxes. After reading the messages, recipients may print, store, or delete them.

11–1 Purpose and Function

E-mail messages are not substitutes for business letters or memorandums. They are used to convey short messages, request information, respond to inquiries, acknowledge receipt of merchandise or mail, or act as cover documents for attached files.

(1) The purpose of e-mail is to convey short messages quickly and easily without incurring long-distance telephone charges or express mailing charges. E-mail messages are not only economical and easily created but also convenient—they may be received in a matter of minutes (more often even seconds) and read at the recipient's discretion.

(2) The e-mail originator composes a message and "sends" it. Messages sent within an organization are directed to the recipient's computer mailbox through the organization's network. Messages directed outside an organizational network are transmitted through the Internet.

(3) E-mail messages do not replace letters or memorandums that are lengthy, need paper copies, require confidentiality, or discuss significant information or issues. Messages of this nature that are for immediate delivery should be prepared on company letterhead or on a memorandum form and sent by fax. Also, the U.S. Postal Service and private mail carriers offer overnight delivery to most cities in the continental United States.

(4) Electronic mail is not protected or private. Because network security is fallible, you must assume that anyone with a computer has the potential to read your message. Be careful not to include any information in e-mail messages that you would not want disclosed publicly or that would cause you embarrassment. Also, remember that with a click of the mouse, you can inadvertently send your message to the wrong person.

11–2 E-Mail Features

Internet service providers (ISPs),[1] employers and colleges,[2] and Internet-based e-mail providers[3] supply users with a comprehensive

---

[1]Examples of Internet service providers are AT&T, Time Warner, Verizon, EarthLink, and MSN.

[2]Employers and colleges provide users with e-mail applications software such as Microsoft Outlook and Lotus Notes. Applications software is used primarily by organizations for both internal and Internet e-mail.

[3]Examples of Internet e-mail providers are Google Gmail, MSN Hotmail, and Yahoo! Mail.

e-mail system. Although these systems may differ in appearance, they basically offer the same features.

a. ***An e-mail address book.*** **In the e-mail address book, you may store e-mail addresses of persons to whom you write on a regular basis. Stored addresses may be inserted directly into an e-mail message, thereby reducing the chance for error.**

(1) Address books provide template forms for recording the name and e-mail address of individuals. Some e-mail address books permit users to include additional information such as company affiliation, address, telephone number, and fax number.

(2) Address books allow users to enter multiple e-mail addresses in a group file. Group files permit you to send the same message simultaneously to all members in the group.

b. ***A message-composition template.*** **This template permits you to create and send e-mail messages. It contains (1) a set of boxes into which you can enter information and (2) a series of icons that permit you to activate e-mail options. A message-composition template is illustrated on page 346.**

E-mail composition templates generally contain the following guides and options:

(1) *The guide word* To:. Clicking on an individual's or a group's name in the address book will enter the recipient's e-mail address (or recipients' addresses) after the guide word *To:*. You may also type in recipient addresses. Do so carefully because one wrong character or space will prevent your message from being delivered—at least to its intended destination.

(2) *The guide abbreviation* Cc:. If you want others to receive courtesy copies of your message, enter their e-mail addresses after the abbreviation *Cc:*—either from your address book or by typing them in.

(3) *The guide abbreviation* Bcc:. Forms provide for sending blind courtesy copies. Copies are sent to the e-mail addresses listed, but all other recipients do not see that the message was also sent to the addresses designated to receive blind courtesy copies.

The blind-copy feature is useful when a message is sent to a large group of individuals. It prevents showing a long list of e-mail addresses before the actual message appears. This feature also respects the privacy of others' e-mail addresses by not displaying them with the message.

(4) *The guide word* Subject:. Type a brief descriptive phrase that summarizes the topic of your e-mail message after the guide

Outlook message-composition template illustration

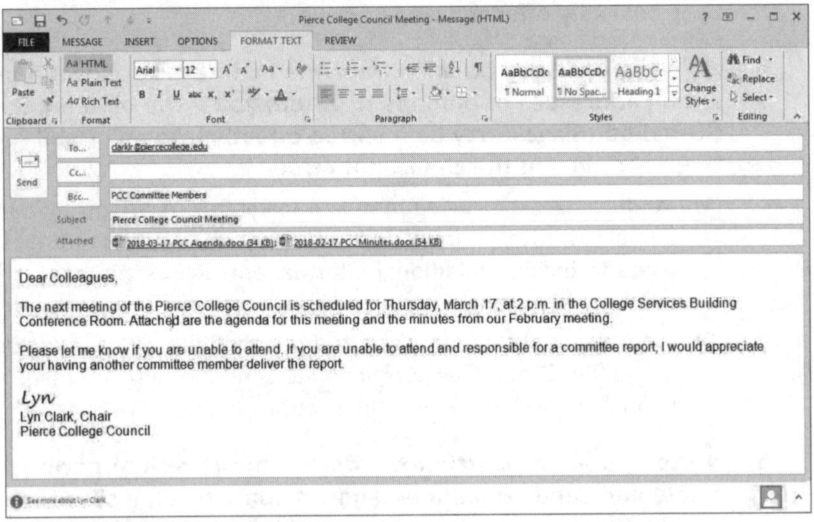

word *Subject:*. Use initial capital letters for each main word[4] in the subject line.

(5) *The message-composition window.* Type your message in the message-composition window. If possible, limit your message to a screenful or two of data. For transmitting lengthy messages and other pertinent data, use attachments.

(6) *The attachments button and window.* You may attach files to be downloaded by the recipient. Keep in mind, though, that the recipient must have the application program in which the file was created to open the file. Use the attachments button and then the attachments window to select (browse) the path and file name of any document or image you wish to send with your e-mail message or to designate a Web site you wish to attach to your message.

(7) *A spell-checker.* Most e-mail systems provide a spell-checker by which you can electronically correct any spelling errors. Some also contain a thesaurus that may be accessed to locate synonyms for words used in your e-mail messages. A few programs provide dictionaries that permit you to look up word meanings as you are composing your message.

(8) *A send button.* The send button routes the message and any attachments to your recipients.

(9) *A save feature.* Most e-mail systems automatically store a copy of your outgoing messages.

---

[4]*Main* words are all words EXCEPT (1) the articles *a, an,* and *the;* (2) the conjunctions *and, but, or, nor,* and *for;* (3) prepositions (e.g., *of, for, on, in, with, through,* etc.); (4) the word *to* in an infinitive (*to purchase, to sign, to negotiate,* etc.); and (5) the word *as*—unless any of these words are the first or last words.

c. ***An in-box.*** **The in-box receives your incoming e-mail messages. From here you are able to open and read the messages sent to you. Your incoming e-mail message is formatted into a template provided by your e-mail system. Information in the template shows the name and/or e-mail address of the sender, the name and/or e-mail address of anyone who received a courtesy copy (not a blind courtesy copy), the subject line, the message, and the file names of any attachments. Three time-saving features appear on templates for incoming messages:**

(1) *A reply-to-sender button.* This reply feature simplifies your providing responses to incoming messages. By clicking the reply-to-sender button within an incoming e-mail message, you will obtain a fresh composition template. The address of the sender is inserted automatically in the address box, and the subject preceded by *Re:* appears in the subject line. All that is needed before you click the send button is your reply in the message-composition window.

(2) *A reply-to-everyone button.* By using this feature, you will obtain a new composition template with all the message recipients' addresses inserted automatically. You may then send your response to the e-mail message originator as well as to all those who received the original message—except those who may have received a blind courtesy copy. Before replying to all recipients, however, make sure that your reply is relevant for everyone.

(3) *A forward button.* By using the forward feature, you may direct a message in your in-box to another person. This feature may be used when another person should see the message contents or when someone else should take responsibility for answering the message because it has been directed to the wrong person. With this feature all attachments are forwarded also.

d. ***A draft folder.*** **This folder option permits you to interrupt composing an e-mail message and store it for editing at another time. Storing an e-mail message temporarily is useful if you need to collect additional information or verify information before sending the message.**

e. ***An e-mail filing cabinet.*** **E-mail systems provide procedures for deleting, saving, and organizing both incoming and outgoing messages.**

(1) Messages in the in-box may be deleted before or after they have been read. Recognizable spam (unwanted, unsolicited e-mail messages or junk mail) may be deleted even before it is opened.

(2) Folders may be created to save and organize incoming and outgoing messages. Messages may later be deleted when they are no longer considered important enough to keep.

f. ***A print feature.*** **You may print incoming and outgoing messages through either a print button or the *File-Print* menu in your e-mail system.**

g. ***Other features.*** **Depending on your software, your e-mail system may allow you to do the following:**

(1) Notify senders that you are unavailable to answer their e-mail messages until a certain date because you are "out of the office."

(2) Create signature files.

(3) Mark messages as "unread" (to be read later).

(4) Use various fonts and font attributes.

(5) Use e-mail stationery.

(6) Paste pictures within messages.

(7) Send messages as greeting cards.

(8) File messages automatically.

(9) Schedule messages to be sent at a later time.

(10) Filter spam (unwanted, unsolicited e-mail messages).

(11) Inform the sender when a message has been delivered.

(12) Inform the sender when a message has been opened and read.

(13) Receive and send messages from a mobile device.

11–3 E-Mail Providers

a. **Large organizations—commercial enterprises, educational institutions, government entities, and other such organizations—provide e-mail capabilities for their employees or for their employees and students.**

(1) E-mail messages within organizations are commonly sent through a computer network established to serve the organization. E-mail messages sent outside an organizational network are transmitted through the Internet.

(2) The organization determines the format of the user's screen name. Usually the format consists of a combination of the individual's first name, last name, and possibly a middle initial. Examples of formats used by organizations are *Jane.Doe@cengage.com* and *DoeJL@piercecollege.edu.*

(3) Access to the e-mail mailbox is generally obtained from a computer located within the organization. Increasingly, however, organizations are furnishing employees Internet access to their organizational e-mail mailboxes from computers outside the organization.

(4) Most large organizations use e-mail applications software (such as Microsoft Outlook or Lotus Notes) for their e-mail systems. See the message-composition template on page 346.

b. Internet service providers (ISPs) provide e-mail services to their clients as part of their subscription fee for Internet access.

(1) Individual users or small businesses obtain access to e-mail messaging through an Internet service provider (ISP). Services that furnish Internet access also provide subscribers from one to a multiple number of e-mail accounts.

(2) Internet service providers supply the connection to the Internet. Examples of commonly known Internet service providers are AT&T, Verizon, Time Warner Cable, Cox, MSN, and EarthLink. Others are scattered in cities throughout the United States and may be easily located through a city's yellow pages under "Internet access."

(3) Internet service providers allow subscribers to select a screen name (a user ID) that is unique for that subscriber. The screen name followed by the *at sign* (@) and the domain name of the Internet service provider make up the subscriber's e-mail address. Examples of e-mail addresses are *davidmonroe@socal.rr.com* and *jslevin@msn.com*.

(4) Messages are sent from one e-mail address to another through the Internet. Subscribers generally have access to their e-mail when they are logged on to their particular Internet service provider. Most Internet service providers also maintain Web sites where subscribers may access their e-mail accounts to read and write mail from any computer connected to the Internet.

(5) Internet service providers furnish an e-mail system with an on-screen form to compose and send messages.

c. A number of Internet sites provide free Internet e-mail accounts to anyone online who requests one.

(1) Internet e-mail accounts are free to anyone worldwide who has an Internet connection, and they may be accessed from any computer that is connected to the Internet. Individuals, then, may communicate with friends, relatives, business associates, colleagues, classmates, and all other persons worldwide—from any connected computer.

(2) Many major sites provide free Internet e-mail accounts. Among the most popular are *MSN Hotmail* at http://www.hotmail.com, *Microsoft Outlook.com* at http://www.microsoft.com/en-us/outlook-com/, *Yahoo! Mail* at http://www.mail.yahoo.com, and *Google Gmail* at https://mail.google.com. Messages are stored on a computer owned by the host (for those sites mentioned—Microsoft, Yahoo!, and Google), not on the computer of an Internet service provider, the message originator, or the message recipient. Consequently, messages may be retrieved, stored, reread, and deleted from any computer as long as it is connected to the Internet.

(3) Messages from an Internet e-mail account may be sent to the mailbox of any e-mail address, regardless of the source of its Internet

access. Conversely, messages from any e-mail address with access to the Internet may be sent to the mailbox of any Internet e-mail account.

(4) Internet e-mail accounts offer features and templates similar to those offered by Internet service providers and organizational e-mail systems.

11–4 Message Preparation

a. Just as business letters and memorandums are forms of one-way communication, so are e-mail messages. Since an e-mail message will not be accompanied by facial expressions or voice inflections, it will be taken at face value. No opportunities exist for the receiver to ask questions, clarify statements, or obtain feedback. Therefore, writers of e-mail messages must plan and write their messages as carefully as they would any other form of written communication.

b. Begin your e-mail message with a friendly greeting. Examples of such greetings follow:

Hi, Bob,	Thank you, Paula,
Hello, Anna,	Dear John Morrow, Dear Mr. Morrow,
Greetings, Don,	Dear Sandra,

c. Use the following guidelines to construct messages. Review your messages to ensure that they are

(1) *Courteous.* Make your message "smile" by using words and phrases such as *please, thank you, appreciate,* and *gladly.* Select positive words to convey your ideas; avoid negative words, innuendos, and accusations. Above all, keep your tone friendly.

(2) *Complete.* Ensure that all the necessary information has been included to achieve the purpose of your e-mail message. Make sure you have not left out any important data.

(3) *Coherent.* Check that all the ideas have been placed in logical order so that one idea flows naturally from the previous one. Ensure that the reader can easily follow your train of thought and that you finish discussing one idea before moving on to the next.

(4) *Clear.* Construct your sentences so that they are worded clearly. Make sure that "who does what" and "what is what" leaves no question in the reader's mind. Avoid long, complicated sentences. Place modifiers as close as possible to the words they modify, and do not use ambiguous pronouns.

(5) *Concrete.* Write in terms of specifics, and use concrete nouns instead of generalities. Dates and times should be expressed explicitly. Likewise, assignments and expectations need to be described in precise terms that are understood similarly by both the writer and the reader.

(6) *Concise.* Use as few words as possible to construct your message, but make sure you have included all the necessary information. Avoid including extra words and extraneous ideas. Remember to keep your e-mail messages as short as possible.

(7) *Correct.* Use the spell-checker of your e-mail software. If your software does not have a spell-checker, keep a dictionary handy as you compose your messages. Proofread your messages carefully for typographical errors, repeated words, omitted words, words used incorrectly, spelling errors, and grammatical errors. E-mail messages represent you as much as any other kind of written communication.

d. Conclude your e-mail message with a "signature," even if it is only your first name. Some people prefer also to sign off with a cordial farewell remark such as *Best wishes,* especially in informal messages to people whom they know.

Signature lines vary in content. Some people may use only their name. Others will include their name, title, organization, and telephone number. Whatever signature lines you choose to use, place the information in no more than five lines.

e. Because e-mail messages are one-way communications, the "Internet community" has developed a series of symbols to express emotion—emoticons, often called "smileys." Some writers of e-mail messages use emoticons to express emotion in their messages. Emoticons should be used only in personal e-mail messages or in e-mail messages to business associates with whom you have a close working relationship. Emoticons may be created through the standard keyboard or by using the extended character set furnished by your e-mail program. Commonly used emoticons are these:

(1) :-) or ☺ This basic smiley is used to show approval or indicate that a statement is made jokingly.

(2) ;-) The wink smiley is flirtatious; it means that what I have just said is a joke.

(3) :-(or ☹ The frowning smiley is used to show disappointment with a situation.

(4) :-I or 😐 The indifferent smiley is used to show that the outcome of a situation makes no difference to the writer.

11–5 E-Mail Netiquette

Netiquette (net etiquette) is a set of behaviors that should be adhered to when using the Internet. Excluding conduct prohibited by federal laws, the Internet community itself has devised etiquette standards for Internet use. Those applying to e-mail follow:

(1) Use e-mail to accomplish a specific purpose. Do not send e-mail messages that are needless or unnecessary. At the same time, send

courtesy copies only to people who will benefit from or who need the information contained in your e-mail message.

(2) Make your reply as succinct as possible when replying to e-mail messages online. If courtesy copies were routed to others, evaluate whether these individuals need your response before sending your reply. Avoid cluttering the network and others' mailboxes with unnecessary replies.

(3) Be courteous in your e-mail messages. Sending rude messages is known as "flaming" and is frowned upon by the Internet community.

(4) Avoid using a series of all capital letters in the body of your message. Besides hindering readability, all capital letters are considered the e-mail equivalent of shouting and may be construed as rude.

(5) Keep your e-mail messages short, generally no more than one or two screenfuls of data. If you send a long message, tell the recipient at the beginning so that he or she has the option to read it later.

(6) Do not send chain letters over the Internet.

Business Letters

Business letters are written primarily to correspond with individuals outside the organization or persons in another organization. They are also written by individuals who wish to communicate with an organization—whether to request information, seek employment, or correct a problem.

In recent years the use of business letters has declined significantly, giving way to e-mail messaging. E-mail messages are less costly in terms of preparation time, supplies, and postage. They are more efficient since they reach the recipient within minutes, sometimes seconds. Only in cases where (1) e-mail is unavailable or inconvenient, (2) the message requires a degree of formality, or (3) the message contains confidential information is a business letter preferred.

Within an organization business letters are generally prepared for customers or clients, prospective customers or clients, suppliers of goods and services, prospective employees, and former employees (recommendations) when e-mail is unavailable or inappropriate.

Business Letter Styles

11-6 Full Block

Business letters may be formatted in several styles.[5] The full block letter is the most streamlined style because all lines begin at the left margin.

full block letter

Gibraltar Insurance Company of America

916 New Britain Avenue
Hartford, Connecticut 06106-2845

Telephone: (203) 743-1200
Toll-free number: (800) 539-8733
Fax: (203) 745-1388

2 inches

June 16, 2017

2–10 blank lines

Prescott & Larsen Insurance Agency
17867 Laurel Canyon Boulevard
Mission Hills, California 91343-2471

1 blank line →

Gentlemen

1 blank line →

SUBJECT: CLAIM NO. AT6509, INSURED ROBERT A. MURPHY

1 blank line →

The claim of your client, Mr. Robert A. Murphy, for $950 to replace the golf clubs that were stolen from him in Scottsdale is covered under his homeowner's policy, No. 2864952.

1 blank line →

To process Mr. Murphy's claim, we must have a copy of the police report filed at the time of the theft. Please contact the police agency handling the theft report and have the agency forward us a copy addressed to my attention.

1 blank line →

As soon as we receive the police report, Mr. Murphy's check will be sent to your office.

1 blank line →

Sincerely yours

1 blank line →

GIBRALTAR INSURANCE COMPANY OF AMERICA

3 blank lines

Annette R. Bushnell

(Mrs.) Annette R. Bushnell, Claims Adjuster

1 blank line →

fd

1 blank line →

cc: Mr. Robert Murphy

[5]All letters appearing in this chapter have been designed by the authors for illustrative purposes. They are not reproductions of actual letters.

11–7 Modified Block

a. The modified block letter with blocked paragraphs is another popular letter style used in business. All lines except the return address (if used), the date, and the closing lines begin at the left margin.

modified block letter with blocked paragraphs

2 inches

Snowflake Crystal, Inc.
1640 Grand Boulevard
Schenectady, New York 12309-1083
Tel: (518) 872-3100, (800) CRYSTAL • Fax: (518) 872-3132

April 17, 2017

2–10 blank lines

EXPRESS MAIL

1 blank line →

The Gift Closet, Inc.
Attention: Ms. Kendra Kriegisch, Buyer
8350 Kensington Avenue
Philadelphia, PA 19149-1452

1 blank line →

Ladies and Gentlemen:

1 blank line →

We appreciate your interest in our crystal creations and would be pleased to have The Gift Closet carry them. I am sure you would find these fast-selling gift items to be a profitable addition to your inventory.

1 blank line →

Our complete line of Snowflake crystal is illustrated in the enclosed catalog. As you will note from the full-page color illustrations, its simple design and exquisite workmanship have made Snowflake crystal one of the most popular lines in the country.

1 blank line →

A complete list of prices and the terms of sale are included in the back pages of the catalog. You will also note that we provide a breakage credit up to 5 percent of purchases on merchandise displayed in your store. Just return any broken pieces, and we will replace the merchandise.

1 blank line →

We hope that we can add your name to the many retailers throughout the country who represent Snowflake crystal. Should you wish to open an account with us, please return the enclosed credit application. If you wish to place a c.o.d. order, we can deliver the merchandise within ten days of the receipt of your order.

1 blank line →

Let Snowflake start earning for you today.

1 blank line →

Sincerely,

3 blank lines *Joshua T. Donovan*

Joshua T. Donovan
Vice President, Marketing

1 blank line →

ma
Enclosures

b. The modified block letter with indented paragraphs is used occasionally. All lines except the first line of each paragraph, the return address (if used), the date, and the closing lines begin at the left margin.

modified block letter with indented paragraphs

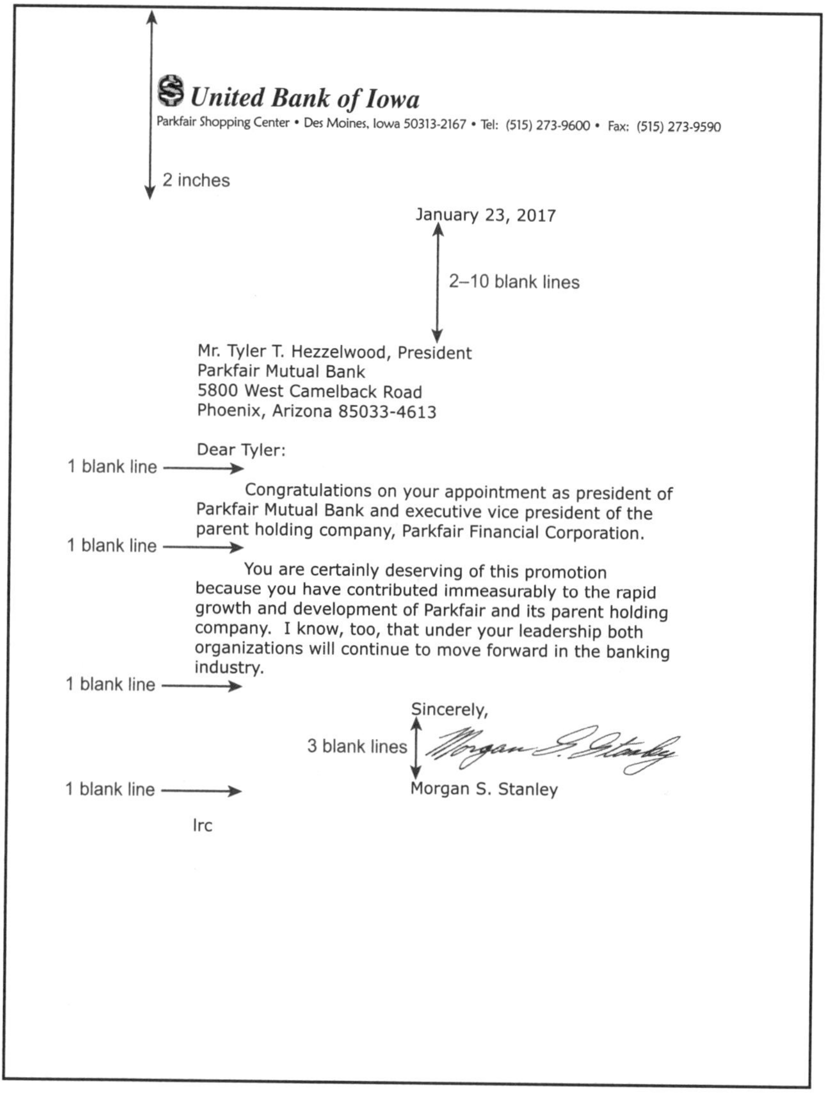

United Bank of Iowa
Parkfair Shopping Center • Des Moines, Iowa 50313-2167 • Tel: (515) 273-9600 • Fax: (515) 273-9590

January 23, 2017

Mr. Tyler T. Hezzelwood, President
Parkfair Mutual Bank
5800 West Camelback Road
Phoenix, Arizona 85033-4613

Dear Tyler:

Congratulations on your appointment as president of Parkfair Mutual Bank and executive vice president of the parent holding company, Parkfair Financial Corporation.

You are certainly deserving of this promotion because you have contributed immeasurably to the rapid growth and development of Parkfair and its parent holding company. I know, too, that under your leadership both organizations will continue to move forward in the banking industry.

Sincerely,

Morgan S. Stanley

lrc

Punctuation Styles

11–8 Mixed Punctuation

The most popular punctuation style for business letters is mixed punctuation. In this format a colon follows the salutation and a comma appears after the complimentary close. No other closing punctuation marks are used except those concluding an abbreviation or ones appearing within the body of the letter.

business letter with mixed punctuation

DALE'S DEPARTMENT STORE

Serving Seattle and the Surrounding Area

1640 Grand Boulevard
Seattle, Washington 98102-1083
Tel: (206) 473-6982 • Fax: (206) 473-6984

2 inches

February 1, 2017

2–10 blank lines

Mr. and Mrs. John Levine
1924 Fulton Avenue
Bothell, WA 98011-1387

1 blank line →

Dear Mr. and Mrs. Levine:

1 blank line →

On Saturday, February 25, 2017, our Bothell location will be closing its doors. Saying goodbye to friends is always sad, and we would like to extend our sincere "thank you" for your support. We are truly honored and grateful to have served the Bothell community for the past 15 years.

1 blank line →

Dale's Department Store will still be here to serve your everyday and special needs at three nearby locations in the cities of Seattle, Kirkland, and Redmond. You may use your Dale's credit card at any one of these locations or for any online purchases.

1 blank line →

You may be wondering what will happen to all the Bothell Dale's associates and whether they will have jobs during these tough economic times. We want to assure you that we value every one of our employees, and they will continue to work at other Dale's Department Stores. Our company is committed to taking care of them as we all consider ourselves family.

1 blank line →

As a token of our appreciation for your patronage and support, we are including some discount coupons for you to use at one of our neighboring Dale's. It has been a pleasure and honor to serve you, and we hope we will see you again soon at one of our other locations.

1 blank line →

Sincerely,

3 blank lines *Peter McDougall*

Peter McDougall
President, Dale's Department Store

1 blank line →

rd
Enclosures

11–9 Open Punctuation

Writers of business letters sometimes use open punctuation. No closing punctuation marks except those concluding an abbreviation appear after the letter parts. The only other ending punctuation marks are ones used within the body of the letter.

business letter with open punctuation

Campbell Vision Institute
Wilshire Medical Plaza • 900 Beverly Drive, Suite 400 • Beverly Hills, CA 90312 • Tel: (310) 371-4200

2 inches

April 14, 2017

2–10 blank lines

Ms. Janice Wellington
17239 Nordhoff Street, Apt. 304
Reseda, CA 91323

1 blank line →

Dear Ms. Wellington

1 blank line →

I hope that you have settled into your new vision and that you are enjoying the results of your LASIK procedure. It was my sincere pleasure to assist with your vision needs and to continue to be of service.

1 blank line →

You might recall that our surgery suite Labrador retriever mascot, "CORNEAlius," may have comforted you during the procedure. As a reminder of the comforts that we are dedicated to providing and in appreciation for trusting us for your care, enclosed is Cornealius's cousin, "Iris." Enjoy!

1 blank line →

On behalf of the entire staff, I wish you the best, and we look forward to seeing you at your next visit with us.

1 blank line →

Sincerely

3 blank lines ↕ *William J. Campbell*

William J. Campbell, MD

1 blank line →

lrc
Enclosure

Letter Format and Placement of Major Parts

11-10 Conventional Margins, Line Spacing, and Vertical Placement with Word Processing Software

a. Use the following guidelines for preparing business letters on letterhead stationery:

(1) Select a sans serif font that is easy to read; for example, Arial, Microsoft Sans Serif, Tahoma, Trebuchet MS, or Verdana. Use a 10-point, 11-point, or 12-point size.

(2) Use a 2-inch top margin for the first page of a business letter printed on letterhead stationery to allow for the letterhead. Any succeeding pages of a business letter have 1-inch top margins. Use left justification.

(3) Set the line spacing to single spacing. In Microsoft Word 2007, 2010, or 2013, reset (or default) the line spacing from 1.15 to 1.0.

(4) Choose the side margins according to the number of words in the letter and the size of the font used. Set the margins after keying the letter and using the word-count feature of your word processing program.

(5) The following tables may be used as guidelines for preparing various length letters. The first table applies to 12-point fonts; the second table applies to 11- and 10-point fonts.

12-point fonts

Margin Settings for Business Letters
12-Point Fonts

Letter Length	*Number of Words*	*Margin Settings*		*Line Length*
		Left	*Right*	
Standard	Up to 200	1.5 inches	1.5 inches	5.5 inches
Long	200 +	1 inch	1 inch	6.5 inches

11- and 10-point fonts

Margin Settings for Business Letters
Printed in 11-Point and 10-Point Fonts

Letter Length	*Number of Words*	*Margin Settings*		*Line Length*
		Left	*Right*	
Short	Up to 150	1.75 inches	1.75 inches	5 inches
Standard	151–200	1.5 inches	1.5 inches	5.5 inches
Long	201–250	1.25 inches	1.25 inches	6 inches
Extra long	251 +	1 inch	1 inch	6.5 inches

b. Leave two or three blank lines between the date and inside address in letters with two or more pages. Balance single-page letters vertically by regulating the number of lines between the date and the inside address. Use the following procedures on your word processing program to achieve this balance after the margins have been set:

(1) Count the number of blank lines between the date and the inside address (e.g., 3 blank lines).

(2) Directly after the *last* line of the letter (usually containing reference initials or an enclosure notation), press the *Enter key* until the page break is reached. Count the number of blank lines from the last line of the letter until the page break (e.g., 6 blank lines).

(3) Total the two line counts (e.g., 3 + 6 = 9). Divide this total by two (e.g., 9 ÷ 2 = 4.5). Disregard any fractional part (e.g., 4 blank lines).

(4) Insert or delete blank lines, if necessary, to ensure that the number of blank lines between the date and the inside address EQUALS the result obtained in Step (3) above. Do not, however, leave fewer than 2 or more than 10 blank lines between the date and the inside address (e.g., Insert 1 additional blank line between the date and the inside address if the result is less than 2).

(5) Delete any extra blank lines at the bottom of the page.

examples for balancing a letter vertically on the page

Blank Lines between Date and Inside Address	*Blank Lines between Letter End and Page Break*	*Sum of Blank Lines*	*Blank Lines Divided by 2 / Remainder Dropped*	*Revised Number of Blank Lines Needed between Date and Inside Address*	*Number of Blank Lines to be Inserted or Deleted*
4	2	4 + 2 = 6	6 ÷ 2 = 3	3	−1
3	7	3 + 7 = 10	10 ÷ 2 = 5	5	+2
4	1	4 + 1 = 5	5 ÷ 2 = 2.5 = 2	2	−2
3	8	3 + 8 = 11	11 ÷ 2 = 5.5 = 5	5	+2
4	−1	4 − 1 = 3	3 ÷ 2 = 1.5 = 1	At least 2	−2

The 240-word business letter shown on page 360 illustrates the margins and vertical placement of a long letter prepared in 11-point Arial font.

11–11 Microsoft Word 2007, 2010, and 2013 Default Margins, Line Spacing, and Font Used for Business Letters

a. Use the following guidelines for preparing business letters on letterhead stationery with the default settings of Microsoft Word 2007, 2010, and 2013:

(1) Use a 2-inch top margin for the first page of a business letter printed on letterhead stationery to allow for the letterhead. Any second and succeeding pages of a business letter should have 1-inch top margins.

(2) Use the default settings of Microsoft Word 2007, 2010, or 2013 to prepare the business letter: side and bottom margins (1 inch), line spacing (1.15), font (11-point Calibri), and paragraph settings (10 points of blank space following each paragraph).

balanced long letter prepared in 11-point font

ABC Global Insurance Company

400 Berkeley Street • Boston, MA 02117 • Tel. (617) 555-3765 • Fax (617) 555-3785

2 inches

June 4, 2017
¶
¶ Letter balanced vertically with 4 blank lines
¶ between date and inside address
¶
Mr. Michael R. Lee
A-1 Insurance Agency
470 West Fairmont Street, Suite 320
Grand Rapids, MI 49502-1036

Dear Mr. Lee:

Subject: ABC Global Policy No. S119294, Insured Duncan R. Hannah

We have completed our investigation of the May 7 accident claim submitted by your agency on behalf of Duncan R. Hannah.

According to our claims adjuster, Mr. Hannah was injured while in the employ of the Millstone Manufacturing Company. His injuries were incurred in an industrial accident on April 27 and are therefore considered job related. Consequently, the expenses for this accident are covered by Workers' Compensation. Only those expenses beyond the amount allowed by Workers' Compensation are covered by our company and eligible for reimbursement.

Please submit a complete listing of Mr. Hannah's expenses in regard to this accident. As soon as we receive verification from the Workers' Compensation Board on the amount allowable in Mr. Hannah's case, we will process the proper claim forms.

If you have any questions or need any additional information, please let me know.

Sincerely,

B. Andrew Ferragamo

B. Andrew Ferragamo, CLU
Vice President

mrd
¶
¶ Letter balanced vertically with 5 blank lines
¶ between last line of the letter and the page break
¶
¶

1-inch margin

b. Prepare the letter according to the following guidelines:

(1) Press *Enter* sufficient times to key the date 2 inches from the top edge of the paper. Do not set a 2-inch top margin as the letter may continue to a second page.

(2) Press *Enter* two times after keying the date.

(3) Press *Shift-Enter* after each line of the inside address, except the last one, to prevent the lines from being formatted as separate paragraphs.

(4) Press *Enter* once after keying the last line in the inside address. Paragraphs are formatted by default to place 10 points of blank space after pressing *Enter.*

(5) Key the salutation, and press *Enter* once.

(6) Key each paragraph in the letter, and press *Enter* only once after each paragraph, including the last paragraph.

(7) Key the complimentary close; press *Enter* two times to provide space for the signature of the letter originator.

(8) Key the signature lines. For multiple lines in the signature block, press *Shift-Enter* after each line (except the last one) to minimize the spacing between lines.

(9) Conclude the letter with any required notations, pressing *Enter* only once after each notation.

c. An example of a business letter with the defaults of Microsoft Word 2007, 2010, and 2013 is illustrated on page 362. This is not a recommended style for business letters nor are the "out-of-the-package" defaults of Microsoft Word 2007, 2010, and 2013 recommended for preparing business documents. The defaults in these last three versions of Microsoft Word may be changed easily to suit the working patterns of individuals and companies. The following default settings are recommended for general business use:

(1) Set the default font as Arial, 11 points. This sans serif font is clear and easy to read.

(2) Change the default line spacing from 1.15 to 1.0. This will eliminate additional spacing between lines.

(3) Change the default spacing after each paragraph from 10 points to 0 points. This will prevent indiscriminately adding 10 points of space each time after pressing *Enter.*

11–12 Return Address

a. No return address is needed, as shown in the letterhead on page 362, for business letters prepared on paper containing a complete company letterhead. Similarly, business letters prepared on word processing programs with a letter template do not require a return address.

business letter prepared using Microsoft Word 2007, 2010, or 2013 defaults

ABC Global Insurance Company

400 Berkeley Street • Boston, MA 02117 • Tel. (617) 555-3765 • Fax (617) 555-3785

2 inches

June 4, 2017

Mr. Michael R. Lee
A-1 Insurance Agency
470 West Fairmont Street, Suite 320
Grand Rapids, MI 49502-1036

Dear Mr. Lee:

Subject: ABC Global Policy No. S119294, Insured Duncan R. Hannah

We have completed our investigation of the May 7 accident claim submitted by your agency on behalf of Duncan R. Hannah.

According to our claims adjuster, Mr. Hannah was injured while in the employ of the Millstone Manufacturing Company. His injuries were incurred in an industrial accident on April 27 and are therefore considered job related. Consequently, the expenses for this accident are covered by Workers' Compensation. Only those expenses beyond the amount allowed by Workers' Compensation are covered by our company and eligible for reimbursement.

Please submit a complete listing of Mr. Hannah's expenses in regard to this accident. As soon as we receive verification from the Workers' Compensation Board on the amount allowable in Mr. Hannah's case, we will process the proper claim forms.

If you have any questions or need any additional information, please let me know.

Sincerely,

B Andrew Ferragamo

B. Andrew Ferragamo, CLU
Vice President

mrd

printed company letterhead

Data
Select
Systems, Inc.

2829 TOWNSGATE RD. #300, WESTLAKE VILLAGE, CA 91361
(805) 446-2090
FAX (805) 446-2089

letterhead produced from a word processing template

b. **When plain bond paper or letterhead paper without a mailing address is used, a return address must be included.**

(1) On plain bond paper, begin the return address so that the date is 2 inches from the top edge of the paper. Although the date appears directly below the last line of the return address, it is not considered part of the return address.

(2) On letterhead paper without a mailing address, begin the return address a double space below the last line in the letterhead or end it so that the date is 2 inches below the top edge of the paper. Select the option that places the return address in the lower position.

c. ***Modified block letter.*** **In the modified block letter, each line of the return address may be centered. Lines in the return address may also (1) begin at the center of the page, (2) begin 0.5 inch to the left of the page center, or (3) align at the right margin.**

Full block letter. **In the full block letter, all lines begin at the left margin.**

return address in modified block letter without letterhead

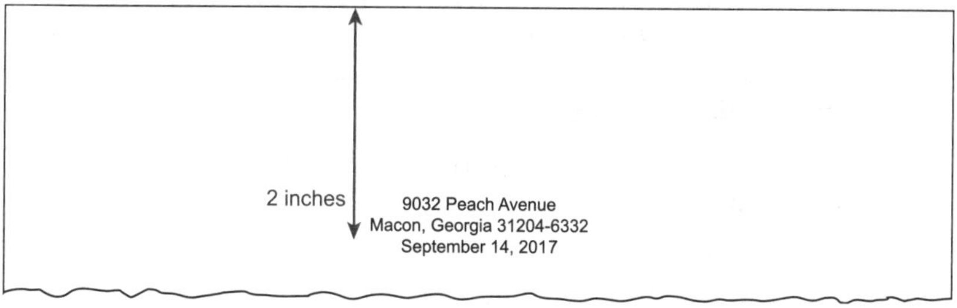

return address in full block letter without letterhead

letterhead with return address ending 2 inches from top edge of paper—modified block letter

letterhead with return address begun a double space below letterhead—full block letter

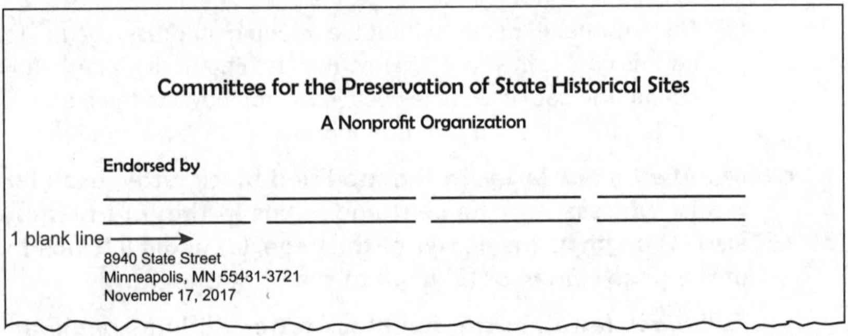

11–13 Date

a. **On letterhead paper with a mailing address, place the date a double space below the last line in the letterhead or allow a 2-inch margin from the top edge of the paper. Select the procedure that places the date in the lower position.**

Modified block letter. **In modified block letters, the date may be positioned as follows:**

(1) Centered

(2) Begun at the center of the page

(3) Aligned with the right margin

Full block letter. **In full block letters, place the date at the left margin.**

date 2 inches below top edge of paper—modified block letter

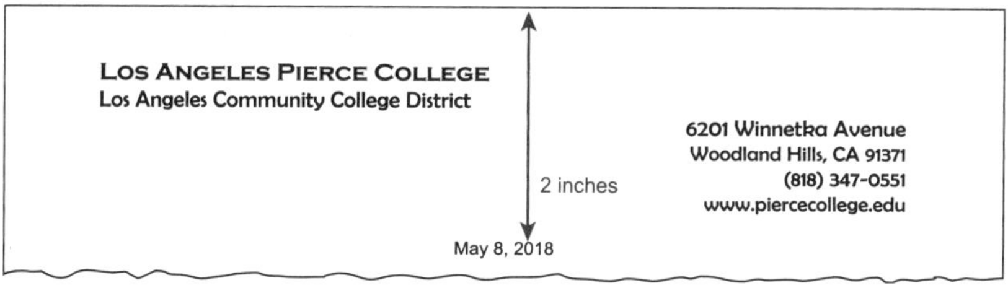

date placed a double space below letterhead—full block letter

b. In letters requiring return addresses, place the date on the line directly below the last line of the return address.

11-14 Addressee and Delivery Notations

a. Addressee notations such as *Personal* and *Confidential* are entered in all capital letters a double space above the inside address.

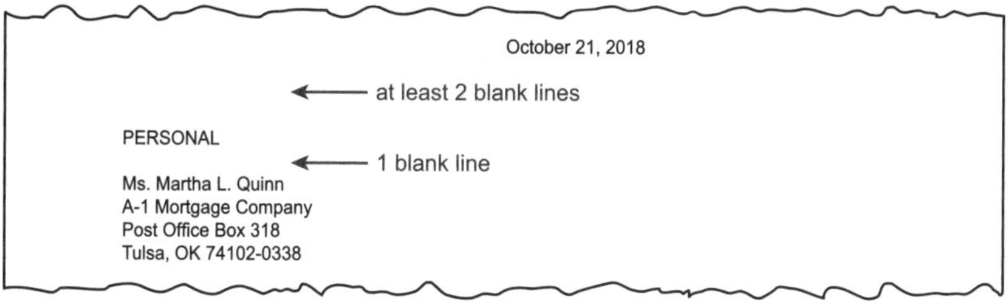

b. Delivery notations such as *Certified Mail, Express Mail, Federal Express, Air Mail, Registered Mail, Fax Transmittal,* and *Messenger Delivery* are entered in all capital letters either (1) a double space above the inside address or (2) a single or double space below the reference initials or enclosure notation, whichever appears last. A delivery notation is illustrated in a complete letter in Section 11–7a, page 354.

delivery notations a double space above inside address

October 21, 2018

← at least 2 blank lines

CERTIFIED MAIL

← 1 blank line

Ms. Anna Torti
Universal Lending Associates
Post Office Box 1330
Tulsa, OK 74102-0338

October 21, 2018

← at least 2 blank lines

FAX TRANSMITTAL

← 1 blank line

Ms. Anna Torti
Universal Lending Associates
Post Office Box 1330
Tulsa, OK 74102-0338

delivery notation after reference initials or enclosure notation

ks
Enclosure
EXPRESS MAIL
copy to Bruce Rosky

c. If an addressee notation and a delivery notation appear in the same letter, place the addressee notation on the third line above the inside address and the delivery notation on the line directly below. Use all capital letters for both notations. Leave *at least* two blank lines between the date and the addressee notation.

January 22, 2018

← at least 2 blank lines

CONFIDENTIAL
EXPRESS MAIL

← 1 blank line

Mr. Michael D. Espinosa
Vice President, Marketing
Creative Choice Toys, Inc.
4000 Washington Boulevard
Chicago, IL 60612-6427

11–15 Inside Address

a. The inside address follows the date and any addressee or delivery notations. It contains some or all of the following:

(1) *Courtesy title and full name.* Place the courtesy title and full name on the first line.

(2) *Professional title and department name.* The professional title and department name have no specific line designations, but they follow the courtesy title and full name. Because the professional title and department name have no specific line designations, they should be positioned to balance with the remaining parts of the inside address.

(3) *Company name.* The company name is placed on a separate line after any professional title or department name.

(4) *Street or mailing address.* The street or mailing address appears on a separate line before the city, state, and ZIP Code.

(5) *City, state, and ZIP Code.* The city, state, and ZIP Code appear on a separate line, which is always the last line of the address.[6]

Single-space and begin at the left margin those parts necessary to direct the letter to the addressee.

Ms. Morgan A. Stanley
Manager, Policy Issue Department
Atlantic-General Insurance Company
400 West Jefferson Boulevard, Suite 100
Charlotte, North Carolina 28212-7610

Mr. Byron Hart, Manager
Department of Human Resources
Citizens Federal Bank
5282 East Ninth Street
Charlotte, NC 28212-4310

b. An inside address may contain from a minimum of two lines to a maximum of six lines. Use the following guidelines to format the various parts of an inside address:

(1) Abbreviate only the courtesy titles *Mr., Mrs.,* and *Dr.* The courtesy title *Ms.* is not an abbreviation; its only form is *Ms.*

(2) Spell out all street designations such as *Street, Avenue,* and *Boulevard. Boulevard* may be abbreviated, however, with exceptionally long street names.

(3) Spell out the state name or use the two-letter post office designation, whichever form achieves balance with the remaining lines. A list of two-letter state and territory designations for the United States may be found in Section 6–12 and on the page opposite the inside back cover.

---

[6] For information on address formats for foreign correspondence, refer to Section 10–8.

two-line inside address
Cedar Creek Inn
Cedar Rapids, IA 52406

six-line inside address
Mr. M. J. Fujimoto
Airline Training Specialist
Division of Personnel Instruction
TransAmerica–Continental Airlines
12700 East Funston Street
Wichita, Kansas 67207-3402

c. The inside address usually follows the date. The number of blank lines between the date and the inside address is determined by the length of the letter. Refer to Section 11–10 for detailed instructions on setting margins and determining the number of blank lines to leave between the date and the inside address.

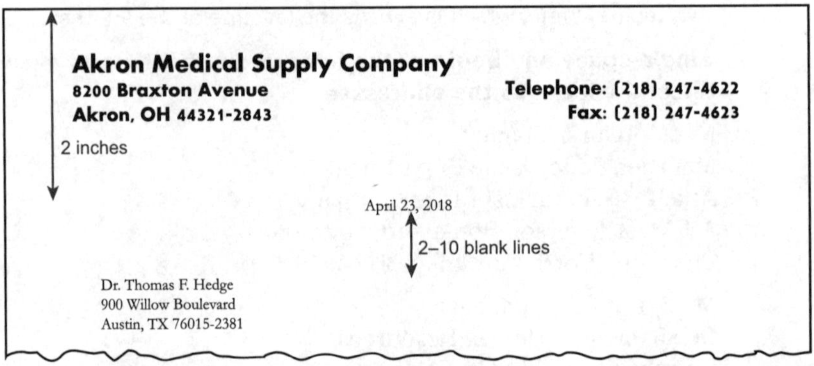

11–16 Attention Line

a. The attention line is used for directing correspondence to an individual or department within a company while still officially addressing the letter to the organization. It is also useful for directing correspondence to a person whose name is unknown.

b. The modern trend is to place the attention line in the inside address directly below the company name and to use the same format for the envelope address.[7] The attention line may also be placed at the left margin a double space below the last line of the inside address.

[7]Correspondence using an attention line is addressed to the company, not an individual. Therefore, the name of the company should appear before the attention line. The U.S. Postal Service recommendation to place the attention line before the company name does not follow this protocol.

Use (1) a combination of initial capital letters and lowercase letters or (2) all capital letters. Using a colon after *Attention* is optional. An attention line is illustrated in a complete letter in Section 11–7a, page 354.

attention line included in inside address

Valley Manufacturing Company
Attention: General Manager
18600 Sierra Bonita Boulevard
San Bernardino, CA 91763-5201

attention line at left margin below inside address

Freestone Rubber Company
1200 North Clybourn Avenue
Chicago, Illinois 60610-1392
1 blank line →
Attention: Director of Human Resources
1 blank line →
Ladies and Gentlemen:
1 blank line →
As an accounting supervisor for a major industrial firm in the greater Detroit area
for the past 13 years, I have had a great deal of experience working with the kinds

11–17 Salutation

a. The format of the salutation depends on to whom the letter is addressed in the inside address and the degree of familiarity between the addressee and the writer (see Section 11–17b–f).[8]

Begin the salutation at the left margin, and place it a double space below the last line of the inside address or the attention line, if used. Conclude the salutation with a colon for the mixed punctuation format; use no ending punctuation mark for the open punctuation format.

Mr. Charles B. Wayama
Empire Check Printing
200 Renaissance Center
Detroit, MI 40610-1392
1 blank line →
Dear Mr. Wayama:
1 blank line →
For the past eight years, our bank has been using your company to print checks for our checking
account customers. During this time we have been pleased with the quality of your service and

b. In letters addressed to individuals, use one of the following salutations, depending upon the degree of formality desired. Use a colon after the salutation if mixed punctuation is used; use no punctuation mark if open punctuation is used.

[8]See Sections 10–11 through 10–14 for additional information on the proper use of formal titles, salutations, and complimentary closes.

informal salutation
Dear Carson: Dear Drew:

standard business letter salutation to a single addressee
Dear Mr. Forrester: Dear Ms. Lopez: Dear Mrs. Chin:

standard business letter salutation for boy or girl younger than 13 years of age
Dear Master Hogan: Dear Miss Jefferson:

standard business letter salutation to two or more men
Dear Mr. Donovan and Mr. Stephenson:

or

Dear Mr. Donovan, Mr. Stephenson, and Mr. Stern:

or

Dear Messrs. Donovan, Stephenson, and Stern:

or

Gentlemen:

***standard business letter salutation to two or more women—courtesy title* Ms.**
Dear Ms. Franklin and Ms. Kellogg:

or

Dear Ms. Franklin, Ms. Horike, and Ms. Kellogg:

or

Dear Mses. Franklin, Horike, and Kellogg:

or

Ladies:

***standard business letter salutation to two or more women—courtesy title* Mrs.**
Dear Mrs. Marsee and Mrs. O'Donnell:

or

Dear Mrs. Bedrosian, Mrs. Marsee, and Mrs. O'Donnell:

or

Dear Mesdames Bedrosian, Marsee, and O'Donnell:

or

Mesdames:

or

Ladies:

standard business letter salutation to two or more persons with different courtesy titles
Dear Ms. Sterling and Mr. Michel:

Dear Mrs. Andrino, Ms. Hopi, Mr. Lopez, and Ms. Mullens-King:

Ladies: [Women only]

Gentlemen: [Men only]

Ladies and Gentlemen:

Dear Colleagues: [Or other appropriate general reference designation]

standard salutations to persons with professional titles

Dear Dr. Marcus:

Dear Professor Bredow:

Dear Colonel Andrews:

formal salutations for certain government officials and religious dignitaries

Sir:

Excellency:

Reverend Sir:

Your Eminence:

c. If the gender of an addressee is unknown, use the full name of the person without a courtesy title. Use the courtesy title *Ms.* for a woman unless another title is specified by the addressee.

full name without courtesy title

Orolyn Ruenz [Dear Orolyn Ruenz:]

Chris Ravetch [Dear Chris Ravetch:]

B. C. Weyenberg [Dear B. C. Weyenberg:]

courtesy title for a woman

Ms. Diana Reember [Dear Ms. Reember:]

Ms. Min Nguyen [Dear Ms. Nguyen:]

d. In correspondence addressed to companies, associations, or other groups, use one of the following salutations:

salutations for groups composed of men and women

Ladies and Gentlemen: Gentlemen and Ladies:

salutation for groups composed entirely of men

Gentlemen:

salutations for groups composed entirely of women

Mesdames: Ladies:

e. Letters addressed to a firm but directed to the attention of an individual within the company receive the salutation used to open a letter to a group: *Gentlemen, Ladies and Gentlemen, Gentlemen and Ladies, Mesdames,* or *Ladies.*

Arroyo Textile Manufacturing Company
Attention Accounts Receivable Manager
2850 Central Avenue, NW
Albuquerque, New Mexico 87105-1742
1 blank line →
Ladies and Gentlemen:
1 blank line →
On September 10 we purchased from your company twelve 50-yard bolts of Royal Luster velvet upholstery fabric (Invoice No. GY-14953). Payment of this invoice was mailed on September 23.

f. Letters to an undetermined individual or group of individuals should generally be avoided. When used, such letters contain no inside address and use *To Whom It May Concern:* as the salutation.

April 7, 2018
↕ 4–12 blank lines
To Whom It May Concern:
1 blank line →
I am pleased to recommend Sharon Hazelbusch for a position as an administrative assistant. For the past five years, Sharon has worked closely with me in the Human

11–18 Subject Line

a. The subject line briefly describes the contents of the letter. Begin the subject line at the left margin a double space below the salutation. Double-space after the subject line.

Use (1) initial capital letters for the main words[9] or (2) all capital letters. The word *Subject* followed by a colon usually introduces the line. The subject line is illustrated in a full block letter in Section 11–6, page 353.

If an attention line appears in the same letter a double space below the inside address, use the same format for both the attention and the subject lines.

subject line at left margin

Dear Mr. Sullivan:
← 1 blank line
Subject: Anticipated Cost Reductions
← 1 blank line
Within the next few weeks, we expect to see significant price reductions in the cost of several raw materials we use for the production of our woven window and patio laminated shades.

Dear Mr. Sullivan:
← 1 blank line
ANTICIPATED COST REDUCTIONS
← 1 blank line
Within the next few weeks, we expect to see significant price reductions in the cost of several raw materials we use for the production of our woven window and patio laminated shades.

---

[9]*Main* words are all words EXCEPT (1) the articles *a*, *an*, and *the*; (2) the conjunctions *and, but, or, nor*, and *for*; (3) prepositions (e.g., *of, for, on, in, with, through*, etc.); (4) the word *to* in an infinitive (*to purchase, to sign, to negotiate*, etc.); and (5) the word *as*—unless any of these words are the first or last words.

two-line subject with book title

Dear Ms. Kellerman:

← 1 blank line

Subject: Alternate Distribution Channels for the Seventh Edition of Our Statistics Textbook,
Statistical Analysis

← 1 blank line

The seventh edition of one of our best-selling textbooks, *Statistical Analysis*, has generated considerable interest among a number of the international business faculty at Southwestern

attention and subject lines in the same letter

Attention: Manager, Human Resources Department

← 1 blank line

Ladies and Gentlemen:

← 1 blank line

Subject: Medical Insurance Programs for Employees

← 1 blank line

Premium expenditures for employee medical, dental, vision care, and life insurance have risen rapidly during the past two years. Besides rising health care costs and the economic decline

b. Insurance companies, financial institutions, attorneys, and government offices often use the abbreviation *Re:* or *In re:* (meaning "in the matter of") in place of the word *Subject:* at the beginning of the subject line.

Re: Policy 489-6342, Insured Michael T. Block

IN RE: TOLBERT VS. FEINBERG

c. When initiating or replying to correspondence that has a special policy number, order number, account number, or other such reference, include this information in a subject line or in a specific reference below and aligned with the date.

If guide words are not printed on the letterhead, supply labels such as *When replying, refer to:, File No.:, In reply to:, Re:, Your reference:, Refer to:*, and so on. These notations are typed in initial capital and lowercase letters; they are placed a double space below the date.

standard subject line

Dear Mr. Urun:

← 1 blank line

Subject: Invoice No. 4398 Dated May 23

← 1 blank line

Four of the seven computer workstations billed on your May 23 invoice, No. 4398, have not yet been installed and are scheduled for installation next week. Our installer will be available to

notation below and aligned with date—modified block letter

October 21, 2018

1 blank line →

In re: Policy 893621P

d. **Some companies prefer to place the subject line above the salutation. In such cases begin the subject line a double space below the inside address. If an attention line follows the inside address, then begin the subject line a double space below the attention line.**

Use (1) initial capital letters with lowercase letters or (2) all capital letters. The caption *Subject, Re,* or *In re* precedes the content and is followed by a colon. If an attention line appears in the same letter, use the same format for both lines.

Double-space after the subject line to begin the salutation.

subject line above salutation

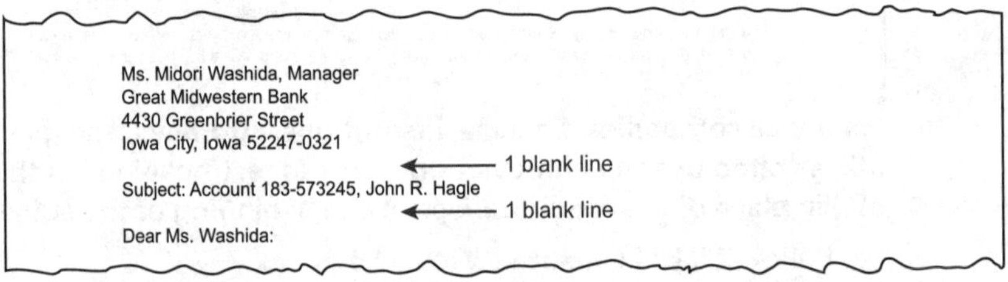

subject and attention lines above salutation

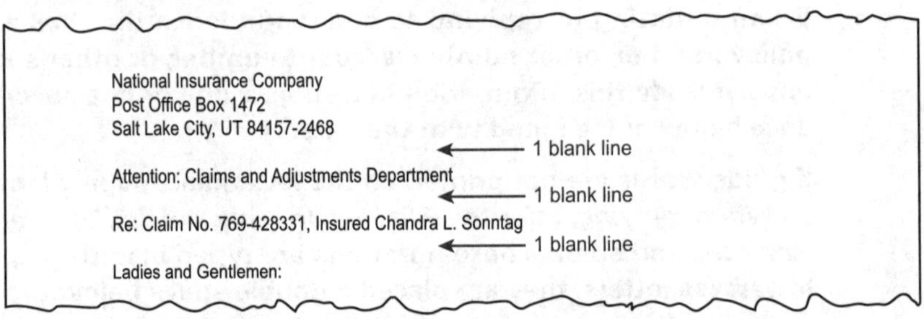

11–19 Body of the Letter

a. **The body of the letter contains the message. It begins a double space below the salutation or the subject line, if used. Single-space paragraphs within the body of the letter and double-space between each paragraph.**

The first line of paragraphs in modified block letters may be either blocked or indented 0.5 inch. Always block the first line of paragraphs in full block letters.

body of letter with blocked paragraphs

Dear Mr. Feinberg:

← 1 blank line

Your Zippo portable sound system arrived yesterday along with your explanation of the needed repairs.

← 1 blank line

As you suggested, the station tuning mechanism has been replaced under the terms of the warranty. In examining your system, however, our service representative noticed that the speaker had been damaged from an apparent jarring or dropping. The installation cost (parts and labor) for a new speaker would be $54.98.

body of letter with indented paragraphs

Dear Mrs. Russell:

← 1 blank line

We learned a great deal from your interesting presentation on the dynamics of color that you gave to Dr. Sullivan's business management class last Friday. Thank you for sharing your valuable ideas with us.

← 1 blank line

The class especially appreciated the material you gave us on the Wilson color wheel. Everyone agreed that this information will certainly be helpful in making color selections for the employee work environment and ensuring comfortable working conditions.

b. Quoted materials, listings, tables, and graphics are often included within the body of a letter between the left and right margins. (See Section 2–25 for instructions on formatting long quotations, Section 12–9 for preparing horizontal and vertical listings, and Section 12–11 for preparing tables and charts.)

listing within the body of a letter

To proceed with the escrow on the property you purchased at 6176 Arroyo Road in Palm Springs, please send in the following items by September 20.

← 1 blank line

- A loan application (form enclosed) completely filled out and notarized ↔ 0.5″ by a bank official.

← 1 blank line

- Verification of employment to include a letter from your employer stating your length of employment and current earnings.

← 1 blank line

- Copies of your last six months' paycheck stubs.

← 1 blank line

- Copies of your federal income tax returns for the previous two years.

← 1 blank line

As soon as we receive these items, we will be able to contact prospective lenders to obtain a loan. Interest rates among lenders vary, but we will attempt to obtain the

quoted material within the body of a letter

recommendations have been based on an economic forecast published in one of our leading trade magazines. The forecast appeared in an article on pages 101–103 of the September issue of *Bankers' Financial World*.

← 1 blank line

> Although interest rates for the next quarter will remain at the same ↔ 0.5″ low rate, building of new homes and commercial buildings will continue ↔ 0.5″ to decline. The large number of bank foreclosures on real property during the past year has driven values down so low that builders are ceasing to develop new projects.

← 1 blank line

The article, "Foreclosures and Their Rippling Effect on the Banking Industry," was written by Joseph L. Langham, a prominent economist and professor at Stanford University. Dr. Langham is noted for his success in predicting trends in the housing

table within the body of a letter

We certainly appreciate your interest in purchasing a catalog that illustrates our fine Foster porcelain figurines.

← 1–2 blank lines

2017–2018 Foster Catalog Set Current Retail Pricing		
Catalog or Supplement	**Price for Members**	**Price for Nonmembers**
Foster Core Catalog	$16.25	$32.50
Foster Limited Edition Catalog	8.75	17.50
Gres Supplement	2.50	5.00
Elite Catalog	10.00	20.00
Limited Edition Gres Catalog	7.50	15.00
Gres Catalog	5.00	10.00
Complete Catalog Set with Price List	$50.00	$100.00

← 1–2 blank lines

Both the *Foster Core Catalog* and the *Foster Limited Edition Catalog* contain color photographs of the figurines currently available. All other catalogs contain black-and-white photographs. As a member of the Foster Collectors' Society, you are

11 Business Messages

11-20 Complimentary Close

a. The complimentary close begins the closing lines of a letter. The complimentary close selected to conclude a business letter must conform to the formality of the salutation. Sample salutations as well as suitable complimentary closes are listed here.

formal correspondence

Salutation	*Complimentary Close*
Dear Mr. President	Respectfully Very truly yours Sincerely yours
Excellency	Respectfully Very truly yours Sincerely yours
Dear Senator Monroe	Respectfully Very truly yours Sincerely yours

general business correspondence

Salutation	*Complimentary Close*
Dear Mr. Solomon	Sincerely yours Sincerely
Dear Ms. Rodriguez	Sincerely yours Sincerely
Dear Dr. Hsueh	Sincerely yours Sincerely
Ladies and Gentlemen	Sincerely yours Sincerely

informal business correspondence

Salutation	*Complimentary Close*
Dear Bill	Sincerely yours Sincerely Cordially yours Cordially
Dear Karen	Sincerely yours Sincerely Cordially yours Cordially

b. Place the complimentary close a double space below the last line of the message. Capitalize only the first word. Conclude the complimentary close with a comma for the mixed punctuation format; use no ending punctuation mark for the open punctuation format.

For modified block letters, begin the closing lines at the center of the page. Begin the closing lines at the left margin for full block letters.

complimentary close begun at page center

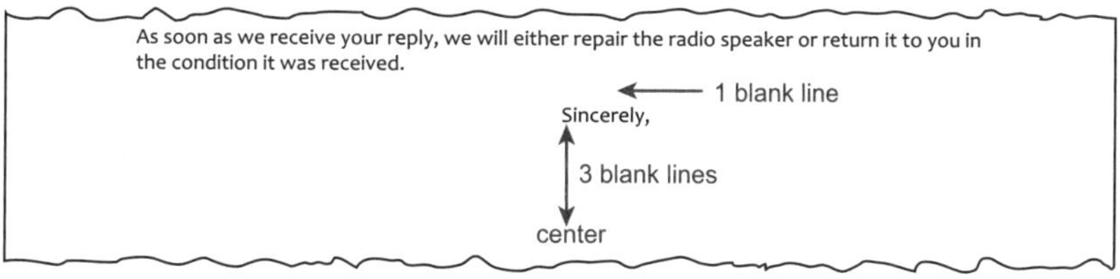

complimentary close begun at left margin

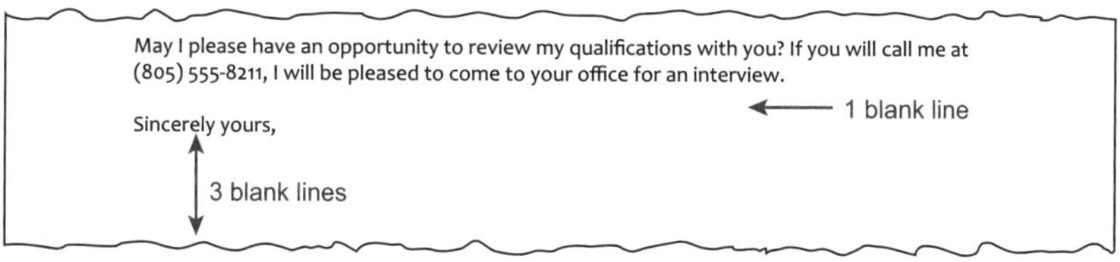

11–21 Signature Block

a. The signature block identifies the writer of the letter by name. In most cases the writer's professional title is also included.

Some business firms include the name of the company in the closing lines. In such cases the name of the company is placed in all capital letters a double space below and aligned with the complimentary close.

Use of the company name in the closing lines is illustrated in a full block letter in Section 11–6, page 353.

company name in modified block letter

Don't delay; act now to receive a copy of *Your Banking Future*—while the supply lasts. Just sign the enclosed postcard and drop it in the mail today.

← 1 blank line

Sincerely yours,

← 1 blank line

BRADSTREET TRAINING INSTITUTE

↕ 3 blank lines

Morgan Riley, Director

company name in full block letter

← 1 blank line

Sincerely yours,

← 1 blank line

REDVIEW TILE COMPANY

↕ 3 blank lines

(Ms.) Gail Fleming, Director
Plant Production

Place the writer's signature line or lines on the fourth line below the previous line, which will be either the complimentary close or the company name. Align the first letter of the individual's name with the first letter of the complimentary close and/or the company name.

signature lines in modified block letter

← 1 blank line

Sincerely yours,

↕ 3 blank lines

David L. Sullivan, Manager
Trust Department

signature lines in full block letter

← 1 blank line

Sincerely,

↕ 3 blank lines

John R. Gregg
Vice President

Place combinations of names, titles, and organizational sectors so that the contents of the signature lines appear balanced. The name and title may appear on the same line or on separate lines, depending upon the length of each unit. Use commas to separate categories within the same line, but do not use commas to conclude any of the signature lines.

single-line signature line

John Wright, President　　　　Sandra R. Bennett, MD

two-line signature line

Deborah T. Washington
Manager, Credit Department

Joshua S. Ross, Supervisor
Data Processing Department

Robert F. Tavelman
Accounts and Sales Representative

three-line signature

Danielle Cooper, EdD
Curriculum Specialist, English
Division of Secondary Education

b. Signature lines containing the names of men are generally not preceded by the courtesy title *Mr.* Only with initials, international names, and gender-equal names should a man use *Mr.* if the addressee does not know him. Mr. may be written with or without parentheses.

If a man has the title *Dr.*, place the abbreviation of the degree after the name of the individual. Separate the abbreviation from the name with a comma.

***signature lines containing name of man to be addressed as* Mr.**

Gordon R. Bezowski
Regional Manager

(Mr.) Huy Cao Nguyen
Assistant Vice President

Mr. R. L. Rothstein
Realtor Associate

(Mr.) Leslie Neible, Manager
Accounting Department

***signature lines containing name of man to be addressed as* Dr.**

Cory V. Thompson, PhD
Professor of Business

Vahi Urun, DDS

Lawrence C. Simi, EdD
Dean, Academic Affairs

Gerald T. Parker, MD

c. Signature lines containing the names of women should be preceded by a courtesy title if the writer prefers to be addressed as *Mrs.* instead of the standard *Ms.* in any return correspondence. Courtesy titles (*Ms.* or *Mrs.*) should also be used before female names that are not readily distinguishable as male or female, names containing only initials, and international names. The title is usually placed in parentheses, but it may appear without them.

If a woman has the title *Dr.*, place the abbreviation of the degree after the name of the individual. Separate the abbreviation from the name with a comma.

signature lines containing name of woman

Sally Abramowitz, Manager
Production Department

Alice H. Duffy, Coordinator
Training and Development

signature lines distinguishing courtesy title of woman

(Mrs.) Miho Tabata Administrative Assistant	*or*	Mrs. Miho Tabata Administrative Assistant
(Mrs.) Kelly Krusee Sales Associate	*or*	Mrs. Kelly Krusee Sales Associate
(Ms.) M. R. Stevens General Manager	*or*	Ms. M. R. Stevens General Manager
(Ms.) Tran Huynh Vice President	*or*	Ms. Tran Huynh Vice President

***signature lines containing name of woman addressed as* Dr.**

Ermonia C. Gevorkian, DBA Associate Professor	Cynthia R. Randall, MD
Alexis Noonan, PhD, Chair Mathematics Department	Sylvia Silva, JD Compliance Officer

d. Correspondence that is signed by a person other than the one whose name appears in the signature line usually shows the initials of the person signing the letter.

e. When more than one signature is required in a business letter, arrange the signature lines in order of rank. If ranking is unimportant, arrange the signature lines in alphabetical order.

(1) *Modified block letter.* In the modified block letter, align multiple signatures vertically beginning at the horizontal center of the page. Leave three blank lines between each signature block.

(2) *Full block letter.* In the full block letter, arrange multiple signatures (a) side by side or (b) aligned vertically at the left margin with three blank lines separating each typed signature block.

multiple signature lines in modified block letter

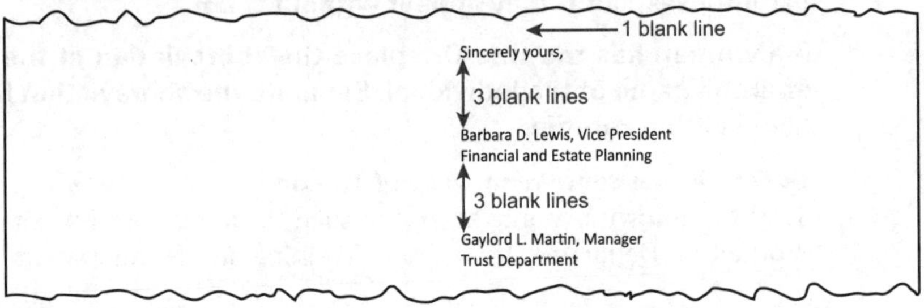

side-by-side signature lines in full block letter

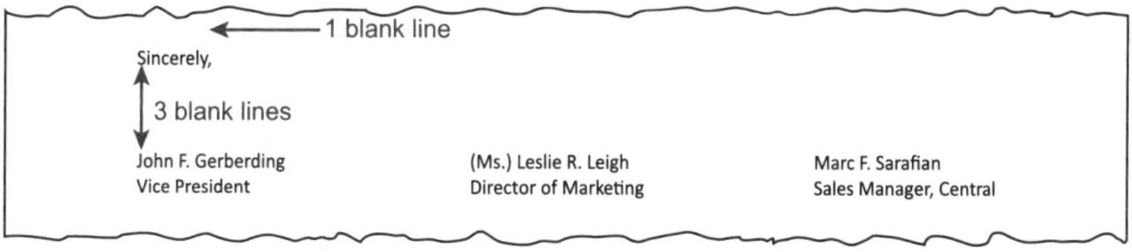

vertically aligned signature lines in full block letter

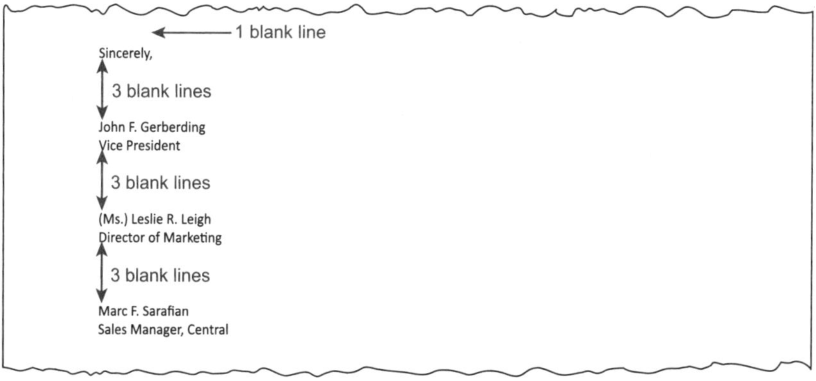

11–22 Reference Initials

a. **Reference initials are used to show who keyed and formatted the letter. The preparer's initials are placed in lowercase letters at the left margin a double space below the last line in the signature block.**

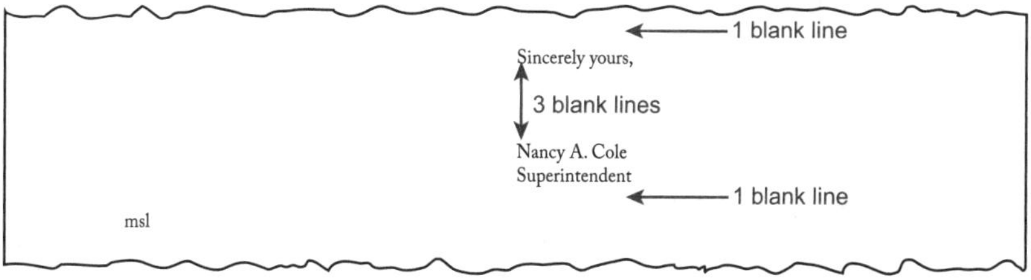

b. **The initials of both the writer and the preparer *may* be included in the reference notation, although the writer's initials are generally omitted. When the person whose name appears in the signature lines is the one who wrote the letter, his or her initials appear in capital letters before the preparer's initials. The initials are separated by a colon or a diagonal line.**

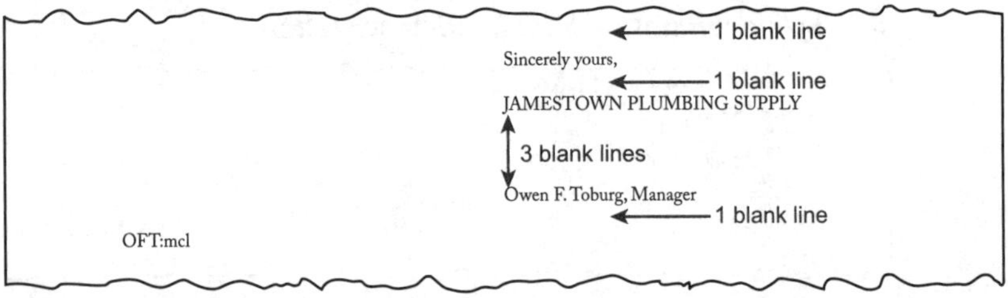

c. **When correspondence is written by a person other than the one whose name appears in the signature lines, the writer's name or capitalized initials precede the initials of the preparer. Separate the name or initials of the writer from the preparer's initials by a colon or a diagonal line.**

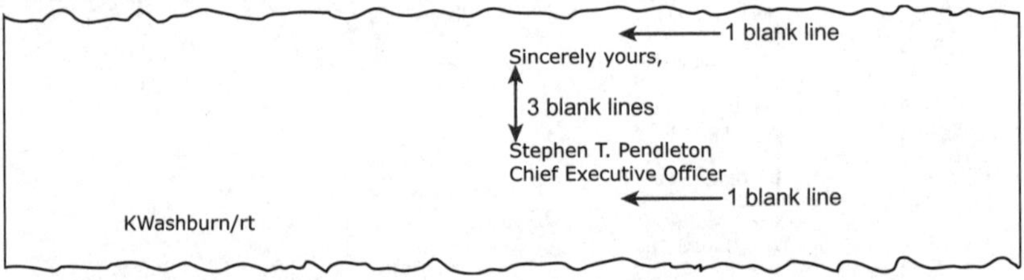

11–23 Enclosure or Attachment Notations

a. **If any enclosures are included with the letter, an enclosure notation is placed on the second line (or the next line to conserve space) below the reference initials. Begin the enclosure notation at the left margin. If more than one enclosure is included, be sure to list them or include the number with the enclosure notation. Following are some examples:**

one enclosure

Enclosure   Enc.   Check enclosed   Enclosure: Wilson Contract

more than one enclosure

Enclosures: Check for $375   2 Enc.   Enc. 2
Copy of Invoice A18743

Enclosures 2   Enclosures (2)   2 Enclosures

b. **When an enclosure is attached to the letter, the word *Attachment* or its abbreviation may be used in place of the enclosure notation. If more than one item is attached, be sure to include a listing or the number with the attachment notation.**

one attachment

Attachment   Att.   Attachment: Meeting Minutes

more than one attachment

Attachments: Application for admission Student information form	Attachments 2
2 Attachments	Att. 2

11-24 Copy Notations

a. When copies of correspondence are directed to individuals other than the addressee, note the distribution at the bottom of the letter. The copy notation is placed on the second line (or the next line to conserve space) following the enclosure notation, if used. Otherwise, the copy notation appears a single or double space below the reference initials. If, however, a delivery notation follows the reference initials or enclosure notation, the copy notation is placed below the delivery notation.

copy notation following reference initials

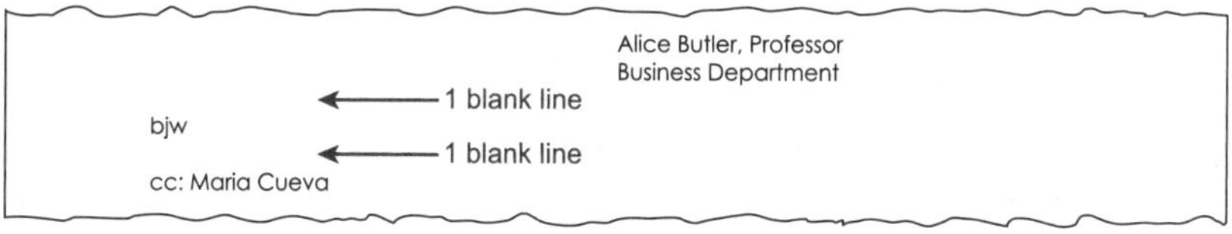

copy notation with additional notations

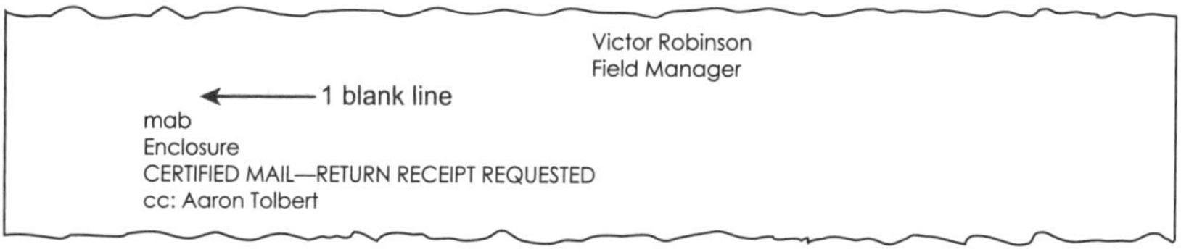

b. Copies of correspondence are prepared with a photocopier or a printer. The traditional *cc* notation, which formerly represented *carbon copy,* now represents *courtesy copy.* This notation is appropriate for copies produced by any method. Some writers use only *c* for *copy.*

Copy notations may include a combination of the courtesy title, name, position, department, company, and complete address of an individual. Following are some examples of appropriate copy notations:

cc: Mr. Kelly T. Mayo
    2432 Grand Avenue
    Oklahoma City, OK 73103

c: Kirby P. Thompson, President, Investments Online

cc Alicia Morley, Escrow Officer

c Vahi Urun

Some companies prefer to note copies made on a photocopier in the following ways:

copy: Ms. Janene Sassine

copies: José Acevedo
Dawn Mellert

c: Marketing Department Staff

C: Mrs. Phuong Nguyen

copy to Mr. Bill Hughes, Plant Manager, Marlborough Paper Company

c. If copies are directed to more than one individual, list the individuals according to rank. If the individuals are equal in rank or ranking is unimportant, alphabetize the list. The list may be prepared either vertically or horizontally.

ranked list
cc: R. F. Gillham, President
T. L. McMillan, Vice President
F. S. Lopez, General Manager

alphabetized list
cc Marcus L. Brendero, Anne S. Langville, David M. Silverman

d. If sending a copy of the letter to other individuals is unnecessary or inappropriate for an addressee to know, use a blind courtesy copy notation (*bcc*) and follow these guidelines:

(1) Place the blind courtesy copy notation only on copies of the letter, not on the original.

(2) Place the blind courtesy copy notation (a) 1 inch from the top edge of the page at the left margin or (b) where the regular copy notation normally appears.

blind courtesy copy notations
bcc: David P. Dougherty

bcc Ms. Marty Hayes

11–25 Postscripts

A postscript may be used to emphasize an idea or add an idea that was unintentionally omitted from the body of the letter. Follow these guidelines in formatting the postscript:

(1) Place the postscript in last position.

(2) Key or handwrite the postscript with or without the abbreviation *PS.*

(3) Treat the postscript like any other paragraph in the letter. If the first line is blocked, then block the first line and all succeeding lines. If the first line is indented, then indent the first line and begin the remaining lines at the left margin.

with abbreviation PS

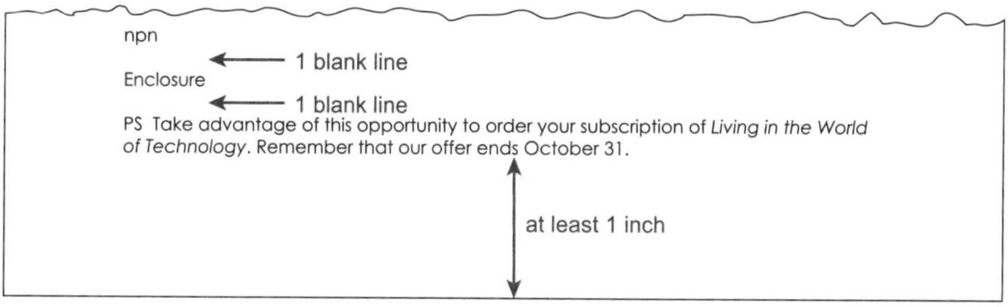

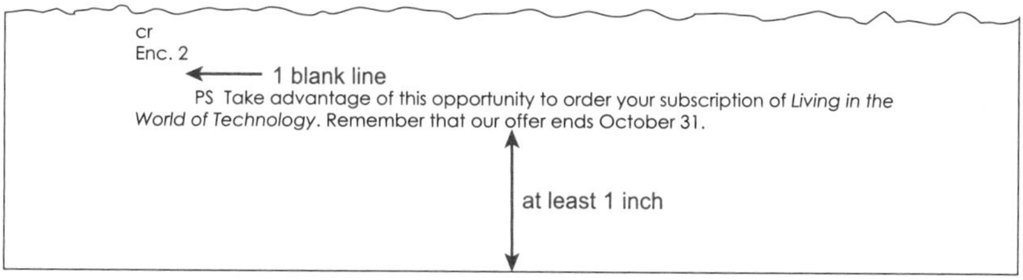

without abbreviation PS

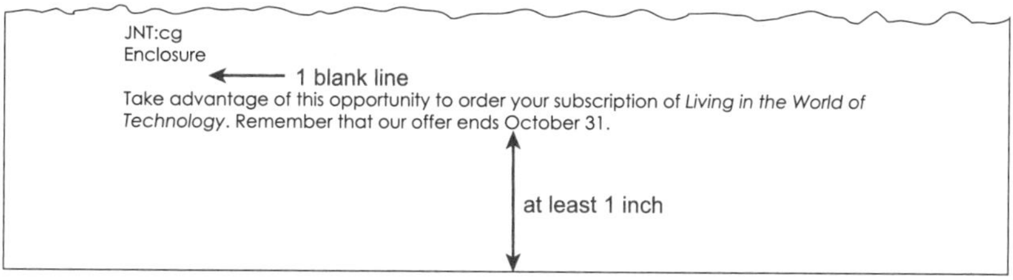

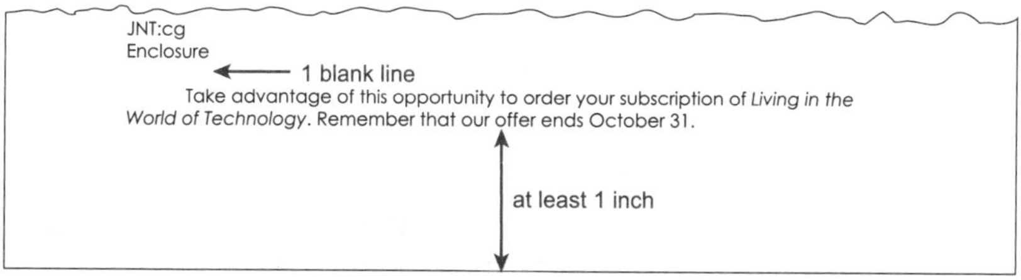

11-26 Computer File Notations

Some companies prefer to place within the document the path and file name of letters produced on word processors. Because these notations are file references, they should appear only on file copies—not on copies sent to the addressee or other recipients. Place computer file notations a single space below the last keyed line of the letter on the file copy only.

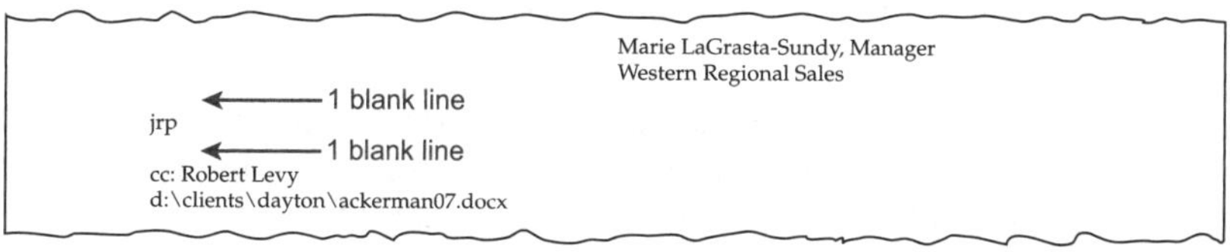

11–27 Second-Page Headings

a. Prepare headings for second and succeeding pages on plain paper using the following guidelines:

(1) Allow a 1-inch top margin, and use the same side margins that appear on the first page.

(2) Include the name of the addressee, the page number, and the date in continuation-page headings. Use either a horizontal or a vertical format.

(3) Space down three lines from the last line of the heading before resuming the message. Two blank lines should separate the heading and the continuation of the message.

horizontal format

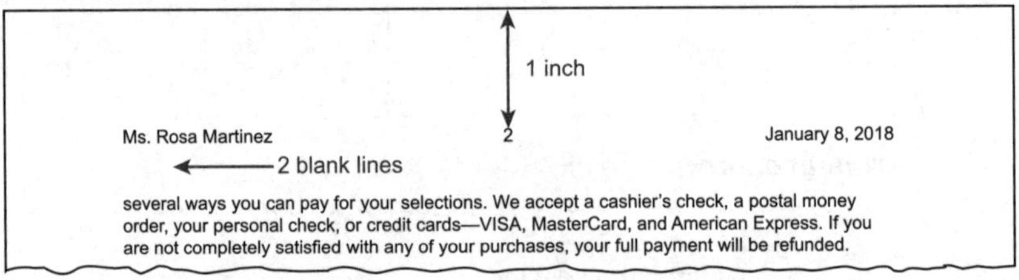

vertical format

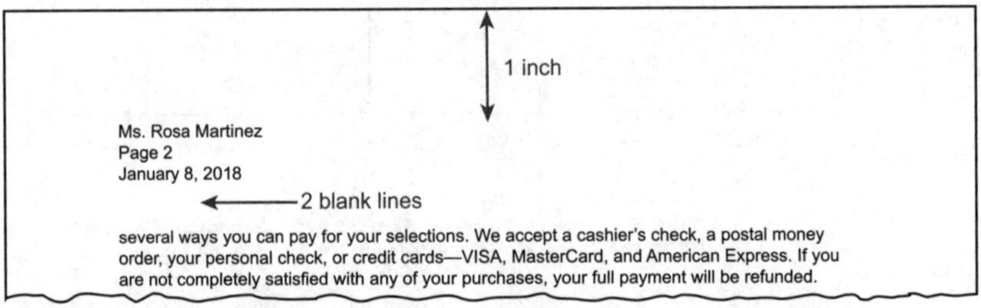

b. If a page does not end at the conclusion of a paragraph, use the following guidelines to break the paragraph:

(1) Use the widow/orphan line protection feature of your word processing program to prevent single lines from a paragraph being isolated at the top or bottom of a page.

(2) Include at least the first two lines of any new paragraph begun at the bottom of the page. Likewise, carry forward to the next page at least the last two lines of a paragraph begun on the previous page.

(3) Do not divide the last word on the page.

(4) Leave at least 1 inch, but no more than 1.5 inches, at the bottom of each page—except, of course, the last one.

c. The closing lines of a business letter should not be isolated on a continuation page. At least two lines of the message must precede the complimentary close and signature lines.

Addressing Envelopes

11–28 Automated Envelope Addressing

Use the envelope feature of your word processing program to prepare envelopes for your correspondence and other mailings. Adapt the default settings to correspond to your needs by following these guidelines:

(1) Select the envelope size from the menu of types provided by your software. If the correct envelope size is not available, create and select it. Be sure that your printer will support the envelope size selected.

(2) Adjust the left and top margin settings of your return address placement to accommodate any lines to be added to a printed return address or to accommodate a keyed return address (see Section 11–29b).

(3) Adjust the left and top margin settings of your mailing address placement to accommodate the envelope size selected. (See Section 11–30 for the margin settings to be used for No. 10 [legal-size] and No. 6¾ [letter-size] envelopes.)

(4) Use the option to insert a bar code, if desired.

envelope printed with envelope feature of a word processing program

Continental Insurance Company
460 North Ashley Drive
Tampa, Florida 33601-1469

CONFIDENTIAL   CERTIFIED MAIL

Mr. Thomas R. Paige, Manager
Allied Insurance Agency
6200 Beachwood Boulevard
Tampa, Florida 33609-2147

11–29 Return Address

a. The return address is usually printed in the upper left corner of the envelope. In large companies the writer's or sender's initials or name and location are placed above the company name and return address. This practice facilitates routing the letter to the sender in case of nondelivery by the post office.

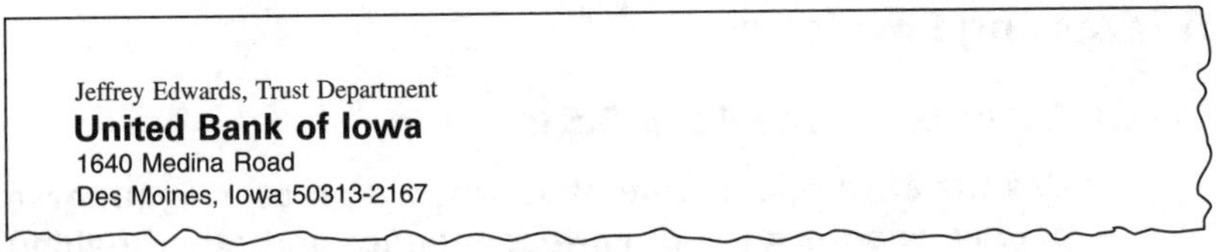

b. **On an envelope without a printed return address, place the return address in the upper left corner. Single-space the lines and include (1) the name of the individual; (2) the title of the individual, if applicable; (3) the company name, if applicable; (4) the mailing address; and (5) the city, state, and ZIP Code. Begin the return address 0.3 inch from the top and 0.4 inch from the left edge of the envelope.**

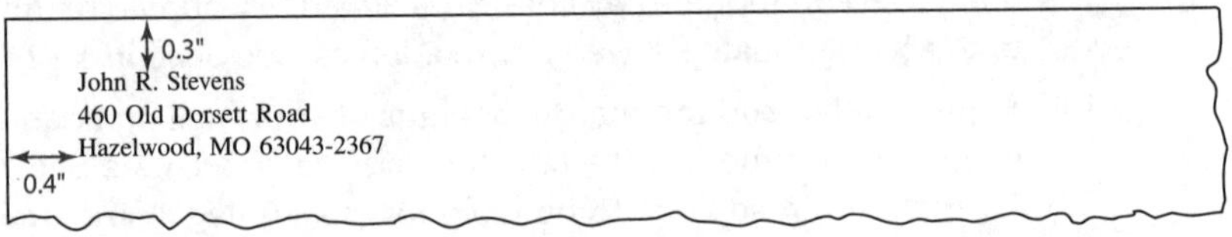

11–30 Mailing Address

a. **Single-space the mailing address, using at least two lines. The last line of the address should contain the city, state, and ZIP Code. If the envelope is used to mail correspondence, key the address exactly as it appears in the inside address.**

b. **On legal-size envelopes, No. 10 envelopes (9.5 by 4.13 inches), allow a 2-inch top margin. Begin the address 4.25 inches from the left edge of the envelope.**

No. 10 envelope

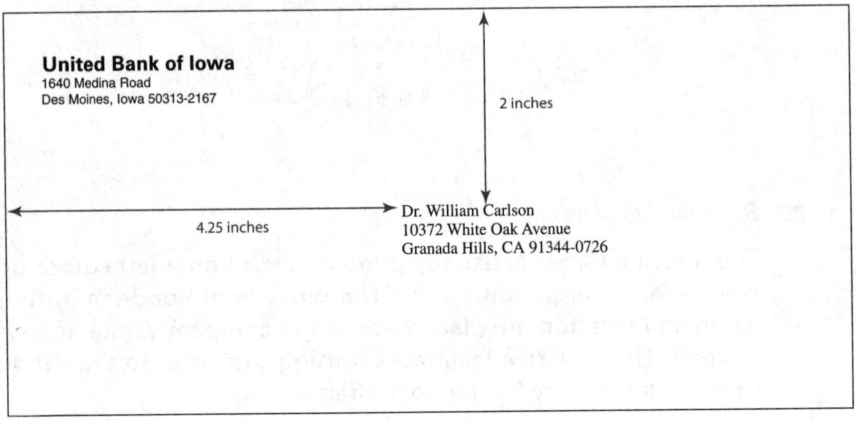

c. On letter-size envelopes, No. 6¾ envelopes (6.5 by 3.63 inches), allow a 1.75-inch top margin. Begin the mailing address 2.5 inches from the left edge of the envelope.

No. 6¾ envelope

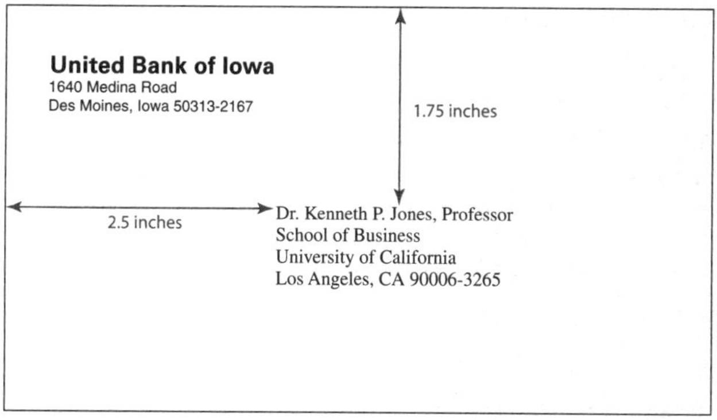

d. Letter-size manila envelopes (9 by 12 inches or 10 by 12 inches) may have the address keyed directly on the envelope or preferably have a label with the address affixed to the envelope. In either case, position the envelope so that the flap and opening are on the right side. Place the first line of the mailing address 4.5 inches (for 9- by 12-inch envelopes) or 5 inches (for 10- by 12-inch envelopes) from the top edge and 4.5 to 5 inches from the left edge, depending upon the length of the address lines.

letter-size manila envelope

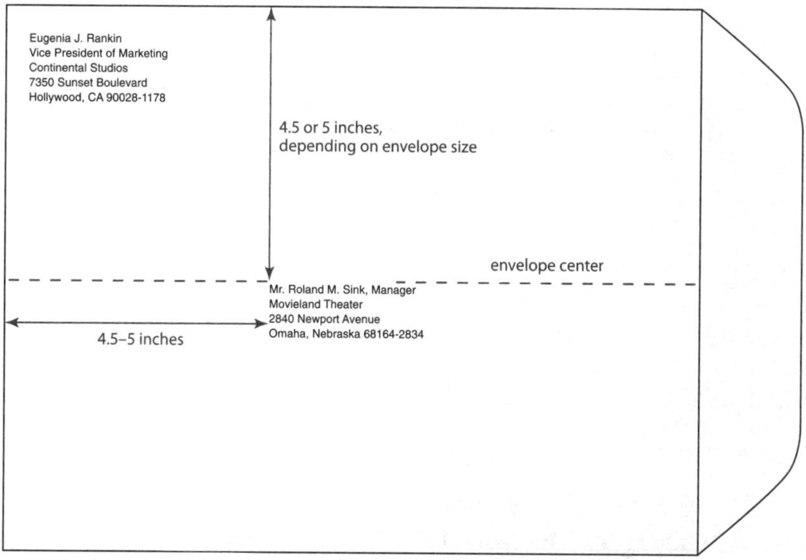

11–31 Addressee Notations

If an attention line appears in the inside address of a letter, include it within the envelope address. If an attention line is placed below the inside address in the letter, treat it the same as you would any other addressee notation.

Place an attention line or an addressee notation such as *Personal, Confidential, Please Forward,* or *Hold for Arrival* a double space below the last line of the return address or 1.5 inches from the top edge of the envelope, whichever position is lower. Begin keying 0.5 inch from the left edge of the envelope, and use all capital letters.

attention line included with mailing address

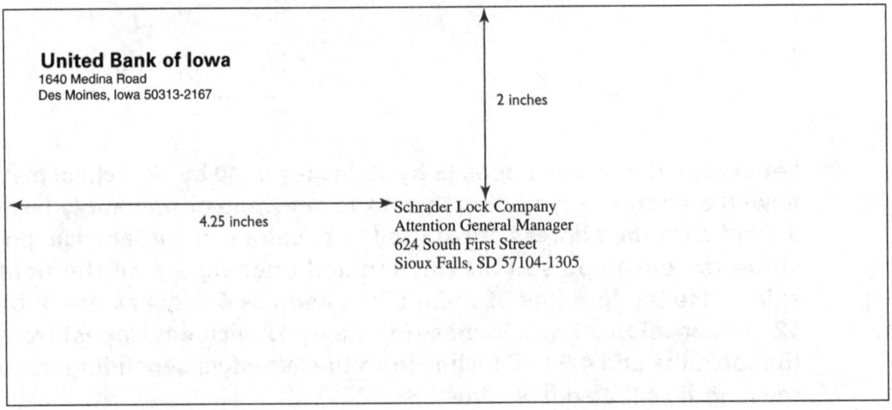

addressee notation below return address

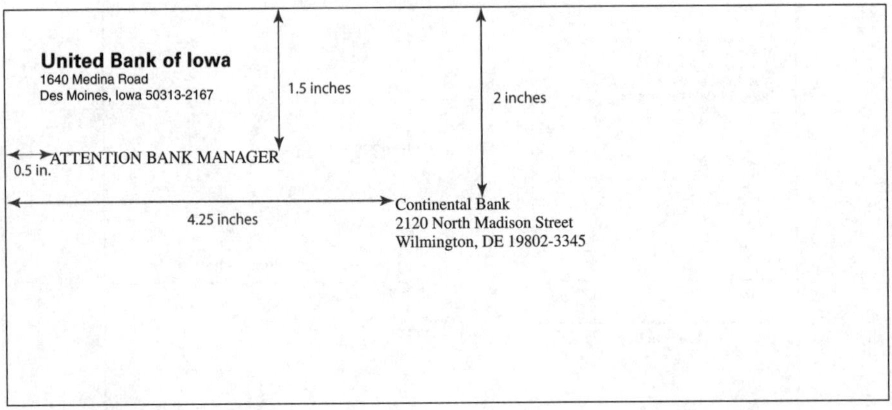

11–32 Delivery Notations

a. **Place the delivery notation *Airmail* (for foreign destinations) below the stamp, 1.5 inches from the top edge of the envelope. End the notation 0.5 inch from the right edge of the envelope. Instead of**

a keyed *Airmail* delivery notation, a self-adhesive *Airmail* label available from the U.S. Postal Service may be substituted.

Envelope delivery notations are less significant than they were previously, except for *Airmail,* which is used exclusively for international mailings. *Express Mail* and other fast-delivery options provided by private courier services have their own supplier-provided envelopes. *Registered Mail* must be presented at the post office for mailing, where it is marked and routed appropriately. *Certified Mail,* too, is usually taken to the post office and marked accordingly.

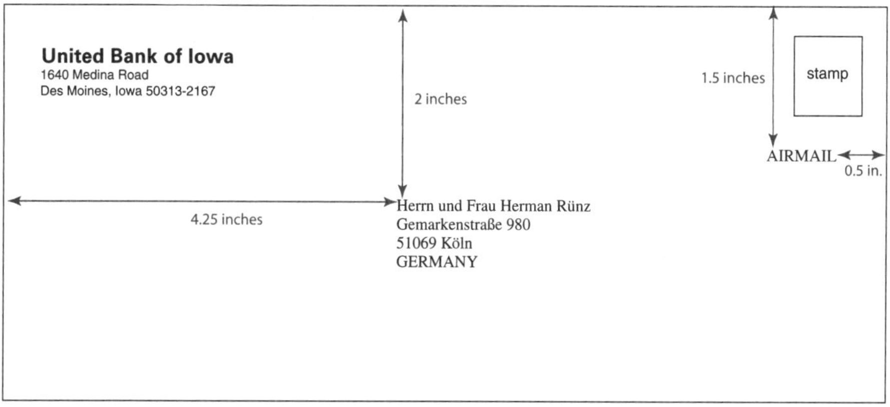

11–33 Computer-Generated Address Labels

Word processing programs as well as database programs can easily generate mailing labels from a database merge file or a database file. Addresses are compiled and formatted for printing on predefined label forms prepared commercially by companies such as Avery or 3M. The following example was prepared on a word processor using an Avery 5162 address label form for a laser printer.

Mr. George R. Simms, Vice President
Great Western Bank
19300 Devonshire Street
Chatsworth, CA 93471-1046

Ms. Elizabeth Candiotti, President
Woodland Hills Chamber of Commerce
20220 Ventura Boulevard, Suite 130
Woodland Hills, CA 91365-3281

Ms. Veronica Richmond, Director
Human Resources Department
Harman International
6200 Balboa Boulevard
Northridge, CA 91324-1954

Dr. Sandra L. Washington, President
California State University, Northridge
18600 Nordhoff Street
Northridge, CA 91327

Mr. Charles E. Buchanan, Manager
Coldwell Banker Realty
8750 Arroyo Parkway
Camarillo, CA 92374-3209

Mr. Anthony Murillo, Vice President
International Operations
Amgen Corporation
30375 Victory Boulevard
Thousand Oaks, CA 94509-1001

11–34 ZIP + 4

a. To process mail faster and more economically, the U.S. Postal Service has assigned four additional digits to the ZIP Codes of mailing addresses. This series of four digits is separated from the ZIP Code with a hyphen.

Tampa, FL 33626-6213	Boise, Idaho 83702-4819
Jackson, MS 39203-1073	Reno, Nevada 89503-2103

b. The use of ZIP + 4 is recommended by the U.S. Postal Service. Bulk mailers may obtain reduced rates for the use of ZIP + 4.

c. ZIP + 4 Codes may be located through various media available for purchase from the U.S. Postal Service[10] and from various private software companies. ZIP + 4 Codes for specific addresses may be retrieved free of charge at the U.S. Postal Service Web site at http://www.usps.com/zip4.

Folding and Inserting Correspondence

11–35 No. 10 Envelopes

a. Fold up one third of the page.

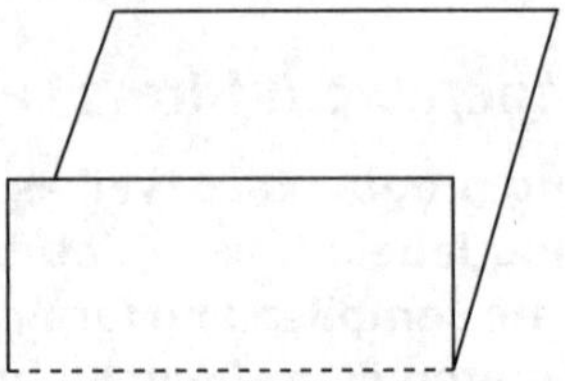

b. Fold down the upper third of the page so that the top edge is approximately 1⁄3 inch above the first fold.

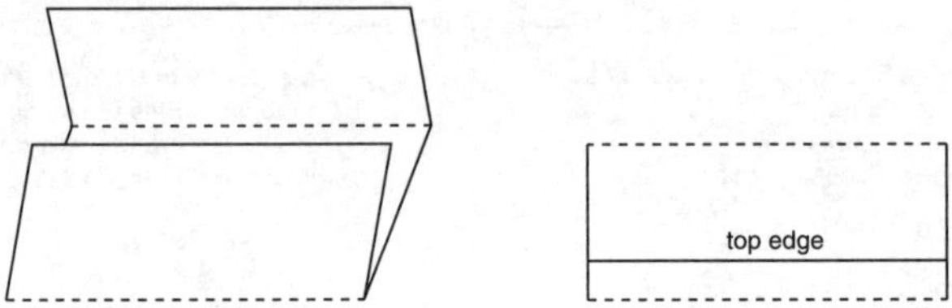

[10]For information about ZIP+4 products, telephone the National Customer Support Center, U.S. Postal Service, (800) 238-3150.

c. Insert the page so that the top edge is near the top edge of the envelope.

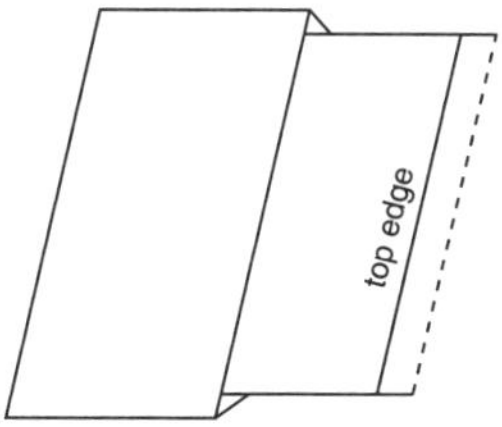

11–36 No. 6¾ Envelopes

a. Fold up one half of the page so that the bottom edge is approximately ⅓ inch below the top edge.

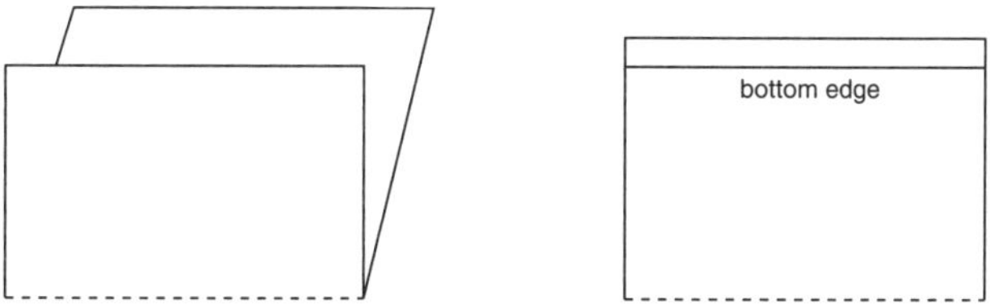

b. From the right side, fold over one third of the page.

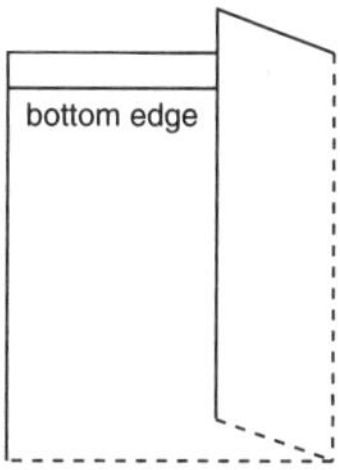

c. Fold over the second third of the page so that the left edge is approximately ⅓ inch from the right fold.

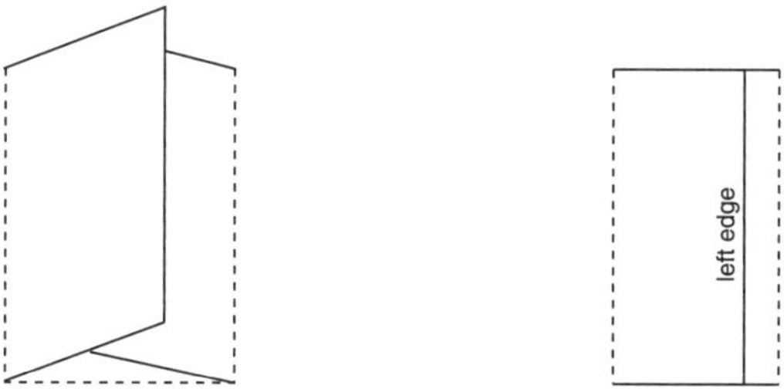

d. Insert the page so that the left edge is near the top edge of the envelope.

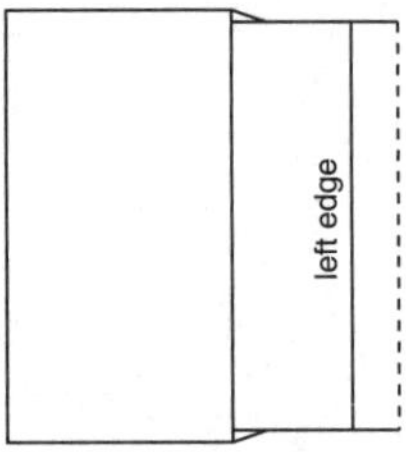

Memorandums

Business letters are generally written for messages that are sent outside the organization. On the other hand, memorandums are used for internal written communication—they are written messages that are sent to another employee or other employees within the organization.

Memorandums, once the major form of internal written communication, have declined in use substantially since the advent of e-mail messaging. Today's organizational employees use memorandums only to convey confidential information, prepare lengthy messages, emphasize ideas or requests, and lend importance to a message.

11–37 Memorandum Forms

a. Most organizations have custom memorandum templates or printed memorandum forms. These templates or forms contain guide words for directing the message to an addressee, specifying the name of the writer, providing the date written, and identifying the subject content. Although the arrangement and design may vary, these basic elements are found in most organizational memorandum templates or printed memorandum forms.

company custom template

Valley Linen Supply, Inc.
Interoffice Memorandum

To:

From:

Date:

Subject:

printed memorandum form

Mattel Toys Memo MAT-3497-8

TO: DATE:

FROM: REFERENCE:

SUBJECT:

b. Organizations that do not have custom templates or printed forms for preparing memorandums use word processing default templates with plain paper, organizational letterhead, or user-created form documents with plain paper.

word processing template[11]

Company Name Here

Memo

To: [Click **here** and type name]
From: [Click **here** and type name]
CC: [Click **here** and type name]
Date: **April 10, 2018**
Re: [Click **here** and type subject]

How to Use This Memo Template

Select text you would like to replace, and type your memo. Use styles such as Heading 1-3 and Body Text in the Style control on the Formatting toolbar. To save changes to this template for future use, choose Save As from the File menu. In the Save As Type box, choose Document Template. Next time you want to use it, choose New from the File menu, and then double-click your template.

[11]Professional Memo template from Microsoft Office Online.

organizational letterhead

Deauville Resort Ranch and Country Club

Marc R. Cohen, General Manager

Executive Offices
Chandler, AZ 85234
Telephone: 602-963-6655
Fax: 602-963-2985

To:

From:

Date:

Subject:

form document printed on plain paper

Los Angeles Pierce College
Computer Applications and Office Technologies Department
clarklr@piercecollege.edu
(818) 710-4244

Date:

To:

From: Lyn Clark

Subject:

Las Vegas Board of Realtors
Memorandum

Date: •

To: •

From: •

Subject: •

11–38 Using Memorandum Forms

a. **Organizations that have developed custom memorandum templates provide fill-in boxes for the preliminary lines of their memo template. These memorandum forms are usually created with form-enabled software such as Adobe Acrobat. Users merely click into the fill-in boxes and enter the necessary information. The message follows the preliminary lines.**

(1) Access the custom memorandum template and save it as a separate file.

(2) Click into the text boxes provided and enter the necessary information.

(3) Key the memorandum message a triple space after the last guide word, usually the subject line.

b. Memorandums are often prepared on preprinted company memorandum forms using word processing software. For standard 8½- by 11-inch printed memorandum forms, create a form document to assist you with completing the preliminary lines: *Date:*, *To:*, *From:*, *Subject:*, and so on. Each time you are required to use the printed form, you can use the form document for placing information after each guide word.

(1) Use 1-inch top and bottom margins and 1.25-inch left and right margins.

(2) Use a ruler to measure the horizontal and vertical position of the first letter to be keyed after each guide word in the memorandum form.

(3) Move your cursor to the horizontal and vertical position (as shown in the ruler and status lines of your program) of the first letter to be keyed after the first guide word; key an asterisk (*). Follow the same procedure for each guide word in the printed form. If any preliminary parts will be completed with standard information, key in this standard information instead of an asterisk.

(4) Triple-space after the asterisk marking the beginning of the last guide word, usually the one that introduces the subject line. Key another asterisk to indicate where the message is to begin.

(5) Save the form document as a separate file.

When a memorandum needs to be prepared, open the form document and save it with a new name. Use the search feature of your program to locate the asterisks and substitute the variable information needed for the current memorandum.

c. For companies that use a word processing template to prepare memorandums, follow these guidelines:

(1) Access the word processing template and save it as a separate file.

(2) Click into the text boxes provided and enter the necessary information.

(3) Key the memorandum message a triple space after the last guide word, usually the subject line.

d. Some companies use their company letterhead to prepare memorandums. In these cases use the following procedures:

(1) Begin the preliminary lines a triple space below the last line of the letterhead for company letterheads printed on 8½- by 11-inch paper.

(2) Use 1.25-inch left and right margins for memorandums prepared on 8½- by 11-inch letterheads.

(3) Key in bold with initial capital letters the guide words ***Date:***, ***To:***, ***From:***, and ***Subject:*** at the left margin. Double-space between the guide words.

(4) Set a tab stop to align the information following the guide words after the colon in the ***Subject:*** guide word.

(5) Place any other guide words the company may wish to use on the same lines after the ***Date:***, ***To:***, or ***From:*** headings; insert the information for those guide words after each one.

(6) Triple-space after the last guide word, which is usually ***Subject:***, and begin keying the body of the memorandum at the left margin.

(7) Create a form document or macro for the preliminary lines of a memorandum if you regularly prepare memorandums on letterhead stationery.

e. For companies that regularly prepare memorandums on blank 8½- by 11-inch paper, create a form document. Use the following procedures:

(1) Set 1-inch top and bottom margins and 1.25-inch left and right margins.

(2) Provide a heading that minimally gives the name of the company and indicates that the document is a "Memo" or "Memorandum."

(3) Begin the preliminary lines a triple space below the last line of the heading.

(4) Key in bold with initial capital letters the guide words ***Date:***, ***To:***, ***From:***, and ***Subject:*** at the left margin. Double-space between the guide words.

(5) Set a tab stop to align the information following the guide words after the colon in the ***Subject:*** guide word.

(6) Place any other guide words the company may wish to use on the same lines after the ***Date:***, ***To:***, or ***From:*** headings.

(7) Key any standard information that will always appear after any of the guide words.

(8) Triple-space after the last guide word, which is usually ***Subject:***.

(9) Save the document; provide a name to indicate that it is a form document for a memorandum; for example, *memoform.*

When a memorandum needs to be prepared, open the form document and save it with a new name. Supply the variable information after each guide word and key the message.

11–39 Memorandum Formats

a. Follow these guidelines to format memorandums:

(1) Use 1.25-inch left and right margins and 1-inch top and bottom margins.

(2) Double-space guide words if they are keyed instead of appearing in templates or on printed forms.

(3) Key the subject line in all capital letters or just capitalize the main words.

(4) Triple-space after the last guide word (usually the subject line) before beginning the message.

(5) Single-space the message, and double-space between paragraphs.

b. Reference initials are used to show who keyed and formatted the memorandum. The preparer's initials are placed in lowercase letters at the left margin a double space below the last line of text.

When a memorandum is written by a person other than the one whose name appears after the *From*: guide word, the writer's name or capitalized initials precede the initials of the preparer. Separate the name or initials of the writer from the preparer's initials by a colon or a slash.

c. If any enclosures or attachments are included with the memorandum, an enclosure or attachment notation is placed on the second line (or next line to conserve space) below the reference initials. Begin the notation at the left margin. If more than one enclosure or attachment is included, be sure to list the items or include the number with the notation. Following are examples of enclosure and attachment notations:

Enclosure	Enc.
Enclosures 2	2 Enc.
Enclosure: Mason Contract	Enc. Directory
Enclosures: Receipt from agent Copy of application	2 Enclosures
Attachment	Att.
Attachments 2	Att. 2
Attachment: Check for $485	Att: Survey results
Attachments: Application for admission Student information form	2 Attachments

d. When copies of memorandums are directed to individuals other than the addressee, note the distribution at the bottom of the memorandum. The copy notation is placed on the second line (or next line to conserve space) following the enclosure notation, if used. Otherwise, it appears a single or double space below the reference initials. For copy notations in memorandums, use the same formats and procedures as shown for business letters in Section 11–23.

cc: Matthew L. Parker, Agent
5600 North Western Avenue
Oklahoma City, OK 73103

c: Donna Huberman   cc Cory Pallini, Supervisor

c Vahi Urun, Vice President, Operations

copy: Ms. Jenell Warren

copies: Bill Acevedo
Kristen Mellert

copy to Mr. Joseph Basil, Manager, Capital Paper Company

cc: R. F. Gillham, President
T. L. McMillan, Vice President
F. S. Brotherton, General Manager

cc Marcus L. Brendero, Anne S. Langville, David M. Silverman

c: Sales Department Staff

C: Mrs. Phuong Nguyen

memorandum prepared on company letterhead

Springfield Department of Water and Power
1400 Washington Boulevard
Springfield, Illinois 62711
(217) 555-8121
(217) 555-8122

2 blank lines →

Memorandum

2 blank lines →

To: Annette Jennings, Public Relations

1 blank line →

From: James D. Bell, Manager, Construction Projects

1 blank line →

Date: May 19, 2018

1 blank line →

Subject: RINALDI-NORTHRIDGE 230-KV TRANSMISSION LINE SEGMENT

2 blank lines →

↔ 1.25 inches

Beginning August 1, 2018, our department will begin constructing a 6.7 mile, 230-kilovolt transmission line segment. This line will be placed between four existing transmission lines that link the DWP's Rinaldi Receiving Station in Springfield with Receiving Station J in Northridge.

↔ 1.25 inches

1 blank line →

The transmission lines will serve the electrical needs of the western portion of Springfield and part of the west Chicago area. The project will include the construction of approximately 45 lattice steel, double-circuit towers and the installation of conductors.

1 blank line →

Before we begin the project, we will need to inform residents affected by this construction of its inception. Notices should be sent by your department to those persons residing south of Rinaldi, east of Wilbur, north of Nordhoff, and west of Zelzah.

1 blank line →

A fact sheet explaining a transmission line and its location should be sent to residents in July. This fact sheet should explain the need for the transmission line segment as well as the source of the power for this segment. Other details that might be included should cover the visual impacts to the surrounding areas, the environmental review process performed, potential health effects of electric and magnetic fields, and the construction schedule.

1 blank line →

The attached report regarding the project provides information that you may wish to use in your fact sheet. If you have any questions about the information contained in the report, I will be pleased to answer them.

1 blank line →

mw

1 blank line →

Attachment

1 blank line →

cc: K. C. Peterson, Vice President, Planning

↕ at least 1 inch

memorandum prepared using an organizational template

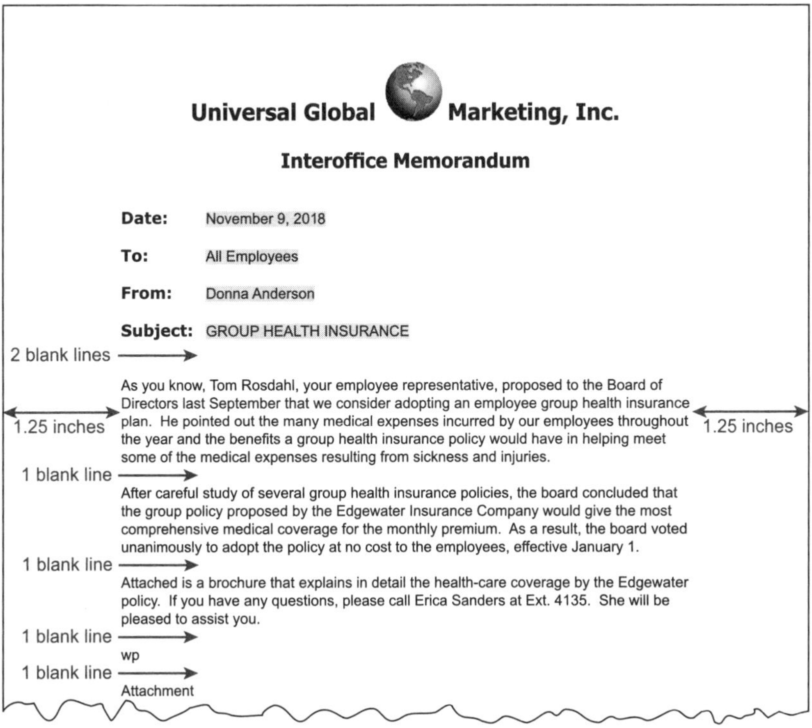

Universal Global Marketing, Inc.

Interoffice Memorandum

Date: November 9, 2018

To: All Employees

From: Donna Anderson

Subject: GROUP HEALTH INSURANCE

As you know, Tom Rosdahl, your employee representative, proposed to the Board of Directors last September that we consider adopting an employee group health insurance plan. He pointed out the many medical expenses incurred by our employees throughout the year and the benefits a group health insurance policy would have in helping meet some of the medical expenses resulting from sickness and injuries.

After careful study of several group health insurance policies, the board concluded that the group policy proposed by the Edgewater Insurance Company would give the most comprehensive medical coverage for the monthly premium. As a result, the board voted unanimously to adopt the policy at no cost to the employees, effective January 1.

Attached is a brochure that explains in detail the health-care coverage by the Edgewater policy. If you have any questions, please call Erica Sanders at Ext. 4135. She will be pleased to assist you.

wp

Attachment

memorandum prepared on blank paper

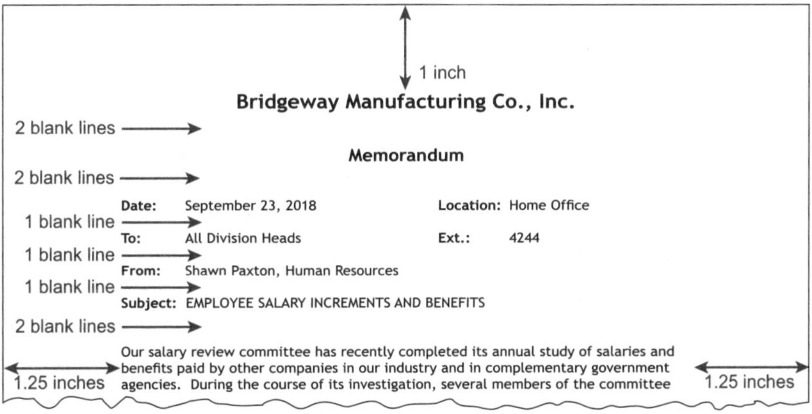

Bridgeway Manufacturing Co., Inc.

Memorandum

Date: September 23, 2018 **Location:** Home Office

To: All Division Heads **Ext.:** 4244

From: Shawn Paxton, Human Resources

Subject: EMPLOYEE SALARY INCREMENTS AND BENEFITS

Our salary review committee has recently completed its annual study of salaries and benefits paid by other companies in our industry and in complementary government agencies. During the course of its investigation, several members of the committee

e. When a memorandum contains more than one page, the heading for the second and succeeding pages should have a 1-inch top margin. The left and right margins should be 1.25 inches—the same as those used for the first page.

In the heading show the name of the person or group to whom the memorandum is addressed, the page number, and the date. This information may be arranged vertically at the left margin or be placed on a single line with the name beginning at the left margin, the page number centered, and the date aligned with the right margin. Triple-space after the heading before continuing the body of the memorandum.

vertical second-page heading

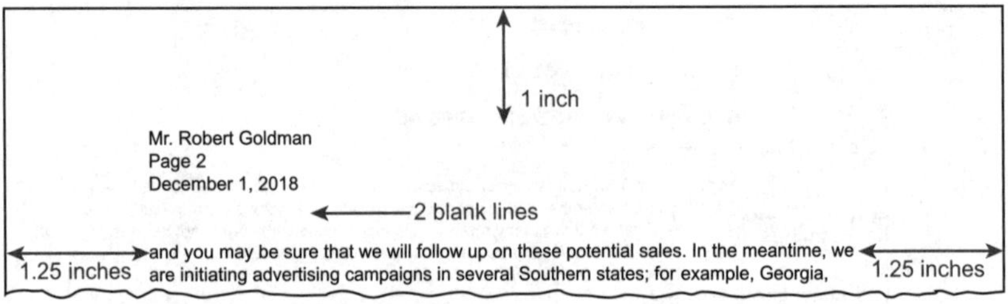

horizontal second-page heading

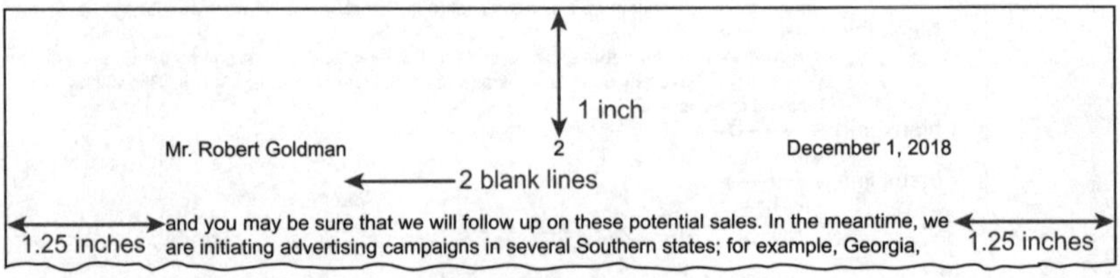

f. If a page does not end at the conclusion of a paragraph, use the following guidelines to break the paragraph:

(1) Use the widow/orphan line protection feature of your word processing program to prevent single lines from a paragraph being isolated at the top or bottom of a page.

(2) Include at least the first two lines of any new paragraph begun at the bottom of the page. Likewise, carry forward to the next page at least the last two lines of a paragraph begun on the previous page.

(3) Do not divide the last word on the page.

(4) Leave at least 1 inch, but no more than 1.5 inches, at the bottom of each page—except, of course, the last one.

12

Reports and Other Business Documents

Reports and Other Business Documents Solution Finder

12 Business Documents

General Formats for Reports and Manuscripts

12-1 Purpose, Content, and General Style

Reports are used in business to convey information, analyze data, or support proposals. Those reports written for public distribution, such as reports to stockholders, are printed and usually appear in booklet form. Other reports, those for internal use or limited distribution, are generated internally using word processing software. Regardless of their final form—printed, desktop published, or keyed and printed from word processing software—the report formats recommended here should be used for the preparation and editing process. Except for printed and desktop published reports, these formats also represent the final product.

All reports and manuscripts contain a title page and the body of the report. Other parts may be added, depending upon the length, complexity, and formality of the document. The parts of a report or manuscript may include the following:

Title page

Letter of transmittal

Summary (or Executive summary)

Table of contents

List of tables (and/or List of illustrations)

Contents of the report (Main body)

Endnotes (If applicable)

Bibliography

Appendix (or Appendixes)

a. Reports or manuscripts may be prepared with *either* 1.25-inch left and right margins *or* 1-inch left and right margins, depending upon the preference of the originator. If the report or manuscript is to be bound on the left, allow an additional 0.25 inch for the left margin. For setting top and bottom margins, follow these guidelines:

(1) Set 1-inch top and bottom margins for the report or manuscript. For top-bound manuscripts, set a 1.25-inch top margin.

(2) Allow a 2-inch top margin, 2.25 inches for top-bound documents, for the first page of major parts (title page, table of contents, bibliography, etc.) and the sections or chapters.

section opener with 2-inch top margin

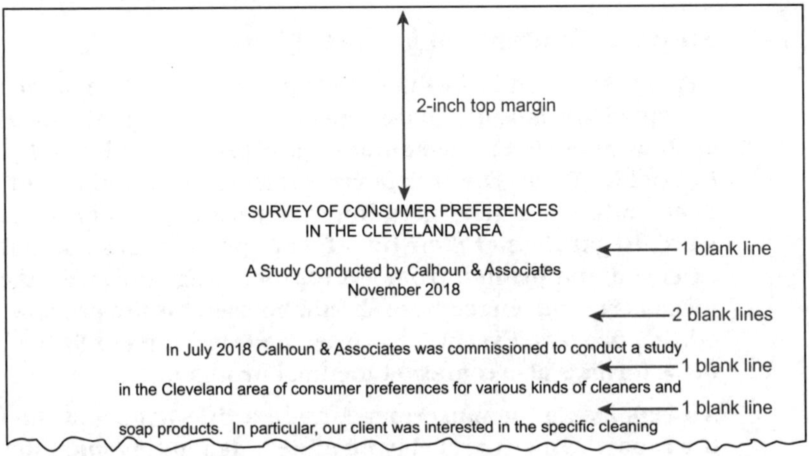

second and succeeding pages with 1-inch top margin

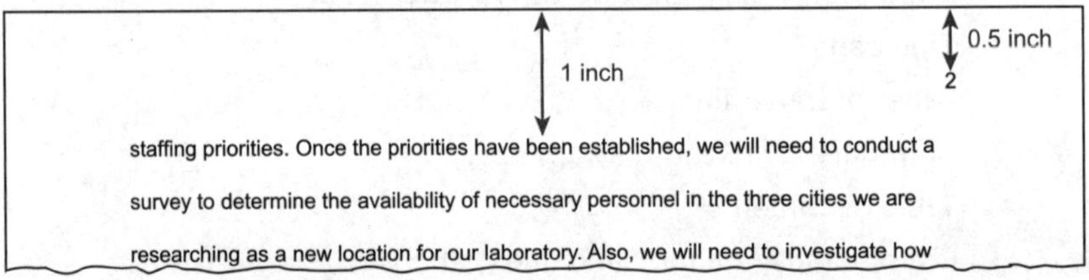

b. If the report or manuscript contains preliminary pages (those preceding the body of the report), number them at the bottom of the page as follows:

(1) Create a footer to use the page numbering feature of your word processing program.

(2) Number the pages consecutively in lowercase Roman numerals (*i, ii, iii, iv, v,* etc.).

(3) Count the title page as page *i* even though no number should be shown. Suppress the footer page numbering on the title page.

(4) Center the page number on a line 0.5 inch from the bottom edge of the paper. Leave at least 0.5 inch separating the page number from the last line of text.

(5) Discontinue the footer or this mode of pagination at the conclusion of the preliminary parts.

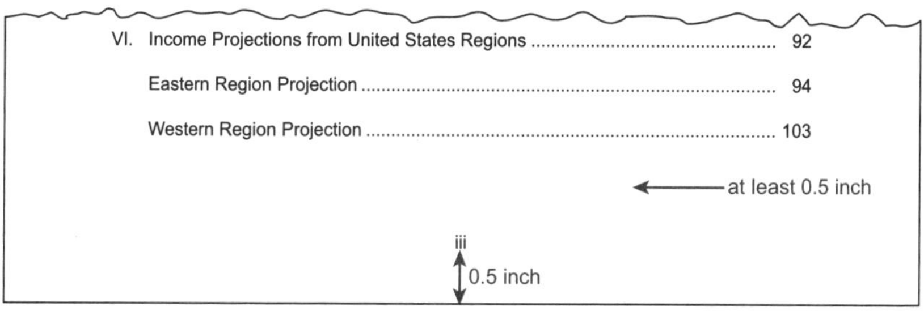

c. In the body of the report, page numbers of major sections are included in the page count but are usually not printed on the page. If a page number is to be included on the section opener, use the following procedures:

(1) Center the page number on a line 0.5 inch from the bottom edge of the paper.

(2) Allow at least 0.5 inch between the last line of text and the page number.

section opener without page number

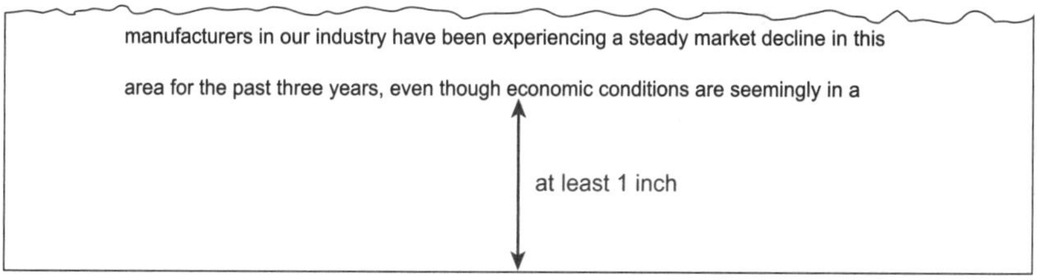

section opener with page number

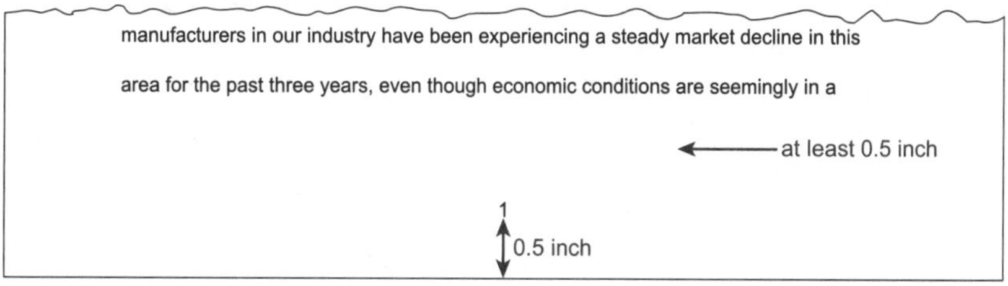

d. For all second and succeeding pages in a section of the report body, the page number begins the page. Use this procedure to number the pages:

(1) Create a header to use the page-numbering feature of your word processing program to number pages.

(2) Place the page number in Arabic numerals 0.5 inch (0.75 inch for top-bound manuscripts) below the top edge of the paper, and align it with the right margin.

(3) Begin the text 1 inch (1.25 inches for top-bound manuscripts) from the top edge of the page.

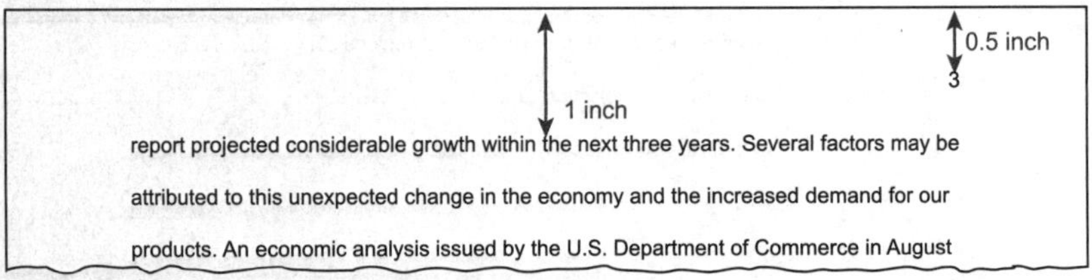

e. In the body of the report, indent the first line of each paragraph 0.5 inch. Indent long quotations and vertical listings 0.5 inch from both the left and right margins.

Use a tab to indent each paragraph and the "left-right indent" feature of your word processing program to indent long quotations and vertical listings.

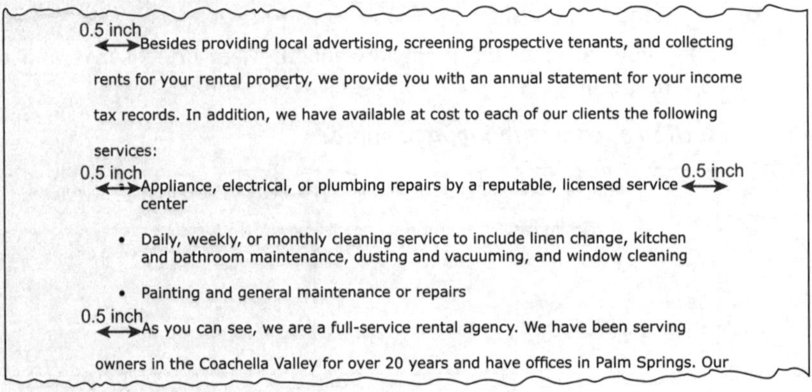

f. If a page ending does not coincide with the end of a paragraph or leaves a text heading as the last line, use the following guidelines to ensure a proper break at the bottom of the page:

(1) Conclude the report or manuscript text between 1 and 2 inches from the bottom edge of the page.

(2) Ensure that *at least* two lines of a paragraph appear at the bottom of a page. A single line that begins a paragraph may not be isolated at the bottom of a page.

(3) Ensure that *at least* two lines of a paragraph begin the next page. A minimum of two lines (one full line and at least one word on a second line) must appear at the top of a page for any paragraphs carried over from a previous page.

(4) Use the widow/orphan line protection feature of your word processing program to prevent single lines of a paragraph from appearing on a separate page, either at the bottom of the page (orphan line) or at the top of a new page (widow line).

(5) Move an isolated text heading from the bottom of the page to the next page. A text heading may not be the last line on the page. Use the line-and-page-break feature of your word processing program to keep lines together and force the heading to the next page.

concluding lines of page

We have been advertising this product line for the past six months in the Dallas area. Internet, television, radio, and newspaper campaigns have focused on various

continuation of paragraph on next page

6

hair-care products in our LustrePlus line. Internet advertising has been confined to featuring only our shampoos and conditioners.

Preliminary results from this advertising campaign show between a 25 and 30 percent increase in sales for the different varieties of LustrePlus shampoo, and a

text heading moved to next page

2

Factors to Be Considered

Several factors may be attributed to this unexpected change in the economy and the increased demand for our products. A recent economic analysis issued by the U.S.

g. In your word processing program, create macros or styles to produce the following results in formatting the report or manuscript.[1] Refer to the illustrations of report pages on pages 410–411.

[1]See the following sections in this chapter for specific instructions and examples for the preparation of report and manuscript parts, main headings, secondary headings, text headings, vertical listings, report or manuscript text (body), tables, and illustrations.

report page with text headings and a table

1-inch top margin

0.5 inch

34

ahead, new 5G deployments are in progress or now being planned for Japan, Brazil, Australia, New Zealand, North America, India, Southeast Asia, Central and South America, and other emerging markets around the globe. The demand for this technology continues to grow not only in the United States but also throughout the world.

Fast and Affordable Wireless Internet Services

Wireless service providers are increasingly looking toward mobile data as a key driver for future growth in revenue and earnings. The quality of service and the cost to deliver data traffic will be key differentiators. To be competitive, operators must quickly select and deploy the most efficient 5G solutions.

Data "throughput" capacity drives network economics, and "peak" data rates affect the user experience. The ability to offer higher throughput and peak data rates at a substantially lower cost creates significant competitive advantage for operators. Figure 1 shows the best user experience for subscribers presently supported by 4G WIRENET WAMA technology:

Figure 1
Best User Experience for Subscribers
WIRENET WAMA Technology
December 2017

Air Interface	Effective Peak Data Rate	Download Time
WSM	.25 mbps	90 seconds
IS-95A WAMA	.5 mbps	50 seconds
WPRS	.75 mbps	30 seconds
IS-95B WAMA	1 mbps	14 seconds
WAMA2000 1X	2 mbps	6 seconds
WWAMA2014	2 .8 mbps	3 seconds
WAMA2015 2XEZ-DO	6 mbps	1 second

Easy Migration Path

From entry-level "voice-only" networks to rich, high-end voice/data solutions, WIRENET supports wireless service providers around the globe by providing flexible technology choices. Engineers in the WIRENET Technology Group include easy migration into the designs of the

at least1 inch

12 Business Documents

report page with text headings and an Excel chart

0.5 inch

1-inch top margin

35

chipsets that are at the heart of network base stations and subscriber devices. Wireless service providers can easily provide the services needed by their clients.

Advances in the Wireless Industry

WIRENET employees innovated and commercialized a revolutionary wireless communication technology called Wireless Application Multiple Access (WAMA). This technology spreads digital radio signals across the spectrum in a unique way that allows multiple users to coexist in the same frequency without time-sharing.

WAMA enables wireless networks to increase their capacity and broaden their coverage areas. Users benefit from higher-quality transmissions with fewer dropped calls, improved voice quality, and enhanced security. The new generation of this technology, called *fifth-generation* or *5G*, is delivering on the promise of the wireless Internet by making always-on, high-speed data both accessible and economical.

Subscriber growth. Since its commercial introduction in 2007, WIRENET's WAMA technology has gained worldwide recognition as an engine for advances in the wireless industry. As shown in Figure 2, WAMA subscribers have grown to more than 297 million within the past ten years.

Figure 2
WAMA Growth History, 2007-2017

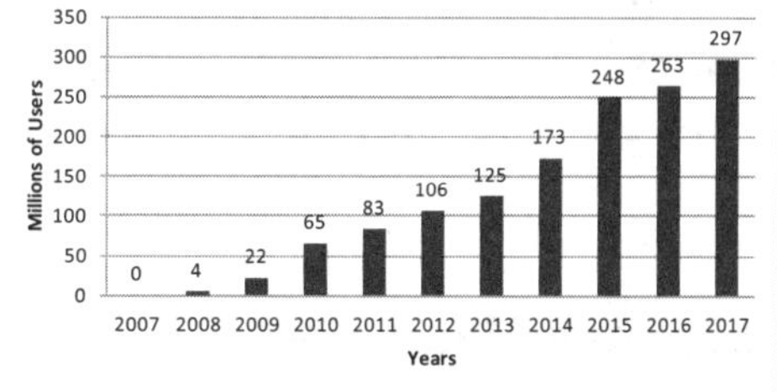

at least 1 inch

(1) Single-space and center main headings (all capital letters). Single-space and center any secondary headings (uppercase and lowercase letters); double-space between the main heading and the secondary heading, if used. Triple-space before beginning the first line of text. Refer to the illustration in Section 12–1a.

(2) Double-space the textual material in the body of the report; indent the first line of each paragraph 0.5 inch.

(3) Double-space before and after first- and second-degree text headings. Third-degree headings are part of the paragraph they introduce and are double-spaced like regular text.

(4) Single-space and indent 0.5 inch from the left and right margins any long quotations; omit the quotation marks. Long quotations are those consisting of more than three lines *or* more than two sentences. Double-space before and after the long quotation.[2]

(5) Vertical listings consisting of single-line items may be single or double spaced. For listings with items containing more than one line, single-space the items and leave one blank line between items. Double-space before and after the vertical listing.

(6) Tables and illustrations should be centered between the left and the right margins. Double-space before and after any tables and illustrations that interrupt the text narrative.

h. Use the spell-checker feature of your word processing program to correct any spelling or typographical errors.

i. If you must frequently prepare manuscripts or reports, use the styles feature of your word processing program to format your reports.

Parts of a Report or a Manuscript

12–2 Title Page

a. The title page generally contains the following information, but its contents are not restricted to these items:

(1) The title of the report or manuscript

(2) The name and the title of the person and/or the name of the group or organization for whom it was written

[2]See Chapter 2, Punctuation, Section 2–48, for an additional example of a long quotation formatted for inclusion in a manuscript or report.

(3) The name and the title of the person and/or the name of the group who wrote it

(4) The date it was submitted

b. Use the following guidelines to prepare a title page. To prepare the title page easily, access the center-page feature of your word processing program.

(1) Allow 2-inch top and bottom margins.

(2) Center all lines horizontally.

(3) Type the title of the report or manuscript in all capital letters. Single-space any titles containing more than one line.

(4) Space equally between the top and bottom margins all other parts following the title.

(5) Count the title page in the pagination, but do not number the page.

An illustration of a title page appears on page 414.

12–3 Letter of Transmittal

a. A letter of transmittal, if used, introduces the reader to the report or manuscript. Although the content of the transmittal letter will depend upon the complexity and scope of the report or manuscript, it should basically tell the reader the following:

(1) What the topic is

(2) Why the report was written

(3) How the report was compiled (method of research)

(4) Who worked on it or helped with its development

(5) What major findings or conclusions resulted (if a synopsis or summary page is not included)

b. A letter of transmittal should be friendly and concise, usually concluding with the writer expressing appreciation for the opportunity to prepare the report or manuscript. Use the following guidelines to format the transmittal letter:

(1) Use any acceptable business letter style.

(2) Place the letter of transmittal after the title page.

(3) Number the page with a lowercase Roman numeral centered at the bottom of the page. Place the page number 0.5 inch from the bottom edge of the page. (See Section 12–1b for further information on the page-numbering formats.)

An illustration of a letter of transmittal appears on page 415.

title page

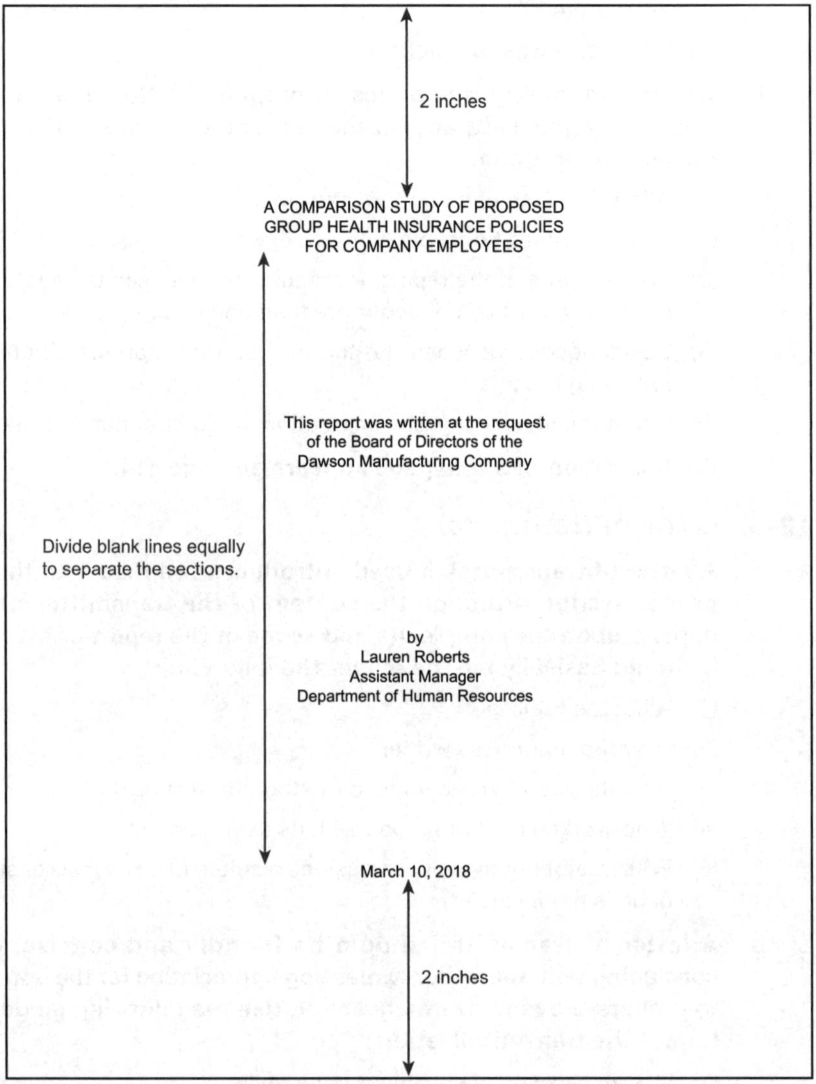
2 inches
A COMPARISON STUDY OF PROPOSED
GROUP HEALTH INSURANCE POLICIES
FOR COMPANY EMPLOYEES
This report was written at the request
of the Board of Directors of the
Dawson Manufacturing Company
Divide blank lines equally
to separate the sections.
by
Lauren Roberts
Assistant Manager
Department of Human Resources
March 10, 2018
2 inches

letter of transmittal

Dawson Manufacturing Company

170 East Parkland Avenue
Dallas, Texas 75214

(214) 363-5757
Fax: (214) 363-5783

March 10, 2018

Mr. Clifford Powell, President
Dawson Manufacturing Company
170 East Parkland Avenue
Dallas, Texas 75214

Dear Mr. Powell:

As requested by the Board of Directors, I have prepared a report comparing the employee group health insurance policies that were submitted by eight companies. The policies were compared in the following ways:

1. Company cost per employee
2. Cost to employees
3. Kinds of illnesses and/or injuries covered
4. Hospital, out-patient, and home-visit coverage
5. Total annual health benefits allowed
6. Miscellaneous coverage such as medicines, X rays, physical therapy, private-duty nursing, etc.
7. Family members covered
8. Annual deductible and copayment

As shown by the summary table on page 19, the Edgewater policy is superior in all categories except one—company cost per employee. The additional $28.16 annual cost per employee is relatively small considering the substantial benefits provided in excess of any of the other less-expensive policies. Consequently, I recommend we select the Edgewater proposal.

Thank you for the opportunity to conduct this study. I appreciate the help and cooperation I received from the employees' representative and from the representatives of the insurance companies.

If you have any questions or if I can be of further assistance, please let me know.

Sincerely,

Lauren Roberts

Lauren Roberts, Assistant Manager
Department of Human Resources

mw

ii

↕ 0.5 inch

12-4 Summary of the Report

Long reports—especially those not including a letter of transmittal or those including a letter of transmittal without a synopsis—usually require a summary, sometimes referred to as an *executive summary*. Use the following guidelines to prepare the summary:

(1) Allow a 2-inch top margin. Center the main heading *SUMMARY* or *EXECUTIVE SUMMARY* in all capital letters. Triple-space after the main heading.

(2) Double-space the text of the summary; indent the first line of each paragraph 0.5 inch. Begin by stating the purpose of the report. Briefly describe the procedures used in preparing the report, and end with a concise presentation of the conclusions and recommendations.

(3) Number the summary page or pages with lowercase Roman numerals centered at the bottom of the page. Place the page number 0.5 inch from the bottom edge of the page (see Section 12–1b).

12–5 Table of Contents

The content and format of a table of contents, illustrated on page 417, vary with the length and complexity of the report or manuscript, but the following guidelines may be used for its preparation:

(1) Allow a 2-inch top margin. Center the main heading *TABLE OF CONTENTS* or *CONTENTS* in all capital letters on the first line.

(2) Place the word *Page* a triple space below the *TABLE OF CONTENTS* heading; align it with the right margin.

(3) Use all capital letters and double-space the listing for the preliminary sections of the report (e.g., *LETTER OF TRANSMITTAL, SUMMARY, or LIST OF TABLES*). Begin at the left margin a double space below *Page*. Although it is counted and paginated with a lowercase Roman numeral, the table of contents is not included in this listing.

(4) Begin the major division heading of the report (e.g., *Chapter, Section, Unit,* or *Topic*) at the left margin. The major division heading may either appear on the same line as *Page* or be placed a double space below the preliminary parts.

(5) Number major sections of the report, if desired, by using uppercase Roman numerals. Align the longest numeral with the left margin, and indent the shorter numerals so the periods following the numerals are aligned. Use a decimal tab in your word processing program to achieve this alignment.

(6) Use all capital letters for listing major sections of the report. Those sections of lesser degree should be indented, placed in capital and lowercase letters, single spaced, and arranged in the same sequence as they appear in the report.

(7) Use leaders (a line of periods) to assist the reader in locating the page number of a particular section, and align vertically the leaders for each section or subsection of the report. Although all major headings must have corresponding page numbers, the assignment of page numbers to subheadings appearing in the table of contents is optional. To obtain leaders in your word processing program, set a right decimal tab with dot leaders adjacent to the right margin.

(8) Number the page or pages containing the table of contents with lowercase Roman numerals centered at the bottom of the page. Place the page number 0.5 inch from the bottom edge of the page. (See Section 12–1b for further information on the page-numbering formats.)

table of contents

2-inch top margin

TABLE OF CONTENTS

← 2 blank lines

Page

← 1 blank line

iii

12–6 List of Tables, List of Figures, or List of Illustrations

a. When a report or a manuscript contains several tables, include as a helpful reference to the reader a list of tables after the table of contents. Guidelines for formatting the list of tables follow:

(1) Use a 2-inch top margin, and center the heading *LIST OF TABLES* in all capital letters on the first line.

(2) Triple-space after the *LIST OF TABLES* heading. Place the word *Table* at the left margin, and align the last letter of the word *Page* with the right margin.

(3) Indent 0.25 inch from the left margin. Key the number of each table followed by spacing of 0.25 inch and the table title. Capitalize the main words,[3] and single-space the lines in each title. Double-space between titles.

(4) Use leaders (a line of periods) to assist the reader in locating the page number of a particular table. To obtain leaders in your word processing program, set a right decimal tab with dot leaders adjacent to the right margin.

(5) Number pages in the list of tables with lowercase Roman numerals centered at the bottom of the page. Place the page number 0.5 inch from the bottom edge of the page. (See Section 12–1b for further information on the page-numbering formats.)

list of tables

LIST OF TABLES

← 2 blank lines

Table		Page
← 1 blank line		
1	Annual Cost per Employee of Health Insurance Policies Submitted by Eight Companies, 2018	8
2	Employer Claims Submitted from 2014 Through 2017 by Three Companies of Equal Size	14
3	Estimated Cost (Without Health Insurance) of Health Care per Employee From 2014 Through 2017	17
4	Cost of Group Insurance Versus Individual Health Policies	25

b. For a listing that contains only figures, use the same format described in the previous section for a list of tables. Change the title to *LIST OF FIGURES*, and substitute the heading *Figure* for *Table* at the left margin.

---

[3]*Main* words are all words except (1) the articles *a*, *an*, and *the*; (2) the conjunctions *and*, *but*, *or*, and *nor*; (3) prepositions (e.g., *of*, *for*, *in*, *on*, *by*, *with*, *through*); (4) the word *to* in infinitives (*to say*, *to enter*, *to look*, etc.); and (5) the word *as*—unless any of these words are the first or last words.

c. **A list of illustrations may be used for a report or a manuscript that contains a combination of tables and figures. Change the title to *LIST OF ILLUSTRATIONS*. Use the following guidelines to format a list of illustrations that contains both tables and figures:**

(1) Center the heading *LIST OF ILLUSTRATIONS* in all capital letters 2 inches from the top edge of the page.

(2) Triple-space after the *LIST OF ILLUSTRATIONS* heading, and center the secondary heading *A. Tables* in capital and lowercase letters. Double-space after the subheading. Place *Table* at the left margin, and align the last letter of the word *Page* with the right margin. Double-space before beginning the listing.

(3) Indent 0.25 inch from the left margin. Key the number of each table followed by a space of 0.25 inch and the table title. Capitalize the main words[4] and single-space each title. Double-space between titles. Use leaders (a line of periods) to assist the reader in locating the page number. To obtain leaders in your word processing program, set a right decimal tab with dot leaders adjacent to the right margin. Triple-space after the last title.

(4) Center the secondary heading *B. Figures* in capital and lowercase letters. Double-space after the secondary heading; place *Figure* at the left margin and align the last letter of the word *Page* with the right margin. Double-space before beginning the listing.

(5) Indent 0.25 inch from the left margin. Key the number of each figure followed by 0.25-inch spacing and the figure title. Capitalize the principal or main words, and single-space each title. Double-space between titles. Use leaders to assist the reader in locating the page number.

(6) Number the list of illustrations with lowercase Roman numerals centered at the bottom of the page. Place the page number 0.5 inch from the bottom edge of the page. (See Section 12–1b for further information on page-numbering formats.)

[4]*Main* words are all words except (1) the articles *a*, *an*, and *the*; (2) the conjunctions *and*, *but*, *or*, and *nor*; (3) prepositions (e.g., *of*, *for*, *in*, *on*, *by*, *with*, *through*); (4) the word *to* in infinitives (*to say*, *to enter*, *to look*, etc.); and (5) the word *as*—unless any of these words are the first or last words.

list of illustrations

LIST OF ILLUSTRATIONS

← 2 blank lines

A. Tables

← 1 blank line

Table		Page
	← 1 blank line	
1	Annual Cost per Employee of Health Insurance Policies Submitted by Eight Companies, 2018	8
	← 1 blank line	
2	Employer Claims Submitted from 2014 Through 2017 by Three Companies of Equal Size	14
	← 1 blank line	
3	Estimated Cost (Without Health Insurance) of Health Care per Employee from 2014 Through 2017	17
	← 1 blank line	
4	Cost of Group Insurance Versus Individual Health Policies	25

← 2 blank lines

B. Figures

← 1 blank line

Figure		Page
	← 1 blank line	
1	Per Capita Dollar Increase in Medical Care for Working-Age Population, 2008–2018	5
	← 1 blank line	
2	Per Capita Dollar Increase of Group Medical Insurance Coverage for Working-Age Population, 2008–2018	6
	← 1 blank line	
3	Assets of Eight Major Health Insurance Carriers (in Millions of Dollars)	28

12 Business Documents

12–7 Preparing the Body of the Report or Manuscript

a. Use the following guidelines to format pages that begin the body of a report or a manuscript or begin major sections of the body:

(1) Allow a 2-inch top margin by adjusting the amount of space between the top margin of the report and the first line of the title. (See Section 12–1a for setting report margins.)

(2) Center the heading in all capital letters; single-space multiple-line main headings.

(3) Double-space after the main heading if it is followed by a secondary heading; triple-space after the main heading if it is not followed by a secondary heading.

b. Secondary headings are often used to explain or elaborate on a main heading.

(1) Begin any secondary heading a double space below the main heading.

(2) Key the heading in capital and lowercase letters.

(3) Center all lines, and single-space multiple lines.

(4) Triple-space after the secondary heading.

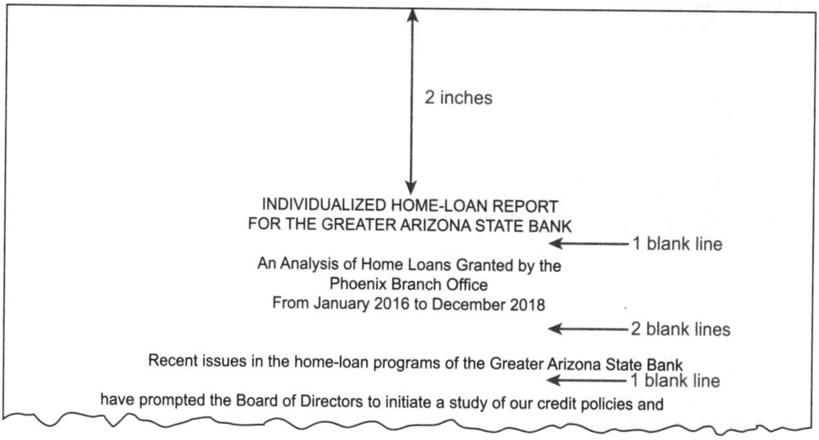

c. Follow these guidelines for preparing the pages of the report body:

(1) Double-space the body of the report or manuscript.

(2) Indent the first line of each paragraph 0.5 inch to offset it clearly from the previous one.

(3) Use the widow/orphan line protection feature of your word processing program to adjust page endings so that single lines from a paragraph are not at the top or bottom of a page. (Single lines are often called *widow* and *orphan lines.*)

(4) Place at least two lines of a new paragraph at the end of the page and carry over at least two lines from the previous paragraph (one complete line and a minimum of one word on a second line) if page and paragraph endings do not coincide.

d. Use the following guidelines to number the pages of the report or manuscript:

(1) For pages with main headings, either omit the page number or center it 0.5 inch from the bottom edge of the page. (See Section 12–1c for further explanation and illustrations.)

(2) For pages without main headings, place the page number 0.5 inch from the top edge of the page aligned with the right margin. (See Section 12–1d for further explanation and illustrations.)

Example pages from the body of a report appear on pages 422 and 423.

body of report

2 inches

SECTION I
INTRODUCTION

2 blank lines

The following report compares employee health and major medical insurance programs submitted by eight insurance companies.

1 blank line

Purpose of the Report

1 blank line

Last January, Jeremy Litchfield, one of the employee representatives of our company, requested that company-sponsored health insurance be considered by the Board of Directors as a supplement to employees' wage and salary schedule.

The Board of Directors subsequently directed the Human Resources Department to (1) contact insurance companies to determine the kinds of health insurance coverage available and (2) compare the kinds of coverage offered to determine which provider would most cost effectively meet our employees' health insurance needs. This report provides an analysis of the available health and medical insurance policies available to our company.

1 blank line

Scope of the Report

1 blank line

The scope of this investigation was limited to an analysis of the written proposals and copies of the proposed insurance policies submitted by the participating insurance companies.

Of the 18 insurance companies contacted, the majority provided only verbal explanations of what the estimated coverage and cost of a group health and major medical insurance program would be for our employees. Only eight of these companies submitted written documents for our consideration. Proposals and policies from these companies were evaluated according to the following criteria:

at least 1 inch

body of report **(continued)**

1 inch top margin

0.5 inch

2

right-margin setting

Company cost per employee
Cost to employee
Kinds of illnesses and/or injuries covered
Hospital, out-patient, and home-visit coverage
Deductibles and dollar amounts of coverage
Exclusions

1 blank line

An explanation of the factors considered in these criteria is provided in the following sections.

1 blank line

Company Cost per Employee

1 blank line

Each health insurance package was analyzed to determine the cost per employee to the company. This analysis took into consideration such variables as discounts for insuring over the minimum number of employees and savings accruing from submitting payments on a monthly basis rather than a quarterly basis.

1 blank line

Cost to Employees

1 blank line

None of the health insurance packages considered in this report included any direct cost to the employees. Some of the policies did, however, provide options whereby individual employees could increase the amount of coverage at their own expense.

1 blank line

Kinds of Illnesses and/or Injuries Covered

1 blank line

Although all the health insurance packages studied in this report covered most of the common types of illnesses and injuries, differences were noted in several specific areas. The most common differences appeared in coverages related to illnesses that result in operations. Other differences occurred in the amounts allowed for childbirth, physical therapy, and recovery in extended-care facilities.

Exclusions also differed among the various policies. Some excluded long-term rehabilitation for neuromuscular disorders; others excluded treatment for psychiatric assistance and/or rehabilitation for alcohol and drug dependencies. Most of the policies excluded chiropractic treatments, and all the policies excluded acupuncture and aspects

at least 1 inch

12–8 Text Headings

a. Text headings of different degrees signal content in a report or manuscript and contribute to its readability. A common classification of text headings includes first-, second-, and third-degree headings. Text headings are usually boldfaced, but they may have a larger font size with or without bolding. Guidelines for formatting each text heading follow and are repeated in the context of its corresponding illustration.

(1) **First-degree text headings.** Center a first-degree text heading, and capitalize the first letter of each main word. The heading may be boldfaced and/or keyed in a larger font size than the report or manuscript text. Double-space before and after a first-degree text heading.

> that main headings and secondary headings introduce the report or a main section of
>
> the report.
>
> 1 blank line ⟶
>
> **Format for a First-Degree Text Heading**
>
> 1 blank line ⟶
>
> A first-degree text heading, also referred to as a "centered heading," is centered
>
> and typed in capital and lowercase letters. The heading may be boldfaced and/or keyed
>
> in a larger font size. Double-space before and after a first-degree heading.

(2) **Second-degree text headings.** Begin the second-degree text heading at the left margin. Capitalize the first letter of each main word. Boldface the heading, or use a larger font size with or without bolding. If enlarged, the font size must be smaller than the one used for first-degree text headings and larger than the one used for the report or manuscript text. Double-space before and after a second-degree text heading.

> may be boldfaced and/or keyed in a larger font size. Double-space before and after a
>
> first-degree heading.
>
> 1 blank line ⟶
>
> **Format for a Second-Degree Text Heading**
>
> 1 blank line ⟶
>
> A second-degree heading is often called a "margin heading" or a "side heading"
>
> because it begins at the left margin. Use capital and lowercase letters. Boldface the
>
> heading, or use a larger font size with or without bolding. If changed, the font size must
>
> be smaller than the one used for first-degree text headings and larger than the one used
>
> for the report or manuscript text. Double-space before and after a second-degree text
>
> heading.

(3) **Third-degree text headings.** The third-degree text heading begins a paragraph, so it is indented from the left margin the same amount of space as the first line of any other paragraph—usually 0.5 inch. Capitalize only the first word and any proper nouns. Boldface the heading and conclude it with a period. Use the same font size as the report or manuscript text. Double-space before a third-degree text heading, and begin keying the paragraph text one or two spaces after the period that concludes the heading.

> than the one used for the report or manuscript text. Double-space before and after a second-degree text heading.
>
> 1 blank line →
>
> **Format for a third-degree text heading.** Because the third-degree heading is part of the paragraph that follows, it is also referred to as a "paragraph heading." Only the first word and proper nouns in the heading are capitalized.
>
> The third-degree heading is boldfaced (in the same typeface and size as the report or manuscript text) and followed by a period. Double-space before a third-degree heading, and begin keying the paragraph on the same line directly after the heading.

b. Text headings indicate divisions of a topic or subtopic; therefore, if a first-, second-, or third-degree heading is used, it must be followed by at least one or more matching headings. For example, if you use one first-degree heading in the report or manuscript, you must use at least one other first-degree heading in the same document.

c. All text headings should be separated by at least two lines of text, regardless of their place in the heading hierarchy. In other words, a lesser-degree text heading may not follow another heading without any intervening text.

d. Text headings must be used in ascending order of degree from first degree to third degree, *but* the first-degree heading may be omitted if only one or two levels of headings are required in a report. The following table illustrates what heading levels may be used based upon the number of levels or divisions required:

Number of Text Headings Required	*Levels of Text Headings to Be Used*
3	First-degree heading, Second-degree heading, and Third-degree heading
2	First-degree heading and Second-degree heading *or* Second-degree heading and Third-degree heading
1	First-degree heading *or* Second-degree heading

12–9 Listings

a. Both vertical and horizontal listings are often used in letters, memorandums, reports, and manuscripts. Whether to use a horizontal or a vertical format depends upon the following:

(1) The number of items in the listing

(2) The number of words contained in each item

(3) The degree of emphasis intended

Vertical listings are more emphatic than horizontal listings. They may be numbered, unnumbered, or bulleted. Lengthy and complex listings are more readily understood in the vertical format.

Horizontal listings are less emphatic. They are generally used with short listings that are few in number. Each item in a horizontal listing is preceded by an Arabic numeral or a lowercase letter enclosed in parentheses.

b. *Numbered vertical listings* are numbered in consecutive order with Arabic numerals. In all business documents, use the following guidelines for listing numbered items vertically:

(1) Introduce a vertical listing with a complete sentence.

(2) Indent the listing 0.5 inch from both the left and right margins. In business letters and memorandums, vertical listings *may* be aligned with the left and right margins of the main text.

(3) Number each item; use the features of your word processing program to align the text approximately two spaces after the period in the number.

(Any second and succeeding lines should begin directly under the first word, not the number, of the item.) Single-space items that contain more than one line.

(4) Use parallel construction; that is, use all complete sentences, all the same kind of phrases, or all single words that begin with the same part of speech and have the same form. Place a period after each item in listings that contain *only* complete sentences. (See Section 8–11 for additional information on parallel construction.)

(5) Capitalize the first word in each listed item.

(6) Double-space before the first item, between items, and after the last item in the listing. Single-space items that contain more than one line.

numbered vertical listing—complete sentences

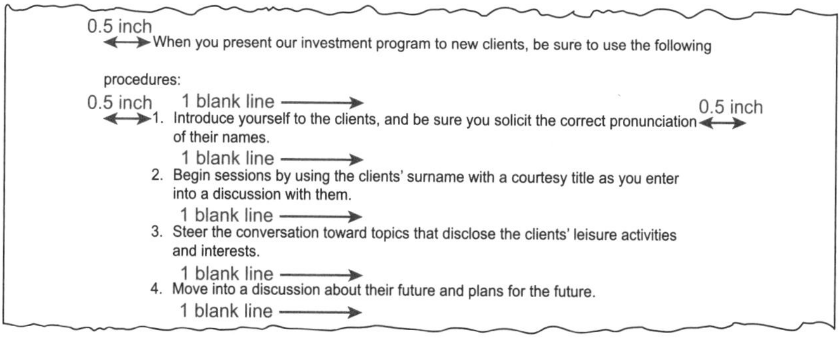

c. ***Unnumbered vertical listings*** **are similar in most respects to numbered vertical listings. Use the following guidelines for listing unnumbered items vertically:**

(1) Introduce a vertical listing with a complete sentence.

(2) Indent the listing 0.5 inch from both the left and right margins.

(3) Use parallel construction; that is, use all complete sentences, all the same kind of phrases, or all single words that begin with the same part of speech and have the same form. Place a period after each item in listings containing *only* complete sentences. (See Section 8–11 for additional information on parallel construction.)

(4) Capitalize the first word in each listed item.

(5) Double-space before the first item, between items, and after the last item in the listing. Single-space items that contain more than one line.

unnumbered vertical listing—complete sentences

0.5 inch
According to our manager, employees closing the store are requested to follow these procedures:
1 blank line
0.5 inch
Place the daily receipts in the vault, close the vault door, and check that the vault is locked.
0.5 inch
1 blank line
Ensure that all other employees except the security guard have left the premises.
1 blank line
Check to make sure that all customer entrances have been locked and bolted.
1 blank line
Engage the alarm system.
1 blank line
Lock the employee entrance upon leaving.
1 blank line

unnumbered vertical listing—words or phrases

0.5 inch
The position requires that the prospective employee be qualified to perform the following duties:
1 blank line
Greet and develop rapport with clients
1 blank line
0.5 inch
Answer questions regarding the many investment opportunities available through our company
0.5 inch
1 blank line
Evaluate clients' investment portfolios and other holdings
1 blank line
Obtain current information and forecasts on investment opportunities
1 blank line

0.5 inch
In our new office complex, all workstations will be equipped with the following computers and peripherals or their equivalents:
1 blank line
0.5 inch
GTA Landmark desktop computer, Model 9750
1 blank line
GTA Windows keyboard
1 blank line
Atlas 21-inch flat-screen monitor
1 blank line
GTA Laser color printer
1 blank line

Unnumbered vertical listings consisting of words or phrases that are keyed on single lines *may* be single spaced, although a double space still appears before and after the listing.

unnumbered vertical listing—words or phrases single spaced

0.5 inch
In our new office complex, all workstations will be equipped with the following computers and peripherals or their equivalents:
1 blank line
0.5 inch
GTA Landmark desktop computer, Model 9750
0.5 inch
GTA Windows keyboard
Atlas 21-inch flat-screen monitor
GTA Laser color printer
1 blank line

d. ***Bulleted listings*** **are similar to numbered listings. Typographic symbols (small solid circles, hollow circles, solid squares, hollow squares, check marks, etc.) replace the numbers. These symbols may be accessed through various options in word processing programs. In all business letters, memorandums, reports, and manuscripts, use the following guidelines for listing bulleted items vertically:**

(1) Introduce a vertical listing with a complete sentence.

(2) Indent the listing 0.5 inch from both the left and right margins. In business letters and memorandums, vertical listings *may* be aligned with the left and right margins of the main text.

(3) Insert the typographical symbol; use the features of your word processing program to align the text approximately two spaces after the typographical symbol. (Any second and succeeding lines should begin directly under the first word, not the symbol, of the item.) Single-space items that contain more than one line.

(4) Use parallel construction; that is, use all complete sentences, all the same kind of phrases, or all single words that begin with the same part of speech and have the same form. Place a period after each item in listings containing *only* complete sentences. (See Section 8–11 for additional information on parallel construction.)

(5) Capitalize the first word in each listed item.

(6) Double-space before the first item, between items, and after the last item in the listing.

bulleted vertical listing—complete sentences

0.5 inch ↔ Please use the following financial guidelines in planning any regional in-service

training conferences for all our personnel:

1 blank line →

0.5 inch ↔ • Speakers' fees (to include all speakers) may be granted up to a maximum ↔ 0.5 inch
of $600 per meeting.

1 blank line →

• Catering expenses, including tax and gratuity, may not exceed $20 per person for breakfast meetings and $30 per person for luncheon meetings.

1 blank line →

• Rental fees for audiovisual equipment may not exceed $300 per meeting.

1 blank line →

• Supplies and printing costs may be incurred up to $150 unless new training manuals must be developed and printed.

1 blank line →

0.5 inch ↔ These financial guidelines are for one-day training conferences that are scheduled to be

held at sites other than one of our company offices. Meetings held at one of our company sites

bulleted vertical listing—words or phrases

0.5 inch ↔ Customers may purchase any of the following four patterns at the sale price of

$49.95 a place setting until October 31:

1 blank line →

0.5 inch ↔ • Princess by Lenox ↔ 0.5 inch

1 blank line →

- Golden Heritage by Mikasa

1 blank line →

- Flower Garden by Noritake

1 blank line →

- Solitaire by Rosenthal

1 blank line →

0.5 inch ↔ These patterns are being offered at savings from 40 to 60 percent. Purchases

are limited by the stock on hand. Once a pattern is sold, it will not be available at the

e. Horizontal listings may be part of a sentence, or they may be introduced by a complete thought followed by a colon. Whenever a horizontal listing contains three or more items, the items are separated by commas or semicolons. Use commas to separate words or phrases; use semicolons to separate complete thoughts or items that contain internal commas. Use the following guidelines for listing items horizontally:

(1) Use a colon to introduce the list *only when it is preceded by a complete thought.*

(2) Capitalize the first word of an item *only if it is a proper noun.*

(3) Identify the listed items by enclosing either numbers or lowercase letters in parentheses before each item. Do not conclude a line with only a number or letter enclosed in parentheses; at least one word of the item must appear after the numeral or letter. Use the nonbreaking space feature of your word processing program to wrap an isolated number or letter to the next line.

horizontal listing—items separated by commas

as requested. Each team will consist of (a) an administrator, (b) a scientist, (c) two

engineers, (d) an administrative assistant, and (e) a secretary. The team will function

under the supervision of our project coordinator, who will ensure that each member

horizontal listing—items separated by semicolons

on Tuesday, June 10. While I am in New York, would you please take care of the

following items: (1) complete the negotiations with AAA Computer System Services for

an additional one-year contract; (2) respond to and follow through on the inquiry from

Medco Financial Services regarding our medical software line; and (3) contact dental

offices to review, test, and evaluate our newly developed line of software for dentists.

If you need assistance with following through on any of these items, please call me on

12–10 Citing Sources

When the source of information or a direct quotation needs to be given in a report or manuscript, the citation may be worked into the surrounding text or put into a footnote, an endnote, or a parenthetical text citation. The format of citations depends upon the style of notation used. The MLA (Modern Language Association) style is generally used in literary writings, and the APA (American Psychological Association) style is used mainly by writers in the social sciences.

Business writers usually use a conventional footnote or endnote style because readers can easily associate the cited information with its source and authenticate its contents. Therefore, the following formats shown for footnotes and endnotes are recommended for use in business reports.[5]

a. Use the footnote feature of your word processing program to ensure that notations and corresponding documentation appear consistently on the same page. Guidelines for preparing footnotes for off-line sources are listed below:

(1) Access the footnote feature of a word processing program to assist you with the automatic format and placement of footnotes. Indicate the presence of a footnote by inserting a superscript figure after the material to be documented. Place the footnote itself at the bottom of the page on which the reference notation appears.

(2) Set off footnotes from the rest of the page with a 2-inch line at the left margin, at least a single space after the last line of text on the page. Begin the footnote a double space after the line separator. These formats may be performed automatically through the footnote feature of a word processing program.

(3) Indent 0.5 inch, and number each footnote consecutively with a superior (slightly raised) figure *or* a full-size number followed by a period. Footnote entries are formatted in a smaller-size font than the font used in the text of the manuscript or report. These formats may be achieved automatically by using the Chicago style citation feature of a word processing program (if available).

(4) Begin the footnote by keying the name of the author or authors, if any, in a first-name, last-name sequence.

---

[5]The formats suggested here for footnotes and endnotes for published and unpublished works are *based on* the format alternatives contained in *The Chicago Manual of Style*, 16th ed. (Chicago: The University of Chicago Press, 2010), Web.

(5) Provide the complete title of the cited reference, and capitalize the main words.[6] Place the titles of magazine articles, sections of books, newspaper columns, and other such section or segment titles in quotation marks. Italicize the titles of books, pamphlets, magazines, newspapers, and other complete works with subdivisions.

(6) Include next, where applicable, the publishing information. Enclose in parentheses the geographical location of the publisher followed by a colon, the name of the publisher, and the date of publication. Eliminate the state name from the geographical location when the city is commonly known; otherwise, use the standard state abbreviation with the city name.

(7) Follow the complete title of journals, magazines, and newspapers with the volume number (if applicable), the issue number (if applicable), and the date of publication (in month and year or in month, day, and year format).

(8) Conclude footnotes with the page location of the cited material. For book titles with multiple volumes, show the volume number first—separate the volume number and the page location with a colon.

(9) Separate the parts of a footnote with commas, except before an opening parenthesis. Conclude the footnote with a period. Single-space all footnotes, and double-space between them.

book, one author

1. Charlene L. Parsons, *Introduction to Computer Concepts and Applications*, 6th ed. (Mason, OH: Cengage South-Western, 2017), 117–132.

book, two authors

2. R. Thomas Paransky and Diane C. Robbins, *Principles of Small Business Management*, 4th ed. (New York: John Wiley & Sons, Inc., 2016), 237.

book, more than two authors

3. Patricia Whitman, David Kane, James L. Wellington, and Ida Mason, *Fundamentals of Finance and Banking* (New York: McGraw-Hill, Inc., 2016), 208–214.

book, editor(s) only

4. Daniel M. Sandalwood and Carol L. Jones, eds., *Readings in Organizational Communication* (Belmont, CA: Wadsworth Publishing Company, 2017), 307–321.

---

[6]*Main* words are all words except (1) the articles *a*, *an*, and *the*; (2) the conjunctions *and*, *but*, *or*, and *nor*; (3) prepositions (e.g., *of*, *for*, *in*, *on*, *by*, *with*, *through*); (4) the word *to* in infinitives (*to say*, *to enter*, *to look*, etc.); and (5) the word *as*—unless any of these words are the first or last words. (See Sections 3–6, 3–7, and 3–8 for further information on the capitalization of titles.)

company memorandum

5. Angela Garcia, "Medical Insurance Programs Available to Employees" (Boston Financial Corporation memorandum, October 25, 2015).

company report—published

6. Sheldon Holtz, "A Partnership in Japan," *Spotlight on Productivity* (Seattle: Star Toy Manufacturing Company, published report, July 2016), 12–14.

company report—unpublished (internal)

7. Terry Thomson, "An Analysis of Current Manufacturing Facilities" (Detroit: General Motors, Chevrolet Division, unpublished report, May 2017), 23–25.

correspondence

8. James R. Bushnell (as chancellor of the East Texas Community College District), response letter to author, September 28, 2015.

digital video disc (DVD), CD, or film

9. *Achieving Effective Global Communication,* DVD (New York: Digital Learning Systems, 2016).

encyclopedia article—signed

10. Richard W. Morton, "Management," *The Global Encyclopedia*, 3rd ed. (Chicago: Global Books, Inc., 2015), 14:108–112.

encyclopedia article—unsigned

11. "Adams, John," *The Global Encyclopedia,* 3rd ed. (Chicago: Global Books, Inc., 2015), 1:203–206.

government publication

12. U.S. Bureau of the Census, *Statistical Abstract of the United States* (Washington, DC: U.S. Government Printing Office, 2010), 296.

interview

13. Jeremy Moore (CEO, Great Western Federal Bank), interview by author, Phoenix, September 14, 2016.

journal article

14. Florence Zelaya, "Inventory Management Programs of Five National Retail Chains," *Journal of Business Research* 112 (2016): 197.

magazine article with author

15. K. T. Stadthaus, "Security Issues Plaguing Wireless Networks for Small Businesses," *Networking*, August 2016, 32–33, 61.

magazine article without author

16. "United States' Increasing Debt in the International Economy," *Business Update*, December 14, 2017, 54–57, 89.

newspaper article with author

17. Andrew R. Murillo, "Current Technology Issues Plaguing Schools," *Los Angeles Times*, San Fernando Valley edition, sec. D, January 16, 2018.

paperback book

18. Janet T. Matthews, *Successful E-commercing for the Small Business Owner* (Upper Saddle River, NJ: Prentice Hall, Inc., 2016), 105.

professional journal article (with volume number)

19. Scott D. Clark, Melissa E. Hogan, Heidi Vithen, and Mark Pracher, "Moving Along on the Information Highway: Integrating Web-Based Resources into the Business Curriculum," *Business Education Quarterly* 63 (March 2016): 37.

radio or television broadcast

20. "United States' Outsourcing: The Impact on Our Economy," *USA Alive* (Dallas: CBS telecast, July 17, 2017).

secondary source citation

21. Robert Willis and Margaret Ellwood, *Succeeding in the International Marketplace* (New York: Penguin Books, 2001), 84, as cited in Michael Crosby, *Nonverbal Communication in a Cross-Cultural Economy* (New York: Random House, Inc., 2003), 109.

table, source in

22. Andrew M. Cogan and Shawn W. Peterson, table "U.S. Merchant Trade Dollars by Country, 2014," *International Trade and Global Marketing* (New York: Random House, Inc., 2015), 147.

unpublished book or booklet

23. John Wooden, "John Wooden Basketball Fundamentals Camp, Player's Notebook" (Unpublished and undated booklet), 9.

unpublished book or booklet without author

24. "A History of Bruin Basketball," The UCLA Alumni Association, Occasional Paper #9 (Unpublished booklet, 1975), 2.

Once a reference has been cited, a shortened form *may be* used when the same reference is shown again. *Ibid.* is used when the reference cited is identical to the one in the preceding footnote. If the reference source is the same but the page numbers differ, use *Ibid.* with appended page numbers.

Ibid.—identical reference

3. Patricia Whitman, David Kane, James L. Wellington, and Ida Mason, *Fundamentals of Finance and Banking* (New York: McGraw-Hill, Inc., 2016), 208–214.

4. Ibid.

Ibid.—same reference but different page number(s)

17. Janet T. Matthews, *Successful E-commercing for the Small Business Owner* (Upper Saddle River, NJ: Prentice Hall, Inc., 2016), 105.

18. Ibid., 134.

When a previously cited work does not directly follow the full-form citation, use a shortened version:

(1) Begin the citation with the last name of the author. For two authors separate the last names with *and*; for three or more authors, add *et al.* after the last name of the first author.

(2) Provide a shortened form of the title, which consists of no more than four consecutive key words.

(3) Conclude with the page number.

3. Patricia Whitman, David Kane, James L. Wellington, and Ida Mason, *Fundamentals of Finance and Banking* (New York: McGraw-Hill, Inc., 2016), 208–214.

4. Janet T. Matthews, *Successful E-commercing for the Small Business Owner* (Upper Saddle River, NJ: Prentice Hall, Inc., 2016), 105.

5. Whitman et al., *Finance and Banking,* 208–214.

6. Paransky and Robbins, *Small Business Management,* 187.

4. Andrew Schultz, *Principles of Success for Small Business Enterprises* (Upper Saddle River, NJ: Prentice Hall, Inc., 2016), 117.

5. Ibid., 134.

6. Philip Freeman and Robert Lyons, *Principles of Small Business Management,* 2nd ed. (New York: John Wiley & Sons, Inc., 2015), 318.

7. Schultz, *Small Business Enterprises,* 147.

Formats for citing electronic sources—Web sites, e-mail messages, Web discussion forum postings, online commercial databases, electronically published books available for download, and so on—have emerged within the past two decades. Current formats

for documenting electronic resources have morphed from a myriad of suggested options into an extension of those recommended for print resources. Use the following guidelines for citing electronic resources:[7]

(1) Use the Chicago style citation feature of a word processing program (if available); and for books, magazines, journals, and newspapers, use the formats suggested for their print counterparts.

(a) Follow the source information with the date of access (month, day, year) preceded by the word *accessed* and the DOI if the source is a Web site.[8] If the site does not have a DOI or the DOI is difficult to locate, provide the complete URL of the Web site. Separate the parts with a comma.

(b) Follow the source information with the platform if the source is electronically published; for example, Kindle edition, PDF e-book, Microsoft Reader e-book, or the name of an online database.

(c) Conclude the citation with a period.

(2) Use the Chicago style citation feature of a word processing program (if available) for documenting other Web resources.

(a) Begin with the author's full name, if known, followed by a comma.

(b) Continue with the full title of the document in quotation marks and the title of the complete work (if applicable) in italics. Separate the items with a comma.

(c) Provide the name of a publisher, a sponsoring body, or a government organization (if applicable) followed by a comma.

(d) Provide the date of publication or last revision followed by a comma.

(e) Provide the date (month, day, year) preceded by the word *accessed* the site was accessed. Place a comma after the accessed date.

(f) Follow the source information with the DOI.[9] If the site does not have a DOI or the DOI is difficult to locate, provide the complete URL of the Web site.

(g) Conclude the citation with a period.

---

[7]The formats suggested here are based upon *The Chicago Manual of Style*, 16th ed. (Chicago: The University of Chicago Press, 2010), Web.

[8]DOI, *digital object identifier*, is a string of digits (e.g., 11.1086/380947) assigned to identify and locate electronic documents. The DOI stores metadata—unique physical aspects about the document such as size, the name of the author, when the document was written, and other such information. This information is more critical in locating documents than URLs because Web addresses may change or documents may be moved. The DOI is unique for each document so the document can be located wherever it may reside on the Internet.

[9]DOI, *digital object identifier*, is a string of digits (e.g., 11.1086/380947) assigned to identify and locate electronic documents. The DOI stores metadata—unique physical aspects about the document such as size, the name of the author, when the document was written, and other such information. This information is more critical in locating documents than URLs because Web addresses may change or documents may be moved. The DOI is unique for each document so the document can be located wherever it may reside on the Internet.

online or digitally delivered book

1. *The Chicago Manual of Style,* 16th ed. (Chicago: The University of Chicago Press, 2010), accessed March 17, 2015. http://www.chicagomanualofstyle.org/home.html.

2. Jack London, *The Valley of the Moon* (New York: The Macmillan Company, 1913), Kindle edition.

3. Jack London, *The Valley of the Moon* (New York: The Macmillan Company, 1913), The Project Gutenberg E-book, produced by Jerry Wann and Dianne Bean, released September 1998, posted September 17, 2008, last updated May 26, 2013, accessed March 17, 2015, http://www.gutenberg.org/cache/epub/1449/pg1449.txt.

general Web site

4. Honor Whiteman, "What Is the Global Economic Burden of Type 2 Diabetes?" *MNT, Medical News Today,* March 17, 2015, accessed March 17, 2015, http://www.medicalnewstoday.com/articles/290948.php.

online article in a magazine

5. David Murphy, "Microsoft Ditching Internet Explorer for 'Project Spartan,'" *PCMag.com,* March 17, 2015, accessed March 18, 2015, http://www.pcmag.com /article2/0,2817,2478396,00.asp.

online government publication

6. "State and County Quick Facts, Washington," *U.S. Census Bureau,* February 5, 2015, accessed March 18, 2015, http://quickfacts.census.gov/qfd/states/53000.html.

online reference source

7. David S.Heidler, "War of 1812," *Encyclopaedia Britannica,* August 4, 2014, accessed March 18, 2015, http://www.britannica.com/EBchecked/topic/181068/War-of-1812.

personal Web site

8. Joseph D. Perret, Web site, *Computer Applications and Office Technologies* Los Angeles Pierce College, 2015, accessed March 18, 2015. http://faculty.piercecollege .edu/perretjd/.

Use the following guidelines for citing e-mail messages:

(1) Use the Chicago style citation feature of a word processing program (if available) to achieve the formats used for other types of sources.

(2) Separate items in the notation with a comma.

(3) Begin with the author's full name.

(4) Place the subject line in quotation marks after the author's name.

(5) Supply the date the message was sent (month, day, year).

(6) Designate the type of message—*personal e-mail, office communication e-mail, distribution list e-mail.*

(7) Conclude the citation with a period.

office communication e-mail

9. Donna-Mae Villanueva, "Technology Report Deadline," February 26, 2017, office communication e-mail.

distribution list e-mail

10. Susan White, "CBEA 2018 Breakout Session Speakers," September 15, 2018, distribution list e-mail.

b. ***Parenthetical text citations*** **may be used as alternatives to formal footnotes. The reference is shown in parentheses at the end of the cited material by listing the (1) last name of the author(s), (2) date of publication, and (3) page number(s). The complete source appears in the bibliography following the body of the paper (see Section 12–12).**

parenthetical text citations

Income has risen 16 percent during the past two years within the industry (Jackson and Aguilar, 2017, 54–57). Small manufacturers have reported that expenses, however, have risen nearly 22 percent within the past six months alone because of increased

c. **Another alternative to footnotes or parenthetical text citations is *endnotes.* Indicate the presence of an endnote by placing a superior figure after the reference material to be documented. Endnotes are placed on a separate page at the end of the body of the report or at the end of each chapter in a long report. Use the endnote feature (Chicago style, if available) of your word processing program and the following guidelines to prepare endnotes:**

(1) Allow a 2-inch top margin. Center the heading *NOTES* or *ENDNOTES* in all capital letters.

(2) Triple-space after the heading. Single-space each note, but double-space between notes.

(3) Number the notes consecutively using Arabic numerals followed by a 0.3-inch left indent.

(4) Use the same content and sequence for endnotes as shown for footnotes in Section 12–10a. Use a footer to number the page at the

bottom, or omit (but count) the page number—select whichever style was used for the beginning pages of other major sections in the body of the report.

(5) Use a 1-inch top margin for any second and succeeding pages. Be sure to follow the same format used for the body of the report.

endnotes page

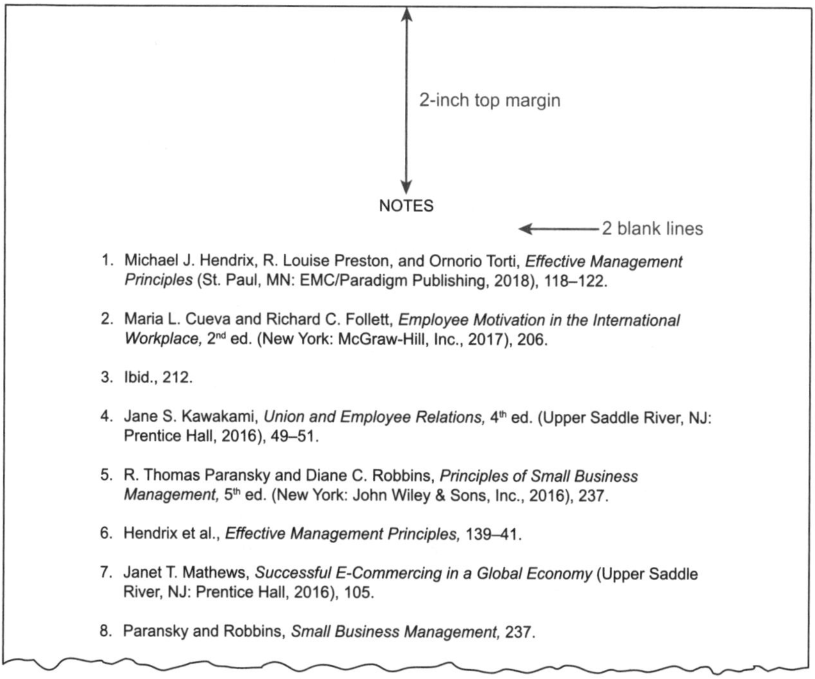

NOTES

1. Michael J. Hendrix, R. Louise Preston, and Ornorio Torti, *Effective Management Principles* (St. Paul, MN: EMC/Paradigm Publishing, 2018), 118–122.

2. Maria L. Cueva and Richard C. Follett, *Employee Motivation in the International Workplace,* 2nd ed. (New York: McGraw-Hill, Inc., 2017), 206.

3. Ibid., 212.

4. Jane S. Kawakami, *Union and Employee Relations,* 4th ed. (Upper Saddle River, NJ: Prentice Hall, 2016), 49–51.

5. R. Thomas Paransky and Diane C. Robbins, *Principles of Small Business Management,* 5th ed. (New York: John Wiley & Sons, Inc., 2016), 237.

6. Hendrix et al., *Effective Management Principles,* 139–41.

7. Janet T. Mathews, *Successful E-Commercing in a Global Economy* (Upper Saddle River, NJ: Prentice Hall, 2016), 105.

8. Paransky and Robbins, *Small Business Management,* 237.

d. Business writers may use a reference style that suits their purpose. In citing sources, though, use a style that meets the following criteria:

(1) The citation can be easily located from its point of reference within the report.

(2) The citation contains sufficient information so that the reader can readily locate the source and authenticate the information cited.

(3) All citations, regardless of media, are complete and expressed in a similar and consistent format.

12-11 Illustrations

Visuals in the form of tables, pie charts, column charts, bar charts, and line charts may be used to illustrate data in a report or manuscript. Where possible, a table or chart should appear on the same

page as the narrative describing it. If there is insufficient space on the same page for the table or chart and its explanation, then the illustration should be placed on the following page. A statement such as "As shown in Table 3 on page 9, . . ." must be used in the narrative to direct the reader to the illustration. The type of illustration used will vary according to the kind of data presented; guidelines for preparing each type of illustration follow:

a. ***Tables*** **arrange data in an orderly fashion by using a system of headings and columns to present information. Either open tables or ruled tables may be used in business documents.**

Although the length, style, and number of table columns will vary according to the type of data presented, use the following general procedures to set up tables:

(1) Use the table feature of your word processing program to create tables. For open tables eliminate the lines and condense the row height. For ruled tables select the line enhancements or one of the preformatted table formats provided by your word processing program.

(2) Leave one blank line before and after a table if it does not appear on a separate page.

(3) Number each table consecutively with Arabic numerals if more than one table or chart appears in the report. Center *Figure* and its corresponding number over the proposed position of the table. (If only one table appears in the report, begin the table with its title.)

(4) Single-space, and then center under the figure number the title of the table. Capitalize the main words.[10] If a subtitle is needed, center and capitalize the main words. Place the subtitle a single space below the main title. Double-space after the last line of either the main title or the subtitle in a table.

(5) Center the entire table between the left and right margins of the report or manuscript. Allow a sufficient amount of space for each column, keeping in mind that the column heading is part of the column.

(6) Use capital and lowercase letters for column headings. Center each column heading and set it in boldface.

(7) Center both horizontally and vertically a table appearing on a separate page.

[10]*Main* words are all words EXCEPT (1) the articles *a*, *an*, and *the*; (2) the conjunctions *and*, *but*, *or*, and *nor*; (3) prepositions (e.g., *of*, *for*, *in*, *on*, *by*, *with*, *through*); (4) the word *to* in infinitives (*to say*, *to enter*, *to look*, etc.); and (5) the word *as*—unless any of these words are the first or last words.

an open table

Figure 1
Monthly Cost per Employee of
Health Insurance Policies
Submitted by Eight Companies
March 3, 2018

1 blank line →

Company	Plan A[1]	Plan B[2]	Plan C[3]
Chicago General	$375.00	$492.50	$545.00
Concord	325.00	450.00	520.00
D & D Life	385.50	485.50	585.50
Edgewater	312.50	443.50	511.50
Lincoln	415.00	500.00	635.00
Morgan	309.34	440.25	524.15
New Jersey	350.00	475.00	530.00
Western	405.60	585.00	620.30

[1]$500,000 maximum coverage
[2]$1,000,000 maximum coverage
[3]$1,500,000 maximum coverage

simple ruled table

Figure 1
Monthly Cost per Employee of
Health Insurance Policies
Submitted by Eight Companies
March 3, 2018

1 blank line →

Company	Plan A[1]	Plan B[2]	Plan C[3]
Chicago General	$375.00	$492.50	$545.00
Concord	325.00	450.00	520.00
D & D Life	385.50	485.50	585.50
Edgewater	312.50	443.50	511.50
Lincoln	415.00	500.00	635.00
Morgan	309.34	440.25	524.15
New Jersey	350.00	475.00	530.00
Western	405.60	585.00	620.30

[1]$500,000 maximum coverage
[2]$1,000,000 maximum coverage
[3]$1,500,000 maximum coverage

enhanced ruled table

Figure 1
Monthly Cost per Employee of
Health Insurance Policies
Submitted by Eight Companies
March 3, 2018

1 blank line →

Company	Plan A[1]	Plan B[2]	Plan C[3]
Chicago General	$375.00	$492.50	$545.00
Concord	325.00	450.00	520.00
D & D Life	385.50	485.50	585.50
Edgewater	312.50	443.50	511.50
Lincoln	415.00	500.00	635.00
Morgan	309.34	440.25	524.15
New Jersey	350.00	475.00	530.00
Western	405.60	585.00	620.30

[1]$500,000 maximum coverage
[2]$1,000,000 maximum coverage
[3]$1,500,000 maximum coverage

b. *Pie charts* are used to illustrate the parts of a whole when that whole represents 100 percent of something. To achieve maximum clarity in this type of visual, do not exceed seven or eight segments in the illustration.

If possible, use the graphics feature of your spreadsheet program to create and import charts into your word processing program. Follow these guidelines to create pie charts:

(1) Begin the figure one blank line below the last line of text.

(2) Number each figure consecutively with Arabic numerals. Center *Figure* and its corresponding number over the proposed position of the pie chart. (If only one chart or table appears in the report, do not number the graphic. Instead, place the chart title on the first line.)

(3) Center the chart title a single space below the figure number. Capitalize the main words. Place any subtitle a single space below the title. Center the subtitle and capitalize the main words.[11]

[11]*Main* words are all words EXCEPT (1) the articles *a, an,* and *the*; (2) the conjunctions *and, but, or,* and *nor*; (3) prepositions (e.g., *of, for, in, on, by, with, through*); (4) the word *to* in infinitives (*to say, to enter, to look,* etc.); and (5) the word *as*—unless any of these words are the first or last words.

(4) Slice the pie in appropriate wedges, showing the largest wedge first. Start at the 12 o'clock position of the circle and move clockwise. The remaining wedges may or may not be in descending order of size, but the size of each wedge should be proportional to the percentage of the whole it represents.

(5) Identify what each wedge represents and its corresponding percentage. If the wedges are too small, use a legend to identify what each wedge represents.

(6) Document any sources directly below the pie chart. Begin the documentation at the left margin with the word *Source* followed by a colon. Place the notation after the colon. Use the guidelines for preparing footnotes contained in Section 12–10a (4)–(9) to cite the reference.

(7) Leave one blank line before resuming the narrative.

simple pie chart

Figure 1
Keystone Products
2017 Area Sales

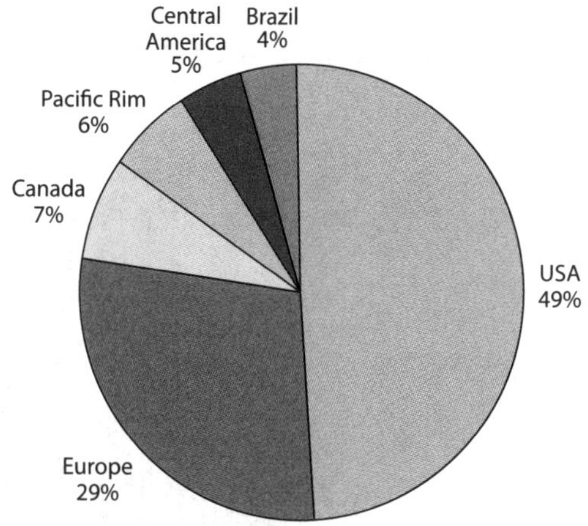

simple pie chart with exploded segment

Figure 2
Rochester Manufacturing Company
Profit and Expense Summary, 2017
Total Sales: $1,547,865

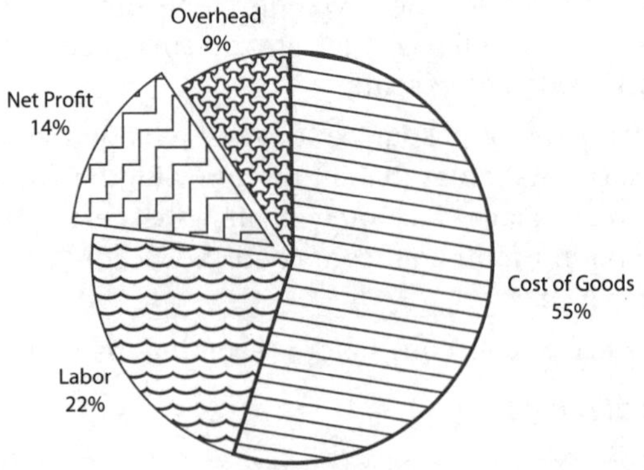

3-D pie chart

Figure 3
Browser Usage on Desktop Computers, February 2015

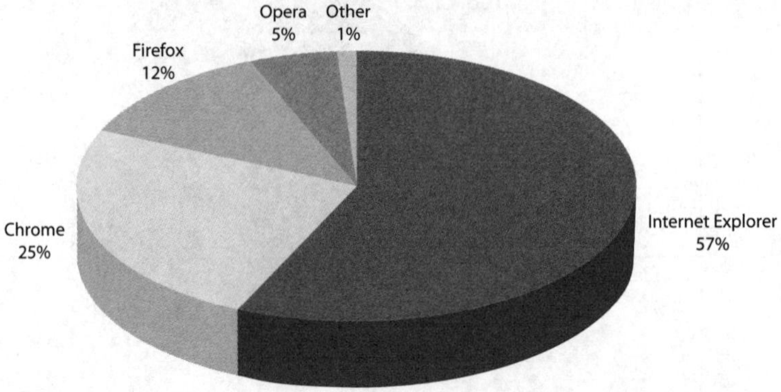

Source: "Desktop Browser Market Share," NETMARKETSHARE, February 2015, accessed March 19, 2015, http://www.netmarketshare.com/browser-market-share.aspx?qprid=0&qpcustomd=0

c. ***Bar charts* and *column charts* are used to compare quantities within a class or over a time period. Bar charts are oriented horizontally, and column charts are oriented vertically. These charts require both a vertical axis and a horizontal axis. One axis represents the quantity, and the other represents the varying items in the class or the time period over which the quantities are measured.**

Use your spreadsheet program and the following guidelines for constructing bar or column charts:

(1) Leave one blank line before and after a column or a bar chart when it interrupts the narrative.

(2) Number each figure consecutively with Arabic numerals. Center *Figure* and its corresponding number over the proposed position of the bar or the column chart. (If only one chart or table appears in the report, do not number the graphic. Instead, place the chart title on the first line.)

(3) Center the chart title a single space below the figure number. Capitalize the main words. Place any subtitle a single space below the title. Center the subtitle and capitalize the main words.[12]

(4) Use the horizontal axis in *bar charts* to represent the different quantities for each variable or time period; use the vertical axis to represent the variables or time periods.

(5) Use the vertical axis in *column charts* to represent the different quantities for each variable or time period; use the horizontal axis to represent the variables or time periods.

(6) Label clearly both the horizontal and the vertical axes.

(7) Document any sources a double space below the bar or the column chart. Begin the documentation at the left margin with the word *Source* followed by a colon. Place the notation after the colon. Use the guidelines for preparing footnotes contained in Section 12–10a (4)–(9) to cite the reference.

[12]*Main* words are all words EXCEPT (1) the articles *a*, *an*, and *the*; (2) the conjunctions *and*, *but*, *or*, and *nor*; (3) prepositions (e.g., *of*, *for*, *in*, *on*, *by*, *with*, *through*); (4) the word *to* in infinitives (*to say*, *to enter*, *to look*, etc.); and (5) the word *as*—unless any of these words are the first or last words.

horizontal 3-D bar chart comparing a single variable

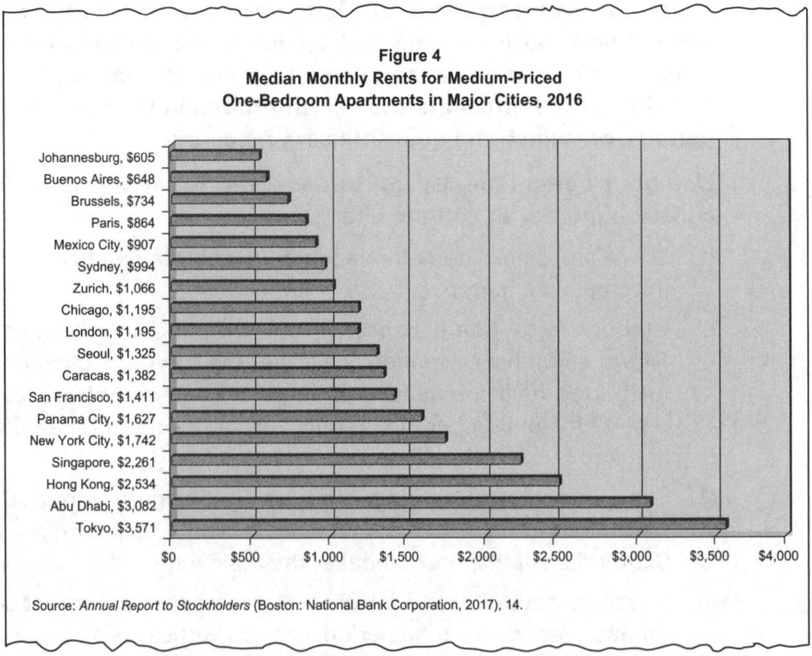

column chart comparing a single variable

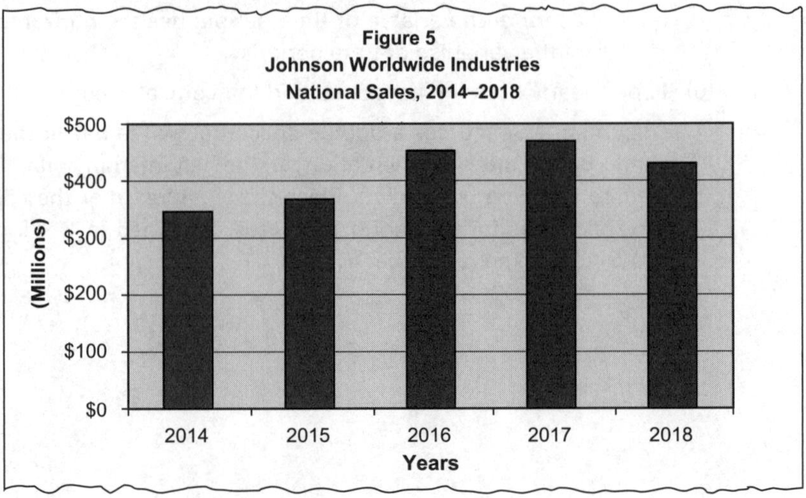

column chart comparing multiple variables

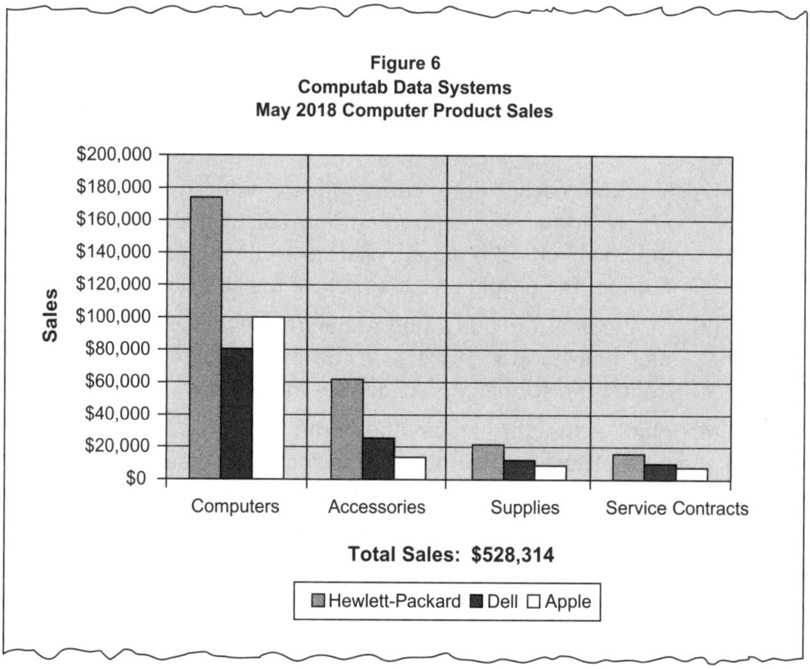

3-D stacked column chart

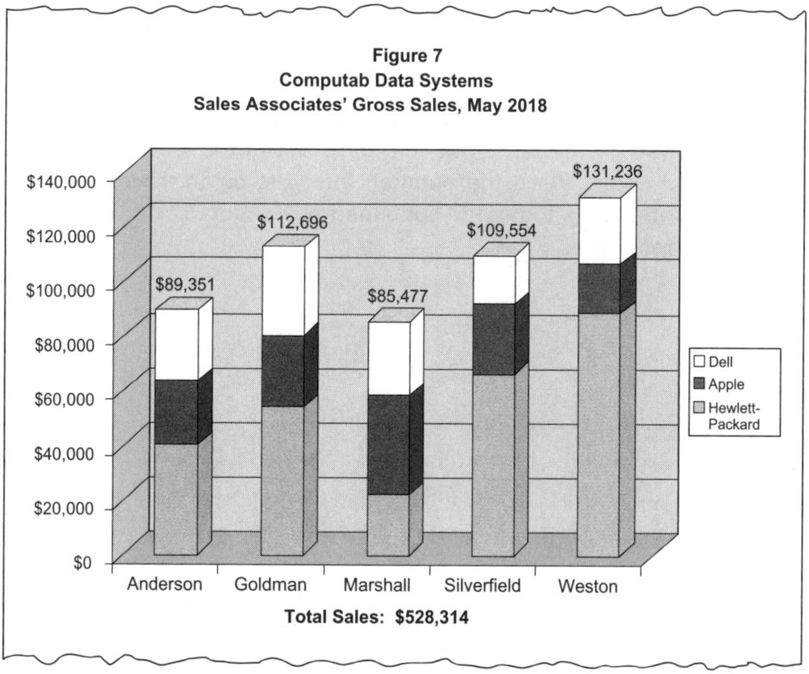

d. ***Line charts*** **are used to illustrate movement or trends over a time period. They may also be used to compare two or more sets of data over a time period.**

Use your spreadsheet program and the following guidelines to construct line charts that plot both single and multiple variables:

(1) Leave one blank line before and after a line chart that interrupts text.

(2) Number each figure consecutively with Arabic numerals. Center *Figure* and its corresponding number over the proposed position of the line chart. (If only one chart or table appears in the report, do not number the graphic. Instead, place the chart title on the first line.)

(3) Center the chart title a single space below the figure number. Capitalize the main words. Place any subtitle a single space below the title. Center the subtitle and capitalize the main words.[13]

(4) Place a straight vertical line at the left of the line chart to portray the quantity scale. The bottom of the scale represents the lowest quantity, and the top of the scale represents the highest quantity.

(5) Place at a right angle to the bottom of the vertical line a horizontal line that extends to the right side of the line chart. This horizontal line represents the time periods covered by the chart.

(6) Mark each quantity and time period equidistantly on its scale.

(7) Plot quantities above their respective time periods. Connect the cross points with a line, mark the cross points with a symbol, or use both symbols and connecting lines. When two or more factors are plotted on the same graph, use a different color, symbol, or line style for each set of data.

(8) Document any sources a double space below the chart. Begin the documentation at the left margin with the word *Source* followed by a colon. Place the notation after the colon. Use the guidelines for preparing footnotes contained in Section 12–10a (4)–(9) to cite the reference.

---

[13]*Main* words are all words EXCEPT (1) the articles *a*, *an*, and *the*; (2) the conjunctions *and*, *but*, *or*, and *nor*; (3) prepositions (e.g., *of*, *for*, *in*, *on*, *by*, *with*, *through*); (4) the word *to* in infinitives (*to say*, *to enter*, *to look*, etc.); and (5) the word *as*—unless any of these words are the first or last words.

line chart plotting a single variable

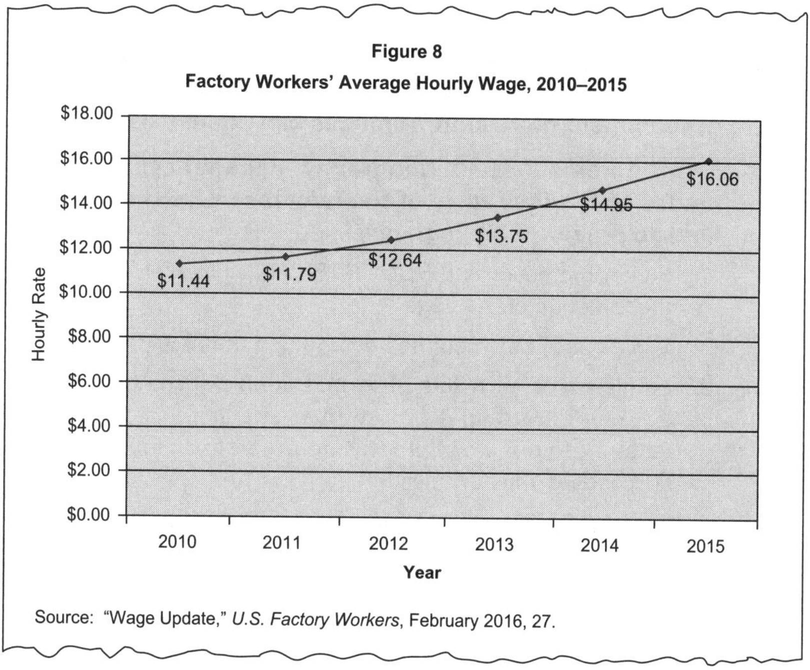

line chart plotting multiple variables

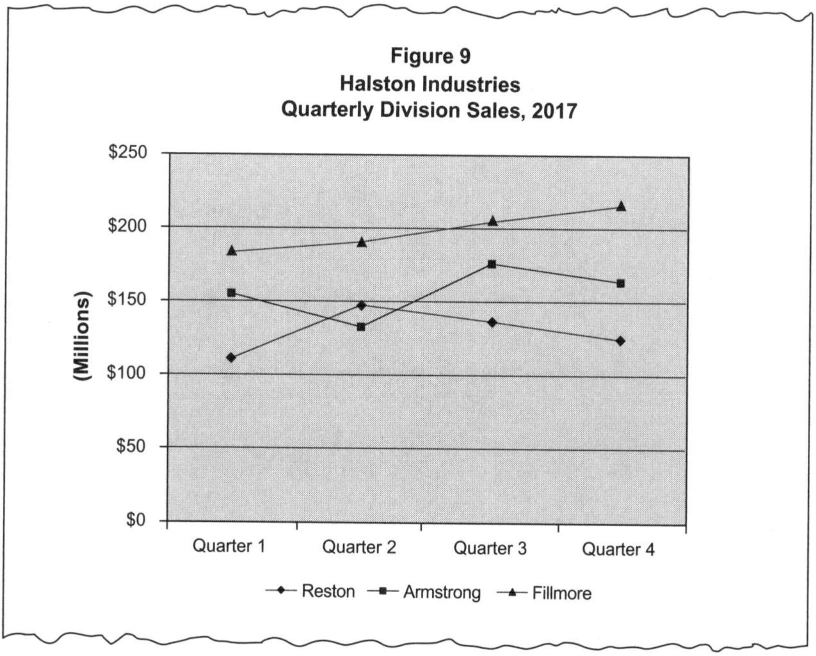

12–12 Bibliography

a. The bibliography[14] follows immediately after the body of the report or manuscript and contains all sources cited in the text. Any source material that is not cited but that has contributed directly to the development of a report or manuscript should also be included.

b. List the items in the bibliography alphabetically by authors' last names or the first entry of the reference. Use the following guidelines to prepare a bibliography:

(1) Center the heading *BIBLIOGRAPHY* in all capital letters 2 inches from the top edge of the page.

(2) Triple-space between the heading and the first reference.

(3) Single-space each reference and double-space between references. If a reference requires more than one line, use the hanging indent feature of your word processing program to indent the second and succeeding lines 0.5 inch.

(4) Type a 0.5-inch underline followed by a period in place of an author's name if he or she has more than one reference listed. Begin this procedure with the second reference for that author.

(5) Alphabetize the reference by title when the author is unknown.

(6) End the citations for magazines, journals, or other such source articles with page references.

(7) Provide the complete uniform resource locator (URL) for Internet sites and the date visited (if needed).

unsigned encyclopedia article

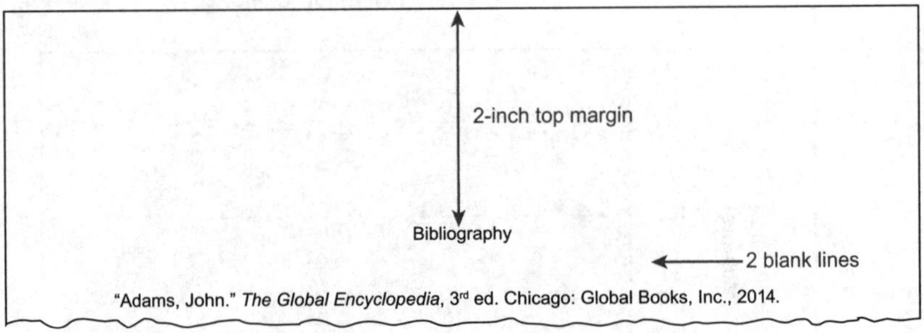

[14]The formats suggested here for bibliographical references are *based* on the traditional format contained in *The Chicago Manual of Style*, 16th ed. (Chicago: The University of Chicago Press, 2010), Web.

digital video disc (DVD), CD, film

Agricultural Production in California's Central Valley. DVD. San Francisco: Digital Learning Systems, 2015.

business correspondence

Bushnell, James R. (as chancellor of the East Texas Community College District). Response letter to author. September 28, 2018.

professional journal article (with volume number)

Clark, Scott D., Melissa E. Hogan, Heidi Vithen, and Mark Pracher. "Moving Along on the Information Highway: Integrating Web-Based Resources into the Business Curriculum." *Business Education Quarterly* 63 (March 2016): 37.

table, source in

Cogan, Andrew M. and Shawn W. Peterson. Table. "U.S. Merchant Trade Dollars by Country, 2014." *International Trade and Global Marketing.* New York: Random House, Inc., 2015. 147.

company memorandum

Garcia, Angela. "Medical Insurance Programs Available to Employees." Boston Financial Corporation memorandum. October 25, 2015.

Internet, World Wide Web

Haviv, Sagi. "How to Design a Logo." *BloombergBusinessWeek.* April 12, 2012. Accessed April 23, 2012. http://www.businessweek.com/articles/2012-04-12/how-to-design-a-logo-sagi-haviv.

unpublished book or booklet without author

"A History of Bruin Basketball." The UCLA Alumni Association. Occasional Paper #9. Unpublished booklet, 1975, 2.

company report—published

Holtz, Sheldon. "A Partnership in Japan." *Spotlight on Productivity.* Published Report. Seattle: Star Toy Manufacturing Company, July 2016.

digitally delivered book

London, Jack. *The Valley of the Moon.* New York: The Macmillan Company, 1913. Kindle edition.

paperback book

Matthews, Janet T. *Successful E-commercing for the Small Business Owner.* Upper Saddle River, NJ: Prentice Hall, Inc., 2016.

interview

Moore, Jeremy (CEO, Great Western Federal Bank). Interview by author. Phoenix. September 14, 2015.

encyclopedia article—signed

Morton, Richard W. "Management." *The Global Encyclopedia.* 3rd ed. Vol. 14. Chicago: Global Books, Inc., 2011.

newspaper article with author

Murillo, Andrew R. "Current Technology Issues Plaguing Schools." *Los Angeles Times.* San Fernando Valley edition. Sec. D. January 16, 2018.

book, one author

Parsons, Charlene L. *Introduction to Computer Concepts and Applications.* 6th ed. Mason, OH: Cengage South-Western, 2017.

book, same author

_____ *Microcomputers: Business and Accounting Spreadsheet Applications.* 2nd ed. Mason, OH: Cengage South-Western, 2018.

book, two authors

Peterson, L. David and Kathleene L. Basil. *Introduction to Real Estate.* 4th ed. (New York: John Wiley & Sons, Inc., 2016.

book, editor(s) only

Sandalwood, Daniel M., and Carol L. Jones, eds. *Readings in Organizational Communication.* Belmont, CA: Wadsworth Publishing Company, 2017.

magazine article with author

Stadthaus, K. T. "Security Issues Plaguing Wireless Networks for Small Businesses." *Networking*, August 2015, 32–33, 61.

government publication

Statistical Abstract of the United States. U.S. Bureau of the Census. Washington, DC: U.S. Government Printing Office, 2015, 296.

company report—unpublished (internal)

Thomson, Terry. "An Analysis of Current Manufacturing Facilities." Detroit: General Motors, Chevrolet Division. Unpublished report, May 2017, 23–25.

magazine article without author

"United States' Increasing Debt in the International Economy." *Business Update*, December 14, 2016, 54–57, 89.

radio or television broadcast

"United States' Outsourcing: The Impact on Our Economy." *USA Alive.* Dallas: CBS telecast, July 17, 2017.

book, more than two authors

Whitman, Patricia, David Kane, James L. Wellington, and Ida Mason. *Fundamentals of Finance and Banking.* New York: McGraw-Hill, Inc., 2016.

secondary source citation

Willis, Robert and Margaret Elwood. *Succeeding in the International Marketplace.* New York: Penguin Books, 2001. As cited in Michael Crosby, *Nonverbal Communication in a Cross-Cultural Economy.* New York: Random House, Inc., 2003.

unpublished book or booklet

Wooden, John. "John Wooden Basketball Fundamentals Camp, Player's Notebook." Unpublished and undated booklet.

journal article

Zelaya, Florence. "Inventory Management Programs of Five National Retail Chains." *Journal of Business Research* 112 (2016): 187–204.

12–13 Appendix

a. The appendix follows the bibliography and contains supportive material. This material may include such items as letters, copies of questionnaires, maps, contracts, lists, tables, and other documents not shown elsewhere.

b. The appendix may be preceded by a page entitled *Appendix* or *Appendixes.*

(1) If the report or manuscript contains one appendix, the name of the appendix may appear a double space below the *Appendix* heading. Center the word *Appendix* and the name of the appendix horizontally and vertically on the page.

(2) If the report or manuscript contains more than one appendix, the introductory page may show a list of the appendixes included. In this case (a) both the title and the listing are centered horizontally and vertically or (b) the title is placed two inches from the top edge of the page with the listing beginning a triple space thereafter.

(3) If the report or manuscript contains more than one appendix, the appendixes should be numbered with their corresponding alphabetic letters.

introductory appendix page

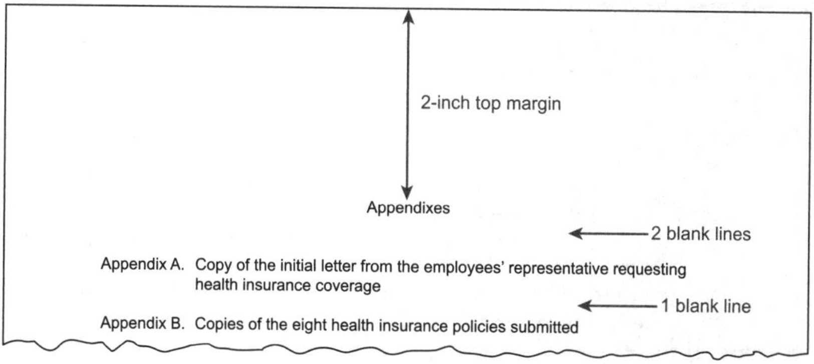

12–14 MLA Report and Documentation Formats

a. The MLA (Modern Language Association) has published a style manual for high school and undergraduate students to assist them with writing research papers. The MLA manual provides guidelines for preparing the research paper and for citing sources—mainly for students in the liberal arts and humanities.[15]

b. Use the following guidelines to set up general formats to prepare the report or manuscript:

(1) Print the report on high-quality 8½- by 11-inch paper.

(2) Use a legible 12-point font. MLA recommends using Times New Roman or a similar font.

(3) Set 1-inch top, bottom, left, and right margins. Set the top header margin at 0.5 inch, and insert a right tab at the right margin in the header to accommodate the page number.

(4) Set all paragraphs for double spacing. Indent paragraphs 0.5 inch; indent long quotations 1 inch.

(5) Set the word processor to space once after periods and other ending punctuation marks.

(6) Ensure that the hyphenation feature of your word processor is turned off.

c. The MLA research report does not begin with a title page. Instead, it opens with a heading that contains the writer's name, the instructor's name, the course name, and the date. Use the following guidelines to prepare the opening page of a research report using the MLA style after you have set the formats described in 12–14b:

(1) Create a header on the first page of your report that aligns with the right margin. Key your last name, press space, and insert the page number code.

(2) Move your cursor to the first line of the body text. Key your first and last name; press **Enter**.

---

[15]For a complete discussion of the preparation of research reports and manuscripts according to the MLA style, consult the *MLA Handbook for Writers of Research Papers*, 7th ed. (New York: The Modern Language Association of America, 2009). The Modern Language Association also publishes a manual intended for graduate students, scholars, and professional writers: *MLA Style Manual and Guide to Scholarly Publishing*, 3rd ed. (New York: The Modern Language Association of America, 2009).

(3) Key the name of your professor, and press **Enter.**

(4) Key the name and number of the course for which you are preparing the research report, and press **Enter.**

(5) Key the date you are submitting the report, and press **Enter.**

(6) Center the title of your report. Capitalize only the main words in the title. Press **Enter**, and return the cursor to a left alignment.

(7) Begin keying the opening paragraph of your research report. Use the tab key to indent the paragraph 0.5 inch, which is the default in most word processing programs.

(8) Indent each subsequent paragraph 0.5 inch from the left margin; continue to use the double-spacing format recommended for the MLA research report style. Double-space all lines in the report.

opening page for research report in MLA style

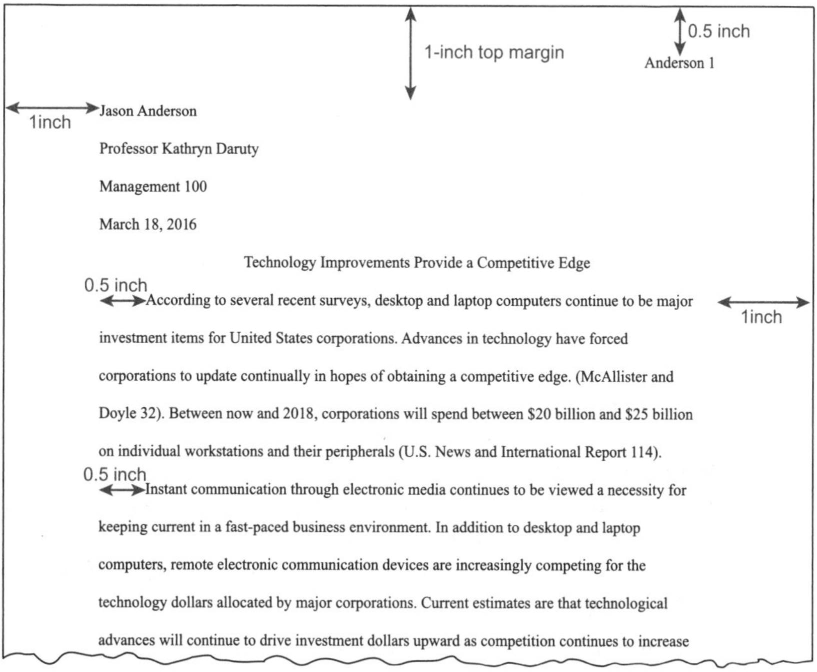

Anderson 1

Jason Anderson

Professor Kathryn Daruty

Management 100

March 18, 2016

Technology Improvements Provide a Competitive Edge

According to several recent surveys, desktop and laptop computers continue to be major investment items for United States corporations. Advances in technology have forced corporations to update continually in hopes of obtaining a competitive edge. (McAllister and Doyle 32). Between now and 2018, corporations will spend between $20 billion and $25 billion on individual workstations and their peripherals (U.S. News and International Report 114).

Instant communication through electronic media continues to be viewed a necessity for keeping current in a fast-paced business environment. In addition to desktop and laptop computers, remote electronic communication devices are increasingly competing for the technology dollars allocated by major corporations. Current estimates are that technological advances will continue to drive investment dollars upward as competition continues to increase

succeeding page with table for research report in MLA style

1-inch top margin

0.5 inch

Anderson 2

desktops, laptops, notebooks, smart phones, and other digital devices compete for the dollars business is able to invest in technology. Investments in these various communication devices are projected to escalate during the next three years. Projections for 2016 through 2018 are contained in the following table:

Table 1

Annual Business Investment Projections 2016–2018 in Computers and Mobile Communication Devices (in Billions of Dollars)

Computers or Mobile Communication Devices	2016	2017	2018
Desktop Computers	$1.2 billion	$1.7 billion	$1.9 billion
Laptop Computers	$1.3 billion	$1.8 billion	$2.0 billion
Notebook Computers	$1.1 billion	$1.2 billion	$1.3 billion
Smartphones	$1.8 billion	$2.1 billion	$2.6 billion
Other Digital Devices	$1.2 billion	$1.4 billion	$1.6 billion

Source: "Business Continues to Invest in Technology," *Business Forecast,* August 2015, 37.

0.5 inch

With advances in technology, costs for desktop computers have declined steadily. Laptop computers and notebook computers have maintained a constant price level during the

d. ***The MLA (Modern Language Association) referencing style*** **is used for citing sources in research reports prepared according to MLA formats. In this style a short description of the source and the pertinent page number(s) appear in parentheses after the information cited. The main purpose of the parenthetical reference is to point the reader to a specific work in the** ***Works Cited,*** **the MLA version of a bibliography.**

Use the following guidelines to cite sources according to the MLA referencing style:

(1) Begin with the last name of the author or authors. If the work has more than three authors, use only the first author's last name followed by *et al.* with no intervening punctuation; for example, Greenburg et al.

(2) Begin the citation with the title of the work or a shortened version of the title—for example, *Employment Trends in Manufacturing* or *Employment Trends*—if a work has no author listed. Italicize the titles of books and magazines.

(3) Follow the author or title reference with the relevant page number(s), but do not use any intervening punctuation.

(4) Place the citation in parentheses directly after the referenced material. Examples of such references would be (Greenburg et al., 113) and (*Employment Trends in Manufacturing* 65–67).

(5) Include only the page number(s) in the citation if the author(s) or source is named in the context of the text.

(6) Provide a full description of all cited sources in the Works Cited.[16]

MLA referencing style

> According to several recent surveys, desktop and laptop computers continue to be major investment items for United States corporations. Advances in technology have forced corporations to update continually in hopes of obtaining a competitive edge. (McAllister and Doyle 32). Between now and 2018, corporations will spend between $20 billion and $25 billion on individual workstations and their peripherals (*U.S. News and International Report* 114).

MLA page reference only

> According to McAllister and Doyle (32), desktop and laptop computers continue to be major investment items for United States corporations. Advances in technology have forced corporations to update continually in hopes of obtaining a competitive edge. Between now and 2018, as reported in *U.S. News and International Report*, corporations will spend between $20 billion and $25 billion on individual workstations and their peripherals (114).

12 Business Documents

e. Reports prepared according to the MLA (Modern Language Association) style title the bibliography Works Cited.[17] References are listed alphabetically as in any other bibliography. Guidelines for formatting the Works Cited follow:

(1) Center the title *Works Cited* 1 inch from the top edge of the page; number the page in the upper right corner, 0.5 inch from the top edge and aligned with the right margin.

(2) Double-space after the heading, and double-space within and between the entries. Begin each entry at the left margin, but use the hanging indent feature of your word processor to indent any subsequent lines 0.5 inch from the left margin.

(3) Italicize the titles of books and magazines.

---

[16]Refer to Section 12-14e of this manual for information on preparing the Works Cited, the MLA version of a bibliography.

[17]For a complete discussion of arrangements and formats for the Works Cited according to the MLA style, consult the *MLA Handbook for Writers of Research Papers*, 7th ed. (New York: The Modern Language Association of America, 2009), Web.

Works Cited—MLA bibliographical style

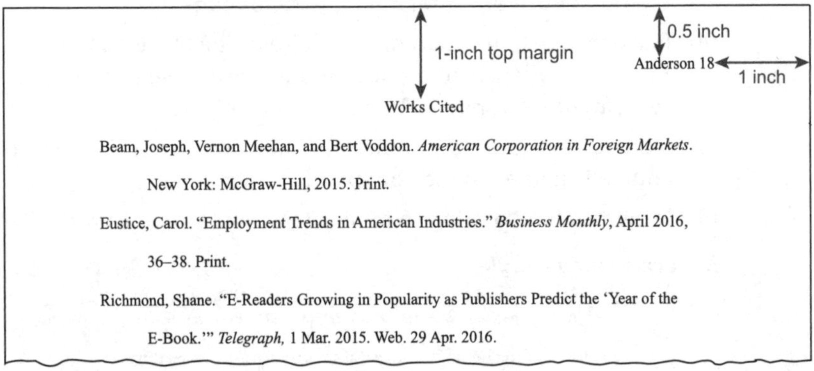

Anderson 18

Works Cited

Beam, Joseph, Vernon Meehan, and Bert Voddon. *American Corporation in Foreign Markets.* New York: McGraw-Hill, 2015. Print.

Eustice, Carol. "Employment Trends in American Industries." *Business Monthly*, April 2016, 36–38. Print.

Richmond, Shane. "E-Readers Growing in Popularity as Publishers Predict the 'Year of the E-Book.'" *Telegraph,* 1 Mar. 2015. Web. 29 Apr. 2016.

12–15 APA Report and Documentation Formats

a. The APA (American Psychological Association) has published a style manual to assist high school students, college students, and professionals in writing research papers. The APA manual provides guidelines for preparing the research paper and for citing sources mainly in the social sciences.

b. Research reports prepared according to the APA style usually contain four parts: a title page, an abstract, the main body, and a list of references. Use the following guidelines to set up general formats to prepare the report or manuscript:

(1) Print the report on high-quality 8½- by 11-inch paper.

(2) Use a legible 12-point font. APA recommends using a serif font such as Times Roman or another similar serif font.

(3) Set 1-inch top, bottom, left, and right margins. Use the default top header margin of 0.5 inch, and insert a right tab at the right margin within the header.

(4) Set all paragraphs for double spacing.

(5) Set the word processor to space once after periods and other ending punctuation marks.

(6) Ensure that the hyphenation feature of your word processor is turned off.

c. The APA research report begins with a title page. All pages of the report, including the title page, contain a page number. Use the following guidelines to prepare the title page:

(1) Create a header on the title page of your report that begins at the left margin and aligns the page number at the right margin. Key "Running Head:" and continue with all capital letters to enter the five

or six words that begin the title of the report. Insert the page number symbol at the right margin.

(2) Space down and key the title of the report in the upper half of the page. Double-space and center the title horizontally in uppercase and lowercase letters using as many lines as necessary to display the title attractively.

(3) Double-space after the title, and insert the applicable author information. Students should provide their name, instructor, class, and educational institution—each centered on a separate line. For scholarly research papers written by professionals, the following lines should contain an "Author Note" that provides additional information and the author's name and affiliation or city and state.

title page of report formatted in APA style

d. The recommended second page of an APA research report consists of an abstract—limited to 120 words. Use the following guidelines to prepare the abstract:

(1) Continue the header from the title page of your report that shows the short title and the page number.

(2) Center in uppercase and lowercase letters the word "Abstract" 1 inch from the top edge of the page.

(3) Press **Enter** after the page title and key the abstract; do not indent the first line of the paragraph. Continue with double spacing for all lines in the blocked paragraph.

abstract page of report formatted in APA style

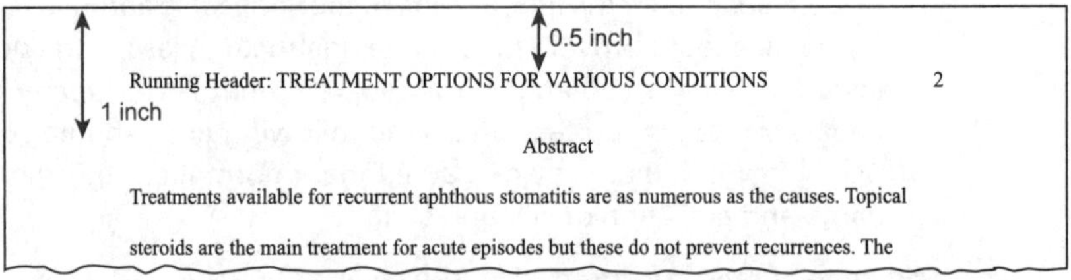

e. The recommended third part of an APA research report consists of the main body. Use the following guidelines to prepare the body of the report:

(1) Begin the main body of the report on a new page. Continue the header from the title page of your report that shows the short title and the page number.

(2) Center in uppercase and lowercase letters the complete title of the report. Begin the title 1 inch from the top edge of the paper. Double-space multiple lines in the title, and double-space after the title to begin the body of the report.

(3) Indent the first line of each paragraph 0.5 inch, and double-space each paragraph.

(4) Center and use uppercase and lowercase letters for first-degree headings within the report body.

(5) Continuation pages in the report body begin below the header 1 inch from the top edge of the page.

main body opening page in APA style

0.5 inch

Running Header: TREATMENT OPTIONS FOR VARIOUS CONDITIONS 3

1 inch

Treatment Options for Various Conditions

Present in Oral Surgery Patients

A number of common conditions present in oral surgery patients have a variety of treatment options. The purpose of this research paper is to present aspects of the condition and explore common successful treatment options.

Recurrent Aphthous Stomatitis

Recurrent aphthous stomatitis is a common oral pathological condition that affects approximately 20 percent of the general population. This condition is characterized by episodes of multiple ulcerations confined to the nonkeratinized mucosa.

The three variations of aphthous stomatitis are minor, major, and herpetiform. Minor aphthous ulcerations are the most common. The ulcers are usually 3 to 10 mm in diameter and generally require from one to two weeks to heal.

Major aphthous ulcerations are larger and take longer to heal. These lesions are 1 to 3 cm in diameter and may take from two to six weeks to heal. Herpetiform ulcers are small, but as many as 100 ulcerations may occur with every episode. They are called herpetiform because of their resemblance to a primary herpes simplex virus infection.

Patients who present with recurrent aphthous stomatitis may have Behcet's syndrome. Behcet's syndrome was first described by a Turkish dermatologist, Dr. Hulusi Behcet in 1937. Behcet's syndrome is characterized by oral, genital, and ocular lesions.

The exact etiology of recurrent aphthous stomatitis is unknown. However, studies have linked recurrent aphthous stomatitis with genetic predisposition, allergies, hematologic abnormalities, hormonal influences, infectious agents, nutritional imbalances, trauma, and continual stress.

at least 1 inch

main body succeeding pages in APA style

> 0.5 inch
>
> Running Header: TREATMENT OPTIONS FOR VARIOUS CONDITIONS 4
>
> 1 inch
>
> The treatments available are as numerous as the causes. Unfortunately, none of them are 100 percent effective. The mainstay of treatment involves topical corticosteroid. Topical steroids help to shorten the length of an acute episode but do not prevent recurrences. Kenalog or Lidex mixed with Orabase may be applied to the individual lesions. Patients with diffuse ulcerations may be given dexamethasone elixir to be used as a mouth rinse.
>
> A recent study showed that Dapsone, an antibacterial medication, can be effective in reducing the recurrence of aphthous stomatitis. Approximately 60 percent of the study group reported either a cessation or reduction in symptoms while taking Dapsone. Before a patient can be placed on Dapsone, the patient must be screened for glucose-6-phosphate dehydrogenase deficiency. Those deficient can develop severe hemolytic anemia when taking Dapsone.

f. APA (American Psychological Association) provides specific guidelines for citing sources.[18] To cite a specific part of a source or a direct quotation in APA style, place in parentheses the (1) last name of the author(s), (2) year of publication, and (3) relevant page number(s) after the information to be cited. To cite a complete source, place in parentheses the last name of the author(s) and the year of publication.

The main purpose of the parenthetical reference is to point the reader to a specific work in the reference list—the APA version of a bibliography. Use the following guidelines to cite sources according to the APA referencing style:

(1) Begin the citation with the last name of the author. If a source has two authors, cite both authors' last names each time the source is referenced. For sources with three to five authors, cite each author's last name in the first reference; additional references require only the first author's last name followed by *et al.*

(2) Join the names in a multiple-author citation with an ampersand (&) instead of the word *and* when they appear in parentheses or in the reference list; for example, (Hendrix, Preston, & Torti, 2016).

(3) Begin the citation with the first two or three words of the entry in the reference list—usually the title of the work—if a work has no author listed. Use quotation marks around titles of articles or chapters; italicize the names of books or magazines. Capitalize the main words; for example, (*Employment Trends*, 2016).

---

[18]For a complete discussion of the preparation of reports and manuscripts according to the APA style, consult *Publication Manual of the American Psychological Association*, 6th ed. (Washington, DC: American Psychological Association, 2010).

(4) Follow the author or title reference with the date of publication. For direct quotations or specific material, include any relevant page number(s) preceded by *p.* or *pp.* Additional examples of such references are (Hendrix et al., 2016) and ("Marketing Aspects," 2017, pp. 87–88).

(5) Include only the date of publication (and any applicable page numbers for direct quotations or specific material) in the citation if the author(s) or source is named in the context of the text. Omit the parenthetical reference for an entire work if both the source and date appear in the text.

(6) Provide a full description of cited sources in the reference list, the APA version of a bibliography.[19] However, personal letters, telephone calls, and other material that cannot be retrieved are not listed in the reference list. These sources are cited only in the text; for example, "B. Baity (personal communication, November 5, 2016) confirmed that . . . ."

APA referencing style

According to several recent surveys, desktop and laptop computers continue to be major investment items for United States corporations. Advances in technology have forced most corporations to update continually in hopes of obtaining a competitive edge (McAllister & Doyle, 2015). "Between now and 2018, corporations will spend between $20 billion and $25 billion on individual workstations and their peripherals" (*U.S. News*, 2015, p. 134).

According to McAllister & Doyle (2015), desktop and laptop computers continue to be major investment items for United States corporations. Advances in technology have forced most corporations to update continually in hopes of obtaining a competitive edge. "Between now and 2018," as reported in *U.S. News and International Reports*, "corporations will spend between $20 billion and $25 billion on individual workstations and their peripherals" (2015, p. 134).

g. The fourth part of a report prepared according to APA style is a list of references. Reports prepared according to the APA (American Psychological Association) style refer to the bibliography as a *reference list*.[20] References are listed alphabetically as in any other bibliography. Guidelines for formatting the reference list follow:

(1) Begin the references of the report on a new page. Continue the header from the title page of your report that shows the short title and the page number.

(2) Place the title "References" 1 inch from the top edge of the paper.

[19]Refer to Section 12–15g of this manual for information on how to prepare a reference list, the APA version of a bibliography.

[20]For a complete discussion of arrangements and formats for the reference list according to the APA style, consult the *Publication Manual of the American Psychological Association*, 6th ed. (Washington, DC: American Psychological Association, 2010), 180–224.

(3) Double-space after the title, and double-space within and between the entries.

(4) Begin the reference at the left margin. Use the hanging indent feature of your word processing program to indent the second and succeeding lines the same amount of space used for paragraphs within the body of the report (usually 0.5 inch).

(5) Provide authors' last names and first initials in inverted order for book entries. Use an ampersand (&) instead of the word *and* to link multiple names. Follow the authors' names with the date of publication enclosed in parentheses.

(6) Capitalize only the first word and any proper nouns in book titles or their subtitles. Italicize the name of complete works.

(7) Provide next the facts of publication, listing the city first. Give the two-letter U.S. Postal Service state designation for little-known cities. The location is followed by a colon and the name of the publisher.

(8) List the names of magazine and journal article authors in the same format used for authors of books. Follow with the publication date enclosed in parentheses. Do not place quotation marks around magazine article titles, and capitalize only the first word or proper nouns. Capitalize all main words and italicize the names of periodicals; include the volume or issue number (if any). Conclude the reference with page numbers.

reference list—APA bibliographical style

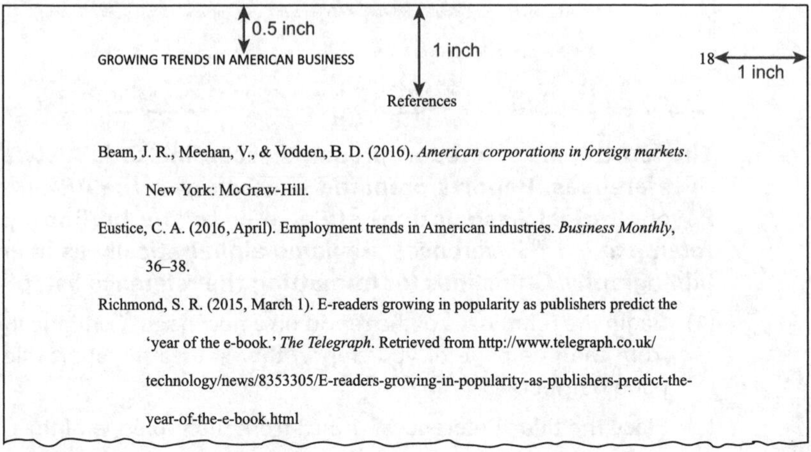

GROWING TRENDS IN AMERICAN BUSINESS 18

References

Beam, J. R., Meehan, V., & Vodden, B. D. (2016). *American corporations in foreign markets.* New York: McGraw-Hill.

Eustice, C. A. (2016, April). Employment trends in American industries. *Business Monthly,* 36–38.

Richmond, S. R. (2015, March 1). E-readers growing in popularity as publishers predict the 'year of the e-book.' *The Telegraph.* Retrieved from http://www.telegraph.co.uk/technology/news/8353305/E-readers-growing-in-popularity-as-publishers-predict-the-year-of-the-e-book.html

Meeting Minutes

12–16 Purpose and Contents

Minutes are compiled to provide a written record of announcements, reports, significant discussions, and decisions that have taken place

during a meeting. Although the degree of formality and extent of coverage may vary, the specific information contained in meeting minutes usually includes the following:

(1) Name of group and meeting

(2) Date, place, and time meeting was called to order; time of adjournment

(3) Names of persons present (if applicable, names of persons absent)

(4) Approval of (or additions to) the agenda

(5) Disposition of any previous minutes

(6) Announcements

(7) Summaries of reports

(8) Motions presented and actions taken on motions

(9) Summaries of significant discussions

(10) Name and signature of person compiling minutes

12–17 Organization and Format of Formal Minutes

a. The organization and format of formal minutes do not follow precise criteria. You may wish, however, to use these guidelines for preparing formal minutes:

(1) Use 8½- by 11-inch white high-quality paper. In your word processing program, use the following page setup:

(a) Set 1-inch left and right margins and 1-inch top and bottom margins.

(b) Single-space the document.

(c) Count the first page in the pagination, but do not number it. Begin page numbering on the second page, and place the number 0.5 inch from the top edge of the page and even with the right margin.

(2) Center and key in boldface the heading for the meeting minutes in capital and lowercase letters. Begin the heading 2 inches from the top edge of the page.

(a) Provide the name of the group and/or meeting as well as the word ***Minutes***. Double-space down.

(b) Follow with the date and scheduled time of the meeting. Double-space down.

(c) Conclude with the place of the meeting.

See page 467 for an illustration of the heading format for meeting minutes.

(3) List the persons attending the meeting after the heading. This listing is placed a triple space below the meeting place. Begin the listing with a phrase such as *Members Present, Managers Present,* or *Persons Present* followed by a colon. Then list the names horizontally or vertically in the order of their importance or in alphabetical order.

(4) Note those regular members absent from a meeting, if appropriate. In this case a separate listing appears a double space below the listing of members present. It is usually preceded by *Members Absent*, *Persons Absent*, or another such designation. Examples of vertical attendance listings appear on page 467.

(5) Begin the first paragraph of the meeting minutes a triple space below the attendance listing or listings. The first paragraph generally opens with a statement giving the exact time the meeting was called to order and by whom. This statement is usually followed by statements indicating approval of the agenda and the disposition of any previous minutes.

(6) List any announcements after the opening paragraph. Use a side heading to introduce the announcements, allowing one blank line above the heading and one blank line below it. Then number and list each announcement made. If only one announcement occurred, show it in paragraph form without a number.

(7) Separate main ideas with topic headings. Many meeting agendas are organized according to old business and new business. These two categories may be used for topic headings (use side headings) in presenting the motions and discussions that have taken place during short meetings. For lengthy meetings, however, readers can more easily locate information in the minutes if the topic headings describe concretely the subject matter discussed, reported, or voted upon.

(8) Note, and in some cases summarize, reports presented at a meeting. The amount of information provided in the minutes will depend upon their purpose, formality, and use. Include with the reference to the report contents the name of the person giving the report as well as its disposition.

(9) Provide the exact wording of motions in the meeting minutes. Persons making and seconding the motions may be named in the motion statement. Include a brief summary of the discussion for each motion. Finally, indicate whether the motion was passed, defeated, or tabled. The number of yeses, noes, and abstentions for each motion should be recorded.

(10) Indicate the time and by whom the meeting was adjourned, even if the meeting was not concluded with a motion for adjournment. This information is placed in the concluding paragraph of the meeting minutes.

(11) Place the typed signature of the person preparing the minutes on the third or fourth line below the concluding paragraph. If the preparer's handwritten signature is required, place the typed signature on the fourth line below the concluding paragraph; otherwise, place the typed signature on the third line. The typed signature line may be placed at the left margin or begun at the page center.

The complimentary closing *Respectfully submitted* may precede the signature line. In this case the entire signature block simulates the signature block of a business letter. Place *Respectfully submitted* a double space below the concluding paragraph, and leave three blank lines for the written signature before displaying the preparer's name. This style of signature block may also begin at the left margin or page center.

b. The major components of formal meeting minutes are illustrated in the following example, which begins below and continues on page 468.

formal meeting minutes

2 inches

State Mutual Life Insurance Company
Monthly Meeting of Home Office Department Managers
Minutes

1 blank line →

April 11, 2017, 2 p.m.

1 blank line →

Room 625, State Mutual Building

2 blank lines →

Persons Present: Louise Brannon, Agency Accounting
Anthony Coletta, Claims
David Haberman, Central Records
Phillip Horowitz, Personnel
Vern Knudsen, Vice President, Operations
Robert Miles, Actuarial
Wayne Nugent, Data Processing
George Ross, Treasurer
David Schultz, Policy Issue
Fred Wyatt, Finance

1 blank line →

Persons Absent: Neil Tsutsui, Group Insurance
Diane Zimmerman, Public Relations

2 blank lines →

The meeting of the home office department managers was called to order by Vern Knudsen at 2:05 p.m. on April 11, 2017, in Room 625 of the State Mutual Building. The agenda was unanimously approved as distributed. Minutes from the previous meeting, held on March 14, 2017, were read and approved unanimously.

1 blank line →

Announcements

1 blank line →

1. Effective June 1 Anthony Coletta will assume the position of administrative assistant to the vice president of operations. John Davis, the present assistant manager of the Claims Department, will assume the role of manager on June 1.

1 blank line →

2. Two new State Mutual agencies will be opened on July 1. The Chadwick Agency (located in Fort Worth, Texas) will become Agency No. 137, and Graff & Phelps (located in Salem, Oregon) will become Agency No. 138.

3. The Norton Agency (located in Albuquerque, New Mexico) will become the Preston Agency effective July 1. Phillip Norton will retire, and he has sold the agency to Donald Preston. The agency will retain its current number—No. 54. Donald Preston plans to move the agency to larger quarters. He will send us his new location once he has moved the offices. He also plans to increase the number of agents in his office from 8 to 12 and also increase the support staff by an additional administrative assistant.

1 inch

***formal meeting minutes* (continued)**

1 inch

0.5 inch

2

1 inch

Financial Report for Period Ending March 31, 2017

1 blank line →

George Ross distributed copies of the 2017 first quarter financial report. He pointed out that overall life insurance sales had increased nearly 8 percent over the same period for last year.

Claims for the period from January 1 to March 31, 2017, increased 6 percent over the same period for last year. This rise has been assessed to be within the statistical projection based on sales and volume presently carried by the company.

Income from other sources rose 4 percent over the last comparable period. Operational expenses during the first quarter increased 12 percent, mainly because of rising prices related to inflationary factors. Net operations income, consequently, for this period decreased 0.5 percent over the same period for last year.

1 blank line →

Progress Report, Central Records Microfilm Conversion

1 blank line →

David Haberman reported that a task force had been formed of representatives from those departments that use or store records in the Central Filing Department. These representatives met to discuss which records should be converted to digital images.

Microfilm readers are centralized in the Central Filing Department and are available in those departments that use microfilm records frequently. Converting frequently used microfilm records to digital images would provide computer access to these records from the network, thus cutting down on the time needed for employees to access information. To convert our critical microfilm records to digital images would require the company to purchase three flatbed scanners for microfilm, which cost approximately $3,000 each. Louise Brannon moved that the company convert critical microfilm records to digital images by purchasing the needed equipment. The motion was seconded by Robert Miles. The motion was passed 8-2-0.

1 blank line →

Employment Freeze on Office Personnel

1 blank line →

Phillip Horowitz reported that in February the company established a Document Processing Group to assist all departments with their written communications. Eight clerical employees plus a supervisor were hired to staff this group, which was placed under the direction of the Information Processing Department.

Wayne Nugent moved that a five-person task force be formed to study the work flow generated to the Document Processing Group and the effect of this delegation on the workloads in all affected departments. The task force is to be charged with making recommendations regarding the staff size of the Document Processing Group and the staff size of clerical employees in other departments. The employment freeze on hiring office personnel is to remain until the task force completes its study and the results have been brought to this body. The motion was seconded by Fred Wyatt. It was passed 7-2-1.

The meeting was adjourned at 3:45 p.m. by Vern Knudsen. The next meeting of the department managers is scheduled for May 10 at 2 p.m. in Conference Room 621-A.

2 blank lines →

Chris Weiser, Secretary

1 blank line →

kc

12 Business Documents

12–18 Organization and Format of Informal Minutes

The organization and format of informal minutes may vary. The only requisite is that the minutes provide an adequate record of the information needed by the group or organization and that this information be presented in an easy-to-understand fashion. Use the tables feature of your word processing program to simplify the formatting of informal minutes.

informal meeting minutes

Computer Applications Advisory Committee
Oakdale Community College
Tuesday, April 4, 2017, 2–4 p.m.
Business 3216

MINUTES

Activity/Discussion	Issues/Relative Information	Resolution
Survey of Classrooms and Laboratories	The faculty familiarized the committee with the equipment presently used for classroom instruction.	Information only.
Language Skills	The faculty described the five departmental courses that meet the requirements for its certificate programs. Two additional courses are required for students completing a degree program in business. The committee emphasized the importance of language skills and how these skills relate to the success of employees in business.	Information only.
Computer Training: Hardware Issues	The committee discussed the specifications the department should use in ordering replacement computers, printers, and other peripheral components. Minimum specifications given for computers include Intel Core 5i processor, 6 GB RAM, 120 GB hard drive, network ready.	**MSP** to replace outdated computers with new computers, ones having the minimum specifications provided by the committee.
	A discussion about printer usage in business indicated that laser printers and color printers are used predominantly. Inkjet printers are generally for home use. All-in-one models are becoming increasingly popular.	**MSP** to replace desktop laser printers with networked laser printers and also acquire a color laser printer.
	The committee felt that students should be competent in the use of the Internet and be able to develop and maintain a simple Web site.	**MSP** to offer classes and a certificate program in Web site design and maintenance.
Computer Training: Software Issues	A discussion about speech-recognition software in the workplace indicated that this tool increased productivity and is being used increasingly in medical offices, legal offices, business, and government.	**MSP** that the department expand its use of voice input into word processing classes.
	A discussion was held concerning the philosophy of upgrading software versions in the business community.	Recommendation: Upgrade software as soon as possible.

***informal meeting minutes* (continued)**

Computer Applications Advisory Committee
MINUTES—April 4, 2017
Page 2

Activity/Discussion	Issues/Relative Information	Resolution
	Knowing more than one software program enhances a student's job opportunities. For example, the student has an advantage if he or she has been trained in at least one word processing program as well as in a spreadsheet, a presentation, and a database program.	Recommendation: Students should be familiar with desktop publishing and graphics software as well.
Job-Related Issues	Entry-level salaries vary from location to location and from specialization to specialization. Students should be trained to be flexible in their expectations and to study the overall package that an employer offers. In our geographical area, entry-level salaries range from $3,250 to $3,650 a month.	Information only.
	Language skills and a knowledge of accounting continue to be requisite skills for entry-level positions and for promotional opportunities. All employers ask for human relations skills at all levels.	Information only.
Recommendations for Future Meetings	Survey technology, software, and business trends by circulating a questionnaire to all advisory committee members prior to the meeting date.	Information only.

Submitted by Barbara Jacobson, Professor
Computer Applications and Administrative Support Department

Format developed by and used with permission of K. Basil and Associates.

12–19 Meeting Agendas

a. Meeting agendas forecast the items to be considered at a scheduled meeting. Basic information that appears on an agenda includes the following:

(1) Name of committee, name of group, or purpose of meeting

(2) Date, time, and location of meeting

(3) Kind of document—*Meeting Agenda* or *Agenda*

(4) List of items to be considered, along with the names of any persons designated to present the item

b. Use the agenda template of your word processing program, the table feature of your word processing program, or plain bond paper to create an agenda. Follow these guidelines to create an agenda:

(1) Use a 1-inch or a 2-inch top margin, depending upon the length of your agenda. Use the default left and right margins of your word processing program.

(2) Center, key in boldface, and place in capital and lowercase letters the name of the committee, the name of the group, or the purpose of the meeting.

(3) Center, key in boldface, and place in capital and lowercase letters *Meeting Agenda* or *Agenda*.

(4) Center, key in boldface, and place in capital and lowercase letters the date, time, and location of the meeting. Triple-space.

(5) Number with Arabic numerals the items to be considered at the meeting. Follow the topic with the name of the presenter, if any.

(a) For agendas prepared on plain bond paper, single-space the items and double-space between them. Use a right tab at the right margin and leaders to separate the name of the presenter from the topic.

(b) For agendas prepared with the table feature of a word processing program, create a table with at least three columns and the number of rows required to accommodate the entries. Adjust the cell margins to provide adequate spacing before and after each agenda item.

agenda created on plain paper

2 inches

Dawson Manufacturing Company
Benefits Committee Meeting
Agenda
February 7, 2017, 2 p.m., Room 240

2 blank lines →

1. Call to order .... Diane Levine

1 blank line →

2. Approval of the agenda .... Diane Levine

1 blank line →

3. Approval of January 6 minutes .... Diane Levine

4. Announcements .... Bob Martinez

5. Progress report on the investigation of health insurance providers for medium-size companies .... Barbara Anderson

6. Unfinished business

   Report to Board of Directors on proposed stock option plans .... Tom Rosdahl

   Review of suggestions proposed by subcommittee on ergonomics and environment .... Evelyn Wong

7. New business

   Projected costs for a comprehensive benefits package .... Dorothy Rupert

   Cost sharing of benefits package .... Dorothy Rupert

8. Adjournment .... Diane Levine

agenda created with table feature

1 inch

Pierce College

Pierce College Council Agenda
Thursday, March 27, 2017, 2–4 p.m.
College Services Building Conference Room

1	Approval of Agenda	Action	Lyn Clark
2	Approval of February 27, 2017, Minutes	Action	Curtis Smith
3	Progress Report on Pierce Building Projects	Information	Ed Cadena
	Old Business		
4	Follow-Up on February Action Items Approval of Facilities Advisory Committee	Information	Kathleen Burke-Kelly
5	PCC Evaluation of Pierce College Strategic Plan, 2014–2017	Information	Lyn Clark
6	Resolution Regarding Bond Program and ADA Transport	Action Item 30	Brian Walsh/Don Sparks
	New Business		
7	Approval of Technology Committee Charter Update	Action Item 27	Wendy Bass/Bruce Rosky
8	Budget Committee Requests Special Events Budget Transfer—2016 Media Arts Radio Budget Transfer Transfer Funds to Cover Financial Aid Deficiencies	Action Items Action Item 20 Action Item 28 Action Item 29	Anna Davies/Don Sparks
9	Update of Electronic Accountability Form	Information	Lyn Clark
	Standing Committee and Other Reports		
10	Accreditation Steering Committee Report	Information	Mia Wood
11	Associated Student Organization Report	Information	Shane Mooney
12	Budget Committee Report	Information	Anna Davies/Don Sparks
13	College Planning Committee Report	Information	Carol Kozeracki
14	Diversity Committee Report	Information	Mitra Hoshiar
15	Enrollment Management Committee Report	Information	Barbara Anderson
16	Facilities Advisory Committee Report	Information	Joy McCaslin
17	Technology Committee Report	Information	Wendy Bass/Bruce Rosky
18	Landscape Task Force Report	Information	Don Sparks

PCC Meeting Dates for Spring 2017	PCC Exec Meeting Dates for Spring 2017
Thursday, January 23, 2017, 2–4 p.m.	Thursday, January 9, 2017, 2–4 p.m.
Thursday, February 27, 2017, 2–4 p.m.	Thursday, February 13, 2017, 2–4 p.m.
Thursday, March 27, 2017, 2–4 p.m.	Thursday, March 13, 2017, 2–4 p.m.
Thursday, April 24, 2017, 2–4 p.m.	Thursday, April 10, 2017, 2–4 p.m.
Thursday, May 22, 2017, 2–4 p.m.	Thursday, May 8, 2017, 2–4 p.m.
Thursday, June 26, 2017, 2–4 p.m.	Thursday, June 12, 2017, 2–4 p.m.

12–20 Itineraries

Itineraries plot out events in a travel plan. Use the table feature of your word processing program and the following guidelines to prepare an itinerary:

(1) Begin the itinerary with a heading that describes the purpose of travel, the name of the person traveling, and the dates of travel.

(2) Use a table or column format with three columns. Set up *Date*, *Time*, and *Activity* as columnar headings.

(3) Specify all airline flights, hotel reservations, car rental reservations, business appointments, and meal reservations. Include addresses, telephone numbers, and confirmation numbers.

itinerary

Meeting With NationsBank Representatives
Tampa, Florida
Itinerary for Kym Freeman
March 17–20, 2017

Date	Time	Activity
Monday, March 17	7:11 a.m.	Depart Burbank airport, American Airlines Flight 1502, beverage service only, Seat 23D
	12:13 p.m.	Arrive Dallas-Fort Worth airport
	2:25 p.m.	Depart Dallas-Fort Worth airport, American Airlines Flight 1564, beverage service only, Seat 19D
	5:46 p.m.	Arrive Tampa airport
		Reservations at the Marriott Airport Hotel; hotel located on airport premises; Tel: (813) 879-5151; Confirmation No. 987T385R
Tuesday, March 18	8:00 a.m.	Obtain rental car at Hertz airport booth, Confirmation No. ZBT4314
	10:00 a.m.	Meet with Robin Fielding and Chris Perez, NationsBank downtown offices, 400 North Ashley Drive, Room 450, (813) 555-2236
	12 noon	Lunch with Robin Fielding, Chris Perez, and Michael Morris at the Tampa Club, Barnett Bank Building, 22nd Floor, 437 North Commonwealth Street, (813) 555-8732
	2:30 p.m.–4:30 p.m.	Conduct orientation session of DLDS computerized loan-tracking system for all members of the Loan Department at NationsBank downtown office
	7:30 p.m.	Dinner with Jeff and Janet Spiegel at the Outrigger Steak House, 814 Bayview Drive, (813) 555-7892
Wednesday, March 19	8:30 a.m.–11:30 a.m.	Conduct training sessions on DLDS computerized loan-tracking system for all members of the Loan Department
	1:00 p.m.–4:00 p.m.	Conduct training sessions on DLDS computerized loan-tracking system for all members of the Loan Department
	6:00 p.m.	Dinner with Robin Fielding and Chris Perez at the University Club, 1320 University Avenue, (813) 555-0930
Thursday, March 20	6:57 a.m.	Depart Tampa airport, American Airlines Flight 1573, beverage service only, Seat 20B
	8:42 a.m.	Arrive Dallas-Fort Worth airport
	9:22 a.m.	Depart Dallas-Fort Worth airport, American Airlines Flight 1465, beverage service only, Seat 15B
	10:43 a.m.	Arrive Burbank airport

12 Business Documents

12-21 Press Releases

Press releases contribute to an organization's visibility and goodwill within the community. Important events and occurrences within an organization should be described on a press release and sent to the news media in the area.

Use the press release template of your word processing program and/or the following guidelines to prepare a press release on your word processor:

(1) Prepare the press release on letterhead or 8½- by 11-inch white bond paper. Use a 2-inch top margin and the default left and right margins of your word processor.

(2) Label the document in large bold letters *Press Release* or *News Release.*

(3) Specify the date for release or use the words *For Immediate Release.*

(4) Include the name, address, telephone number, and fax number of the contact person.

(5) Provide a headline (centered and in all capital letters) that summarizes the content of the press release. Triple-space before and after the headline.

(6) Double-space the text. Begin the opening paragraph with the city, state, and date. State immediately the essence of your news—who, what, when, where, and why. Follow with the details in subsequent paragraphs.

(7) Number multiple-page press releases with Arabic numbers in the upper right corner beginning with page 2. Center the word *-more-* at the bottom of the first page and all other pages except the last.

(8) Conclude the press release by centering (a double space below the last line) one of the following: *-30-*, -# # #-, or *-end-*.

(9) Place at the left margin a double space below the concluding notation the date (month, day, year) the press release was released.

press release prepared on company letterhead

Paramount Textile Company

170 East Parkland Avenue
Dallas, Texas 75214
(214) 383-5757
(800) 392-5481
Fax: (214) 383-5783

2 inches

Press Release

For Immediate Release

From Sandra Dubin
Phone: (214) 383-5726
Fax: (214) 383-5727

2 blank lines →

JEREMY K. COLE NEW PRESIDENT OF PARAMOUNT TEXTILE COMPANY

2 blank lines →

Dallas, Texas, March 6. The Board of Directors of Paramount Textile Company announced yesterday the appointment of Jeremy K. Cole as its new president, effective June 1.

Mr. Cole, 49, has been with Paramount Textile Company for seven years. He is presently serving as vice president of operations, a position he has held since joining the company in 2010. During this time the company has increased its sales 32 percent and expanded operations into New Mexico, Oklahoma, and Louisiana.

Before joining Paramount, Mr. Cole was vice president of marketing for Dresler Furniture Company, a nationally known furniture manufacturer in South Carolina. Mr. Cole resides with his wife and two children in Dallas.

Mr. Cole will replace William R. Byrd, who will retire on May 31. Mr. Byrd has served as president of Paramount Textile Company for the past nine years.

-30-

March 6, 2017

12–22 Fax Transmittal and Cover Letter

Fax transmittal and cover letters accompany documents that are sent by fax to ensure that the faxed materials are directed to the correct individual upon arriving at their destination. They also provide feedback to the destination in case not all parts of the document arrive or they are illegible. Consequently, fax transmittals must contain complete information for the sender and complete information for routing the materials to their destination.

Use the fax transmittal template of your word processing program or the following guidelines to prepare a fax transmittal and cover letter on company letterhead:

(1) Prepare the fax transmittal and cover letter on letterhead paper. Use a 2-inch top margin and the default left and right margins of your word processor.

(2) Center in large bold letters *Fax Transmittal and Cover Letter.* Triple-space.

(3) Begin at the left margin and double-space the following guide words:

  (a) Date:

  (b) To:

  (c) Firm:

  (d) City:

  (e) Fax No.:

  (f) From:

  (g) Message:

(4) Provide a footer that indicates the number of pages in the fax transmittal and a request to telephone you if all the pages are not received.

fax transmittal template—Microsoft Professional

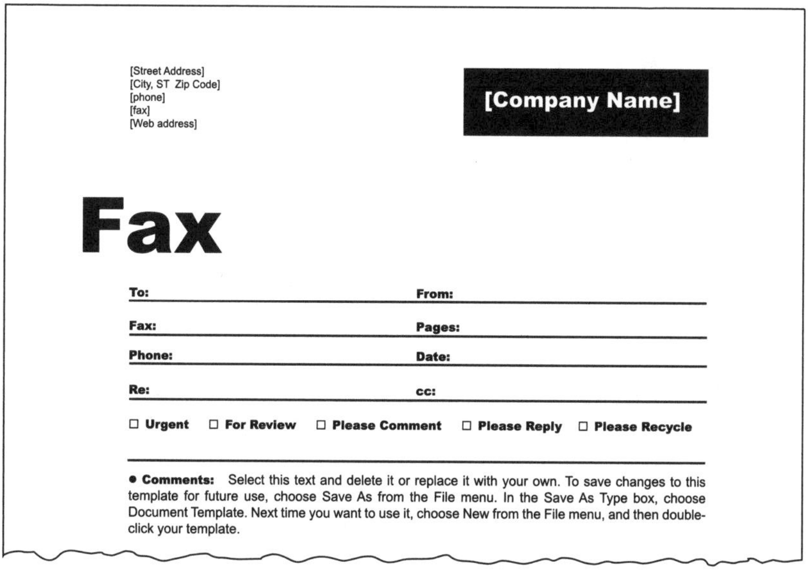

[Street Address]
[City, ST Zip Code]
[phone]
[fax]
[Web address]

[Company Name]

Fax

To: **From:**

Fax: **Pages:**

Phone: **Date:**

Re: **cc:**

☐ **Urgent** ☐ **For Review** ☐ **Please Comment** ☐ **Please Reply** ☐ **Please Recycle**

• **Comments:** Select this text and delete it or replace it with your own. To save changes to this template for future use, choose Save As from the File menu. In the Save As Type box, choose Document Template. Next time you want to use it, choose New from the File menu, and then double-click your template.

Used with permission from Microsoft.

fax transmittal and cover letter on letterhead

Paramount Textile Company

170 East Parkland Avenue
Dallas, Texas 75214
(214) 383-5757
(800) 392-5481
Fax: (214) 383-5783

2 inches

Fax Transmittal Cover Letter

2 blank lines →

Date:

1 blank line →

Please deliver the following pages to

1 blank line →

Name:

1 blank line →

Firm:

City:

Fax No.:

From:

Message:

We are transmitting page(s) (including this cover letter). If you do not receive all the pages, please call us as soon as possible.

13

Employment Application Documents

Solution Finder for Employment Application Documents

13 Employment Application

The job-seeking process has taken on different dimensions during the past several years. Locating employment through online social networking sites as well as traditional networking has been cited as the major vehicle used by a growing percentage of successful candidates. Social networking sites such as LinkedIn, Facebook, and Twitter are gaining in importance in the job-seeking process. On the other hand, mega online job boards, such as Monster and CareerBuilder, with literally thousands of listings are declining as a source of hire (SOH) for employers. This trend is attributed to companies' hesitation to hire "strangers." This same hesitation keeps alive the "temp-to-hire" process that has become popular within the last decade and has stimulated the growth in internships offered to new graduates. Even with social networking, temp-to-hire, and internships, candidates are still confronted with preparing employment application documents.

Anyone seeking employment is faced with preparing several kinds of documents: a résumé, a letter of application, an application form, reference request letters, and follow-up letters. Candidates may prepare each of these documents or just one or two before obtaining a position.

The initial document prepared by a job seeker is usually the résumé. A résumé provides the prospective employer with a capsulized visual of an applicant's qualifications. Its chart-like features summarize for the busy employer the attributes a candidate will bring to the position.

Résumés may have various formats and be organized in different ways. Commonly recognized résumé styles are chronological and functional. In addition, candidates must take into consideration that their résumé may be subjected to a computer scan before it is ever read by human eyes. Increasingly, too, companies are requiring candidates to submit résumés online, and they are providing the candidates with form documents to do so. Some companies will require online applicants to complete an assessment (general and/or skills based) during the online application process.

Today's job seekers need to prepare their résumés in two formats—one in a traditional format and another suitable for online transmission and assessment by an automated applicant tracking system. The traditional format may be a chronological résumé, which is the most popular, or a functional résumé. Those résumés for online transmission or applicant tracking systems should be in chronological format.

The Chronological Résumé

13–1 Information to Include in the Chronological Résumé

The résumé is often the only document an employer will use to screen individuals for an interview; therefore, it must summarize your abilities and present you in a favorable light. The résumé style favored by most employers is the *chronological résumé* because it is easy to follow and assess. Guidelines for preparing this résumé style follow:

(1) Select carefully the information you include in your résumé so that the information can be presented on a single page. Only in situations where an applicant has considerable experience or other qualifications related specifically to a position should the résumé exceed one page.

(2) Organize the information you wish to include in the résumé. Start with your name and contact information and provide an employment or career objective. Incorporate into the résumé facts about your education, employment background, abilities, achievements, and awards. Other information may include college extracurricular activities, professional memberships, and willingness to relocate if they are related to the qualifications for the job. Omit from the résumé personal statistics (age, height, weight, gender), marital status, race, religion, ethnicity, birthplace, high school grades and activities, church responsibilities, hobbies, and interests—unless they relate specifically to the job for which you are applying. Do not include references on the résumé, but be prepared to provide them at the interview.

(3) Begin your résumé with a main heading (name, address, telephone number, cell phone number, fax number [if applicable], and e-mail address) followed by your career objective. Whether you begin the presentation of your credentials with a profile of your educational history and performance, special skills and aptitudes, or work experience depends upon where your greatest strengths lie. Launch the display of your abilities with the category that is most likely to get you the job. Follow up with other categories in the order of their importance to the career objective stated initially. Use text headings such as the following for the categories in your résumé:

Objective or *Career Objective*

Education, Educational Background, Academic Preparation, or Professional Training

Employment, Experience, or Employment Experience

Skills and Abilities

Activities; Honors and Awards; or Honors, Awards, and Activities

References

13–2 Main Heading

The main heading opens the résumé and displays your name, address, telephone number, cell phone number, and e-mail address. If you have a fax number, include it also. Follow these guidelines for the main heading:

(1) Set up the main heading so that a prospective employer can easily spot your name and where to reach you for an interview.

(2) Include the addresses and telephone numbers for your *temporary* and *permanent* residences if you have both a college and a home residence. If you know an ending date for your temporary residence, indicate it in the heading also.

main heading showing single residence

Morgan D. Schultz
2430 Brockton Drive
Upper Marlboro, Maryland 20772
(301) 555-4374
Cell: (301) 368-5947
E-mail: mdschultz483@aol.com

main heading showing temporary and permanent residences

Taylor R. Garvey

Temporary Residence:	Permanent Residence:
830 Willow Street, Apt. 6	5460 Roundtree Circle
Columbia, South Carolina 29207	Atlanta, Georgia 30315
Cell phone: (803) 555-7863	(404) 555-9066
E-mail: trgarvey1983@yahoo.com	

13–3 Career or Employment Objective

a. Include in your résumé a career or an employment objective so that prospective employers know the kind of position you are seeking. Prepare an objective related to a specific job or one that would make you employable in a number of job categories, depending upon your qualifications and interests.

specific employment objective

Objective: To obtain a position as a legal office assistant in a medium-size legal office where I can use my skills and knowledge to contribute to the operations of the office.

general employment objective

Career Objective

To begin a career in marketing with exposure to retail sales, customer relations, market research, and advertising.

13 Employment Application

b. Prepare separate résumés if you have more than one employment area in which you wish to apply. Write the career objective to pertain to each of the positions in which you are interested, and tailor the other sections to emphasize the position stated in your objective.

13–4 Educational History and Performance

Résumés furnish the opportunity to provide prospective employers with information substantiating an applicant's academic preparation to perform the job for which the person is applying. Use these guidelines to present your academic qualifications in the chronological résumé:

(1) Begin this section with the college, university, or other postsecondary institution you attended most recently. Include the name and location of the institution, school or department within the institution, major and minor fields of study, degrees or diplomas received, and dates of attendance. If you expect to earn a degree, list the degree and include the expected date or a statement such as *to be granted May 2017.*

(2) Provide your grade-point average (GPA) within this section. You may wish to provide your overall grade-point average and/or a grade-point average in your major courses of study. Include the scale on which the grade-point average is based—for example, 3.65/4.00. If you do not include a grade-point average, either for your overall work or for your major courses, the prospective employer may think your course work has been less than satisfactory.

(3) Avoid listings of courses completed. Furnish only those course names and other educational experiences that are directly related to performing successfully in the desired position.

(4) List all collegiate or other postsecondary institutions attended. Include your high school education only if your postsecondary education has not resulted in a degree, an anticipated degree, a diploma, or a certificate.

example of educational background entry in a résumé

Education

- University of Southern California, Los Angeles, Graduate School of Business Administration, Master of Science Degree in Management of Human Resources to be awarded May 2017, 3.9/4.0 grade-point average

  Courses in management of human resources, management-union relations, contract negotiations, and international resource development

- University of Montana, Missoula, Montana, College of Engineering, Bachelor of Science in Mechanical Engineering, June 2014, 3.2/4.0 grade-point average

13–5 Work Experience

Reportings of successful work experiences tell prospective employers that applicants have been productive in the work environment. This section gives you an opportunity to show that you respond positively to supervision, have good work habits, and work well with others.

a. If your work experience is limited, include all the positions you have held—even though they do not relate to the position for which you are applying. They indicate to the employer that you are familiar with the work world and have performed successfully in its environment.

b. If your work experience is vast and varied, include only those positions that are most recent and/or are related to the job for which you are applying.

c. In the chronological résumé, list your work experience in reverse chronological order, that is, your most recent employment first. Provide the following information for each position listed:

(1) *Employer's or company's name and location.* Include only the city and state for the address.

(2) *Dates of employment.* State the month and year you began work and the month and year you terminated. You need not state a reason for leaving or provide salary information.

(3) *Job title.* Supply only the title of the most important or the last position held before leaving the employer.

(4) *Significant duties, activities, accomplishments, and promotions.* Use parallel construction and action verbs to describe succinctly and concretely the activities involved in your employment. Use action verbs such as *composed, conducted, created, designed, initiated, maintained, organized, prepared,* and *upgraded.* For ongoing employment activities, use the present tense; for previous employment activities, use the past tense. As much as possible, select those responsibilities and accomplishments that feature your attributes for the position you are seeking.

d. In cases of part-time employment, indicate the part-time status in parentheses after the dates of employment. No notation is necessary for positions held as a full-time employee.

example of work experience entry in a résumé

Work Experience

Freestone Industries, Inc., Portland, Oregon, *Payroll Accountant,* July 2014–present
Enter and maintain payroll records using QuickBooks
Issue weekly and monthly payroll checks
Complete payroll and tax reports for local, state, and federal agencies
Submit withholding and other payroll taxes

Ritter's Clothing Emporium, Eugene, Oregon, *Bookkeeper-Accountant,* September 2011–March 2014 (part-time)
Entered daily sales receipts and expense disbursements using Excel
Prepared checks for signature
Maintained payroll records using Excel

Barton-Hagan Ice Cream Parlor, Eugene, Oregon, *Service Representative,* September 2010–August 2011 (part-time)
Served and packed ice cream
Cashiered customer purchases

3-6 Skills and Abilities

a. **Your educational background and work experience may not show all the talents and abilities that relate to the job you are seeking. Qualities that fall into the skills and abilities category include knowledge of specific computer programs or the ability to speak a foreign language. In some cases extensive travel in another country or knowledge pertaining to another culture might prove of value. Include here only skills and abilities that pertain to your job objective. Omit this section in your chronological résumé if the information can be incorporated into another part.**

b. **Follow these guidelines to list your skills and abilities:**

(1) Begin, if possible, each item in the listing with an action verb stated in the present tense.

(2) Use parallel construction to list your special abilities.

example of skills and abilities entry in a résumé

Skills and Abilities

Use proficiently the following computer application programs: Word, Excel, Access, PowerPoint, Outlook, QuickBooks, Adobe Photoshop, Adobe Dreamweaver and Flash, and Adobe Illustrator

Access and navigate the Internet to retrieve needed information

Use social networking sites to promote business and business relationships

Speak and write Spanish fluently

13-7 Awards, Honors, and Activities

a. **Combine your awards, honors, and activities into one category. If, however, you have at least three awards and honors and also at least three collegiate extracurricular activities, you may wish to show these items in two categories (*Honors and Awards* and *Activities*).**

b. **If your career experiences are more important than your educational awards and activities in obtaining the desired position, this category may well be replaced by a listing of your activities in professional and community organizations.**

c. **Use these guidelines to present any activities, honors, or awards in the chronological résumé:**

(1) Begin with the most recent occurrence.

(2) List the names of the honors and awards and the dates they were earned or received. Provide a brief explanation of an honor or an award if it is not commonly known.

(3) List the name of the organization, any offices held, and the dates of participation for each activity.

example of honors, awards, and activities entry in a résumé

Honors, Awards, and Activities

The Wall Street Journal scholarship award for academic excellence, May 2016

Dean's Honor Roll—Spring 2015, Fall 2015, and Spring 2016 semesters

Fenton College Student Council, Associated Student Body Representative, Business Department, Fall 2015 and Spring 2016 semesters

Alpha Gamma Sigma, honor society—Spring 2015, Fall 2015, and Spring 2016 semesters

Phi Beta Lambda, business fraternity, Fall 2014 semester–Present
- Treasurer, Spring 2015 semester
- Vice President, Fall 2015 semester
- President, Spring 2016 semester

13-8 References

a. **Including references in the chronological résumé or the statement *References furnished upon request* is not necessary. Prospective employers assume that at the point of interview you will furnish references from former professors and/or employers who are able to provide firsthand information about you.**

b. **Select your references carefully. A bad reference is worse than no reference at all. Before giving the name of a reference, check with that person to ensure that he or she is agreeable to giving you a recommendation. Give each reference a copy of your résumé.**

c. **Use the following guidelines for preparing a separate listing of your references:**

(1) Prepare a separate listing of your references that begins with the same heading as you used for your résumé.

(2) Limit the number of references to two or three.

(3) Provide the name and the title of the individual, the name of the organization, the address, and the telephone number for each reference cited.

listing of references

Morgan D. Schultz
2430 Brockton Drive
Upper Marlboro, Maryland 20772
(301) 555-4374
Cell: (301) 368-5947
E-mail: mdschultz483@aol.com

References

Robert W. Bugliosi, CPA
100 Commonwealth Avenue
Boston, MA 02118
(617) 555-8172

Dr. Andrew Fernandez, Professor
Fisher School of Accounting
University of Florida
Gainesville, FL 32611
(352) 555-2020

13 Employment Application

chronological résumés

MARISSA A. SCHULTZ

Temporary Address:
3220 SW 15th Street, #8
Gainesville, FL 32608
(904) 555-3250, Cell: (904) 555-2630
E-mail: Schultz187@yahoo.com

Permanent Address:
332 Shawmut Avenue
Boston, MA 02118
(617) 555-4028

Objective	To begin a career in accounting with the immediate objective to gain experience for certification as a Certified Public Accountant	
Education	**Master of Accounting (3/2 program)**	May 2017
	Bachelor of Science in Accounting	May 2016
	Fisher School of Accounting	
	University of Florida, Gainesville, Florida	
	GPA 3.74/4.0 (accounting), 3.82/4.0 (overall)	
Honors	Beta Alpha Psi	Spring 2015–present
	Becker CPA Review Scholarship	Spring 2015
	Golden Key Honor Society	Spring 2015
	Dean's List	Summer 2014–present
	President's Honor Roll	Spring 2014
Activities	**Beta Alpha Psi**	
	Treasurer	Spring 2015–present
	Fisher School of Accounting Council	
	President	Spring 2015–Spring 2016
	Audit Team	Spring 2015
	Student Representative to Programs Board	Spring 2015
	Class Representative	Fall 2014–Spring 2015
	Becker CPA Review	
	Student Representative	May 2015–present
	Florida Accounting Association	Fall 2015–present
	American Marketing Association	
	Recording Secretary	Fall 2015
Work Experience	**James W. Brenner, CPA,** Boston, Massachusetts	Summer 2013
	Accounting Clerk	
	• Reconciled monthly bank statements and daily deposits	
	• Recorded and updated billable time for accounting fees	
	• Prepared clients' monthly bills	
	• Updated clients' financial files	
	Mimi's Cafe, Server, Boston, Massachusetts	Summer 2012
	Boston Eye Clinic, Boston, Massachusetts (part-time)	August 2011–May 2012
	Front Office Assistant	
	• Updated patients' files	
	• Scheduled patients' appointments	
Computer Knowledge	Excel, QuickBooks, Microsoft Word, Access, PowerPoint	

chronological résumé

DANIEL LEE

6201 Woodley Avenue • Northridge, California 91325 • (818) 555-9770
Cell: (818) 555-8142 • E-mail: DanielinCA@earthlink.net

Objective

To obtain a responsible and challenging position as an administrative assistant in which my education and work experience will be of value

Education

Los Angeles Pierce College Woodland Hills, California Certificate in Computer Applications and Office Technologies, General Administrative	June 2016
Associate in Arts degree, Quality Control Engineering	June 2010
Associate in Arts degree, Landscape Maintenance	June 2008

Work Experience

Los Angeles Pierce College Woodland Hills, California Computer Laboratory Assistant Assist students with computer assignments Provide instructional support during evening classes Maintain equipment in working order	August 2015– May 2016 (part-time)
Remington Industries, Inc. Van Nuys, California CNC Operator Assembled and operated CNC (Computerized Numerical Control) machine Checked and modified CNC program Assembled and bonded parts for commercial airplane galleys	July 2011– August 2014

Computer Skills

Training in the following computer programs with emphasis on the production of documents used in business and office applications:
Microsoft Word, Excel, Access, PowerPoint, Outlook, Adobe Dreamweaver and Flash, Adobe Photoshop, QuickBooks, Dragon NaturallySpeaking
Ability to access Internet resources and maintain Web sites
Ability to type 60 wpm

The Functional Résumé

13-9 Preparation of the Functional Résumé

Functional résumés, shown on pages 491–494, focuses on an applicant's skills, abilities, and accomplishments. Rather than beginning with an education or an employment history, the functional résumé presents competencies and accomplishments in special categories.

a. You may wish to use a functional résumé if you have changed jobs frequently or if there are gaps in your employment history. Applicants with no or little full-time employment experience also find this form of résumé appealing.

b. Although the functional résumé emphasizes abilities, it should also include information about a candidate's education; previous employment; and any pertinent honors, activities, and affiliations. Use the following guidelines to prepare a functional résumé:

(1) Begin with a main heading that displays your name, address, and telephone number. Include also your cell phone number and an e-mail address—along with a fax number if you have one. Follow the main heading with your employment objective.

(2) Continue the functional résumé with a listing of your significant abilities, skills, activities, and accomplishments. As much as possible, select items that feature your attributes for the position you are seeking. Group the items into meaningful categories, and use a descriptive heading for each category.

(3) Use parallel construction and action verbs to describe succinctly and concretely the items in your listing. Use action verbs such as *assisted, compiled, coordinated, developed, edited, established, managed, planned,* and *translated.* For present skills and abilities, use the present tense; for previous accomplishments, use the past tense.

(4) Include in the functional résumé a history of your academic preparation (see Section 13-4) and an account of your previous employment (see Section 13-5).

(5) Conclude the functional résumé with a listing of any awards, extracurricular activities, or professional affiliations (see Section 13-7).

functional résumé—entry-level applicant

Rocio Martinez
136 Rose Lane • Encino, California 91326 • Cell: (818) 555-6497 • rmart@aol.com

OBJECTIVE

To obtain a secretarial or an administrative assistant position with opportunity for advancement

SKILLS AND ABILITIES

- *Use proficiently the following software programs:*
  Microsoft Word, Excel, Access, PowerPoint
  Adobe Photoshop, Illustrator, InDesign, and Acrobat
- Transcribe and proofread business documents accurately
- Compose and prepare routine correspondence
- Perform computerized accounting functions using QuickBooks
- Use the Internet to obtain information
- Speak and write English and Spanish fluently
- Key 65 words a minute

ACCOMPLISHMENTS

- Trained and supervised student workers
- Performed database entries using FileMaker Pro on a Macintosh computer and Microsoft Access on a Windows-based computer
- Reorganized instructional media for easier access and availability to faculty
- Maintained audio and video equipment
- Filed invoices and catalogs
- Answered telephone inquiries and took reservations for equipment loans
- Duplicated audiocassettes for students

EDUCATION

Los Angeles Pierce College, Woodland Hills, California. Associate in Arts degree, May 2016, Computer Applications and Office Technologies—General Administrative. Overall GPA 3.9/4.0

EXPERIENCE

Instructional Media Center, Los Angeles Pierce College, Woodland Hills, California. August 2014 to present (part-time)

HONORS AND AWARDS

- Certificate of Recognition from Alpha Gamma Sigma, the scholastic honor society, for "Outstanding Scholarship and Placement" on the Dean's List each semester
- Frances M. Heinze Memorial Scholarship for outstanding scholastic achievement, May 2015
- Teresa A. Caruana Memorial Award for overall outstanding achievement, May 2016
- Computer Applications and Office Technologies Department, Highest GPA Award, May 2016

functional résumé—entry-level applicant with minimum experience

Deborah Ann Campbell

640 Winnetka Avenue • Encino, CA 91371 • (818) 555-4210 • camp24@yahoo.com

EMPLOYMENT OBJECTIVE

To obtain a paralegal position offering challenge, responsibility, and personal growth

CAPABILITIES AND SKILLS

- Draft complaints/answers
- Compose interrogatories/answers
- Prepare motions
- Conduct legal research
- Access and use WESTLAW
- Compose and prepare business correspondence
- Operate proficiently Microsoft Word, Excel, QuickBooks, Access, and WordPerfect
- Type 70 words a minute
- Operate the numeric 10-key pad proficiently

EDUCATION

University of California, Los Angeles, Extension, Attorney Assistant Training Program. Certificate in Litigation, November 2013. This program is offered in cooperation with the UCLA School of Law and is approved by the American Bar Association.

Los Angeles Pierce College, Woodland Hills, Associate in Arts degree, Computer Applications and Office Technologies—Legal Office, June 2013

EXPERIENCE

July 2013–Present

Litigation Assistant, Martinson & Myers, Los Angeles

Perform automated document management on multiple projects
Review documents and prepare information for discovery
Investigate facts and case law

February 2013–July 2013 (part-time)

Legal Secretary, Law Offices of Donald Monroe, Encino

Composed and prepared correspondence
Managed documents for personal injury cases
Transcribed dictation
Maintained business calendars

HONORS

Dean's Honor Roll, 2010–2013
The National Dean's List Award, 2010–2013
Teresa A. Caruana Memorial Award, May 2013
2,000 Notable American Women Award

AFFILIATIONS

Phi Theta Kappa International Honor Society
UCLA Extension Attorney Assistant Alumni Association
Los Angeles Paralegal Association
National Association for Female Executives
National Association of Legal Assistants

functional résumé—applicant returning to the workforce (page 1)

Shannon Cates

4780 Angus Avenue—Clarkston, Michigan 48348—(248) 555-8870
Cell: (248) 553-2381—E-mail: ShannonCates@earthlink.net

Objective

To work in sales or marketing within the automotive industry

Summary of Qualifications

Background includes practical experience and education, which have provided solid working knowledge of these key areas:

- Direct and indirect sales
- New business development
- Wholesaler responsibility
- Local marketing and advertising
- Representative training
- New product-line introductions
- Account service and management
- Product support
- Presentation skills and experience

Relevant Experience

2006-2012 Account Manager, Kraft Foods, Fresno, California
1999-2006 Sales Representative, Kraft Foods, Fresno, California

Managed business for Kraft Foods at wholesale level. Managed Fleming Foods, Fresno, and Market Wholesale, Fresno, for Kraft Foods. Duties and responsibilities:

- Managed from $12 million to $20 million in food sales annually
- Maintained inventory levels of more than 400 items for wholesalers who served more than 700 grocery stores throughout Central Valley of California
- Supervised and facilitated all levels of paperwork; that is, invoicing, pricing, billing, terms, price protection, advertising, and promotional dollars
- Managed $80,000-$100,000 of advertising dollars per year for local marketing at the retail level to increase sales through advertising, new product introductions, presentations, merchandising, and distribution activities

functional résumé—applicant returning to the workforce (page 2)

Shannon Cates Résumé Page 2

- Developed unique sales presentations and strategies for selling direct shipments to independent chain stores
- Assisted independent retail stores with shelf layout of merchandise, and instructed store personnel on consumer shopping and buying patterns

Accomplishments

- 2006 winner of Award of Excellence for Western Region, most prestigious award
- 2005 candidate for Award of Excellence
- Met or exceeded sales target every year since employed
- Wrote custom computer programs (mid-2000s) that increased sales, reduced labor, and provided efficient shipment/delivery system for direct shipments
- Established and expanded new accounts, which increased direct volume at retail level by 190 percent since 2009
- Secured extensive competitive information for corporate research and knowledge
- Cultivated and maintained effective business relationships while increasing trade and brand franchises over a long-term basis
- Implemented many creative local-marketing events; for example, sold world's largest cereal display three years in a row. Submitted to *Guinness Book of World Records* (2004-2007)
- Coordinated local Hispanic events, for example, Cinco de Mayo celebration
- Worked closely with corporate marketing to launch successful air show sponsorship at Lemoore Naval Air Force Base
- Obtained free television spot on nightly news for world's largest cereal display
- Proficient with computer application programs: Excel, Microsoft Word, PowerPoint, and Access
- Attended many self-development, management, and sales seminars

Education

Masters of Business Administration—2012
Emphasis: International Marketing
California State University, Fresno
GPA 3.5/4.0

Bachelor of Science—1999
Emphasis: Marketing
California State University, Humboldt
GPA 3.5/4.0

Conventional Résumé Formats

13–10 Formats for Résumés

The appearance of your résumé creates the first impression a prospective employer forms of you. If the résumé is well designed and well written, it is more likely to be read and to lead to an interview. Use the following guidelines to prepare your résumé:

(1) Use 24-pound high-quality white paper to prepare your résumé. Ensure that the print quality is high density, equal to that of a laser printer.

(2) Strive for optimal top, bottom, left, and right margins—1 inch. Use no less than 0.75 inch for each of these margins.

(3) Select a font with a typeface that is easy to read, such as Arial. Use no smaller than an 11-point font, and do not condense the line spacing so that the copy becomes difficult to read.

(4) Use headings for each of your major categories. Differentiate through size and/or attribute (bold and/or italic) these text headings from the regular text. Use regular second-degree text headings as shown in Section 12–8a and the example résumés on pages 489 and 493–494 or parallel headings as shown in the example résumés on pages 488, 491, and 492.

(5) Use font attributes (**bold**, *italic*, ***bold italic***, ALL CAPITAL LETTERS, SMALL CAPITALS) to make your résumé more attractive and easily comprehensible. Be careful, though, not to overuse these attributes and to apply them consistently for the same features.

(6) Single-space the items listed within each section, but double-space between the items. Use parallel construction for all entries within a section, and place a period only at the end of complete sentences. Use no punctuation mark to conclude incomplete word groups unless they are followed by complete sentences or another word group.

Automated Applicant Tracking Systems

13–11 Preparation for Computerized Résumé Searches

a. **Large companies are increasingly relying on automated applicant tracking systems (ATS) to screen candidates. These computers are not programmed to assess personal skills, initiative, motivation, drive, attitude, disposition, or other such attributes based on a résumé. Instead, they look for the marketable skills possessed by a candidate. Automated applicant tracking systems generally operate in the following way:**

(1) Online résumés are loaded directly into the tracking system. A paper résumé is scanned, and its scanned image is sent to a computer equipped with optical character recognition (OCR) software. The computer quickly reads, classifies, and stores each résumé.

(2) When a job opening occurs, the employer tells the tracking system the keywords for the position. The computer looks for keywords (nouns that match the candidates' education, experience, skills, abilities, and knowledge with the job requirements).

(3) Applicants' résumés are selected and ranked according to the number of keywords appearing in the résumé. Only applicants whose résumés contain the keywords are candidates for the interview. These résumés are then subjected to human scrutiny for a decision on whether the applicant will be invited for an interview.

(4) Automated applicant tracking systems generate response letters to prospective job candidates—interview offers, acknowledgments, and rejections. Most résumés are stored for a stipulated period of time before they are purged from the system.

b. Keywords are the core of automated applicant tracking systems. Computers identify what a person can *do*. They look for substantiated facts, definitive quantities, and concrete nouns that describe specific skills and accomplishments.

Keywords *differ* for each job title and each industry. Some companies will use keywords for the specific job opening and other keywords to assess familiarity with terms in the industry. Consider the following examples:

(1) A company looking for a tax accountant with at least two years' experience with a Big 4 accounting firm might search for the following keywords:

BA in Accounting	public accounting
BS in Accounting	Excel
Masters of Accounting	computer skills
Masters of Tax Law	communication skills
CPA	years' experience
auditing	income tax
tax accounting	Deloitte Touche Tohmatsu
tax law	Ernst & Young
corporate tax	PricewaterhouseCoopers
tax return preparation	KPMG

(2) A major pharmaceutical company posted the following job opening for an "Administrative Coordinator" (April 2, 2015) at its Web site.

Administrative Coordinator
Auto Req #: XXXXXX
Career Categories: Administrative
(Company Name) Job Description

The Administrative Coordinator (AC) will be primarily responsible for complex administrative support activities, supporting executive directors, directors, and other staff.

Key responsibilities include:

- Extensive administrative support to CBSS staff at three sites
- Primary contact for CBSS ASF
- Providing backup support to additional department ACs
- Making travel arrangements & preparing expense reports as requested
- Coordinating visitor arrangements
- Scheduling and coordinating candidate interviews
- Providing meeting support for cross-functional teams, to include scheduling, agenda preparation, collection/distribution of pre-reads, and meeting start-up as appropriate
- Organizing departmental events and meetings including logistics, catering, supplies and equipment needs
- Independently responding to routine correspondence
- Determining best approach and presentation when preparing and formatting correspondence, memoranda, reports, and presentations
- Assisting with training, guidance, and orientation of new staff members
- Obtaining office space, equipment, and supplies for new staff members and setting up offices prior to start date
- Assisting with exit process for departing staff members
- Coordinating staff moves
- Assisting with clerical biorepository functions as needed
- Coordinating mailings and courier/deliveries
- Arranging purchase orders
- Maintaining general office supplies inventory
- Submitting IS Help Desk work orders, as needed
- Assisting staff members with Office software and (Company Name) systems
- Assisting with maintaining SharePoint sites; coordinating current content with staff
- Coordinating and managing documents in EDM Teams and SharePoint
- Providing systems training to staff as needed
- Creating efficient and user-friendly templates for procedures and reports
- Identifying process-improvement opportunities
- Making decisions based on knowledge of staff needs and available resources
- Using the latest technology to solves business problems

Basic Qualifications

Associate's degree & 2 years of Administrative experience
OR
High school diploma / GED & 4 years of Administrative experience

Preferred Qualifications

- Excellent skills in Word, Excel, PowerPoint, and SharePoint
- Ability to manage large data sets
- Operational Efficiency: Process Improvement / Project Management and Support

From the job description provided, an applicant might assume that the employer would suggest the following keywords for the automated applicant tracking system.

administrative support	multitasking
travel arrangements and expense reports	SharePoint
agendas	meeting planning
correspondence, reports, presentations	team player
college degree	four years' experience
MS Office	Excel
orientation and training	organizing, scheduling, and planning events
Word	
PowerPoint	

Additional industry-specific keywords this employer may look for include these:

pharmaceutical	research
health	infections
biology	chemistry
science	anatomy
medical terminology	life science

Match your qualifications with those of the posted job before applying for a job, and place your listing of keywords within your résumé. Be sure, however, that the keywords you use match your qualifications.

c. **Check with prospective employers to see if your résumé will be evaluated by an automated applicant tracking system. If so, devise a list of keywords from your qualifications that you think may be used by the employer to select people for the position in which you are interested.**

After the personal information (name, address, telephone number, cell phone number, e-mail address, fax number) in your résumé, begin your listing of qualifications with a *Summary of Qualifications* or a *Professional Profile*. Use the following guidelines to prepare this section of your résumé:

(1) Label the section *Summary of Qualifications* or *Professional Profile*. Use no font attributes such as boldface, italics, or underlining.

(2) Place keywords in phrases to feature what you can do or what you have accomplished.

(3) Begin the listing with the most important qualifications, and follow with those keywords having a lesser significance.

(4) Use variants of the keywords in the main text of your résumé to increase your chances of matching the keyword images of the optical character reading (OCR) software; for example, substitute *Associate Degree* for *Associate in Arts degree, spreadsheet* for *Excel,* or *administrative assistant* for *secretary.*

Summary of Qualifications

Previous experience and education have provided solid working knowledge in these key areas:

- Proficiency in using Microsoft Word, Excel, SharePoint, Access, and PowerPoint
- Experience in making travel arrangements, reporting business expenses, preparing agendas, arranging meetings, preparing meeting minutes
- Ability to work under pressure in a fast-paced industry requiring team coordination, multitasking, and confidentiality
- Gained four years' experience in administrative support after obtaining a college degree
- Apply English grammar skills in preparing correspondence, reports, and meeting minutes
- Knowledge of anatomical terms based on science courses taken in college

d. Paper résumés submitted to automated applicant tracking systems are scanned and forwarded to computers with optical character reading (OCR) software for reading. Examples of résumés prepared for scanning are shown on pages 500 and 504. So that your résumé is read correctly, you need to ensure that it meets the following criteria:

(1) Use black print equal to the quality of a laser or an inkjet printer on 24-pound, 8½- by 11-inch high-quality smooth-surfaced white paper.

(2) Use standard fonts (11 to 13 points in size) in which none of the characters touch each other (Arial, Univers, Helvetica, New Century Schoolbook), and avoid attributes such as underscores, italics, or shadows that are hard for optical scanning equipment to read. You may use boldface and/or all capital letters for section headings and emphasis as long as the letters do not touch each other.

(3) Keep your résumé free of graphics, boxed text, and shading; you may use solid bullets or asterisks for a listing, but leave a space after them. Confine your résumé to a single-column format; multiple columns often run together in translations by OCR software.

(4) Place your name on the first line of the résumé. Following lines should include your complete address and telephone number. Include also your cell phone number, e-mail address, and fax number, if applicable.

(5) Begin your description of qualifications with a summary that contains keywords (nouns used by the computer to match candidates' traits with job requirements).

(6) Continue to employ keywords to describe specifically what you can do in relation to the job for which you are applying. Examples are (1) perform bookkeeping and accounting functions such as payroll, accounts receivable, and accounts payable; (2) use computer programs such as Microsoft Word, Excel, PowerPoint, Outlook, and Access; (3) work in retail sales and customer relations; and (4) prepare, edit, and proofread reports.

(7) Avoid using abbreviations unless they are common to your profession or only after you have spelled them out in full.

(8) Send the résumé in a large envelope, and be sure to include a cover letter. Do not fold or staple the pages; fasten them with a paper clip.

résumé prepared for an automated applicant tracking system

Corey T. Roberts
2380 Vista Avenue
Tampa, Florida 33626
(813) 553-2196 • Cell: (813) 555-3841 • CoreyRob2@msn.com

Summary of Qualifications

Previous experience and education have provided solid working knowledge in these key areas:

- Proficiency in using Microsoft Word, Excel, Outlook, Access, and PowerPoint
- Experience in making travel arrangements, reporting business expenses, preparing agendas, arranging meetings, preparing meeting minutes
- Ability to work under pressure in a fast-paced industry requiring team coordination, multitasking, and confidentiality
- Gained four years' experience in administrative support after obtaining a college degree
- Apply English grammar skills in preparing correspondence, reports, and meeting minutes
- Knowledge of anatomical terms based on science courses taken in college

Objective

Administrative support position in a large national or international corporation

Experience

2012 to Present, ABCO Resource and Consulting Services, Administrative Assistant to the General Manager, Tampa Office

- Handle phones and incoming calls on Help Desk
- Schedule meetings, prepare agendas, take minutes, and prepare meeting minutes
- Make travel arrangements and prepare itineraries
- Use word processing software to prepare documents and answer routine correspondence
- Use spreadsheet software for budget and expense reports
- Use presentation software to assist staff in developing sales presentations
- Maintain a database of current and potential contract employees
- Maintain the branch Web site
- Maintain a filing system
- Process incoming mail

2011 to 2012, Salvation Corps, Tampa, Administrative Clerk

- Handled all incoming phone calls and greeted visitors
- Scheduled pickup of nonmonetary donations
- Used spreadsheet software to track donations, prepare budgets, and record expenses
- Used a Macintosh to prepare flyers
- Processed all incoming mail and handled the filing system

2009 to 2011, Tampa, Assistant to Professor Linda Atkinson (part-time)

- Used a word processing program to prepare manuscript for publication
- Proofread page proof

Education

Associate in Arts degree, Office Administration, Office Automation option, Brookview Community College, Tampa, 2011

Online Career Resources

Online career centers, also known as job boards, continue to play a role in the job-seeking process, although not as dominantly as in previous years. Online career centers (1) post job openings in organizations throughout the United States, (2) allow applicants to apply for openings online, and (3) permit job-seeking candidates to post résumés.These career sites also offer suggestions for preparing résumés and provide general career advice.

Most major corporations that maintain Web sites have established a career center within their site. Here they list job openings within their organization and provide opportunities for interested candidates to submit their résumés online.

13–12 Locating Career Centers on the Internet

The Internet furnishes access to a variety of career centers and services. Career centers usually provide information about employers, post employment opportunities, assist candidates in placing their résumés online, and grant employers access to candidates' résumés. Many of these career centers are free of charge to the prospective employee and employer, but others charge the employer or both the employer and employee. Follow these guidelines to locate various career sites on the Internet:

(1) Use a search site (Google,Yahoo!, etc.) to locate a listing of career centers and services for your area of interest and expertise—business, health services, law, entertainment, computing, and so on.

(2) Explore a number of the career centers and services your search produces to determine the one or ones suitable for you. Consider job classifications, location of opportunities, kinds of applicants targeted, kinds of employers, scope of coverage, and cost (if any). You may also wish to visit the following Web site that contains links to a large number of career centers and services on the Internet or the second Web site that provides articles on a number of topics relevant to job seekers:

Careers.Org. http://www.careers.org. This site provides job advice, career articles, and links organized by topic—including links to Web sites with a significant number of job listings. (Registration required)

U.S. News & World Report—Money—Careers. http://money.usnews.com/money/careers. This site provides up-to-date information on the best jobs available, interview and presentation tips, and advice to the beginning worker who is employed. (No registration required)

(3) Visit well-known, popular job boards that post job openings and candidates' résumés. Some of these are listed here:

CareerBuilder. http://www.careerbuilder.com. Striving to be a valuable source to both the employer and the job seeker, this Web site posts job openings, posts résumés, and provides career information for job seekers. No fee; registration required for résumé posting.

LinkedIn. https://www.linkedin.com. This site began as a business-oriented social networking service. Although it still maintains the same service, it has also taken on the functions of a job board. Employers may post job openings for a fee and job seekers may post résumés. If job seekers wish to have their résumés moved up, they may do so for a monthly fee.

Monster. http://www.monster.com. This popular Web site for job seekers offers a variety of services. The Monster network posts job openings, posts résumés, and provides career advice. No fee; registration required for résumé posting.

MonsterCollege. http://college.monster.com/. MonsterCollege, a division of Monster, specializes in listings for recent college graduates. It assists recent college graduates and college students to get started in their career. This site provides entry-level job listings, internship listings, job search tips, an opportunity to post a portfolio, and a career contact network. No fee; registration required.

TrueCareers. http://www.truecareers.com. TrueCareers connects educated, diverse job seekers with employers who want well-educated, diverse candidates. This Web site posts job openings and résumés. It also provides career advice. No fee; registration not required to view postings.

13–13 Accessing Corporate Online Career Centers

a. Major corporations generally include career centers on their Web sites. Here they describe career opportunities and post job openings in their organization. If you are interested in employment

with a particular organization, visit its Web site, view its advertised positions, and submit your résumé if you qualify for one of the positions listed.

b. Most company Web sites may be accessed by entering *www .[companyname].com* in the address box of your browser. Specific examples are *www.dole.com* and *www.amgen.com*. If this strategy does not produce the desired result, use these procedures:

(1) Use a search site (Google, Yahoo!, etc.) to locate the company Web site you wish to access.

(2) Access *FORTUNE*, "Fortune Rankings," http://fortune.com/rankings/, (April 6, 2015), for a listing of the Fortune 500 companies, the 100 best companies to work for, the 100 fastest-growing companies, and a number of other listings. Fortune ranks annually the top companies and the top executives. Descriptions are available without charge.

c. Some companies accept résumés only for the positions that are advertised. Others accept all résumés and store them for a specified time. Should an opening occur that requires the qualifications of an applicant on file, the applicant may then be considered for the position.

Résumés submitted online are routed into an automated applicant tracking system. Follow the procedures described in Section 13–11 to prepare your résumé; keywords will be used to determine your qualifications for openings in the organization. In addition, follow the procedures outlined in Section 13–14 to prepare your résumé in ASCII format (text format) or RTF format (rich text format) for transmission over the Internet. Do not send your resume in PDF format.

13–14 Preparing and Posting an Online Résumé

a. Select one or more sites on which to post your résumé. Use the chronological style résumé described in Section 13–1, and prepare a version of your résumé in ASCII format or RTF format. Cut and paste from this version to accommodate any templates that may be required by an Internet career center or a company career site. A résumé prepared in ASCII format is shown page 504.

résumé prepared in ASCII format

```
JORDAN W. J. SAVAGE
6683 Kreag Road
Pittsford, NY 14536
(716) 555-8438
jwjsavage@telis.org

OBJECTIVE
To obtain a position that allows me to use my skills as a Web site designer
and HTML programmer

EMPLOYMENT HISTORY
February 2015 - present, Webmaster, Moran Food Corporation, Albany,
New York
** Design all pages for Web site of Moran Food Corporation, domestic and
international
** HTML code all Web pages for Moran Food Corporation
** Maintain all Web sites for Moran Food Corporation

June 2014 - January 2015, Graphic Designer, Moran Food Corporation,
Albany, New York
** Created magazine ads for national magazines
** Created multimedia presentations for the marketing staff
** Created designs for recipe booklets and other promotional materials
** Provided integration assistance between the art and information
processing departments

August 2013 - May 2014, Assistant Graphic Designer, Wilmont College,
Boston, Massachusetts (part-time)
** Assisted in the development of advertising materials including
an Adobe Director presentation
** Designed flyers for promotional events
** Assisted in producing mechanicals

EDUCATION
BS in Computer Science, major in computer science and minor in
graphic design, Wilmont College, Boston, Massachusetts, 2014,
GPA: 3.7/4.0

ADDITIONAL SKILLS
** Programming/Scripting Languages: C++, COBOL, HTML, PHP,
and XML
** Operating Systems: MacOS, UNIX, Windows Server 2003 SP2,
Windows Server 2008 R2, Windows 7, and Windows 8
** Software: Adobe Creative Suite, Design Premium (Dreamweaver,
Flash, Photoshop, InDesign, Illustrator, and Acrobat), Microsoft Word,
Excel, PowerPoint, Access, Outlook, Project, and SharePoint Designer
```


You may also use your prepared résumé as a guide to complete the fill-in blanks of a résumé builder or template provided by an Internet career center or company career site.

b. Use the following guidelines to prepare your résumé for posting on an Internet career center or for online transmission to a company career site:

(1) Prepare your résumé in ASCII text. To create an ASCII résumé, key your résumé in a word processing program and save it as a *Plain Text* file (*.txt). This choice of file type should be available in your *Save as*

type: option box. You may also use a simple text program to compose your résumé.

(2) Use a 5-inch typing line. Align all text at the left margin. Use the space bar, not the tab key, for any indentions.

(3) Use hard returns for line breaks; do not rely on the word wrap feature of your word processing program.

(4) Avoid special characters and font attributes such as italics, underlining, and bolding. Fonts will become whatever a computer uses as its default typeface and size.

(5) Use the spell-checker, and carefully proofread your résumé before you save it as an ASCII file.

The Application Letter

Although the application letter functions as a cover letter in the transmittal of your résumé, its importance must not be minimized. This document is your initial introduction to the employer, so care must be taken to make a good first impression. This letter represents you. If it is prepared poorly, there is a good chance that your résumé will not be read.

13–15 Contents of the Application Letter

a. Begin the application letter with a statement that attracts the interest of the reader and is related to the purpose of the letter. If an opening has been announced and applications are being solicited, use a direct approach. If, on the other hand, you are investigating whether an opening may exist, use a different strategy by approaching your purpose indirectly.

direct opening for solicited application

> The opening for an administrative assistant in your Publications Department that you filed with the Loma Vista College Career Center appears to be interesting and challenging. As you can see by the enclosed résumé, my specialty in the computer applications/office administration area has been desktop publishing.

indirect opening for unsolicited application

> My high regard for Allerman Corporation and its products has prompted me to inquire whether you could use the services of a knowledgeable administrative assistant who has two years' successful experience in computer applications and office administration.

b. Continue the letter of application with information that explains the purpose of your letter and convinces the reader to consider your qualifications further. Do not summarize your résumé; instead, amplify and briefly explain one or two of your strongest qualifications and

relate them to the job for which you are applying. Refer the reader to the enclosed résumé.

body of application letter

> My formal study of computer application programs—word processing, desktop publishing, Web page construction, spreadsheet, and database—at Loma Vista College culminated with an internship program at Data Select. Here I was able to use my word processing and desktop publishing skills to produce a 170-page instructional manual for one of the company's new software programs.
>
> In addition to my course work and experience in applications software, courses in business English and business communication have enabled me to develop the writing, editing, and proofreading skills needed to produce error-free business documents. Information regarding my other qualifications is included in the enclosed résumé.

c. **A request for action closes the application letter. Usually the action requested is an invitation for an interview. It may, however, merely be that the reader mail an employment application or refer your letter and résumé to a local office or representative. Whatever the request may be, preface it with *please* or another such polite expression.**

In asking for an interview, make it easy for the reader to reply by furnishing your telephone number and the times you may be reached. Serious job seekers mostly rely on cell phones so they are readily reachable when opportunities arise. However, be sure you have some kind of messaging service should you be temporarily unavailable.

Applicants should also furnish an e-mail address through which they may be contacted, should the prospective employer prefer this method of responding to the letter of application. If you furnish an e-mail address, be sure to check your in-box frequently or have your e-mail messages forwarded to your cell phone.

closing for application letter

> May I have an opportunity to discuss my qualifications with you further? To arrange an interview, please call me on my cell phone at (212) 555-5865. I can be reached personally before 10 a.m. and after 3 p.m. and through my messaging service between 10 a.m. and 3 p.m. I can arrange to meet with you anytime that is convenient for you.

13–16 Preparation of the Application Letter

Like the résumé, the application letter represents you and forms a first impression. To form a favorable first impression, follow these guidelines:

(1) Use 24-pound high-quality white paper to prepare your application letter. Ensure that the print quality is high density, equal to that of a laser printer. Select a typeface and font size that complement the ones used in your résumé.

(2) Use one of the three following business letter formats: full block, modified block with blocked paragraphs, or modified block with indented paragraphs. Instructions for preparing letters in these formats are contained in Sections 11–6 and 11–7. An example application letter is shown below.

letter of application

1116 East 59th Street, Apt. 301
Chicago, IL 60615-3022
March 1, 2016

Ms. Denise R. Cueva, Vice President
Human Resources and Development
First National Bank of Arizona
10370 Camelback Road
Phoenix, Arizona 85030-1900

Dear Ms. Cueva:

As a growing bank in the Phoenix area, does First National have a need for a qualified representative in its trust and estate planning area?

In June I will earn a bachelor of science degree in business finance from Chicago State University. Besides fulfilling all the requirements for the regular curriculum in finance, I have completed additional course work in estate planning, trust initiation and management, tax law for trusts, and ethics in trust management.

As you can see by the enclosed résumé, for the past year the knowledge gained in my course work has been applied in a part-time position at Illinois Federal Bank. Here I met with new clients and assisted in setting up trusts to meet their individual needs. I also worked closely with trust officers in reviewing and maintaining present clients' trusts.

May I have an opportunity to discuss with you how my education and experience can be put to work for First National? I plan to be in Phoenix from April 12 to 16 and would appreciate your scheduling an interview during that time. You may reach me by e-mail at rgferreira1531@msn.com, on my cell phone at (312) 555-8732, or by mail at the above address. I look forward to hearing from you.

Sincerely,

Robert Ferreira

Robert Ferreira

Enclosure

(3) Limit your application letter to one page. Keep in mind that it is a transmittal letter for your résumé and, in most cases, a request for an interview. Highlight and expand only one or two of your major qualifications. Letters that are too long are less likely to be read.

Similarly, letters prepared in fonts smaller than 11 points will receive less attention.

(4) Be sure to begin the application letter with a return address. Although your address and other contact information are prominently displayed in the résumé, your address must also appear on the application letter.

(5) Other parts of a business letter to be used include an inside address, a salutation, the letter body, a complimentary close, a signature line, and an enclosure notation. Specific instructions for the placement and format of these letter parts are contained in Sections 11–10 through 11–23.

The Application Form

Some organizations require candidates to complete formal application forms even though they have submitted résumés. Application forms permit employers to obtain and organize standardized information about applicants—and those whom they hire as employees.

13–17 Procedures for Completing Application Forms

Use the following guidelines to assist you in completing application forms efficiently and completely:

(1) Carry with you a copy of your résumé when visiting prospective employers' offices. Much of the information contained in your résumé will be needed to complete the application form.

(2) Write on the reverse side of your résumé copy any information that may be needed for the application form but is not included on your résumé. Such information may include the following:

Social Security number

Driver's license number

Beginning and ending dates of *all* employment

Salary history

Name, title, complete address, and telephone number of all former supervisors

Name, title, complete address, and telephone number of all references

(3) Read all the questions before you begin to answer any. Write neatly and legibly. If you have poor handwriting, print your responses. If the prospective employer has an electronic or online version of the employment application, use this form. In this way you can edit your responses and also ensure that the application is legible and neat.

(4) Answer all questions on the application form. If a question is not applicable to your situation, respond with a statement such as *Not applicable.*

(5) Write *Negotiable* or *Open* on application forms that contain questions regarding the salary you expect to earn. This strategy is best used when you are uncertain what others in comparable positions are earning.

Reference Requests

13–18 Reference Requests

a. Prospective employers will undoubtedly ask you to furnish two or three references, persons who can verify your abilities and/or former employment. Provide the names of former professors or employers who will present you in a favorable light. Do not provide "character" references from family friends, personal friends, or relatives.

b. Request permission from potential references to use their names; select people who you feel will enthusiastically endorse you. Remember that a poor recommendation is worse than no recommendation at all.

c. Solicit the recommendation endorsement in person, by telephone, or by e-mail—and follow up a *yes* response with an acknowledgment. Use the following guidelines for writing an acknowledgment e-mail or a letter:

(1) Express appreciation for the person's willingness to provide you with a recommendation should a prospective employer contact him or her.

(2) Provide a description of the job for which you are applying. If appropriate, relate one of your accomplishments or skills (that the person has observed personally) to the qualifications for the job.

(3) Attach (or include) and refer to a copy of your résumé.

(4) Invite the reference to contact you if he or she has any questions.

reference acknowledgment e-mail

Dear Professor Simons:

I appreciate your willingness to provide me with a reference for a position as a legal assistant should you be contacted by a prospective employer.

My immediate objective is to obtain a position in a large legal firm where I will have an opportunity for advancement. The courses I took from you—word processing, legal office procedures, and legal document preparation—certainly prepared me well to begin my career in a legal office.

After graduating from Dawson College, I continued my education in the area of legal assisting. As you can see by the attached résumé, I enrolled in the Attorney Assistant Training Program at the University of Oregon, Portland, Extension. Here I earned a Certificate in Litigation.

Thank you for your support. If you have any questions or wish any additional information, please let me know.

Maria Cessante

Follow-Up Letters

Follow-up letters may be written when no response is received to an application letter or form. They are also written after an interview. The follow-up letter reminds the prospective employer that you are interested in a position with that employer or company.

13–19 Application Follow-Up Letter

If you have not received a response to an application letter or an application form within a reasonable period of time, you may wish to send an application follow-up letter. Such a letter shows serious interest and reminds the human resource officer of your qualifications.

(1) Use 24-pound high-quality white paper to prepare your application follow-up letter. Ensure that the print quality is high density, equal to that of a laser printer. Select a typeface and font size that complement the ones used in your application letter and résumé.

(2) Use one of the following three business letter formats: full block, modified block with blocked paragraphs, or modified block with indented paragraphs. Instructions for preparing letters in these formats are contained in Sections 11–6 and 11–7. Be sure to begin the application follow-up letter with a return address. Other parts of a business letter to be used include an inside address, a salutation, the letter body, a complimentary close, and a signature line. Specific instructions for the placement and format of these letter parts are contained in Sections 11–10 through 11–22.

(3) Begin the application follow-up letter with a statement reaffirming your interest in the job for which you formerly applied. Remind the addressee of your letter or application and mention one of your qualifications—or provide any new information that may enhance your likelihood of obtaining the position. Anticipate that you will hear from the addressee and provide all your contact information.

(4) An example application follow-up letter is shown on page 511.

application follow-up letter

1116 East 59th Street, Apt. 301
Chicago, IL 60615-3022
March 21, 2016

Ms. Denise R. Cueva, Vice President
Human Resources and Development
First National Bank of Arizona
10370 Camelback Road
Phoenix, Arizona 85030-1900

Dear Ms. Cueva:

As I mentioned in my March 1 letter, I am interested in discussing with you the opportunities for a qualified representative in your trust and estate planning area. First National is a growing bank in the Phoenix area, and I would be pleased to have a few minutes of your time to see if I can fit in with your plans for expansion.

In June I will earn a bachelor of science degree in business finance from Chicago State University. For the past year, I have worked part-time at Illinois Federal Bank. Here I met with new clients and assisted in setting up trusts to meet their individual needs. I also worked closely with trust officers in reviewing and maintaining present clients' trusts.

My continued interest in becoming part of the First National team stems from my respect for First National and its operations. Consequently, may I have an opportunity to discuss with you how my education and experience can be put to work for First National? I still plan to be in Phoenix from April 12 to 16 and would appreciate your scheduling an interview during that time. If these dates do not coincide with your schedule, I can arrange to meet with you on a different date.

You may reach me by e-mail at rgferreira1531@msn.com, on my cell phone at (312) 555-8732, or by mail at the above address. I look forward to hearing from you.

Sincerely,

Robert Ferreira

Robert Ferreira

13-20 Interview Follow-Up Letter

After you have been interviewed, send a brief letter of appreciation to the interviewer. This courtesy will not only express your thanks for the interviewer's time but also remind that person of your meeting. Sending a follow-up letter will reaffirm your interest in the position and at the same time distinguish you from the other candidates. More than likely, others will not take this extra step.

(1) Write and send the interview follow-up letter immediately after the interview. A delay will impair its effectiveness. In addition to

expressing appreciation and thanks, remind the interviewer of a topic discussed during your conversation and conclude with a positive statement indicating your interest in the position.

(2) Use one of the following three business letter formats: full block, modified block with blocked paragraphs, or modified block with indented paragraphs. Instructions for preparing letters in these formats are contained in Sections 11–6 and 11–7. An example interview follow-up letter is shown below.

(3) Be sure to begin the interview follow-up letter with a return address. Other parts of a business letter to be used include an inside address, a salutation, the letter body, a complimentary close, and a signature line. Specific instructions for the placement and format of these letter parts are contained in Sections 11–10 through 11–22.

interview follow-up letter

1116 East 59th Street, Apt. 301
Chicago, IL 60615-3022
April 19, 2016

Ms. Denise R. Cueva, Vice President
Human Resources and Development
First National Bank of Arizona
10370 Camelback Road
Phoenix, Arizona 85030-1900

Dear Ms. Cueva:

Thank you for meeting with me in Phoenix last week. My interview with you and Mr. Sebastian has convinced me even more that I would like to become part of the First National Bank of Arizona staff.

Since there are no openings in your Estate Planning and Trust Department at the present time, I appreciate your suggesting the management training program in the interim. Please consider me for an opening in this program.

Because of my experience at Illinois Federal Bank, I believe I could be a productive member of your staff. I look forward to receiving your decision about my entering the management training program at First National.

Sincerely,

Robert Ferreira

Robert Ferreira

14

The Internet and Its Resources

The Internet and Its Resources Solution Finder

The Internet and the World Wide Web

The Internet, an extensive system of connected computers, comprises a vast number of networks that are made up of millions of host computers. This online global network, which is accessible worldwide, promotes information exchange between almost every segment of our society.

From major universities and giant corporations to the single user at a home computer or handheld device, all may access the wealth of information that the Internet provides. Businesspeople need to gather information for general operations, decision making, and document preparation. Online resources play a major role in providing access to the information needed by today's fast-paced business environment.

E-commerce, the sale of goods and services through Web sites, has had a major impact on the purchasing patterns of both consumers and businesses. Fledgling enterprises and long-established business organizations have flocked to the Internet to capture a part of this burgeoning consumer marketplace.

14–1 Using the Internet

a. Major business interests today rely on accessing the Internet's World Wide Web (WWW) and its exploding abundance of vital resources. The Internet with its World Wide Web provides the following kinds of information often needed for research, planning, and implementation:

(1) General references such as dictionaries, encyclopedias, thesauri, atlases, telephone white and yellow pages (national directories), currency exchange rates, world time-zone charts, measurement conversions, calendars, and directories of reference materials

(2) Stock and bond market quotations, company profiles, industry trends, management advice, online banking, and a multitude of other business and financial resources

(3) Travel information and resources—airline schedules and reservations, hotel reservations, rental cars, restaurants, attractions and events, mapped driving routes, train schedules, and bus schedules

(4) Current news and weather—local, national, and international

(5) Articles published in major newspapers and magazines worldwide

(6) Services, rates, and tracking for domestic and international mail service providers such as the United States Postal Service, United Parcel Service, FedEx, and other private carriers

(7) Products and services provided by companies throughout the world

(8) Career services and company career centers

(9) Government information and services

b. Individuals, small businesses, and major corporations use the Internet to market products and services. By creating Web sites and advertising their addresses (uniform resource locators [URLs]), they are soliciting sales through e-commerce.

14–2 Accessing the World Wide Web

a. Using the World Wide Web requires a Web browser. Popular browsers—Microsoft Internet Explorer, Google Chrome, Firefox, Safari, Opera, and Torch—are available for free download.

b. Locating information through your Web browser may be accomplished in several ways:

(1) *Through an Internet address.* Any Internet site may be reached through its address (uniform resource locator [URL]). Each Web page has a specific address, and by typing the correct address in the appropriate box shown on your Web browser screen, you will be transported to that site.

Most World Wide Web addresses begin with *http://* (HyperText Transfer Protocol) or *https://* (Hyper Text Transfer Protocol Secure); the succeeding letters, numbers, and symbols must be entered exactly as shown to access the site. In most cases you need not key *http://*. By keying the remaining letters in the address box, you can access the site. For example, *http://www.usps.com* may be accessed by keying www.usps.com instead of the full address.[1]

Internet addresses in running copy may often appear with commas that relate to the sentence punctuation or periods that conclude a sentence. Remember that a URL has no spaces or commas. It does not end with a period or any other punctuation mark—except perhaps a slash (/).

(2) *Through a search site.* Web browsers have available at least one search site, or search sites may be accessed through their own Web sites. Search sites permit you to locate information by entering keywords.

If you were trying to find job listings on the Internet using a search site, you might enter *employment jobs resumes career postings.* This search string will give you the information you need; it relies on a series of keywords to capture the various employment-related information that is available. From the list produced by this search, you can connect directly to any of the sites listed.

(3) *Through a link in a Web site.* Hypertext permits Web sites to link to other Web sites. By clicking on an icon, underlined text, or highlighted text, you can be transported from one information source to another. Related

[1]Although the complete URL is shown here, these sites may be accessed without keying *http://* in the address bar. Some browsers permit users to access these sites (and other *www. . . . .com* sites) by keying only the domain name and then pressing *Ctrl + Enter*.

information is frequently linked through hypertext, so often you can locate needed information through a link. Hypertext permits you to (a) migrate easily to documents, graphics, or other Web pages; (b) connect to other kinds of Internet resources such as newsgroups; and (c) download text, graphics, photos, sounds, music, and movies to a computer.

c. **Search sites provide access to locating information on the Internet. Specific search sites may be accessed by entering their addresses (URLs) in the address box of your browser. These resources use various means for classifying sites, and they produce results based upon search strings entered in a search box. From the same search string, different search sites commonly produce different results. That is why persons researching a topic often rely on more than one search site to gather information.**

Learn to use search sites to gather the information you need. Bookmark sites that you use frequently or that you feel will be useful to you sometime in the near future. Continually search for Web sites that will assist you in carrying out your responsibilities.

Several of the popular and reliable search sites, along with their Internet addresses (URLs), include the following:

(1)	Google	http://www.google.com
(2)	Bing	http://www.bing.com
(3)	Yahoo!	http://www.yahoo.com
(4)	Ask	http://www.ask.com
(5)	AOL	http://www.aol.com

d. **Google is the most popular search site on the Web. Besides its intuitive, powerful search engine, Google has a number of features that simplify locating information on the Internet:**

(1) Contains a "define" operator that allows searchers to obtain definitions of words and abbreviations; for example, *define: WYSIWYG.*

(2) Allows a number of natural language questions; for example, *population of the United States* and *governor of Oregon* and *When was Barack Obama born?*

(3) Provides weather information and access to current features (such as movie schedules) using natural language. Information is displayed in what is called "onebox" results. Examples include *weather in Seattle, Washington,* and *movie schedule in Granada Hills for Home* (2015 movie).

(4) Provides a built-in calculator that solves basic arithmetic as well as complicated math problems, converts units of measure, and converts currency. Simply enter the query in the search box; for example, *144/12, sqrt(64), half a cup in tablespoons, 13.5 feet × 12.8 feet in square yards, 1,000 USD in euros,* and *1,000 USD in GBP.*

Web Resources

The wealth of information available on the Internet is overwhelming. Not all of it is valid or reliable—and not all of it is obtainable free of charge. The Internet user must use good judgment and discretion in selecting sources. Also, the Internet user must decide whether the fees to access certain kinds of information are worthwhile. The sites recommended here are just a sampling of the vast traditional resources available on the World Wide Web.

14–3 Reference Sources

a. Reference sources such as dictionaries, thesauri, encyclopedias, almanacs, and atlases are available for access on the Internet. A number of such sites follow. The dates in parentheses show when the information for these sites was last confirmed.

Acronym Finder. Acronym Finder, 2015. http://www.acronymfinder.com (accessed April 7, 2015). A search site that locates the meaning of acronyms, abbreviations, or initialisms or locates the acronym, abbreviation, or initialism for terms.

Encyclopædia Britannica Online. Encyclopædia Britannica, Inc., 2015. http://www.britannica.com/ (accessed April 7, 2015). A Web-based subscription encyclopedia.

Encyclopedia.com. HighBeam Research, Inc., 2015. http://www.encyclopedia.com (accessed April 8, 2015). A free online encyclopedia containing articles, pictures, facts, and biographies along with information about the arts, science, sports, medicine, accounting, management, and similar topics.

FindLaw. FindLaw, 2015. http://www.findlaw.com (accessed April 8, 2015). Contains links to numerous legal resources that provide information on various aspects of law.

Howe, Denis. *FOLDOC: Free On-Line Dictionary of Computing*. Imperial College Department of Computing, February 8, 2015. http://foldoc.org (accessed April 8, 2015). A dictionary of computer terms with more than 15,000 entries.

Martindale's: The Reference Desk. Jim Martindale, 2015. http://www.martindalecenter.com (accessed April 8, 2015). Provides a large collection of links to reference resources, including language centers, agriculture, calculators, maps, mathematics, and science tables.

Merriam-Webster. Springfield, Mass.: Merriam-Webster, Incorporated, 2015. http://www.m-w.com (accessed April 8, 2015). Provides free access to *Merriam-Webster Online Dictionary*, *Merriam-Webster Online Thesaurus*, and *Merriam-Webster Online Medical Dictionary*—along with a number of other valuable language resources.

NetLingo. NetLingo, 2015. http://www.netlingo.com (accessed April 8, 2015). An extensive, comprehensive glossary of Internet terms, along with definitions of online jargon that is also known as *text-messaging shorthand* and *chat acronyms*.

OneLook Dictionary Search. n.d. http://www.onelook.com (accessed April 8, 2015). A dictionary search site that accesses multiple sources to locate words and allows users to insert wildcard symbols to locate spellings. Provides a reverse dictionary.

Refdesk.com. Refdesk.com, 2015. http://www.refdesk.com (accessed April 8, 2015). Links to a comprehensive variety of reference sources; for example, dictionaries, encyclopedias, atlases, calendars, currency calculators, newspapers, magazines, columns, and personal entertainment sources.

The World Factbook. Washington, DC: Central Intelligence Agency, 2015. https://www.cia.gov/library/publications/the-world-factbook/index.html (accessed April 8, 2015). Links to current information on countries throughout the world. This site is updated weekly, and a new edition is published each year.

YourDictionary.com. LovetoKnow, Corp., 2015. http://www.yourdictionary.com (accessed April 8, 2015). Provides an online English dictionary (with spelling, definitions, pronunciation, and usage examples), a thesaurus, grammar assistance, vocabulary building support, and a series of famous quotations.

14-4 News and Weather

News and weather sources—news channels, weather channels, newspapers, and magazines—are available online. Several sites are listed here:

AccuWeather.com. AccuWeather, Inc., 2015. http://www.accuweather.com (accessed April 8, 2015). Provides local and worldwide weather forecasts and weather news.

Bloomberg Business. Bloomberg L.P., 2015. http://www.bloomberg.com (accessed April 8, 2015).

CNN. Cable News Network, Turner Broadcasting System, Inc., 2015. http://www.cnn.com (accessed April 8, 2015).

Intellicast.com. The Weather Company, 2015. http://www.intellicast.com (accessed April 8, 2015). Provides worldwide weather reports and ten-day forecasts.

The New York Times. The New York Times Company, 2015. http://www.nytimes.com (accessed April 8, 2015).

Newsweek. Newsweek LLC, 2015. http://www.newsweek.com/ (accessed April 8, 2015).

TIME. Time Inc., 2015. http://www.time.com/time (accessed April 8, 2015).

USA TODAY. USATODAY, 2015. http://www.usatoday.com (accessed April 8, 2015).

U.S. News & World Report. U.S. News & World Report LP, 2015. http://www.usnews.com/ (accessed April 8, 2015).

THE WALL STREET JOURNAL. Dow Jones & Company, Inc., 2015. http://www.wsj.com (accessed April 8, 2015).

The Weather Channel. The Weather Channel, LLC, 2015. http://www.weather.com (accessed April 8, 2015).

14–5 Government Information

Government offices provide information through the Internet. Mailing, tax, and census information, as well as other resources, may be obtained at the following sites:

CONGRESS.GOV. Washington, DC: The Library of Congress, n.d. https://www.congress.gov (accessed April 9, 2015). Provides a listing of members in the United States Senate and House of Representatives, information regarding dates when bodies are in session, videos explaining the various legislative stages, access to current and previous legislation, and a variety of other information related to the U.S. Congress.

FEDWORLD.GOV. Alexandria, VA: U.S. Department of Commerce, National Technical Information Service, April 9, 2015. http://fedworld.ntis.gov/ (accessed April 9, 2015). Serves as the online locator for a comprehensive inventory of information disseminated by the federal government.

IRS. "Forms & Publications." Washington, DC: Department of the Treasury, Internal Revenue Service, March 29, 2015. http://www.irs.gov/Forms-&-Pubs (accessed April 9, 2015). Permits download of federal income tax forms.

The Library of Congress THOMAS. Washington, DC: The Library of Congress, n.d. http://thomas.loc.gov/home/thomas.php (accessed April 9, 2015). Provides continual legislative updates.

United States Postal Service. Washington, DC: USPS, 2015. http://www.usps.com (accessed April 9, 2015). Provides information on the services provided by the U.S. Postal Service.

U.S. Census Bureau. Washington, DC: U.S. Department of Commerce, n.d. http://www.census.gov (accessed April 9, 2015). Posts up-to-date projections since the official 2010 United States census. Provides information on current population, housing, business, and other topics.

"ZIP Code Lookup." *United States Postal Service*. Washington, DC: USPS, 2015. https://tools.usps.com/go/ZipLookupAction_input (accessed April 9, 2015). Provides access to nine-digit ZIP Codes for addresses. Quick access may also be obtained through a link on the U.S. Postal Service home page, http://www.usps.com.

14-6 Private Delivery Services

Private delivery services maintain Web sites that allow package tracking and provide information about their services. Web site addresses for several such providers are listed below:

DHL. DHL International GmbH, 2015. http://www.dhl-usa.com (accessed April 9, 2015).

FedEx. FedEx, 2015. http://www.fedex.com (accessed April 9, 2015).

UPS. United Parcel Service of America, Inc., 2015. http://www.ups.com (accessed April 9, 2015).

14-7 Online Directories and Locators

Online directories provide addresses, telephone numbers, fax numbers, e-mail addresses, Web site addresses (URLs—uniform resource locators), and other similar types of information for individuals, businesses, organizations, and government agencies. A select list of online locators follows:

Google Maps. Google, 2015. https://www.maps.google.com (accessed April 9, 2015). Provides area maps as well as mapping, photos, and turn-by-turn directions for driving from one location to another throughout the United States.

MapQuest. MapQuest, 2015. http://www.mapquest.com (accessed April 9, 2015). Provides mapping and turn-by-turn directions for driving from one location to another throughout the United States.

Superpages.com. Dex Media, Inc., 2015. http://www.superpages.com (accessed April 9, 2015). Provides a lookup service for business addresses and phone numbers.

Switchboard.com. WhitePages Inc., 2015. http://www.switchboard.com (accessed April 9, 2015). Offers white pages, yellow pages, an area code locator, and a ZIP Code locator.

14-8 Career Centers

Job searches are no longer dominated by the traditional résumé and letter of application. Most major companies today maintain career centers on their Web sites and accept résumés online. In addition, the Internet hosts a number of career centers that post job openings, post résumés, permit online applications for job postings, and offer career advice. The following sites are among the most popular ones on the Internet:

CareerBuilder. CareerBuilder, LCC, 2015. http://www.careerbuilder.com (accessed April 10, 2015). *CareerBuilder* posts job openings, posts résumés, and provides career information for job seekers. No fee; registration required for résumé posting.

Monster. Monster, 2015. http://www.monster.com (accessed April 10, 2015). This popular Web site for job seekers offers a variety of services. The Monster network posts job openings, posts résumés, and provides career advice. No fee; registration required for résumé posting.

MonsterCollege. MonsterCollege, 2015. http://college.monster.com (accessed April 10, 2015). *MonsterCollege*, a division of Monster, specializes in listings for recent college graduates. It assists recent college graduates and college students to get started in their career. This site provides entry-level job listings, internship listings, job search tips, an opportunity to post a portfolio, and a career contact network. No fee; registration required.

TrueCareers. True Careers Inc., 2015. http://www.truecareers.com (accessed April 10, 2015). *TrueCareers* connects educated, diverse job seekers with employers who want well-educated, diverse candidates. This Web site posts job openings and résumés. It also provides career advice. No fee; registration required for résumé posting.

14–9 Travel Arrangements

The Web contains a large number of sites that may be used to make travel arrangements. A few of the more popular ones are listed here:

Expedia.com. Expedia, Inc., 2015. http://www.expedia.com (accessed April 10, 2015). A popular site for making worldwide travel reservations.

Fodor's. Fodor's Travel, 2015. http://www.fodors.com (accessed April 10, 2015). A well-known Web site that provides information and bookings for hotels and cruises. Provides information on restaurants in various cities. Hosts forums and blogs. A source for purchasing Fodor's guidebooks.

Hotels.com. Hotels.com, L.P., 2015. http://www.hotels.com (accessed April 10, 2015). Specializes in making hotel reservations in major cities worldwide.

hotels & travel.com. WebScope, 2013. http://www.hotelstravel.com (accessed April 10, 2015). A site for making travel reservations worldwide.

Orbitz. Orbitz, LLC, 2015. http://www.orbitz.com (accessed April 10, 2015). A site for making travel reservations.

Travelocity.com. Travelocity, Inc., 2015. http://www.travelocity.com (accessed April 10, 2015). A popular site for making travel reservations.

tripadvisor. TripAdvisor LLC, 2015. http://www.tripadvisor.com (accessed April 10, 2015). Provides travel advice and makes travel reservations worldwide.

14–10 Internet Resources

A variety of Internet browsers are available for free download. Some of these sites offer other free downloads in addition to their browser.

Chrome. Google, n.d. https://www.google.com/chrome (accessed April 10, 2015). Provides a free download for the Internet browser Google Chrome.

Downloads. Apple Inc., 2015. https://support.apple.com/downloads/safari (accessed September 21, 2015). Provides access to a download for the Internet browser Safari. Contains links to other Apple products and resources.

Microsoft Download Center. Microsoft, 2015. http://windows.microsoft.com/en-us/internet-explorer/download-ie (accessed September 21, 2015). Provides access to downloading the browser Internet Explorer (and updates) without charge.

Mozilla. Mozilla, 2015. http://www.mozilla.org/en-US (accessed April 10, 2015). Provides a free download for the Web browser Firefox.

14–11 Other Resources

Several other kinds of free information sources on the Internet that may be of value to persons involved in business, industry, or government are listed below:

timeanddate.com. Time and Date AS, 2015. http://www.timeanddate.com/ (accessed April 10, 2015). Provides a world clock, date-to-date calculators, calendars, weather conditions and forecasts, calendars, and information regarding the sun and moon phases. Permits individuals to create free calendars for any year.

VPCalendar.net. VPCalendar.net, 2011. http://vpcalendar.net/ (accessed April 10, 2015). Provides free perpetual calendars for the 21st century.

xe.com. XE.com, 2015. http://www.xe.com (accessed April 10, 2015). Provides international currency rates of exchange and a currency converter.

Yahoo! Yahoo! Inc., 2015. http://www.yahoo.com (accessed April 10, 2015). Contains up-to-date news items, and provides links to a number of valuable resources.

Web 2.0

The Internet continues to be dynamic. As its information sources grow, new Web sites will emerge as others disappear. Some Web sites will be updated almost daily, some periodically, and others not at all. Not every source contains valid information, so evaluate

judiciously its contents and origin. In recent years a number of Web sites have appeared that are a departure from the traditional Web presence. They solicit user participation and are exponentially attracting adherents as they increase networking capabilities and provide new services through the Web. This dramatic departure from tradition has become known as *Web 2.0.* Web 2.0 is focused on the capacity for people to collaborate and share information online.

14–12 Blogs

a. A Web log is a Web page that contains the publicly accessible journal of an individual or company. Shortened to *blog,* this Web page contains personal insights that reflect the personality of its originator and is updated on a regular basis. Although blogs are written in chronological order, they appear to the reader in reverse order. They are written by companies to provide information on their products and services, by individuals interested in various topics or sharing information, and public service agencies to provide information. Blogs for a company or an organization may be accessed from a link in its Web site.

b. In its earlier stages, the Web required the knowledge of HTML or a complex software to create Web pages. Currently, a number of sites offer the tools free of charge for individuals to develop Web pages and create their personal blogs. These tools are easy to use and do not require the high skill level for creating Web pages that was needed earlier. Virtually "anyone" can use these tools to create a blog that contains both text and graphics.

Each blog has its own URL and can be accessed by anyone who has access to the Internet. Some sites offer free hosting, but all charge for separate domains. Most sites also have premium plans for larger storage, wider bandwidth, enhanced themes, specialized templates, and e-commerce features. Although there are a large number of Web page development sites on the Internet, not all of them suit everyone's needs. Anyone interested in developing a blog should check carefully the sites available before committing to one. Popular development and/or hosting sites follow:

(1) *Blog.com.* Offers themes with different layouts, connectivity to the blogger's social networking sites, posting from any Internet-connected device, multiauthoring blogs, multimedia support, and help from a support team. If not already taken, individuals may have their names as their URL; for example, *yourname.blog.com.* Basic services are free for up to 2 GB of storage, and free blogs will have ads placed on the page. For minimal annual fees, however, individuals can request no ads (or their ad) and purchase additional storage space. These and other premium services along with their costs are described on the Blog.com Web site. http://www.blog.com/ (accessed April 14, 2015).

(2) *Blogger.* Provides free blogs with features for customizing templates and designs, collecting and sharing things users find interesting, connecting with and receiving responses from anyone who reads the work, initiating a group blog, restricting access to the blog, posting photographs easily, reading the blog from mobile devices, and uploading text and photos from a mobile device. Users may have up to 100 blogs per account, but there is no limit as to how many pages you may have on one blog. Individual Web pages are limited to 1 MB in size, which equals several hundred pages of text. Photos are limited to 1 GB of total storage. http://www.blogger.com/ (accessed April 17, 2015).

(3) *Google+.* Recommended for social networking. Contains millions of photographs and a "hangout" feature. Permits authorship, Gmail integration, chat, mobile chat, and mobile publishing. The site is free. https://plus.google.com/ (accessed April 26, 2015).

(4) Millburn, Joshua Fields. "How to Start a Successful Blog Today." *TheMinimalists.* April 6, 2015. http://www.theminimalists.com/blog/ (accessed April 11, 2015). Provides a step-by-step process to initiate a blog.

(5) *Penzu.* Provides a free personal journal or online diary. Entries are private and available everywhere, including iOS and Android. Reminders are available should you forget to write. Penzu has a premium service with a fully customizable diary, military-grade security, and a comprehensive journal search feature. https://penzu.com/ (accessed April 19, 2015).

(6) *Wix.* Offers a free Web site development service with hundreds of templates, unlimited pages, and top-grade free hosting. This site also has premium plans that may be purchased for a monthly fee. http://www.wix.com/ (accessed April 26, 2015).

(7) *WordPress.com.* Offers a free blogging service with customizable themes, 3 GB of storage, restricted or unrestricted entry, statistics on the number of visitors, writing tools, photo uploads, video uploads, spam blocker, and other features. If not already taken, users may have *yourname.wordpress.com* as their site address. Provides a premium service for a fee. https://wordpress.com/ (accessed April 17, 2015).

14–13 Wikis

A wiki is a Web site in which users may add, delete, or modify content through a Web browser and a piece of server software that allows users to create and edit Web page content. A wiki allows a group of people to enter and collectively edit bits of text. Wikis are open to the public, open to viewing by the public with restricted editing access, or open only to invited members. Anyone who enters a public wiki may participate by entering or editing text. By clicking an "edit" button, individuals may change whatever they wish in the article they are reading. The most well-known wiki is *Wikipedia*.

Wikis have been created for people who have an interest in a specific topic. Other wikis have been created for individuals to collaborate on a project or an activity. Specific Web sites are available that allow users to participate in existing wikis or create new wikis. Several are listed here:

(1) *Front Page.* Creates content wikis in which collaboration generates and develops new ideas. This site provides instruction and practice in initiating and participating in wikis. It has a "sandbox" to practice, instructions for beginners, text formatting rules, and a link to existing wikis on this Web site. http://c2.com/cgi/wiki (accessed April 28, 2015).

(2) *Google Docs.* Provides a free Web site for collaboration. Google Docs is an online word processor that allows users to create and format text documents and collaborate with others in real time. Users may upload a Word document and convert it to a Google document, adding formats and attributes. They may invite other people to collaborate on the document by providing editing access. Initiators may view the document history and roll back to any previous version. https://docs.google.com/ (accessed April 29, 2015).

(3) *Wikispaces.* Offers wikis for education, businesses, nonprofits, community groups, and individuals. It features Wikispaces Classroom, a social writing platform for education. Teachers may create a classroom workspace where they and their students can communicate and work on writing projects alone or in teams. This service is free to teachers and students. Collaborative sites for schools or school districts, colleges or universities, businesses or nonprofit organizations, and individuals are charged according to the amount of space and the number of users. http://www.wikispaces.com/ (accessed April 29, 2015).

14–14 Social Networking Sites

Social networking sites focus on building social relationships among people who share interests, engage in similar activities, have like backgrounds, or commonplace connections. Sites are Web based and provide tools for users to interact over the Internet, such as e-mail and messaging. They allow users to set up a user profile and add social links to their page. Social networking sites permit users to share activities, ideas, events, and interests within their individual networks.

Social networking sites differ from community networking sites in that they center around an individual; community networking sites, for example wikis, are group centered. The Internet contains nearly two hundred, exclusive of dating sites, active social networking sites. Seven are particularly popular in the United States, having

more than 100 million estimated unique monthly visitors.[2] Web 2.0, however, is fickle; what may be popular today may not exist tomorrow.

(1) *Facebook*. Facebook, 2015. With more than 900 million unique monthly visitors,[3] Facebook is the largest social networking site worldwide. Users create profiles and develop relationships with other people and companies on the network. They are able to share text, photos, and videos through this social connection as well as play games. Users' sites may be restricted to those who have permission to view the site or may be open to any person with access to Facebook. More and more, however, prospective employers are asking to view the Facebook pages of applicants. Recruiters are warning applicants not to place anything on their Facebook pages that could cost them the opportunity of obtaining a job in which they are interested. There are no costs to join and use Facebook, but users must be over 13 years of age. https://www.facebook.com/ (accessed April 30, 2015).

(2) *Google+*. Google, 2015. According to an April 2015 usage report,[4] Google+ ranked fifth among social networking sites with 120 million unique monthly visitors worldwide. When users set up their profile in Google+, they can include a picture of themselves, a background picture that depicts them or where they live, and other background information—such as where they have gone to school or worked—that will make locating them easier for their friends. By adjusting their privacy settings, users can control who can see their profile, tag them in photos, comment on their posts, and send them notifications. The "Circles" feature enables users to share the right things with the right people; with Circles, users can share some things with their family and other things with their close friends. They may share comments, photographs, videos, links, or whatever they wish. Google+ is free. Participants may use the share box on any Google site or the +1 buttons across the Web. https://plus.google.com/ (accessed April 30, 2015).

(3) *Instagram*. Instagram, 2015. With 100 million estimated unique monthly visitors worldwide,[5] Instagram ranks seventh among social networking sites. It is a free online mobile photo-sharing, video-sharing, and social networking service that enables users to take pictures and videos and share them on a variety of social networking platforms such as Facebook, Twitter, and Flickr. Instagram provides filters that transform mobile photos into professional-looking snapshots. https://instagram.com/ (accessed April 30, 2015).

[2]"Top 15 Most Popular Social Networking Sites/April 2015." *EBizMBA*. eBizMBA Inc., April 2015. http://www.ebizmba.com/articles/social-networking-websites (accessed April 29, 2015).

[3]Ibid.

[4]Ibid.

[5]Ibid.

(4) *LinkedIn.* LinkedIn 2015. LinkedIn, rated the third most popular social networking site in April 2015, was reported to have 255 million estimated unique monthly visitors.[6] It claims to be the world's largest professional social networking site. This free professional networking site allows members to establish business contacts, search for jobs, and find potential clients. Participants create a professional profile that may be viewed by others in their network. Likewise, they may view the profiles of their contacts. LinkedIn supports the formation of interest groups, the majority of which are employment related—mainly around professional and career issues. https://www.linkedin.com/ (accessed April 30, 2015).

(5) *Pinterest.* Pinterest 2015. Ranked fourth among the most popular social networking sites in April 2015,[7] Pinterest was reported to have 250 million estimated unique monthly visitors. Pinterest is a free site that provides "boards" on which members may "pin" ideas from around the Web. Members may gather photographs, videos, articles, recipes, and any other information that may interest them to save in one place for future reference. Users merely "pin" the item and it is transferred to a board in their account. Pinterest also maintains a giant database of videos and articles contributed by members in a variety of fields of interest. Users may access these materials and pin them to one of their boards. https://www.pinterest.com/ (accessed April 30, 2015).

(6) *Tumblr.* Tumblr, 2015. Tumblr is basically a series of blogs. It is rated as the sixth most popular social networking site with 110 million estimated unique monthly visitors in April 2015.[8] Tumblr is noted for its ease in displaying videos, music, and images on a Tumblr profile and its numerous ways to showcase them. Provides opportunities for people to "re-blog" owner's posts, thus creating a larger group of followers and a fan base. https://www.tumblr.com/ (accessed April 26, 2015).

(7) *Twitter.* Twitter, 2015. Next to Facebook, Twitter in April 2015 was the second most popular social networking site with 310 million estimated unique monthly visitors.[9] This free online social networking and microblogging service permits its users to send and read text-based postings, known as "tweets," up to 140 characters. Twitter is used by individuals to give snippets of their activities to friends and by businesses for advertising and to hone in on any problems that may exist with their products or services. Members may follow individuals, groups, or businesses. They may also add photographs and videos to their tweets. https://twitter.com/ (accessed April 30, 2015).

---

[6]Ibid.

[7]Ibid.

[8]Ibid.

[9]Ibid.

14–15 Cloud Computing

Cloud computing **refers to storing files on a remote server so that they may be accessed through an Internet connection. By storing files remotely and accessing them through the Internet, you can upload and retrieve information from any computer anytime as long as you have access to the Internet. The advantage of cloud computing is that the files you have at home are also available to you in the office. End users may access files through a Web browser and a computer or a mobile app while the business software and the data are stored on servers in different locations.**

Some services permit companies to upload the business software needed, and employees then use the software on the remote site. Other services provide their own generic software, and still others have end users use the software on their own devices and just provide storage services. Services are available that provide a minimum amount of storage space free. Additional gigabytes of storage are available for monthly or annual fees.

(1) *ADrive.* ADrive LLC, 2015. ADrive offers cloud storage for both business and personal use. The personal basic plan provides 50 GB of free online cloud storage with anytime access to the data. Users may log in to their ADrive account through any device to store, share, or edit files online as long as they have Internet access. ADrive permits sharing large files online by creating a unique link for the file, which may be transmitted by e-mail directly from the ADrive account. Through Zoho technology ADrive users may edit their word processing documents, spreadsheets, and presentations online. They can open, edit, and save documents all from within ADrive. ADrive permits file transfers from external Web sites remotely; once transferred, files may be downloaded or shared. ADrive also provides a search tool for locating files. Besides the basic service, users may upgrade to obtain additional storage and features for a monthly or annual fee. http://www.adrive.com/ (accessed May 1, 2015).

(2) *Dropbox.* Dropbox, 2015. Dropbox provides free file storage for up to 2 GB. This service enables users to synchronize their computers and mobile devices so that up-to-date files are readily available no matter which device they use. Dropbox functions as a folder on the computers or mobile devices, and any changes made to a file in Dropbox are automatically stored in Dropbox and reflected on all devices connected to Dropbox. Users may also access their Dropbox folder from computers not connected to their network by accessing the Web site and providing their password. Shared folders may be created by users for people to collaborate and work together on the same documents and projects. Users may create photo galleries for selective viewing, and they may send a link to any file in their Dropbox

through a public folder. Apps are available for iPhone, iPad, Android, and BlackBerry. Additional storage of 1 TB or unlimited storage may be purchased. https://www.dropbox.com/ (accessed May 1, 2015).

(3) *Google Drive.* Google, 2015. Google Drive provides 15 GB of storage space free. This feature of Google contains many of the tools offered by Google. Google Drive permits users to create new documents, spreadsheets, and presentations online. Individuals may work together on the same document at the same time. Besides accessing Google Drive from a desktop or laptop, users may download apps for their mobile devices—Android or iOS smartphones and tablets. Files may be created, opened, and shared from a variety of apps directly in Google Drive. All photos stored in Google + will also be stored in Google Drive. Premium plans are available to purchase up to 100 GB or 1 TB of storage. https://drive.google.com/ (accessed May 1, 2015).

(4) *OneDrive.* Microsoft, 2015. OneDrive is one of the services of Windows Live, and access is available through a Hotmail or Live e-mail account. OneDrive provides 15 GB of free storage space. With a free OneDrive app, important files and photos are always with the user. Users can synchronize their computer with other computers and mobile devices so that changes made in a file on any computer or mobile device will be reflected in the OneDrive file, which later may be accessed from a linked computer and mobile device. Users may create new files or edit files with Microsoft Word, Excel, and PowerPoint as well as create a OneNote notebook from OneDrive. Folders are set up for private and public access. https://onedrive.live.com/ (accessed May 1, 2015).

14–16 Communication Resources

Among the many resources in Web 2.0, two additional free resources stand out: (1) Skype, an Internet telephone service that permits users to view each other during the conversation and (2) Google Sites, a service that allows individuals to create and maintain Web sites.

(1) *Skype.* Skype, 2015. Skype is an Internet telephone service that promotes communication worldwide. It not only supports voice calls but also face-to-face conversations with live video. Subscribers may have free around-the-world video calling from their computer screen as long as they have a built-in microphone, a webcam, and are connected to the Internet. Contacts, too, must be subscribers and have a built-in microphone, a webcam, and be connected to the Internet to receive a call. Group video calls may include from three to ten people, but Skype recommends five or fewer for the best quality. Subscribers may make video calls to friends on mobile phones as long as the phones are compatible. The latest version of Skype offers high-definition capability as long as everyone on the call has an HD-quality webcam. The free service permits Skype-to-Skype calls, one-to-one video calls, instant messaging, and screen sharing. Additional services

are available through various pay programs that are described on the site. http://www.skype.com/en/ (accessed May 1, 2015).

(2) *Google Sites.* Google, 2015. Google Sites is an easy-to-use way to make your own Web site—free. This site contains dozens of prebuilt templates, or users may just start from a blank page. Sites may contain multiple pages, and Google Sites even provides layout strategies. Plain text, photographs, and videos—all may be used easily to develop the Web site. Instructions are available on how to substitute images and videos for placeholders. Web sites may be developed for groups, family, individuals, and even company intranets. They may be private or public. The Web site is hosted by Google at no cost. http://www.sites.google.com/ (accessed May 1, 2015).

14–17 Evaluating Web Resources

The World Wide Web maintains a valuable collection of information. As it has grown, however, the Web has accumulated outdated, inaccurate, and biased sites. Resourceful Internet users should evaluate objectively the information contained in the sites they visit.

In 1998 Jim Kapoun suggested five criteria for evaluating Web pages.[10] Since then other authors have patterned their criteria after his.[11] Still others have incorporated Kapoun's criteria but have expanded their perspective to include additional standards.[12] The following criteria to evaluate Web sites are based on those devised by Jim Kapoun and the other authors cited here:

(1) *Purpose of use.* If the site is for research, business, or educational use, stricter standards should be applied than if the site is for entertainment or personal interests.

- Assess the purpose of the Web page or site.
- Consider whether the Web site fits in with your purpose.

(2) *Creditability of Web documents.* Review the document to determine the creditability of the authors and the host.

[10]Jim Kapoun, "Teaching Undergrads WEB Evaluation: A Guide for Library Instruction," *C&RL News*, July/August 1998 as reprinted and revised in "Five Criteria for Evaluating Web Pages." Olin & Uris Libraries, Cornell University Library, updated June 28, 2010. Revised and updated again February 5, 2015. http://guides.library.cornell.edu/c.php?g=32334&p=203767 (accessed May 2, 2015).

[11]*Evaluating Web Pages: Techniques to Apply and Questions to Ask.* UC Berkeley—Teaching Library Internet Workshops. University of California, Berkeley, 2012. http://www.lib.berkeley.edu/TeachingLib/Guides/Internet/Evaluate.html (accessed May 2, 2015).

[12]*Evaluating Information.* "Evaluating Internet Resources." The Sheridan Libraries. John Hopkins University, May 2, 2015. http://guides.library.jhu.edu/c.php?g=202581&p=1334997 (accessed May 2, 2015).

- Determine who authored the document and whether that person is separate from the webmaster.
- Check to see whether the author has any credentials listed on the Web page. If so, do they meet your standards for the purpose of your visit? If no credentials are listed, are they available from another source?
- Determine whether the author has provided an e-mail address or other contact information.
- Evaluate the category of the domain (the extension of the domain name). Is the document hosted by an educational institution (*.edu*), a government agency (*.gov*), a nonprofit organization (*.org*), an Internet service provider (*.net*), a military organization (*.mil*), or a commercial organization (*.com*)? Critique the organizational information available—or the absence of information about the organization sponsoring the site.

(3) *Accuracy of information in Web documents.* Assess the purpose of the Web document and the reason it was produced as you evaluate its accuracy.

- Determine whether the purpose of the site is clear and the content reflects its purpose. Is the site meant to entertain, persuade, educate, or sell?
- Determine whether the subject matter is covered adequately.
- Assess the quality of the content and whether it compares favorably with other sources in the field.
- Determine whether the facts are similar to those reported in related print materials or other online sources. Are the facts well researched and documented?
- Determine whether the page contains original work, not simply links to external sources. Do those links in the site lead to quality sources that complement the theme of the Web document?
- Check whether appropriate copyright information is available.
- Assess whether the spelling, grammar, and punctuation are correct.

(4) *Objectivity of Web documents.* Determine whether the author provides opinions instead of facts—or is the site a mask for advertising?

- Assess the intended audience. Why was this page written and for whom?
- View the page as you would any television infomercial to determine whether the site is free of bias.
- Assess the document to determine what opinions (if any) are expressed by the author.
- Determine whether the information is primary or secondary in origin.

- Identify whether the site exhibits objective writing by presenting controversial issues from more than one viewpoint.
- Count the number of embedded advertisements in the site as well as pop-up advertisements that occur upon accessing and viewing pages in the site.

(5) *Currency of Web documents.* Determine whether the information contained in the Web page is up-to-date.

- Determine when the Web page was first produced by locating any information related to a creation date at the bottom of the page. Note specifically when the page was last updated.
- Determine whether the information on the page is outdated.
- Assess the currency of any links contained on the page.
- Determine whether there are any dead links on the page. If so, how many?

(6) *Design and usability of the page or site.* Determine how easily the page may be accessed and the information can be located.

- Determine whether the page has a proper title and other information that permits it to be cited properly.
- Determine whether the site organization is logical and easy to maneuver. Does it provide a search feature?
- Evaluate the format of pages in terms of text, graphics, and background. Is there a balance of text and images? Does the background enhance readability or detract from it?
- Learn whether access to the page is free or charges apply.
- Evaluate the reading level of the page in terms of its intended audience.
- Determine what add-ins are required, if any, to view the page.

14–18 Evaluating Social Media Sites

The rise in the number of social media sites on the Web and the large number of adherents to these sites deserve attention in terms of assessing the reliability of the sites and the information posted. As social networking has grown on the Web, it has produced a few bogus sites and spread some inaccurate information. Resourceful social media advocates should evaluate carefully the sites they join and the information broadcast by others.

Social media can report news faster than traditional sources. Rumors and misinformation can travel quickly through social media channels such as Facebook and Twitter—long before they can be contradicted through regular channels. This makes it even

more important to determine the reliability of posts and tweets. Use these guidelines to assess the authenticity and accuracy of information:[13]

(1) *Location of source.* Are the persons supplying the news located in the place they are posting or tweeting about?

(2) *Reliability of network.* Who is in the network and who are their followers? Are you familiar with the network?

(3) *Accuracy of the content.* Can the information be corroborated from other sources?

(4) *Contextual updates.* Does the person usually post or tweet on this topic? If so, are the previous posts or tweets related to the topic, or do they provide details?

(5) *Age of the account.* Has the account been created recently? Be aware that the account may have been created by an Internet robot (bot).

(6) *Reliability.* Is the source of information reliable?

[13]*Evaluating Information.* "Evaluating Social Media." The Sheridan Libraries. John Hopkins University, May 2, 2015. http://guides.library.jhu.edu/c.php?g=202581&p=1335031 (Accessed May 3, 2015).

15

Manual and Electronic File Management

Manual and Electronic File Management Solution Finder

The Paper Filing Process

15–1 Purpose of Indexing

You may need to set up communication indexes (e.g., names, addresses, telephone numbers, etc.), customer or client files, patient files, vendor files, or some other kind of paper files involving individuals and/or organizations. To organize names or files so that they can be located easily, you will first need to place the separate words in each name in a sequence to be alphabetized. This process is known as *indexing*. Once placed in the proper order, the units may be alphabetized.

So that filed names may be located (retrieved) easily, names must be indexed and alphabetized the same way; that is, you need to follow the same set of guidelines in preparing each name for filing. The general rules presented here can be applied to all systems because of their widespread acceptance and use. These standard rules use the "unit-by-unit" filing method.

15–2 Standard Filing Rules

The rules presented here for indexing and alphabetizing individual and organizational names are the standard filing rules endorsed by ARMA International, an association of professionals involved in records and information management.[1]

The ARMA International publication for alphabetic filing explains accepted deviations from the standard filing rules but cautions that these deviations must be documented for all users. Otherwise, inconsistencies in indexing records for alphabetizing will lead to difficulties in locating and retrieving records.

The following rules and examples are based solely on the standard filing rules.

Indexing and Alphabetizing

15–3 Indexing and Alphabetizing the Names of Individuals

a. To index the names of individuals, arrange the units (words and initials) in each name in the following order:

(1) Complete last name as written (includes hyphenated last names and *all* prefixes such as *D', Da, De, Del, De La, Della, Den, Des, Di, Du, El,*

[1] *Establishing Alphabetic, Numeric and Subject Filing Systems*. Overland Park, Kans.: ARMA International, 2005, 10 and 17–22. (Copies are available at the ARMA International online bookstore, which may be accessed through http://www.arma.org/.) https://members.arma.org/eweb/browse.aspx?site=armastore&webcode=product&id=227f33ba-cce4-4259-85fb-97c6337bd046&category=Filing#.VWuwwZXbK1I (accessed May 31, 2015).

15 Electronic File Management

Fitz, L', La, Las, Le, Les, Lo, Los, M', Mac, Mc, O', Saint, San, St., Ste., Te, Ten, Ter, Van, Van de, van Der, Von, and *Von der*). Variations in the capitalization of these prefixes are treated the same.

(2) Complete first name or initial (includes two-word first names such as *Jo Ann, Mary Ellen, John Paul,* and *Billy Bob*)

(3) Complete middle name(s) or initial(s)

Use suffixes and titles as filing units only if they are needed to distinguish between or among identical names. Titles and suffixes include the following:

(1) Seniority suffix (rank designated by a Roman numeral or the abbreviation *Jr.* or *Sr.*)

(2) Professional suffix (position designated by a certification such as *CPA, PhD,* or *RN*)

(3) Title (such as *Mr., Mrs., Ms., Dr., Professor, Sergeant, Dean,* or *Governor*)

Index titles followed only by a first name or a last name in the order they are written. Examples of such names are *Queen Elizabeth, Brother John,* and *Mr. Damico*.

complete names of individuals placed in indexing order

Last (Unit 1)	*First (Unit 2)*	*Middle (Unit 3)*	*Suffixes and Titles (Unit 4)*
Clark	James	L.	Jr.
Clark	James	L.	Sr.
Hunter	Han Nang	Kim	Mrs.
Hunter	Harold	Michael	Mr.
Clark	William	James	Mr.
Clark	William	James	Dr.
Cueva	Maria Elena		
Hunter	Hannah	Kim	Ms.
Clark	Wm.	Bradley	
Clark-Hunter	Karen	Lynelle	Ms.
Clemson	B.	Thomas	II
Ho	Hung		Mr.
Clemson-Clark	Alice	Marie	
Harper	Mary		Sister
Hunter	Betty-Ann	Harris	
Hunter	Betty Lou	H.	Ms.
Hertig	Thomas	J.	Major
De Hertog	Thos.	I.	RN
De Hertog	Thomas	James	
Hertig	Thomas	J.	Mr.
Clemson	B.	Thomas	III
Hunter	Harold	Conrad Milton	Mr.
Hunter	Harry	Michael	MD
Debrosian	John	T.	
Delano	Marisa	Torti	Mrs.
Hunter	Billy Bob	Scot	

title with first or last name only

Title (Unit 1)	*First or Last (Unit 2)*
Sister	Mary
Mr.	Hunter
General	Clark

b. Indexed names are alphabetized in indexing order. In alphabetizing names, use the following guidelines:

(1) Place nothing before something.

(2) Place numerals before alphabetic letters. Arabic numbers (1, 2, 3, etc.) come before Roman numerals (I, II, III, IV, etc.).

(3) Place initials before names beginning with that letter.

(4) Treat as a single word all compound names (those containing more than one word) whether they are hyphenated or separated by a space.

(5) Disregard all punctuation marks such as periods, apostrophes, hyphens, and commas.

(6) Alphabetize abbreviated and shortened names such as *Wm.* and *Sandy* as they are written.

indexed names of individuals alphabetized

Unit 1	*Unit 2*	*Unit 3*	*Unit 4*
Clark	James	L.	Jr.
Clark	James	L.	Sr.
Clark	William	James	Dr.
Clark	William	James	Mr.
Clark	Wm.	Bradley	
Clark-Hunter	Karen	Lynelle	Ms.
Clemson	B.	Thomas	II
Clemson	B.	Thomas	III
Clemson-Clark	Alice	Marie	
Cueva	Maria Elena		
Debrosian	John	T.	
De Hertog	Thomas	James	
De Hertog	Thos.	I.	RN
Delano	Marisa	Torti	Mrs.
General	Clark		
Harper	Mary		Sister
Hertig	Thomas	J.	Major
Hertig	Thomas	J.	Mr.
Ho	Hung		Mr.
Hunter	Betty-Ann	Harris	
Hunter	Betty Lou	H.	Ms.
Hunter	Billy Bob	Scot	
Hunter	Hannah	Kim	Ms.
Hunter	Han Nang	Kim	Mrs.
Hunter	Harold	Conrad Milton	Mr.

Unit 1	Unit 2	Unit 3	Unit 4
Hunter	Harold	Michael	Mr.
Hunter	Harry	Michael	MD
Mr.	Hunter		
Sister	Mary		

15–4 Indexing and Alphabetizing the Names of Organizations

a. Words in organizational names, even the full names of individuals, are arranged in the order in which they are written. Each word—including articles, prepositions, conjunctions, and symbols—is a separate unit. Except for the word *The* appearing as the first word, index the words in the order they are written. When the word *The* begins an organizational name, consider it the last filing unit. In addition, use the following guidelines:

(1) Spell out any symbols such as & (*and*), $ (*dollar*), or # (*number*).

(2) Disregard all punctuation marks such as hyphens, apostrophes, periods, commas, question marks, or quotation marks.

(3) Close up any letters or words containing hyphens, apostrophes, or periods; index them as a single unit.

organizational names containing articles, lowercase words, and symbols

Organizational Name	Unit 1	Unit 2	Unit 3	Unit 4	Unit 5
Fortune $ Saver	Fortune	Dollar	Saver		
Jane Ryan & Associates	Jane	Ryan	and	Associates	
Jane Ryan and Sons	Jane	Ryan	and	Sons	
The Jane Ryan Realty Company	Jane	Ryan	Realty	Company	The
Rings and Things	Rings	and	Things		

organizational names containing punctuation

Organizational Name	Unit 1	Unit 2	Unit 3	Unit 4	Unit 5
Dr. Ryan's Hospital and Clinic	Dr	Ryans	Hospital	and	Clinic
In-and-Out Burger King	InandOut	Burger	King		
Mark C. Ryan Tires	Mark	C	Ryan	Tires	
Ryan, Irwin, Kirk, and Janns	Ryan	Irwin	Kirk	and	Janns
Ryan-Foreman Furniture	RyanForeman	Furniture			
Ryan's Automotive Repair	Ryans	Automotive	Repair		
R.Y.'s Steakhouse	RYs	Steakhouse			

15 Electronic File Management

b. Single letters separated by spaces in business and other organizational names are considered separate indexing units. Index as single units (1) single letters written without spaces, (2) letters representing the full organizational name (such as IBM, GM, and YMCA), (3) acronyms (names made from initial letters such as MADD and DARE), and (4) call letters for radio and television stations.

letters indexed as separate units

Organizational Name	*Unit 1*	*Unit 2*	*Unit 3*	*Unit 4*	*Unit 5*
A B C Linen Service	A	B	C	Linen	Service
A to Z Rentals	A	to	Z	Rentals	
H LT Express	H	L	T	Express	

letters indexed as a single unit

Organizational Name	*Unit 1*	*Unit 2*	*Unit 3*	*Unit 4*	*Unit 5*
ABC Learning Systems	ABC	Learning	Systems		
ARMA International	ARMA	International			
A-to-Z Data Systems	AtoZ	Data	Systems		
ITT	ITT				
KABC Radio	KABC	Radio			
KNXT Television	KNXT	Television			
TRW	TRW				
ZZZ Freight Express	ZZZ	Freight	Express		

c. **In business and other organizational names, all abbreviated words such as *Inc.*, *Co.*, and *Mfg.* are indexed as written. Names of cities appearing in business and other organizational names are also indexed as written; however, city names with prefixes such as *San*, *Los*, and *St.* (see Section 15–3a) are indexed as one unit.**

abbreviations indexed as written

Organizational Name	*Unit 1*	*Unit 2*	*Unit 3*	*Unit 4*	*Unit 5*
A & A Paper Co.	A	and	A	Paper	Co
The Clothing Factory, Ltd.	Clothing	Factory	Ltd	The	
Mrs. Ryan's Cookies, Inc.	Mrs	Ryans	Cookies	Inc	

cities indexed as written or combined with prefixes

Organizational Name	*Unit 1*	*Unit 2*	*Unit 3*	*Unit 4*	*Unit 5*
El Centro Produce Market	ElCentro	Produce	Market		
Ft. Lauderdale Resorts, Inc.	Ft	Lauderdale	Resorts	Inc	
The Kansas City Inn	Kansas	City	Inn	The	
Las Vegas Credit Bureau	LasVegas	Credit	Bureau		
Los Angeles Flower Exchange	LosAngeles	Flower	Exchange		
New York Stock Exchange	New	York	Stock	Exchange	
Newark Yellow Cab Co.	Newark	Yellow	Cab	Co	
San Diego Gas and Electric Co.	SanDiego	Gas	and	Electric	Co
San Francisco Travel Agency	SanFrancisco	Travel	Agency		
South Pasadena Cleaners	South	Pasadena	Cleaners		
St. Louis Flowers and Gifts	StLouis	Flowers	and	Gifts	
Terre Haute Pharmacy	Terre	Haute	Pharmacy		

Organizational Name	*Unit 1*	*Unit 2*	*Unit 3*	*Unit 4*	*Unit 5*
West Covina Pet Hospital	West	Covina	Pet	Hospital	
The West Haven Motor Lodge	West	Haven	Motor	Lodge	The
The Westfield Motor Lodge	Westfield	Motor	Lodge	The	

d. Spelled-out numbers in business and other organizational names are treated as any other word in alphabetizing names. Arabic numerals, however, precede all alphabetic letters in arranging indexing units. Roman numerals follow directly after any Arabic numerals—before any alphabetic letters. Arrange the numerals in ascending order, and disregard any ordinal endings such as *st, nd,* or *rd*.

spelled-out numbers

Organizational Name	*Unit 1*	*Unit 2*	*Unit 3*	*Unit 4*	*Unit 5*
Twelfth Street Café	Twelfth	Street	Cafe		
Twentieth Century Insurance	Twentieth	Century	Insurance		
Two-for-One Sundries	TwoforOne	Sundries			

Arabic or Roman numerals

Organizational Name	*Unit 1*	*Unit 2*	*Unit 3*	*Unit 4*	*Unit 5*
5 Star Realty	5	Star	Realty		
20th Century Realtors, Inc.	20	Century	Realtors	Inc	
$1 Outlet	1dollar	Outlet			
2-for-1 Photos	2for1	Photos			
99¢ Store	99cent	Store			
A1 Photos	A1	Photos			
Aaron Bros. Art Studios	Aaron	Bros	Art	Studios	
Pier 1 Imports	Pier	1	Imports		
Pier I Food Imports	Pier	I	Food	Imports	
Sixth Avenue Pharmacy	Sixth	Avenue	Pharmacy		
Star 4 Studios	Star	4	Studios		
Star III Studios	Star	III	Studios		

e. Names of federal government entities are indexed under the level of government—*United States Government*. Use the following guidelines to index departments, agencies, and military installations:

(1) Limit the indexing levels to three, if possible.

(2) Index first under *United States Government.*

(3) Index second on the main word or words that identify the department or agency. If necessary, invert the name in order to file by the distinctive word or words.

(4) Index third on the main word or words of any department or agency subdivisions.

(5) Place terms such as *Department of* or *Bureau of* after the main words. Place words such as *of* and *of the* in parentheses because they are not considered in the filing process.

(6) Index military locations in the second level.

federal government entities

Unit 1	*Unit 2*	*Unit 3*
United States Government	Agriculture Department (of)	
United States Government	Commerce Department (of)	Census Bureau (of the)
United States Government	Commerce Department (of)	Economic Development Administration
United States Government	Commerce Department (of)	International Trade Administration
United States Government	Edwards Air Force Base	
United States Government	Fort Bragg	
United States Government	General Services Administration	Citizen Services Office (of)
United States Government	Historic Preservation Advisory Council (on)	
United States Government	Homeland Security Department (of)	Customs (and) Border Protection
United States Government	Homeland Security Department (of)	Federal Emergency Management Agency
United States Government	Homeland Security Department (of)	Transportation Security Administration
United States Government	Library of Congress (the)	United States Copyright Office
United States Government	National Aeronautics (and) Space Administration	
United States Government	State Department (of)	Consular Affairs Bureau (of)
United States Government	Transportation Department (of)	Federal Aviation Administration
United States Government	Transportation Department (of)	Federal Highway Administration
United States Government	Treasury Department (of the)	Alcohol (and) Tobacco Tax (and) Trade Bureau
United States Government	Treasury Department (of the)	Internal Revenue Service
United States Government	Treasury Department (of the)	Public Debt Bureau (of)

f. State and local governments or political divisions are filed by their distinctive names. To avoid confusion, include official terms such as *State of* or *County of* in the indexing process: (1) [state name] State of, (2) [county name] County of, (3) [city name] City of, or (4) [village name] Village of. Each word in the name and the name of any departments or agencies is considered an indexing unit.

state and local government entities

Unit 1	*Unit 2*	*Unit 3*	*Unit 4*	*Unit 5*	*Unit 6*	*Unit 7*
California	City	Economic	Development	Corporation		
California	State	of	Consumer	Affairs	Department	of
California	State	of	Employment	Development	Department	
Glendale	City	of	Community	Development	and	Housing
Los Angeles	City	of	Public	Works	Department	of
Los Angeles	County	of	Health	Services	Department	of
Los Angeles	Water	and	Power	Department	of	
Mission	Viejo	City	Council			
Oxnard	City	of	Community	Development	Department	

g. Index government agencies in foreign countries first by their country. To prevent confusion, use English names. If appropriate, index any additional units in the country name; for example, *China, Republic of.* States, colonies, provinces, cities, and other such government entities follow, with their names spelled in English.

foreign government entries

Unit 1	*Unit 2*	*Unit 3*	*Unit 4*	*Unit 5*	*Unit 6*	*Unit 7*
Australia	Commonwealth	of	Human	Services	Department	of
China	Republic	of	Foreign	Affairs	Ministry	of
South	Korea	Seoul	City	of		

15–5 Handling Identical and Alternate Names

a. Use the address to determine the correct filing order of identical individual or organizational names. Compare addresses in the following order: (1) city names, (2) state names, (3) street names (with numbered street names appearing first), and (4) house or building numbers. Use these address components in the order listed only until the names are distinguished.

identical names

Name	*City*	*State*	*Street*	*House No.*
John R. Smith	Springfield	Connecticut		
John R. Smith	Springfield	Illinois	23rd Street	
John R. Smith	Springfield	Illinois	Dover Avenue	910
John R. Smith	Springfield	Illinois	Dover Avenue	3640

b. Individuals or organizations that could be indexed by more than one name should be cross-referenced. These second (and even third) names are an additional filing entry that is indexed in the order of the alternate name. When persons look for an entry under the alternate name, the cross-reference entry refers them to the original record.

Cross-referencing is used to simplify the location of (1) unusual names, (2) persons or organizations having more than one name, (3) abbreviated names, and (4) foreign individual and business names.

cross-reference entry

IAAP See: International Association of Administrative Professionals

examples of cross-referenced names

Thomas Howard	See:	Howard, Thomas
Hung Ho	See:	Ho, Hung
Duncan, Thelma R.	See:	Nicklin, Thelma R. Duncan
Yama Motors	See:	Matsuyama Motor Imports, Inc.
ABC	See:	Association for Business Communication
Bonn Chemische Fabrik AG	See:	Bonn Chemical Works Inc.

Organizing and Maintaining Computer Data Files

Computer program files and data files are organized into folders for easy access. These folders may be likened to folders you will find in a traditional file cabinet and are sequenced automatically in alphabetical order. A Windows program, Windows Explorer or File Explorer, is used to manage the folders and files contained on computer hard drives, auxiliary drives, remote drives on remote servers, USB pocket drives, and CD-ROMs—although most software applications have a number of data management capabilities also.

You may create folders to group files that are related to the same topic or project. Additional folders may be created for subdivisions of the topic or project. You may then save and store data and image files under their respective topics or projects.

15-6 Creating File Folders for Data Files

Program files install automatically with a hierarchy of folders and files. Rarely does the user need to reorganize the structure of program files and folders to use the software.

Windows automatically comes with a folder specifically for the storage of files created by the user—*Documents*. If you were to use this folder to store all the files you created, it would soon become so full that you would be unable to locate easily files you might need. Therefore, you need to create your own file cabinet—additional folders—to store your data files.

a. Create file folders for the major categories of information that make up your data files. Use the following procedures to determine the names and the number of folders you will need:

(1) Make a comprehensive list of the major categories of information with which you deal. Your categories may be function based, client based, department based, or a combination of major areas for which you are responsible.

(2) Under each major category, list any subcategories that would ultimately contain sufficient files to warrant a separate folder.

(3) List under any subcategories additional subcategories that may be appropriate. Attempt to keep your listing hierarchy to no more than three levels.

b. Access Windows Explorer or File Explorer. All the present drives and folders on your computer are listed. If you choose to store your documents in the *Documents* folder, access this folder. If you have additional drives on your computer and wish to store your documents in one of them, access the drive. You should then be in the root directory of your selected folder or drive and ready to create folders to store your data files. The Windows Explorer or File Explorer address bar at the top of the screen is your navigation bar as it shows you the path you are taking as you create new folders and add files. Follow these procedures to create new folders in the root directory:

(1) To create a new folder in the root directory, click *New folder* on the menu bar. In the name box that appears next to the new folder, key a name that will describe its contents and then press *Enter*. Use as few words as possible, but not so few that you will not be able to recognize easily the subject matter of the folder. Begin the main words in the name of each folder with a capital letter.

(2) To create a new folder within a folder that is in the root directory, you must first open the existing parent folder. Do so by double-clicking it with the left mouse button. When the folder is open, you may create additional folders within this major category. Follow the same steps you did in Step (1) to create a folder. Name the new folder with a descriptive title.

(3) To create a new folder within a subcategory folder, first open the subcategory folder by double-clicking it with the left mouse button. Follow the procedure you used in Step (1) to create any additional folders in this subcategory.

c. As you create files in separate software applications such as Microsoft Word, Excel, PowerPoint, Access, QuickBooks, Adobe Photoshop, Adobe InDesign, and so on, be sure to save your file in the folder that best categorizes the information in the file. To do

so in the software application, click the *File* tab on the menu bar and click *Save as*. Navigate to the folder in which you wish to store the file if the folder name is not displayed and then click the *Save* option.

d. You may manage your files from Windows (or File) Explorer or from your applications software. Folders and files, however, are managed more efficiently through Windows (or File) Explorer.

15–7 Selecting Folders and Files

a. Selecting a folder permits you to open it, delete it, move it to another location, or copy it to another location. Select a folder by left-clicking it. Double-clicking the left mouse button on a folder opens the folder and displays its contents.

b. Selecting a file permits you to open it, delete it, move it to another location, or copy it to another location. Select a file by left-clicking it. Double-clicking the left mouse button on a file in Windows (or File) Explorer opens the file in the program in which it was created, provided that the program is resident on your computer.

c. Multiple folders or files may be selected simultaneously. Use the following procedures to select contiguous and noncontiguous files or folders simultaneously:

(1) Contiguous folders or files, those appearing one after another, may be selected simultaneously by left-clicking the first folder or file, holding down the *Shift* key, and then left-clicking the last folder or file in the series to be selected. Release the *Shift* key. The series of selected items will be highlighted.

(2) Noncontiguous folders or files, those not appearing directly one after another, may be selected simultaneously by left-clicking the first folder or file, holding down the *Ctrl* key, and then left-clicking each folder or file to be selected. Release the *Ctrl* key when your selection has been completed. The selected items will be highlighted.

15–8 Deleting Folders and Files

Folders and files that are no longer needed occupy valuable space on the computer hard drive and slow down its operation. Proper maintenance procedures require that any obsolete folders and files be removed. Follow these procedures to delete any unwanted folders or files:

(1) Select the folders or files to be deleted by following the procedures described in Section 15–7.

(2) Place the mouse pointer anywhere in the highlighted selection and press the *Delete* key on the keyboard. You may, as an alternative, right-click the mouse and select the *Delete* option from the drop-down menu.

15–9 Copying Folders and Files

Copying folders or files to another location—in another folder on the hard drive, to a USB pocket drive, to an external drive, or to a CD—leaves the folders or files in their original location and places a copy in the designated location. Procedures for copying folders and files to another location are not limited to one. The following procedure is just one of several that may be used in Windows (or File) Explorer:

(1) Select the folders or files to be copied by following the procedures described in Section 15–7.

(2) Place the mouse pointer anywhere in the highlighted selection and press *Ctrl+C* (the keyboard copy command). You may, as an alternative, right-click the mouse and select the *Copy* option from the drop-down menu.

(3) Navigate to the location where the files are to be copied, and double-click the left mouse button on that drive or folder to open it.

(4) Place the pointer in the open destination drive or folder and press *Ctrl+V* (the keyboard retrieve [paste] command) to place a copy of the folders or files in the desired location. You may, as an alternative, right-click the mouse and select the *Paste* option from the drop-down menu.

(5) Copied folders and files may initially appear at the bottom of the listing but will be sorted correctly once a drive or folder has been closed and reopened. A copied folder is copied with all its contents.

15–10 Moving Folders and Files

Moving folders and files to another location removes the folders and files from the original location and places them in a new drive or folder. Procedures for moving folders and files to another location are not limited to one. The following procedure is just one of several that may be used in Windows (or File) Explorer. It permits folders and files to be moved easily to a designated location.

(1) Select the folders or files to be moved by following the procedures described in Section 15–7.

(2) Place the mouse pointer anywhere in the highlighted selection and press *Ctrl+X* (the keyboard move [cut] command). You may, as an alternative, right-click the mouse and select the *Cut* option from the drop-down menu.

(3) Navigate to the location where the files are to be moved, and double-click the left mouse button on that drive or folder to open it.

(4) Place the pointer in the open destination drive or folder and press *Ctrl+V* (the keyboard retrieve [paste] command) to transfer the folders

or files to their new location. You may, as an alternative, right-click the mouse and select the *Paste* option from the drop-down menu.

(5) Moved folders and files may initially appear at the bottom of the listing but will be sorted correctly once a drive or folder has been closed and reopened. A moved folder is moved with all its contents.

Glossary

Grammatical Terms Used in *A Handbook for Office Professionals*

Abbreviation
A shortened form of a word or word group. Examples: *in.* for *inches*, *AMA* for *American Medical Association*, and *CAD* for *computer-aided design*. Compare with **Acronym** and **Initialism**.

Absolute adjective
An adjective that cannot be compared because it represents a definite and exact state. Examples: *dead*, *perfect*, *unique*, *complete*, and *full*.

Acronym
A kind of abbreviation (a shortened form of a word or word group) that may be pronounced as a word. Examples: *PIN* for *personal identification number*, *RAM* for *random access memory*, and *NATO* for *North Atlantic Treaty Organization*. Compare with **Initialism**.

Action verb
A verb that shows or represents movement. Examples: *run*, *talk*, *write*, and *breathe*.

Active voice
A method of constructing sentences that identifies who does what. The person or thing performing the action is the subject of the sentence. Examples: The *stockholders* rejected the proposal. *We* signed a one-year lease.

Adj.
Abbreviation of *adjective*.

Adjective
A word or word group that describes a noun or pronoun. It tells what kind, which one, or how many. Examples: *good* investment, *this* bank, and *three* employees.

Adverb
A word that describes a verb, an adjective, or another adverb. It tells when, where, how, or to what degree. Many adverbs end in *ly*. Examples: arrive *early*, consider *carefully*, drive *safely*, come *here*, and *too* small.

Adverbial clause
A word group containing a subject and a verb that begins with a subordinating conjunction such as *if*, *when*, *since*, *because*, or *as*. An adverbial clause modifies the verb in the main clause. Example: *If you wish to make an appointment,* please *call* me.

Ampersand

A symbol (&) meaning *and* used mainly in organizational names. Example: We have signed a contract with Robert White & Associates.

Animate object

Any person, any living thing, or any group composed of persons or living things. Examples: *manager*, *tree*, *company*, and *flock of sheep*. Compare with **Inanimate object**.

Antecedent

A noun or an indefinite pronoun to which a pronoun or any number of pronouns refer. Examples: Our last newsletter asked all *clients who* are interested in bond investments to indicate *their* willingness to attend a free seminar by phoning me. *Anyone* in the office *who* is interested in carpooling should submit *his* or *her* name to our manager.

Apostrophe

A symbol (') used to show noun possession, the omission of letters in contractions, and the beginning and ending of quotations within quotations. Examples: (1) *Carol's* salary; (2) we *haven't*; and (3) He asked, "Have you read my latest article, 'Western Travels'?"

Apposition, Appositive, Appositive expression

A word or word group that renames or explains the noun or pronoun it follows. These descriptive words usually add extra information. Example: Ms. Johnson, *our new manager*, has been with the company for three years.

Article

The words *a*, *an*, and *the*. These words are used as adjectives. Examples: *a* method, *an* interesting tour, *the* stock market.

Being verb

A form of the verb *to be* when it is used as a main verb, that is, when it appears alone or as the last verb in a verb phrase. These forms are *am*, *is*, *are*, *was*, *were*, *be*, and *been*. Examples: (1) Jill *was* here yesterday. (2) He *will be* available for an interview tomorrow.

Being verb helper

A form of the verb *to be* when it is used in a verb phrase as a helping verb. These forms are *am*, *is*, *are*, *was*, *were*, *be*, and *been*. Example: A large selection of toys *have been ordered* to stock our shelves for the holiday season.

Cardinal number

A number such as *3* (three), *10* (ten), *32* (thirty-two), *541*, or *1,856* that is used in simple counting.

Case form

A category used to classify nouns and pronouns in a sentence as subjective (also called *nominative*), objective, or possessive.

Clause

A word group that contains a subject and a verb. Example: before *you leave* the office.

Collective noun
A noun composed of individual persons or things. Examples: *committee*, *team*, *jury*, *class*, and *herd*.

Colon
A punctuation mark (:) used to indicate that the following words explain further the word or word group appearing before the punctuation mark. Example: Our company specializes in the manufacture of the following women's clothing accessories: shoes, boots, handbags, and belts.

Command
A sentence in which the subject *you* is not stated but is implied. The sentence directs the understood subject *you* to perform (or refrain from) an action. Examples: (1) (You) E-mail this information to me as soon as possible. (2) (You) Do not mail these payments until April 29.

Common noun
A noun that does not name a specific person, place, or thing. Examples: *supervisor*, *building*, *city council*, *university*, and *company*.

Common noun element
That part of a proper noun that is not a specific name. Examples: *university* in Rutgers University, *building* in Tishman Building, and *city council* in Miami City Council.

Comparative form
The spelling or form of an adjective or an adverb when it compares two nouns or pronouns or two conditions. Examples: (1) This year's sales are *greater* than last year's. (2) We have progressed *more slowly* in this area than we had hoped. Compare with **Superlative form.**

Complement pronoun
A pronoun that completes a *being* verb. It follows a form of the verb *to be—am*, *is*, *are*, *was*, *were*, *be*, and *been*. Example: The contest winners were *they*, Karen and Bill.

Complete thought
A word group that contains a subject and a verb. The word group must make sense and be able to stand alone as a complete sentence. A complete thought is also known as an *independent clause*. Examples: I will interview the three applicants on Monday. Mr. Oliver signed a five-year lease for a suite in our office building.

Complex sentence
A sentence that contains a dependent clause and an independent clause. Example: As soon as we receive your reply, we will send you a replacement or issue a credit to your account.

Complimentary close
The first closing line of a business letter. Example: *Sincerely yours*.

Compound adjective
Two or more words acting together as a single thought to describe or modify a noun or pronoun. Examples: *part-time* job and *year-end* sale. Same as *compound modifier*.

Compound modifier
See **Compound adjective**.

Compound noun
Two or more words used as a single unit to name a person, place, or thing. Examples: *sister-in-law*, *notary public*, *high school*, *community college*, *word processing*, and *income tax*.

Compound number
A number requiring more than one word when written in word form. Examples: *twenty-seven*, *ninety-eight*, *one hundred*, and *two hundred fifty*.

Compound sentence
A sentence containing two independent clauses (complete thoughts) joined by (1) a semicolon; (2) a transitional expression (such as *therefore*, *consequently*, or *nevertheless*); or (3) the conjunction *and*, *but*, *or*, or *nor*. Examples: (1) Please call me when the shipment arrives; I will pick it up immediately. (2) The Model 432 cart you ordered has been discontinued; *however*, our Model 434 cart has all the specifications you listed for a laptop computer cart. (3) The manufacturer has agreed to send us another shipment of these sheet protectors by next week, *and* we will fill your order immediately upon its arrival.

Compound subject
A subject that contains two or more nouns or pronouns joined by *and*, *or*, or *nor*. Example: *Ellen and Jack* have already reached their quotas for this month's sales.

Compound verb
Two or more words combined to produce a single thought unit that functions as a verb. Compound verbs appear as one word, as two words, or hyphenated. Examples: *upgrade*, *mark up*, *double-space*.

Compound-complex sentence
A sentence containing two or more independent clauses (complete thoughts) and one or more dependent clauses. Example: This suite of offices is currently available for occupancy, and we will release the keys to you as soon as you return the signed lease agreement with a certified check for $3,000.

Conjugation
The various forms of a verb that show person. Examples: I *see*, he or she *sees*, we *see*, you *see*, they *see*; I *am*, he or she *is*, we *are*, you *are*, they *are*.

Conjunction
A part of speech that serves as a connector of words or word groups within a sentence. Examples: *and*, *but*, *or*, *nor*, *either . . . or*, and *not only . . . but also*.

Conjunctive adverb
An adverb—such as *consequently*, *however*, or *therefore*—that connects the main clauses of a compound sentence. Example: Most of our advertising budget has already been allocated; *therefore*, we are unable to take advantage of your offer.

A Conjunctive pair
A class of connecting words—conjunctions—that link contrasting or dependent ideas. These connectors consist of two parts. Examples: *either . . . or, neither . . . nor, if . . . then*, and *not only . . . but also*.

Consonant
Any letter of the alphabet other than *a, e, i, o*, and *u*.

Contingent expression
An expression that depends upon a similar expression for completion. Example: *The sooner* you take advantage of this offer, *the more often* you will be able to enjoy your personal home movie selections.

Contraction
Shortened forms in which an apostrophe is used to show the omission of letters or numbers. These shortened forms may be applied to certain words, verb phrases, and dates. Examples: *internat'l* for *international, doesn't* for *does not*, and *'18* for *2018*.

Coordinating conjunction
A part of speech (conjunction) that joins words or word groups with the same grammatical construction. Examples: *and, but, or*, and *nor*. The students *and* their professor attended the special lecture on employment opportunities in the health-care industry. All the applicants have bachelor's degrees, *but* most of them have no full-time work experience in business-related organizations.

Courtesy title
A title used to address individuals. Examples: *Mr., Ms., Mrs., Miss, Master*, and *Dr.*

Dangling modifier or participle
A short phrase at the beginning of a sentence followed by a noun or pronoun that does not relate to the opening phrase. In most cases the sentence results in a silly meaning. Example: *Filling with water, Bill* was fearful the broken pipe would damage further the carpeting, computers, and furniture in the office. (Bill would look funny filling with water.) Bill was fearful the broken pipe, as the *office continued filling with water*, would damage further the carpeting, computers, and furniture. (The second sentence shows correctly that the office is filling with water.)

Dash
A mark of punctuation (— or --) used to precede summary statements or to set off words or word groups. The em dash (—) is used in computer-based and printed copy. In e-mail and typewritten copy, the dash is formed by keying two hyphens consecutively (--); no space appears before or after the hyphens. Examples: (1) Sofas, chairs, bedroom suites, dining room sets—we have a large variety of styles and brands from which you may choose. (2) Three employees--Clyde Jones, Janice Lee, and Dennis Martinez--have agreed to work overtime next week. Compare with **En Dash**.

Decimal
A small dot (.) used in numbers to separate a whole number from a portion of the next number in the sequence. Examples: *12.5, 0.07, 147.38, 6.75 percent*, and *$1.4 million*.

Declarative sentence

A complete sentence that makes a statement. Example: Our company president announced our merger with Cory Industries yesterday.

Dependent adverbial clause

A word group that (1) contains a subject and a verb and (2) begins with a subordinating conjunction such as *if*, *when*, *since*, *because*, or *as*. An adverbial clause modifies the verb in the main clause. Examples: *When the shipment arrives,* we will *call* you immediately. We will *call* you immediately *when the shipment arrives*.

Dependent clause

A word group that contains a subject and a verb but cannot stand alone as a complete sentence. Example: John told me last week *that he expects to win this month's sales contest*. Same as a *subordinate clause*.

Direct address

The act of calling a person by name, title, or classification in written or oral communication *with that person*. Examples: (1) Thank you, *Ms. Burwell*, for responding so promptly. (2) Yes, *Professor*, we will have this textbook available for use during the spring semester. (3) Only you, *fellow citizens*, can prevent a further decline of schools in this city.

Direct object

A noun or pronoun acted upon by the subject and verb of a sentence. Example: Our accountant mailed the *check* yesterday.

Direct quotation

The exact words spoken or written by a person or a group. Example: According to the committee's report, "The building was sold in 2014 for $28,950,000."

Ellipsis

A series of three periods (. . .)—with spaces before, between, and after the periods—used to show omissions in quoted material or hesitations in other printed material. Example: According to his latest journal article, Professor Haley concludes, "Social conditions will continue to improve in this area . . . unless the government withdraws its funding commitment."

Em Dash

A symbol (—) that represents a dash in word processing and printed documents. In word processing programs, the symbol is accessed through the extended character set. No space appears before or after the em dash. Example: All our accessories—purses, belts, scarves, and so on—will be on sale at discounts from 25 percent to 40 percent this weekend. Compare with **En Dash**.

En Dash

A symbol (–) that represents the words *through* or *to* in word processing and printed documents. In word processing programs, the symbol is accessed through the extended character set. No space appears before or after the en dash. Examples: Information on this Excel function may be found on pages 27–32. Applications for admission will be accepted November 1–April 30. Compare with **Em Dash**.

Essential subordinate clause

A word group that contains a subject and a verb but cannot stand alone as a complete sentence. The word group is needed to complete the main idea of the sentence by furnishing *who, what, which one, when, why, how, whether*, or *to what degree*. Example: Dr. Logan is the professor *who is in charge of preparing the accreditation report*. An *essential subordinate clause* is the same as a *restrictive clause*, a *restrictive dependent clause*, or a *restrictive subordinate clause*.

Exclamation mark

A mark of punctuation (!) used to show strong feeling or emotion. Example: Take advantage of our free offer today—while this letter is in front of you!

First person

I or *we* used as subjects; *me* or *us* used as objects; and *my*, *mine*, *our*, or *ours* used as possessives in writing or speaking. Examples: After analyzing the specimen, *we* contacted several contagious disease specialists. Please e-mail *me* the specifications for the processor. *Ours* was the last case on the court docket for that day.

Fraction

A part of a whole number expressed in proportion to the whole. Example: The legislature is proposing a 0.5 percent increase in our state's sales tax.

Future perfect tense

A verb phrase used to express an action that will occur before a certain time in the future. This tense is formed by using the helping verbs *will have* and the past participle of a verb. Example: If donations continue to be made at this same rate, we *will have paid* for this new hospital wing before its completion.

Future progressive tense

A verb phrase used to express an action that will be ongoing in the future. This tense is formed by using the helping verbs *will be* and the present participle of a verb. Example: Our volunteers *will be calling* other alumni during the next month to solicit donations for the newly formed college foundation.

Future tense

A verb phrase used to express an action that will happen in the future. This tense is formed by using the helping verb *will* and the present part of a verb. Example: I *will call* you next week.

Gender

A term used to refer to the classification of nouns, pronouns, and their modifiers. Classifications include *feminine*, *masculine*, and *neuter*. Examples: (1) *Maria* lost *her* purse. (2) *He* sold all *his* stock. (3) The *company* has just purchased dental insurance for all *its* employees.

Gerund

A verb form ending in *ing* that functions as a noun in a sentence. Example: His *refusing* our offer came as a surprise to all of us.

Helping verb

A verb that appears with the present part, present participle, or past participle of another verb. Examples: *will* go, *are* planning, *has been* employed.

Horizontal listing

A listing of items that continue across the page like ordinary text. Example: Check the following sources for current employment opportunities: *(a) classified ads appearing in your local newspaper, (b) postings in your college or university employment office, and (c) listings provided by career centers on the Internet.* Compare with **Vertical listing**.

Hyphen

A mark of punctuation (-) used (1) to join two or more words that function as a single idea, (2) to divide words at the end of a line, and (3) to represent *through* when placed between two numbers and an en dash is unavailable. Examples: *mother-in-law*, *up-to-date*, *password-protected* files, and pages *34-37*.

Hyphenated compound

A word group joined by hyphens that functions as a single thought unit. Examples: *trade-in*, *self-employment*, *well-to-do*.

Imperative sentence, Imperative statement

A complete sentence in which the subject *you* is not stated; it is understood. Example: (You) Please mail your check in the enclosed envelope today.

Implied verb

An intended verb that is not stated. Examples: (1) If possible (If it *is* possible), we would appreciate your shipping this order by July 10. (2) John has more seniority with the firm than I (I *have*). Compare with **Stated verb**.

Inanimate object

A nonliving thing. Examples: *computer*, *lease*, and *pen*. Compare with **Animate object**.

Indefinite pronoun

A pronoun that does not represent a specific person, place, or thing. Examples: *everybody*, *anyone*, and *something*.

Independent adjective

An adjective that describes a noun without relying on other adjectives to enhance its meaning. Two or more independent adjectives modifying a noun are separated by commas. Examples: an *intelligent*, *conscientious* student. Note that in the phrase *large bold print*, the first adjective modifies the second adjective and noun as a unit (*bold print*); the adjectives are not independent and therefore are not separated by a comma.

Independent clause

A word group that (1) contains a subject and a verb and (2) can stand alone as a complete sentence. Example: Although he was at first reluctant, *Senator Richards has agreed to seek reelection for a third term*. An *independent clause* is the same as a *main clause*.

Independent phrase
A word group that represents a complete sentence although it is not. Example: *Now to the point.*

Independent question
A word group stated in question format that stands alone as a complete sentence. Example: Who is responsible for closing the office on Friday evenings?

Indirect object
A noun or pronoun acted upon by a subject, a verb, and a direct object. Example: Chris gave *him* the check yesterday.

Indirect question
A statement that describes the content of a question or questions. Example: Several customers have asked whether we will extend our shopping hours during the holiday season.

Indirect quotation
A statement that describes written or spoken words of another person or source but does not use the exact words of that person or source. Example: Sharon said that if she is not promoted within the next three months, she will begin to look for another position.

Infinitive
The present part of a verb preceded by the word *to*. Example: You will probably need *to work* overtime *to finish* this project by its deadline date.

Infinitive phrase
A word group beginning with an infinitive and ending with a noun or pronoun. Example: *To obtain more information,* just mail the enclosed card.

Initialism
A kind of abbreviation (a shortened form of a word or word group) that is derived from the first letters of a word group and is pronounced by its letters. Examples: *ATM* for *automated teller machine*, *LCD* for *liquid crystal display*, and *IBM* for *International Business Machines.* Compare with **Abbreviation** and **Acronym**.

Inside address
The part of a business letter that lists the addressee's name, professional title (if any), company name (if any), street address or post office box, city, state, and zip code.

Intransitive verb
A verb that does not have a direct or an indirect object. Examples: (1) The governor will *campaign* heavily in the southern part of the state next week. (2) Responsibility for the success of this project *lies* with the project manager. (3) As gasoline prices *rise*, we can expect consumers to purchase more hybrid vehicles. Compare with **Transitive verb**.

Introductory clause, Introductory dependent clause
A word group that (1) contains a subject and a verb and (2) starts with a subordinating conjunction such as *if*, *when*, *since*, *because*, or *as*. The word group begins the sentence, ends with a comma, and is followed by the main clause. Example: *Because we are no longer able to obtain the Designer DogCondo,* we are returning your check.

Introductory phrase

A word group without a subject and corresponding verb that starts with a preposition, an infinitive, or a participle. Such word groups that begin a sentence and appear directly before the main clause are introductory. Examples: (1) *By this time next year*, we will have moved our offices to Louisville. (2) *To receive your free copy*, simply sign and mail the enclosed card. (3) *Lured by the promise of large profits*, investors poured millions of dollars into this fraudulent development project.

Introductory prepositional phrase

A word group that starts with a preposition but does not contain a subject or a verb. The word group begins the sentence and is followed directly by the main clause. Example: *During this time* we will need to gather more information about the economic conditions of this area.

Irregular verb

A verb that does not form its parts in the usual way, that is, by adding *ed* to the present part to form the past part and the past participle. Examples: *eat*, *ate*, *eaten*; *go*, *went*, *gone*; and *sing*, *sang*, *sung*.

Limiting adverb

A word or word group that restrains, confines, or negates the meaning of a verb. Examples: *not*, *barely*, *scarcely*, and *hardly*.

Limiting expression

A word group that restrains or confines another word group. Example: You may petition for a grade change, *but only for a valid reason*.

Linking verb

A form of the verb *to be* used as a main verb or a form of another nonaction verb. Examples: (1) She *is* a conscientious employee. (2) I *feel* bad that our manager is being transferred.

Lowercase

Refers to the format of alphabetic characters; letters that are not capitalized. Examples: *a*, *d*, *m*, and *u*.

Main clause

A word group that (1) contains a subject and a verb and (2) can stand alone as a complete sentence. Example: When we receive your signed contract, *we will order the equipment needed for your installation*. A *main clause* is the same as an *independent clause*.

Main verb

A single verb or the last verb in a verb phrase. Examples: (1) Please *call* me tomorrow. (2) The display *was* too large to fit into a suitcase. (3) Only three candidates have been *called*. (4) Our manager was *disappointed* with the results of the advertising campaign.

Main word

The most descriptive or definitive word in a compound noun. Examples: *mother*-in-law, personnel *manager*, *notary* public, and vice *president*.

Main words in a heading or title to be capitalized

All words except (a) the articles *a*, *an*, and *the*; (b) the conjunctions *and*, *but*, *or*, *nor*, or *for*; (c) all prepositions; (d) the word *to* in an infinitive such as *to* apply, *to* invest, and *to* communicate; and (e) the word *as* unless any of these words appear as the first or last word. Examples: (1) Normal Climate Conditions in the Northeastern Part of the United States, (2) Corporate Goals and Strategies for 2018, (3) An Analysis of Marketing Strategies Used by an Independent Mail-Order House, (4) How to Invest Wisely on a Minimum Budget, (5) Trends in Economic Globalization as the World Turns.

Misplaced modifier

A word or phrase in a sentence that results in misunderstanding because it has been placed incorrectly within the sentence. Examples: (1) After the luncheon *only John attended the financial seminar*. After the luncheon *John only attended the financial seminar*. In the first example, John was the only one who attended the seminar; in the second example, he attended just the single seminar. (2) *Covered with dirt and debris, Mary* requested the maintenance crew to vacuum the hallway carpeting. Mary requested the maintenance crew to vacuum the *hallway carpeting, which was covered with dirt and debris*. In the first example, Mary is covered with dirt and debris whereas the second example is expressed correctly—the carpeting is covered with dirt and debris.

Modifier

An *adjective* that describes a noun or pronoun. An *adverb* that describes or limits a verb, an adjective, or another adverb.

N.

An abbreviation for *noun*.

Nominative case, Nominative case form

A noun or pronoun used as the subject of a sentence, the complement of a *being* verb, or the object of the infinitive *to be* when this infinitive has no subject. Nouns always maintain the same form; pronouns require a specific form: *I*, *he*, *she*, *you*, *we*, *they*, *who*, *whoever*. Examples: (1) *We* called you yesterday. (2) The winner was *she*, Joyce Moore. (3) I would not want to be *he* when the mistake is discovered. Same as *subjective case*, *subjective case form*.

Nonaction verb

A verb that does not demonstrate action. Examples: *am*, *is*, *was*, and *were*.

Nonessential subordinate clause

A word group that (1) contains a subject and a verb and (2) starts with a subordinating conjunction such as *if*, *when*, *as*, *after*, or *although* or a relative pronoun such as *who* or *which*. This word group provides an additional thought unit that does not change or modify the main clause of the sentence. Examples: (1) Our major advertising campaign will begin on November 1, *after all our dealers nationwide have the new product line in their stores.* (2) Jan Davidson, *who has been with our company for four years,* has been placed in charge of the project. It is the same as a *nonrestrictive clause* or a *nonrestrictive subordinate clause.*

Nonrestrictive

A word or word group that is not essential to the meaning of the main idea.

Nonrestrictive clause

A word group that (1) contains a subject and a verb and (2) appears with a main clause. This word group is subordinate to the main idea and does not alter its meaning. It complements the main idea by adding additional information. Examples: (1) This proposal, *as I explained to you earlier*, has not yet been approved by the Board of Directors. (2) The profit and loss statement for this project was shown in our last annual report, *which was distributed to the stockholders on March 1.* A *nonrestrictive clause* is the same as a *nonessential subordinate clause* or a *nonrestrictive subordinate clause*.

Nonrestrictive phrase

A word group that (a) begins with a preposition, an infinitive, or a participle; (b) does not contain a subject with a corresponding verb; and (c) ends with a noun or pronoun. This word group does not affect the meaning of the main clause; it adds an additional idea that does not modify the main idea. Examples: (1) You cannot, *in my estimation*, expect a greater return on your investment at this time. (2) Susan and Randy, *to name at least two people*, were among those staff members in our department who were affected by the closing of our child-care center. (3) Our president, *concerned about the steady sales decline*, has decided to invest more heavily in research and development.

Nonrestrictive subordinate clause

See **Nonessential subordinate clause**.

Noun

A person, place, thing, animal, quality, concept, feeling, action, measure, or state. Examples: *employee*, *city*, *chair*, *cat*, *sincerity*, *democracy*, *love*, *swimming*, *inch*, and *happiness*.

Object

A noun or pronoun acted upon by another part of speech, for example, a verb or a preposition. Examples: (1) Scott sent *me* the *check* yesterday. (2) For the next three *months*, you will receive a free trial *subscription*.

Object of a preposition

The noun or pronoun that follows a preposition. Examples: of our *clients*, for the past few *months*, from *her*, and through your *efforts*.

Objective case, Objective case form

A noun or pronoun used as the object of a verb, the object of a preposition, the subject or object of an infinitive other than *to be*, or the object of the infinitive *to be* when this infinitive has a subject. Nouns always maintain the same form; pronouns require a specific form: *me*, *him*, *her*, *you*, *us*, *them*. Examples: (1) You may *contact me* at this number after 3 p.m. (2) Please send this information *to me* directly. (3) I do not want *to give her* too much information about our new product. (4) I would not want our new *supervisor to be him*.

Open compound
Two or more words used to represent a single idea. The words appear as separate words and are not hyphenated. Examples: *information processing, golf club*, and *vice president.*

Ordinal number
A number form that indicates order in a series. Cardinal numbers such as *3, 10*, and *246* are numbers used in counting; ordinal numbers such as *first (1st), second (2nd)*, and *twenty-fourth (24th)* indicate order or position in a series. Examples: Our sales report for the *fourth* quarter must be ready by January 15. According to the published list, Don is *12th* on the list to be hired by the New York City Police Department.

Parallel structure
Words or word groups used in a similar fashion that are expressed in the same format. Parallel structure applies to words joined by a conjunction, joined by a conjunctive pair, appearing in a series, and appearing in a listing. Examples: (1) Our receptionist's main duties are to *answer the telephone* and *greet office visitors*. (2) You may order supplies from not only *our standard supply catalog* but also *Kalleen's Computer Supply Catalog*. (3) The whole day was spent *returning phone calls, reading the mail*, and *responding to e-mail messages.*

Parenthesis
A mark of punctuation signifying the beginning [( ] of a side thought and the ending [ )] of a side thought. Example: Please request copies of any ancillary materials (at least an instructor's manual and key) that may accompany the text.

Parenthetical element, Parenthetical expression, Parenthetical remark
A word or word group that does not contribute to the meaning of the main clause but merely acts as a transitional thought or provides an additional idea. Examples: (1) *Therefore*, we are returning this order for credit. (2) The meeting scheduled for October 24, *as you probably already know*, has been canceled.

Participial phrase
A word group beginning with a past or present participle. Examples: (1) *Encouraged by last month's increased sales*, our Advertising Department has decided to extend the present campaign another month. (2) *Hoping to sell the property immediately*, Mr. Rice agreed to drop the price by $10,000.

Parts of a verb
The forms of a verb that are used to construct tenses, that is, spellings of a verb used in expressing time periods. The parts of a verb include the *infinitive, present part, past part, present participle*, and *past participle*. Examples: *to send, send, sent, sending, sent.*

Passive voice
A form of sentence construction in which the doer of the action is not the subject of the sentence. This form is used primarily to deemphasize the person performing the action by focusing instead on the results. It is often used to convey negative ideas or to avoid placing blame. The passive voice is constructed by using a form of the verb *to be* as a helper and the past participle of the main verb. Examples: Since these insurance claims *were not filed* within a year's time, they are not eligible for reimbursement. The back gate *was left* unlocked last night.

Past part

One of the five verb parts used in constructing tenses. For most verbs this part is formed by adding *ed* to the present part, the form listed in the dictionary. Examples: *call* (call+ed), *discuss* (discuss+ed), and *answer* (answer+ed). The past part for verbs not following this pattern is shown in the dictionary directly after the main entry. Examples: *see* (*saw*), *write* (*wrote*), and *go* (*went*).

Past participle

One of the five verb parts used in constructing tenses. The past participle is always used with a helping verb. For most verbs this part is formed by adding *ed* to the present part, the form listed in the dictionary. Examples: *call* (call+ed), *discuss* (discuss+ed), and *answer* (answer+ed). The past participle for verbs not following this pattern is shown in the dictionary directly after the main entry. Examples: *see* (seen), *write* (written), and *go* (gone).

Past perfect tense

Used to describe a past action that has taken place before another past action. This tense is formed by using the helping verb *had* and the past participle of the main verb. Example: The applicant *had accepted* another position before he *received* our offer.

Past progressive tense

Used to describe an ongoing action that took place in the past. This tense is formed by using the helping verb *was* or *were* with the present participle of the main verb. Example: Last year our company *was hiring* additional personnel; this year the company is reducing its staff in all departments.

Past tense

Used to report a single past action or occurrence. This tense is formed by using the past part of a verb. Example: We *finished* the report last Friday. The customer *paid* his outstanding balance yesterday.

Perfect tense

Describes the present, past, or future by using a form of *have* as a helping verb and the past participle of the main verb. Examples: *have completed*, *had completed*, and *will have completed*. Amy *has* already *completed* all her assignments for this week. Fundraisers *had reached* their goal to finance the new hospital wing before the deadline date. Matt *will have completed* all the requirements for a bachelor's degree before his older brother.

Permanent compound

A dictionary entry consisting of more than one word to represent a single idea. Examples: *air-conditioning*, *high school*, *community college*, *up-to-date*, and *full-time*.

Person

A grammatical category based on the relationship between the writer (or speaker) and the reader (or listener). There are three grammatical persons:

(1) *First person*, which includes dialogue in which the writer refers to himself or herself in the singular or as part of a group; the pronouns *I* and *we* are in the first person.

(2) *Second person*, which refers specifically to the individual addressed; the pronoun *you* is in the second person.
(3) *Third person*, which refers to the individual or thing spoken of; all other pronouns and nouns used as the subject of a sentence are in the third person.

Examples: (1) *We* expect to complete the salary analysis of major occupations in Cook County by June. (2) *You* have been nominated to receive the company "Employee of the Month" award. (3) This *applicant* appears to have all the qualifications we specified for the opening in our Accounting Department.

Personal pronoun
A word that substitutes for the name of a person or thing. Examples: *I*, *he*, *she*, *it*, *we*, *they*, *you*, *me*, *him*, *her*, *us*, and *them*.

Phrase
A group of two or more grammatically related words that act upon one another in a modifying, coordinating, or composite relationship. The word group does not have a subject and a verb. Examples: (1) Our sales have increased *during the past few months*. (2) Mr. Lee requested the custodial crew *to wash the windows*, *vacuum the carpeting*, and *set up the chairs*. (3) Our supply *of printer toner cartridges* is diminishing rapidly.

Plural
More than one. Nouns, pronouns, and verbs have plural forms.

Plural noun
More than one person, place, or thing. These nouns usually require a special form and appear with a plural verb. Examples of different formats for forming plural nouns: *employees* (employee), *losses* (loss), *companies* (company), *curricula* (curriculum), and *potatoes* (potato).

Polite request
A command worded like a question that requests the reader or listener to perform a specific action. A polite request in written form ends with a period. Example: Will you please send us your remaining application materials by November 16.

Possessive
A noun or pronoun that shows ownership. Examples: (1) The *company's* liability has not yet been determined. (2) The company awarded all *its* employees a bonus.

Possessive case, Possessive case form
The spelling of a noun or pronoun that shows ownership. Examples: *Sally's* desk, an *accountants'* convention, *his* books, *your* paycheck, and *their* tickets.

Predicate
That part of a sentence that includes the verb or verb phrase and all its modifiers—all parts of the sentence except the complete subject. Example: All parts in this assembly *will need to be replaced within the next few months*.

Prefix
A syllable attached to the beginning of a word that forms a derivative word or an inflectional form. Examples: *un*able, *dis*cover, *mis*pronounce, and *ful*fill. Compare with **Suffix.**

Preposition
A part of speech that links a noun or pronoun to another word in the sentence. Examples: *of*, *for*, *behind*, *in*, *through*, *during*, *around*, *above*, *between*, and *except*.

Prepositional phrase
A word group that begins with a preposition and ends with a noun or pronoun. The phrase modifies another noun or pronoun or a verb in the sentence. Examples: (1) Our new line *of office desks* may be purchased online. (2) Do not park *between these posts*.

Present part
One of the five verb parts used in constructing tenses. This part is the form shown as the main dictionary entry of the verb. Examples: *call*, *discuss*, *answer*, *see*, *write*, and *go*.

Present participle
One of the five verb parts used in constructing tenses. For most verbs this part is formed by adding *ing* to the present part, the form listed in the dictionary. Examples: *call* (call+ing), *discuss* (discuss+ing), and *answer* (answer+ing). The present participle for verbs not following this pattern is shown in the dictionary directly after the main entry. Examples: *omit* (omit+ting), *write* (writ+ing), and *star* (star+ring).

Present perfect tense
Used to describe an action that began in the past but has continued during the time leading to the present. This tense is formed by using the helping verb *has* or *have* and the past participle of the main verb. Example: We *have sent* this client at least three reminders about his past-due account.

Present progressive tense
Used to describe an action in progress during the present time. This tense is formed by using the helping verb *am*, *is*, or *are* and the present participle of the main verb. Example: We *are* now *taking* applications for this position.

Present tense
Used to describe an ongoing action or an existing condition. This tense is formed by using the present part of the verb. Examples: (1) Lisa *drives* 20 miles each day to work. (2) Your company *has* too many employees.

Principal parts of a verb
See **Parts of a verb**.

Principal word
The word in a compound noun that describes or defines the noun most explicitly. Examples: *brother*-in-law, *sergeant* at arms, lieutenant *colonel*, and high *school*.

Principal words in a heading or title to be capitalized
See **Main words in a heading or title to be capitalized**.

Professional title
A title related to a person's employment. Examples: *Professor* Scot Ober, *Governor* Joyce Arntson, *Dean* Carole Delgado, *Vice President* Norlund, *General* Rodriguez, and *Mayor* Bradley.

Progressive tenses
Used to describe actions in progress during various time periods. Describes the present, past, or future by using a form of *to be* as a helping verb and the present participle of the main verb. Examples: *are processing*, *were processing*, and *will be processing*.

Pronoun
A word that functions as the substitute for a noun. Examples: *I*, *her*, and *their*; *that* and *who*; and *this*, *each*, and *everyone*.

Proper noun
The name of a specific person, place, or thing. Examples: *Janet Thompson*, *Empire State Building*, and *San Francisco Bay Bridge*.

Question mark
A mark of punctuation (?) used to end a word group or complete sentence that is a direct question. Example: Have you received any further information about the proposed project*?*

Quotation marks
A pair of punctuation marks (" ") used primarily to set off the exact words spoken or written by another person. Example: The author stated in his article, "As interest rates decline, investments in the municipal bond market become less attractive."

Reflexive pronoun
A pronoun ending with *self* or *selves* that refers back to or is acted upon by another noun or pronoun in the sentence. Examples: *Tom himself* was unsure of the date when the property was sold. *We* can certainly give *ourselves* a pat on the back for this major accomplishment.

Regular verb
A verb that forms its parts by adding standard endings to the present form; that is, by adding *ed* for the past part, *ed* for the past participle, and *ing* for the present participle. Example: *check*, *checked*, *checked*, *checking*.

Relative clause
A word group (containing a subject and a verb) introduced by a pronoun that refers back and relates to a noun or pronoun in the main clause. Relative clauses are introduced by *who*, *whoever*, *whom*, *whomever*, *that*, or *which*. Same as *relative pronoun clause*. Example: Dr. Williams is the physician *who will handle your case*.

Relative pronoun
The noun substitutes *who*, *whoever*, *whom*, *whomever*, *that*, and *which* used to introduce a clause that refers back and relates to a noun or pronoun in the main clause. Example: The *subsidiary* of our company *that* handles this product is Belegrath Tool & Die.

Relative pronoun clause
A word group containing a subject and a verb that appears with a main clause; it begins with *who*, *whom*, *whoever*, *whomever*, *that*, or *which*. Example: Heritage Inc. is the real estate agency *that is handling the sale of our Springfield warehouse*. Same as *relative clause*.

Restrictive

A word or word group that contributes substantially to the main idea of the sentence and is needed for it to convey the same meaning. Without the word or word group, the meaning of the sentence would be changed or incomplete.

Restrictive appositive

A word or word group used to rename or describe a previous noun or pronoun. The word or word group is needed to identify *which one*. Example: The *book The Pentagon Heroes* has been on the best-seller list for the past eight weeks.

Restrictive clause

A word group that (1) contains a subject and a verb and (2) appears with a main clause. Although this word group is subordinate to the main idea, it does clarify, limit, or otherwise affect its meaning. Examples: (1) This order will be shipped *as soon as I receive approval from our Credit Department*. (2) The only person *who can approve this request* is the vice president of financial services. A *restrictive clause* is the same as an *essential subordinate clause*, a *restrictive dependent clause*, or a *restrictive subordinate clause*.

Restrictive dependent clause

See **Restrictive clause.**

Restrictive phrase

A word group beginning with a preposition or an infinitive and ending with a noun or pronoun. This word group affects the meaning of the main clause by answering such questions as *who*, *what*, *which one*, *when*, *why*, *how*, *whether*, or *to what degree*. Examples: (1) We increased the advertising budgets *for several of our new products*. (2) Please mail the enclosed postcard *to obtain further information*.

Restrictive subordinate clause

See **Restrictive clause.**

Return address

The complete address of the person writing a business letter that is not prepared on letterhead stationery. On envelopes addressed for mailing, the complete address of the person mailing the envelope and its contents.

Roman numeral

One of a sequence of numbering based on the ancient Roman system. In business this system is used primarily for numbering the major divisions in an outline, the chapters in a report, and the preliminary pages of a report. Examples: *I*, *II*, *III*, *IV*, *V* and *i*, *ii*, *iii*, *iv*, *v*.

Salutation

The opening greeting in a business letter. Examples: *Gentlemen*, *Ladies and Gentlemen*, *Dear Dr. Gates*, *Dear Ms. Howell*, and *Dear Bob*.

Semicolon

A mark of punctuation (;) used primarily to join two complete thoughts in a sentence. Example: We have not received any responses to our advertisement for an accountant; therefore, please do not renew our ad in the *Valley Star*.

Sentence fragment
A word group ending with a period, question mark, or exclamation mark that is not a complete sentence or does not represent a complete thought. Example: As a charge customer, you are invited to the presale for our Jubilee Discount Weekend. *Our greatest money-saving event of the year.*

Series
Three or more words or word groups that have the same structure within a sentence. Items in a series consist of words, phrases, or clauses. The last item is joined to the others with a coordinating conjunction: *and*, *or*, or *nor*. Example: You may *telephone, fax, or e-mail* your orders.

Signature block
In a business letter, the lines that contain the signature of the writer, the typewritten name of the writer, and the title of the writer, if any.

Simple fraction
Any portion of a whole number that is less than *one*. Examples: ¼ or *one fourth*, ⅔ or *two thirds*, and ⅝ or *five eighths*.

Simple noun
The name of a person, place, or thing that consists of one word. Examples: *Mary*, *desk*, *computer*, and *manager*.

Simple sentence
A word group that contains only one subject and one verb (or verb phrase) and makes sense. Example: I received the package of materials yesterday.

Simple subject
The single word in the main clause of a sentence that answers *who* or *what* in relation to the verb. Example: All *employees* in our division *have received* copies of the employee newsletter.

Simple tenses
The present, past, and future tenses. Examples: (1) He *writes* well. (2) He *wrote* this letter yesterday. (3) He *will write* the letter tomorrow.

Singular
A mode or form of nouns, pronouns, and verbs signifying *one*. Examples: *truck* (vs. *trucks*), *she* (vs. *they*), and *drives* (vs. *drive*).

Singular noun
The form used to name a person, place, or thing that signifies *one*. Examples: *supervisor*, *country*, and *bank*.

Slash
A symbol (/) used primarily for expressing fractions and certain expressions. Examples: *3½*, *c/o* (in care of), and *and/or*. Same as a *solidus* and a *virgule*.

Solidus
See **Slash.**

Stated verb

A verb expressed orally or in written format. Examples: (1) If this *is* so, please *call* me. (2) He *is* older than I *am*. Compare with **Implied verb**.

Statement

A sentence that presents facts or ideas. It is concluded with a period. Example: Our company was established in 1987.

Subject

The word or word group in the main or subordinate clause of a sentence that answers *who* or *what* in relation to the verb. Examples: (1) The *stockholders* of the corporation *approved* the merger last month. (2) Both *answers and explanations* for these test questions *are contained* in the instructor's manual. (3) *We will notify* you when your *order arrives.*

Subject complement

The noun, pronoun, or adjective following a *being* verb (*am*, *is*, *are*, *was*, *were*, *be*, *been*) that either renames or describes the subject. Examples: (1) The former *manager* of our department *is* the new *vice president.* (2) The *paintings* in this exhibition *are* exceptionally *valuable.*

Subject of a clause

The word or word group in the subordinate clause of a sentence that answers *who* or *what* in relation to the verb. Example: If *you are interested* in this position, please send us your résumé.

Subject of a sentence

The word or word group in the main clause of a sentence that answers *who* or *what* in relation to the verb. Example: As I mentioned in my previous memorandum, any further *delays* in the completion of this contract *will cost* the company thousands of dollars.

Subject of an infinitive

A noun or pronoun that appears directly before an infinitive. Example: I did not expect *him to have* the authority to release this kind of information.

Subjective case, Subjective case form

A noun or pronoun used as the subject of a sentence, the complement of a *being* verb, or the object of the infinitive *to be* when this infinitive has no subject. Nouns always maintain the same form; pronouns require a specific form: *I*, *he*, *she*, *you*, *we*, *they*, *who*, *whoever*. Examples: (1) *They* signed the contract this morning. (2) The only person who responded was *he*. (3) I would not want to be *she* when our manager discovers her errors. Same as *nominative case*, *nominative case form*.

Subjunctive mood

Used to describe events that cannot or probably will not happen and conditions that are not true or highly unlikely. The plural form *were* is used with *if*, *as if*, *as though*, or *wish* for singular subjects when the situation described is not true or is unlikely. Examples: (1) *If* I *were* you, I would refer this letter to my attorney. (2) During the meeting Tina acted *as if* she, not Ms. Elliott, *were* the department manager. (3) I wish it *were* possible to replace the photocopier in the Accounting Department, but funds are not available in this year's budget.

Subordinate clause

A word group that contains a subject and a verb but cannot stand alone as a complete sentence. Example: Please notify our office *if you need any additional sales literature.* Same as a *dependent clause.*

Subordinating conjunction

A specific kind of conjunction used to introduce a dependent or subordinate word group that contains a subject and a verb. Examples: *if, as, when, because*, and *since.*

Suffix

A syllable attached to the ending of a word or word root that forms a derivative word or an inflectional form. Examples: invest*ment*, account*ant*, fruit*ful*, walk*ing*, and child*ren*. Compare with **Prefix**.

Superlative form

The spelling or form of an adjective or an adverb when it compares more than two nouns or pronouns or more conditions than two. Examples: (1) Your firm is the *most* highly *respected* firm in the industry. (2) Sales figures for this year are the *highest* in our company's history. Compare with **Comparative form**.

Suspending hyphen

A hyphen following the first word (or multiple words) of a compound adjective in which the last word of the compound adjective appears later. Examples: (1) Rolls of this carpeting may be purchased in *10-*, *12-*, and 15-foot widths. (2) Most of our automobile loans extend over a *four-* or five-year period.

Syllable

A unit of spoken language used to make up words. Syllables are marked off in the main entries of the dictionary; a small dot separates each syllable. Written words may be divided at the end of a line only between syllables. Examples: *syl•la•ble*, *di•vi•sion*, and *ir•re•vo•ca•ble*.

Temporary compound

A compound adjective not appearing in the dictionary. This compound is hyphenated only when it precedes the noun it modifies. Examples: (1) These *easy-to-follow instructions* were written by our supervisor. (2) These *instructions* are *easy to follow.*

Tense

The form of a verb that places an action or a condition in a time frame.

Transitional expression, Transitional word

A word or phrase that does not contribute to the meaning of a sentence but takes the listener or reader smoothly from one concept to another by bridging two ideas or signaling a turn in thought. Examples: (1) We are unable to obtain the Harwood china by Lexington that you ordered; *therefore*, we are crediting your account for $227.47. (2) You may, *on the other hand*, wish to upgrade the computer memory to 8 gigabytes.

Transitive verb

A verb that has an object. Examples: (1) Mr. Morris *called me* yesterday. (2) Please *place the book* on the table. (3) Our supervisor *gave her* an excellent *rating*. Compare with **Intransitive verb**.

Uppercase

Capital letters. Examples: *A*, *M*, and *IBM*.

Verb

A part of speech that shows action or movement or describes a situation or condition. Examples: *write*, *listen*, *send*, *be*, *appear*, and *look*.

Verb phrase

A verb part combined with helpers such as *was*, *have*, *did*, and *will* to form tenses. Examples: *were divided*, *had reached*, *does work*, *will have finished*, and *may be reached*.

Vertical listing

A listing of items in which each item begins a new line on the page. The following entries are an example of a vertical listing:

Use the following sources to locate current employment opportunities:

Classified ads
College employment office
Company online career centers
Internet career centers
State employment office

Compare with **Horizontal listing**.

Virgule

See **Slash.**

Vowel

Letters of the alphabet *a*, *e*, *i*, *o*, and *u*.

Index

A

Index

B

Index

C

Index

D

F

G

Index

H

I

J

K

L

M

N

Index

Q

R

Index

S

Y

Z

Two-Letter State Postal Designations

State or Territory	Two-Letter Postal Designation	Standard Abbreviation
Alabama	AL	Ala.
Alaska	AK	—
American Samoa	AS	—
Arizona	AZ	Ariz.
Arkansas	AR	Ark.
California	CA	Calif.
Colorado	CO	Colo.
Connecticut	CT	Conn.
Delaware	DE	Del.
District of Columbia	DC	DC
Florida	FL	Fla.
Georgia	GA	Ga.
Guam	GU	—
Hawaii	HI	—
Idaho	ID	—
Illinois	IL	Ill.
Indiana	IN	Ind.
Iowa	IA	—
Kansas	KS	Kans.
Kentucky	KY	Ky.
Louisiana	LA	La.
Maine	ME	—
Maryland	MD	Md.
Massachusetts	MA	Mass.
Michigan	MI	Mich.
Minnesota	MN	Minn.
Mississippi	MS	Miss.
Missouri	MO	Mo.
Montana	MT	Mont.
Nebraska	NE	Neb., Nebr.
Nevada	NV	Nev.
New Hampshire	NH	NH
New Jersey	NJ	NJ
New Mexico	NM	N. Mex.
New York	NY	NY
North Carolina	NC	NC
North Dakota	ND	N. Dak.
Ohio	OH	—
Oklahoma	OK	Okla.
Oregon	OR	Ore., Oreg.
Pennsylvania	PA	Pa.
Puerto Rico	PR	PR
Rhode Island	RI	RI
South Carolina	SC	SC
South Dakota	SD	S. Dak.
Tennessee	TN	Tenn.
Texas	TX	Tex.
Utah	UT	—
Vermont	VT	Vt.
Virgin Islands	VI	VI
Virginia	VA	Va.
Washington	WA	Wash.
West Virginia	WV	W. Va.
Wisconsin	WI	Wis., Wisc.
Wyoming	WY	Wyo.